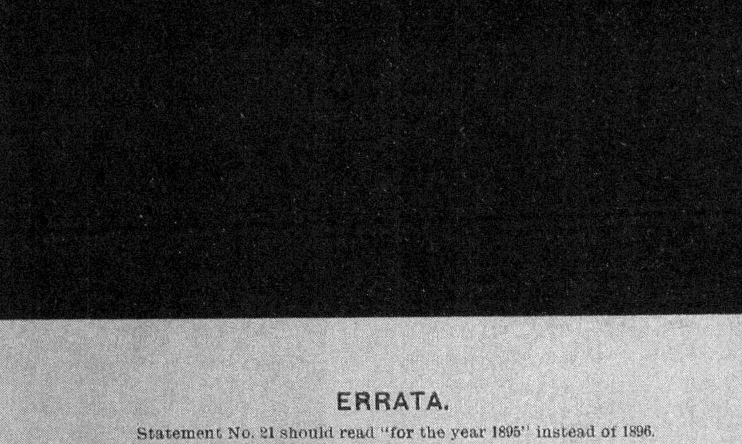

ERRATA.

Statement No. 21 should read "for the year 1895" instead of 1896.

BIENNIAL REPORT

OF THE

Auditor of Public Accounts

TO THE

GOVERNOR OF ILLINOIS.

NOVEMBER 1, 1896.

SPRINGFIELD, ILL.:
PHILLIPS BROS., STATE PRINTERS.
1897.

BIENNIAL REPORT.

AUDITOR'S OFFICE,
November 1, 1896.

To His Excellency, JOHN P. ALTGELD, *Governor of Illinois:*

SIR:—I have the honor to submit herewith a report of the transactions of the revenue department of this office, together with brief mention of other departments connected with the office, from which quarterly or annual reports are required by law, and have been made from time to time.

The arrangement is by tabular statements, as follows:

1. Receipts and disbursements of General Revenue Fund.
2. Receipts and disbursements of Special State Funds.
3. Detail of warrants drawn on the Treasury for all purposes.
4. Recapitulation of warrants drawn on the Treasury.
5. Table of balances of Appropriations made by the Thirty-eighth General Assembly, unexpended October 1, 1894, amount of warrants since drawn thereon, and amounts which lapsed into Treasury September 30, 1895.
6. Table of appropriations made by the Thirty-ninth General Assembly, showing amount of warrants drawn thereon, respectively, and balances unexpended September 30, 1896.
7. Warrants outstanding October 1, 1894, and September 30, 1896.
8. Condition of School, College and Seminary Funds.
9. Summary of the State Treasurer's account with the several State funds.
10. School Tax Fund and Interest on the School Fund, distributed to the several counties, for the years 1894 and 1895.
11. Aggregate amount of State taxes charged on tax books for the year 1894, the amount of abatements, commissions, etc., the net amount collected, and the amount received at the State Treasury on account thereof.
12. Aggregete amount of State taxes charged on tax books for the year 1895, the amount of abatements, commissions, etc., the net amount collected, and the amount received at the State Treasury on account thereof.
13. School Fund tax charged on the tax books of 1894, showing the abatements and net amount collected and amount paid each county.

14. School Fund tax charged on the tax books of 1895, showing the abatements and net amount collected and amount paid each county.

15. State, County and Local taxes charged on the tax books of 1894.

16. State, County and Local taxes charged on the tax books of 1895.

17. Statement showing the per cent. of forfeitures and insolvencies on account of State tax, for the years 1894 and 1895, in the various counties.

18. Statement showing per cent. of total amount of State tax collected for the years 1874 to 1895, inclusive, paid by each of the various counties.

19. Statement showing the average rate of taxation in the several counties for the years 1888 to 1895, inclusive.

20. Statement of property assessed in the several counties for the year 1895.

21. Rate per cent. of addition to or deduction from the assessed value of each class of property in each county of the State, as determined by the State Board of Equalization, on the assessment of 1895.

22. Railroad property in the several counties, as assessed and equalized for 1895.

23. Aggregate equalized assessment of railroad property for the year 1895.

24. "Capital Stock" assessments made by the State Board of Equalization for the year 1895.

25. Statement of the equalized assessment of all taxable property in the several counties for the year 1895.

26. Statement of property assessed in the several counties for the year 1896.

27. Rates per cent. of addition to or deduction from the assessed value of each class of property in each county in the State, as determined by the State Board of Equalization, on the assessment of 1896.

28. Statement showing the proportion of the total equalized assessments of taxableable property in the various counties, for the years 1884 to 1895, inclusive, assessed on *Real* and *Personal* property, respectively.

29. Statement of the aggregate equalized assessment of taxable property in the several counties in the State for the years 1873 and 1884 to 1896, inclusive.

30. Railroad property in the several counties as assessed and equalized for the year 1896.

31. Aggregate equalized assessment of railroad property for the year 1896.

32. "Capital Stock" assessments made by the State Board of Equalization for the year 1896.

33. Statement of the equalized assessment of all taxable property in the several counties for the year 1896.

34. Statement of Bonds issued by Counties, Townships, Cities and Towns, registered in the Auditor's office, in pursuance of an act entitled "An act to fund and provide for paying the Railroad Debts of Counties, Townships, Cities and Towns," in force April 16, 1869.

35. Statement of Bonds registered in pursuance of the original act of February 13, 1865.

36. Statement of Bonds registered in pursuance of the act of February 13, 1865, as amended by acts of April 27, 1877, and June 4, 1879.

37. Statement of Drainage District Bonds registered in pursuance of the act of June 27, 1885.

38. Statement of Bonds issued by Commissioners of Sny Island Levee (of Adams, Pike and Calhoun counties) in pursuance of act of April 24, 1871, and registered in the Auditor's office under act of April 9, 1872.

39. Abstract of the accounts of the State Treasurer with the several Local Registered Bond Funds of Counties, Townships, Cities and Towns.

40. Aggregate amount of taxes charged on account of Local Bond Funds, the amount of abatements, commissions, etc., and the amount paid over by Collectors for each locality, for the year 1894.

41. Aggregate amount of taxes charged on account of Local Bond Funds, the amount of abatements, commissions, etc., the net amount collected, the amount paid State Treasurer, and the amount remaining unpaid for each locality, for the year 1895.

42. Statement of the condition of Trust Companies as shown by report of examinations.

43. Statement showing resources and liabilities of each State Bank before the commencement of business September 1, 1896, being the date of the last call made by the Auditor prior to the date of this report. Also total resources and liabilities of all State Banks as reported under each quarterly call during the past biennial period.

Summary of Receipts and Disbursements of State Treasury.

Fund.	Amount in State Treasury October 1, 1894.	Amount received from October 1, 1894, to September 30, 1896, inclusive.	Amount disbursed from October 1, 1894, to September 30, 1896, inclusive.	Amount in Treasury September 30, 1896.
Revenue	$1,293,173 44	$6,746,067 62	$7,675,511 54	$363,729 52
State School	144,794 04	2,009,011 89	2,135,251 90	18,554 03
Unknown and Minor Heirs	11,334 24		53 71	11,280 53
Aggregate State Funds	$1,449,301 72	$8,755,079 51	$9,810,817 15	$393,564 08
Local Bond Funds	474,160 35	2,763,513 58	2,744,891 88	492,782 05
Totals	$1,923,462 07	$11,518,593 09	$12,555,709 03	$886,346 13

Warrants Drawn on Treasury.

On the first day of October, 1894, there were Treasury warrants outstanding amounting to	$41,562 45
During the two years ending September 30, 1896, 18,893 warrants were drawn on the several funds, aggregating	12,569,753 21
Total	$12,611,315 66
Of the above the State Treasurer paid prior to October 1, 1896	12,555,709 03
Leaving warrants outstanding October 1, 1896	$55,606 63

The warrants drawn may be classified as follows:

Agricultural and Horticultural	$196,653 66
Charitable	3,129,603 45
Canal Commissioners	12,345 00
Commerce, Mining and Labor Statistics	20,738 47
Commission of Claims—expenses and awards paid	2,781 00
Cotton States Exposition	14,995 00
Conveying convicts	78,085 55
Educational	2,894,900 11
Executive	294,812 62
Factory and workshop inspection	26,963 68
Fugitives from justice, and rewards	15,138 84
Fish Commission	21,958 50
Judicial	692,758 02
Legislative	375,256 69
Local Bond Fund	2,741,086 86
Military	711,479 86
Minor Heirs' Fund	53 71
Miscellaneous	135,986 61
Monumental and Lincoln Homestead	33,123 14
Penal and Reformatory	879,117 66
Prevention of cruelty to animals	7,200 00
Public printing and binding, printing paper and stationery, and salary of Printer Expert and assistant	128,153 91
Railroad and Warehouse Commission	45,262 72
State Board of Arbitration	5,850 00
State Board of Equalization	22,295 46
State Board of Health	18,337 81
State Board of Live Stock Commissioners and State Veterinarian	52,255 67
World's Columbian Exposition	12,559 21
Total	$12,569,753 21

Balance of all Funds in State Treasury October 1, 1896.

Trust Funds.		
Local Bond Funds	$492,782 05	
Unknown and Minor Heirs' Fund	11,280 53	
		$504,062 58
State Funds.		
General Revenue Fund	$363,729 52	
State School Fund	18,551 03	
		382,283 55

Estimated Expenses of the State Government from October 1, 1896, to July 1, 1897.

For the pay of members and officers, and expenses of the 40th General Assembly; the Executive Departments, for pay of officers, clerk hire, office expenses, etc., and for the Judicial Department, for salaries of judges and attorneys, and expenses of the Supreme and Appellate Courts	....	$635,499 24
For balance of appropriations to State charitable, educational, penal and reformatory institutions	....	1,519,312 47
For balance of miscellaneous appropriations, including Board of Public Charities, Board of Railroad and Warehouse Commissioners, State Board of Equalization, State Horticultural Society, Historical Society and Natural History Museum, Bureau of Labor Statistics, State Board of Health, Live Stock Commissioners, conveying convicts to and from penitentiary and reformatory, fugitives from justice, Fish Commissioners, Illinois Dairymen's Association, Farmers' County Institutes, and special appropriations	$271,516 52	
For expenses of Illinois National Guard	78,832 20	
		350,348 72
For services and expenses of County Superintendents of Schools, clerk hire and office expenses of State Superintendent of Public Instruction	....	97,282 97
		$2,602,443 40
*The above expenses are payable from funds as follows, viz:		
General Revenue Fund	$2,505,160 43	
State School Fund	97,282 97	
		$2,602,443 40

*See table No. 6 for unexpended balances of existing appropriations.

Assessment and Equalization.

Statements No. 20 and 26 detail the assessments by local assessors for the years 1895 and 1896.

The following tables show the aggregate assessments for those years:

FOR THE YEAR 1895.

	Assessed in Counties by Local Assessors.			Assessed by State Board of Equalization.		Total.
	Personal property.	Lands.	Town and city lots.	Railroads.	Capital stock of corporations.	
Assessed	$130,108,200	$332,738,585	$280,993,368	$79,319,385	$4,782,509	$827,942,047
Equalized	128,742,115	322,171,959	298,172,499	79,319,385	4,782,509	833,188,467

FOR THE YEAR 1896.

	Assessed in Counties by Local Assessors.			Assessed by State Board of Equalization.		Total.
	Personal property.	Lands.	Town and city lots.	Railroads.	Capital stock of corporations.	
Assessed	$121,117,667	$329,914,878	$280,182,943	$78,996,324	$4,030,384	$814,242,196
Equalized	121,639,720	311,050,565	300,962,627	78,996,324	4,030,384	816,679,620

Comparison of the Assessment of Live Stock for the years 1895 and 1896.

Year......	Horses.		Cattle.		Mules and Asses.		Sheep.		Hogs.	
	No.	Assessed value.	No.	Assessed value.	No.	Assess'd value.	No.	Assessed value.	No.	Assess'd value.
1895..	1,169,360	$15,014,342	1,593,755	$10,642,105	97,428	$1,348,815	615,718	$523,614	2,072,922	$2,937,581
1896..	1,112,094	12,599,782	1,547,156	10,036,926	94,066	1,142,860	515,816	410,531	1,823,155	2,294,822

STATE TAXES LEVIED.

The Thirty-ninth General Assembly, by an act to provide the necessary revenue for State purposes, which became a law by limitation June 26, 1895, authorized taxation to raise for general State purposes two millions five hundred thousand dollars on the assessment of 1895, and two millions five hundred thousand dollars on the assessment for the year 1896, and for State school purposes one million dollars on the assessment for each of the years 1895 and 1896. At a subsequent and extraordinary session of the 39th General Assembly an act was passed and approved August 2, 1895, authorizing taxation for an additional sum of five hundred thousand dollars for the year 1895 and a like amount for the year 1896, making the total amount of taxation authorized for general State purposes three million dollars for the year 1895 and three million dollars for the year 1896. The rate per cent. required to produce the amounts thus authorized to be raised were in accordance with the provisions of said acts computed by the Governor and Auditor as follows: On each one hundred dollars of the equalized assessment for the year 1895 for general State purposes thirty-nine cents; for State school purposes thirteen cents; on each one hundred dollars of the equalized assessment for the year 1896 for general State purposes forty-one and one-fourth cents, for State school purposes thirteen and three-fourth cents, thus making the aggregate rate of tax for the year 1895 fifty-two cents and for the year 1896 fifty-five cents.

The Aggregate Amount of Taxes Charged on the Tax Books for the Years 1894 and 1895.

	1894.	1895.
State taxes	$2,615,747 33	$4,375,551 40
County taxes	5,595,129 61	5,745,687 12
Registered bond fund taxes	1,411,119 84	1,279,035 01
City taxes	9,342,373 23	9,695,979 32
District school taxes	13,841,200 55	15,976,235 85
Town, district, etc., taxes	7,935,933 40	10,474,390 67
Totals	$40,741,503 96	$47,546,879 37

The principal of the bonded debt outstanding October 1, 1896, was $18,500. Said amount consists of the following bonds which have been called in by the Governor's proclamation and have ceased to draw interest, but have not been surrendered:

New internal improvement stock	$4,000
New internal improvement interest stock payable after 1877	500
One old internal improvement bond	1,090
Thirteen canal bonds	13,000
Total	$18,500

ILLINOIS CENTRAL RAILROAD FUND—REPORTS OF GROSS RECEIPTS AND PAYMENTS TO THE STATE.

The following figures will show the amount of gross receipts of the Illinois Central Railroad, and the amount of five and seven per cent. thereon, paid into the State Treasury for each six months, beginning with the first report and payment and embracing all subsequent semi-annual reports and payments which have been made by said Company up to the date of this report:

Time.	Gross Receipts.	Per Cent.	Amount paid into the State Treasury.
From March 24, 1855, to October 31, 1855	$595,031 86	5	$29,751 59
For six months ending April 30, 1856	630,580 02	5	31,529 00
" " October 31, 1856	922,053 30	5	46,102 66
" " April 30, 1857	925,386 69	5 and 7	59,196 82
" " October 31, 1857	1,234,986 00	7	86,449 02
" " April 30, 1858	860,796 56	7	60,255 76
" " October 31, 1858	1,024,996 78	7	71,749 77
" " April 30, 1859	830,538 42	7	58,137 68
" " October 31, 1859	1,056,668 35	7	73,966 78
" " April 30, 1860	1,151,608 00	7	80,612 56
" " October 31, 1860	1,384,923 67	7	96,944 66
" " April 30, 1861	1,213,348 00	7	84,934 36
" " October 31, 1861	1,318,906 47	7	92,323 45
" " April 30, 1862	1,063,790 61	7	74,465 34
" " October 31, 1862	1,967,275 18	7	137,709 26
" " April 30, 1863	1,809,068 97	7	126,634 83
" " October 31, 1863	2,482,282 12	7	173,759 75
" " April 30, 1864	2,429,358 23	7	170,055 08
" " October 31, 1864	3,363,699 48	7	235,458 96
" " April 30, 1865	3,436,483 38	7	240,553 84
" " October 31, 1865	3,656,228 56	7	255,936 00
" " April 30, 1866	2,935,738 55	7	205,501 70
" " October 31, 1866	3,165,343 63	7	221,574 05
" " April 30, 1867	2,959,566 99	7	207,169 70
" " October 31, 1867	3,383,400 57	7	236,838 04
" " April 30, 1868	2,780,043 05	7	194,603 01
" " October 31, 1868	3,339,921 01	7	233,794 47
" " April 30, 1869	2,999,196 41	7	209,943 75
" " October 31, 1869	3,642,708 06	7	254,989 56
" " April 30, 1870	3,068,850 81	7	214,819 56
" " October 31, 1870	3,568,070 85	7	249,764 96
" " April 30, 1871	3,026,072 73	7	211,825 09
" " October 31, 1871	3,595,540 32	7	251,687 82
" " April 30, 1872	3,158,597 62	7	221,101 83
" " October 31, 1872	3,167,924 49	7	221,754 71
" " April 30, 1873	2,932,653 13	7	205,285 72
" " October 31, 1873	3,189,882 63	7	223,288 28
" " April 30, 1874	2,535,046 43	7	177,453 25
" " October 31, 1874	3,098,760 13	7	216,913 21
" " April 30, 1875	2,575,133 82	7	180,259 37
" " October 31, 1875	2,792,952 20	7	195,506 65
" " April 30, 1876	2,519,443 07	7	176,361 01
" " October 31, 1876	2,566,351 07	7	179,644 57
" " April 30, 1877	1,996,359 60	7	139,745 17
" " October 31, 1877	2,522,953 86	7	176,606 77
" " April 30, 1878	2,160,421 90	7	151,229 54
" " October 31, 1878	2,417,773 81	7	169,202 17

Statement—Concluded.

Time.		Gross Receipts.	Per Cent.	Amount paid into the State Treasury.
For six months ending	April 30, 1879	$2,137,648 88	7	$149,635 42
" "	October 31, 1879	2,512,028 08	7	175,841 96
" "	April 30, 1880	2,368,395 46	7	165,787 68
" "	October 31, 1880	2,893,728 27	7	202,560 98
" "	April 30, 1881	2,517,346 22	7	176,214 24
" "	October 31, 1881	2,976,689 73	7	208,368 28
" "	April 30, 1882	2,681,463 17	7	187,702 42
" "	October 31, 1882	2,976,195 60	7	208,333 69
" "	April 30, 1883	2,601,497 13	7	182,104 80
" "	October 31, 1883	2,951,977 00	7	206,638 39
" "	April 30, 1884	2,458,148 86	7	172,070 42
" "	October 31, 1884	2,637,274 35	7	184,609 20
" "	April 30, 1885	2,491,886 22	7	174,432 03
" "	October 31, 1885	2,762,241 28	7	193,356 89
" "	April 30, 1886	2,468,711 57	7	172,809 81
" "	October 31, 1886	2,941,495 56	7	205,904 69
" "	April 30, 1887	2,720,148 23	7	190,410 38
" "	October 31, 1887	3,199,488 47	7	223,964 19
" "	April 30, 1888	2,816,877 41	7	191,181 41
" "	October 31, 1888	3,253,921 12	7	227,774 48
" "	April 30, 1889	3,013,271 90	7	210,929 03
" "	October 31, 1889	3,561,651 68	7	249,315 62
" "	April 30, 1890	3,272,311 40	7	229,061 80
" "	October 31, 1890	3,674,561 85	7	257,219 33
" "	April 30, 1891	3,647,096 62	7	255,296 76
" "	October 31, 1891	4,038,698 75	7	282,708 91
" "	April 30, 1892	3,967,543 71	7	277,728 06
" "	October 31, 1892	4,453,685 09	7	311,757 96
" "	April 30, 1893	4,327,012 90	7	302,890 90
" "	October 31, 1893	6,431,090 53	7	450,176 34
" "	April 30, 1894	3,959,747 87	7	277,182 35
" "	October 31, 1894	3,953,273 36	7	276,729 14
" "	April 30, 1895	4,238,911 18	7	296,723 26
" "	October 31, 1895	4,565,681 83	7	*318,264 39
" "	April 30, 1896	4,541,521 02	7	†317,600 91
Total amount paid State				$15,726,677 25

* Less $1,333.33, being 4 per cent. on $250,000, from Oct. 15 to Dec. 2, 1895, inclusive, advanced to State.

† Less $305.56, being 5 per cent. on $200,000, for 11 days advanced to State.

BONDS REGISTERED IN AUDITOR'S OFFICE UNDER ACTS OF APRIL 16, 1869, FEB. 13, 1865, APRIL 27, 1877, JUNE 4, 1979, AND JUNE 27, 1885.

Bonds registered under act of 1869, outstanding September 30, 1896.	....	$2,713,817 15
Apportioned as follows:		
Sixteen counties	$1,289,700 00	
Fifty-seven townships	1,266,717 15	
Seven cities	127,300 00	
Four incorporated towns	30,100 00	
*Bonds registered under original act of 1865, outstanding September 30, 1896—Four cities	....	912,625 40
Bonds registered under act of 1865, as amended by the acts of April 27, 1877, and June 4, 1879, outstanding September 30, 1896	....	9,210,862 00
Apportioned as follows;		
Twenty-six counties	$3,175,350 00	
Ninety-six townships	2,889,490 53	
Twenty-four cities	2,981,921 47	
Ten incorporated towns	132,100 00	
Three school districts	32,000 00	
Drainage district bonds registered under the act of June 27, 1885, outstanding September 30, 1896	....	469,300 00
Total	....	$13,306,604 55
Of the foregoing .... $479,000 00 bear 4 per cent. interest.		
" " .... 907,000 00 " $4\frac{1}{2}$ " "		
" " .... 3,636,400 00 " 5 " "		
" " .... 30,000 00 " $5\frac{1}{4}$ " "		
" " .... 72,000 00 " $5\frac{1}{2}$ " "		
" " .... 5,267,037 40 " 6 " "		
" " .... 874,150 00 " 7 " "		
" " .... 7,590 00 " $7\frac{3}{10}$ " "		
" " .... 793,800 00 " 8 " "		
" " .... 1,239,717 15 " 10 " "		
The average rate of interest being 6.11 per cent.		
Bonds registered under the drainage and levee law of April 9, 1872.	....	$648,500 00
(The Supreme Court has held that the law of April 9, 1872, under which these bonds were issued, is in violation of the State constitution. See Table No. 38.)		

*** Note—Bonds which were registered under the act of 1865, and have been re-registered under the act of 1869, remaining in Table No. 35, viz.:**

City of Quincy	$121,000 00
" Galena	57,000 00
" Warsaw	14,900 00
Total	$192,900 00

TRUST COMPANIES.

There are now nine trust companies operating in this State, which have qualified by making the deposit with the Auditor of Public Accounts, in accordance with the requirements of "An act to provide for and regulate the administration of trusts by trust companies," approved June 17, 1887, as amended by an act approved June 1, 1889, and are competent to act as trustee, receiver, assignee, guardian, conservator, executor or administrator. They are as follows:

Chicago Title and Trust Company, Chicago.
Illinois Trust and Savings Bank, Chicago.
The American Trust and Savings Bank, Chicago.
The Equitable Trust Company, Chicago.
The Northern Trust Company, Chicago.
Title Guarantee and Trust Company, Chicago.
State Bank of Chicago, Chicago.
Royal Trust Company, Chicago.
Security Title and Trust Company, Chicago.

The two last named companies have qualified for business during the past two years, since our last report.

Annual reports have been filed in this office and abstracts of same have been published as required by law. The annual examinations, conducted by this department, have shown these companies all to be in satisfactory condition and their affairs to be conducted in accordance with the requirements of the trust act, under which they are operating.

In Statement No. 42 will be found table giving more complete information as to the results of such examinations.

BANKING CORPORATIONS.

Statement 43, appended to this report, shows a list of the banking corporations now doing business, which are organized under the Act of 1887, governing corporations with banking powers, together with a statement of their condition on September 1, 1896.

The previous good reputation of banks organized under the laws of this State has been fully sustained, no bank having suspended its business with the loss of a dollar to its depositors, and but one bank having suspended, namely: Central Trust and Savings Bank of Chicago. We desire to repeat and emphasize the necessity of the enactment of proper legislation, as set out in our last report. The legislation believed to be necessary is set forth as follows:

1. That a minimum reserve, below which a bank shall not allow its available cash to fall, be required, at least one-third of which shall be on hand in current funds, and the remainder with banks approved by the Auditor as reserve agents.

2. That dividends shall not be declared until all expenses, losses, interest, taxes and other legitimate charges are first provided for.

3. That a surplus fund which shall equal twenty per per cent. of the capital shall be created by setting aside from the net earnings annually at least one-tenth part thereof until such amount of surplus shall have been accumulated.

4. That directors shall have a stock qualification, owning at least ten shares of the bank's capital stock.

5. That a limit be placed upon the amount which a bank may loan on real estate security, restricting same to a certain per cent. of the capital, and that the power to loan on real estate located outside of this State be duly restricted.

6. That banks shall not loan on their own stock, nor be permitted to invest their funds in the stock of any other bank or corporation or employ its moneys in trade or commerce.

7. That directors be required to give personal attention to the affairs of the bank, and that in addition to the cashier's affidavit to quarterly statements, at least three directors be required to attest same.

8. That no officer or employè of a bank be permitted to borrow funds without first obtaining the consent of the board of directors.

9. That adequate penalties be provided in case of failure to comply with any of the requirements of the law or for refusal to submit to inspection, or to disclose any obtainable information concerning their affairs called for by the Auditor, or to amend irregular or unsafe methods after due notice from said Auditor.

10. That a failure to organize for one year after a permit is granted shall work a forfeiture of such permit and leave the name of the bank free to be taken by other applicants.

11. That all information resulting from examinations of banks be required to be kept secret by all examiners and persons connected with or about the work of supervision, except in so far as their public duty shall require them to report upon or take official action regarding the affairs of same.

12. That in case of insolvency or a failure to make good an impairment of the capital after due notice, the Auditor be authorized to take possession of the bank and keep the same in custody until a receiver shall be appointed by the court.

AWARDS OF COMMISSION OF CLAIMS.

Section 5 of "An Act to create a Commission of Claims and prescribe its powers and duties," approved May 29, 1887, as amended by act approved June 3, 1889, provides that the Auditor shall submit with his biennial report a statement of the awards of said commission.

Since the date of the last report awards have been made by the commission as follows, viz.:

On the 24th day of January, 1895, an award was made in favor of Patrick R. Bannon, claimant against the State of Illinois for the sum of twenty-one hundred dollars, the same being for damages to property caused by overflow of the waters of the Illinois and Michigan Canal at Joliet; and the further sum of one hundred and fifty-eight dollars and eighty-five cents costs of suit.

On the same day an award was made to John Scanlan against the State of Illinois for the sum of seven hundred and fifty dollars and costs, the same being for injuries received by falling down an elevator shaft at armory, at No. 23 Lake street, Chicago, while a member of Company H, 7th Regiment, Illinois National Guard.

On the 29th day of January, 1896, an award was made to Frederick Klor against the State of Illinois for the sum of one thousand five hundred dollars for damages on account of destruction of crops and fences by Illinois troops at Camp Butler during 1861.

Respectfully submitted,

DAVID GORE,
Auditor of Public Accounts.

No. 1.

Statement of Receipts and Disbursements of the General Revenue Fund from October 1, 1894, to September 30, 1896, inclusive.

GENERAL REVENUE FUND.	Amount.
RECEIPTS.	
From taxes, 1893	$54,640 09
From taxes, 1894	1,479,102 57
From taxes, 1895	2,918,103 30
From 7 per cent on gross receipts of Illinois Central Railroad for six months ending October 31, 1894	276,729 14
From 7 per cent on gross receipts of Illinois Central Railroad for six months ending April 30, 1895	296,723 78
From 7 per cent on gross receipts of Illinois Central Railroad for six months ending October 31, 1895	318,264 39
From 7 per cent on gross receipts of Illinois Central Railroad for six months ending April 30, 1896	317,600 91
From John P. Altgeld, Governor of Illinois, being amount received by him from the U. S. Government in aid of the Soldiers and Sailors' Home from October 1, 1894, to June 30, 1896, inclusive	239,075 00
From W. H. Hinrichsen, Secretary of State, fees collected by him from April 1, 1894, to March 31, 1896, inclusive	195,134 87
From W. H. Hinrichsen, Secretary of State, being amount received for rent of house on Monroe street, belonging to State, from April 1, 1894, to March 31, 1896, inclusive	735 00
From David Gore, Auditor of Public Accounts, being fees collected by him from October 1, 1894, to March 31, 1896, inclusive	773 90
From B. K. Durfee, Superintendent of Insurance, being fees collected by him from July 20, 1893, to December 31, 1895, inclusive	328,475 42
From the United States Government for endowment and support of colleges for the benefit of agriculture and mechanical arts, Act of Congress approved August 30, 1890, from October 1, 1894, to September 30, 1896, inclusive	43,000 00
From Marcia Louise Gould, being proceeds of sale of furniture, etc., by Illinois Women's Exposition Board	42 50
From H. E. Billings, being amount of overpayment to McDonough County Farmers' County Institute	24 40
From M. H. Gollon, being amount realized from sale of land in Peoria county	2,746 56
From Dr. A. M. Miller, Superintendent of asylum for feeble-minded children, being amount of unexpended balance of appropriation	12,373 55
From Louis H. Holmes, Treasurer Illinois Charitable Eye and Ear Infirmary, being amount of unexpended balance of appropriation	2,750 11
From Philip Freiler, Treasurer Northern Hospital for Insane, being amount of unexpended balance of appropriation	23,555 77
From M. V. Eaves, Treasurer Southern Hospital for Insane, being amount of unexpended balance of appropriation	81,299 36
From M. F. Dunlap, Treasurer Central Hospital for Insane, being amount of unexpended balance of appropriation	51,900 59
From B. P. McDaniel, Acting Superintendent of Illinois Soldiers and Sailors' Home, being amount of unexpended balance of appropriation	13,073 68
From A. J. Barr, Treasurer Illinois Soldiers' Orphans' Home, being amount of unexpended balance of appropriation	16,218 92
From Wm. K. Ackerman, Treasurer Home for Juvenile Female Offenders, being amount of unexpended balance of appropriation	16,000 00
From W. V. Choisser and E. C. Kramer, Trustees of Illinois Asylum for Insane Criminals, being amount of unexpended balance of appropriation	4,546 20
From Hendrick V. Fisher, being purchase money for E. ½ N. W. ¼ Sec. 11, T. 18 N. R. 3 E. of 4th P. M.	560 00
From Chas. P. Burton, being amount of salary as janitor for President *pro tem.* of Senate 39th General Assembly, turned back into treasury	210 00
From John N. Welch, Treasurer Canal Commissioners, being fees from Illinois and Michigan Canal	50,000 00
From R. H. H. Hampton, being purchase money for S. W. ¼ S. E. ¼, Sec. 2, T. 9 S., R. 1 E., 3d P. M.	600 00
From George Schilling, Secretary, etc., being fees collected by State Board of Examiners	807 62
Amount carried foward	$6,745,067 63

No. 1—Continued.

GENERAL REVENUE FUND.		Amount.
Amount brought forward		$6,745,067 63
From J. E. Craine, Treasurer, etc., being fees collected from candidates examined for mine managers		685 00
From David Gore, Auditor of Public Accounts, being amount refunded on warrant No. 17620, account overdrawn		01
From W. E. Peabody, Treasurer of Christian county, being amount of inheritance tax from the estate of Robert B. Berriman, deceased		314 98
Total amount received		$6,746,067 62
DISBURSEMENTS.		
Amount of Revenue Fund warrants issued for all purposes (see Statement No. 3)	$7,693,368 05	
Amount of Revenue Fund warrants outstanding October 1, 1894	33,192 43	
Total	$7,726,560 48	
Amount of Revenue Fund warrants outstanding October 1, 1896	51,048 94	
		7,777,609 42
Excess of disbursements over receipts		$1,031,541 80

No. 2.

Statement of Receipts and Disbursements of Special State Funds from October 1, 1894, to September 30, 1896, inclusive.

STATE SCHOOL FUND.		Amount.
RECEIPTS.		
From taxes, 1893		$36,918 96
From taxes, 1894		999,392 57
From taxes, 1895		972,700 36
Total amount received		$2,009,011 89
DISBURSEMENTS.		
Amount paid for salary, Superintendent of Public Instruction	$7,875 00	
Amount paid for clerk hire, janitor, porter, etc., in office of Superintendent of Public Instruction	8,925 00	
Amount paid for refurnishing office and library of Superintendent of Public Instruction	83 10	
Amount paid for office expenses, including stationery, etc., of Superintendent of Public Instruction	3,270 62	
Amount of "School Tax Fund orders" for 1894 and 1895, paid counties	1,750,201 00	
Amount of "School Tax Fund interest orders" for 1894 and 1895, paid counties	113,874 62	
Amount paid County Superintendents of Schools for services and expenses	251,015 25	
Amount of School Fund warrants outstanding October 1, 1894	4,565 00	
Total	$2,139,809 59	
Amount of School Fund warrants outstanding October 1, 1896	4,557 69	
Total amount disbursed by Treasurer		2,135,251 90
Excess of disbursements over receipts		$126,240 01

No. 3.

Detailed Statement of Warrants drawn on State Treasury from October 1, 1894, to September 30, 1896, inclusive.

ACCOUNTS.	App.	Amount.	Total.
APPROPRIATIONS—SPECIAL.			
Samuel Warren— Damages for physical injuries received while stopping a runaway elevator in the State capitol at Springfield, Illinois, in February, 1893, in which elevator were three small children unattended....	1895	$3,000 00	
Clarence P. Johnson.. Balance of salary due him as former secretary of State Board of Live Stock Commissioners for six months ending June 30, 1893, and awarded him by the Commission of Claims........................	"	200 00	
Mark Clark— Damages for physical injuries received on account of the explosion or blowing out of a steam valve in the Institution for the Blind, at Jacksonville, Illinois, in the month of November, 1894..........	"	1,000 00	
George Hunt, Attorney, Etc.— Damages for physical injuries received by John Scanlan, who, while in the line of duty as a soldier of Company H, 7th Regiment, Illinois National Guard, on the night of October 3, 1893, fell down an open elevator shaft in a dark hall at the Armory of said regiment, at No. 23 Lake street, Chicago, as awarded him by the Commission of Claims....	"	750 00	
William E. Henry— Relief on account of the loss of a part of one foot and other permanent and serious injuries received while in the discharge of his duties as corporal of Company A, 3d Regiment, Illinois National Guard.	"	2,500 00	
Patrick R. Bannon— Damages and costs in full sustained by him as owner of certain real estate and property overflowed by waters gathered from a dam constructed by the Canal Commissioners of Illinois, awarded by the Commission of Claims	"	2,258 85	
J. A. Cowlin— Damages for injury sustained by him while in actual service as member of Company G, 3d Regiment, Illinois National Guard, at the World's Fair, August 24, 1893, which caused the amputation of one of his legs..................................	"	2,500 00	
E. B. Whennan (should be E. B. Sherman)— Taking testimony as master-in-chancery in the cause of the People of the State of Illinois vs. Illinois Central Railroad Company, as directed by the Supreme Court of the United States...........	"	387 20	
John R. O'Connor— Taking testimony as stenographer in the case of the People of the State of Illinois vs. Elizabeth Cooling, et al..	"	800 00	
C. C. Walker (should be C. E. Walker)— Taking testimony as stenographer in the case of the People of the State of Illinois vs. Continental Investment and Loan Society	"	600 00	
Amount carried forward..		$13,996 05	

Statement 3—Continued.

Accounts.	App.	Amount.	Total.
Amount brought forward	....	$13,996 05	
APPROPRIATIONS—SPECIAL—*Continued.*			
Charles Mills Rogers (should be George Mills Rogers)— Taking testimony as master-in-chancy in the case of the People of the State of Illinois vs. Elizabeth Cooling, et al.	1895	450 00	
Thomas Taylor, Jr.— Taking testimony as master-in-chancery in the case of the People of the State of Illinois vs. Continental Investment and Loan Society	"	600 00	
Charles Fetzer, City Treasurer— Amount paid by the city of Springfield for paving the east side of Fifth street, in front of the State Arsenal, in part as per account filed in the Auditor's office	"	288 60	
Edward L. Merritt— Balance due him as member of committee, 38th General Assembly, for services rendered under a joint resolution of the 38th General Assembly	"	25 40	
Joseph W. Drury— Balance due him as member of committee, 38th General Assembly, for services rendered under a joint resolution of the 38th General Assembly	"	25 40	
Mary, Hiram, Ada, William, Darwin and Marquis McLaughlin, heirs at law of L. W. McLaughlin, deceased— Damages on account of overflow of lands by water caused by the Copperas Creek dam, in full satisfaction of all matters claimed by said claimants in their statement before the Commission of Claims, at its session of 1892	"	400 00	
Greely-Carleson Company, Surveyors— Cost incurred in the case of the People, *ex rel.* Attorney General vs. Lincoln Park Commissioners *et al.*, for survey of the inner breakwater between Oak and Pearson streets, Chicago, making plat showing same, also shore lines of 1883 and 1888, calculations, etc	"	75 00	
Triebel & Sons— For the erection of a suitable monument to the memory of Thomas Ford, late Governor of the State of Illinois, and for securing from the authorities of the cemetery where the grave is located the attentions provided for by the rules of said cemetery association	"	1,200 00	$17,060 45
APPROPRIATIONS—GENERAL.			
CANAL COMMISSIONERS.			
Alt Gerdes, commissioner, per diem	1893.	$2,285 00	
John M. Welch, " "	"	2,285 00	
W. A. S. Graham, " "	"	2,285 00	
Alt Gerdes, " "	1895.	1,830 00	
John M. Welch, " "	"	1,830 00	
W. A. S. Graham, " "	"	155 00	
Thomas H. Cannon, " "	"	1,675 00	12,345 00
To amount paid from appropriation of 1893.... $6,855 00			
" " " 1895.... 5,490 00			
COMMISSION OF CLAIMS.			
William H. Dawdy, member of commission— 30 days' per diem, session of 1894	1893.	$450 00	
Henry G. Reeves, member of commission— 30 days' per diem, session of 1894	"	450 00	
Samuel Alschuler, member of commission— 30 days' per diem, session of 1894	"	450 00	
Fred. E. Whitmer, bailiff— 23 days' per diem, session of 1894	"	69 00	
Amounts carried forward	....	$1,419 00	$29,405 45

Statement 3—Contiinued.

Accounts.	App.	Amount.	Total.
Amounts brought forward	....	$1,419 00	$29,405 45
COMMISSION OF CLAIMS—*Continued.*			
William H. Dawdy, member of commission—30 days' per diem, sessions of 1895 and 1896	1895.	450 00	
Henry G. Reeves, member of commission—30 days' per diem, sessions of 1895 and 1896	"	450 00	
Samuel Alschuler, member of commission—27 days' per diem, sessions of 1895 and 1896	"	405 00	
Fred. E. Whitmer, bailiff—19 days' per diem, sessions of 1895 and 1896	"	57 00	
To amount paid from appropriation of 1893.... $1,419 00 " " " 1895.... 1,362 00			2,781 00
COMMISSION TO MARK POSITION OF ILLINOIS TROOPS AT CHICKAMAUGA, ETC.			
John B. Turchin—Traveling expenses, etc., as commissioner to mark position of troops	1893.	$67 00	
H. E. Rives—Traveling expenses, etc., as commissioner to mark position of troops	"	35 53	
Smith D. Atkins—Traveling expenses, etc., as commissioner to mark position of troops	"	77 39	
E. A. Blodgett—Traveling expenses, etc., as commissioner to mark position of troops	"	45 25	
W. E. Carlin—Traveling expenses, etc., as commissioner to mark position of troops	"	42 50	
J. G. Everest—Traveling expenses, etc., as commissioner to mark position of troops	"	32 45	
Edgar D. Swain—Traveling expenses, etc., as commissioner to mark position of troops	"	48 75	
James A. Connolly—Traveling expenses, etc., as commissioner to mark position of troops	"	46 10	
First National Bank—Monuments and markers furnished by The Culver Stone Company for marking the positions of the several commands of Illinois Volunteers engaged in the battles of Chickamauga, Georgia; Lookout Mountain and Missionary Ridge, Tennessee	1895.	18,500 00	
The Culver Stone Company—Monuments and markers furnished for marking the positions of the several commands of Illinois Volunteers engaged in the battles of Chickamauga, Georgia; Lookout Mountain and Missionary Ridge, Tennessee	"	5,247 04	
To amount paid from appropriation of 1893.... $394 97 " " " 1895.... 23,747 04			24,142 01
COMMISSIONERS OF LABOR STATISTICS.			
George A. Schilling, Secretary—Salary	1893	$1,875 00	
Amount paid for current expenses of the Board of Commissioners of Labor, as per vouchers rendered, viz.:			
For clerical services	"	3,088 77	
For postage	"	141 00	
For expressage	"	63 87	
For janitor	"	35 00	
For special work on tax report	"	55 30	
For traveling expenses, etc., Secretary	"	114 90	
For traveling expenses, etc., Charles F. Seib, Clerk	"	172 00	
Amounts carried forward	....	$5,545 84	$56,328 46

Statement 3—Continued.

Accounts.	App.	Amount.	Total.
Amounts brought forward	....	$5,545 84	$56,328 46
COMMISSIONERS OF LABOR STATISTICS—*Continued.*			
George A. Schilling, Secretary—			
For traveling expenses, etc., Gertrude Green, Clerk.	1893	28 00	
For traveling expenses, etc., Catherine Fitzgerald, Clerk	"	28 00	
For extra clerical services of Marian Hamilton	"	25 00	
For special investigations and work by John Ehlert, Agent	"	118 00	
For special investigations and work by M. V. Smith, Agent	"	68 50	
For special investigations and work by Mary O'Hara, Agent	"	13 00	
For special investigations and work by J. M. Craine, Agent	"	33 33	
For special investigations by Weigley's Real Estate Ownership Co	"	625 00	
For special investigations by Chicago Index Co	"	1 06	
For per diem as Commissioner, to C. G. Stiver	"	50 00	
For per diem as Commissioner, to W. E. R. Kell	"	50 00	
For miscellaneous office expenses, including telephone rental, repairs, books, newspapers, stationery, furniture, binding reports, printing blanks, etc	"	143 42	
George A. Schilling, Secretary—			
Salary	1895	2,500 00	
Amount paid for current expenses of the Board of Commissioners of Labor, as per vouchers rendered, viz.:			
For clerical services	"	5,424 50	
For postage	"	683 75	
For expressage	"	1,025 78	
For janitor	"	184 00	
For traveling expenses, Secretary, etc	"	331 58	
For expenses of Charles F. Seib, in Chicago	"	23 00	
For extra clerical services of Charles F. Seib	"	100 00	
" " J. D. Roper	"	50 00	
" " Marian Hamilton	"	50 00	
" " Carrie Johnson	"	14 00	
For amount paid Chas. J. Riefler, for reading proof of 8th Biennial Report	"	90 00	
For special investigations and work by Chicago Index Co	"	151 44	
For special investigations and work by James Malcolm	"	176 64	
For special investigations and work by M. V. Smith	"	27 50	
For special investigations and work by Clinton B. Evans	"	40 00	
For special investigations and work by Louis F. Post	"	500 00	
For special investigations and work by Gertrude Green	"	18 00	
For special investigations and work by J. G. Vehe.	"	25 00	
For special investigations and work by F. L. Conroy	"	25 00	
For special investigations and work by Felix L. Senff	"	351 95	
For special investigations and work by John Ehlert	"	110 50	
For special investigations and work by W. G. Eggleston	"	50 00	
For special investigations and work by Mabel Gray	"	4 00	
For special investigations and work by A. L. Green	"	20 00	
For special investigations and work by George Strebel	"	60 00	
For per diem as Commissioner, to J. C. Lutz	"	63 40	
" " W. E. R. Kell	"	210 14	
" " C. G. Stiver	"	210 50	
" " Louis F. Lumaghi	"	157 45	
Amounts carried forward:	....	$19,407 28	$56,328 46

Statement 3—Continued.

Accounts.	App.	Amount.	Total.
Amounts brought forward	....	$19,407 28	$56,328 46
COMMISSIONERS OF LABOR STATISTICS—*Continued*,			
George A. Schilling, Secretary— For miscellaneous office expenses, including telephone rental, repairs, books, newspapers, stationery, furniture, binding reports, printing blanks, etc	1895	1,331 19	
To amount paid from appropriation of 1893.... $6,729 15 " " " 1895.... 14,009 32			20,738 47
COMMISSIONERS OF PUBLIC CHARITIES.			
Boerne Bettman— Expenses as commissioner	1893	$140 50	
George W. Curtis— Expenses as commissioner	"	109 13	
James McNabb— Expenses as commissioner	"	144 78	
D. W. Andrews— Expenses as commissioner	"	221 00	
Julia C. Lathrop— Expenses as commissioner	"	92 24	
George F. Miner— Salary as Secretary	"	1,250 00	
George F. Miner, Secretary— Amount paid for office expenses, express, telegrams, etc	"	358 06	
George F. Miner, Secretary— Amount paid for traveling expenses	"	50 58	
George F. Miner, Secretary— Amounts paid as follows, viz.: C. E. Gilpin, assistant on biennial report.. $87 50 E. McLaughlin, assistant in office.......... 152 10 Assistant in office.......... 68 75 Mary L. Rogers, stenographer.......... 25 00	"	333 35	
Arthur R. Reynolds— Expenses as commissioner	1895	83 70	
George W. Curtis— Expenses as commissioner	"	475 37	
James McNabb— Expenses as commissioner	"	236 17	
D. W. Andrews— Expenses as commissioner	"	16 88	
Julia C. Lathrop— Expenses as commissioner	"	426 74	
Henry Wulff, State Treasurer— Amount paid Arthur R. Reynolds for expenses as commissioner.......... $102 00 Amount paid Julia C. Lathrop, for expenses as commissioner.......... 150 00	"	252 00	
Annie R. Sheridan— Two weeks services assisting on report	"	25 00	
H. A. Rice, M. D.— Tabulating records of Cook County Insane Asylum and work on poor-house record	"	50 00	
R. E. Todd— Work on schedules and traveling expenses incurred	"	37 25	
H. H. Hart, General Secretary, etc.— 100 copies, Report of National Conference of Charities and Corrections, 1895, furnished	"	112 50	
The Johns Hopkins Press— Reports of International Congress of Charities and Corrections, and volumes on Hospitals	"	31 50	
George F. Miner— Salary as Secretary	"	3,500 00	
Mary L. Rogers— Salary of Assistant Secretary	"	1,050 00	
Amounts carried forward	....	$8,996 75	$77,066 93

Statement 3—Continued.

Accounts.	App.	Amount.	Total
Amounts brought forward	....	$8,996 75	$77,066 93
COMMISSIONERS OF PUBLIC CHARITIES—*Continued.*			
George F. Miner, Secretary— Amount paid for office expenses, including express charges, telegrams, telephone, janitor, etc.	1895	453 43	
George F. Miner, Secretary— Amount paid for traveling expenses incurred	"	229 04	
George F. Miner, Secretary— Expense incurred completing census of counties, conference and office expenses	"	521 42	10,200 64
To amount paid from appropriation of 1893.... $2,699 64 " " " 1895.... 7,501 00			
CONTINGENT FUND OF GOVERNOR.			
William F. Dose— Incidental expenses incurred as Private Secretary of Governor	1893	$50 00	
Benjamin Rosenberg— Investigation of values of school leases and furnishing information in regard to value of other leases, etc	"	75 00	
R. M. Ridgely, Postmaster— Amount due for postage stamps furnished Governor's office	"	30 00	
William H. Colvin— Cash paid for securing valuations and evidence in relation to value of certain school properties, in Chicago	"	240 00	
George F. Miner, Secretary— Expenses incurred by Commissioners of Public Charities investigating State Home for Juvenile Female Offenders	"	228 95	
Western Union Telegraph Co.— Time service and telegrams furnished Governor's office	"	23 44	
Postal Telegraph Cable Co.— Telegraphic services rendered Governor's office	"	2 95	
The Citizen's Newspaper Co.— Two years subscription to Governor's office	"	4 00	
Willett and Pashley— Professional services as architects in visiting Anna and preparing estimates, etc., for reconstruction of buildings of Southern Insane Hospital, destroyed by fire	"	150 00	
John M. Striffler— Amount due for ice furnished Governor's office	"	8 25	
Henry Abels— Balance due on typewriter furnished Governor's office	"	50 00	
E. A. Richardson— Attorney fees; investigating troubles at Danville	"	25 00	
John P. Altgeld, Governor— Traveling expenses, etc., at Milwaukee, Atlanta, etc., in discharge of official duties for the State of Illinois	1895	169 00	
Alzina P. Stevens— Expenses as assistant Inspector of Factories and Workshops, during trip east in line of duty, investigating, etc	"	54 60	
J. P. Lindsey, Agent— 1,000 mile railroad ticket furnished L. B. Larmoor by Chicago and Alton Railroad Co	"	25 00	
L. B. Larmoor— Salary as Superintendent and Inspector of Eastern Normal School and other buildings, $47.25; moneys expended in revising Eastern Normal plans for building, $271.55	"	318 80	
Amounts carried foward	....	$1,454 99	$87,267 57

Statement 3—Continued.

Accounts.	App.	Amount.	Total.
Amounts brought foward	....	$1,454 99	$87,267 57
CONTINGENT FUND OF GOVERNOR—*Concluded.*			
L. B. Larmoor— Per diem, $249.42; expenses, $72.35; revising Eastern Normal plans for building	1895	$321 77	
Harry H. Weatherwax— Per diem, $30,00; expenses, $22.50; as Architect and Draughtsman, Illinois University Building	"	52 50	
L. S. Anderson— 5 copies, photo of Eastern Normal School Building	"	10 00	
George F. Miner— Services rendered at Quincy, at instance of Governor	"	19 51	
Volney Hickox— Attendance as stenographer, Illinois State Farmers' Institute, January 7, 8, 9, 1896, and making transcript of 40,000 words	"	100 00	
C. S. Darrow, Attorney— Expenses at Springfield, $50.00; payment for printing briefs, $25.00; and Stenographer, $25.00—in the matter of the appointment of justices of the peace in the City of Chicago	"	100 00	
Elmer Allen Kimball— Investigations and examinations relating to public maters of the State of Illinois	"	1,735 00	
Ridgely National Bank— Services rendered by W. G. Eggleston in investigations of matters of the State of Illinois	"	40 00	
L. and P. Trumbull— Legal services rendered the State of Illinois in suit in Circuit Court of Cook County	"	200 00	
Rosenthal, Kurtz and Hirschl— Legal services rendered the State of Illinois as assistants to L. and P. Trumbull, in suits of State	"	50 00	
To amount paid from appropriation of 1893.... $887 59 To amount paid from appropriation of 1895.... 3,196 18			4,083 77
CONVEYING CONVICTS TO PENITENTIARY.			
Sheriff of Adams county for conveying 9 convicts	1893	$352 35	
" Alexander " " 5 "	"	149 80	
" Carroll " " 4 "	"	91 50	
" Cass " " 1 "	"	44 50	
" Champaign " " 7 "	"	178 35	
" Clinton " " 1 "	"	21 50	
" Coles " " 5 "	"	165 90	
" Cook " " 129 "	"	500.50	
" DeKalb " " 6 "	"	67 60	
" DeWitt " " 2 "	"	45 60	
" Douglas " " 2 "	"	72 00	
" DuPage " " 3 "	"	23 40	
" Edgar " " 4 "	"	96 60	
" Effingham " " 3 "	"	79 95	
" Franklin " " 2 "	"	24 40	
" Grundy " " 1 "	"	6 00	
" Hamilton " " 3 "	"	48 50	
" Hancock " " 4 "	"	123 60	
" Hardin " " 1 "	"	36 25	
" Henry " " 1 "	"	33 25	
" Jackson " " 11 "	"	83 25	
" Jasper " " 4 "	"	87 60	
" Jefferson " " 7 "	"	81 25	
" Jersey " " 8 "	"	198 00	
" Jo Daviess " " 2 "	"	65 20	
" Johnson " " 4 "	"	61 80	
" Kane " " 11 "	"	68 15	
" Kankakee " " 5 "	"	42 50	
" Kendall " " 2 "	"	12 40	
" Knox " " 9 "	"	185 90	
" Lake " " 3 "	"	46 15	
" La Salle " " 6 "	"	50 60	
Amounts carried forward	....	$3,144 35	$91,351 34

Statement 3—Continued.

Accounts.	App.	Amount.	Total.
Amounts brought forward	....	$3,144 35	$91,351 34
CONVEYING CONVICTS TO PENITENTIARY—*Continued.*			
Sheriff of Lee county for conveying 3 convicts	1893	57 20	
" Livingston " " 1 "	"	14 25	
" Macon " " 20 "	"	519 75	
" Macoupin " " 3 "	"	88 40	
" Madison " " 26 "	"	521 75	
" Mason " " 1 "	"	37 50	
" Massac " " 4 "	"	67 80	
" McDonough " " 5 "	"	128 10	
" McLean " " 13 "	"	259 35	
" Menard " " 3 "	"	76 00	
" Monroe " " 2 "	"	29 50	
" Montgomery " " 2 "	"	55 60	
" Morgan " " 4 "	"	137 60	
" Moultrie " " 1 "	"	39 50	
" Ogle " " 1 "	"	40 50	
" Peoria " " 12 "	"	179 20	
" Pike " " 6 "	"	243 60	
" Pope " " 4 "	"	94 80	
" Pulaski " " 3 "	"	74 10	
" Randolph " " 1 "	"	50	
" Richland " " 2 "	"	52 40	
" Rock Island " " 3 "	"	71 50	
" Sangamon " " 17 "	"	487 50	
" Scott " " 1 "	"	40 75	
" Shelby " " 1 "	"	36 50	
" St. Clair " " 20 "	"	302 40	
" Stephenson " " 2 "	"	44 80	
" Tazewell " " 5 "	"	102 00	
" Union " " 3 "	"	50 80	
" Vermilion " " 6 "	"	143 75	
" Wabash " " 3 "	"	68 00	
" Warren " " 5 "	"	111 30	
" Washington " " 1 "	"	21 40	
" Whiteside " " 11 "	"	233 10	
" Will " " 4 "	"	2 00	
" Winnebago " " 5 "	"	94 50	
" Adams " " 34 "	1895	1,376 50	
" Alexander " " 44 "	"	870 40	
" Bond " " 2 "	"	51 50	
" Boone " " 9 "	"	131 40	
" Brown " " 5 "	"	190 50	
" Bureau " " 9 "	"	119 00	
" Calhoun " " 4 "	"	123 00	
" Carroll " " 1 "	"	30 50	
" Cass " " 2 "	"	74 80	
" Champaign " " 25 "	"	920 45	
" Christian " " 23 "	"	786 45	
" Clark " " 3 "	"	112 45	
" Clay " " 9 "	"	252 90	
" Clinton " " 1 "	"	21 50	
" Coles " " 16 "	"	526 15	
" Cook " " 659 "	"	2,674 00	
" Crawford " " 6 "	"	218 25	
" Cumberland " " 2 "	"	76 00	
" DeKalb " " 3 "	"	33 80	
" DeWitt " " 10 "	"	367 30	
" Douglas " " 6 "	"	223 60	
" DuPage " " 6 "	"	54 00	
" Edgar " " 18 "	"	528 85	
" Edwards " " 1 "	"	29 75	
" Effingham " " 8 "	"	196 80	
" Fayette " " 2 "	"	50 00	
" Ford " " 7 "	"	126 10	
" Franklin " " 5 "	"	70 15	
" Fulton " " 7 "	"	208 60	
" Gallatin " " 7 "	"	156 80	
" Greene " " 12 "	"	331 20	
" Grundy " " 4 "	"	18 00	
" Hamilton " " 7 "	"	121 25	
" Hancock " " 13 "	"	515 00	
" Hardin " " 4 "	"	145 00	
" Henry " " 6 "	"	152 95	
Amounts carried forward	....	$19,556 95	$91,351 34

Statement 3—Continued.

Accounts.	App.	Amount.	Total.
Amounts brought forward	....	$19,556 95	$91,351 34
CONVEYING CONVICTS TO PENITENTIARY—*Continued.*			
Sheriff of Iroquois county for conveying 5 convicts	1895	78 00	
" Jackson " " 18 "	"	346 50	
" Jasper " " 4 "	"	131 40	
" Jefferson " " 12 "	"	152 75	
" Jersey " " 11 "	"	313 50	
" Jo Daviess " " 7 "	"	252 65	
" Johnson " " 14 "	"	262 65	
" Kane " " 18 "	"	116 00	
" Kankakee " " 7 "	"	57 50	
" Kendall " " 1 "	"	7 75	
" Knox " " 33 "	"	793 65	
" Lake " " 6 "	"	92 30	
" LaSalle " " 18 "	"	174 80	
" Lawrence " " 4 "	"	137 70	
" Lee " " 8 "	"	149 60	
" Livingston " " 4 "	"	51 30	
" Logan " " 7 "	"	315 00	
" Macon " " 24 "	"	828 90	
" Macoupin " " 19 "	"	591 60	
" Madison " " 29 "	"	626 75	
" Marion " " 23 "	"	444 80	
" Marshall " " 2 "	"	34 80	
" Mason " " 5 "	"	242 65	
" Massac " " 9 "	"	163 85	
" McDonough " " 5 "	"	228 75	
" McHenry " " 2 "	"	26 00	
" McLean " " 18 "	"	373 10	
" Menard " " 1 "	"	48 75	
" Mercer " " 2 "	"	78 00	
" Montgomery " " 4 "	"	118 25	
" Morgan " " 4 "	"	172 00	
" Moultrie " " 8 "	"	205 40	
" Ogle " " 3 "	"	60 75	
" Peoria " " 51 "	"	1,024 80	
" Perry " " 3 "	"	20 80	
" Piatt " " 10 "	"	308 50	
" Pike " " 11 "	"	436 45	
" Pope " " 8 "	"	244 90	
" Pulaski " " 11 "	"	400 50	
" Putnam " " 1 "	"	20 00	
" Randolph " " 7 "	"	2 80	
" Richland " " 10 "	"	203 05	
" Rock Island " " 26 "	"	715 00	
" Saline " " 8 "	"	246 00	
" Sangamon " " 56 "	"	1,955 20	
" Schuyler " " 1 "	"	46 50	
" Scott " " 3 "	"	105 95	
" Shelby " " 8 "	"	175 20	
" Stark " " 1 "	"	30 75	
" St. Clair " " 48 "	"	836 75	
" Stephenson " " 13 "	"	313 60	
" Tazewell " " 8 "	"	198 00	
" Union " " 7 "	"	93 60	
" Vermilion " " 48 "	"	1,737 75	
" Wabash " " 5 "	"	122 40	
" Warren " " 10 "	"	278 25	
" Washington " " 7 "	"	112 60	
" Wayne " " 2 "	"	40 80	
" White " " 14 "	"	315 90	
" Whiteside " " 26 "	"	588 30	
" Will " " 34 "	"	13 80	
" Williamson " " 11 "	"	205 00	
" Winnebago " " 16 "	"	297 00	
" Woodford " " 1 "	"	24 00	
Total number of convicts............. 2,249			
Amounts carried forward	....	$38,348 50	$91,351 34

Statement 3—Continued.

ACCOUNTS.	App.	Amount.	Total.
Amounts brought forward	....	$38,348 50	$91,351 34
CONVEYING CONVICTS FROM AND TO PENITENTIARY FOR NEW TRIAL OR TO BE USED AS WITNESSES.			
Sheriff of Cook county for conveying 2 convicts	1893	38 50	
" Massac " " 1 "	"	62 15	
" Cook " " 6 "	1895	89 25	
" Johnson " " 2 "	"	61 80	
" Scott " " 2 "	"	179 30	
Total number of convicts............. 13			38,779 50
To amount paid from appropriation of 1893.... $7,772 70			
" " " 1895.... 31,006 80			
CONVEYING CONVICTS TO REFORMATORY.			
Sheriff of Menard county for conveying 6 convicts (in part)	1893	$1 45	
Sheriff of Adams county for conveying 16 convicts	1895	658 95	
" Alexander " " 68 "	"	3,650 70	
" Bond " " 4 "	"	142 20	
" Brown " " 2 "	"	65 60	
" Bureau " " 4 "	"	84 00	
" Carroll " " 5 "	"	158 70	
" Cass " " 1 "	"	30 25	
" Champaign " " 13 "	"	203 50	
" Christian " " 17 "	"	397 50	
" Clark " " 1 "	"	37 75	
" Clay " " 4 "	"	150 30	
" Clinton " " 1 "	"	44 50	
" Coles " " 25 "	"	622 30	
" Cook " " 771 "	"	8,298 40	
" Crawford " " 1 "	"	44 75	
" Cumberland " " 4 "	"	99 75	
" DeKalb " " 3 "	"	69 75	
" DeWitt " " 11 "	"	116 85	
" Douglas " " 4 "	"	85 50	
" DuPage " " 2 "	"	46 50	
" Edgar " " 22 "	"	634 50	
" Edwards " " 1 "	"	51 25	
" Effingham " " 5 "	"	147 00	
" Fayette " " 6 "	"	196 00	
" Ford " " 5 "	"	52 00	
" Franklin " " 9 "	"	168 75	
" Fulton " " 3 "	"	65 00	
" Gallatin " " 6 "	"	347 20	
" Greene " " 12 "	"	379 20	
" Grundy " " 4 "	"	56 00	
" Hamilton " " 7 "	"	260 40	
" Hancock " " 6 "	"	243 00	
" Hardin " " 10 "	"	523 55	
" Henderson " " 2 "	"	73 50	
" Henry " " 4 "	"	115 00	
" Iroquois " " 8 "	"	95 40	
" Jackson " " 20 "	"	1,085 70	
" Jefferson " " 8 "	"	307 20	
" Jersey " " 10 "	"	386 40	
" JoDaviess " " 2 "	"	71 20	
" Johnson " " 10 "	"	548 00	
" Kane " " 14 "	"	292 40	
" Kankakee " " 11 "	"	110 40	
" Kendall " " 3 "	"	44 20	
" Knox " " 12 "	"	226 80	
" Lake " " 2 "	"	64 00	
" LaSalle " " 28 "	"	225 00	
" Lawrence " " 4 "	"	199 00	
" Lee " " 6 "	"	104 65	
" Logan " " 8 "	"	117 00	
" Macon " " 32 "	"	534 30	
" Macoupin " " 9 "	"	270 60	
" Madison " " 18 "	"	697 06	
" Marion " " 16 "	"	554 60	
" Marshall " " 3 "	"	39 00	
" Mason " " 5 "	"	111 55	
Amounts carried forward	....	$24,405 95	$130,150 84

Statement 3—Continued.

Accounts.	App.	Amount.	Total.
Amounts brought forward	....	$24,405 95	$130,150 84
CONVEYING CONVICTS TO REFORMATORY—*Continued.*			
Sheriff of Massac county for conveying 13 convicts	1895	766 80	
" McDonough " " 6 "	"	195 00	
" McHenry " " 1 "	"	30 50	
" McLean " " 21 "	"	176 75	
" Menard " " 6 " (in full)	"	104 15	
Sheriff of Mercer county for conveying 3 convicts	"	89 70	
" Monroe " " 1 "	"	52 50	
" Montgomery " " 10 "	"	296 70	
" Morgan " " 7 "	"	192 20	
" Moultrie " " 4 "	"	75 75	
" Ogle " " 3 "	"	82 50	
" Peoria " " 58 "	"	581 15	
" Perry " " 3 "	"	156 00	
" Piatt " " 3 "	"	52 50	
" Pike " " 6 "	"	229 60	
" Pope " " 11 "	"	651 45	
" Pulaski " " 28 "	"	1,280 40	
" Randolph " " 2 "	"	119 50	
" Richland " " 2 "	"	87 50	
" Rock Island " " 7 "	"	211 20	
" Saline " " 6 "	"	305 00	
" Sangamon " " 32 "	"	651 00	
" Schuyler " " 4 "	"	119 70	
" Scott " " 2 "	"	57 60	
" Shelby " " 4 "	"	93 00	
" Stark " " 4 "	"	90 00	
" St. Clair " " 43 "	"	1,356 75	
" Stephenson " " 8 "	"	241 30	
" Tazewell " " 10 "	"	140 70	
" Union " " 16 "	"	864 30	
" Vermilion " " 28 "	"	559 35	
" Wabash " " 2 "	"	85 60	
" Warren " " 8 "	"	206 25	
" Washington " " 8 "	"	351 00	
" White " " 23 "	"	888 75	
" Whiteside " " 6 "	"	159 60	
" Will " " 26 "	"	324 50	
" Williamson " " 12 "	"	551 25	
" Winnebago " " 8 "	"	207 40	
" Woodford " " 6 "	"	51 30	
Total number of convicts..............1,734			
CONVEYING CONVICTS FROM AND TO REFORMATORY FOR NEW TRIAL OR TO BE USED AS WITNESSES.			
Sheriff of Cook county, for conveying 8 convicts	1895.	335 80	
" Henry " " 1 "	"	63 25	
" Macoupin " " 1 "	"	72 60	
" Massac " " 1 "	"	156 20	
" Williamson " " 1 "	"	134 75	37,904 75
Total number of convicts.............. 12			
To amount paid from appropriation of 1893.... $1 45			
" " " 1895.... 37,903 30			
CONVEYING JUVENILE FEMALE OFFENDERS TO STATE HOME.			
Sheriff of Alexander county, for conveying 1 offender	1895.	$91 25	
" Coles " " 1 "	"	55 00	
" Cook " " 47 "	"	351 00	
" Edgar " " 2 "	"	78 00	
" Henderson " " 1 "	"	48 50	
" Jersey " " 1 "	"	71 25	
" Kane " " 1 "	"	10 00	
" Macon " " 3 "	"	135 85	
" Mercer " " 1 "	"	37 50	
Amounts carried forward	....	$878 35	$168,035 59

Statement 3—Continued.

ACCOUNTS.		App.	Amount.	Total.
Amounts brought forward		....	$878 35	$168,035 59
CONVEYING JUVENILE FEMALE OFFENDERS TO STATE HOME—*Continued.*				
Sheriff of Moultrie county, for conveying 1 offender		1895.	43 90	
" Richland " " 2 "		"	106 80	
" Sangamon " " 4 "		"	221 00	
" Schuyler " " 2 "		"	113 50	
" Warren " " 1 "		"	37 75	
Total number female juvenile offenders. 68				1,401 30
COSTS AND EXPENSES OF STATE SUITS.				
E. A. Snively, Clerk of Supreme Court—Costs in cases in Supreme Court, viz.; David Gore, Auditor P. A., vs. Peoria Mercantile Library Association	$10 00			
David Gore, Auditor P. A., vs. Young Men's Christian Association	10 00			
Copy of opinion of Supreme Court in case of Distilling and Cattle Feeding Co. vs. The People, *ex rel.*	19 75			
Costs of appellees of Supreme Court in case of Distilling and Cattle Feeding Co. vs. The People *ex rel*	33 05	1893	72 80	
M. T. Moloney, Attorney General—Expenses of M. L. Newell, Asst. Attorney General, in state suit viz.: The Bank of Marion, etc., No. 59, October Term of Supreme Court, 1894, traveling and hotel expenses from Springfield to Ottawa and return	$18 54			
Moneys advanced for costs and expenses in State suits viz.: To Frank Gaulter, Clerk of the Circuit Court of Cook County, for records in cases of The People vs. Comrs. of Lincoln Park, *et al*, and The People vs. Pullman's Palace Car Co.	79 00	"	97 54	
David Gore, Auditor of Public Accounts—Amount paid Samuel P. Wheeler, Attorney at Law, for opinion in the matter of the refusal of the Attorney General to proceed against the Illinois Building and Loan Association; for legal services in case of the People of the State of Illinois on the relation of David Gore, Auditor Public Accounts, vs. Maurice T. Moloney, Attorney General; mandamus in Circuit Court of Sangamon County, Illinois, to compel defendant to proceed against Illinois Building and Loan Association to close up its business	$200 00			
Amount paid L. W. Young and H. A. Sauer, expert witnesses in cases of The People *ex rel.* vs. The Continental Investment and Loan Society	245 00	"	445 00	
George W. Jones, Clerk of Appellate Court—Balance of costs due in the case of The People, etc., *ex rel.* David Gore vs. The Illinois Building and Loan Association		"	12 70	
H. G. Reeves, Attorney at Law—Legal services and expenses on account thereof, rendered to Auditor of Public Accounts, in case of The People *ex rel.* vs. National Home Building and Loan Association		1895	14 00	
J. H. Leaton, Clerk of Circuit Court, McLean County—Copy of Record furnished in case of The People *ex rel.* vs. National Home Building and Loan Association		"	14 00	
Amounts carried forward		....	$656 04	$169,436 89

Statement 3—Continued.

Accounts.		App.	Amount.	Total.
Amounts brought forward			$656 04	$ 169,436 89
COSTS AND EXPENSES OF STATE SUITS—*Continued.*				
E. A. Snively, Clerk of Supreme Court—				
Advance costs in case of The People *ex rel.* vs. The National Home Building and Loan Association	$10 00			
Copy of Record in Supreme Court in case of Dement *et al*, Comrs., vs. Rokker *et al*	25 00	1895	$35 00	
M. T. Moloney, Attorney General—				
Expenses to Chicago, taking depositions, etc., in case of Rokker *et al* vs. The State of Illinois	$19 50			
Amounts paid for costs in suits as follows, viz.:				
People vs. Inter-Ocean H. & L. Association	18 50			
People vs. Fidelity Ins. Trust and Safety Deposit Co	165 00			
People vs. United States Leather Co	2 50			
People vs. American Sugar Refining Co	2 50			
People vs. Independent Order Odd Fellows of Canada	10 00			
Catherine Cutting vs. The People	5 40			
People vs. Spring Valley Coal Co. (for J. L. Murphy)	100 00			
People vs. Spring Valley Coal Co. (for Jeff Durley)	22 00			
People vs. Illinois Steel Co	60 00			
People vs Ryan *et al*, and People vs. Heisen *et al* (services of J. P. Mahoney, Master in Chancery)	200 00			
People vs. Ryan *et al*, and People vs. Heisen *et al* (services of stenographer)	100 00	"	705 40	
T. J. Scofield, Assistant Attorney General—				
Costs advanced in case of People *ex rel.* vs. National Home Building and Loan Association		"	2 65	
To amount paid from appropriation of 1893	$628 04			1,399 09
To amount paid from appropriation of 1895	771 05			
COTTON STATES AND INTERNATIONAL EXPOSITION.				
Willis J. Abbot, Secretary—				
Erection of State building on the grounds of the Cotton States and International Exposition, held at Atlanta, Georgia, in 1895, for use and comfort of Illinois visitors; furnishing and maintaining the same; expenses of commissioners to said exposition, and salaries of secretary and assistants		1895	$14,995 00	14,995 00
COURT—APPELLATE—FIRST DISTRICT.				
Incidental expenses, including stationery, postage, express charges, printing, repairs, ice, etc		1893	$1,330 43	
Librarian		"	416 68	
Rent of court rooms		"	6,666 67	
Purchase of law books		"	1,014 60	
Incidental expenses, including stationery, postage, express charges, printing, repairs, ice, etc		1895	1,616 73	
Librarian		"	583 32	
Rent of court rooms		"	8,333 33	
Purchase of law books		"	1,159 26	
Re-binding law books		"	959 50	22,080 52
COURT—APPELLATE—SECOND DISTRICT.				
Incidental expenses, including stationery, postage, express charges, fuel, printing, ice, etc		1893	$1,406 39	
Sheriff's per diem for attendance on court		"	66 00	
Amounts carried forward			$1,472 39	$207,911 50

Statement 3—Continued.

Accounts.	App.	Amount.	Total.
Amounts brought forward	....	$1,472 39	$207,911 50
COURT—APPELLATE—SECOND DISTRICT—*Continued.*			
Janitor's salary	1893	400 00	
Incidental expenses, including stationery, postage, express charges, fuel, printing, ice, etc	1895	1,382 03	
Sheriff's per diem for attendance on Court	"	105 00	
Janitor's salary	"	400 00	
			3,759 42
COURT—APPELLATE—THIRD DISTRICT.			
Incidental expenses, including stationery, postage, repairs, telephone, express charges, printing, etc	1893	$622 52	
Sheriff's per diem for attendance on court	"	114 00	
Janitor's salary	"	400 00	
Incidental expenses, including stationery, postage, telephone rental, express charges, printing, etc	1895	620 63	
Sheriff's per diem for attendance on court	"	93 00	
Janitor's salary	"	400 00	
			2,250 15
COURT—APPELLATE—FOURTH DISTRICT.			
Incidental expenses, including stationery, postage, repairs, records, printing, lights, gasoline, etc	1893	$874 95	
Sheriff's per diem for attendance on court	"	48 00	
Janitor's salary	"	400 00	
Incidental expenses, including stationery, postage, repairs, records, printing, fuel, lights, etc	1895	938 36	
Sheriff's per diem for attendance on court	"	51 00	
Janitor's salary	"	300 00	
			2,612 31
COURT—SUPREME—CENTRAL GRAND DIVISION.			
Incidental expenses, including stationery, postage, express charges, law books, telephone rental, ice, repairs, etc	1893	$818 80	
Sheriff's per diem for attendance on court	"	21 00	
Librarian's salary	"	1,000 00	
Janitor's salary	"	333 34	
Incidental expenses, including stationery, postage, express charges, law books, telephone rental, ice, repairs, etc	1895	1,197 55	
Sheriff's per diem for attendance on court	"	48 00	
Librarian's salary	"	1,000 00	
Janitor's salary	"	466 66	
			4,885 35
COURT—SUPREME—NORTHERN GRAND DIVISION.			
Incidental expenses, including stationery, postage, express charges, gas, repairs, fuel, etc	1893	$3,001 43	
Sheriff's per diem for attendance on court	"	87 00	
Librarian's salary	"	500 00	
Janitor's salary	"	400 00	
Law books and binding	"	78	
Repairs on court house	"	81 00	
Incidental expenses, including stationery, postage, express charges, gas, repairs, fuel, etc	1895	1,265 08	
Sheriff's per diem for attendance on court	"	48 00	
Librarian's salary	"	500 00	
Janitor's salary	"	400 00	
Law books and binding	"	198 77	
			6,482 06
COURT—SUPREME—SOUTHERN GRAND DIVISION.			
Incidental expenses, including stationery, postage, express charges, printing, repairs, ice, fuel, light, etc	1893	$1,111 96	
Sheriff's per diem for attendance on court	"	24 00	
Librarian's salary	"	500 00	
Janitor's salary	"	400 00	
Amounts carried forward	....	$2,035 96	$227,900 79

Statement 3—Continued.

Articles.	App.	Amount.	Total.
Amounts brought forward	....	$2,035 96	$227,900 79
COURT—SUPREME—SOUTHERN GRAND DIVISION—*Cont'd.*			
Incidental expenses, including stationery, postage, express charges, printing, repairs, ice, fuel, light, etc.	1895	2,093 35	
Sheriff's per diem for attendance on court	"	27 00	
Librarian's salary	"	500 00	
Janitor's salary	"	400 00	
			5,056 31
EXECUTIVE MANSION.			
E. N. Davenport—Services in care of mansion and grounds	1893	$175 00	
Ella Bullough—Services in care of mansion and grounds	"	17 33	
Alice Byrd—Services in care of mansion and grounds	"	103 98	
Samuel Earl—Services in care of mansion and grounds	"	150 00	
William Parker—Services in care of mansion and grounds	"	225 75	
Champ Singleton—Services in care of mansion and grounds	"	30 00	
Central Union Telephone Co.—Rental of telephone, service, etc	"	22 50	
Springfield Gas Light Co.—Gas furnished mansion	"	128 00	
Springfield Water Works—Water furnished mansion and grounds	"	93 31	
Capital Coal Co.—Coal furnished and labor storing same	"	210 50	
Evening Telegram—Subscription to daily publication	"	5 00	
Illinois State Register—Subscription to daily publication	"	5 20	
Morning Monitor—Subscription to daily publication	"	9 00	
United States Express Co.—Express charges on packages	"	8 85	
Armstrong & Schanbacher—Paint, oil, wall paper, shellac, etc., furnished	"	21 80	
E. S. Gard—Groceries and merchandise furnished	"	33 30	
Charles H. Long—Garden and flower seeds, furnished	"	3 85	
Payne & Sons—Hardware supplies furnished	"	23 07	
William M. Payne—Hardware supplies furnished	"	6 10	
Louis Unverzagt—Flowers furnished mansion	"	106 75	
Brown & Canfield—Roses, lilies, jardiniere furnished, express charges paid	"	18 05	
Pitkin & Brooks—Trays, brushes, knife rests, etc., furnished	"	81 80	
J. M. Striffler—Coal and ice furnished	"	56 02	
J. M. Rippey—Material and labor furnished—repairing grates, lamp, pipe, etc	"	57 67	
Frank Simmons—Frame furnished mansion	"	2 25	
R. L. Barry—Rent of piano, tuning same, etc	"	35 00	
William Durry—Hauling ashes, manure, etc., from grounds	"	15 00	
C. H. Edmands—Curtain rings, hinges, repairs, etc., furnished	"	5 35	
Reisch & Thoma—Amount due for merchandise furnished	"	20 06	
Hall & Herrick—Amount due for merchandise furnished	"	5 00	
Amounts carried forward	....	$1,675 49	$232,957 10

Statement 3—Continued.

Accounts.		App.	Amount.	Total.
Amounts brought forward		....	$1,675 49	$232,957 10
EXECUTIVE MANSION—*Continued.*				
John N. Murphy— Radiators and packless valves furnished		1893	21 00	
Charles Ryan— Soap, moth balls, ammonia, etc., furnished		"	21 65	
R. F. Herndon & Co.— Balance on acc., ribbons, cloth, violets, etc., furnished		"	14 30	
A. Dirksen & Sons— Amount due for furniture for mansion		"	66 60	
C. W. Buscher— Canvassing mansion floors for receptions		"	17 00	
August Claus— Repairing iron clock at mansion		"	4 50	
B. H. Ferguson— Jardiniere furnished and hire on candelabras		"	7 20	
Charles F. Hawk— Top jar for No. 7 stone filterer, and express charges paid		"	3 00	
C. A. Power— Repairs and material furnished for mansion		"	26 35	
August Leroy— Repairs and material furnished for mansion		"	21 50	
William Parker— Services rendered cleaning mansion		"	10 80	
Mandel Brothers— Amount due for merchandise furnished		"	91 02	
Guthman Brothers— Amount due for merchandise furnished		"	3 20	
Henry Wulff, State Treasurer— Amounts paid as follows, viz.:				
To Champ Singleton for services in care of mansion and grounds	$130 00			
To Henry Wilson for services in care of mansion and grounds	50 00			
To Villiam Parker for services in care of mansion and grounds	75 00			
To E. N. Davenport for services in care of mansion and grounds	125 00			
To Alice Byrd for services in care of mansion and grounds	86 67			
To Central Union Telephone Co., for telephone rental, etc., to mansion	7 50			
To Capital Coal Co., for coal furnished mansion	44 56			
To Springfield Gas Light Co., for gas furnished mansion	97 90			
To Springfield Water Works, for water furnished mansion	24 49			
To Illinois State Register, subscription to daily	5 20			
To L. Smith, for work done at mansion	11 00			
To August Leroy, for material and repairs furnished	2 25			
To Wm. M. Payne, for hardware, etc., furnished	22 10			
To John M. Strifler, for ice furnished mansion	13 84			
To M. Zwicky's Sons, for soap furnished mansion	3 85			
To Armstrong & Schanbacher, for repairs, etc., furnished	3 25			
To C. H. Edmunds, for merchandise furnished	2 30			
To J. M. Rippey, for repairs, etc., furnished	38 00			
To E. S. Gard, for merchandise furnished	35 15			
To Reisch & Thoma, for merchandise furnished	9 84			
To J. D. Snoden, for hauling for mansion	1 50	"	789 40	
Amounts carried foward		....	$2,773 01	$232,957 10

Statement 3—Continued.

Accounts.	App.	Amount.	Total.
Amounts brought forward	....	$2,773 01	$232,957 10
EXECUTIVE MANSION—*Continued.*			
E. N. Davenport— Services rendered in care of mansion and grounds.	1893	299 30	
Alice Byrd— Services rendered in care of mansion and grounds.	"	190 63	
William Parker— Services rendered in care of mansion and grounds.	"	224 25	
Champ Singleton— Services rendered in care of mansion and grounds.	"	375 50	
William H. Bates— Services rendered in care of mansion and grounds.	"	6 20	
Henry Wilson— Services rendered in care of mansion and grounds.	"	75 00	
Allie Singleton— Services rendered in care of mansion and grounds.	"	18 00	
A. Smith— Amount due for work at mansion	1895	6 00	
Central Union Telephone Co.— Amount due for telephone rental, etc., to mansion..	"	30 00	
Springfield Gas Light Co.— Amount due for gas furnished mansion	"	168 50	
Springfield Water Works— Amount due for water furnished mansion	"	54 89	
Freeman Transfer Co.— Freight charges due on vases and bulbs	"	72	
Capital Coal Co.— Amount due for coal furnished	"	151 32	
Evening Telegram— Subscription to daily issue of paper	"	10 40	
J. M. Rippey— Plumbing repairs and material furnished	"	16 95	
A. Dirksen & Sons— Amount due for furniture furnished	"	56 55	
B. H. Ferguson— Sherbets, teas, cement and freezer, $16.80; lamps, plates, tumblers, etc., $8.10	"	24 90	
E. S. Gard— Oil, starch, soap, etc., furnished mansion	"	48 80	
R. F. Herndon & Co.— Linen, centre piece, doylies, etc., furnished	"	58 76	
H. L. Phelps— Amount due for flowers furnished	"	25 50	
Reisch & Thoma— Knitting silk, napkins, cloth, comforts, crash, etc., furnished	"	31 01	
The John Bressmer Co.— Muslin, shade, thread, mats, etc.. furnished	"	29 54	
R. M. Armbruster— Hammock and mammoth stands and canopies	"	25 50	
Emma F. Altgeld— Amount due for furniture bought for mansion	"	1,458 00	
Armstrong & Schanbacher— Touching up and repairing walls of mansion	"	12 00	
R. F. Kinsella— Papering rooms and hall and glass furnished	"	18 35	
August LeRoy— Keys, wire and repairs furnished mansion	"	7 50	
Charles Matthews— Amount due for labor, cutting grass, etc	"	3 00	
Brown & Canfield— Amount due for flowers furnished mansion	"	10 00	
R. L. Berry— Rent of piano, tuning piano, etc	"	23 00	
John M. Striffler— Amount due for ice furnished mansion	"	61 02	
Sherman Smith— Amount due for hauling rubbish	"	3 50	
Frank Simmons— Shelf and tissue paper furnished	"	50	
G. N. Davenport— One set decorated dishes furnished	"	25 00	
Amounts carried forward	....	$6,329 10	$232,957 10

Statement 3—Continued.

Accounts.	App.	Amount.	Total.
Amounts brought forward	....	$6,329 10	$232,957 10
EXECUTIVE MANSION—*Continued.*			
George Simmons— Lumber, labor on steps, putting up storm door, strips for windows, sash locks, cedar posts, repairs on roof, etc., furnished mansion	1895	13 45	
J. J. Clark— Repairing carpet sweepers at mansion	"	2 00	
J. H. Edington— Amount due for load of straw, etc., furnished	"	4 11	
C. H. Edmunds— Sash cord, paint, nails, etc., furnished	"	5 80	
William M. Payne— Hardware supplies, etc., furnished mansion	"	13 71	
Louis Unverzagt— Flowers, plants, sod and sodding furnished	"	344 25	
J. A. Mussillon & Bro.— Work on locks, adjusting electric bell, etc	"	3 25	
Frank Hinrichs— Amount due for load of hay furnished	"	14 80	
O. Hanratty— Plumbing supplies and labor furnished	"	23 20	
Patrick Higgins— Amount due for freight and drayage paid	"	75	$6,754 42
To amount paid from appropriation of 1893.... $1,983 61 " " " 1895.... 4,770 81			
FACTORY AND WORKSHOP INSPECTORS.			
Florence Kelley, Inspector— Salary $1,125.00, expenses $446.53	1893	$1,571 53	
Alzina P. Stevens, Assistant Inspector— Salary $749.97, expenses $161.79	"	911 76	
Sarah Cunningham, Deputy Inspector— Salary $562.50, expenses $45.08	"	607 58	
Emma Jamieson, Deputy Inspector— Salary $500.00, expenses $35.13	"	535 13	
Fannie M. Jones, Deputy Inspector— Salary $562.50, expenses $25.90	"	588 40	
Mary Moran, Deputy Inspector— Salary $562.50, expenses $47.30	"	609 80	
Belle M. Powell, Deputy Inspector— Salary $562.50, expenses $57.80	"	620 30	
Abraham Bisno, Deputy Inspector— Salary $562.50, expenses $163.50	"	726 00	
Joseph Farris, Deputy Inspector— Salary	"	562 50	
James Hickey, Deputy Inspector— Salary $562.50, expenses $129.20	"	691 70	
P. Ewald Jenson, Deputy Inspector— Salary $565.50, expenses $96.75	"	659 25	
John Merz, Deputy Inspector— Salary $562.50, expenses $414.52	"	977 02	
Andrew A. Bruce, attorney at law— Legal services and expenses	"	529 15	
Jane Addams— Rent of office, 247 W. Polk st., Chicago	"	180 00	
Lizzie Evans— Amount due for cleaning office	"	10 00	
Wm. C. Hollister & Bro.— Circulars, letter-heads, schedules and envelopes	"	67 25	
Lanz, Owen & Co.— Leather rolls furnished deputy inspectors	"	18 00	
A. H. Andrews & Co.— Special oak book case furnished office	"	70 00	
Florence Kelley, Inspector— Salary $1,875.00, expenses $554.59	1895	2,429 59	
Amounts carried forward	....	$12,364 96	$239,711 52

Statement 3—Continued.

Accounts.	App.	Amount.	Total.
Amounts brought forward	....	$12,364 96	$239,711 52
FACTORY AND WORKSHOP INSPECTORS—*Continued.*			
Alzina P. Stevens, Assistant Inspector— Salary $1,249.95, expenses $294.63	1895	1,544 58	
Sarah Cunningham, Deputy Inspector— Salary $937.50, expenses $150.32	"	1,087 82	
Emma Jamieson, Deputy Inspector— Salary $937.50, expenses $113.41	"	1,050 91	
Fannie M. Jones, Deputy Inspector— Salary $937.50, expenses $111.50	"	1,049 00	
Mary Moran, Deputy Inspector— Salary $937.50, expenses $116.55	"	1,054 05	
Belle M. Powell, Deputy Inspector— Salary $937.50, expenses $640.75	"	1,578 25	
Frances Bracken, Deputy Inspector— Salary	"	125 00	
Ida P. Gibson, Deputy Inspector— Salary $327.50, expenses $24.90	"	352 40	
Joseph Farris, Deputy Inspector— Salary	"	116 67	
Abraham Bisno, Deputy Inspector— Salary $937.50, expenses $378.51	"	1,316 01	
James Hickey, Deputy Inspector— Salary $187.50, expenses $76.66	"	264 16	
P. Ewald Jensen, Deputy Inspector— Salary $937.50, expenses $387.54	"	1,325 04	
John Merz, Deputy Inspector— Salary $937.50, expenses $170.08	"	1,107 58	
John Martin, Deputy Inspector— Salary $562.50, expenses $315.64	"	878 14	
Jane Addams— Rent of office for use of inspectors	"	393 00	
L. C. Huck— Rent of office for use of inspectors	"	140 00	
Lizzie Evans— Cleaning and taking care of office	"	169 50	
Andrew A. Bruce, attorney at law— Legal services rendered, railroad expenses, etc	"	635 51	
F. W. Havill, Clerk of Supreme Court— Two copies of decision of Supreme Court, in case of Ritchie vs. The People, etc	"	28 00	
Chicago Legal News— Eleven copies of "Legal News" furnished	"	1 10	
Wm. C. Hollister & Bro.— Printing cards, performing job work, etc	"	40 25	
International Association of Factory Inspectors— One thousand copies of proceedings furnished	"	250 00	
Hannan, Geng & Co.— Two hundred cards furnished deputy inspectors	"	1 50	
A. H. Andrews & Co.— Merchandise, etc., furnished inspector	"	10 25	
Evan H. Davis— Two hundred copies of proceedings, International Association	"	80 00	
			26,963 68
To amount paid from appropriation of 1893.... $9,935 37			
" " " 1895.... 17,028 31			
FARMER'S COUNTY INSTITUTES.			
To amounts paid, on account of appropriations, to the following counties for expenses incurred in holding institutes, viz.:			
Joseph A. Nevins, Treasurer, Adams county	1893	$50 00	
F. Dresser, " Bond "	"	50 00	
Joseph W. Becker, " Calhoun "	"	42 50	
Conrad Lamp, " Carroll "	"	47 18	
H. M. Dunlap, " Champaign "	"	50 00	
Henry Grundy, " Christian "	"	46 90	
Edward Henbest, " Clark "	"	50 00	
J. P. Jones, " Coles "	"	23 00	
Amounts carried forward	....	$359 58	$266,675 20

Statement 3—Continued.

Accounts.				App.	Amount.	Total.
Amounts brought forward				....	$359 58	$266,675 20
FARMERS' COUNTY INSTITUTES—*Continued.*						
J. W. Sullivan,	Treasurer,	Dewitt	county	1893	$50 00	
Slocum Harvey.	"	Effingham	"	"	50 00	
Frederick Johnson,	"	Ford	"	"	50 00	
Carrol Moore,	"	Franklin	"	"	23 45	
E. A. Belknap,	"	Green	"	"	50 00	
C. M. McMillan,	"	Hancock	"	"	26 00	
Frank Moore,	"	"	"	"	17 75	
William Love.	"	Henry	"	"	50 00	
J. W. Dixon,	"	Iroquois	"	"	50 00	
T. C. Moss,	"	Jefferson	"	"	50 00	
John J. Steele,	"	JoDaviess	"	"	50 00	
Julius Reinhart,	"	Madison	"	"	50 00	
H. C. Burnham,	"	Mason	"	"	50 00	
H. E. Billings,	"	McDonough	"	"	50 00	
George W. Reid,	"	"	"	"	24 80	
W. L. Candor,	"	Mercer	"	"	50 00	
Ed. Blackburn,	"	Morgan	"	"	42 22	
Charles Walkup,	"	Ogle	"	"	50 00	
T. L. Williams,	"	Perry	"	"	50 00	
G. A. Burgess,	"	Piatt	"	"	50 00	
W. R. Wilsey,	"	Pike	"	"	50 00	
Thomas Campbell,	"	Rock Island	"	"	40 75	
C. L. DeWitt,	"	Schuyler	"	"	30 65	
A. P. Grout,	"	Scott	"	"	47 45	
Fred. Helms,	"	St. Clair	"	"	50 00	
Frank B. Walker,	"	Stephenson	"	"	50 00	
Thomas S. McClanahan,	"	Warren	"	"	30 54	
Healy H. Alexander,	"	Will	"	"	50 00	
George Williams,	"	Winnebago	"	"	50 00	
John C. Pearce,	"	Adams	"	1895	50 00	
F. Dresser.	"	Bond	"	"	50 00	
R. W. Morgan,	"	Boone	"	"	38 11	
John E. Watson,	"	Calhoun	"	"	49 40	
Conrad Lamp,	"	Carroll	"	"	50 00	
Z. R. Genung,	"	Champaign	"	"	50 00	
George Large,	"	Christian	"	"	50 00	
Edward Henbest,	"	Clark	"	"	36 00	
J. P. Jones,	"	Coles	"	"	18 40	
C. Y. Miller,	"	DeWitt	"	"	50 00	
George Calloway,	"	Douglas	"	"	29 82	
John Christia,	"	DuPage	"	"	50 00	
John O'Hannold,	"	Edgar	"	"	44 25	
Joseph White,	"	Edwards	"	"	37 50	
William Dyke,	"	Effingham	"	"	50 00	
Frederick Johnson,	"	Ford	"	"	50 00	
Carrol Moore,	"	Franklin	"	"	46 50	
Wm. A. Peeples,	"	Gallatin	"	"	50 00	
B. C. Hodges,	"	Greene	"	"	50 00	
J. K. Ely,	"	Grundy	"	"	50 00	
C. N. Dennis.	"	Hancock	"	"	40 41	
Hal. W. Steward,	"	Henderson	"	"	21 72	
R. W. Fleming,	"	Henry	"	"	50 00	
James A. Hasbrouck,	"	Iroquois	"	"	50 00	
W. R. Carrico,	"	Jasper	"	"	36 15	
T. C. Moss,	"	Jefferson	"	"	50 00	
J. W. Becker,	"	Jersey	"	"	49 40	
John J. Steele,	"	JoDaviess	"	"	50 00	
H. M. Sisson,	"	Knox	"	"	50 00	
H. B. Corkins,	"	LaSalle	"	"	50 00	
W. E. Neal,	"	Lawrence	"	"	9 00	
John L. Lord,	"	Lee	"	"	50 00	
O. S. Westervelt,	"	Livingston	"	"	50 00	
A. B. Nicholson,	"	Logan	"	"	48 00	
Charles Scott,	"	Macon	"	"	50 00	
Julius Reinhart,	"	Madison	"	"	50 00	
Lee S. Dorsey,	"	"	"	"	50 00	
Wm. H. Parkinson,	"	Marshall	"	"	47 55	
Wm. H. Parkinson,	"	"	"	"	45 25	
H. C. Burnham,	"	Mason	"	"	26 50	
Geo. W. Reid,	"	McDonough	"	"	25 00	
Geo. W. Reid,	"	"	"	"	25 00	
Amounts carried forward				....	$3,467 15	$266,675 20

Statement 3—Continued.

Accounts.			App.	Amount.	Total.
Amounts brought forward			....	$3,467 15	$266,675 20
FARMERS' COUNTY INSTITUTES—*Continued.*					
L. E. Skaggs,	Treasurer,	McLean county	1895	50 00	
W. S. McCreight,	"	Mercer "	"	50 00	
A. A. K. Sawyer,	"	Montgomery "	"	50 00	
A. H. Sturtevant,	"	Morgan "	"	48 00	
Charles Walkup,	"	Ogle "	"	50 00	
T. L. Williams,	"	Perry "	"	50 00	
F. P. Anderson,	"	" "	"	50 00	
C. W. Moore,	"	Piatt "	"	50 00	
R. A. Anderson,	"	Pike "	"	50 00	
H. K. Smith,	"	Putnam "	"	50 00	
J. H. Moreland,	"	Randolph "	"	25 50	
John J. Vanderslice,	"	Rock Island "	"	50 00	
L. H. Coleman,	"	Sangamon "	"	50 00	
L. H. Coleman,	"	" "	"	50 00	
J. E. Thompson,	"	Schuyler "	"	7 85	
W. R. Smithson,	"	Scott "	"	46 88	
A. J. Finley,	"	Stark "	"	34 10	
Fred. Helms,	"	St. Clair "	"	50 00	
Frank B. Walker,	"	Stephenson "	"	50 00	
James L. Reid,	"	Tazewell "	"	49 00	
James Mahon,	"	Wabash "	"	50 00	
Thos. S. McClanahan,	"	Warren "	"	50 00	
J. B. Cable,	"	Wayne "	"	35 23	
H. L. Ewing,	"	Whiteside "	"	50 00	
Healy H. Alexander,	"	Will "	"	50 00	
Geo. W. Collins,	"	Winnebago "	"	50 00	
John M. Stonebraker,	"	Woodford "	"	48 21	
					4,711 92
FIRE APPARATUS FOR STATE CAPITOL BUILDING.					
W. H. Hinrichsen, Secretary of State—Traveling expenses to Chicago, etc., on account of fire apparatus for State Capitol Building			1895	$27 00	
					27 00
FISH COMMISSIONERS.					
George W. Langford, Commissioner—Amount paid for sundry expenses of commission, including supplies for office and expenses of storage boat, as per vouchers furnished			1893	$7,789 52	
John C. Mathis—Legal services rendered in case of the People vs. James Bridges, for violation of fish laws			"	100 00	
George W. Langford, Commissioner—Amount paid for personal and traveling expenses in enforcing the laws relative to fishways over dams, for the protection of fish, etc			"	2,079 84	
George W. Langford, Commissioner—Amount paid for sundry expenses of commission, including supplies for office and expenses of storage boat, as per vouchers furnished			1895	8,927 27	
George W. Langford, Commissioner—Amount paid for personal and traveling expenses in enforcing the laws relative to fishways over dams, for the protection of fish, etc			"	2,082 80	
S. P. Bartlett—Amount paid for sundry expenses of commission, including supplies for office and expenses of storage boat, as per vouchers furnished			"	767 17	
S. P. Bartlett—Amount paid for personal and traveling expenses in enforcing the laws relative to fishways over dams, for the protection of fish, etc			"	211 90	
					21,958 50
To amount paid from appropriation of 1893.... $9,959 36					
" " " 1895.... 11,989 14					
Amount carried forward					$293,372 62

Statement 3—Continued.

Accounts.	App.	Amount.	Total.
Amount brought forward	....	....	$293,372 62
FLAGS FOR DOME OF STATE HOUSE.			
Mrs. W. E. Richardson— Repairing flags of Capitol Building	1895	$5 00	
F. N. Harris— Work and material on flags and bunting	"	23 50	
Wm. M. Payne— Flags, couplings and rope furnished State	"	363 90	392 40
FUGITIVES FROM JUSTICE—EXPENSES FOR APPREHENSION AND DELIVERY.			
John W. Vancil— Returning fugitive from justice to Adams county	1893.	$87 55	
A. F. Roth— Returning fugitive from justice to Adams county	"	47 39	
D. W. Shankland— Returning fugitive from justice to Brown county	"	39 05	
Samuel A. Tate— Returning fugitive from justice to Carroll county	"	19 70	
W. T. Baker— Returning fugitive from justice to Christian county	"	52 55	
Allen Hurst— Returning fugitive from justice to Clark county	"	110 11	
Michael Loftus— Returning fugitive from justice to Cook county	"	152 47	
Michael Loftus— Returning fugitive from justice to Cook county	"	86 00	
W. J. Welbasky— Returning fugitive from justice to Cook county	"	154 95	
W. J. Welbasky— Returning fugitive from justice to Cook county	"	148 95	
W. J. Welbasky— Returning fugitive from justice to Cook county	"	97 67	
Charles J. Niggemeyer— Returning fugitive from justice to Cook county	"	36 06	
Charles J. Niggemeyer— Returning fugitive from justice to Cook county	"	39 93	
James McCarthy— Returning fugitive from justice to Cook county	"	84 00	
James McCarthy— Returning fugitive from justice to Cook county	"	155 92	
John T. Rafferty— Returning fugitive from justice to Cook county	"	58 65	
John T. Rafferty— Returning fugitive from justice to Cook county	"	49 50	
John T. Rafferty— Returning fugitive from justice to Cook county	"	98 60	
George F. Braxton— Returning fugitive from justice to Cook county	"	28 95	
George F. Braxton— Returning fugitive from justice to Cook county	"	28 95	
Louis Bock— Returning fugitive from justice to Cook county	"	102 50	
John W. Regan— Returning fugitive from justice to Cook county	"	37 40	
Joseph Spiegel— Returning fugitive from justice to Cook county	"	47 25	
John A. Elliott— Returning fugitive from justice to Cook county	"	72 75	
John A. Elliott— Returning fugitive from justice to Cook county	"	60 92	
Charles B. Hearle— Returning fugitive from justice to Cook county	"	49 50	
William Nelson— Returning fugitive from justice to Cook county	"	67 78	
Charles Arnstein— Returning fugitive from justice to Cook county	"	36 99	
Charles S. Berry— Returning fugitive from justice to Cook county	"	48 50	
William Nolan— Returning fugitive from justice to Cook county	"	49 30	
Amounts carried forward	....	$2,149 84	$293,765 02

Statement 3—Continued.

Accounts.	App.	Amount.	Total.
Amounts brought forward	....	$2,149 84	$293,765 02
FUGITIVES FROM JUSTICE—*Continued.*			
William Nolan— Returning fugitive from justice to Cook county....	"	49 30	
George M. Porteous— Returning fugitive from justice to Cook county....	"	121 50	
George M. Porteous— Returning fugitive from justice to Cook county....	"	127 00	
C. Foley— Returning fugitive from justice to Cook county....	"	39 50	
Samuel Zellenka— Returning fugitive from justice to Cook county....	"	120 30	
Thomas Duffy— Returning fugitive from justice to Cook county....	"	69 75	
William K. Green— Returning fugitive from justice to Cook county....	"	59 50	
Cass Smith— Returning fugitive from justice to Cook county....	"	63 75	
C. W. Wright— Returning fugitive from justice to Cook county....	"	25 15	
Timothy McKeough— Returning fugitive from justice to Cook county....	"	63 30	
Timothy McKeough— Returning fugitive from justice to Cook county....	"	55 80	
Timothy McKeough— Returning fugitive from justice to Cook county....	"	123 60	
H. J. Stark— Returning fugitive from justice to Cook county....	"	70 50	
Thomas Cronin— Returning fugitive from justice to Cook county....	"	51 50	
Guy V. Burton— Returning fugitive from justice to Cook county....	"	114 00	
Joseph C. Fleming— Returning fugitive from justice to Cook county....	"	121 00	
Andrew Rohan— Returning fugitive from justice to Cook county....	"	133 00	
James McCormick— Returning fugitive from justice to Cook county....	"	99 20	
C. A. McDonald— Returning fugitive from justice to Cook county....	"	55 10	
Charles H. Hærle— Returning fugitive from justice to Cook county....	"	98 75	
Charles H. Hærle— Returning fugitive from justice to Cook county....	"	47 50	
Charles H. Hærle— Returning fugitive from justice to Cook county....	"	81 20	
John V. Sederburg— Returning fugitive from justice to Cook county....	"	67 50	
Gideon S. Thompson— Returning fugitive from justice to Cook county....	"	119 74	
William F. Smith— Returning fugitive from justice to Cook county....	"	24 00	
Peter C. Dick— Returning fugitive from justice to Cook county....	"	68 75	
Sol. H. Marks— Returning fugitive from justice to Cook county....	"	72 55	
Anton Albrecht— Returning fugitive from justice to Cook county....	"	38 50	
C. R. Gorham— Returning fugitive from justice to DuPage county.	"	132 55	
B. F. Mason— Returning fugitive from justice to Ford county....	"	101 37	
R. G. Robinson— Returning fugitive from justice to Greene county..	"	35 20	
M. E. Buck— Returning fugitive from justice to Hamilton county	"	31 87	
E. J. Dorothy— Returning fugitive from justice to Hancock county.	"	210 54	
E. A. Wells— Returning fugitive from justice to Jackson county.	"	38 40	
Thomas M. Gray— Returning fugitive from justice to Jefferson county.	"	26 93	
Amounts carried forward,........	....	$4,907 94	$293,765 02

Statement 3—Continued.

ACCOUNTS.	App.	Amount.	Total.
Amounts brought forward	....	$4,907 94	$293,765 02
FUGITIVES FROM JUSTICE—*Continued.*			
John R. Ward— Returning fugitive from justice to Jefferson county	1893	106 86	
E.W. Faxon, Attorney in fact for Samuel Normandine— Returning fugitive from justice to Kendall county.	"	105 77	
Thomas Hanley— Returning fugitive from justice to LaSalle county.	"	50 61	
R. H. Haltzwan— Returning fugitive from justice to Livingston county	"	131 31	
A. T. Hays— Returning fugitive from justice to Logan county.	"	39 14	
S. M. Holmes— Returning fugitive from justice to Macon county...	"	66 55	
W. W. Mason— Returning fugitive from justice to Macon county...	"	61 42	
F. D. Bagley— Returning fugitive from justice to Macon county...	"	53 36	
J. P. Nicholson— Returning fugitive from justice to Macon county...	"	75 15	
Henry D. O'Neil— Returning fugitive from justice to Macoupin county	"	21 18	
Jacob Kuhn— Returning fugitive from justice to Madison county.	"	37 15	
A. W. Hope— Returning fugitive from justice to Madison county.	"	62 70	
Michael J. Helm— Returning fugitive from justice to Marion county..	"	200 15	
John W. Evers— Returning fugitive from justice to Massac county..	"	30 50	
John W. Evers— Returning fugitive from justice to Massac county..	"	24 69	
Thomas Furlong— Returning fugitive from justice to Sangamon county	"	98 50	
Edward A. Baxter— Returning fugitive from justice to Sangamon county	"	57 97	
Edward A. Baxter— Returning fugitive from justice to Sangamon county	"	47 78	
Edward A. Baxter— Returning fugitive from justice to Sangamon county	"	18 85	
Edward A. Baxter— Returning fugitive from justice to Sangamon county	"	58 10	
Henry J. Marks— Returning fugitive from justice to Sangamon county	"	60 44	
J. W. Norvell— Returning fugitive from justice to Sangamon county	"	51 10	
Joseph D. Henson— Returning fugitive from justice to Scott county....	"	69 86	
J. D. Langley— Returning fugitive from justice to St. Clair county.	"	23 18	
James McNamara— Returning fugitive from justice to Stephenson county	"	12 45	
John D. Mount— Returning fugitive from justice to Tazewell county.	"	42 09	
John E. Andrew— Returning fugitive from justice to Vermilion county	"	160 91	
John W. Newton— Returning fugitive from justice to Vermilion county	"	114 66	
George Gerrard— Returning fugitive from justice to Vermilion county	"	57 40	
James Sloan— Returning fugitive from justice to Vermilion county	"	39 62	
A. B. Holliday— Returning fugitive from justice to Warren county.	"	91 73	
W. N. Dickey— Returning fugitive from justice to Wayne county..	"	33 48	
Eugene Ackman— Returning fugitive from justice to White county...	"	25 70	
John B. Hutchens— Returning fugitive from justice to White county..	"	35 40	
H. M. Parks— Returning fugitive from justice to Williamson county	"	24 83	
Amounts carried forward	....	$7,098 53	$293,765 02

Statement 3—Continued.

Accounts.	App.	Amount.	Total.
Amounts brought forward	....	$7,098 53	$293,765 02
FUGITIVES FROM JUSTICE—*Continued.*			
Henry Wulff, State Treasurer— Amount paid Edwin F. Uhl, Acting Secretary of State of the United States, for expenses of Theodore Runyon, United States Ambassador to Germany, in returning Clarence F. Rix, fugitive from justice, from Germany to State of Illinois...	1893	73 01	
A. F. Roth— Returning fugitive from justice to Adams county..	1895	63 25	
A. F. Roth— Returning fugitive from justice to Adams county..	"	48 65	
A. F. Roth— Returning fugitive from justice to Adams county..	"	32 96	
L. H. Myers— Returning fugitive from justice to Alexander county	"	22 00	
George L. Aderton— Returning fugitive from justice to Calhoun county.	"	51 52	
D. D. Cannon— Returning fugitive from justice to Champaign county	"	55 03	
Ira Coburn— Returning fugitive from justice to Christian county	"	65 05	
Ira Coburn— Returning fugitive from justice to Christian county	"	59 97	
Ira Coburn— Returning fugitive from justice to Christian county	"	65 88	
Ira Coburn— Returning fugitive from justice to Christian county	"	62 36	
E. S. Edmonds— Returning fugitive from justice to Christian county	"	80 85	
S. D. Roseberry— Returning fugitive from justice to Christian county	"	50 20	
John W. Lewis— Returning fugitive from justice to Clark county ...	"	39 35	
Wm. M. Checkley— Returning fugitive from justice to Coles county....	"	32 59	
A. H. Messer— Returning fugitive from justice to Coles county....	"	44 18	
A. H. Messer— Returning fugitive from justice to Coles county....	"	81 95	
A. H. Messer— Returning fugitive from justice to Coles county....	"	41 30	
A. H. Messer— Returning fugitive from justice to Coles county....	"	106 43	
Harry McCaffery— Returning fugitive from justice to Cook county....	"	51 00	
Charles McNulty— Returning fugitive from justice to Cook county....	"	45 00	
John M. Tierney— Returning fugitive from justice to Cook county....	"	41 50	
George Grunnett— Returning fugitive from justice to Cook county	"	6 50	
Joseph Carolan— Returning fugitive from justice to Cook county	"	131 72	
Charles Arnstein— Returning fugitive from justice to Cook county	"	88 15	
James A. Patton— Returning fugitive from justice to Cook county....	"	285 15	
Peter C. Dick— Returning fugitive from justice to Cook county....	"	66 50	
Peter C. Dick— Returning fugitive from justice to Cook county....	"	175 50	
Peter C. Dick— Returning fugitive from justice to Cook county....	"	20 95	
William Plunkett— Returning fugitive from justice to Cook county....	"	129 75	
Louis Bock— Returning fugitive from justice to Cook county....	"	118 50	
John D. Hartford— Returning fugitive from justice to Cook county....	"	70 50	
John F. Kiley— Returning fugitive from justice to Cook county....	"	41 75	
Amounts carried forward	....	$9,447 53	$293,765 02

Statement 3—Continued.

Accounts.	App.	Amount.	Total.
Amounts brought forward	....	$9,447 53	$293,765 02
FUGITIVES FROM JUSTICE—*Continued.*			
John W. Norton— Returning fugitive from justice to Cook county....	1895	108 79	
James McCarthy— Returning fugitive from justice to Cook county....	"	60 00	
Edward Wallner— Returning fugitive from justice to Cook county....	"	62 64	
John Tobin— Returning fugitive from justice to Cook county....	"	36 29	
John H. Tobin— Returning fugitive from justice to Cook county....	"	49 29	
Charles S. Berry— Returning fugitive from justice to Cook county....	"	179 00	
Frank Stible— Returning fugitive from justice to Cook county....	"	74 73	
F. K. Buckminster— Returning fugitive from justice to Cook county....	"	61 35	
F. K. Buckminster— Returning fugitive from justice to Cook county....	"	89 75	
Wm B. Shope— Returning fugitive from justice to Cook county....	"	71 00	
J. E. Cornick— Returning fugitive from justice to Cook county....	"	24 95	
David Kipley— Returning fugitive from justice to Cook county....	"	43 00	
Peter Fitzpatrick— Returning fugitive from justice to Cook county....	"	130 75	
Wm. J. Burke— Returning fugitive from justice to Cook county....	"	56 67	
James N. Shafter— Returning fugitive from justice to DeKalb county.	"	63 30	
James N. Shafter— Returning fugitive from justice to DeKalb county.	"	49 15	
Minor B. Neal— Returning fugitive from justice to DeWitt county..	"	91 94	
Minor B. Neal— Returning fugitive from justice to DeWitt county..	"	62 09	
Minor B. Neal— Returning fugitive from justice to DeWitt county..	"	8 94	
Minor N. Neal— Returning fugitive from justice to DeWitt county..	"	20 80	
Minor B. Neal— Returning fugitive from justice to DeWitt county..	"	41 42	
Frank D. Bagley— Returning fugitive from justice to Douglas county.	"	20 22	
Edward O. Reed— Returning fugitive from justice to Ford county....	"	73 46	
M. E. Buck— Returning fugitive from justice to Hamilton county	"	64 55	
E. A. Wells— Returning fugitive from justice to Jackson county.	"	42 30	
E. A. Wells— Returning fugitive from justice to Jackson county.	"	39 24	
A. R. Chappell— Returning fugitive from justice to Jersey county..	"	130 30	
A. R. Chappell— Returning fugitive from justice to Jersey county..	"	108 15	
Edward Clark— Returning fugitive from justice to JoDaviess county....	"	66 60	
A. J. Gray— Returning fugitive from justice to Johnson county.	"	12 45	
C. B. Sherman— Returning fugitive from justice to Kankakee county....	"	27 14	
O. J. Aldrich— Returning fugitive from justice to Knox county....	"	126 82	
O. J. Aldrich— Returning fugitive from justice to Knox county....	"	38 39	
Daniel Thorn— Returning fugitive from justice to Lawrence county....	"	50 55	
Amounts carried forward	....	$11,633 51	$293,765 02

Statement 3—Continued.

Accounts.	App.	Amount.	Total.
Amounts brought forward	....	$11,633 51	$293,765 02
FUGITIVES FROM JUSTICE—*Continued.*			
Norman E. Jewett— Returning fugitive from justice to Lee county	1895	85 51	
W. H. Luke— Returning fugitive from justice to Livingston county	"	62 68	
H. K. Midkiff— Returning fugitive from justice to Macon county	"	41 31	
P. C. Davenport— Returning fugitive from justice to Macoupin county	"	100 70	
P. C. Davenport— Returning fugitive from justice to Macoupin county	"	43 80	
P. C. Davenport— Returning fugitive from justice to Macoupin county	"	52 00	
E. A. Burke— Returning fugitive from justice to Madison county	"	54 25	
John W. Evers— Returning fugitive from justice to Massac county	"	26 30	
M. H. Watson— Returning fugitive from justice to McDonough county	"	57 53	
John T. Dawdy— Returning fugitive from justice to Moultrie county	"	53 30	
Charles Lansden— Returning fugitive from justice to Moultrie county	"	56 36	
Charles Lansden— Returning fugitive from justice to Moultrie county	"	40 28	
Charles P. Sloan— Returning fugitive from justice to Peoria county	"	32 78	
Ira Dubois— Returning fugitive from justice to Peoria county	"	98 95	
L. O. Tripp— Returning fugitive from justice to Peoria county	"	39 79	
David Kerr— Returning fugitive from justice to Peoria county	"	52 64	
John Kinsey— Returning fugitive from justice to Peoria county	"	77 45	
C. A. Shively— Returning fugitive from justice to Piatt county	"	34 97	
Samuel Knox— Returning fugitive from justice to Pike county	"	108 39	
Edward A. Baxter— Returning fugitive from justice to Sangamon county	"	70 05	
Edward A. Baxter— Returning fugitive from justice to Sangamon county	"	50 71	
Edward A. Baxter— Returning fugitive from justice to Sangamon county	"	156 20	
Edward A. Baxter— Returning fugitive from justice to Sangamon county	"	75 63	
Joseph W. Norvell— Returning fugitive from justice to Sangamon county	"	96 42	
Evan T. Jones— Returning fugitive from justice to Sangamon county	"	60 50	
John Doocy— Returning fugitive from justice to Sangamon county	"	64 59	
William Maloney— Returning fugitive from justice to Sangamon county	"	347 25	
Herman Barniekol— Returning fugitive from justice to St. Clair county	"	25 65	
James Sloan— Returning fugitive from justice to Vermilion county	"	70 25	
James Sloan— Returning fugitive from justice to Vermilion county	"	129 42	
James Sloan— Returning fugitive from justice to Vermilion county	"	51 47	
James Sloan— Returning fugitive from justice to Vermilion county	"	50 90	
James Sloan— Returning fugitive from justice to Vermilion county	"	76 89	
Amounts carried forward	....	$14,078 43	$293,765 02

Statement 3—Continued.

Accounts.	App.	Amount.	Total.
Amounts brought forward	....	$14,078 43	$293,765 02
FUGITIVES FROM JUSTICE—*Continued.*			
A. B. Pershin— Returning fugitive from justice to Warren county.	1895	101 64	
A. B. Holliday— Returning fugitive from justice to Warren county.	"	88 70	
A. B. Holliday— Returning fugitive from justice to Warren county.	"	138 30	
Fred U. Glass— Returning fugitive from justice to Warren county.	"	26 24	
Louis Petty— Returning fugitive from justice to Will county.....	"	61 72	
Moses H. Luke— Returning fugitive from justice to State Reformatory	"	43 81	
			14,538 84
To amount paid from appropriation of 1893.... $7,171 54 " " " 1895.... 7,367 30			
FUGITIVES FROM JUSTICE—REWARDS FOR ARREST AND CONVICTION.			
C. C. Huthmacher— Reward for arrest, delivery to Jackson county, and conviction of Louis A. Miller, for the murder of Joseph Schielle	1893	$200 00	
Lawrence Morrissey— Reward for arrest, delivery to LaSalle county, and conviction of Grant Sims, for the murder of Barney Finnegan	1895	200 00	
John Hall— Reward for arrest, delivery to Vermilion county, and conviction of Andrew Unhorse, for murder ..	"	200 00	
			600 00
To amount paid from appropriation of 1893.... $200 00 " " " 1895.... 400 00			
GENERAL ASSEMBLY.			
Members of the Senate—Regular Session— Per diem, mileage, compensation for postage, stationery, etc	1893	$44,032 20	
Officers of the Senate—Regular Session— Per diem	"	5,199 00	
Members of the House of Representatives—Regular Session— Per diem, mileage, compensation for postage, stationery, etc	"	132,181 10	
Officers of the House of Representatives—Regular Session— Per diem	"	6,283 00	
Expenses of Senate Committee incurred in part payment of costs of contested election—Wilson vs. McKinlay—Regular session	"	1,000 00	
Nellie M. Day— Copying laws, journals, etc., in part	"	350 00	
George R. Paullen— Distributing laws, journals, etc., in full	"	30 00	
James H. Curtis— Distributing laws, journals, etc	"	135 00	
McCosky & Holcomb— Wiring rooms for electric lighting of State House.	"	215 00	
Adams Express Co.— Express charges on laws, journals, etc	"	41 82	
American Express Co.: Express charges on laws, journals, etc	"	74 49	
United States Express Co.— Express charges on laws, journals, etc	"	76 24	
Fort Wayne Electric Co.— Express charges paid on armature received	"	6 00	
Amounts carried forward	....	$189,623 85	$308,903 86

Statement 3—Continued.

Accounts.	App.	Amount.	Total.
Amounts brought forward		$189,623 85	$308,903 86
GENERAL ASSEMBLY—*Continued.*			
R. M. Ridgely, P. M.— Postage stamps furnished for distributing laws, journals, etc	1893	453 38	
P. H. Kelly, P. M.— Postage stamps furnished for distributing laws, journals, etc	"	100 00	
J. W. Barrett— Amount paid for postage on election returns	"	39 21	
Patrick Higgins— Amount paid for freight and drayage on public documents	"	16 98	
W. F. Downs— Amount paid for freight and drayage on public documents	"	3 00	
Members of the Senate—Extraordinary Session— Per diem, mileage, compensation for postage, stationery, etc	"	13,942 20	
Officers of the Senate—Extraordinary Session— Per diem	"	1,524 00	
Members of the House of Representatives—Extraordinary Session— Per diem, mileage, compensation for postage, stationery, etc	"	41,761 50	
Officers of the House of Representatives—Extraordinary Session— Per diem	"	1,656 00	
Employés of the Senate—Regular Session— Per diem	1895	34,386 00	
Employés of the House of Representatives—Regular Session— Per diem	"	30,971 50	
Employés Appointed by Secretary of State—Regular Session— Per diem	"	42,098 00	
Temporary Officers of the Senate—Regular Session— Per diem	"	11 00	
Temporary Officers and Employés of the House of Representatives—Regular Session— Per diem	"	60 00	
Temporary Employés of the House of Representatives Appointed by the Secretary of State—Regular Session— Per diem	"	138 00	
Employés of the Senate—Extraordinary Session— Per diem	"	2,413 50	
Employés of the House of Representatives—Extraordinary Session— Per diem	"	3,707 50	
Employes Appointed by Secretary of State—Extraordinary Session— Per diem	"	574 00	
Balance of expenses of Senate committee incurred in contested election—Wilson vs. McKinlay—Regular session	"	1,964 82	
Expenses of Senate and House committees incurred in traveling, etc.—Regular session	"	6,692 82	
Expenses of Senate and House committees incurred in traveling, etc.—Extraordinary session	"	638 25	
Nellie M. Day— Copying laws, journals, etc., in full	"	81 50	
James H. Curtis— Distributing laws, journals, etc	"	135 00	
R. M. Ridgely, P. M.— Postage stamps furnished for distributing laws, journals, etc	"	975 00	
P. H. Kelly, P. M.— Postage stamps furnished for distributing laws, journals, etc	"	200 00	
Frank Fleury— Postage stamps furnished for distributing laws, journals, etc	"	36 00	
Amounts carried forward		$374,203 01	$308,903 86

Statement 3—Continued.

Accounts.	App.	Amount.	Total.
Amounts brought forward	....	$374,203 01	$308,903 86
GENERAL ASSEMBLY—*Continued.*			
Adams Express Co.— Express charges paid on laws, journals, etc	1895	141 41	
American Express Co.— Express charges paid on laws journals, etc	"	400 90	
Pacific Express Co.— Express charges paid on laws, journals, etc	"	25 13	
United States Express Co.— Express charges paid on laws, journals, etc	"	441 31	
Wabash Railroad Co.— Freight charges paid on paper	"	9 20	
John W. Barrett— Postage paid on election returns	"	15 72	
Barkley & Lax— Amount paid for hauling public documents	"	7 75	
Patrick Higgins— Express charges paid on books, and drayage	"	12 26	
			375,256 69
To amount paid from appropriation of 1893.. $249,129 12 " " " 1895.. 126,136 57			
HEATING AND LIGHTING.			
M. F. DeSouza— Repairs on pump and work on electric engine	1893	15 50	
Wm. M. Payne— Hardware supplies furnished heating and lighting departments	"	452 68	
Ætna Foundry and Machine Co.— Repairs and material furnished heating and light-departments	"	369 03	
Springfield Gas Light Co.— Gas furnished for lighting State house, etc	"	1,550 85	
Springfield Water Works— Water furnished State house, heating department, etc	"	734 07	
The National Carbon Co.— Amount due for carbons furnished	"	90 00	
John M. Striffler— Ice furnished heating department	"	22 00	
Crane Company— Asbestos, hanfelt covering and other material furnished heating department	"	25 93	
Hellweg & Hopkins— Repairs and material furnished heating department	"	293 98	
Blakesley & Son— 1 bbl. boiler purger furnished heating department	"	27 60	
M. Zwicky's Sons— 5 boxes "Uncle Tom" tar soap furnished heating department	"	25 00	
McCord & Stewart— Repairs and material furnished heating and lighting department	"	8 90	
J. C. Moorhead— Repairs and material furnished heating and light-departments	"	15 75	
D. A. Stuart & Co.— Scale dissolvent, machine and dynamo oil, elevator grease, waste, boiler purger and Japan varnish furnished heating and lighting departments	"	314 99	
F. P. Sullivan, Administrator of the estate of D. A. Stuart, deceased— Scale dissolvent and valve oil furnished heating and lighting departments	"	77 60	
Ridgely National Bank— Amount due for gas furnished for lighting State house, etc., by Springfield Gas Light Co	"	216 20	
Capital Coal Co.— 2230.49 tons of coal furnished heating department on contract	"	2,230 49	
Amounts carried forward	....	$6,470 57	$684,160 55

Statement 3—Continued.

Accounts.	App.	Amount.	Total.
Amounts brought forward	....	$6,470 57	$684,160 55
HEATING AND LIGHTING—*Continued.*			
R. Haas Electric and Manufacturing Co.— Chamois, brass connections, porcelain knobs, wire, tape and battery zincs furnished lighting department	1893	30 07	
Packless Valve Co.— 1 No. 16 valve furnished heating department	"	5 22	
Patrick Higgins— Freight and drayage paid on carbons for lighting department	"	5 30	
O. Hanratty— Repairing water pipes, moving and repairing pipes at pump, fittings, radiator air valves, brasses, etc., furnished, on account of heating and lighting departments	"	129 70	
Fort Wayne Electric Corporation— Opal globes, cask and 825 lbs. Amer brushes furnished lighting department	"	9 75	
A. H. Merkel— Paint, oil, brushes and gasoline furnished lighting department	"	2 60	
William Drake— Calking boiler of heating department	"	1 50	
P. Vredenburgh— Lumber, etc., furnished heating department	"	6 61	
Charles J. Bretz— Oil furnished heating department	"	2 00	
Adam Hoff— Part payment for services as fireman at heating department	"	30 00	
John Stroub— Part payment for services as fireman at heating department	"	40 00	
John T. Rittman— Part payment for services as fireman at heating department	"	130 00	
C. H Otto— 7 days' services as fireman at heating department	"	14 00	
Mike White— 9 days' services as fireman at heating department	"	18 00	
John Graham— 9 days services as fireman at heating department	"	18 00	
Adolph Leutenmayer— 9 days services as fireman at heating department	"	18 00	
James Calligan— 7 days services as fireman at heating department	"	14 00	
John Dillon— 8 days services as fireman at heating department	"	16 00	
James Fitzpatrick— Part payment for services as fireman at heating department	"	10 00	
Joseph Creed— Part payment for services as fireman at heating department	"	60 00	
J. H. McDonnell— Part payment for services as weigher at heating department	"	205 00	
Richard Wolfsberg— Part payment for services as electrician at lighting department	"	110 01	
W. F. Bretz— Part payment for services as electrician at lighting department	"	15 00	
W. F. Bretz, et al, employès of lighting department— Amount in part paid for services as electrician and janitor of lighting department, as per pay-roll of W. H. Hinrichsen, Secretary of State	"	135 00	
August Bartling, et al, employès of heating and lighting departments— Amount paid for services as per pay-rolls of W. H. Hinrichsen, Secretary of State	"	6,915 00	
Amounts carried forward	....	$14,396 33	$684,160 55

Statement 3—Continued.

Accounts.	App.	Amount.	Total.
Amounts brought foward	......	$14,396 33	$684,160 55
HEATING AND LIGHTING—*Continued.*			
Capital Coal Co.— 4,679.31 tons of coal furnished heating department, on contract	1895	4,679 31	
Ætna Foundry and Machine Co.— Repairs and material furnished heating and lighting departments	"	948 05	
Springfield Water Works— Water furnished State House, heating department, etc	"	1,293 72	
Springfield Gas Light Co.— Gas furnished for lighting State House, etc	"	653 70	
Capital Electric Co.— Electric lighting of State House	"	1,834 60	
Fort Wayne Electric Corporation— Opal globes for American arc lamps, and casks	"	4 75	
Chicago Edison Co.— Electrical merchandise furnished	"	206 31	
R. Haas Electric and Manufacturing Co.— Electric bell, switches, batteries, pushes, tubes and Westinghouse fan motors furnished lighting department	"	54 55	
National Carbon Co.— 5,000 ½x12 C. C., and 1,000 ½x7 C. C. med. furnished lighting department	"	55 00	
Electric Appliance Co.— Megnetic bell pliers and handles, staples and carbon batteries, furnished lighting department	"	15 39	
Central Electric Co.— 8 Lungen bells, and box for packing, furnished lighting department	"	3 93	
Bechtold & Parker Electric Co.— American lamp parts furnished lighting department	"	32 87	
McCosky & Holcomb— Part payment for wiring State House for electric lighting	"	1,300 00	
Fred Rauth— Repairing boiler, material, etc., furnished heating department	"	148 00	
William M. Payne— Hardware supplies, etc., furnished heating and lighting departments	"	1,277 93	
D. A. Stuart & Co.— Japan varnish, boiler purger, dynamo oil, elevater grease, valve oil, white waste, etc., furnished heating and lighting departments	"	653 27	
M. Zwicky's Sons— Soap furnished heating department	"	20 00	
Charles J. Bretz— Oil furnished heating department	"	5 75	
McCord & Stewart— Repairs and material furnished heating department	"	2 65	
Charles V. Hickox— Premiums on policies 40,004, 119,813 and 127,288 of heating department	"	355 00	
A. H. Merkel— Paint, lead, brush, moulding, etc., furnished heating department	"	6 25	
J. C. Moorhead— Repairing oil can, tin cups and sprinkler furnished heating department	"	3 30	
W. C. Moorhead— Repairing oil cans, etc., for heating department	"	3 15	
R. McCord— Keys and batteries furnished heating department	"	4 75	
John M. Striffler— Ice furnished heating department	"	24 20	
M. F. DeSouza— Work on electrical engine, making piston, wrench furnished, etc., for heating and lighting departments	"	47 09	
Amounts carried forward	......	$28,044 85	$684,160 55

Statement 3—Continued.

ACCOUNCTS.	App.	Amount.	Total.
Amount brought forward	....	$28,044 85	$684,160 55
HEATING AND LIGHTING—*Continued.*			
Patrick Higgins— Freight and drayage charges on carbons for lighting department	1895	7 28	
Packless Valve Co.— Packless valves, steam pipe, trap, etc., furnished heating department	"	145 74	
William Drake— Examining and repairing boilers and flues, charcoal and drayage furnished, on account of heating department	"	19 25	
L. A. Graham— Soap, oil, candles, brooms, etc., furnished heating department	"	24 90	
Moorhead & Atteberry— Lamp covers, repairs and gaskets furnished heating and lighting departments	"	9 75	
August Bartling— Part payment of salary as chief engineer, heating department	"	52 80	
L. A. Graham— Part payment of salary as assistant engineer, heating department	"	150 00	
Perry White— Part payment of salary as assistant engineer, heating department	"	45 00	
Richard Wolfsberg— Part payment of salary as electrician of lighting department	"	710 00	
John Ahern— Salary as fireman, heating department, in full	"	60 00	
James Fitzpatrick— Part payment of salary as fireman, heating department	"	490 00	
W. F. Bretz— Part payment of salary as electrician of lighting department	"	135 00	
Adam Hoff— Part payment of salary as fireman, heating department	"	260 00	
John T. Rittman— Part payment of salary as fireman of heating department	"	120 00	
John Stroub— Part payment of salary as fireman, heating department	"	130 00	
P. H. Durkin— Part payment of salary as fireman, heating department	"	10 00	
Charles McGuire— Part parment of salary as fireman, heating department	"	20 00	
Charles E. Crum— Part payment of salary as elevator conductor, on account, heating department	"	120 00	
Hellweg & Hopkins— Labor, material, plumbing, etc., furnished heating department	"	10 61	
Louis Unverzagt— Sod furnished for sodding boiler house grounds, heating department	"	4 00	
J. C. Koch— Sundry supplies furnished lighting department	"	16 30	
A. Leschen & Sons Rope Co.— Two hundred feet of iron rope furnished heating department	"	17 00	
August Bartling et al., employés of heating and lighting departments— Amount paid for services as per pay-rolls of W. H. Hinrichsen, Secretary of State	"	11,462 20	
Amounts carried forward	....	$42,064 58	$684,160 55

Statement 3—Continued.

Accounts.	App.	Amount.	Total.
Amounts brought forward	....	$42,064 58	$684,160 55
HEATING AND LIGHTING—*Continued.*			
Henry Wulff, State Treasurer— Amount paid employés for services as per pay-rolls of W. H. Hinrichsen, Secretary of State, on account of heating department	1895	1,405 00	
M. F. Dunlap— Balance paid McCosky & Holcomb for wiring State House for electric lighting	"	990 87	44,460 55
To amount paid from appropriations of 1893 for heating, fuel, etc. $10,997 49			
To amount paid from appropriation of 1895 for heating, fuel, etc. 22,644 82			
To amount paid from appropriation of 1893 for lighting State House, etc. 3,413 84			
To amount paid from appropriation of 1895 for lighting State House, etc. 5,113 53			
To amount paid from appropriation of 1895 for heating State House, for wiring building for electric lighting 300 00			
To amount paid from appropriation of 1895 for lighting State House, for wiring building for electric lighting 1,990 87			
ILLINOIS DAIRYMEN'S ASSOCIATION.			
E. E. Garfield, Treasurer— Compiling, publishing and distributing 21st Annual Report of Association	1895	$1,000 00	
G. H. Gurler, President— Compiling, publishing and distributing 22d Annual Report of Association	"	1,000 00	2,000 00
ILLINOIS STATE HISTORICAL SOCIETY.			
Josephine P. Cleveland— Salary as librarian	1893	$500 00	
Josephine P. Cleveland— Expenses attending meeting of the American Library Association	"	110 50	
Josephine P. Cleveland— Expenses paid on account of library	"	158 68	
R. A. Gray— Expenses as trustee of society, postage, etc., paid	"	98 96	
Rufus Blanchard— Historical Atlas of United States furnished	"	15 00	
Charles L. Woodward— Historical publications furnished	"	56 25	
The Robert Clarke Co.— Historical publications furnished	"	16 65	
Eva Munson Smith— Historical publications furnished	"	4 50	
David Gore, for Bernard Quaritch, London, England— Historical publications furnished and express charges paid	"	4 48	
A. C. McClurg & Co.— Historical publications furnished	"	4 93	
T. L. Cole— Historical publications furnished	"	10 25	
A. J. Ludlam— Geological and Adjutant General's reports furnished	"	22 50	
The Bancroft Co.— Sections 1, 2, 3, 4 and 5, Book of the Fair, furnished	"	37 50	
David G. Francis— Annals of Congress, Register of Debates, Congression Globe and Record, 282 vols., boxes and cartage, furnished	"	230 25	
W. H. Lowdermilk & Co.— Historical publications furnished	"	110 25	
Amounts carried forward	....	$1,380 70	$730,621 10

Statement 3—Continued.

Accounts.	App.	Amount.	Total.
Amounts brought forward	......	$1,380 70	$730,621 10
ILLINOIS STATE HISTORICAL SOCIETY—*Continued.*			
John Moses— Moses' History of Chicago furnished	1893	22 50	
E. S. Walker— Historical publications and map of Springfield, furnished	"	17 50	
William Hanna— History of 50th Regiment, Illinois Infantry Vols., furnished	"	3 00	
J. L. Pickering— 1 Legislative Directory, 1895, furnished	"	5 00	
The Bowen-Merrill Co.— Thompson's Personal Recollections and other historical publications furnished	"	12 25	
Dodd-Mead Co.— Historical publications furnished	"	127 00	
Elizabeth Bryant Johnson— George Washington Day by Day, furnished	"	2 50	
J. L. Stocking— 1 set, 5 vols., Larned's History for Ready Refer-fence, furnished	"	37 50	
Rand, McNally & Co.— World's Fair Album (Art) furnished	"	8 50	
Cyrus Adler— 1 vol. American Jewish Historical Society, furnished	"	1 50	
Martin I. J. Griffin— Subscription to The American Catholic Historical Research for 1895	"	1 00	
Archaeologist Publishing Co.— Subscription to Archaeologist for year ending December 31, 1895	"	1 00	
E. W. Smith & Co.— Maps, atlases, box, etc., furnished	"	63 50	
Thomas Kane & Co.— One Rudolph Indexer, complete, furnished	"	150 00	
A. Dirksen & Sons— 8 bookcases for library furnished	"	104 00	
Josephine P. Cleveland— Salary as librarian	1895	750 00	
Josephine P. Cleveland— Expenses paid on account of library	"	94 45	
Caroline L. Tozier— Dusting and marking books in library, 20 days	"	25 00	
John Britnell— Garneau History of Canada furnished	"	3 43	
Library Bureau— Letter files and other supplies furnished	"	29 97	
E. S. Walker— Atlas of Sangamon county and historical publications furnished and rebinding volume	"	10 90	
H. E. Barker— Atlasses of Logan and Hancock counties, life etc. of Andrew Jackson furnished	"	14 00	
American Express Co.— Express charges, etc., on box of books from London, England	"	12 67	
The Robert Clarke Co.— Historical publications furnished	"	26 14	
Burrows Brothers Co.— Historical publications furnished	"	19 89	
Bernard Quaritch— Historical publications furnished	"	193 62	
Rufus Blanchard— Historical publications furnished	"	21 50	
Slyvia Schermerhorn— Typewriting letters, envelopes, etc	"	12 50	
William L. Newlin— History of 125th Regt. Ill. Vol. Infantry	"	1 25	
A. Dirksen & Sons— Balance due from bookcases, etc., furnished	"	94 25	
Dodd-Mead Co.— One copy John Cabot furnished	"	7 50	
Amounts carried forward	......	$3,254 52	$730,621 10

Statement 3—Continued.

Accounts.	App.	Amount.	Total.
Amounts brought forward	....	$3,254 52	$730,621 10
ILLINOIS STATE HISTORICAL SOCIETY—*Continued.*			
Stephen D. Pelt— 3 volumes American Antique furnished and subscription paid	1895	$13 50	
A. C. McClurg & Co.— Historical publications furnished	"	68 85	
Martin I. J. Griffin— Subscription to American Catholic Historical Researches	"	1 00	
A. J. Rudolph— Typewriting and preparing indexes, Rudolph indexer, express charges paid	"	23 65	
Robert A. Gray— Traveling expenses, etc., as Trustee of Society	"	50 00	
Houghton, Mifflin & Co.— One copy Mississippi Basin furnished	"	3 20	
Joseph J. Casey— Index to Herring's Statute furnished	"	4 50	
Harper's Brothers— One copy American Congress furnished	"	2 40	
The MacMillan Co.— One copy Bruce's Virginia furnished	"	5 80	
A. S. Clark— Historical publications furnished	"	15 04	
Willsey & Wood— One copy Harper's Book of Facts furnished	"	8 00	
F. M. Crouse— Historical publications furnished	"	4 50	
C. S. Burrows— Historical publications furnished	"	6 85	
			3,461 81
To amount paid from appropriation of 1893.... $1,937 45 " " " 1895.... 1,524 36			
ILLINOIS STATE HORTICULTURAL SOCIETY.			
Arthur Bryant, Treasurer— Appropriation for advancing the growth and development of the horticultural interests of the State of Illinois	1893	$2,000 00	
Arthur Bryant, Treasurer— Appropriation for advancing the growth and development of the horticultural interests of the State of Illinois	1895	4,000 00	
			6,000 00
ILLINOIS STATE NATIONAL GUARD.			
Eml. Salzenstein— Horses furnished and straw, oats and hay supplied during encampment of 1894, as per contract	1893	$2,254 85	
Eml. Salzenstein— Boarding State horse, and veterinary services rendered thereto	"	86 00	
Springfield Consolidated Railway Co.— Transporting troops to and from Camp Lincoln during encampment of 1894	"	9 28	
H. L. Hampton— Commissary stores furnished troops at Camp Lincoln during encampment of 1894	"	44 19	
Major J. C. Cabanis, A. A. Q. M.— Amount paid for freight on public property during encampment of 1894	"	3 63	
E. S. Gard— 2 dozen brooms furnished, encampment of 1894	"	5 50	
Barkley & Lax— Hauling public property, encampment of 1894	"	67 50	
R. F. Kinsella— Paint furnished and painting, encampment of 1894	"	47 70	
McGrue & Powell— 500 oak tent pins furnished encampment of 1894	"	17 50	
Amounts carried forward	....	$2,536 15	$740,082 91

Statement 3—Continued.

Accounts.	App.	Amount.	Total.
Amounts brought forward	....	$2,536 15	$740,082 91
ILLINOIS NATIONAL GUARD—*Continued.*			
W. B. Miller & Son— Hardware supplies furnished encampment of 1894	1893	$15 62	
B. H. Ferguson— 8½ dozen knives furnished encampment of 1894	"	4 75	
Col. H. L. Turner— Active duty of members 1st Regt. Camp Detail at Camp Lincoln during encampment of 1894	"	44 00	
B. Franz & Bro.— Subsistence furnished troops at Camp Lincoln encampment of 1894	"	413 36	
C. A. Power— Carpenter work at Camp Lincoln, encampment of 1894	"	56 42	
Henson Robinson Co.— Pipe and elbows for 45 cooking ranges and quartermaster's stores furnished encampment of 1894	"	350 90	
Springfield Coöperative Coal Mining Co.— Coal furnished troops at Camp Lincoln, encampment of 1894	"	27 72	
John W. Bunn & Co.— Commissary stores furnished troops, encampment of 1894	"	132 06	
Robert D. Loose— Milk furnished troops, encampment of 1894	"	15 68	
Charles Pfeffer— Bread furnished troops, encampment of 1894	"	18 30	
M. Zwicky's Sons— Soap and candles furnished troops, encampment of 1894	"	11 60	
The John Bressmer Co.— Supplies furnished troops, encampment of 1894	"	55 77	
Major J. C. Cabanis— Amount of pay-rolls of civil employés at Camp Lincoln	"	786 37	
Peter Vredenburgh— Lumber, shingles, etc., furnished for repairs at Camp Lincoln	"	115 97	
Davidson & Henley— Stiff tongue put in sprinkler wagon at Camp Lincoln	"	3 00	
E. F. Gehlman— Labor and material furnished at Camp Lincoln	"	50 79	
Wm. Ihlenfeldt— Keys for lock on gate at Camp Lincoln furnished	"	2 50	
J. M. Striffler— Ice furnished troops at Camp Lincoln	"	32 34	
Zimmerman & Prouty— Paste brush furnished for Camp Lincoln	"	1 75	
Richard Beet— Pump furnished and repairs made at Camp Lincoln	"	10 30	
Clark Cabanis— Two days' labor performed at Camp Lincoln	"	3 00	
John W. Elliott— Trimming hedge and repairing fence at Camp Lincoln	"	10 00	
Fred H. Solle— Coal oil furnished for use at Camp Lincoln	"	2 55	
J. W. Dilks— Services as watchman, 1 night, at Camp Lincoln	"	1 50	
Hellweg & Hopkins— Plumbing work done at Camp Lincoln and office of Adjutant General	"	41 88	
Springfield Electric Light and Power Co— Lights, wire, lamps, etc., used at Camp Lincoln	"	175 00	
Edward Fitzgerald— Amount due for labor performed at Camp Lincoln	"	25 00	
Studebaker Brothers Mfg Co.— Sprinkler, with Niagara valve, furnished Camp Lincoln	"	410 00	
Allen Enos— Surveying, etc., east line of Camp Lincoln	"	8 40	
Amounts carried forward	....	$5,362 68	$740,082 91

Statement 3—Continued.

Accounts.	App.	Amount.	Total.
Amounts brought forward	......	$5,362 68	$740,082 91
ILLINOIS STATE NATIONAL GUARD—*Continued.*			
The Granolithic Pavement Co.— Repairing and re-cementing swimming pool at Camp Lincoln	"	624 49	
Central Union Telephone Co.— Rental of telephone, and services, at Camp Lincoln	"	20 00	
John E. White— Carpenter work done at Camp Lincoln	"	60 45	
Captain Robert H. Aiken— Amount of pay-roll of civil employés at Camp Lincoln	"	431 74	
Brigadier General H. A. Wheeler— Amount paid for expenses of Logan Rifle Range	"	1,449 14	
Springfield Boiler and Mfg. Co.— Fourteen sets silhouette figures for rifle practice at Logan Rifle Range	"	100 76	
V. H. Sweinhart— Salary as Range officer, reloading shells, freight paid, and supplies furnished Logan Rifle Range	"	1,061 17	
Raymond Lead Co.— Pig lead and tin furnished Logan Rifle Range	"	354 69	
Brigadier General H. A. Wheeler— Services of T. H. Rust, custodian, Logan Rifle Range	"	25 00	
E. S. Rice— Twenty-five kegs rifle powder furnished Logan Rifle Range	"	81 25	
Rogers & Wells— Receipt book furnished for Logan Rifle Range	"	10 75	
Marshall Field & Co.— Cloth, etc., for targets, furnished Logan Rifle Range	"	53 03	
Standard Oil Co.— One barrel oil furnished Logan Rifle Range	"	5 56	
Captain R. H. Aiken— Amount paid for expenses, Logan Rifle Range	"	692 64	
Captain R. H. Aiken— Salary as Range officer, Logan Rifle Range	"	300 00	
John Spence— Cleaning wells on Rifle range and parade ground, and new pump furnished	"	17 50	
Central Union Telephone Co.— Rental and telephone service at State Arsenal	"	48 00	
Postal Telegraph-Cable Co.— Amount due for telegraphic service rendered	"	1 90	
Western Union Telegraph Co.— Time service and telegraphic service rendered	"	92 79	
Adams Express Co.— Express charges due on public property	"	132 23	
American Express Co.— Express charges due on public property	"	1,103 92	
United States Express Co.— Express charges due on public property	"	771 56	
Baltimore & Ohio Southwestern Railway Co.— Amount due for freight charges on public property	"	26 31	
Chicago & Alton Railroad Co.— Amount due for freight charges on public property	"	43 29	
Chicago, Peoria & St. Louis Railroad Co.— Amount due for freight charges on public property	"	8 24	
Illinois Central Railroad Co.— Amount due for freight charges on public property	"	114 01	
Wabash Railroad Co.— Amount due for freight charges on public property	"	14 39	
F. D. Comstock, Treasurer— Cleveland, Cincinnati, Chicago & St. Louis Railroad, transportation of officers on tour of inspection	"	2 69	
T. D. Hinchcliffe, Auditor— Chicago, Peoria & St. Louis Railroad, transportation of troops during strike of 1894	"	76 94	
C. O. Patier— Commissary stores furnished troops at Mounds, 1894 strike	"	620 31	
Amounts carried forward	......	$13,707 43	$740,082 91

Statement 3—Continued.

Accounts.	App.	Amount.	Total.
Amounts brought forward	....	$13,707 43	$740,082 91
ILLINOIS STATE NATIONAL GUARD—*Continued.*			
J. A. Orendorff— Services in quartermaster's department at Decatur, during strike 1894, and expenses under orders, Chicago	1893	83 40	
Major J. C. Cabanis— Personal expenses under orders and Arsenal expenses paid, $141.94; freight charges on tents at Galesburg, $4.30; expenses at Chicago on account of disbandment of Illinois Naval Militia and amount paid for labor in moving and transferring State property from battleship, Illinois, etc., $79.85	"	226 09	
Captain H. M. Smith— Services in quartermaster's department at Chicago, etc., during strike of 1894	"	35 00	
Morehouse, Wells & Co.— Quartermaster's stores furnished troops at Decatur during strike of 1894	"	12 94	
Captain E. H. D. Couch— Services of T. F. Sheehan, musician, to Co. L, 5th Regt., during strike of 1894 at Danville	"	14 00	
Colonel Hugh E. Bayle— Expenses under orders in discharge of duties as Assistant Adjutant General, 1894 strike, etc	"	710 25	
General Alfred Orendorff— Expenses under orders in discharge of duties as Adjutant General, during strike of 1894, revision of Military Code at Chicago, etc	"	731 75	
Brigadier-General H. A. Wheeler— Stationery furnished and other expenses incurred on account of Headquarters, 1st Brigade, $513.40; and expenses at Chicago revising Military Code, $10.00	"	523 40	
Colonel Francis T. Colby— Amount paid on account of 7th Regiment for janitors, postage, hauling, gas, water, coal, cleaning uniforms, repairs, telephone charges, commissary stores furnished, and transportation, and services of private, Thomas Davis, Co. D, 7th Regiment, etc	"	2,624 10	
Price Clothing House— Blouses and trousers furnished troops on contract.	"	1,783 75	
Lieutenant Frank B. Gilder— Amount due for rent of Armory	"	87 50	
George S. Connolly & Co.— Subsistence furnished troops at Wabash shops, Springfield, Camp Lincoln and Chicago, during strike of 1894	"	360 56	
W. B. Miller & Son— Hardware supplies furnished State Arsenal	"	29 88	
Dr. Wm. A. Hickman— Medical stores furnished troops during strike of 1894, and camphor and moth balls furnished State Arsenal	"	48 03	
C. A. Power— Gun rack, gun carriages, etc., furnished Memorial Hall on contract	"	33 40	
Fred L. Schlierbach— Services as quartermater at Spring Valley during strike of 1894	"	36 65	
John W. Webster— Wood furnished troops at Danville, strike of 1894	"	9 30	
Vance and Dooling— Insurance premiums on insurance of public property	"	789 90	
Major E. J. Lang— Amount due Field, staff and non-commissioned staff, 4th Regimen, for services rendered during strike of 1894, at Chicago, as per pay-roll	"	254 32	
Captain Ed. E. Elliott— Amount due members of Co. A, 4th Regiment, for services rendered during strike of 1894, at Chicago, as per pay-roll	"	1,123 68	
Amounts carried forward	....	$23,225 33	$740,082 91

Statement 3—Continued.

Account.	App.	Amount.	Total.
Amounts brought forward	....	$23,225 33	$740,082 91
ILLINOIS NATIONAL GUARD—*Continued.*			
Captain E. W. Hersch— Amount due members, Co. B, 4th Regiment, for services rendered during strike of 1894, at Chicago, as per pay-roll	1893	1,073 09	
Captain Charles E. Rudy— Amount due members, Co. E, 4th Regiment, for services rendered during strike of 1894, at Chicago, as per pay-roll	"	1,185 76	
Captain McFarren Davis— Amount due members, Co. H, 4th Regiment, for services rendered during strike of 1894, at Chicago, as per pay-roll	"	1,315 30	
Captain W. N. Rickard— Amount due members, Co. L, 4th Regiment, for services rendered during strike of 1894, at Chicago, as per pay-roll	"	1,350 94	
Colonel J. S. Culver— Amount due field, staff and non-commissioned staff, 5th Regiment, for services rendered during strike of 1894, while stationed at Chicago, Decatur, Pekin and Danville, as per pay-roll	"	717 13	
Captain C. E. Collier— Amount due members, Co. E, 5th Regiment, for services rendered during strike of 1894, at Chicago, as per pay-roll	"	1,311 64	
Colonel D. Jack Foster— Amount due field, staff and non-commissioned staff, 6th Regiment, for services rendered during strike of 1894, at Chicago, as per pay-roll	"	1,851 56	
Captain J. W. Meloy— Amount due members, Co. D, 6th Regiment, for services rendered during strike of 1894, at Chicago and Springfield, as per pay-roll	"	1,940 39	
James Dillon— Hauling for troops at Chicago, 1894 strike	"	5 00	
James Griffin— Hauling for troops at Chicago, 1894 strike	"	1 00	
James H. Etheridge— 3 trunks furnished for medicines and surgical dressings, 1894 strike	"	21 60	
George Mitchell— Teaming for troops at Chicago, 1894 strike	"	5 00	
C. E. Masters— Teaming for troops at Chicago, 1894 strike	"	5 00	
Lakin & Co.— Teaming for troops at Chicago, 1894 strike	"	9 00	
Charles Litzinge— Teaming for troops at Chicago, 1894 strike	"	3 50	
Colonel D. J. Foster— Expenses, ordering and massing troops at Chicago, telegrams, etc., 1894 strike	"	22 32	
N. F. Ratty— Teaming for troops at Chicago, 1894 strike	"	10 00	
K. H. Hendrickson— Quartermaster's stores furnished troops, Chicago strike, 1894	"	2 40	
Armour & Co.— Commissary stores furnished troops, Chicago strike, 1894	"	336 89	
A. F. Whittemore— Commissary stores furnished troops, Chicago strike, 1894	"	220 81	
The Wm. Schmidt Baking Co.— Commissary stores furnished troops, Chicago strike, 1894	"	74 56	
The Heissler & Jurage Co.— Commissary stores furnished troops, Chicago strike, 1894	"	72 00	
D. T. Collins— Commissary stores furnished troops, Chicago strike, 1894	"	46 20	
Amounts carried forward	....	$34,806 42	$740,082 91

Statement 3—Continued.

Accounts.	App.	Amount.	Total.
Amounts brought foward	....	$34,806 42	$740,082 91
ILLINOIS STATE NATIONAL GUARD—*Continued.*			
Consumer's Pure Ice Co.— Commissary stores furnished troops, Chicago strike, 1894	1893	43 17	
Edward Koenig— Medical supplies furnished troops, Chicago strike, 1894	"	13 88	
D. J. Stewart— Commissary and quartermaster's stores furnished troops, Chicago strike, 1894	"	887 94	
Jones & Laughlin, (Limited)— Iron work furnished for Logan Rifle Range	"	10 23	
E. S. Rice, Agent— 20 kegs rifle powder furnished Logan Rifle Range	"	65 00	
Meacham & Wright— 6 bbls. Portland cement furnished Logan Rifle Range	"	17 40	
Raymond Lead Co.— 2 small pigs lead furnished Logan Rifle Range	"	11 22	
Chicago Paper Co.— 720 lbs. manila paper furnished Logan Rifle Range	"	35 67	
Hibbard, Spencer, Bartlett & Co.— Roofing paper, rifle cartridges and primers furnished Logan Rifle Range	"	263 13	
Raymond Lead Co.— Pig lead and tin furnished Logan Rifle Range	"	89 58	
Lyon & Healy— 2 drums furnished 7th Regiment, 1894 strike	"	28 40	
E. S. Rice, Agent— 23 kegs powder and reloading shells, 1894 strike	"	74 75	
Morin & Son— Ice furnished troops at Danville, 1894 strike	"	16 56	
Hollister & Son— Quartermaster's stores furnished troops at Danville, 1894 strike	"	40 50	
W. T. Dickson— Commissary stores furnished troops at Danville, 1894 strike	"	295 23	
J. C. Morehouse— Commissary stores furnished troops at Danville, 1894 strike	"	291 68	
C. B. Fenton— Commissary stores furnished troops at Danville, 1894 strike	"	28 25	
Danville Transfer Co.— Quartermaster's stores furnished troops at Danville, 194 strike	"	48 25	
Hercer Brothers— Commissary stores furnished troops at Spring Valley, 1894 strike	"	39 85	
S. M. Horner— Subsistence furnished troops at Spring Valley, 1894 strike	"	8 75	
J. B. Callan— Subsistence furnished 5th Regt., enroute from Chicago, 1894 strike	"	38 00	
Captain T. Leslie McGirr— Amount paid on account of medical attendance on troops at Spring Valley, stenographer, telegrams and teaming, expenses at Pekin, transportation, etc., strike of 1894	"	40 25	
C. F. Meyer & Co.— Straw furnished troops at Mounds, strike of 1894	"	8 00	
Captain Charles P. Collier— Subsistence, livery hire and amounl paid for medical attention to Co. E, 5th Regt., strike of 1894	"	33 75	
Amounts paid the following named persons and firms for medical supplies, commissary and quartermaster's stores, teaming, transportation, services, express charges, etc., furnished and rendered troops during the strike of 1894, at Chicago, viz:			
L. E. Howard	"	97 00	
Swift & Co.	"	94 83	
Amounts carried foward	....	$37,427 69	$740,082 91

Statement 3—Continued.

Accounts.	App.	Amount.	Total.
Amounts brought forward	....	$34,806 42	$740,082 91
ILLINOIS STATE NATIONAL GUARD—*Continued.*			
Horatio L. Wait	1893	94 07	
Consumer's Pure Ice Co	"	92 55	
Armour & Co	"	91 43	
Franklin McVeagh & Co	"	84 15	
J. G. Gahagan	"	83 15	
C. L. Roy	"	81 75	
Siegel, Cooper & Co	"	74 76	
D. F. Bremner	"	70 88	
Sprague, Warner & Co	"	69 92	
T. L. Reynolds	"	56 85	
L. A. Budlong	"	56 00	
W. R. Shiel	"	50 67	
W. Morris & Sons	"	47 70	
Lockwood & Strickland	"	40 59	
P. K. Howard	"	40 00	
Hibbard, Spencer, Bartlett & Co	"	39 20	
Wallace R. Martin	"	39 00	
Capt. Paul B. Lino	"	38 97	
C. Y. Transfer Co	"	34 60	
M. Bracken	"	33 75	
Union Stock Yards and Transit Co,	"	32 50	
Robert Stevenson & Co	"	31 88	
Henry Hoffman	"	31 85	
J. H. M. Schroeter	"	30 15	
F. L. Lade	"	30 00	
Symonds, Tyrrell & Co	"	29 25	
John M. Smyth & Co	"	28 32	
Hibbard, Spencer, Bartlett & Co	"	27 06	
Thomas & Browne	"	26 00	
Capt. A. L. Bolté	"	25 03	
Aldrich Baking Co	"	24 84	
Knickerbocker Ice Co	"	23 25	
Joseph Morey	"	22 40	
E. O. Studley	"	22 00	
W. R. Shiel	"	21 00	
Anderson Transfer Co	"	21 00	
Joseph T. Leimert	"	20 75	
Aldrich Baking Co	"	20 55	
E. H. Schloeman	"	20 00	
Charles D. Bennett	"	19 90	
F. E. Coyne	"	19 10	
W. R. Shiel	"	18 90	
Carey & Ryder	"	18 00	
C. Y. Transfer Co	"	18 00	
A. M. Chamberlin	"	17 43	
Charles E. Sherwood	"	17 00	
D. Ayers	"	16 85	
Col. Leroy T. Steward	"	16 05	
Capt. Joseph Leiter	"	15 55	
John J. Magee	"	15 35	
Stock Yards Lumber and Coal Co	"	15 00	
Daube Bros. & Co	"	15 00	
Frank Parmalee	"	15 00	
Sprague, Warner & Co	"	14 69	
L. P. Anderson	"	14 25	
Geo. L. Hinckley	"	14 00	
S. D. Kimbark	"	12 75	
Metropolitan Restaurant	"	11 75	
Frank Eschbacker	"	10 25	
D. J. O'Brien	"	10 25	
Lieut. W. J. Lloyd	"	10 00	
B. M. Shaffner	"	9 75	
Adams & Westlake Co	"	9 25	
Humiston, Keeling & Co	"	8 72	
Hibbard, Spencer, Bartlett & Co	"	8 41	
Capt. Willis J. Wells	"	7 25	
William Hunt	"	7 00	
Louis B. Marks	"	6 78	
Chas. Truax, Greene & Co	"	6 62	
J. W. Slough	"	6 47	
Amounts carried forward	....	$39,540 83	$740,082 91

Statement 3—Continued.

Accounts.	App.	Amount.	Total.
Amounts brought forward	....	$39,540 83	$740,082 91
ILLINOIS STATE NATIONAL GUARD—*Continued.*			
Morgan & Wright	1893	6 25	
T. R. Randall & Co	"	6 15	
A. Booth Packing Co	"	6 00	
George Nelson	"	6 00	
Metropolitan Restaurant Co	"	5 86	
Swift & Co	"	5 55	
Capt. George Meehan	"	5 45	
Metropolitan Restaurant Co	"	5 41	
Harvey L. Goodall	"	4 50	
Miller & Shariger	"	4 25	
D. O'Connell	"	4 00	
P. Miller	"	3 75	
W. Doody	"	3 00	
Shark & Smith	"	2 75	
A. H. McNeal	"	2 70	
P. A. Johnson	"	2 50	
Andrew Hartman	"	2 50	
J. S. Cessna	"	2 45	
J. J. O'Brien	"	2 15	
A. Booth Packing Co	"	2 00	
Harrison C. Hopper	"	1 80	
Capt. W. B. Alexander	"	1 75	
The Heissler & Jauge Co	"	1 44	
Lieut. E. B. Eddy	"	1 30	
Worrants were issued to the following named persons and firms in payment for services rendered, or articles furnished to the Illinois National Guard during the strike of 1894, in and about Chicago, viz.:			
Major B. B. Griffith—Pay of rank while under orders	"	18 75	
Capt. A. W. Buttler, Co. C, 5th Regiment—Livery hire assembling command	"	12 50	
Dr. Louis Thexton—Surgical operation on Guy Stickle, Co. D, 3rd Regiment	"	14 50	
Capt. C. Andel, Co. D, 4th Regiment—Ammunition, freight, teaming, etc., paid for	"	23 90	
Capt. W. P. Butler, Troop B, Cavalry—Subsistence and hauling paid for	"	20 30	
Capt. L. H. Gillett, Co. M, 5th Regiment—Livery hire, rations, transportation, etc	"	41 66	
C. G. Brush—Subsistence, etc., furnished Co. C, 4th Regiment.	"	12 00	
Capt. W. H. Glasgow, Co. M, 6th Regiment—Livery, etc., assembling command	"	8 50	
Capt. W. D. Clark, Co. B, 6th Regiment—Rations furnished while en route	"	14 00	
Capt. Fred. W. Pearson, Co. B, 3d Regiment—Livery, etc., assembling command	"	5 50	
Daniel V. McCarthy—Livery, etc., assembling Co. B, 3rd Regimend	"	2 00	
John McFadden—Livery, etc., furnished troops	"	3 00	
John V. Bronk—Livery, etc., furnished troops	"	1 50	
Postal Telegraph Cable Co.—Telegraphic services rendered	"	33	
Western Union Telegraph Co.—Telegraphic services rendered	"	12 46	
East Side Livery Co.—Horse furnished for troops	"	1 00	
Baskerville Brothers—Hauling for troops	"	3 00	
Donald Danked—Medical supplies furnished troops	"	1 75	
Capt. Chas. E. Rudy, Co. E, 4th Regiment—Livery, etc., assembling command	"	8 50	
Capt. Fred. H. Muench, Co. F, 6th Regiment—Rations furnished while en route	"	7 60	
Capt. C. E. Gardner, Co. M, 3rd Regiment—Livery, etc., assembling command	"	14 50	
Amounts carried forward	....	$39,857 19	$740,082 91

Statement 3—Continued.

Accounts.	App.	Amount.	Total.
Amounts brought forward	....	$39,857 19	$740,082 91
ILLINOIS STATE NATIONAL GUARD—*Continued.*			
Capt. W. H. Brogunier, Co. H, 3rd Regiment—Livery, etc., assembling command	1893	17 71	
Capt. W. F. Lawrie, Co. E, 6th Regiment—Rations furnished while en route	"	25 15	
Capt. J. N. St. Clair, Co. A, 3rd Regiment—Livery, etc., assembling command	"	13 50	
Capt. W. C. Eichelberger, Co. G, 3rd Regiment—Livery, etc., assembling command	"	13 50	
Barkley & Lax—Amount due for hauling public property	"	61 00	
T. C. Smith—Teaming for troops during strike, 1894, at Chicago	"	167 50	
Kent Koerner—Translations from Belleville Arbeiter Zeitung	"	5 00	
W. H. Roberts—Typewriter work, copying reports	"	45 45	
A. H. McNeal—Subsistence during tour of duty in Chicago	"	10 35	
Charles Truax, Greene & Co.—Medical and surgical supplies furnished during strike of 1894	"	1,517 95	
The Votzenburg Co.—Medical supplies furnished troops, strike of 1894	"	2 70	
John Olmstead—Shoeing horses for Troop A, at Chicago	"	7 50	
Captain Phil Yeager—Rations, drayage, repairs on harneso, etc., furnished Battery D, during strike of 1894	"	28 55	
Henry Hoffman—Medical supplies furnished troops at Chicago, 1894 strike	"	7 85	
Leroy Payne—Horses furnished Battery A during strike at Chicago	"	8 00	
A. F. Stolle—Sprinkling grounds at Camp Hopkins, Chicago	"	47 25	
Captain M. L. Vanderkloot—Transportation furnished Company E, 2d Regt., 1894 strike	"	1 80	
Colonel Geo. M. Moulton—Transportation, etc., furnished signal corps, 2d Regt., 1894 strike	"	4 35	
P. K. Howard—Hauling for troops at Chicago during strike, 1894, and on account of disbandment of Illinois Naval Militia	"	34 50	
J. M. Striffler—Ice furnished State Arsenal	"	3 50	
D. A. King—Commissary stores furnished troops at Carbondale during strike of 1894	"	9 75	
Shea, Smith & Co.—Stationery furnished 1st Brigade	"	10 65	
O. F. Stebbins—Hardware supplies furnished State Arsenal	"	1 67	
Otto H. Winneborg—6 days' labor at State Arsenal	"	9 00	
Illinois State Register—Official paper, envelopes, etc., furnished companies, Adjutant General, etc	"	316 34	
Charles P. Kane, Agent—Rent of land adjoining Camp Lincoln for one year, March 1, 1894, to March 1, 1895	"	175 00	
Ihlenfeldt & Wiedlocher—Feed for State horse and flour furnished	"	41 90	
J. W. Dilks—Material and repairs for lockers at State Arsenal	"	10 55	
Lyon & Smith—Teaming during June and July, 1894	"	96 75	
Lieutenant D. G. Baker, Jr., U. S. Army—Expenses under orders at Chicago	"	26 25	
Amounts carried forward	....	$42,578 16	$740,082 91

Statement 3—Continued.

Accounts.	App.	Amount.	Total.
Amounts brought forward	....	$42,578 16	$740,082 91
ILLINOIS STATE NATIONAL GUARD—*Continued.*			
Captain W. F. Knoch— Services as private, Edward Gebert, Co. E, 1st Regt.	1893	14 00	
A. L. Toun— Repairs on roof of State Arsenal	"	18 85	
W. H. Newlin— Services with tents, September, 1894	"	3 10	
Charles H. Lanphier, Jr.— Wiring State Arsenal for electric lighting	"	120 00	
Captain W. S. Campbell— Clerical services rendered Headquarters 5th Regt.	"	25 00	
Robert Finnegan— Services as watchman at State Arsenal	"	15 00	
Brand & Groenke— Spring wagon furnished State Arsenal	"	65 00	
William B. Barry— Amount due for shoeing State horse	"	2 00	
Springfield Gas Light Co.— Gas furnished State Arsenal to December 31, 1894	"	1 70	
Hotel Livery Co.— Livery hire from July 14 to August 14, during strike of 1894	"	16 50	
Springfield Water Works— Water furnished Arsenal to July 1, 1895	"	11 00	
Schlierbach & Blucke— 1 set of harness furnished to State horse	"	21 75	
Colonel J. S. Culver— Expenses under orders at Jacksonville, and amount paid Adjutant, postage, record and pen	"	44 48	
Springfield Electric Light and power Co.— Electric light furnished State Arsenal	"	8 76	
George Hodge— Repairing tent poles and shoeing State horse	"	3 25	
Flanders & Zimmerman— Plans and specifications furnished for altering Armory, etc., 7th Regiment, superintending the fitting up quarters for 4th Regiment Armory, Michigan avenue, moving fixtures from 23 Lake street, professional services rendered, etc	"	130 00	
Brigadier General J. H. Barkley— Expenses under orders in Chicago on Board for Revision of Military Code	"	10 00	
Brigadier General Andrew Welch— Expenses under orders in Chicago on Board for Revision of Military Code	"	10 00	
Lieutenant Colonel Leroy T. Steward— 22 days' service inspecting 1st Brigade	"	220 00	
Work Brothers & Co.— 266 military overcoats furnished troops	"	3,045 70	
Captain Fred W. Pearson— Painting lockers and cards on locker doors of Co. B., 3d Regiment	"	7 50	
Colonel Don R. Frazer— Expenses as Assistant Adjutant General, 2nd Brigade, Camp Altgeld, near Chicago	"	25 00	
Dillon & Steamer— Amount due for shoeing State horse	"	2 00	
Edward F. Hartmann— Report blanks, etc., furnished	"	69 25	
Rand, McNally & Co.— Four thousand military maps of Illinois furnished	"	590 00	
A. Aldrich— Packing arms on account of disbandment of Illinois Naval Militia	"	2 00	
C. G. Harrison— Packing arms on account of disbandment of Illinois Naval Militia	"	2 00	
Dr. Albert Babb— Medical attention rendered State horse	"	4 50	
West End Coal Co.— Coal furnished State Arsenal	"	3 74	
Edward J. Remick—			
Amounts carried forward	....	$47,070 24	$740,082 91

Statement 3—Continued.

Accounts.	App.	Amount.	Total.
Amounts brought forward	....	$47,070 24	$740,082 91
ILLINOIS STATE NATIONAL GUARD—*Continued.*			
Moving lockers, etc., for 7th Regiment	1893	67 76	
Springfield Paper Co.— Paper furnished State Arsenal	"	3 10	
William J. Warner— Services as custodian of State property, battleship "Illinois."	"	200 00	
Major W. F. Colladay— Expenses under orders, inspecting 3d Battalion, 5th Regiment	"	4 00	
Major W. T. Channon— Expenses under orders, inspecting 2nd Battalion, 7th Regiment	"	4 50	
Congress Construction Co.— Furnishing and putting up lockers and gun-racks for 7th Regiment, as per contract	"	913 00	
George E. Platt— Medical attention to State horse	"	1 00	
The H. and D. Folsom Arms Co.— 12 sets of reloading tools furnished	"	15 31	
Tunney & Jones— Amount due for shoeing State horse	"	6 00	
August Leroy— Repairing lock and rifle	"	1 00	
S. Karpen & Brothers— Packing State property at 2d Regiment Armory for shipment to Springfield	"	3 00	
Army and Navy Journal— Advertising proposals for uniforms, and subscription to April 13, 1895	"	24 00	
Army and Navy Register— Advertising proposals for uniforms, and subscription to April 13, 1895	"	13 40	
Captain W. D. Clark— Insurance on State property to January 19, 1895	"	11 50	
Wickham & Burns— Amount due for clipping State horse	"	2 50	
Harry Withrow— Repairing fire hydrant at State Arsenal	"	7 00	
Colonel Fred Bennitt— Amounts paid Geo. Mitchell, $6, and Ed. Carroll, $4, for hauling for 3d Regiment	"	10 00	
George H. Williams & Co.— Subsistence furnished 7th Regiment, strike of 1894	"	12 00	
W. C. Lindsay— Subsistence furnished troops, strike of 1894	"	206 60	
Edward Koenig— Medical supplies furnished troops, strike of 1894	"	118 16	
Chicago Ship Building Co. Housing and wintering steam launch and two cutters	"	75 76	
James J. Power— Plumbing at State Arsenal	"	8 25	
R. N. Dodds— Medical supplies furnished troops, strike of 1894	"	32 30	
Klaholt & Fogarty— 2,000 pairs regulation canvass leggins furnished troops	"	1,100 00	
Thorsen & Cassady Co.— Expressage paid on guns shipped to Sheriff Kankakee county	"	5 87	
Illinois State Journal Co.— Advertising proposals for stores for troops	"	2 50	
E. J. Garland— Removing naval equipments from Chicago to State Arsenal	"	26 00	
Charles Hiltwein— Labor, moving stores from 2d Regiment Armory	"	2 00	
W. J. Downey— Labor, moving stores from 2d Regiment Armory	"	1 50	
Amounts carried forward	....	$49,948 25	$740,082 91

Statement 3—Continued.

Accounts.	App.	Amount.	Total.
Amounts brought forward	....	$49,948 25	$740,082 91
ILLINOIS STATE NATIONAL GUARD—*Continued.*			
L. V. Gillespie—			
Labor, moving stores from 2d Regiment Armory....	1893	2 00	
Robert Ford—			
Labor, moving stores from 2d Regiment Armory....	"	2 00	
J. Zahn—			
Labor, moving stores from 2d Regiment Armory....	"	2 00	
E .Francis—			
Labor, moving stores from 2d Regiment Armory....	"	2 00	
To amounts paid for armory rent, fuel, light, etc., for various commands, for six months ending July 1, 1894, viz.:			
Brig. Gen. Andrew Welch, 3d Brigade Headquarters	"	55 88	
Capt. W. P. Butler, Troop B, Cavalry	"	387 60	
Col. Henry L. Turner, 1st Regiment	"	4,500 00	
" Fred Bennitt, 3d " Headquarters	"	194 05	
Lieut. Col. Wm. Wildt, 3d " "	"	586 76	
Capt. S. R. Blanchard, Co. C, 3d Regiment	"	386 70	
" A. W. Siddell, Co. D, "	"	409 93	
" Anthony Wiltheis, Co. E, "	"	234 25	
" Enos. A. Smith, Co. L. "	"	43 33	
" E. E. Elliott, Co. A, 4t, Regiment	"	196 00	
" W. O. Bryden, Co. C, "	"	188 50	
" Charles E. Rudy, Co. E, "	"	274 89	
" Alfred Adams, Co. F, "	"	142 70	
" McFarren Davis, Co. H, "	"	213 85	
" W. N. Rickard, Co. L, "	"	166 78	
" Fred T. Whipp, Co. C, 5th Regiment	"	216 15	
" W. D. Courtney, Co. D, "	"	201 58	
" C. E. Collier, Co. E, "	"	213 74	
" W. F. CoLaday, Co. H, "	"	298 92	
" E. E. Vickery, Co. I, "	"	289 85	
" J. E. Watkins, Co. K, "	"	203 25	
Col. D. J. Foster, 6th Regiment Headquarters	"	150 00	
Capt. E. M. Cook, Co. A, 6th Regiment	"	254 49	
" W. D. Clark, Co. B, "	"	176 28	
" T. L. McGirr, Co. C, "	"	229 64	
" W. F. Lawrie, Co. E, "	"	292 00	
" F. H. Muench, Co. F, "	"	278 16	
" W. F. Colebaugh, Co. I, "	"	225 00	
Major John G. Gammon			
Expenses under orders, inspecting 1st Battalion, 3d Regiment	"	14 00	
Major Edward J. Sill—			
Expenses under orders, inspecting 2d Batallion, 3d Regiment	"	4 50	
Major Fred A. Jackson—			
Expenses under orders, inspecting 3d Battalion, 3d Regiment	"	4 85	
Major Louis E. Bennett—			
Expenses under orders, inspecting 1st Battalion, 4th Regiment	"	7 75	
Major S. A. D. McWilliams—			
Expenses under orders, inspecting 2d Battalion, 4th Regiment	"	14 00	
Major E. J. Lang—			
Expenses under orders, inspecting 3d Battalion, 4th Regiment	"	8 75	
Major J. C. Cabanis—			
Expenses under orders, inspecting 1st Battalion, 5th Regiment	"	5 75	
Major Fred B. Nichols—			
Expenses under orders, inspecting 2d Battalion, 5th Regiment	"	2 00	
Major Charles H. Ingalls—			
Expenses under orders, inspecting 1st Battalion, 6th Regiment	"	3 00	
Major David E. Clarke—			
Expenses under orders, inspecting 3d Battalion, 6th Regiment	"	14 15	
Amount carried forward	....	$61,045 28	$740,082 91

Statement 3—Continued.

ACCOUNTS.	App.	Amount.	Total
Amounts brought forward	....	$61,045 28	$740,082 91
ILLINOIS STATE NATIONAL GUARD—*Continued.*			
To amounts paid for Armory rent, fuel, light, etc., for various commands, for six months ending Dec. 31, 1894, viz.:			
Brig.-Gen. J. H. Barkley, 2d Brigade Headquarters	1893	134 50	
" Andrew Welch, 3d " "	"	54 90	
Capt. Phil. Yeager, Battery A, Artillery	"	355 10	
" Paul B. Lino, Troop A, Cavalry	"	44 82	
" W. P. Butler, Troop B, "	"	356 20	
Col. Henry L. Turner, 1st Regiment	"	4,500 00	
" George M. Moulton, 2d "	"	4,500 00	
" Fred Bennitt, 3d Regiment Headquarters.........	"	190 40	
Lieut.-Col. Wm. Wildt, Cos. H & K, 3d Regiment......	"	496 89	
Major E. J. Sill, 3d Battalion, etc., "	"	129 46	
Capt. J. N. St. Clair, Co. A, "	"	300 00	
" F. W. Pearson, Co. B, "	"	315 25	
" S. R. Blanchard, Co. C, "	"	404 65	
" A. W. Siddall, Co. D, "	"	413 50	
" Anthony Wiltheis, Co. E, "	"	230 30	
" Alfred Adams, Co. F, "	"	....	
" W. C. Eichelberger, Co. G, "	"	200 69	
" W. H. Brogunier, Co. H, "	"	24 55	
" R. J. Shand, Co. K, "	"	31 17	
" Enos A. Smith, Co. L, "	"	275 00	
" Charles E. Gardner, Co. M, "	"	184 70	
Col. R. M. Smith, 4th Regiment Headquarters......	"	204 00	
Capt. E. E. Elliott, Co. A, 4th Regiment......	"	196 00	
" E. Wood Herech, Co. B, "	"	178 14	
Lieut. E. E. Burton, Co. C, "	"	185 00	
Capt. Cassimir Andel, Co. D, "	"	415 10	
" Charles E. Rudy, Co. E, "	"	296 84	
" Alfred Adams, Co. F, "	"	134 22	
" Claude E. Ryman, Co. G, "	"	181 25	
" McFarren Davis, Co. H, "	"	213 76	
" S. S. Houston, Co. I, "	"	182 90	
" S. G. Burdick, Co. K, "	"	216 50	
" W. N. Rickard, Co. L, "	"	123 15	
Lieut. F. B. Grider, Co. M, "	"	55 57	
Capt. George Barber, Co. A, 5th "	"	452 71	
" J. E. Hogan, Co. B, "	"	230 00	
" Fred T. Whipp, Co. C, "	"	228 06	
" W. R. Courtney, Co. D, "	"	142 80	
" Charles R. Collier, Co. E, "	"	213 86	
" Frank Rothgeb, Co. F, "	"	141 87	
" Eugene Sheer, Co. G, "	"	260 80	
" J. Frank Cassell, Co. H, "	"	279 61	
" E. C. Vickery, Co. I, "	"	288 39	
" James E. Watkins, Co. K, "	"	202 50	
" E. H. D. Couch, Co., L, "	"	253 15	
" L. H. Gillett, Co. M, "	"	342 00	
Col. D. J. Foster, 6th Regiment headquarters.......	"	117 50	
Capt. Edwin M. Cook, Co. A, 6th Regiment..........	"	224 76	
" W. D. Clark, Co. B, "	"	158 13	
" T. Leslie McGirr, Co. C, "	"	252 03	
" J. W. Meloy, Co. D, (1year) "	"	314 70	
" W. F. Lawrie, Co. E, "	"	292 50	
" Fred H. Muench, Co. F, "	"	256 15	
" W. E. Baldwin, Co. G, "	"	173 42	
" W. W. Shields, Co. H; "	"	235 83	
" W. F. Colebaugh, Co. I, "	"	214 50	
" A. T. Tourtillott, Co. K, "	"	206 42	
" Charles B. King, Co. L, "	"	227 75	
" W. H. Glasgow, Co. M. "	"	135 00	
Col. Francis T. Colby, 7th Regiment headquarters..	"	184 99	
J. M. Bush—			
Amount due for Armory rent account Co. A, 5th Regiment, to Dec. 31, 1894.........................	"	158 10	
S. D. Childs & Co.—			
Shooting decorations furnished for the season of 1894..	"	632 80	
Amounts carried foward............................	....	$83,590 12	$740,082 91

Statement 3—Continued.

Accounts.	App.	Amount.	Total.
Amounts brought forward		$83,590 12	$740,082 91
ILLINOIS STATE NATIONAL GUARD—*Continued.*			
Amounts paid for services rendered by the following commands during the strike of 1894, at Chicago, as per pay-rolls $202,150.07, and interest $7,369.94, said interest being computed at the rate of six per cent. per annum from the date of the assignment of said pay-rolls until paid, viz.:			
John J. Mitchell, Trustee, Etc., Chicago—Amount of pay-rolls $108,032.91, and interest $3,907.19, for services of commanding general, staff, etc., of 1st Brigade; field, staff, etc., of 1st and 2d Regiments; Companies A, B, C, D, E, F, G, H, I, K, L and M, 1st Regiment, and Companies A, B, C, D, E, F, G, H, I, K, L and M, 2d Regiment.	1895	111,940 10	
Illinois National Bank, Springfield—Amount of pay-roll $836.49, and interest $30.65, for services of commanding general, staff, etc., 2nd Brigade	"	867 14	
First National Bank, Springfield—Amount of pay-roll $1,584.68, and interest $59.17 for services of commanding general, staff, etc., of 3rd Brigade	"	1,643 85	
Will County National Bank, Joliet—Amount of pay-roll $2,475.28, and interest $91.60, for services of field, staff etc., of 3rd Regiment.	"	2,566 88	
Fred. W. Eads, Streator—Amount of pay-roll $2,506.61, and interest $94.82, for services of Co. A, 3rd Regiment	"	2,601 43	
First National Bank, Springfield—Amount of pay-roll $2,214.83, and interest $84.92, for services of Co. B, 3rd Regiment	"	2,299 75	
Al. F. Schock, Ottawa—Amount of pay-roll $2,621.17, and interest $97.42, for services of Co. C, 3rd Regiment	"	2,718 59	
First National Bank, Springfield—Amount of pay-roll $2,540.26, and interest $94.83, for services of Co. D, 3rd Regiment	"	2,635 09	
Ridgely National Bank, Springfield—Amount of pay-roll, $2,003.32, and interest, $77.12, for services of Co. E, 3d Regiment	"	2,080 44	
Corn Belt Bank, Bloomington—Amount of pay-roll, $2,340.69, and interest, $86.19, for services of Co. F, 3d Regiment	"	2,426 88	
John J. Murphy, Woodstock—Amount of pay-roll, $2,438.89, and interest, $97.56, for services of Co. G, 3d Regiment	"	2,536 45	
First National Bank, Springfield—Amount of pay-roll, $2,440.69, and interest, $93.13, for services of Co. H, 3d Regiment	"	2,533 82	
First National Bank, Springfield—Amount of pay-roll, $2,676.25, and interest, $99.91, for services of Co. I, 3d Regiment	"	2,776 16	
First National Bank, Springfield—Amount of pay-roll, $2,738.76, and interest, $104.96, for services of Co. K, 3d Regiment	"	2,843 72	
William Stocking & Co., Rochelle—Amount of pay-roll, $2,582 43, and interest, $96.40, for services of Co. M, 3d Regiment	"	2,678 83	
R. T. Hicks, Cashier, Etc., Pittsfield—Amount of pay-roll, $1,341.45, and interest, $48.28, for services of Co. A, 5th Regiment	"	1,389 73	
Ridgely National Bank, Springfield—Amount of pay-roll, $1,002.28, and interest, $38.08, for services of Co. C, 5th Regiment	"	1,040 36	
Champaign National Bank, Champaign—Amount of pay-roll, $1,377.33, and interest, $52.10, for services of Co. D, 5th Regiment	"	1,429 43	
L. C. Schwerdtfeger, Cashier, Etc., Lincoln—Amount of pay-roll, $1,071.21, and interest, $40.52, for services of Co. G, 5th Regiment	"	1,111 73	
Amounts carried forward		$233,710 50	$740,082 91

Statement 3—Continued.

Accounts.	App.	Amount.	Total.
Amounts brought forward	....	$233,710 50	$740,082 91
ILLINOIS STATE NATIONAL GUARD—*Continued.*			
Illinois National Bank, Springfield— Amount of pay-roll, $983.55, and interest, $37.03, for services of Co. K, 5th Regiment	1895	1,020 58	
Illinois National Bank, Springfield— Amount of pay-roll, $1,204.68, and interest, $45.75, for services of Co. M, 5th Regiment	"	1,250 43	
Hiram Wilson, Cashier, Etc., Geneseo— Amount of pay-roll, $1,958.26, and interest, $73.10, for services of Co. B, 6th Regiment	"	2,031 36	
Henry Wulff, State Treasurer— Amount of pay-roll, $2,181.77, and interest, $83.64, for services of Co. E, 6th Regiment	"	2,265 41	
First National Bank, Moline— Amount of pay-roll, $1,721.68, and interest, $63.42, for services of Co. F, 6th Regiment	"	1,785 10	
Dixon National Bank, Dixon— Amount of pay-roll, $2,307.77, and interest, $86.55, for services of Co. G, 6th Regiment	"	2,394 32	
F. W. Harding, Cashier, Etc., Monmouth— Amount of pay-roll, $2,164.08, and interest, $76.82, for services of Co. H, 6th Regiment	"	2,240 90	
Leander Smith & Son, Morrison— Amount of pay-roll, $1,778.08, and interest, $60.76, for services of Co. I, 6th Regiment	"	1,838 84	
John R. Woods, LaMoille— Amount of pay-roll, $2,473.19, and interest, $86.97, for services of Co. K, 6th Regiment	"	2,560 16	
First National Bank, Freeport— Amount of pay-roll, $2,133.58, and interest, $81.42, for services of Co. L, 6th Regiment	"	2,215 00	
Galena National Bank, Galena— Amount of pay-roll, $1,645.77, and interest, $61.45, for services of Co. M, 6th Regiment	"	1,707 22	
John J. Mitchell, Trustee, Chicago— Amount of pay-rolls, $20,194.80, and interest, $730.37, for services of field, staff, etc., and Companies, A, B, C, D, E, F, G and H, of 7th Regiment	"	20,925 17	
The Palmer National Bank, Danville— Amount of pay-roll, $1,176.15; and interest, $28.43; for services of Battery A, Artillery	"	1,204 58	
John J. Mitchell, Trustee, Chicago— Amount of pay-roll, $5,470.24; and interest, $197.84; for services of Battery D, Artillery	"	5,368 08	
John J. Mitchell, Trustee, Chicago— Amount of pay-roll, $3,558.83; and interest, $128.71; for services of Troop A, Cavalry	"	3,687 54	
Corn Belt Bank, Bloomington— Amount of pay-roll, $2,015.04; and interest, $75.24; for services of Troop B, Cavalry	"	2,090 28	
John J. Mitchell, Trustee, Chicago— Amount of pay-rolls, $4,357.07; and interest, $157.59; for services of Commanding Officer and Staff, and First, Second, Third and Fourth Divisions, First Battalion, Illinois Naval Militia	"	4,514 66	
Charles F. Halbe Baking Co— Subsistence stores furnished troops during strike of 1894, at Chicago	"	190 37	
Amounts paid for subsistence, commissary and quartermaster's stores, medical supplies, stationery, ice, teaming, expressage, telegrams, etc., furnished to the troops during the strike of 1894, (at Aurora, Brighton Park, Chicago, Elgin, Elsdon, Harvey, Joliet, Ottawa, Riverdale, Rockford, Streator and Woodstock) at Chicago, Illinois, by the following persons and firms, viz.:			
Coptain A. W. Siddall	"	21 45	
C. Iverson	"	1 75	
Charles H. Slack	"	66 39	
Wm. Thompson & Co	"	40 50	
W. Morris & Sons	"	14 00	
The Kotzenberg Co	"	13 50	
John F. Higgins	"	6 00	
Amounts carried forward	....	$293,464 09	$740,082 91

Statement 3—Continued.

Accounts.	App.	Amount.	Total.
Amounts brought forward	....	$293,464 0[illegible]	$740,082 91
ILLINOIS STATE NATIONAL GUARD—*Continued.*			
Washington Ice Co	1895	5 85	
Edward Mulhern	"	1 50	
H. Bartel	"	2 50	
C. Y. Transfer Co	"	111 00	
S. P. Russell	"	54 00	
Dr. F. W. Roha	"	39 00	
Herman Fry	"	14 70	
Brink's Chicago Express Co	"	1 50	
John Dillon	"	12 00	
Captain Geo. W. Connell	"	2 25	
Captain Anthony Wiltheis	"	8 60	
D. C. Cory	"	19 95	
W. A. Tait, M. D	"	13 00	
Riordan & Ellis	"	14 65	
James Caldwell	"	9 00	
H. B. Veerhusen	"	4 86	
Lieutenant H. B. Smith	"	50	
Captain Fred W. Pearson	"	8 40	
W. B. Stewart, M. D	"	2 00	
Colonel Fred Bennitt	"	2 15	
Captain John B. Shaw	"	80	
J. H. Goodspeed	"	17 20	
Thomas Brothers	"	72 58	
J. C. Adler & Co	"	71 16	
E. C. Shaw	"	45	
Thomas McCreevy	"	22 61	
Dahlem Brothers	"	3 25	
Daptain S. R. Blanchard	"	13 28	
L. W. Trumbull	"	33 00	
G. A. Schmidt	"	1 70	
Captain R. J. Shand	"	5 80	
Major W. L. Smith	"	2 25	
Captain J. N. St. Clair	"	10 00	
Captain W. C. Eichelberger	"	46 95	
Amounts paid to the following named persons and firms for telephone poles used as firewood, ammunition, cooks and waiters' services, telegrams, quartermaster's and commissary stores, rent of building, shoes, horses, express charges, medical supplies, forage, rent of horses and wagons, blankets, etc., furnished troops during the strike of 1894, at Chicago, viz.:			
Chicago Telephone Co	"	80 00	
Hibbard, Spencer, Bartlett & Co	"	477 75	
Lieut. A. L. Bell	"	934 10	
Neal Brothers	"	110 25	
Arnold Brothers	"	117 00	
A. Booth Packing Co	"	122 72	
The Union Stock Yards & Transit Co	"	2,752 15	
H. H. Kohlsaat & Co	"	131 40	
D. T. Collins	"	141 20	
A. F. Whittemore	"	1,949 62	
C. Jevne & Co	"	150 00	
Phelps, Dodge & Palmer Co	"	154 00	
John MacRae	"	157 00	
Sprague, Warner & Co	"	484 96	
The Columbia Co	"	178 00	
Harry Horner & Co	"	180 74	
American Biscuit and Manufacturing Co	"	199 12	
Col. Geo. M. Moulton	"	746 40	
D. R. Dyche & Co	"	251 46	
F. L. Reynolds	"	310 76	
Capt. Alfred Russell	"	336 98	
The Heissler & Junge Co	"	914 92	
Hess & Pfaelzer	"	368 58	
John Ford	"	385 00	
Selz, Schwab & Co	"	393 25	
R. G. Clarke, Manager	"	744 00	
C. Y. Transfer Co	"	906 50	
J. T. Cartan & Co	"	908 00	
Magner & Winslow	"	3,947 26	
Armour & Co	"	2,558 92	
Amounts carried forward	....	$315,184 57	$740,082 91

Statement 3—Continued.

Accounts.	App.	Amount.	Total.
Amounts brought forward	....	$315,184 57	$740,082 91
ILLINOIS STATE NATIONAL GUARD—*Continued*,			
L. E. Howard, Manager	1895	1,423 01	
D. J. Stewart	"	2,020 86	
Capt. Paul B. Lino	"	3,067 00	
Marshall Field & Co	"	3,449 77	
C. M. Henderson & Co	"	604 70	
Herman Werner	"	188 45	
Amounts paid for transportation of troops, and telegraphic services rendered during the strike of 1894, at Chicago and other points in the State of Illinois, viz.:			
E. Wilder, Treasurer, Atchison, Topeka & Santa Fé R. R. Co	"	108 51	
C. H. Foster, Treasurer, Chicago & Alton R. R. Co.	"	1,331 28	
W. J. Fabian, Cashier, Chicago, Burlington & Quincy R. R. Co	"	1,149 59	
C. W. Hillard, Treasurer, Chicago & Eastern Illinois R. R. Co	"	668 45	
M. M. Kirkman, 2nd Vice-President, Chicago & Northwestern R. R. Co	"	441 67	
Chicago, Milwaukee & St. Paul R. R. Co	"	1 84	
Chicago, Rock Island & Pacific R. R. Co	"	572 02	
Illinois Central R. R. Co	"	4,770 96	
R. H. Hill, Acting Auditor, Lake Shore & Michigan Southern R. R. Co	"	62 00	
W. E. Jones, Treasurer, Baltimore & Ohio Southwestern Ry. Co	"	33 77	
F. D. Comstock, Treasurer, Cleveland, Cincinnati, Chicago & St. Louis R. R. Co	"	91 00	
W. J. Lewis, Treasurer, Peoria, Decatur & Evansville R. R. Co	"	132 73	
C. W. McGuire, Auditor, Peoria, Decatur & Evansville R. R. Co	"	105 03	
W. S. Roney, Auditor, Vandalia Line Ry	"	67 50	
H. T. Nash, Auditor, St. Louis, Alton & Terre Haute R. R. Co	"	150 71	
F. L. O'Leary, Treasurer Wabash R. R. Co	"	2,209 83	
Western Union Telegraph Co	"	476 40	
Col. J. S. Culver—			
Amount, in part, said for clerk and cook, at headquarters, 5th Regiment	"	41	
I Price Clothing House—			
Amount due for 1,700 blouses and trousers, 2,389 uniform suits and 18 packing cases furnished troops on contract	"	23,869 60	
Work Brothers & Co.—			
Amount due for 4,004 overcoats furnished troops on contract	"	33,787 00	
Klaholt & Fogarty—			
Amount due for 1,500 pairs of leggins furnished troops on contract	1895	825 00	
Thomas C. Orendorff, Government Contractor—			
Amount due, in part payment for 1,000 United States regulation belts and 600 woven cartridge belts furnished troops	"	1,288 40	
G. F. Foster, Son & Co.—			
Amount due for 3,000 forage caps furnished troops on contract	"	1,350 00	
W. L. DeRemer—			
Amount due for 1,000 United States regulation campaign hats furnished troops	"	880 00	
C. A. Power—			
Repairing tent floors, making tent pins, etc., at Camp Lincoln	"	215 58	
Garner Wright—			
Fencing furnished at Camp Lincoln	"	276 00	
Inez Dilks—			
Mending 128 straw ticks for Camp Lincoln	"	5 12	
Ætna Foundry and Machine Co.—			
Brass and iron work furnished Camp Lincoln	"	52 60	
H. W. Rokker—			
Score sheets for rifle practice furnished Camp Lincoln	"	50 50	
Amounts carried forward	....	$400,911 86	$740,082 91

Statement 3—Continued.

Accounts.	App.	Amount.	Total.
Amounts brought forward	....	$400,911 86	$740,082 91
ILLINOIS STATE NATIONAL GUARD—*Continued.*			
Barkley & Lax—			
Hauling public property, etc., at Camp Lincoln.....	1895	21 00	
W. B. Miller & Son—			
Hardware, supplies, etc., furnished Camp Lincoln.	"	7 75	
Hellweg & Hopkins—			
Repairing water pipes at Camp Lincoln............	"	63 23	
The Dr. Hickman Drug Co.—			
Drugs, etc., furnished State Arsenal and Camp Lincoln	"	8 95	
Wm. D. Morgan—			
Labor with team at Camp Lincoln..................	"	16 90	
Charles P. Kane, Attorney, etc.—			
Rent of 60 acres of ground north of Camp Lincoln to March 1, 1896, in part	"	58 33	
C. D. Roberts & Co.—			
Laundry work and bed sack furnished Camp Lincoln........	"	13 70	
A. Dirksen & Sons—			
Amount due for repairing cots at Camp Lincoln....	"	15 35	
Raymond Lead Co.—			
Pig lead and tin furnished Logan Rifle Range......	"	151 05	
Vance & Dooling—			
Insurance premiums paid on State property........	"	122 50	
Western Union Telegraph Co.—			
Time service and telegrams furnished	"	14 01	
Springfield Iron Co.—			
Iron furnished for use at State Arsenal	"	5 43	
Springfield Electric Light and Power Co.—			
Electric light furnished State Arsenal	"	2 49	
Springfield Gas Light Co.—			
Gas furnished State Arsenal, in part	"	60	
Tunny & Jones—			
Shoeing State horses during June, 1895............	"	8 00	
Marshall Field & Co.—			
Amount due for 27 flags furnished, as per contract.	"	106 60	
Adams Express Co.—			
Express charges on public property...............	"	7 80	
American Express Co.—			
Express charges on public property	"	4 77	
United States Express Co.—			
Express charges on public property	"	4 90	
Illinois Central Railroad Co.—			
Freight charges on public property................	"	46 65	
Illinois State Register—			
Letterheads and envelopes furnished companies...	"	55 60	
P. K. Howard—			
Hauling Illinois Naval Militia stores to Illinois Central Railroad depot at Chicago....................	"	7 50	
Amounts paid for Armory rent, fuel, light, etc., on account of various commands, for six months ending July 1, 1895, viz:			
Brig.-Gen. H. A. Wheeler, Headquarters 1st Brigade	"	500 00	
" J. H. Barkley, " 2d "	"	128 75	
" Andrew Welch, " 3d "	"	250 00	
Col. Henry L. Turner, 1st Regiment	"	4,500 00	
" George M. Moulton, 2d Regiment...............	"	4,500 00	
" Fred Bennitt, Headquarters 3d Regiment	"	192 35	
Lieut.-Col. Wm. Wildt, Headquarters 3d Regiment.	"	601 01	
Major E. J. Sill, 2d Battalion, 3d Regiment........	"	571 28	
Capt. J. N. St. Clair, Co. A, "	"	300 00	
" Fred W. Pearson, Co. B, "	"	318 25	
" S. R. Blanchard, Co. C, "	"	438 82	
" Joseph B. Caughey, Co. E, "	"	232 00	
" W. C. Eichelberger, Co. G, "	"	179 42	
" W. H. Brogunier, Co. H, "	"	31 60	
" R. J. Shand, Co. K, "	"	14 75	
" Enos A. Smith, Co. L, "	"	275 00	
" Charles E. Gardner, Co. M, "	"	187 85	
Col. Relly M. Smith, Headquarters 4th Regiment...	"	204 00	
Capt. E. E. Elliott, Co. A, "	"	196 00	
" E. Wood Hersch, Co. B, "	"	173 31	
" J. T. Galbraith, Co. C, "	"	202 00	
Amounts carried forward	....	$415,651 36	$740,082 91

Statement 3—Continued.

Accounts.	App.	Amount.	Total.
Amounts brought forward	....	$415,651 36	$740,082 91
ILLINOIS STATE NATIONAL GUARD—*Continued.*			
Capt. E. P. Rogers, Co. D, 4th Regiment	1895	196 95	
" Charles E. Rudy, Co. E, "	"	279 82	
" John F. Harris, Co. F, "	"	131 50	
" C. E. Ryman, Co. G, "	"	187 80	
" McFarren Davis, Co. H, "	"	233 56	
" S. S. Houston, Co. I, "	"	194 65	
" Geo. D. Sherwin, Co. K, "	"	211 50	
" E. N. Steward, Co. L, "	"	117 00	
" George Barber, Co. A, 5th Regiment	"	197 50	
" Charles A. Parish, Co. B, "	"	238 60	
" A. W. Butler, Co. C, "	"	354 60	
" W. R. Courtney, Co. D, "	"	155 35	
" James C. Walter, Co. E, "	"	204 60	
" A. E. Harding, Co. F, "	"	323 70	
" Eugene Sheer, Co. G, "	"	259 10	
" J. Frank Cassell, Co. H, "	"	301 56	
" E. C. Vickery, Co. I, "	"	295 08	
" James E. Watkins, Co. K, "	"	219 50	
" E. H. D. Couch, Co. L, "	"	251 19	
" L. H. Gillett, Co. M, "	"	364 50	
Col. D. J. Foster, Headquarters 6th Regiment	"	175 40	
Capt. E. M. Cook, Co. A, 6th Regiment	"	222 00	
" W. D. Clark, Co. B, "	"	171 65	
" T. Leslie McGirr, Co. C, "	"	259 75	
" John W. Meloy, Co. D, "	"	127 50	
" W. F. Lawrie, Co. E, "	"	281 87	
" F. H. Muench, Co. F, "	"	260 74	
" W. E. Baldwin, Co. G, "	"	173 50	
" W. W. Shield, Co. H, "	"	237 26	
" H. T. Guffin, Co. I, "	"	277 19	
" A. T. Tourtillott, Co. K, "	"	190 94	
" C. B. Kling, Co. L, "	"	210 50	
" W. H. Glasgow, Co. M, "	"	140 00	
Col. Francis T. Colby, Headquarters and 7th Reg't.	"	3,863 92	
Kehm Bros. & Mertz— Repairing boiler and hot water attachments at 7th Regiment Armory	"	31 97	
Col. J. S. Culver— Amount, in full, paid for clerk and cook at 5th Regiment headquarters	"	46 59	
Col. Fred R. Hanlon— Expenses under orders, holding election of Co. I, 6th Regiment	"	1 50	
Col. Hugh E. Bayle— Expenses under orders, May and June, 1895	"	180 15	
Gen. Alfred Orendorff— Expenses under orders, May and June, 1895	"	147 00	
Capt. W. S. Campbell— Expenses under orders, June, 1895	"	29 50	
Major J. C. Cabanis— Expenses under orders, April, 1895	"	6 00	
S. D. Childs & Co.— One sharpshooter's bar, season of 1893, furnished	"	1 56	
Col. Francis T. Colby— Supplies furnished 7th Regiment by Gale & Blocki .... $73 10 Supplies furnished 7th Regiment by Hibbard, Spencer, Bartlett & Co., Chicago strike, 1894. 6 53	"	79 63	
E. Knapp & Co.— Subsistence furnished troops during strike of 1894, at Mounds	"	75 25	
A. G. Meserve— Transportation paid, Robinson to Chicago and return	"	12 32	
Capt. McFarren Davis— Transportation furnished 1 man to Chicago, strike of 1894	"	4 85	
Hibbard, Spencer, Bartlett & Co.— 1,000 Smith & Wesson cartridges furnished during strike of 1894, at Chicago	"	9 12	
Amounts carried forward	....	$427,587 08	$740,082 91

Statement 3—Continued.

Accounts.	App.	Amount.	Total.
Amounts brought forward	....	$427,587 08	$740,082 91
ILLINOIS STATE NATIONAL GUARD—*Continued.*			
Keith Brothers & Co.— Hats supplied troops at Chicago, during strike of 1894	1895	91 00	
Hibbard, Spencer, Bartlett & Co.— Ordnance stores furnished 1st Regiment during Strike at Chicago in 1894	"	401 50	
Toledo, Peoria & Western Railroad Co.— Transportation of troops during strike of 1894, at Minonk	"	103 08	
Louisville, Evansville & St. Louis Railroad Co.— Transportation of troops during strike of 1894	"	43	
Edward Wilder, Treasurer, Atchison, Topeka & Santa Fé Railroad Co.— Transportation of troops during strike of 1894	"	2 12	
W. E. Jones, Treasurer, Baltimore & Ohio Southwestern Railroad Co.— Transportation of troops during strike of 1894, at Pana, etc	"	27 52	
F. D. Comstock, Treasurer, Cleveland, Cincinnati, Chicago & St. Louis Railroad Co.— Transportation of troops during strike of 1894	"	1 91	
W. G. Purdy, Treasurer, Chicago, Rock Island & Pacific Railroad Co.— Transportation of troops during strike of 1894	"	107 54	
J. F. Titus, Local Treasurer, Illinois Central Railroad Co.— Transportation of troops during strike of 1894	"	6 04	
W. J. Dickinson, Auditor, Louisville & Nashville Railroad Co.— Transportation of troops during strike of 1894	"	1 29	
J. E. Griffiths, Cashier, Michigan Central Railroad Co.— Transportation of troops during strike of 1894	"	1 10	
T. H. McKnight, Treasurer, Pennsylvania Railroad Co.— Transportation of troops during strike of 1894	"	2 62	
H. T. Nash, Auditor, St. Louis, Alton & Terre Haute Railroad Co.— Transportation of troops during strike of 1894	"	99	
E. D. Usner, Auditor, Toledo, Peoria & Western Railroad Co.— Transportation of troops during strike of 1894	"	3 19	
J. J. Clark— Repairs on water pipe at 7th Regiment armory	"	274 99	
Ihlenfeldt & Wiedlocher— Feed, etc., furnished for state horse	"	20 00	
Oscar F. Stebbins— Hardware furnished Memorial Hall and State Arsenal, etc	"	37 62	
Schlierbach & Blucke— Harness and horse equipments, repairs, etc	"	2 45	
E. C. Cook & Bro.— Headquarters tent, mattress covers and flag brackets furnished	"	122 38	
J. Irving Pearce— Rooms used as headquarters for Governor and staff during trip to Atlanta, Ga., etc	"	43 50	
Unity Company— Rent of office to Col. Hugh E. Bayle, A. A. G., to July 1, 1895	"	150 00	
Capt. Paul B. Lino, Troop A, Cavalry— Armory rent, fuel, light, etc., for 6 months, to July 1, 1895	"	547 96	
Capt. W. P. Butler, Troop B, Cavalry— Armory rent, fuel, light, etc., for 6 months, to July 1, 1895	"	408 45	
Capt. Phil Yeager, Battery A, Artillery— Armory rent, fuel, light, etc., for 6 months, to July 1, 1895	"	367 30	
Amounts carried foward	....	$430,312 06	$740,082 91

Statement 3—Continued.

Accounts.	App.	Amount.	Total.
Amounts brought forward	....	$430,312 06	$740,082 91
ILLINOIS STATE NATIONAL GUARD—*Continued.*			
Captain Robert H. Aiken—			
Amount of pay-rolls of civil employés at Camp Lincoln	1895	1,713 19	
Major J. C. Cabanis—			
Amount of pay-rolls of civil employés at Camp Lincoln	"	7,820 03	
C. W. Eaton & Co.—			
Twenty perfection frames and targets, complete, furnished Rifle Range at Camp Lincoln	"	1,176 00	
McGrue & Powell—			
Brackets and sockets for danger signals in rifle pits at Camp Lincoln furnished	"	6 00	
John E. White—			
Carpenter work performed at Camp Lincoln	"	13 70	
C. A. Power—			
Carpenter work, improvements, repairs, ice boxes furnished, building abutments at Camp Lincoln Rifle Range, and material furnished, at Camp Lincoln, on contract	"	3,531 43	
W. J. Ralph—			
Guttering on commissary house at Camp Lincoln, on contract	"	14 55	
R. H. Hargraves—			
Tents, rope slides, powder bags, flags, repairs on tents, etc., furnished Camp Lincoln, on contract	"	475 15	
R. F. Kinsella—			
Painting, etc., at Camp Lincoln and State Arsenal	"	613 94	
M. Jones, M. D.—			
Medical services rendered troops at Camp Lincoln	"	25 00	
George F. Fisher—			
Labor in Rifle Range at Camp Lincoln	"	27 00	
A. M. Chamberlin—			
Services on special detail, General headquarters, Camp Lincoln	"	28 00	
J. A. Tillotson—			
Labor and material furnished at Camp Lincoln	"	11 50	
John Kessler—			
Labor, putting in bridges at Camp Lincoln	"	8 75	
Amounts paid for services during tour of instruction at Camp Lincoln, July 6 to 27, 1895, both inclusive, of Illinois National Guard, warrants issued, viz.;			
Lieutenant Colonel W. D. Hotchkiss, Cavalry, Troop A	"	362 00	
Captain Alfred Russell, Artillery, Battery D	"	480 00	
Lieutenant Colonel George V. Lauman, field, staff, non-commissioned staff, band and unassigned, 1st Regiment	"	328 00	
Captain B. F. Patrick, Jr., 1st Regiment, Co. A	"	525 00	
" W. J. Sanderson, " Co. B	"	378 00	
" Anson L. Bolté, " Co. C	"	596 00	
" Joseph H. Barnett, " Co. D	"	397 00	
" William F. Knoch, " Co. E	"	424 00	
" Sherman W. Smith, " Co. F	"	496 00	
" George W. Bristol, " Co. G	"	445 00	
" Timothy M. Kennedy, " Co. H	"	406 00	
" Charles B. Sandham, " Co. I	"	352 00	
" Thomas W. Cole, " Co. K	"	445 00	
" A. M. Daniels, " Co. L	"	356 00	
" E. H. Switzer, " Co. M	"	684 00	
Lieutenant-Colonel W. D. Hotchkiss, field, staff, non-commissioned staff and band, 2nd Regiment	"	335 00	
Lieutenant-Colonel W. D. Hotchkiss, 2nd Regiment, Co. A	"	469 00	
Lieutenant-Colonel W. D. Hotchkiss, 2nd Regiment, Co. B	"	433 00	
Captain Thomas J. Mair, 2nd Regiment, Co. C	"	576 00	
Lieutenant-Colonel W. D. Hotchkiss, 2nd Regiment, Co. D	"	507 00	
Lieutenant-Colonel W. D. Hotchkiss, 2nd Regiment, Co. E	"	512 00	
Amounts carried forward	....	$455,282 30	$740,082 91

Statement 3—Continued.

Accounts.	App.	Amount.	Total.
Amounts brought forward	....	$455,282 30	$740,082 91
ILLINOIS STATE NATIONAL GUARD—*Continued.*			
Captain Joseph I. Kelly, 2nd Regiment, Co. F....	1895	470 00	
" Willis McFeely, " Co. G....	"	466 00	
" John J. Garrity, " Co. H....	"	405 00	
Lieutenant-Colonel W. D. Hotchkiss, 2nd Regiment, Co. I....	"	400 00	
Captain Alben A. Benning, 2nd Regiment, Co. K....	"	507 00	
Lieutenant-Colonel W. D. Hotchkiss, 2nd Regiment, Co. L....	"	430 00	
Lieutenant-Colonel W. D. Hotchkiss, 2nd Regiment, Co. M....	"	408 00	
Colonel Francis T. Colby, field, staff, non-commissioned staff and band, 7th Regiment....	"	255 00	
Colonel Francis T. Colby, 7th Regiment, Co. A....	"	319 00	
" " " Co. B......	"	419 00	
" " " Co. C......	"	408 00	
" " " Co. D......	"	360 00	
" " " Co. E......	"	480 00	
" " " Co. F......	"	416 00	
" " " Co. G......	"	424 00	
" " " Co. H......	"	275 00	
" " " Co. I......	"	616 00	
" " " Co. K......	"	392 00	
" " " Co. L......	"	296 00	
" " " Co. M......	"	476 00	
R. H. Armbruster— Repairing tents, etc., at Camp Lincoln....	"	115 65	
Prather, McCoy & Co.— Supplies furnished troops at Camp Lincoln....	"	75	
Ætna Foundry and Machine Co.— Door frame and grate for melting furnace at Camp Lincoln....	"	3 50	
Captain Alfred Russell— Hauling guns and baggage of Battery D to Camp Lincoln, and ration furnished troops enroute...	"	34 43	
E. J. Garland— Clerical services rendered general headquarters, Camp Lincoln....	"	52 50	
R. F. Herndon & Co.— Table linen, towels, etc., furnished general headquarters, Camp Lincoln....	"	53 68	
Amount paid for services during tour of instruction at Camp Lincoln, July 27 to August 17, 1895, both inclusive, of Illinois National Guard, warrants issued, viz.:			
Captain W. P. Butler, Cavaly, Troop B....	"	356 00	
Lieutenant Mort. Graham, Artillery, Battery A....	"	520 00	
Colonel Relly M. Smith, 4th Regt., Field, Staff, etc.	"	332 00	
Captain Ed. E. Elliott, 4th Regt., Co. A....	"	424 00	
" E. W. Hersch, " Co. B....	"	480 00	
" John T. Galbraith, " Co. C....	"	465 00	
" E. P. Rogers, " Co. D....	"	536 00	
" Chas. E. Rudy " Co. E....	"	495 00	
" John F. Harris, " Co. F....	"	496 00	
" C. E. Ryman, " Co. G....	"	496 00	
" McFarren Davis, " Co. H....	"	430 00	
" S. S. Houston, " Co. I....	"	488 00	
" Geo. D. Sherwin, " Co. K....	"	517 00	
" Edgar N. Steward, " Co. L....	"	472 00	
Colonel J. S. Culver, 5th Regt., Field, Staff, etc....	"	448 00	
Captain Geo. Barber, 5th Regt., Co. A....	"	371 00	
" C. A. Parish, " Co. B....	"	392 00	
" A. W. Bulter, " Co. C....	"	414 00	
" Wm. R. Courtney, " Co. D....	"	357 00	
" J. C. Walters, " Co. E....	"	303 00	
" A. E. Harding, " Co. F....	"	290 00	
" Eugene Sheer, " Co. G....	"	264 00	
" J. F. Cassell, " Co. H....	"	526 00	
" E. C. Vickery, " Co. I....	"	368 00	
" James E. Watkins, " Co. K....	"	383 00	
" E. H. D. Couch, " Co. L....	"	358 00	
" L. H. Gillett, " Co. M....	"	484 00	
Amounts carried forward	....	$475,229 81	$740,082 91

Statement 3—Continued.

Accounts.	App.	Amount.	Total.
Amounts brought forward	....	$475,229 81	$740,082 91
ILLINOIS STATE NATIONAL GUARD—*Continued.*			
Colonel D. J. Foster, 6th Regt., Field, Staff, etc.	1895	293 00	
Lieutenant Will. Johnston, 6th Regt., Co. A	"	453 00	
Captain W. D. Clark, " Co. B	"	352 00	
" T. L. McGirr, " Co. C	"	820 00	
" J. W. Meloy, " Co. D	"	392 00	
" W. F. Laurie, " Co. E	"	376 00	
" F. H. Muench, " Co. F	"	356 00	
" Wm. E. Baldwin, " Co. G	"	448 00	
" W. W. Shields, " Co. H	"	466 00	
" H. T. Guffin, " Co. I	"	342 00	
" A. T. Tourtillott, " Co. K	"	395 00	
" Charles B. Kling, " Co. L	"	396 00	
" Wm. H. Glasgow, " Co. M	"	424 00	
Peter Vredenburgh—Lumber, lime, etc., for permanent improvements at Camp Lincoln	"	1,232 88	
Central Union Telephone Co.—Rental of instruments and services at general headquarters, rifle pits and range, Camp Lincoln, and at State Arsenal	"	130 05	
Capital Electric Co.—Electric light furnished at Camp Lincoln, on contract	"	309 80	
M. Zwicky's Sons—Soap and candles for troops at Camp Lincoln	"	111 75	
Capt. Paul B. Lino—Use of 77 horses for Cavalry Troop A, and amount paid for janitor, hauling, postage, etc., during tours of instruction at Camp Lincoln, in 1895 and 1896	"	907 37	
Capt. W. P. Butler—Use of 42 horses for Cavalry Troop B, during tour of instruction at Camp Lincoln, in 1895	"	420 00	
H. L. Hampton—Butter, commissary stores, etc., furnished general headquarters, troops and commissary department during 1895 and 1896 tours of instruction at Camp Lincoln	"	2,908 33	
Fitzgerald Plaster Co.—Six bags of plaster for use at Camp Lincoln	"	3 80	
John W. Bunn & Co.—Commissary stores furnished troops at Camp Lincoln	"	1,680 25	
Robert D. Loose—Milk furnished troops at Camp Lincoln	"	550 10	
Springfield City Laundry—Laundry work for Camp Lincoln	"	71 32	
William M. Payne—Powder, primers and revolver cartridges furnished, plumbing and permanent improvements, at Camp Lincoln	"	406 85	
Geo. S. Connelly & Co.—Commissary stores furnished troops at Camp Lincoln	"	2,129 68	
Illinois Produce Co.—Lemons, vegetables, etc., furnished troops at Camp Lincoln	"	587 15	
P. H. Giblin—Commissary stores furnished troops at Camp Lincoln	"	1,279 87	
Barkley & Lax—Merchandise, quartermaster stores and enamel furnished, hauling public property, hire and loss of furniture, and repairing desk of 5th Regiment Headquarters, at Camp Lincoln, etc	"	1,457 31	
E. S. Gard—Groceries and quartermaster's stores furnished troops at Camp Lincoln	"	41 65	
The John Bressmer Co.—Sheeting, flannel and other quartermaster's stores furnished troops at Camp Lincoln	"	176 97	
Amounts carried forward	....	$495,147 94	$740,082 91

Statement 3.—Continued.

Accounts.	App.	Amount.	Total.
Amounts brought forward	....	$495,147 94	$740,082 91
ILLINOIS STATE NATIONAL GUARD—*Continued.*			
Fred. H. Solle— Coal oil, can, etc., furnished troops at Camp Lincoln	1895	22 85	
W. B. Miller & Son— Hardware, etc., furnished troops at Camp Lincoln	"	138 82	
Peter Nisin— Kegs furnished Camp Lincoln	"	2 35	
Scherer Bros.— Hauling tents for 3d Regiment on tour of instruction	"	10 00	
Hellweg & Hopkins— Repairing water pipes, plumbing, etc., at Camp Lincoln and State Arsenal	"	75 76	
B. Franz Brothers— Meats, ham, lard, etc., furnished troops at Camp Lincoln	"	8,941 22	
Henson Robison Co.— Hardware, quartermaster's stores, tin, fire-pot and covering platform at Camp Lincoln, tin label for Memorial Hall, repairing roof at State Arsenal, etc	"	373 55	
The Dr. Hickman Drug Co.— Drugs, etc., furnished troops at Camp Lincoln and State Arsenal	"	49 36	
Capt. A. T. Tourtillott— Rations furnished troops en route to Camp Lincoln	"	20 00	
John M. Striffler— Ice and sawdust furnished troops at Camp Lincoln and State Arsenal	"	1,363 50	
Blakely & Co.— Medical supplies furnished troops at Camp Lincoln	"	47 90	
Springfield Coal Mining and Tile Co.— Coal furnished troops at Camp Lincoln	"	55 95	
John W. Elliott— Trimming hedge at Camp Lincoln	"	10 00	
Maurice O. Smith— Services as Drum Major, 5th Regiment, at Camp Lincoln	"	12 00	
C. D. Roberts & Co.— Gloves furnished staff officers, laundry work and bed sacks furnished, at Camp Lincoln	"	144 10	
Myers Brothers— Gloves furnished bullet moulder at Camp Lincoln	"	1 00	
Otto Miller— Carpenter work done at Camp Lincoln	"	24 85	
Emil Salzenstein— Horses for General staff, Brigade and Regimental Staffs, and troops—services of superintendent and hostlers—horses killed and crippled—oats, hay and straw—carriages, attention, etc., furnished during encampments of 1895 and 1896, at Camp Lincoln	"	10,937 79	
Springfield Evening News— Advertising for proposals for furnishing troops commissary, etc., supplies during encampments at Camp Lincoln	"	7 50	
Illinois State Register— Advertising for proposals for furnishing troops commissary, etc., supplies during encampments at Camp Lincoln	"	30 35	
Illinois State Journal— Advertising for proposals for furnishing troops commissary, etc., supplies during encampments at Camp Lincoln	"	31 85	
W. D. Morgan— Labor with team at Camp Lincoln	"	16 90	
Captain T. L. Hartigan— Transportation from Chicago to Springfield	"	4 75	
Charles P. Kane, Attorneys, etc.— Rent of 60 acres of ground north of Camp Lincoln for use of troops, etc	"	116 67	
Amounts carried foward	....	$517,586 96	$740,082 91

Statement 3—Continued.

Accounts.	App.	Amount.	Total.
Amounts brought forward	....	$517,586 96	$740,082 91
ILLINOIS STATE NATIONAL GUARD—*Continued.*			
B. H. Ferguson— China, glassware, knives, forks, etc., furnished quartermasters department at Camp Lincoln	"	164 91	
R. N. Dodds— Medical supplies furnished troops at Camp Lincoln	"	56 25	
John W. Dilks— Labor and material for dining tents, and labor on house, at Camp Lincoln	"	13 20	
Dawson Brick & Tile Co.— Tile furnished Camp Lincoln	"	1 20	
C. H. Edmands— Oil stove furnished reloading room at Camp Lincoln	"	2 50	
John Ford— Commissary stores furnished 7th Regiment enroute to Camp Lincoln	"	30 66	
T. J. Murray— Commissary stores furnished troops at Camp Lincoln	"	28 40	
John H. McCreery— Services as superintendent headquarters, and commissary stores furnished troops at Camp Lincoln.	"	247 10	
Lyon & Smith— Hauling baggage for troops at Camp Lincoln	"	125 50	
Samuel L. Willis— Commissary stores furnished troops at Camp Lincoln	"	11 00	
Springfield Transfer Co.— Carriages furnished, and hauling baggage for officers and troops at Camp Lincoln—hauling desk from State House to Arsenal	"	134 25	
H. Kloppenberg & Bro.— Brick and sand furnished Camp Lincoln	"	5 75	
P. Hagle— Rent of grond for stacking hay at Camp Lincoln	"	5 00	
Brown & Canfield— Grass seed furnished Camp Lincoln	"	27 50	
Lieutenant A. L. Bell, Q. M., 1st Regiment— Freight paid on clothing, netting and frame to Camp Lincoln	"	15 31	
John Gadert & Son— Commissary stores furnished troops at Camp Lincoln	"	43 45	
James VanDoren— Labor performed at Camp Lincoln	"	2 00	
S. D. Childs & Co.— Shooting decorations for 1895 furnished Camp Lincoln	"	500 55	
G. M. Houston— Trimming maple trees at Camp Lincoln	"	14 00	
The Granolithic Pavement Co.— Repairs at Camp Lincloln, on contract	"	149 37	
Oscar F. Stebbins— Hardware, etc., furnished Camp Lincoln, State Arsenal and Memorial Hall	"	103 94	
Thomas C. Orendorff— 1,000 woven cartridge belts, U. S. Reg., furnished.	"	1,250 00	
Price Clothing House— 1,000 bed sacks furnished Camp Lincoln; 21 packing cases, and 400 uniforms furnished troops on contract	"	2,959 75	
Tunney & Jones— Shoeing State horse	"	26 50	
Anna Hosturann— Rent of 40 acres of ground and labor and material repairing fences after field exercises by troops at Camp Lincoln	"	48 00	
Stroud & Mahoney— Blacksmith work at Camp Lincoln	"	16 20	
Springfield Junction Coal Co.— Coal furnished troops at Camp Lincoln	"	54 93	
Amounts carried forward	....	$523,624 18	$740,082 91

Statement 8—Continued.

Accounts.	App.	Amount.	Total.
Amounts brought forward	....	$523,624 18	$740,082 91
ILLINOIS STATE NATIONAL GUARD—*Continued.*			
John R. Booth, Jr.— Milk furnished troops at Camp Lincoln	1895	379 18	
F. J. Hogan— Hay furnished troops at Camp Lincoln	''	428 93	
John Foster— Straw furnished troops at Camp Lincoln	''	131 20	
Charles Pfeffer— Bread furnished troops at Camp Lincoln	''	834 68	
Amounts paid for services of Illinois National Guard and Illinois Naval Militia during tour of instruction at Camp Lincoln, encampment of 1896, and for services rendered by Illinois National Guard at East St. Louis, on account of cyclone May, 1896, warrants issued, viz.:			
Brig. Gen. James H. Barkley and staff, 2d Brigade	1895	144 00	
Brig. Gen. Andrew Welch and staff, 3d Brigade	''	128 00	
Major Edward C. Young, field and staff, cavalry squadron	''	294 00	
Capt. Paul B. Lino, Troop A, cavalry	''	402 00	
'' W. P. Butler, '' B, ''	''	364 00	
'' M. L. C. Funkhouser, Troop C, cavalry	''	733 00	
Major Alfred Russell, artillery battalion	''	46 00	
Capt. Wm. Austin, Battery D, Artillery	''	552 00	
'' Joseph I. Kelly, engineer corps	''	96 00	
P. M. Horatio L. Wait, Comdr. and staff, naval militia	''	38 00	
P. M. F. W. Gould, Comdr., staff and band, 2d Batt., naval militia	''	203 00	
P. M. Horatio L. Wait, staff, 1st Batt., naval militia	''	38 00	
'' '' 1st Div. '' ''	''	188 00	
'' '' 2d Div. '' ''	''	265 00	
'' '' 3d Div. '' ''	''	302 00	
'' '' 4th Div. '' ''	''	382 00	
P. M. F. W. Gould, 1st Div., 2d Batt., ''	''	392 00	
'' '' 2d Div. '' ''	''	343 00	
'' '' 3d Div. '' ''	''	400 00	
Lieut.-Col. Geo. V. Lauman, field staff, non-com. staff, band, etc., 1st Regiment	''	348 00	
Capt. B. F. Patrick, Co. A, 1st Regiment	''	351 00	
'' Wm. J. Sanderson, Co. B, ''	''	384 00	
'' Anson L. Bolte, Co. C, ''	''	480 00	
'' Joseph H. Barnett, Co. D, ''	''	400 00	
'' Wm. F. Knock, Co. E, ''	''	400 00	
'' Oliver D. Stelle, Co. F, ''	''	482 00	
'' Charles T. Wilt, Jr., Co. G, ''	''	374 00	
'' Wallace H. Whigham, Co. H, ''	''	329 00	
Sergt. David P. Barrett, Co. I, ''	''	338 00	
Capt. Thos. W. Cole, Co. K, ''	''	388 00	
'' A. M. Daniels, Co. L, ''	''	436 00	
'' E. A. Switzer, Co. M, ''	''	576 00	
Lieut.-Col. W. D. Hotchkiss, field, staff, non-commissioned staff and band, 2nd Regiment	''	356 00	
Lieut.-Col. W. D. Hotchkiss, Co. A, 2nd Regiment	''	461 00	
'' '' Co. B, ''	''	544 00	
'' '' Co. C, ''	''	784 00	
Capt. W. A. Chadwick, Co. D, ''	''	480 00	
Lieut.-Col. W. D. Hotchkiss, Co. E, ''	''	436 00	
'' '' Co. F, ''	''	439 00	
'' '' Co. G, ''	''	452 00	
'' '' Co. H, ''	''	440 00	
'' '' Co. I, ''	''	429 00	
'' '' Co. K, ''	''	376 00	
'' '' Co. L, ''	''	318 00	
Capt. John McFadden, Co. M, ''	''	480 00	
Col. Fred Bennitt, field, staff, non-commissioned staff, etc., 3rd Regtment	''	427 00	
Col. Fred Bennitt, band, 3rd Regiment	''	456 00	
Capt. J. M. St. Clair, Co. A, 3rd Regiment	''	416 00	
'' F. W. Pearson, Co. B, ''	''	474 00	
'' S. R. Blanchard, Co. C, ''	''	496 00	
'' John L. Graves, Co. D, ''	''	430 00	
Amounts carried forward	....	$544,688 17	$740,082 91

Statement 3—Continued.

Accounts.	App.	Amount.	Total.
Amounts brought forward		$544,683 17	$740,082 91
ILLINOIS STATE NATIONAL GUARD—*Continued.*			
Capt. J. B. Caughey, Co. E, 3d Regiment	1895	384 00	
" A. J. Renoe, Co. F, "	"	472 00	
" W. C. Eichelberger, Co. G, "	"	386 90	
" Wm. H. Brogunier, Co. H, "	"	478 00	
" Edwin M. Harris, Co. I, "	"	489 00	
" R. J. Shand, Co. K, "	"	514 00	
" Enos A. Smith, Co. L, "	"	436 00	
" E. A. Ward, Co. M,	"	336 00	
Major Louis E. Bennitt, 1st Battalion, 4th Regiment	"	135 63	
Capt. E. P. Rogers, Co. D. 4th Regiment, at East St. Louis	"	1,582 56	
Major Louis E. Bennitt, Co. F, 4th Regiment, at East St. Louis	"	1,355 16	
Col. J. S. Culver, field, staff and band, 5th Regiment	"	500 00	
" " detachments, 5th Regiment	"	208 00	
Capt. Geo. Barber, Co. A, 5th Regiment	"	400 00	
" C. A. Parish, Co. B, "	"	381 00	
" M. F. O'Brien, Co. C, "	"	364 00	
" E. .Y Miller, Co. D, "	"	563 00	
" J. C. Walters, Co. E. "	"	315 00	
" A. E. Harding, Co. F, "	"	434 00	
" E. L. Conklin. Co. G, "	"	352 00	
" J. F. Cassell. Co. H, "	"	320 00	
" E. C. Vickery, Co. I, "	"	344 00	
" James E. Watkins, Co. K, "	"	360 00	
" E. H. D. Couch, Co. L, "	"	440 00	
" F. D. Tanquary, Co. M,	"	392 00	
Col. D. J. Foster, field. staff and band, 6th Regiment	"	311 00	
Capt. John J. McConochie, Co. A, 6th Regiment	"	403 00	
" John W. Reig, Co. B "	"	400 00	
" T. L. McGirr, Co. C, "	"	680 00	
" Neal F. Pavey, Co. D, "	"	424 00	
" W. F. Lawrie, Co E, "	"	616 00	
" Frank J. Clendenin, Co. F, "	"	345 00	
" Philip McGrath, Co. G, "	"	445 00	
" W. W. Shields, Co. H. "	"	382 00	
" Wm. F. Colebaugh, Co. I, "	"	360 00	
" A. T. Tourtillott, Co. K, "	"	376 00	
" Charles B. Kling, Co. L, "	"	352 00	
" W. H. Glasgow, Co. M "	"	448 00	
Major John C. Buckner, field, staff and band, 9th Battalion	"	248 00	
Capt. John R. Marshall, Co. A, 9th Battalion	"	688 00	
" Adolph Thomas, Co. B, "	"	776 00	
" Charles L. Hunt, Co. C "	"	640 00	
" Robert R. Jackson, Co. D, "	"	824 00	
R. Haas Electric and Manufacturing Co.— Amount due for repairing bits	"	3 00	
Col. Robert H. Aiken— Salary as range officer. $1,315.00; expenses, $273.36; enpenses under orders, $76.25; pay-roll of civil employés, $1,580.55; boring artesian well, $239.13; masonry work and building chimney, $37.60; purchasing 15 perfection targets, $900.00; subsistence furnished naval militia, $714.60, at and for Logan rifle range	"	5,136 49	
Kenosha Lumber Co.— Lumber furnished Logan Rifle Range	"	175 46	
C. A. Dewey— Hardware furnished Logan Rifle Range	"	34 16	
Bullard & Gormley— Hardware furnished Logan Rifle Range	"	129 71	
Crocker Chair Co.— 10 dozen chairs furnished	"	35 00	
M. O'Connor— 12 water casks furnished Camp Lincoln	"	12 00	
Col. J. S. Culver, 5th Regiment— Dishes and mess chests for headquarters and battalions, use of horse at Camp Lincoln, clerical work paid for headquarters, amount paid for postage	"	233 42	
Amounts carried forward		$571,107 66	$740,082 91

Statement 3—Continued.

Accounts.	App.	Amount.	Total.
Amounts brought forward	....	$571,107 66	$740,082 91
ILLINOIS STATE NATIONAL GUARD—*Continued.*			
Secretary U. S. Infantry and Cavalry School, Leavenworth, Kan.— Instruction books furnished	1895	6 50	
Brig.-Gen. J. H. Barkley, 2d Brigade— Armory rent, fuel, light, etc., furnished headquarters for 6 months ending June 30, 1896	"	687 82	
Brig.-Gen. Andrew Welch, 3d Brigade— Use of horses at Camp Lincoln, armory rent, fuel, light, etc., for year ending June 30, 1896, and express charges paid on public property	"	574 59	
Capt. W. C. Eichelberger— Amount paid for repairs on uniforms	"	5 70	
Capt. J. N. St. Clair, Co. A, 3d Regiment— Armory rent, fuel, light, etc., for 6 months ending June 30, 1896	"	300 00	
Capt. C. E. Ryman— Rations furnished Co. G, 4th Regiment, en route to Camp Lincoln	"	12 60	
Capt. T. L. McGirr, Co. C, 6th Regiment— Armory rent, fuel, lights, etc., for 6 months ending June 30, 1896	"	236 10	
Capt. A. T. Tourtillott— Rations furnished Co. K, 6th Regiment en route to Camp Lincoln	"	9 40	
Lieut.-Com. A. A. Michelson, Naval Militia— Armory rent paid, May 1, to June 30, 1896	"	583 33	
Rickard & Hamilton— Survey and plat of rifle range at Camp Lincoln	"	15 00	
Springfield Electric Light & Power Co.— Lighting Camp Lincoln, encampment 1896	"	353 80	
St. Nicholas Hotel— Rations furnished details of 4th and 5th Regiments	"	10 00	
Capt. W. S. Campbell— Clerical services to headquarters 5th Regiment, to Dec. 31, 1895, Quartermaster's stores and attention to State horse paid for, and red shale, postage, hauling, etc., furnished	"	109 00	
C. W. Busher— Rent of tents for troops at Camp Lincoln	"	27 00	
August Wolf— Commissary stores furnished troops at Camp Lincoln	"	13 50	
Louis Unverzagt— Decorations for Governor's car to Peoria	"	5 60	
Gen. C. C. Hilton— Expenses under orders as Adjutant General	"	364 10	
Gen. Alfred Orendorff— Expenses under orders as Adjutant General	"	596 50	
Col. Hugh E. Bayle— Expenses under orders as Asst. Adjutant General	"	1,065 55	
Henry Wulff, State Treasurer— Amount paid Col. Hugh E. Bayle, Asst. Adjutant General, for expenses	"	410 60	
Col. Fred Bennitt— Expenses under orders	"	10 75	
Lieut.-Col. Chas. G. Averill— Expenses under orders	"	60 00	
Lieut.-Col. Walter S. Frazer, Jr.— Expenses under orders, etc	"	139 95	
Major J. C. Cabanis— Expenses under orders as A. A. Q. M	"	243 80	
Capt. W. S. Campbell— Expenses under orders	"	39 00	
Capt. Lincoln Dubois— Expenses under orders	"	50 00	
Capt. J. H. McDonnell— Expenses under orders	"	2 00	
Lieut. D. J. Baker, Jr., U. S. Army— Expenses under orders, etc	"	339 35	
Lieut. J. C. Grimes— Expenses under orders	"	28 20	
Amounts carried forward	....	$577,407 40	$740,082 91

Statement 3—Continued.

Accounts.	App.	Amount.	Total.
Amounts brought forward	....	$577,407 40	$740,082 91
ILLINOIS STATE NATIONAL GUARD—*Continued.*			
Sergeant J. C. Grimes— Expenses under orders	"	97 00	
Adams Express Co.— Express charges on public property	"	238 62	
American Express Co.— Express charges on public property	"	126 38	
United States Express Co.— Express charges on public property	"	159 44	
Western Union Telegraph Co.— Telegraphic services rendered	"	294 81	
Postal Telegraph Cable Co.— Telegraphic services rendered	"	10 34	
Chicago & Alton Railroad Co.— Freight charges on public property	"	574 77	
Baltimore & Ohio Southwestern Railway Co.— Freight charges on public property	"	71 22	
Illinois Central Railroad Co.— Freight charges on public property	"	384 38	
Wabash Railroad Co.— Freight charges on public property	"	247 36	
Chicago, Burlington & Quincy Railroad Co.— Freight charges on public property	"	167 85	
Chicago, Peoria & St. Louis Railroad Co.— Freight charges on public property	"	188 75	
Baltimore & Ohio Southwestern Railway Co.— Special train furnished Governor and staff to Charleston	"	148 93	
Toledo, Peoria & Western Railroad Co.— Transportation of troops	"	22 90	
Elgin, Joliet & Eastern Railroad Co.— Transportation of troops	"	54 74	
Peoria, Decatur & Evansville Railroad Co.— Transportation of troops	"	28 36	
Chicago, Peoria & St. Louis Railroad Co.— Transportation of troops	"	3 09	
Chicago & Alton Railroad Co.— Transportation of troops	"	5,004 62	
Chicago, Burlington & Quincy Railroad Co.— Transportation of troops	"	1,579 09	
Chicago & North Western Railroad Co.— Transportation of troops	"	196 44	
Rock Island & Peoria Railroad Co.— Transportation of troops	"	142 31	
Vandalia Line Railway— Transportation of troops	"	1 57	
Jacksonville, Louisville & St. Louis Railroad Co.— Transportation of troops	"	15 68	
Louisville, Evansville & St. Louis Railroad Co.— Transportation of troops	"	1 85	
Cleveland, Cincinnati, Chicago & St. Louis Railroad Co.— Transportation of troops	"	3 95	
Baltimore & Ohio Southwestern Railway Co.— Transportation of troops	"	3 51	
Indiana, Illinois & Iowa Railroad Co.— Transportation of troops	"	109 53	
St. Louis, Alton & Terre Haute Railroad Co.— Transportation of troops	"	1 84	
Wabash Railroad Co.— Transportation of troops	"	3,696 31	
F. C. Ramsey, Treasurer, Chicago, Milwaukee & St. Paul Railroad— Transportation of troops	"	75	
H. T. Nash, Auditor— St. Louis, Alton & Terre Haute Railroad, transportation of troops	"	10 46	
F. D. Comstock, Treasurer— Cleveland, Cincinnati, Chicago & St. Louis, R. R., transportation of troops	"	6 18	
Amounts carried forward	....	$591,000 43	$740,082 91

Statement 3—Continued.

Accounts.	App.	Amount.	Total.
Amounts brought forward	....	$591,000 43	$740,082 91
ILLINOIS STATE NATIONAL GUARD—*Continued.*			
W. E. Jones, Treasurer— Baltimore & Ohio Southwestern Railway, transportation of troops	1895	1,077 36	
W. D. Tucker, Auditor— Chicago, Peoria & St. Louis Railroad, transportation of troops	"	217 74	
E. D. Usner, Auditor— Toledo, Peoria & Western Railroad, transportation of troops	"	12 89	
W. S. Roney, Treasurer— Vandalia Line Railway, transportation of troops	"	97 84	
J. F. Titus, Local Treasurer— Illinois Central Railroad, transportation of troops	"	5,094 54	
Captain W. J. Lloyd— Freight and drayage on signal outfit, Springfield to Chicago	"	10 89	
Geo. Foster— Instrument chest furnished Signal Corps	"	12 50	
Erickson Brothers— Lockers furnished Naval Militia and Cavalry Troop A	"	1,281 00	
A. F. Hussander— Services as architect, Naval Militia and Cavalry Troop A	"	64 05	
Robert A. Douglas— Services as janitor to Springfield Armory	"	199 94	
Joseph Blankenship— Services as Janitor to Springfield Armory	"	33 32	
Amount paid services of troops during tour of duty in 1895, Aurora to Ottawa, warrants issued, viz.:			
Colonel Fred Bennitt, Field, Staff, etc., 3d Regt.	"	682 00	
Captain J. N. St. Clair, Co. A, 3d Regiment	"	306 00	
" W. F. Pearson, Co. B, " "	"	400 00	
" S. R. Blanchard, Co. C, " "	"	532 00	
" John L. Graves, Co. D, " "	"	425 00	
" Joseph B. Caughey, Co. E, " "	"	407 00	
" W. H. Wilson, Co. F, " "	"	444 00	
" W. C. Eichelberger, Co. G, " "	"	413 00	
" W. H. Brogunier, Co. H, " "	"	361 00	
" Edwin M. Harris, Co. I, " "	"	464 00	
" R. J. Shand, Co. K, " "	"	432 00	
" Enos A. Smith, Co. L, " "	"	368 00	
Lieutenant, F. E. Dresser, Co. M, " "	"	240 00	
Amount paid for services rendered, or articles furnished to the 3d Regiment, during their tour of duty, from Aurora to Ottawa in 1895, and warrants issued, viz.:			
W. H. Riale & Co.— Commissary stores furnished	"	49 57	
The Fox River Butter Co.— Butter furnished	"	136 54	
W. M. Boughner— Horses furnished, freight paid and services of Supt	"	101 58	
F. E. Royeton & Co.— Commissary stores furnished	"	221 11	
W. D. Leser— Commissary stores furnished	"	32 58	
David Hamison— Wood furnished	"	7 00	
E. W. Schreeb— Milk furnished	"	6 00	
Duncan & Perkins— Medicines furnished	"	3 25	
Fredenburg & Riale— Commissary stores furnished	"	12 60	
Geo. W. Barnhardt— Water furnished and hauling	"	12 00	
P. O. Beikland— Supplies furnished	"	6 30	
F. W. McClaery— Ice furnished	"	9 45	
Amounts carried forward	....	$605,174 48	$740,082 91

Statement 3—Continued.

Accounts.	App.	Amount.	Total.
Amounts brought forward	....	$605,174 48	$740,082 91
ILLINOIS STATE NATIONAL GUARD—*Continued.*			
Emile Hess— Supplies furnished	1895	1 60	
Richard Von Buskirk— Supplies furnished	"	13 00	
John Dolder— Wood furnished	"	3 50	
B. S. Armstrong— Oats furnished	"	6 10	
H. Weddenk— Shoeing horses	"	1 75	
Louis Ericksen— Milk furnished	"	3 50	
Frank DeBolt— Repairs to wagon and fences injured	"	10 40	
E. Belrose— Eggs and ice furnished	"	5 75	
J. G. Nichols— Milk furnished	"	1 55	
Hartman Saxton— Wagon repairs furnished	"	1 75	
Hallack & Ruby— Drugs furnished	"	45	
A. & E. Tarbox— Wood furnished	"	3 50	
A. Schlanbusch— Oil cans, globe and wicks furnished	"	65	
J. D. Marco— Ice furnished	"	9 80	
Joseph Jackson— Wood furnished	"	5 25	
Sam Hurd— Cleaning grounds	"	18 00	
Ely, Hinman & Co.— Bread furnished	"	152 66	
Armour & Co.— Ham and bacon furnished	"	242 39	
Edwards Brothers— Meat furnished	"	342 44	
C. W. Marshall & Co.— Potatoes and onions furnished	"	28 40	
D. L. Goodale— Use of horse	"	10 00	
M. Otto— Sprinkling, and saddle horse furnished	"	15 00	
J. R. Sorg— Wagon spring broken paid for	"	8 00	
J. R. Sorg— Teaming, Aurora to Ottawa	"	24 00	
O. M. Rundle— Teaming, Aurora to Ottawa	"	24 00	
C. Lewis— Teaming, Aurora to Ottawa	"	24 00	
Fred S. Lord— Teaming, Autora to Ottawa	"	24 00	
E. Logan— Teaming, Aurora to Ottawa	"	21 00	
George C. Day— Teaming, Aurora to Ottawa	"	18 00	
T. Wilson— Teaming, Aurora to Ottawa	"	36 00	
N. D. Otto— Teaming, Aurora to Ottawa	"	18 00	
Edward English— Teaming, Aurora to Ottawa	"	24 00	
Curtis Lord— Teaming, Aurora to Ottawa	"	3 00	
E. Dano— Teaming, Aurora to Ottawa	"	21 00	
W. F. Cleveland— Teaming, Aurora to Ottawa	"	24 00	
D. L. Goodale— Teaming, Aurora to Ottawa	"	18 00	
Amounts carried forward	....	$606,338 92	$740,082 91

Statement 3—Continued.

Accounts.	App.	Amount.	Total.
Amounts brought forward	....	$606,338 92	$740,082 91
ILLINOIS STATE NATIONAL GUARD—*Continued.*			
E. A. Smith— Teaming, Aurora to Ottawa	1895	24 00	
W. Haywood— Teaming, Aurora to Ottawa	"	21 00	
T. W. Swarthout— Teaming, Aurora to Ottawa	"	24 00	
R. A. Evans— Oats and hay furnished	"	4 80	
Western Union Telegraph Co.— Telegraphic services	"	1 93	
E. W. Thompson & Co.— Teaming, and saddle horse furnished	"	62 50	
A. L. Gillett— Teaming, Aurora to Ottawa	"	7 00	
J. K. Bullock— Saddle horse furnished	"	10 00	
Robert Donaldson— Teaming, Aurora to Ottawa	"	1 50	
E. J. Pease & Co.— Oats and hay furnished	"	10 89	
Ellery A. Summers— Horse and buggy furnished Major Cabanis	"	2 50	
J. F. Harrol— Four cords sawed wood furnished	"	32 00	
E. S. Rice, Agent— Rifle powder furnished	"	68 75	
Jeter & Boston— Bags and oats furnished	"	18 00	
Weaver & Hallock— Hay and ice furnished	"	18 75	
John P. Halleck— Milk furnished	"	1 50	
Frank Weaver— Teaming, Yorkville to Ottawa	"	30 00	
C. R. Cornell— Teaming, Yorkville to Ottawa	"	15 00	
George H. Nichols— Hay furnished	"	23 75	
Major J. C. Cabanis— Taking down tents at Ottawa	"	18 25	
George Marve— Hauling to Yorkville	"	3 00	
Anton Demetross— Hauling to Yorkville	"	3 00	
Frank Hill— Milk furnished	"	5 48	
Aurora Pure Ice and Cold Storage Co.— Milk furnished	"	9 93	
Hichcox & Vansickle— Saddle horses, etc., furnished	"	62 25	
Chicago, Rock Island & Pacific R. R. Co.— Freight on wagon, Ottawa to Joliet	"	6 64	
James J. Dwyer— Shoeing horses for troops	"	1 15	
Fred Schott— Lettering company wagons	"	2 50	
C. C. Glover— Ice furnished	"	5 00	
Ralph W. Gridley— Lime, hay and cartage	"	15 50	
Frank Randolph— Teaming, Aurora to Ottawa	"	16 00	
Frank Zimmerman— Teaming, Aurora to Ottawa	"	8 00	
C. Grampp & Co.— 9 water barrels furnished	"	9 00	
Joseph M. Frey— 6 water barrels furnished	"	6 00	
Standard Oil Co.— One barrel of oil furnished Logan Rifle Range	"	4 85	
Amounts carried forward	....	$606,893 34	$740,082 91

Statement 3—Continued.

Accounts.	App.	Amount.	Total.
Amounts brought forward	....	$606,893 34	$740,082 91
ILLINOIS STATE NATIONAL GUARD—*Continued.*			
The Kenosha Lumber Co.— Lumber, etc., furnished for repairs to Logan Rifle Range	1895	309 67	
Raymond Lead Co.— Lead and tin furnished for bullets, Logan Rifle Range	"	177 74	
C. W. Eaton & Co.— Shell trays, melting pots, furnaces, rifle shells, etc., furnished Logan Rifle Range	"	223 15	
Robert Steveson & Co.— 100 lbs. bees wax furnished Logan Rifle Range	"	34 00	
E. W. Blatchford & Co.— Lead and tin furnished Logan Rifle Range	"	695 73	
Chicago Dye and Machine Works— Shell extractor, repairs, labor, etc., Logan Rifle Range	"	255 51	
E. S. Rice— Rifle Powder furnished Logan Rifle Rage	"	84 50	
The Massey Vise Co.— Two vises furnished Logan Rifle Range	"	9 60	
Wells & Masier— Repairing bullet moulds for Logan Rifle Range	"	3 42	
B. Franz & Bro.— 50 lbs. tallow furnished Logan Rifle Range	"	4 00	
E. S. Rice— Powder furnished Logan Rifle Range and Camp Lincoln	"	220 00	
John W. Dilks— Cutting timber and bracing bullets stops, Logan Rifle Range	"	13 25	
Truesdell & Bellamore— Coal, etc., furnished Logan Rifle Range	"	11 36	
F. Bairstow— Cement and brick furnished Logan Rifle Range	"	6 50	
Brig. Gen. H. A. Wheeler— Amount paid S. H. Rust, custodian, Logan Rifle Range	"	35 00	
The Keith Lumber Co.— Lumber furnished Logan Rifle Range	"	347 44	
Jones & Laughlin, Limited— Hardware furnished Logan Rifle Range	"	59 06	
Springfield Electric Light and Power Co.— Light furnished State Arsenal	"	8 63	
Springfield Gas Light Co.— Light furnished State Arsenal	"	2 41	
Springfield Paper Co.— Wrapping paper furnished State Arsenal	"	4 65	
Springfield Water Works— Water furnished State Arsenal	"	11 00	
Eugene McLaughlin— Clerical services at State Arsenal	"	36 00	
The Dr. Hickman Drug Co.— Cleaning material furnished State Arsenal	"	5 61	
August LeRoy— Repairing lawn mower for State Arsenal	"	1 00	
West end Coal Co.— 65 lbs coal furnished State Arsenal	"	3 90	
L. E. Wheeler— Coal furnished State Arsenal	"	2 52	
Peter Vredenburg— Lumber furnished State Arsenal	"	4 01	
Vance & Dooling— Insurance on State property in hands of company commanders, etc	"	2,335 84	
Ihlenfieldt & Wiedlocker— Feed furnished for State horse, etc	"	64 85	
John Foster— Clipping State horse	"	2 50	
R. McCord— 1,000 bayonet holders furnished	"	22 50	
Amounts carried forward	....	$611,888 80	$740,082 91

Statement 3—Continued.

Accounts.	App.	Amount.	Total.
Amounts brought forward	....	$611,888 80	$740,082 91
ILLINOIS STATE NATIONAL GUARD—*Continued.*			
Winchester Repeating Arms Co.— Blank cartridges and primers furnished	1895	2,761 25	
The Heisler & Junge Co.— Bread furnished troops during Chicago strike, 1894.	"	152 00	
J. Cook— Commissary stores furnished troops during Chicago strikee, 1894	"	10 00	
Collier Shot Tower Works— 50 bags round bullets furnished troops	"	17 50	
United States Army and Navy Journal— Subscription for year ending April 13, 1897	"	6 00	
Brueck Brothers— Cleaning and repairing uniforms of troops	"	153 60	
John S. Cooper— Horses and feed furnished during Chicago strike, 1894	"	1,837 50	
Army and Navy Register— Subscription to April 15, 1896	"	3 00	
P. K. Howard— Hauling State property	"	9 25	
Alexander Lumber Co.— Lumber furnished lockers, etc., Co. I, 3d Regiment.	"	47 01	
N. B. Wiggins— Commissary stores furnished Governor and staff	"	34 88	
P. Carroll Teaming Co.— Hauling property for naval militia	"	33 50	
E. A. Armstrong Manufacturing Co.— Uniform furnished as per contract	"	10 00	
Carey & Loranger— Cleaning, blocking and pressing 12 doz. and cleaning 44 campaign hats for troops	"	47 00	
Roberts Brothers— One tent, 9x9 furnished troops	"	8 28	
A. F. Hassander— Architect's fees for inspecting Chicago armories, etc	"	101 05	
St. Luke's Hospital— Board and attention to Nimrod Killem, etc	"	27 00	
Julian P. Friez— Heliographs, U. S. army standard, furnished	"	110 00	
Graham-Meyer T. & L. L. Co.— Army signal kits and poles furnished	"	100 00	
Whitman Saddle Co.— Saddle and bridle furnished	"	55 50	
Levy, Dreyfus & Co.— Aluminum field glasses furnished	"	81 00	
Thompson C. Dill & Co.— 4 sets 3 joint signal corps staff furnished	"	14 00	
Lieut. W. J. Lloyd— Expenses of signal corps at Carlinville	"	14 25	
Hartley & Graham— Ammunition for Krag-Jorgenson rifles furnished	"	30 00	
Geo. B. Carpenter & Co.— National flag and regimental flag furnished 6th Regiment	"	110 00	
John L. Pickering— Advertising proposals for furnishing military stores in Evening Telegram	"	6 00	
McCord & Stewart: 2100 bayonet holders and field belts furnished	"	42 00	
Whitman Saddle Co.— Saddles, blankets, bridles, breast plates furnished.	"	437 55	
C. Hiltwein— Packing and shipping condemned clothing to Springfield	"	7 50	
Illinois State Register— Letter heads and envelopes furnished companies, etc	"	277 31	
J. C. Klaholt— Cleaning and packing trophy	"	13 00	
George Sponsler— Labor at State arsenal	"	21 75	
Amounts carried forward	....	$618,467 48	$740,082 91

Statement 3—Continued.

Accounts.	App.	Amount.	Total.
Amounts brought forward	......	$618,467 48	$740,082 91
ILLINOIS STATE NATIONAL GUARD—*Continued.*			
Marshall Field & Co.— Shields furnished and decorating car of commander in chief and staff for trip to Chattanooga; bunting furnished and draping Governor's car for trip to Cotton States and International Exposition at Atlanta, Ga	"	94 75	
T. B. Blair— Making and painting 50 lockers for 7th Regiment	"	378 00	
J. B. Frink— Shields furnished for decorating cars, trip of Governor and staff to Atlanta, Ga	"	20 00	
Phillips Brothers— 1,000 company reports furnished	"	17 50	
Hotel Livery Co.— Carriages furnished Governor and staff	"	30 50	
Army and Navy Journal— 300 manuals of guard duty furnished	"	56 25	
John G. Schubert, Manager— Gallagher Floral Co., decorations of car of Governor and staff, trips to Milwaukee, Wis., and Atlanta, Ga	"	15 00	
Hensler & Dunham Towing and Wrecking Co.— Towing small boats from Jackson Park to shipyard at South Chicago	"	15 00	
The Crocker Uniform Co.— Caps furnished troops on contract	"	21 50	
Mat Wright— Moving boats, etc., Naval Militia, to South Chicago	"	45 00	
Frak Mellen— Moving boats, etc., Naval Militia, to South Chicago	"	11 25	
Alexander St. Peter— Moving boats, etc., Naval Militia, to South Chicago	"	6 75	
Dennis St. Peter— Moving boats, etc., Naval Militia, to South Chicago	"	6 75	
Edward Chambers— Moving boats, etc., Naval Militia, to South Chicago	"	2 25	
J. Irving Pearce— Rooms used as headquarters, Governor and staff, trip to Atlanta, Ga., etc	"	18 00	
Moody & Fritze— Transportation furnished Hugh E. Bayle, A. A. G.	"	5 00	
Williams & Newman— Commissary stores furnished staff car on trip to Atlanta, Ga., etc	"	15 00	
G. J. Little— Rent of Armory at Springfield, as per lease	"	450 00	
Work Brothers & Co.— 1,000 overcoats furnished troops on contract	"	3,250 00	
Wright's Livery— Transportation furnished	"	4 00	
T. C. Orendorff, government contractor— 500 U. S. reg. belts furnished troops	"	561 60	
C. A. Power— Boxes for saddles furnished Major Cabanis, and 45 lockers furnished 4th Regiment Band at Springfield Armory	"	186 50	
Schlierbach & Blucke— Harness and horse equipments, repairs, etc., furnished	"	70 80	
B. Westermann & Co.— 50 Wagner service, and organization, of security	"	200 00	
E. F. Hartmann & Co.— Stationery furnished	"	11 00	
S. D. Childs & Co.— Badges furnished	"	2 28	
Hibbard, Spencer, Bartlett & Co.— No. 45 cal. round bullets furnished	"	371 03	
Charles Truax, Greene & Co.— Medical supplies furnished 5th and 6th Regiments	"	51 67	
J. Capps & Sons, Limited— 530 wool blankets furnished, on contract	"	1,855 00	
Amounts carried forward	......	$626,239 86	$740,082 91

Statement 3—Continued.

Accounts.	App.	Amount.	Total.
Amounts brought forward	....	$626,239 86	$740,082 91
ILLINOIS STATE NATIONAL GUARD—*Continued.*			
Brig. Gen. H. A. Wheeler—			
Armory rent, headquarters 1st Brigade, to December 31, 1895	1895	500 00	
Col. Henry S. Turner—			
Armory rent, etc., 1st Regiment, to December 31, 1895	"	4,500 00	
Col. George M. Moulton—			
Armory rent, etc., 2nd Regiment, to December 31, 1895	"	4,500 00	
Amount of pay-roll for armory rent, fuel, light, etc., of Illinois National Guard and Naval Militia, for six months ending December 31, 1895, warrants issued, viz.:			
Brig. Gen. J. H. Barkley, headquarters, 2nd Brigade	"	103 45	
Major Alfred Russell, Artillery, Battery D	"	500 00	
Capt. Philip Yeager, Artillery, Battery A	"	358 70	
Capt. Will P. Butler, Cavalry, Troop B	"	394 75	
Lieut. Com. D. C. Daggett, 2nd Bat'n, Naval Militia	"	150 00	
Col. Fred Bennett, headquarters, 3d Regiment	"	221 30	
Lieut. Col. Wm. Wildt, " "	"	568 95	
Major Edward J. Sill, " "	"	541 61	
Capt. J. N. St. Clair, Co. A, "	"	300 00	
" F. W. Pearson, Co. B "	"	302 75	
" S. R. Blanchard, Co. C, "	"	435 98	
" J. B. Caughey, Co. E, "	"	249 25	
" W. C. Eichelberger, Co. G, "	"	180 96	
" W. H. Brogunier, Co. H, "	"	30 65	
" R. J. Shand, Co. K, "	"	27 15	
" Enos A. Smith, Co. L, "	"	275 00	
" E. A. Ward, Co. M, "	"	176 05	
" R. M. Smith, Headquarters, 4th Regiment	"	100 00	
" E. E. Elliott, Co. A, 4th Regiment	"	201 00	
" E. Wood Heroch, Co. B, "	"	185 35	
" E. P. Rogers, Co. D, "	"	229 03	
" Chas. E. Rudy, Co. E, "	"	290 60	
" Claude E. Ryman, Co. G, "	"	175 63	
" McFarren Davis, Co. H, "	"	227 61	
" S. S. Houston, Co. I, "	"	181 10	
" Geo. D. Sherwin, Co. K, "	"	223 61	
" Geo. Barber, Co. A, 5th Regiment	"	202 20	
" C. A. Parish, Co. B, "	"	230 00	
" W. R. Courtney, Co. D, "	"	144 50	
" A. E. Harding, Co. F, "	"	272 80	
" E. Sheer, Co. G, "	"	255 40	
" E. C. Vickery, Co. I, "	"	280 33	
" J. E. Watkins, Co. K, "	"	218 97	
" E. H. D. Couch, Co. L, "	"	258 70	
" L. H. Gillett, Co. M, "	"	342 60	
Col. D. J. Foster, Headquarters, 6th Regiment	"	149 65	
Capt. E. M. Cook, Co. A, 6th Regiment	"	222 00	
" W. F. Lawrie, Co. E, "	"	288 37	
" Wm. E. Baldwin, Co. G, "	"	151 22	
" W. W. Shields, Co. H, "	"	237 41	
" A. T. Tourtillott, Co. K, "	"	213 22	
" Chas. B. Kling, Co. L, "	"	225 00	
Col. Francis T. Colby, Headquarters, 7th Regiment	"	333 04	
Col. Francis T. Colby—			
Company clothing boxes and field desk furnished 7th Regiment	"	207 35	
Col. Francis T. Colby—			
Amount paid for janitors, postage, office supplies, etc., for 7th Regiment headquarters	"	652 82	
Col. Francis T. Colby—			
Amount of supplemental pay-roll, Co. A, 7th Regiment, and amount paid for janitors, gas, coal, repairs, etc., for 7th Regiment	"	269 34	
J. T. Carton & Co.—			
Rent of Armory to 9th Battalion, Jan., 1896	"	25 00	
Capt. F. W. Pearson—			
Fitting up rifle range, Co. B, 5th Regiment	"	30 00	
Gen. H. A. Wheeler—			
Labor of Jos. F. Lee, cleaning guns in 7th Regiment Armory	"	12 50	
Amounts carried forward	....	$647,592 76	$740,082 91

Statement 3—Continued.

Accounts.	App.	Amount.	Total.
Amounts brought forward	....	$647,592 76	$740,082 91
ILLINOIS STATE NATIONAL GUARD—*Continued.*			
Capt. J. C. Walters— Armory rent, fuel, light, etc., Co. E, 5th Regiment, for six months, ending Dec. 31, 1895	1895	217 11	
Capt. W. D. Clark— Armory rent, fuel, light, etc., Co. B, 6th Regiment, for 6 months ending Dec. 31, 1895	"	158 28	
Capt. F. H. Muench— Armory rent, fuel, light, etc., Co. F, 6th Regiment, for 6 months ending Dec. 31, 1895	"	295 32	
Col. Francis T. Colby— Janitor's service, fuel, light, etc., furnished 7th Regiment	"	261 58	
Col. Francis T. Colby— Armory rent, etc., furnished 7th Regiment to Dec. 31, 1895	"	2,000 00	
Capt. W. H. Glasgow— Armory rent, fuel, light, etc., Co. M, 6th Regiment, for 6 months ending Dec. 31, 1895	"	135 00	
Lieut.-Col. Leroy T. Steward— Per diem as Asst. Inspector General, 1st Brigade	"	390 00	
Capt. Wm. R. Courtney— Armory rent, fuel, light, etc., Co. M, 4th Regiment, for 6 months ending Dec. 31, 1895	"	11 39	
Capt. T. Leslie McGirr— Armory rent, fuel, light etc., Co. C, 6th Regiment, for 6 months ending Dec. 31, 1895	"	260 44	
Capt. Harry T. Griffin— Armory rent, fuel, light, etc., Co. I, 6th Regiment, for 6 months ending Dec. 31, 1895	"	273 82	
Major John C. Buckner— Armory rent, etc., 9th Battalion, for 2 months ending March 31, 1896	"	750 00	
Capt. Thomas L. McGirr— Amount paid for freight and cartage on public property	"	6 65	
Capt. Harry M. Smith— Labor and material furnished shooting gallery, Springfield Armory	"	49 86	
Capt. Henry S. Parker— Moving State property from old to new Armory, Springfield	"	3 50	
Lieut.-Col. J. Milton Oliver— Expenses of general court martial, convened by Adjutant General's order, July 1, 1895	"	135 03	
Major E. A. Sill— Gas furnished Armory 3d Regiment and omitted in previous voucher	"	39 75	
Brig.-Gen. H. A. Wheeler— Rent of headquarters, 1st Brigade, to March 31, 1896, and expenses headquarters, 1st Brigade	"	500 00	
Capt. Harry M. Smith— Expenses attending election of Co. M, 5th Regiment, at Canton	"	5 50	
Capt. John F. Harris— Armory rent, fuel, light, etc., Co. F, 4th Regiment, for 6 months ending Dec. 31, 1895	"	132 60	
Capt. S. G. Burdick— Expenses of Co. K, 4th Regiment, during strike at Centralia in 1894	"	13 75	
Amounts paid on account of Co. L, 4th Regiment, as follows, viz.:			
John Schmid, Armory rent to Dec. 31, 1895	"	75 00	
E. Murray, light furnished "	"	7 80	
Isadore Brassie, coal " "	"	4 00	
Daniel Allen, janitor's services, etc., to Dec. 31, 1895	"	27 50	
Col. Henry L. Turner— Armory rent, fuel, light, etc., 1st Regiment, for 6 months ending June 30, 1896	"	4,500 00	
Col. Geo. M. Moulton— Armory rent, fuel, light, etc., 2d Regiment, for 6 months ending June 30, 1896	"	4,500 00	
Amounts carried forward	....	$662,346 64	$740,082 91

Statement 3—Continued.

Accounts.	App.	Amount.	Total.
Amounts brought forward	....	$662,346 64	$740,082 91
ILLINOIS STATE NATIONAL GUARD—*Continued.*			
Capt. J. F. Cassell— Armory rent, fuel, light, etc., Co. H, 5th Regiment, for 6 months ending Dec. 31, 1895	1895	430 81	
Capt. John W. Meloy— Armory rent, fuel, light, etc., Co. D, 6th Regiment, for 6 months ending Dec. 31, 1895	"	165 50	
Capt. Eugene Sheer— Armory rent, drayage, etc., to March 24, 1896, for Co. G, 5th Regiment	"	97 35	
Nelson W. Graham— Electric light furnished Armory of Co. C, 4th Regiment, to Dec. 31, 1895	"	30 00	
W. G. Batron— Salary as janitor of Armory, Co. C, 4th Regiment, to Dec. 31, 1895	"	15 00	
J. M. Johnson— Rent of Armory to Co. C, 4th Regiment, to Dec. 31, 1895	"	150 00	
C. Broady— Janitor's service to 7th Regiment Armory for March, 1896	"	36 00	
Wm. B. Chiddick— Office supplies, postage and janitor's services furnished 7th Regiment Armory, Feb. and March, 1896	"	111 25	
Thomas W. Piercy— Janitor's services to 7th Regiment Armory, Feb. and March, 1896	"	100 00	
J. C. Craig, Supt.— Water furnished 7th Regiment Armory to March 17, 1896	"	13 50	
Fred Nelson— Hauling ashes from 7th Regiment Armory in March, 1896	"	9 00	
L. Gould & Co.— Mops and mop sticks furnished 7th Regiment Armory	"	2 25	
C. H. Mears & Co.— Lumber furnished 7th Regiment Armory	"	4 50	
Ætna Fuel Co.— Coal furnished 7th Regiment Armory	"	65 79	
Chicago Gas Light Co.— Gas furnished 7th Regiment Armory	"	63 63	
Sullivan Oil Co.— Oil, benzine and water furnished 7th Regiment Armory	"	2 05	
J. F. Carton & Co.— Rent, 9th Battalion, for February, 1896	"	5 25	
S. D. Childs & Co.— Stationery furnished 1st Brigade	"	18 00	
Lieut.-Col. Walter S. Frazer, Jr.— Postage furnished 3d Brigade	"	3 60	
Capt. John L. Graves— Postage and drayage furnished Co. D, 3d Regiment	"	2 75	
Major Will T. Channon— Stationery, postage, etc., furnished 2d Battalion, 6th Regiment	"	4 50	
C. C. Howorth— Frames and glass furnished 5th Regiment, for rifle reports	"	1 50	
Capt. Paul B. Lino— Cavalry guidon furnished Troop C, on contract	"	6 50	
Col. Marcus Kavanaugh— Janitor's services, water rent, postage, etc., furnished 7th Regiment	"	254 02	
Major S. A. D. Williams— Postage furnished 4th Regiment	"	20 00	
Lieut.-Col. Wm. Wildt— Decorating, furniture, etc., for Armory, 3d Regiment	"	200 00	
Amounts carried forward	....	$664,159 39	$740,082 91

Statement 3—Continued.

Accounts.	App.	Amount.	Total.
Amounts brought forward	....	$664,159 39	$740,082 91
ILLINOIS STATE NATIONAL GUARD—*Continued.*			
Lieut.-Col. Daniel Moriarity— Gas, janitor, etc., for 7th Regiment, April and May, 1896	1895	166 34	
Major John C. Buckner— Armory rent, etc., 9th Battalion, to June 30, 1896	"	750 00	
J. G. Lobstein— Lockers, etc., furnished 9th Battalion, on contract	"	1,243 00	
Davlin, Mueller & Co.— Truck wagon and United States scale furnished	"	138 00	
W. L. DeRemer— 1,000 campaign hats furnished on contract	"	910 00	
Michael Burke— 2 loads of straw furnished 4th Regiment	"	10 00	
Springfield Electric Light and Power Co.— Electric light furnished State Arsenal	"	2 92	
Brand & Groenke— Repairing wagon and sprinkler	"	28 15	
Capt. John H. McCreery— Subsistence and lodging, officers attending School of Instruction	"	22 35	
W. W. Sweet, Jr.— Cabbage and quartermaster's stores for troops at Camp Lincoln	"	80 85	
John D. Lamken— Use of grounds for battle tactics, as per contract	"	20 00	
A. T. Booth— Meals furnished troops at East St. Louis, account of cyclone, May, 1896	"	162 75	
Henry F. Bader— Medical supplies furnished troops at East St. Louis, account of cyclone, May, 1896	"	8 15	
John Gerth— Meals furnished troops at East St. Louis, account of cyclone, May, 1896	"	133 25	
Frank Tuttle— Meals furnished troops at East St. Louis, account of cyclone, May, 1896	"	676 50	
S. A. Enloe— Rent of office for battalion headquarters, account of cyclone, May, 1896	"	5 00	
Scherer & Son— Rent of quarters for troops, account of cyclone, May, 1896	"	110 00	
Lieut. W. A. Phillips— Freight on horse from Galesburg to Springfield	"	9 40	
Amounts paid for Armory rent, fuel, light, etc., to the various commands of Illinois State National Guard, for 6 month ending June 30, 1896, viz.:			
Capt. W. P. Butler, Troop B, Cavalry	"	375 45	
" M. L. C. Funkhouser, Troop C, Cavalry	"	400 00	
" Phil. Yeager, Battery A, Artillery	"	379 45	
" Wm. Austin, " D, "	"	500 00	
Lieut.-Col. Wm. Wildt, Headquarters 3d Regiment	"	679 50	
Capt. F. W. Pearson, Co. B, 3d Regiment	"	415 50	
" S. R. Blanchard, Co. C, "	"	435 40	
" J. B. Caughey, Co. E, "	"	250 50	
" W. C. Eichelberger, Co. G, "	"	161 70	
" E. A. Ward, Co. M, "	"	198 60	
Col. R. M. Smith, Headquarters 4th Regiment	"	100 00	
Capt. E. E. Elliott, Co. A, "	"	200 00	
" E. W. Hersch, Co. B, "	"	196 05	
" Dick C. Wiliams, Co. C, "	"	195 00	
" E. P. Rogers, Co. D, "	"	202 50	
" C. E. Reedy, Co. E, "	"	282 62	
——— Ike Norman, Co. F, "	"	125 00	
Capt. C. E. Ryman, Co. G, "	"	215 95	
" W. H. Slanker, Co. H, "	"	227 79	
" S. S. Houston, Co. I, "	"	188 45	
" Geo. D. Sherwin, Co. K, "	"	216 50	
" W. R. Courtney, Co. M, "	"	121 62	
Amounts carried forward	....	$674,703 83	$740,082 91

Statement 3—Continued.

Accounts.	App.	Amounts.	Total.
Amounts brought forward	....	$674,703 83	$740,082 91
ILLINOIS STATE NATIONAL GUARD—*Continued.*			
" C. A. Parish, Co. B, 5th Regiment	1895	230 00	
" J. C. Walters, Co. E, "	"	260 02	
" A. E. Harding, Co. F, "	"	277 50	
" J. F. Cassell, Co. H, "	"	448 85	
" E. C. Vickery, Co. I, "	"	296 17	
" J. E. Watkins, Co. K, "	"	217 50	
" E. H. D. Couch, Co. L, "	"	259 60	
" F. D. Tanquary, Co. M, "	"	352 25	
Col. D. J. Foster, Headquarters 6th Regiment	"	60 00	
Capt. J. J. McConochie, Co. A, "	"	222 00	
" J. W. Reig, Co. B, "	"	159 94	
" W. F. Lawrie, Co. E, "	"	283 00	
" Phil. McGrath, Co. G, "	"	153 60	
" W. W. Shields, Co. H, "	"	236 43	
Lieut. Edward Lawton, Co. I, "	"	224 61	
Capt. A. T. Tourtillott, Co. K, "	"	206 31	
" Charles B. Kling, Co. L, "	"	204 75	
" W. H. Glasgow, Co. M, "	"	135 00	
Col. Marcus Kavanaugh, Headquarters 7th Regiment	"	196 43	
Amounts paid the following named persons and firms for articles furnished, or services rendered the Illinois National Guard and Naval Militia, viz.:			
Major Edward C. Young, 1st Cavalry—			
Standard colors and guidon	"	100 00	
Capt. W. J. Lloyd—			
Tools for signal corps	"	8 55	
Capt. W. J. Lloyd—			
Reel cart for signal corps	"	20 00	
Capt. W. P. Butler, Troop B—			
Use of 43 horses at Camp Lincoln	"	516 00	
Capt. Joseph I. Kelly—			
Blue print maps, etc	"	9 55	
Capt. Wm. Austin—			
Use of 3 horses at Camp Lincoln	"	42 00	
Lieut.-Col. J. B. Washburn, 4th Regiment—			
Expenses under orders, Olney and Mt. Vernon	"	6 79	
Col. Geo. M. Moulton, 2d Regiment—			
42 dozen campaign hats purchased	"	458 64	
Major F. B. Nichols, 5th Regiment—			
Postage furnished 2d Battalion	"	7 82	
Major Will S. Channon, 6th Regiment—			
Postage and election notices	"	5 25	
Major David E. Clarke, 6th Regiment—			
Postage	"	4 50	
Lieutenant Commander R. S. Critchell, N. M.—			
Cash paid for storage of boats	"	75 00	
Lieutenant Commander R. S. Critchell, M. M—			
Telegraphic services Logan Rifle Range	"	28 50	
Lieutenant Commander D. C. Daggett—			
Painting and repairing boats	"	110 00	
John W. Bunn & Co.—			
Commissary stores for troops at Camp Lincoln	"	1,686 30	
LaFayette Smith Grocer Co.—			
Commissary stores for troops at Camp Lincoln	"	121 98	
M. Zwicky's Sons—			
Soap for troops at Camp Lincoln	"	64 25	
Jonathan Cashmore—			
Brick furnished Logan Rifle Range	"	15 00	
T. H. Russ—			
Grading and sodding Logan Rifle Range	"	150 00	
A. Willey—			
Permanent improvements Logan Rifle Range	"	96 85	
C. F. G. Stender—			
16 sets artillery harness furnished	"	2,827 18	
H. H. Hopkins—			
Material for improvement of Logan Rifle Range	"	125 00	
Henion & Hubbell—			
Material for improvement of Logan Rifle Range	"	28 78	
Jones & Laughlin, Ltd.—	"		
3 kegs nails for Logan Rifle Range	"	10 45	
Amounts carried forward	....	$685,645 98	$740,082 91

Statement 3—Continued.

Accounts.	App.	Amounts.	Total.
Amounts brought forward	....	$685,645 98	$740,082 91
ILLINOIS STATE NATIONAL GUARD—*Continued.*			
E. C. Cook & Bro.— Tents and flys, as per contract	1895	1,521 39	
A. Ortmayer & Son— Pack saddles for engineer's corps	"	35 50	
Red Line City Express Co.— Teaming—forage caps	"	20 36	
Keuffell& Esser Co.— Supplies for engineer's corps	"	144 77	
E. A. Armstrong Manufacturing Co.— Uniforms, silk neckerchiefs, etc., for naval militia	"	1,449 45	
Barber Asphalt P. Co.— Material for improvement of Logan Rifle Range	"	22 00	
S. D. Childs & Co.— Shooting decorations and field order books	"	72 87	
Marshall Field & Co.— Material for targets Logan Rifle Range	"	76 44	
Chas. Truax, Green & Co. Refitting and refurnishing seamens' medical and surgical chests	"	880 26	
Eugene Dietzgen Co.— Supplies furnished engineers' corps	"	227 90	
Crerar, Adams & Co.— Supplies furnished engineers' corps	"	256 95	
N. W. Wire Mattress Co.— 125 mattress springs for Logan Rifle Range	"	88 75	
Wadsworth, Howland Co.— Material for improvement at Logan Rifle Range	"	92 85	
Keuffel & Esser Co.— Blue print paper for maps	"	23 50	
Mrs. C. Grant— Material for targets at Logan Rifle Range	"	10 00	
Mrs. C. Grant— Lumber furnished Logan Rifle Range	"	272 46	
Kenosha Lumber Co.— Lumber furnished Logan Rifle Range	"	557 06	
Kenosha Lumber Co.— Lumber for targets Logan Rifle Range	"	59 98	
Kentucky Wagon Manufacturing Co.— Red cross army ambulance, complete	"	350 00	
M. C. Lilly Co.— 6,000 forage caps furnished	"	4,800 00	
Winchester Repeating Arms Co.— 25,000 blank cartridges furnished	"	311 85	
Capt. Geo. Barber— Armory rent, fuel, light, etc., Co. A, 5th Regiment, for 6 months ending June 30, 1896	"	197 00	
Amounts paid for services of Illinois National Guard during tour of instruction at Camp Lincoln, encampment of 1896—Warrants issued, viz:			
Col. R. M. Smith, field, staff, etc., 4th Regiment	"	337 00	
Capt. Ed. E. Elliott, Co. A, 4th Regiment	"	387 00	
" E. W. Hersch, Co. B, "	"	472 00	
" Dick C. Williams, Co. C, "	"	449 00	
" Eddy P. Rogers, Co. D, "	"	496 00	
" Chas. E. Rudy, Co. E, "	"	440 00	
" Chas. G. Ryman, Co. G, "	"	508 00	
" W. H. Slanker, Co. H, "	"	399 00	
" S. S. Houston, Co. I, "	"	496 00	
" Geo. D. Sherwin, Co. K, "	"	423 00	
" Franz Muench, Co. L, "	"	360 00	
" Wm. R. Courtney, Co. M, "	"	376 00	
N. W. Wire Mattress Co.— 100 cots furnished on contract	"	127 60	
A. Willey— 1 oven and 1 coffee tank furnished	"	55 30	
The Wm. Zapf Drug Store— Medical supplies furnished troops at Camp Lincoln	"	241 16	
Lee Hickox— Use of 200 acres of land for field exercises, encampment of 1896, on contract	"	1,000 00	
Amounts carried forward	....	$703,684 38	$740,082 91

Statement 3—Continued.

Accounts.	App.	Amounts.	Total.
Amounts brought forward	....	$703,684 38	$740,082 91
ILLINOIS STATE NATIONAL GUARD—*Continued.*			
Major Edward J. Sill— Armory rent, fuel, light, etc., for 6 months ending June 30, 1896—Co. D, $282.20; Co. I, $282.20—3d Regiment	1895	564 40	
Brig.-Gen. H. A. Wheeler— Use of 3 horses at Camp Lincoln, encampment 1896	"	36 00	
Brig.-Gen. H. A. Wheeler— Services, as per pay-roll, of headquarters 1st Brigade, at Camp Lincoln, encampment 1896	"	112 00	
Col. Marcus Kavanaugh— Services, as per pay-rolls, of 7th Regiment, during tour of instruction at Camp Lincoln, encampment of 1896, viz.:			
Field, staff, non-commissioned staff, band, etc. $320 00			
Co. A 328 00			
" B 372 00			
" C 431 00			
" D 434 00			
" E 387 00			
" F 416 00			
" G 272 00			
" H 320 00			
" I 286 00			
" K 360 00			
" L 430 00			
" M 439 00		4,795 00	
Lieut.-Col. Geo. M. Skelly— Use of horse at Camp Lincoln, encampment 1896	"	12 00	
Lieut.-Col. Wm. F. Dose— Use of horse at Camp Lincoln, encampment 1896	"	12 00	
Lieut.-Col. Frank L. Hatch— Use of horse at Camp Lincoln, encampment 1896	"	12 00	
Major Geo. N. Kreider— Use of horse at Camp Lincoln, encampment 1896	"	12 00	
Lieut. John A. Orendorff— Use of horse at Camp Lincoln, encampment 1896	"	9 00	
W. L. Rankin— Horse furnished General Barkley at Camp Lincoln, encampment 1896	"	9 00	
Capt. Enos A. Smith— Armory rent, fuel, light, etc., Co. L, 3d Regiment, for 6 months ending June 30, 1896	"	275 00	
Capt. T. J. Clendenin— Armory rent, fuel, light, etc., Co. F, 6th Regiment, for 6 months ending June 30, 1896	"	268 04	
Elevator Milling Co.— Corn meal furnished troops at Camp Lincoln, encampment 1896	"	14 80	
Springfield Water Works— Laying new water pipe at Camp Lincoln	"	118 99	
Keefe & Son— 200 pounds rock salt furnished troops	"	1 30	
John N. Murphy— Plumbing at State arsenal	"	4 05	
W. R. Strode— Rent of camping ground to 6th Regiment at Chickapin bridge	"	5 00	
Thomas Reed— Washing 400 bed sacks for troops	"	33 35	
B. H. Smith— Hauling State property, encampment 1896	"	51 00	
Ihlenfeldt & Wiedlocher— Flour and feed furnished	"	109 70	
Little & Son— Hire of saddles for troops, encampment 1896	"	50 00	
Major E. J. Lang— Postage furnished 3d Battalion, 4th Regiment	"	12 00	
Amounts carried forward	....	$710,201 01	$740,082 91

Statement 3—Continued.

Accounts.	App.	Amounts.	Total.
Amounts brought forward	....	$710,201 01	$740,082 91
ILLINOIS STATE NATIONAL GUARD—*Continued.*			
Crpt. Phil. Yeager— Services of Battery A, Artillery, during tour of instruction at Camp Lincoln, encampment 1896	1895	385 00	
A. B. Nokes— Rent of 4 acres of ground for field exercises, encampment 1896	"	10 00	
Wm. R. Strode— Commissary stores furnished troops at Camp Lincoln	"	15 00	
C. Jeone & Co.— Commissary stores furnished troops at Camp Lincoln	"	130 00	
Major J. C. Cabanis— Sundry expenses incarred at Camp Lincoln	"	8 00	
P. Hagle— Rent of ground for field exercises, encampmeht 1896	"	27 50	
Capt. Phil. Yeager— Use of horses at Camp Lincoln, $588; use of horses at Danville, $96; feed furnished, $12.85; hauling State property, $6.50; Battery A, Artillery, at Camp Lincoln	"	703 35	
To amount paid from appropriation of 1893.. $83,590 12 " " " 1895.. 627,889 74			711,479 86
ILLINOIS STATE ASYLUM FOR FEEBLE-MINDED CHILDREN.			
Appropriation for ordinary expenses	1893	$63,750 00	
" repairs and improvements	"	2,000 00	
" maintenance of library	"	200 00	
" ordinary expenses	1895	100,000 00	
" repairs and improvements	"	2,000 00	
" maintenance of library	"	196 97	
" school house	"	10,000 00	
" new boiler	"	1,000 00	
			179,146 97
ILLINOIS STATE ASYLUM FOR INCURABLE INSANE.			
Appropriation for the purchase of grounds for a suitable site; for the erection of buildings and completion of the whole, and for the purchase of furniture and fixtures	1895	$65,000 00	
			65,000 00
ILLINOIS STATE ASYLUM FOR INSANE CRIMINALS.*			
Appropriation for ordinary expenses	1893	$22,500 00	
" repairs and improvements	"	750 82	
" maintenance of library	"	73 59	
" building road to asylum	"	300 00	
" water supply	"	592 36	
" surgical instruments and apparatus	"	44 00	
" electric lighting	"	979 85	
" furniture and repairs	"	3,649 90	
" ordinary expenses	1895	32,500 00	
" repairs and improvements	"	1,936 37	
" maintenance of library	"	44 00	
" water supply	"	600 00	
" electric lighting	"	400 00	
" addition to building	"	20,000 00	
" furnishing addition to building	"	686 90	
			85,057 79
Amounts carried forward	....	....	$1,780,767 53

Statement 3—Continued.

Accounts.	App.	Amount.	Total.
Amounts brought forward	....	....	$1,780,767 53
ILLINOIS STATE CHARITABLE EYE AND EAR INFIRMARY			
Appropriation for ordinary expenses	1893	$22,500 00	
" repairs and improvements	"	927 79	
" maintenance of library	"	100 00	
" ordinary expenses	1895	32,500 00	
" repairs and improvements	"	2,665 71	
" maintenance of library	"	55 82	
" furniture	"	912 45	
" clothing and bedding	"	594 88	
" instruments and apparatus	"	663 31	
" reconstruction of annex	"	1,000 00	
" household expenses	"	536 11	
			62,456 07
ILLINOIS STATE HOME FOR JUVENILE FEMALE OFFENDERS.			
W. K. Ackerman, Treasurer; Appropriation for ordinary expenses	1893	$32,000 00	
Mayo & Curry; Plans and specifications furnished of buildings	"	333 33	
Lewis M. Curry; Services as superintendent in construction of buildings	"	1,125 00	
Mangson & Davis; Contractors work on buildings erected	"	55,347 98	
Wm. Prentiss, Trustee: Contractors Mangson and Davis, certificate of Aug. 10, 1895, for work on buildings	"	7,499 47	
Chicago Terra Cotta Roof and Siding Tile Co.; Contractors, Mangson and Davis, certificate of June 27, 1895, for work on buildings	"	1,800 00	
W. H. Pease: Services surveying, estimating number of acres, locating, etc., State home	"	33 50	
W. C. Vosburgh Manufacturing Co.; Electric light fixtures, etc., furnished State home, as per contract	"	745 00	
Appropriation for ordinary expenses	1895	15,000 00	
" horse	"	75 00	
" carriage	"	138 00	
" farm implements	"	22 00	
" furnishing building	"	337 90	
" maintenance of library	"	215 73	
" stable and other improvements	"	1,000 00	
" improvement of grounds	"	360 16	
			116,033 07
ILLINOIS STATE HOME FOR SOLDIERS' ORPHANS.			
Appropriation for ordinary expenses	1893	$54,000 00	
" repairs and improvements	"	1,162 83	
" maintenance of library	"	481 58	
" ordinary expenses	1895	65,625 00	
" repairs and improvements	"	1,956 51	
" maintenance of library	"	158 90	
" painting	"	507 20	
" building and furnishing addition to school house	"	1,769 15	
			125,661 17
ILLINOIS STATE HOME FOR SOLDIERS AND SAILORS.			
Appropriation for ordinary expenses	1893	$101,250 00	
" repairs and improvements	"	5,000 00	
" maintenance of library	"	549 13	
" improvement of grounds	"	3,467 75	
" roads, walks and stone gutters	"	2,000 00	
" painting	"	1,877 03	
" ordinary expenses	1895	186,875 00	
" repairs and improvements	"	4,181 50	
" maintenance of library	"	200 38	
" improvement of grounds	"	421 71	
Amount carried forward	....	....	$2,084,917 84

Statement 3—Continued.

Accounts.	App.	Amount.	Total.
Amount brought forward	....	....	$2,084,917 84
ILLINOIS STATE HOME FOR SOLDIERS AND SAILORS—*Continued.*			
Appropriation for painting	1895	$344 39	
" storage house for vegetables	"	315 00	
" cottage annex to hospital	"	18,000 00	
			324,481 89
ILLINOIS STATE HOME FOR SOLDIERS' WIDOWS.			
Appropriation for purchase of necessary site and buildings, and to furnish said buildings and maintain said home, viz.:			
Amount paid for purchase of site and buildings	1895	$5,000 00	
Amount paid for maintenance and furnishing of Home for year beginning July 1, 1895, and ending June 30, 1896	"	5,000 00	
Amount paid for maintenance and furnishing of Home for quarter (of year beginning July 1, 1896, and ending June 30, 1897) ending September 30, 1896	"	2,500 00	
			12,500 00
ILLINOIS STATE HOSPITAL FOR INSANE—CENTRAL.			
Appropriation for ordinary expenses	1893	$133 200 00	
" repairs and improvements	"	4,134 76	
" maintenance of library	"	343 25	
" ordinary expenses	1895	206,250 00	
" repairs and improvements	"	6,000 00	
" maintenance of library	"	400 00	
" painting	"	2,000 00	
" rebuilding old reservoir	"	5,000 00	
" new engine for electric light plant, etc	"	4,000 00	
" new boilers	"	3,000 00	
			364,328 01
ILLINOIS STATE HOSPITAL FOR INSANE—EASTERN.			
Appropriation for ordinary expenses	1893	$222,000 00	
" repairs and improvements	"	6,806 07	
" maintenance of library	"	347 78	
" painting	"	2,767 78	
" furniture and fixtures	"	2,744 28	
" pipe covering	"	83 26	
" improvement of water supply	"	58 41	
" furnaces, changing hot water tanks, laundry extension, etc	"	4,280 53	
" roads, walks, improvement of grounds and additional stock	"	874 22	
" ordinary expenses	1895	385,000 00	
" repairs and improvements	"	14,192 95	
" maintenance of library	"	217 02	
" painting	"	6,297 13	
" furniture and fixtures	"	7,140 97	
" reconstruction and improvement of heating and power plants	"	3,969 09	
" reconstruction and improvement of plumbing	"	2,154 67	
" material and work repairing slate roofs	"	2,239 85	
" addition for dining room	"	983 92	
" dairy house and material and work repairing barns	"	2,470 73	
" equipment and support of patholog- laboratory	"	2,401 28	
" cement walks	"	1,472 20	
" additional live stock	"	1,956 50	
" refitting basements for dining rooms	"	4,485 89	
" roads and improvement of grounds	"	746 31	
			675,690 84
Amount carried forward	....	....	$3,461,918 58

Statement 3—Continued.

Accounts.	App.	Amount.	Total.
Amount brought forward	......	....	$3,461,918 58
ILLINOIS STATE HOSPITAL FOR INSAND—NORTHERN.			
Appropriation for ordinary expenses	1893	$111,000 00	
" repairs and improvements	"	4,910 54	
" improvement of grounds	"	486 67	
" purchase of cows, etc	"	998 00	
" purchase of gas machine for laundry	"	700 00	
" addition to main and annex kitchens, removal of steamer, etc	"	42 00	
" construction of iron porches	"	1,500 00	
" ordinary expense	"	187,500 00	
" repairs and improvements	1895	8,005 79	
" maintenance of library	"	547 03	
" improvement of grounds	"	1,315 36	
" purchase of cows, etc	"	1,964 54	
" painting	"	1,979 92	
" concrete walks	"	1,500 00	
" new boilers, etc., in main building	"	5,999 32	
" new apparatus in laundry	"	499 38	
" repairs to oven and purchase of dough-mixer	"	500 00	
			329,448 55
ILLINOIS STATE HOSPITAL FOR INSANE—SOUTHERN.			
Appropriation for ordinary expenses	1893	$99,900 00	
" repairs and improvements	"	5,055 65	
" maintenance of library	"	464 14	
" laying water pipe	"	984 22	
" new roads and improvement of grounds	"	949 00	
" covering steam pipes, additional machinery, bridge repairs and wire fencing	"	396 92	
" erection of cottage for consumptives, etc	"	7,985 00	
" painting	"	815 26	
" refurnishing center building	"	22 50	
" additional stock and implements for farm	"	393 65	
" ordinary expenses	1895	156,250 00	
" repairs and improvements	"	3,706 26	
" maintenance of library	"	29 75	
" painting	"	456 94	
" rebuilding the south dormitories and wings, and administration building destroyed by fire, including cost of improvement, etc	"	171,970 00	
" reservoir and improvement of water supply	"	2,605 16	
" hot water tank and two pumps	"	421 06	
" improvement of roads	"	49 68	
" furniture and equipment of new building	"	1,912 31	
			454,397 50
ILLINOIS STATE HOSPITAL FOR INSANE—WESTERN.			
Appropriation for purchase and locotion of site for said Hospital and construction of appropriate fire-proof buildings to accommodate patients, with all necessary heating, lighting, ventilating, water supply and drainage appliances, and all necessary furniture and furnishings, and maintenance until appropriations of next General Assembly are available	1895	$28,822 26	28,822 26
ILLINOIS STATE INDUSTRIAL HOME FOR THE BLIND.			
Appropriation for running expenses	1895	$20,000 00	
" working capital	"	10,000 00	
" completion of dormitory	"	7,000 00	
			37,000 00
Amount carried forward	......	....	$4,311,586 89

Statement 3—Continued.

Accounts.	App.	Amount.	Total.
Amounts brought forward	....	....	$4,311,586 89
ILLINOIS STATE INSTITUTION FOR THE EDUCATION OF THE BLIND.			
Appropriation for ordinary expenses	1893	$33,750 00	
" repairs and improvements	"	1,466 62	
" maintenance of library	"	564 09	
" erection of work shop, etc	"	1,042 07	
" brick paving in yard	"	68 44	
" ordinary expenses	1895	65 000 00	
" repairs and improvements	"	1,966 94	
" maintenance of library	"	365 89	
" repairs to organ	"	500 00	
" gymnasium and drill hall	"	9,905 35	
" piano and musical instruments	"	1,000 00	
" new boilers	"	3,000 00	
" changing steam fittings and plumbing	"	2,000 00	
" relaying floors, changing stairways, building wagon sheds and repairing roof	"	5,000 00	
			125,629 40
ILLINOIS STATE INSTITUTION FOR THE DEAF AND DUMB.			
Appropriation for ordinary expenses	1893	$75,000 00	
" repairs and improvements	"	3,290 76	
" maintenance of library	"	256 84	
" new radiators and coil steam fittings	"	551 55	
" material and tools for teaching wood carving	"	364 94	
" ordinary expenses	1895	125,000 00	
" repairs and improvements	"	7,911 10	
" maintenance of library	"	541 08	
" improvement of trades school and purchase of printing press	"	1,366 09	
" cottage and furnishing	"	20,000 00	
" otological laboratory	"	200 00	
" water supply	"	8,000 00	
" bathing facilities and plumbing	"	5,000 00	
" boilers and repairs	"	2,000 00	
" ice house	"	300 00	
			249,782 36
ILLINOIS STATE NORMAL SCHOOL—EASTERN.			
M. P. Rice—Amount paid for personal and traveling expenses as Trustee	1895	$580 00	
F. M. Youngblood—Amount paid for personal and traveling expenses as Trustees	"	660 00	
M. J. Walsh—Amount paid for personal and traveling expenses as Trustee	"	680 00	
C. L. Pleasants—Amount paid for personal and traveling expenses rs Trustee	"	640 00	
A. J. Barr—Amount paid for personal and traveling expenses as Trustee	"	600 00	
Isaiah H. Johnson, Treasurer—Amount paid for erection of building, improvements, etc	"	30,000 00	
			33,160 00
Amounts carried forward	....	....	$4,720,158 65

Statement 3—Continued.

Accounts.	App.	Amount.	Total.
Amounts brought forward	....	....	$4,720,158 65
ILLINOIS STATE NORMAL UNIVERSITY—NORMAL.			
Appropriation for ordinary expenses	1893	$23,620 17	
" " "	1895	43,750 00	
" renewing heating plant and equipping main building	"	7,000 00	
" erection of building for physical training, heating, equipping etc...	"	40,000 00	
			114,370 17
ILLINOIS STATE NORMAL SCHOOL—NORTHERN.			
J. H. Lewis, Treasurer— Amount paid for erection of building, improvements, etc	1895	$30,000 00	
			30,000 00
ILLINOIS STATE NORMAL UNIVERSITY—SOUTHERN			
Appropriation for ordinary expenses	1893	$21,457 50	
" " "	1895	35,762 50	
" library, museum, etc	"	17,314 42	
			74,534 42
ILLINOIS STATE PENITENTIARY—JOLIET.			
Appropriation for maintenance of library	1893	$975 28	
" contingent expenses	1895	50,000 00	
" painting, relaying floors, etc	"	25,000 00	
" artesian well	"	5,000 00	
" new hospital building, fixtures, furniture, etc	"	25,000 00	
" construction of building and walls for female convicts	"	75,000 00	
			180,975 28
ILLINOIS STATE PENITENTIARY—SOUTHERN.			
Appropriation for ordinary expenses	1893	$70,000 00	
" maintenance of library	"	280 81	
" ordinary expenses	1895	80,000 00	
" contingent expenses	"	10,000 00	
" repairs and furnishing	"	5,000 00	
" pump and fixtures	"	1,500 00	
" maintenance of library	"	250 00	
" knitting machine and fixtures	"	2,500 00	
" dust extractor and heater for pearl button factory	"	1,700 00	
" material and construction of additional brick kilns	"	15,000 00	
" material and construction of tramway and clay sheds	"	2,000 00	
" material and construction of stone wall around prison	"	10,000 00	
" excavating and removing earth and useless stones from penitentiary yard	"	2,500 00	
			200,730 81
ILLINOIS STATE REFORMATORY—PONTIAC.			
Appropriation for ordinary expenses	1893	$58,750 00	
" barn for horses, etc	"	1,000 00	
" additional ordinary expenses	1895	56,128 50	
" ordinary expenses	"	146,750 00	
" repairs and improvements	"	7,000 00	
" maintenance of library	"	500 00	
" discharge and parole of prisoners	"	16,250 00	
" school books, maps and charts	"	1,500 00	
" team, wagon and farm implements	"	1,500 00	
" stand pipe and connections	"	2,500 00	
" addition to new cell house	"	55,000 00	
" completion of power house, including engine and dynamo room	"	7,000 00	
Amounts carried forward	....	$353,878 50	$5,320,769 33

Statement 3—Continued.

Accounts.	App.	Amount.	Total.
Amounts brought forward	....	$353,878 50	$5,320,769 33
ILLINOIS STATE REFORMATORY—PONTIAC—*Continued*			
Appropriation for boiler, with improved furnace, cost setting, etc.	1895	4,500 00	
" additional engines, dynamo and arc light service	"	10,000 00	
" maintenance and repairs of electric light service	"	500 00	
" additional beds, bedding, furniture, etc.	"	1,500 00	
" equipment and maintenance of trade schools	"	6,000 00	
" material to be used in trade instruction	"	3,000 00	
" additional cooking, bakery and laundry machinery appliances	"	2,000 00	
			381,378 50
ILLINOIS STATE UNIVERSITY—CHAMPAIGN.			
Appropriation for payment of taxes	1895	$3,200 00	
" salaries, maintenance and repairs, ordinary expenses, etc	"	180,000 00	
" addition to libraries	"	6,000 00	
" addition to apparatus and appliances	"	6,000 00	
" material for shop practice	"	3,000 00	
" increase of scientific cabinets and collections	"	2,000 00	
" completing the fitting and furnishing of Engineering Hall.l	"	5,000 00	
" extending equipment of college en-engineering, etc	"	30,000 00	
" improvement in chemical laboratory	"	5,000 00	
" laboratory for vegetable physiology.	"	2,000 00	
" equipment and material for fire protection	"	2,000 00	
" Biological Experiment Station on Illinois River and half the operating expenses thereof	"	5,500 00	
" library building, industrial and zoölogical collections	"	150,000 00	
" astronomical observatory and equipment thereof	"	15,000 00	
" paving streets and laying walks	"	9,300 00	
" agriculture and mechanic arts by United States	"	43,000 00	
" propagation of vaccine virus	"	3,000 00	
Amounts paid on account of appropriations to State Laboratory of Natural History, viz.:			
Appropriation for field work, office and incidental expenses	"	3,000 00	
" improvement of library	"	2,000 00	
" salaries and assistance	"	7,300 00	
" publication of bulletins	"	1,000 00	
" illustration of biennial reports of State Entomologist	"	500 00	
" expenses of experimental investigation of contagious diseases of insects	"	3,000 00	
" one-half of operating expenses of Biological Station on Illinois River	"	3,000 00	
			489,800 00
INCIDENTAL EXPENSES.			
Richter & Doland— 3 stone posts furnished, and drayage paid	1893	$10 00	
F. O. Elledge— Hauling sand for State	"	3 00	
Thomas McMurry— Hauling chairs from Fair Grounds to State House.	"	15 00	
Allen F. Goodfellow— Tile furnished, and repairing floor in Auditor's office	"	50 00	
Amounts carried forward	....	$78 00	$6,191,947 83

Statement 3—Continued.

Accounts.	App.	Amount.	Total.
Amounts brought forward	....	$78 00	$6,191,947 83
INCIDENTAL EXPENSES—*Continued.*			
P. M. Lax— Ice cooler and mirror furnished Secretary State	1893	93 50	
Michael Doyle— 25 elm trees furnished State House grounds	"	50 00	
W. F. Downs— Freight and drayage on furniture to Jacksonville	"	5 89	
John W. Bunn & Co.— Buffalo powder and soap furnished	"	7 25	
Illinois Institution for Education of Blind— 6 doz. No. 2 velvet brooms furnished	"	13 50	
Wm. White's Sons Co.— 26 load of dirt furnished State House grounds	"	3 90	
F. H. Solle— 10 gal. gasoline furnished	"	1 30	
John Underfanger— Hauling chairs from G. A. R. hall, and returning same	"	3 00	
Pillo & Kenneth— Blacksmithing for State	"	2 00	
E. Collins— 2 doz. brooms furnished	"	4 50	
James O'Brien— Cucumber soap and brooms furnished	"	14 25	
Richard Beet— 4½ lbs. sash L. cord furnished	"	1 50	
Good & Davenport— 65 boxes for packing furnished	"	9 75	
John Bird— 2 white wash brushes furnished	"	4 00	
Joseph Dalton— 12½ doz. brooms furnished	"	25 00	
Little & Son— Horse and wagon furnished, 2 days	"	3 00	
W. H. Hinrichsen, Secretary State— Amount paid for expenses to Chicago, and for expenses serving on Board of Review at Chicago	"	145 75	
Barkley & Lax— Hauling flags from Fair Grounds, and for room 6; amount paid for freight and drayage; rolling State House grounds; teaming; hauling furniture; part payment for rent of chairs, etc	"	61 87	
William M. Payne— Hardware supplies furnished janitor's department; door bell, pump, etc., furnished Monroe street residence, etc	"	292 43	
Brown & Canfield: Blue grass and white clover seed, etc., furnished State House grounds	"	7 70	
Peter Vredenburgh— Pipe, shingles, lumber, etc., furnished	"	31 82	
L. Sommer & Son— White lead, varnish, paint, drug supplies, etc., furnished	"	59 15	
Henson Robinson Co.— Cash boxes, brackets and box furnished	"	15 20	
S. D. Grant— Concentrated lye, Pearline, brushes, mop sticks, mop holders, scrub brushes, etc., furnished janitor's department	"	48 00	
R. H. Hargrave.— Awnings furnished, hanging, repairs, putting up awnings for Secretary State, etc	"	127 50	
John M. Striffler— Ice furnished State House	"	217 75	
William Uhlenfeldt— Lawn mowers, lock and key furnished; sharpening lawn mower, repairs, etc	"	40 35	
J. C. Moorhead— Repairs on State residence, Monroe street	"	8 00	
Amounts carried forward	....	$1,357 00	$6,191,947 83

Statement 3—Continued.

Accounts.	App.	Amount.	Total.
Amounts brought forward	....	$1,375 00	$6,191,947 83
INCIDENTAL EXPENSES—*Continued.*			
Ætna Foundry and Machine Co.—			
Iron strips, etc., furnished; making chair screws, centre, jaw for saw clamps, welding screw drivers, etc.	1893	7 25	
R. F. Kinsella—			
Plate-glass, gold bronze, wall-paper, etc., furnished	"	63 45	
A. Dirksen & Co.—			
5 rolls of leather gimp furnished	"	3 75	
R. McCord—			
Stencil, ink, brush, bell, battery, wire, etc., furnished	"	4 85	
Amounts paid for temporary services, as janitors and janitresses at the State House, of the following named persons, viz.:			
Robert Tobin, 11 days	"	22 00	
John Fitzpatrick, 11 days	"	22 00	
James McBurnie, 11 days	"	22 00	
James W. Smith, 10 days	"	20 00	
Martin Murphy, 5 days	"	10 00	
Clarence Glysson, 5 days	"	10 00	
McClellan Pangle, 3 days	"	6 00	
George Trotter, 9 days	"	18 00	
Peter McCoy, 8 days	"	16 00	
John Hughes, 9 days	"	18 00	
Thomas Walsh, 7 days	"	14 00	
John Burke, 5 days	"	10 00	
Charles Brown, 5 days	"	10 00	
John Dressendorfer, 5 days	"	10 00	
Frank Delaney, 5 days	"	10 00	
John Fix, 5 days	"	10 00	
Gus Cunningham, 3 days	"	6 00	
Henry D. Kinsella, 10 days	"	20 00	
John White, 5 days	"	10 00	
Samuel Cohen, 8 days	"	16 00	
Ed. McBride, 12 days	"	24 00	
John Walsh, 10 days	"	20 00	
Charles Green, 5 days	"	10 00	
Wm. Schevers, 5 days	"	10 00	
Isaac Wheaton, 5 days	"	10 00	
Charles Saner, 10 days	"	20 00	
James Kelly, 5 days	"	10 00	
John Kilday, 5 days	"	10 00	
Ida Johnson, 5 days	"	5 00	
Amanda Wilson, 9 days	"	9 00	
Annie Topp—			
Part payment of salary as janitress	"	75 00	
P. H. Durkin—			
Part payment of salary as janitor	"	70 00	
S. M. Davidson—			
Part payment of salary as janitor	"	135 00	
James D. Stacy—			
Part payment of salary as janitor	"	10 00	
T. K. Ball—			
Part payment of salary as janitor	"	15 00	
D. T. Sullivan et. al.—			
Amount paid for services as janitors of the State House, as per monthly pay-roll of W. H. Hinrichsen, Secretary of State	"	242 00	
S. M. Davidson et al.—			
Amount paid for services as janitors of the State House, as per monthly pay-roll of W. H. Hinrichsen, Secretary of State	"	4,439 00	
Geo. Westenberger—			
2 bunches of cane furnished, and caning chairs	1895	3 30	
Klaholt & Fogarty—			
100 wooden boxes furnished for packing	"	15 00	
Bauman Bros.—			
2 doz. metal and rubber combs furnished	"	2 25	
Amounts carried forward	....	$6,869 71	$6,191,947 83

Statement 3—Continued.

Accounts.	App.	Amount.	Total.
Amounts brought forward	....	$6,869 71	$6,191,947 83
INCIDENTAL EXPENSES—*Continued.*			
T. VanWelch— 6 doz. shoe brushes, 1½ doz. chamois skins, toilet and buttermilk soap furnished	1895	48 00	
Reisch & Thoma— Green cloth, cotton flannel, flannel, felt and ducking furnished	"	12 66	
H. Williams— Floral designs, satin crepe, pins, ribbon, tacks, etc., furnished House of Representatives, 39th General Assembly, on account of death of John Meyer, Speaker	"	91 50	
Myers & Co.— Cuspidors, tumblers and 10 doz. flags furnished	"	12 75	
Fred Smith— Material, labor and repairs furnished	"	7 00	
John W. Bunn & Co.— 1 case of concentrated lye furnished	"	2 90	
Dillon & Steamer— Skid trusses and bolts furnished	"	3 50	
E. A. Jones— Hauling sawdust for State House	"	6 50	
Charles Hoffman— 5 days' services as janitor and 6 days' work painting roof of State House	"	22 00	
J. C. Klaholt— Clocks, seals and repairing	"	49 50	
Wm. H. Dietz— Merchandise furnished Hon. Timothy Hogan, member of House of Representatives, 39th General Assembly, May 27, 1895	"	4 25	
R. F. Kinsella— Wall paper and hanging, glass, paint, putty, etc	"	83 95	
McCasky & Holcomb: Part payment for wiring State House for electric lighting	"	400 00	
S. A. Fairbanks— 41¼ yards carpet furnished	"	30 95	
L. E. Lawson— Repairing State House floor	"	9 00	
C. S. Fowler & Co.— Dustless oil furnished	"	4 00	
Ridgely National Bank— Services rendered by John G. Drennan, attorney at law, in case of Columbia Construction Co. vs. Wm. H. Hinrichsen, Sec'y State	"	250 00	
M. F. Dunlap— Extra electric lights furnished in State House by McCasky & Holcomb	"	450 00	
O. P. Thompson— Services as attorney at law in case of Columbia Construction Co. vs. W. H. Hinrichsen, Sec'y State	"	250 00	
C. F. Smith, by Julius Myers— Cementing and repairing cistern	"	5 00	
Henson Robinson Co.— Hardware and repairs; labor and material furnished	"	213 75	
John Farmer— Cleaning carpets for Secretary of State	"	5 25	
Philip Kress— Making 7 mops for State House	"	5 00	
J. S. Fisher— 242 lbs. hydrochloric acid furnished	"	10 29	
Springfield Gas Light Co.— 3 Welsbach gas burners furnished	"	6 75	
The John Bressmer Co.— Rugs and carpet furnished	"	17 50	
Stacy, Herbst Co.— Soap, brushes, combs, mops, etc., furnished	"	76 87	
George E. Brennan— Services of R. M. Harris in relation to the Columbia Construction Co. vs. Sec'y State	"	25 00	
J. B. Brown— 2 gal. mixoline furnished	"	2 00	
Amounts carried forward	....	$8,975 58	$6,191,947 83

Statement 3—Continued.

Accounts.	App.	Amount.	Total.
Amounts brought forward	....	$8,975 58	$6,191,947 83
INCIDENTAL EXPENSES—*Continued.*			
Charles Hoffman— 35 days' work painting for State	1895	70 00	
Geo. S. Connelly & Co.— Soap furnished	"	9 75	
P. H. Giblin— Brushes and pearline furnished	"	11 25	
Barkley & Lax— Furniture furnished, rent of chairs, repairing desk, hauling for State, broken chairs paid for, repairing chairs, drayage, etc	"	1,290 80	
John M. Striffler— Ice furnished State House	"	266 66	
L. Sommer & Son— Drugs, sponges, chamois skins, oil, putty, ammonia, acids, dusters, etc	"	149 03	
L. F. W. Sommer & Bro.— Benzine, ammonia, drugs, sponges, dusters, etc	"	155 67	
S. D. Grant— Pearline, oil, brushes, salt., etc., furnished	"	113 20	
William M. Payne— Hardware supplies, etc., furnished janitor's department	"	806 68	
James Furlong— Crash towels, brushes, cotton flannel and felt	"	98 29	
Brown & Canfield— Clover and blue grass seed furnished	"	4 15	
Wm. H. Hinrichsen, Secretary of State— Traveling expenses to Chicago, etc	"	23 00	
Miller & Staley— 60 boxes for packing furnished	"	9 00	
Capital Coal Co.— 561.48 tons of coal furnished State	"	561 48	
C. A. Power— Plate and stained glass, glass, putty, lumber, labor, etc., furnished	"	205 50	
R. H. Armbruster— Desk stool and rod awning hinges furnished	"	6 10	
R. H. Hargraves— Awnings furnished and repairs on library and other awnings	"	85 50	
McCord & Stewart— Repairs and material furnished	"	4 60	
R. McCord— Grinding mower, repairs on locks and keys, and locks, keys, etc., furnished	"	39 75	
Hellweg & Hopkins— Material furnished, plumbing, repairs, etc	"	355 91	
Peter Vredenburgh— Lime, lumber blinds, shingles, cement, etc	"	133 23	
Amounts paid for temporary services, as janitors and janitresses at the State House, of the following named persons, viz.:			
Denny J. Hartnett, 5 days	"	10 00	
Peter McCoy, 10 days	"	20 00	
Dennis Gahan, 5 days	"	10 00	
John Burke, 5 days	"	10 00	
C. Sanners, 5 days	"	10 00	
Amandy Wilson, 10 days	"	10 00	
Anna Vantrese, 11½ days	"	11 50	
Susie E. Thompson, 15 days	"	15 00	
P. H. Durkin— Part payment of salary as janitor	"	190 00	
Annie Topp— Part payment of salary as janitress	"	225 00	
Wm. B. Fink— Part payment of salary as janitor	"	195 00	
Charles E. Perdue— Part payment of salary as watchman	"	10 00	
James R. Cross— Part payment of salary as janitor	"	60 00	
Amounts carried forward	....	$14,091 63	$6,191,947 83

Statement 3—Continued.

Accounts.	App.	Amount.	Total.
Amounts brought forward	....	$14,091 63	$6,191,947 83
INCIDENTAL EXPENSES—*Continued.*			
F. M. McKendrick— Part payment of salary as janitor	1895	110 00	
T. K. Ball— Part payment of salary as janitor	"	20 00	
Adam Hoff— Part payment of salary as fireman	"	30 00	
John Stroub— Part payment of salary as fireman	"	30 00	
John T. Rittman— Part payment of salary as fireman	"	20 00	
L. A. Graham— Part payment of salary as assistant engineer	"	75 00	
Perry White— Part payment of salary as assistant engineer	"	10 00	
Bev. Wiltshire et al.— Amount paid for services as janitors, etc., of State House, as per monthly pay-rolls of W. H. Hinrichsen, Secretary of State	"	2,015 00	
T. K. Ball et al.— Amount paid for services as janitors, etc., of State House, as per monthly pay-rolls of W. H. Hinrichsen, Secretary of State	"	5,844 00	
Henry Wulff, State Treasurer— Amount paid for services as janitors, etc., of State House, as per monthly pay-rolls of W. H. Hinrichsen, Secretary of State	"	1,161 66	
C. C. Leavitt et al.— Amount paid for services as janitors, etc., of State House, as per monthly pay-rolls of W. H. Hinrichsen, Secretary of State	"	4,200 00	
To amounts paid on account of incidental expenses of 39th General Assembly, viz.:			
John W. Hedenberg— 1 load of sawdust furnished	"	3 00	
The Evening Telegram— India Ink sketch of capitol and electros	"	21 00	
L. Sommer & Son— Acids, ammonia, etc., furnished	"	156 96	
Frank Simmons— 1 diary, 1 Challenge eyelet press, fountain pens, calendars, stands, and stationery furnished	"	43 40	
William M. Payne— Hardware, sash cord, etc., furnished	"	763 62	
Baumann Brothers— Ink, thermometers, brushes and combs fsrnished	"	11 25	
J. D. O'Keefe— 1 Remington typewriter, No. 6, furnished	"	97 50	
R. M. Ridgely, P. M.— Postage stamps furnished	"	78 00	
McCord & Stewart— 1 Remington typewriter, 1 Remington typewriter, cabinets and covers, letter press bath and Remington typewriter, Remington typewriter and oak cabinet, Century, oak cabinet, repairing typewriter and new parts furnished	"	579 40	
Henry Abels— 2 Premier typewriters, 1 typewriter and desk, 1 Smith-Premier typewriter, services rendered in preliminary organization of Senate, 39th General Assembly, and 1 Smith-Premier typewriter furnished	"	533 00	
Fidelity and Casualty Co.— Premium on insurance policy No. 28,880	"	125 00	
S. D. Grant— Pearline, soap, brushes, etc	"	35 25	
Hellweg & Hopkins— Labor as plumbers, etc	"	197 00	
Jessie L. Wilson— Copies of bill amendment to election laws	"	3 80	
O. C. Blakely— Hair brushes and combs	"	7 00	
Amounts carried forward	....	$30,322 47	$6,191,947 83

Statement 3—Continued.

Accounts.	App.	Amount.	Total.
Amounts brought forward	....	$30,322 47	$6,191,947 83
INCIDENTAL EXPENSES—*Continued.*			
R. Wolfsberg— Salary as assistant electrician	1895	30 01	
Halliday & Kessberger— Print of State House	"	10 00	
Henson Robinson Co.— Galvanized iron pan and tin boxes	"	5 45	
C. F. Weisenmeyer— 1 mail pouch furnished	"	5 00	
R. J. McDonald— 6 dozen Bunk's disinfectant	"	25 00	
Wyckoff, Seamans & Benedict— 1 No. 6 Remington typewriter and cover	"	100 00	
M. E. Ehrsam— Type, rubber stamps, ink, pads, fonts and pica dates	"	31 16	
Dearborn Duster Co.— 5 doz. 16 car., $13, less 50x$\frac{3}{10}$x5 per cent	"	25 02	
S. A. Fairbanks— Carpets, fitting and repairs; carpet sweepers, padded papers, sewing and fitting; carpets, filling, and sweepers furnished	"	1,908 45	
Fort Wayne Electric Corporation— Winding armature, etc	"	133 30	
T. Van Welch— Soap, brushes, combs, sponges, vaseline, express charges, chamois skins, combs and brushes	"	97 95	
Dr. H. Lee Hatch— Soap, brushes, combs and whisk brooms	"	15 40	
Reisch & Thoma— Flannel and ducking furnished	"	27 36	
Rockwell & Rupel Co.— Blue cobweb carbon paper, copy holders and onion skin paper, etc	"	25 32	
Chicago Legal News Co.— 186 Hurd's Statutes, 1893, furnished,	"	418 50	
Arcola Broom Co.— 6 doz. brushes furnished	"	6 00	
F. P. Sullivan— 1 barrel Spl. sperm machine oil	"	25 75	
F. P. Sullivan, Administrator— 1 barrel scalt dissolvent furnished	"	33 76	
Myers & Co.— Baskets, tumblers, pitchers, soap dishes, cuspidors, etc	"	111 75	
E. S. Gard— 2 cases of matches, 2 gross Lamb's wool toilet soap, matches and soap, Lamb's wool soap	"	45 25	
James Furlong— Towels, muslin, flannel and oil cloth	"	80 78	
Anna Stewart— Washing and ironing 17 5-6 doz. towels	"	14 38	
Ætna Foundry and Machine Co.— Labor, material and repairs furnished	"	82 91	
Susie E. Thompson— 7 days services rendered as janitress	"	7 00	
Barkley & Lax— Hauling boxes, etc	"	6 25	
J. B. Brown— Office knives, falcon files, file spindles, hair and cloth brushes, inkstands, knives, pens, ink, eyelet press, stationery, Carter's commercial inkstand, etc	"	229 45	
Wm. Ihlenfeldt— Repairs on locks; tumblers, keys, etc., furnished	"	106 00	
Louis Unverzagt— 100 yds. wreathing, and work of two men	"	9 50	
R. H. Hargraves— Repairing flags	"	8 50	
Lawson Clay— Washing towels for Senate and House	"	61 05	
Amounts carried forward	....	$34,008 72	$6,191,947 83

Statement 3—Continued.

Accounts.	App.	Amount.	Total.
Amounts brought forward	....	$34,008 72	$6,191,947 83
INCIDENTAL EXPENSES—*Continued.*			
J. C. Moorhead— Repairs on pump, solder and copper furnished for engine, galvanized iron, etc	"	9 00	
R. F. Kinsella— Glass, putty, turpentine, etc., furnished	"	76 02	
National Carbon Co.— 2 pairs, ½x1, 207 C. C. Mtg	"	30 00	
J. P. Radcliff— 1 doz. chair seats furnished	"	1 20	
W. E. Savage— Yost writing machine and cabinet	"	130 00	
Frank E. Hills— Cash paid for engrossing 6 extra copies of Senate resolutions; engrossing copies of resolution on the death of Hons. Jason Rogers and Sherwood Dixon; 2 copies of engrossed resolutions on flags for Senator H. H. Kingsbury, 39th General Assembly	"	40 00	
E. M. Kreigh— Water buckets and slop pails	"	57 85	
Springfield Trunk Factory— 1 trunk furnished for ballots	"	24 00	
Adams Express Co.— Express charges on packages	"	6 65	
American Express Co.— Express charges on packages	"	14 73	
United States Express Co.— Express charges on packages	"	12 19	
Frank Hudson— 13 days' service as assistant proof-reader	"	26 00	
John Riordan & Co.— Merchandise furnished	"	26 00	
Graeser & Fitzgerald— Hair brushes and combs furnished	"	25 00	
D. Bahan— 2 second-hand typewriters furnished	"	84 00	
Jacquin-Oden Book and Music Co.— Stationery furnished	"	30 00	
Klaholt & Fogarty— Repairing mail bags and furnishing file strings	"	3 70	
Wm. A. Ramplin— Copies of engrossed resolutions furnished	"	35 00	
Springfield Gas Light Co.— 6 mantles, and gas furnished	"	522 80	
R. Haas Electric and Mfg Co.— Electric lights in conference rooms and judges' chambers, Supreme Court	"	38 54	
Capital Coal Co.— Coal furnished	"	1,457 04	
Barkley & Lax— Furniture furnished	"	3,008 85	
			39,667 29
To amount paid from appropriation of 1893, for incidental expenses of Secretary of State... $6,849 16			
To amount paid from appropriation of 1895, for incidental expenses of Secretary of State... 20,818 13			
To amount paid from appropriation of 1895, for incidental expenses of 39th General Assembly... 12,000 00			
JOINT COMMISSION ON STATE REVISION.			
Ethelbert Callahan— Services rendered as member of commission	1895	$2,000 00	
Free P. Morris— Services rendered as member of commission	"	2,000 00	
Reed Green— Services rendered as member of commission	"	2,000 00	
Clayton E. Crafts— Services rendered as member of commission	"	2,000 00	
Amounts carried forward	....	$8,000 00	$6,231,615 12

Statement 3—Continued.

Accounts.	App.	Amount.	Total.
Amounts brought forward	....	$8,000 00	$6,231,615 12
JOINT COMMISSION ON STATE REVISION—*Continued.*			
Orville F. Berry— Services rendered as member of commission	1895	2,000 00	
Alex. J. Jones— Services rendered as stenographer of commission	"	2,000 00	
H. R. Mitchell— Services rendered as proof-reader for commission	"	185 00	
J. McCan Davis— Services rendered as proof-reader for commission	"	185 00	
			12,370 00
LABORERS, JANITORS, WATCHMEN AND POLICEMEN OF THE STATE HOUSE.			
Charles McBride et al.— Amount paid for services as chief janitor, carpenter and watchmen, as per monthly pay-rolls of W. H. Hinrichsen, Secretary of State	1893	$3,797 26	
Julius Myers— Part payment of salary as watchman	"	20 00	
Charles McBride— Part payment of salary as chief janitor	"	200 00	
J. M. Morrow et al.— Amount paid for services as carpenter and watchmen, as per monthly pay-rolls of W. H. Hinrichsen, Secretary of State	"	363 32	
Charles McBride et al.— Amount paid for services as chief janitor, assistant carpenter and watchmen, as per monthly pay-rolls of W. H. Hinrichsen, Secretary of State	1895	2,831 00	
J. M. Morrow et al.— Amount paid for services as carpenter and watchmen, as per monthly pay-rolls of W. H. Hinrichsen, Secretary of State	"	1,439 00	
J. H. Hodges, et. al.— Amount paid for services as assistant chief janitor, carpenter, and watchmen, as per monthly pay-rolls of W. H. Hinrichsen, Secretary of State	"	2,063 35	
Charles McBride— Part payment of salary as chief janitor	"	900 00	
J. H. Hodges— Part payment of salary as assistant chief janitor	"	333 30	
Julius Myers— Part payment of salary as watchman	"	260 00	
James T. Smith— Part payment of salaay as watchman	"	150 00	
D. T. Sullivan— Part payment of salary as watchman	"	310 00	
Jesse Mays— Part payment of salary as watchman	"	60 00	
Thomas Walsh— Part payment of salary as watchman	"	60 00	
			12,787 23
To amount paid from appropriation of 1893.... $4,380 58 " " " 1895.... 8,406 65			
LINCOLN HOMESTEAD TRUSTEES.			
Herman Hofferkamp— Salary as custodian from September 1, 1894, to June 30, 1895, inclusive	1893	$833 34	
Herman Hofferkamp— Lumber furnished, plastering and other repairs made	"	163 88	
Springfield Water Works— Water furnished for year ending June 30, 1895	"	10 00	
Herman Hofferkamp— Salary as custodian from July 1, 1895, to August 31, 1896, inclusive	1895	700 00	
Amounts carried forward	....	$1,707 22	$6,256,772 35

Statement 3—Continued.

Accounts.	App.	Amount.	Total.
Amounts brought forward	....	$1,707 22	$6,256,772 35
LINCOLN HOMESTEAD TRUSTEES—*Continued.*			
Henson Robinson Co.— 1 No. 50 Gilt Edge furnace furnished	1895	150 00	
Springfield Water Works— Water furnished for year ending June 30, 1896	"	10 00	
Vance & Dooling— Premiums on insurance policy No. 2161	"	25 00	
Henson Robinson Co.— Labor and material furnished	"	20 90	
To amount paid from appropriation of 1893.... $1,007 22			1,913 12
" " " 1895.... 905 90			
LINCOLN MONUMENT COMMISSIONERS.			
E. S. Johnson— Salary as custodian from August 1, 1895, to August 31, 1896, inclusive	1895	$1,083 30	
George W. Trotter— 6 days' service as custodian	"	15 25	
The Culver Stone Co.— Work and material furnished in erection of dwelling for custodian	"	2,500 00	
First National Bank— Work, material, etc., furnished for preserving, repairing and beautifying monument, grounds and approaches by the Culver Stone Co	"	3,146 31	
The Culver Stone Co.— Expenses incurred by Major E. S. Johnson, custodian, in preserving, repairing and beautifying monument, grounds and approaches	"	63 55	
E. S. Johnson— Expenses incurred in preserving, repairing and beautifying monument, grounds and approaches.	"	209 85	
Samuel M. Inglis, Secretary— Amount paid for merchandise, etc., furnished for preserving, repairing and beautifying monument, grounds and approaches	"	30 50	
Springfield Water Works— Water furnished custodian's residence and for preserving, repairing and beautifying monument, grounds and approaches	"	19 25	
			7,068 01
MINE INSPECTORS.			
T. S. Cumming— Salary $2,250.00, and expenses $9.99, as inspectors	1893	$2,348 39	
Edward Fellows— Salary $1,800.00 as inspector	"	1,800 00	
James A. Keating— Salary $1,800.00 as inspector	"	1,800 00	
John Keay— Salary $2,250.00, and expenses $97.60, as inspector	"	2,347 60	
Hugh J. Hughes— Salary $2,250.00, and expenses $109.66, as inspector	"	2,359 66	
T. S. Cumming— Salary $1,800.00, and expenses $249.53, as inspector	1895	2,049 53	
Edward Fellows— Salary $115.00, and expenses $192.40, as inspector	"	307 40	
James A. Keating— Salary $1,800.00, and expenses $285.40, as inspector.	"	2,085 40	
John Keay— Salary $1,800.00, and expenses $257.82, as inspector	"	2,057 82	
Hugh J. Hughes— Salary $115.00, and expenses $506.81, as inspector	"	621 81	
Charles Duncan— Salary as inspector	"	1,685 00	
James B. Bennett— Salary as inspector	"	1,685 00	
Robert Pickett— Salary as inspector	"	1,685 00	
Amounts carried forward	....	$22,832 61	$6,265,753 48

Statement 3—Continued.

Accounts.	App.	Amount.	Total.
Amounts brought forward	......	$22,832 61	$6,265,753 48
MINE INSPECTORS—*Continued.*			
Henry E. Malloy— Salary as inspector	1895	1,685 00	
Walter Rutledge— Expenses as inspector	"	490 65	
Thomas Hudson— Expenses as inspector	"	282 27	
James Freer— Expenses as inspector	"	365 30	
Quintin Clark— Expenses as inspector	"	739 63	
John G. Massie— Expenses as inspector	"	538 45	
J. D. Roper— Amount paid heirs of Elisha Beadle, deceased, for expenses of said Elisha Beadle, as inspector	"	78 01	
To amount paid from appropriation of 1893... $10,655 65 " " " 1895... 16,356 27			27,011 92
MONEY REFUNDED.			
Albert W. Wells, for S. L. Roe— Amount of taxes, 1894, Adams Co., refunded on account of double assessment	1893	$4 11	
Albert Walters, County Collector— Amount paid on account of error in over payment of taxes, 1894, refunded to Hamilton county	"	25 81	
Henry Wulff, State Treasurer— Amount paid by W. J. Baldridge, county collector of McLean county, on account of error in over payment of taxes, 1894, to be applied to deficiency in bond tax of said county	"	27 14	
George W. Day, County Collector— Amount paid on account of error in over payment of taxes, 1894, refunded to Union county	"	54 61	
			111 67
OFFICE OF GOVERNOR.			
Private secretary, stenographer, etc	1893	$4,500 01	
Porter	"	525 01	
Express charges, freight and drayage	"	29 51	
Stationery, newspapers, etc	"	100 87	
Rental of telephone, etc	"	37 61	
Time service and telegrams	"	155 89	
Ice	"	36 40	
Postage stamps, newspaper wrappers, etc	"	195 00	
Laundry work	"	6 59	
Miscellaneous articles furnished	"	1 40	
Recharging battery in office	"	1 00	
Private secretary, stenographer, etc	1895	7,500 00	
Porter	"	875 00	
Rental of telephone, etc	"	58 39	
Stationery, newspapers, etc	"	149 81	
Ice	"	37 75	
Janitor's service, washing walls, taking up carpets, etc	"	50 00	
New carpet	"	71 25	
Express charges, freight and drayage	"	352 88	
Time service and telegrams	"	491 36	
Laundry work	"	15 05	
Postage stamps, newspaper wrappers, etc	"	250 00	
Fares, carriage hire, calls, etc	"	87 00	
Traveling expenses of Governor in discharge of duties	"	230 00	
Expenses of W. F. Dose, Private Secretary, traveling under orders	"	185 00	
Articles furnished, repairs, etc	"	31 10	
			15,973 91
To amount paid from appropriation of 1893.... $5,589 29 " " " 1895.... 10,381 62			
Amounts carried forward	....	....	$6,308,850 98

Statement 3—Continued.

Accounts.	App.	Amount.	Total.
Amounts brought forward	....	....	$6,308,850 98
OFFICE OF SECRETARY OF STATE.			
Clerk hire	1893	9,103 78	
Porter and messenger	"	1,168 10	
Indexing records	"	2,258 84	
Stenographer and typewriter	"	750 01	
Care of document library	"	399 92	
Expenses enforcing Anti-Trust Law	"	4,065 04	
Wireing document library room for electric lighting	"	95 11	
Wireing Anti-Trust Law room for electric lighting	"	319 66	
Stationery, newspapers, etc	"	168 14	
Old State law books	"	125 00	
Janitor's services	"	620 00	
Washing towels for office, etc	"	36 89	
Messenger's traveling expenses (special)	"	40 00	
Traveling expenses of Secretary of State (official bus.)	"	15 00	
Furniture	"	214 25	
Telegraphic services	"	90 52	
Telephone rental, etc	"	96 00	
Express charges, drayage, etc	"	152 38	
Merchandise and other incidentals	"	126 13	
Repairs, pictures, typewriter, etc	"	136 00	
Postage	"	546 57	
Clerk hire	1895	24,674 93	
Extra clerk hire	"	1,890 00	
Stenographers and typewriters	"	2,500 00	
Porter and messenger	"	1,750 00	
Postage and newspaper wrappers	"	813 46	
Telegraphic services	"	104 92	
Express charges, freight and drayage	"	38 79	
Telephone rental, etc	"	96 00	
Stationery, newspapers, etc	"	204 36	
Brooms, matches, soap, combs and other merchandise	"	355 35	
Washing towels for office, etc	"	114 12	
Repairs and articles furnished	"	40 70	
Incidentals	"	21 60	
Furniture	"	527 75	
Carpets, rug, lace curtains, silk, etc	"	300 85	
Trees for State House grounds	"	182 50	
Steel boxes with locks, handles and keys	"	91 50	
Traveling expenses of Secretary of State (official bus.)	"	82 00	
Wireing State House for electric lighting	"	815 00	
Electric lighting of State House	"	200 00	
Gas furnished State House	"	36 60	
Salaries of watchmen	"	120 00	
Salaries of janitors	"	331 00	
Salaries of firemen	"	30 00	
Painting State House	"	16 00	
			55,914 77
To amount paid from appropriation of 1893....$20,577 34			
" " " " 1895.... 35,337 43			
OFFICE OF AUDITOR OF PUBLIC ACCOUNTS.			
Clerk hire	1893	5,736 67	
Stenographer and typewriter	"	749 70	
Porter and messenger	"	1,049 40	
Newspapers, stationery, etc	"	64 41	
Telephone rental, etc	"	40 90	
Time service and telegrams	"	141 11	
Express charges, etc	"	78 39	
Postage	"	313 00	
Ice	"	30 25	
Laundry work	"	11 85	
Incidentals	"	51 04	
Pole and carpet	"	224 82	
Traveling expenses of Auditor of Public Accounts (official business)	"	11 75	
Clerk hire	1895	9,375 00	
Extra clerk hire	"	1,530 00	
Stenographer and typewriter	"	1,250 00	
Porter and messenger	"	1,750 00	
Newspapers, stationery, etc	"	99 48	
Amounts carried forward	....	$22,507 77	$6,364,765 75

Statement 3—Continued.

Accounts.	App.	Amount.	Total.
Amounts brought forward	....	$22,507 77	$6,364,765 75
OFFICE OF AUDITOR OF PUBLIC ACCOUNTS—*Continued.*			
Telephone rental, etc.	1895	$54 90	
Time service and telegrams	"	267 16	
Express charges, etc.	"	304 77	
Postage	"	1,442 30	
Ice	"	46 00	
Laundry work	"	30 60	
Gas stove, Statute, City Directory, carpet and Smith-Premier typewriter	"	90 31	
Incidentals	"	140 16	
			24,883 97
To amount paid from appropriation of 1893.... $8,503 29			
" " " 1895.... 16,379 68			
OFFICE OF STATE TREASURER.			
Clerk hire	1893	$3,000 00	
Clerk and messenger	"	600 00	
Stenographer and typewriter	"	562 50	
Watchmen	"	2,400 00	
Desk, chair, inkstand and freight	"	185 25	
Advertising State Treasurer's notice by L. D. Morse Advertising Agency	"	12 50	
Newspapers, advertising, etc.	"	309 35	
Telegrams and telephone charges	"	150 60	
Express charges	"	319 80	
Postage	"	80 20	
Extra labor	"	10 00	
Incidentals	"	157 01	
Clerk hire	1895	9,375 00	
Clerk and messenger	"	1,000 00	
Watchmen	"	4,000 00	
Newspapers, advertising, etc.	"	108 14	
Telegrams and telephone charges	"	147 65	
Express charges	"	35 63	
Postage	"	100 14	
Repairs	"	108 70	
Labor and material	"	584 81	
Laundry work	"	4 30	
Incidentals	"	241 36	
			23,493 03
To amount paid from appropriation of 1893.... $7,787 30			
" " " 1895.... 15,705 73			
OFFICE OF ATTORNEY GENERAL.			
First Assistant Attorney General	1893	$1,875 01	
Second Assistant Attorney General	"	1,350 00	
Stenographer and typewriter	"	1,050 02	
Porter and messenger	"	525 01	
Clerical work paid for on account of suits, etc.	"	6 00	
Expenses of M. L. Newell, Second Assistant, attending Supreme Court, etc.	"	51 55	
Supreme Court records and opinions	"	39 11	
Court fees paid Appellate Court	"	10 00	
Telegraphic services	"	9 45	
Express charges	"	12 27	
Postage	"	35 00	
Stationery	"	3 25	
Ice	"	22 00	
Personal expenses of M. T. Moloney, Attorney General, in Chicago and elsewhere, attending to State matters	"	1,190 00	
Personal expenses of T. J. Scofield, First Assistant Attorney General, in Chicago and elsewhere, attending to State matters	"	615 00	
Miscellaneous office supplies, etc.	"	16 08	
First Assistant Attorney General	1895	3,125 00	
Second Assistant Attorney General	"	2,250 00	
Amounts carried forward	....	$12,184 75	$6,413,142 75

Statement 3—Continued.

Accounts.	App.	Amounts.	Total.
Amounts brought forward	....	$12,184 75	$6,413,142 75
OFFICE OF ATTORNEY GENERAL—*Continued.*			
Stenographer and typewriter	1895	1,750 00	
Porter and Messenger	"	875 00	
Legal and other incidental expenses incurred in relation to Building, Loan and Homestead Associations	"	3,901 67	
Legal and other incidental expenses incurred in relation to Insurance Laws	"	7,383 00	
Personal expenses of M. T. Moloney, Attorney General, in Chicago and elsewhere, attending to State matters	"	1,975 00	
Personal expenses of T. J. Scofield, First Assistant Attorney General, in Chicago and elsewhere, attending to State matters	"	250 00	
Personal expenses of M. L. Newell, Second Assistant Attorney General attending Supreme Courts, etc.	"	140 54	
Express charges	"	112 94	
Postage	"	134 40	
Telegraphic services	"	21 82	
Ice	"	51 00	
Records and certificate	"	2 50	
Awning, directory and binderfiles	"	8 50	
Repairs, fixtures and office supplies	"	48 55	
			28,830 67
To amount paid from appropriation of 1893.... $6,809 75			
" " " 1895.... 22,029 92			
OFFICE OF THE ADJUTANT GENERAL.			
Clerk hire	1893	$2,500 00	
Acting Assistant Quartermaster General	"	800 00	
Custodian, Memorial Hall	"	466 64	
Stenographer and typewriter	"	487 17	
Ordnance Sergeant	"	400 00	
Extra clerk hire	"	420 00	
Rental of telephone, etc	"	48 00	
Newspapers, office suplies, etc	"	122 48	
Time service and telegrams	"	17 24	
Express charges	"	85 32	
Postage	"	300 00	
Ice for office and State Arsenal	"	31 00	
Painting and renovating Memorial Hall and office	"	21 85	
Repairs on vault	"	1 75	
Standard Dictionery and stationery	"	26 35	
Janitor and messenger services, Memorial Hal and office	"	51 00	
Carpet sweeper and hat rack	"	17 00	
Typewriter and numbering machine	"	73 50	
Rugs for office	"	63 00	
Incidentals	"	75 91	
Clerk hire	1895	4,687 50	
Acting Assistant Quartermaster General	"	1,500 00	
Custodian, Memorial	"	875 00	
Stenographer and typerwriter	"	1,250 00	
Ordnance Sergeant	"	750 00	
Messenger	"	750 00	
Rental of telephone, etc	"	48 00	
Newspapers, office supplies, etc	"	102 87	
Postage	"	305 00	
Time service and telegrams	"	10 17	
Stationery	"	64 35	
Ice	"	58 40	
Laundry work	"	9 00	
Extra janitor's service	"	2 50	
Water cooler and city directory	"	9 00	
Walnut gun rack for Memorial Hall	"	7 00	
Small arms practice and range manuals	"	300 00	
Storage, repairs and putting up awnings	"	29 50	
Amounts carried forward	....	$16,766 50	$6,441,982 42

Statement 3—Continued.

Accounts.	App.	Amount.	Total.
Amounts brought forward	....	$16,766 50	$6,441,982 42
OFFICE OF THE ADJUTANT GENERAL—*Continued.*			
Compiling records of Illinois Sailors who served in the United States Navy—War of 1861-5	1895	85 00	
Incidentals	"	65 36	
			16,916 86
To amount paid from appropriation of 1893.... $6,008 21			
" " " 1895.... 10,908 65			
OFFICE OF INSURANCE SUPERINTENDENT.			
Clerk hire	1893	$11,541 70	
Postage	"	3,837 00	
Expenses attending Annual Convention of Insurance Commissioners	"	145 72	
Legal expenses of the Insurance Department	"	7,955 59	
Expenses of examinations and investigations of insurance companies	"	6,209 83	
Traveling expenses of Insurance Superintendent	"	4 56	
Use of typewriter, ribbons, and repairs furnished	"	37 50	
Time service and telegrams	"	85 36	
Express charges	"	44 77	
Newspapers, office supplies, etc	"	48 12	
Laundry work	"	7 10	
Telephone rental, etc	"	39 00	
Ice	"	22 00	
Newspaper publications revoking licenses of insurance companies	"	36 00	
Incidentals	"	30 25	
Clerk hire	1895	17,172 04	
Stenographer and typewriter	"	1,400 00	
Porter and messenger	"	875 00	
Printing blank forms, etc., for Farmers' National Insurance Company	"	1,000 00	
Expenses attending Annual Convention of Insurance Commissioners	"	250 00	
Expenses of examinations and investigations of insurance companies	"	955 09	
Furniture bought	"	1,200 00	
New furniture	"	800 00	
Vault, and metal cases	"	1,999 00	
Fittings for office	"	493 55	
Transferring records from Auditor's to Insurance Office	"	34 00	
Preparing tabular statements	"	40 00	
Proof reading, 28th Annual Insurance Report	"	200 00	
Burroughs' Registering Accountant	"	375 00	
Tate's Improved (16 figure) Artihmometer	"	375 00	
Globe reversible envelopes	"	200 00	
Making file case, millwork, painting, carpenter work, material furnished, and numbering boxes	"	162 50	
Window screens	"	30 00	
Special services of Lucie Wright, indexing	"	150 00	
Traveling expenses of B. K. Durfee, Insurance Superintendent	"	553 14	
Traveling expenses of H. A. Niehoff, clerk, office of Insurance Superintendent	"	15 20	
Typewriters furnished, repairs, and other articles	"	216 80	
Telephone rental, etc	"	60 00	
Time service and telegrams	"	105 23	
Postage	"	450 00	
Newspapers, stationery, etc	"	170 31	
Express charges	"	138 89	
Ice	"	37 75	
Laundry work	"	1 20	
Painting floors, lettering transoms, and small glass furnished	"	47 50	
Newspaper publications revoking licenses of insurance companies	"	45 00	
Publishing proceedings of National Convention	"	20 00	
Palmer, Shutt, Drennan & Lester—attorneys' fees	"	100 00	
Amounts carried forward	....	$59,716 70	$6,458,899 28

Statement 3—Continued.

Accounts.	App.	Amount.	Total.
Amounts brought forward	....	$59,716 70	$6,458,899 28
OFFICE OF INSURANCE SUPERINTENDENT—*Continued.*			
Copies of charters	1895	5 00	
Awnings for office	"	23 50	
Incidentals	"	111 43	
			59,856 63
To amount paid from appropriation of 1893.. $30,044 50 " " " 1895.. 29,812 13			
PAVING AND CURBING STREETS AROUND CAPITOL GROUNDS AND EXECUTIVE MANSION.			
J. W. Vance— Building sidewalk, curbing, grubbing trees, etc	1895	767 47	
George Trotter— Sod furnished around cement walk	"	50 00	
T. C. Wood— Completing work on cement walk	"	5 40	
Ben. M. Kirlin— Hauling sod and removing rubbish	"	14 00	
Richard Egan— Services inspecting paving around Capitol building	"	237 00	
John F. Bretz & Son— Paving around Capitol grounds and Executive Mansion	"	6,488 64	
Henry Nelch— 263 yards paving—extension on Monroe street, etc	"	278 78	
Charles McBride— Services superintending paving, curbing and walk building, etc	"	100 00	
			7,941 29
PRINTER EXPERT.			
A. L. Hereford— 365 days' services as Printer Expert	1893	$2,190 00	
Ella Guiney— 365 days' services as Assistant to Printer Expert	"	1,095 00	
Ivan Sumerlin— 196 days' services as bill proof reader, 39th General Assembly	"	588 00	
A. L. Hereford— 366 days' services as Printer Expert	1895	2,196 00	
Ella Guiney— 366 days' services as Assistant to Printer Expert	"	1,098 00	
			7,167 00
To amount paid from appropriation of 1893.... $3,873 00 " " " 1895.... 3,294 00			
PRINTING PAPER AND STATIONERY.			
The J. M. W. Jones Stationery and Printing Co.— Stationery furnished offices of Governor and Secretary of State, on contract	1893	$370 00	
Jacquin-Oden Book and Music Co.— Stationery furnished Secretary of State, on contract	"	6,721 61	
The Transcript Co.— Stationery furnished Secretary of State, on contract	"	1,242 70	
Graham Paper Co.— Paper furnished Secretary of State, on contract	"	3,401 69	
George E. Bardeen— Paper furnished Secretary of State, on contract	"	1,007 77	
Charles J. Ambs & Co.— Paper furnished Secretary of State, on contract	"	3,214 94	
J. Furlong— 216 yards of muslin furnished	"	15 12	
Frank Simmons— Frame, ink, penholders, eyelets and presses, office knives, fountain pens, inkstands, stationery, etc	"	146 55	
Amounts carried forward	....	$16,120 38	$6,533,864 20

Statement 3—Continued.

Accounts.	App.	Amount.	Total.
Amounts brought forward	....	$16,120 38	$6,533,864 20
PRINTING PAPER AND STATIONERY—*Continued.*			
Rockwell & Rupel Co.— Oil boards, pigeon-hole boxes and onion skin paper	1893	15 80	
Edward F. Hartman— 3½ reams French folio and 115 pounds enameled book furnished	"	16 15	
B. F. Methven— Binding files for use of legislature	"	451 50	
J. B. Brown— Inkstands, pens, pen racks, paper knives, stationery, letter clips, combs, etc	"	126 20	
McCord & Stewart— 100 blue carbons and 3 dozen fountain pens	"	58 00	
P. F. Pettibone & Co.— 30 dozen Dixon's sketching crayon furnished	"	13 13	
George E. Brennan— Expenses to Peoria, adjusting contract with Jacquin-Oden Book and Music Co	"	10 00	
George E. Brennan— Salary as bookkeeper	"	74 97	
J. D. O'Keefe— Salary as custodian	"	600 00	
Jacquin-Oden Stationery Co.— Stationery furnished Secretary of State, on contract	1895	8,087 47	
The Transcript Co.— Stationery furnished Secretary of State, on contract	"	2,912 45	
Graham Paper Co.— Paper furnished Secretary of State, on contract	"	1,291 26	
George E. Bardeen— Paper furnished Secretary of State, on contract	"	2,192 42	
Charles J. Ambs & Co.— Paper furnished Secretary of State, on contract	"	7,170 03	
J. B. Brown— Stationery, fountain pens, paper fasteners, paper cases, paper files, wax tapers, envelopes, etc	"	358 45	
McCord & Stewart— Fountain pens	"	9 00	
Ralph McCord— Fountain pens, rubbers and long hand brushes	"	136 80	
Frank Simmons— Eyelets and presses, office knife, pens, card case and 3 24-inch rulers	"	12 50	
P. F. Pettibone & Co.— Fountain pens and blade erasers	"	126 00	
W. W. Swinger— Stamp, large air cushion, ink pad, etc	"	5 40	
Henry Abels— Typewriter ribbons furnished	"	3 00	
Rockwell & Rupel Co.— Blue cobweb carbons, stencil, silks, varnish, brush, blotters, ribbons for stamp dater, etc	"	11 53	
Edward F. Hartman & Co.— Envelopes, tubes, mailing clasp, envelopes, stationery, paper fasteners, penholders, etc	"	769 35	
George E. Brennan— Salary as bookkeeper	"	124 97	
J. D. O'Keefe— Salary as custodian	"	1,125 00	
			41,821 76
To amount paid from appropriation of 1893....$17,486 13			
" " " 1895.... 24,335 63			
PUBLIC PRINTING.			
Edward F. Hartman, Contractor— For public printing	1893	$7,394 86	
Thomas Rees, Contractor— For public printing	"	3,400 00	
Phillips Bros., Contractors— For public printing	"	1,850 00	
H. W. Rokker, Contractor— Balance for public printing	"	1,249 40	
Amount carried forward	....	$13,894 26	$6,575,685 96

Statement 3—Continued.

Accounts.	App.	Amount.	Total.
Amounts brought forward	....	$13,894 26	$6,575,685 96
PUBLIC PRINTING—*Continued.*			
Quincy Herald— Printing advertisement for proposals for State contracts	1893	55 81	
Herald Publishing Co.— Printing advertisement for proposals for State contracts	"	55 03	
Chicago Dispatch— Printing advertisement for proposals for State contracts	"	56 58	
Cairo Publishing Co. (Limited)— Printing advertisement for proposals for State contracts	"	51 88	
Illinois State Register— Printing brief in contested apportionment case and publishing Governor's proclamations	"	225 40	
Illinois State Journal— Publishing notice to contractors	"	4 00	
Evening Telegram— Publishing Governor's proclamations	"	169 70	
Morning Monitor— Publishing Governor's proclamations	"	134 25	
Illinois Printing Co.— Registry book furnished Sec'y State	"	6 25	
James T. Roney— Services and expenses as expert before the Committee on Contracts	"	15 60	
Geo. E. Doying— Services and expenses as expert before the Committee on Contracts	"	14 00	
Edward F. Hartman, Contractor— For public printing	1895	28,905 14	
Thomas Rees, Contractor— For public printing	"	2,825 03	
Phillips Bros., Contractors— For public printing	"	2,500 00	
Phillips Bros.— Printing blanks, etc., for Sec'y State	"	33 43	
Illinois Printing Co.— Printing and binding election registers, etc	"	205 50	
Illinois State Register— Publishing Governor's proclamations, notice to contractors, notice of awards, etc	"	654 42	
Evening Telegram— Publishing Governor's proclamations and notice to contractors	"	62 10	
Chicago Dispatch— Publishing proposals for paving streets, notice of incorporation of North Kankakee, notice of proposals for State contracts, etc	"	438 07	
S. A. Miller— Drawing and engraving 8 plates for illustrating bulletins 8 and 9	"	160 00	
Democrat Publishing Co.— Publishing notice of change of name of North Kankakee to Bradley City	"	5 00	
Patrick Higgins— Freight and drayage on election registers	"	16 20	
John C. Neltnor— Publishing notice of change of name of Turner to West Chicago	"	7 50	
T. W. S. Kidd— Publishing proposals for State contracts, and local matter in Weekly Monitor	"	363 32	
Peoria Journal— Publishing proposals for State contracts	"	97 65	
Cairo Printing Co. (Limited)— Publishing proposals for State contracts	"	97 65	
Amounts carried forward	....	$51,143 77	$6,575,685 96

Statement 3—Continued.

Accounts.	App.	Amount.	Total.
Amounts brought forward	....	$51,143 77	$6,575,685 96
PUBLIC PRINTING—*Continued.*			
D. Wilcox & Sons— Publishing proposals for State contracts	1895	96 87	
Freié Presse— Advertising for State, etc	"	77 50	
Wm. F. E. Gurley— Illustrating bulletins of Illinois Museum of Natural History	"	300 00	
To amount paid from appropriation of 1893....$14,682 76 " " " " 1895.... 36,935 38			51,618 14
PUBLIC BINDING.			
H. W. Rokker, Contractor— For public binding	1893	$14,313 27	
H. W. Rokker, Contractor— For public binding	1895	13,233 74	27,547 01
RALROAD AND WAREHOUSE COMMISSIONERS.			
W. S. Cantrell— Salary as commissioner .... $3,500 00 Expenses as commissioner 675 00	1893	$4,175 00	
Charles F. Lape— Salary as commissioner .... $2,916 68 Expenses as commissioner 415 00	"	3,331 68	
Thomas Gahan— Salary as commissioner .... $3,500 00 Expenses as commissioner 215 00	"	3,715 00	
J. W. Yantis— Salary as secretary .... $1,500 00 Expenses as secretary 228 80	"	1,728 80	
D. R. Levy— Salary as assistant secretary .... $1,125 00 Expenses as assistant secretary 90 00	"	1,215 00	
R. P. Morgan & Son— Salary as civil engineer	"	2,250 00	
James Miller— Salary as Janitor .... $720 00 Washing paid as janitor 3 00	"	723 00	
J. W. Yantis, Secretary— Postage furnished office and on schedules	"	325 00	
W. S. Cantrell, Commissioner— Stenographer fees of Miss Murdock in case of the People vs. St. L., A. & T. H. Railroad Co., and court costs advanced in said case	"	120 00	
E. A. Snively, Clerk Supreme Court— Court costs in case of the People vs. St. L., A. & T. H. Railroad Co	"	10 40	
G. B. Shaw, Clerk— Costs in Circuit Court, Franklin Co. vs. St. L., A. & T. H. Railroad Co., on mandamus	"	124 50	
T. W. S. Kidd— Subscription to Morning Monitor	"	11 50	
The Standard— Printing abstract for case in Supreme Court	"	160 00	
Myers Brothers— Merchandise furnished office	"	3 00	
Frank Simmons— Newspapers, desk brackets, stationery, leader files, and daily papers	"	36 30	
Railway Age— Subscription paid	"	8 00	
Railway Purchasing Agents Co.— Subscription paid	"	3 00	
Amounts carried forward	....	$17,940 18	$6,654,851 11

Statement 3—Continued.

Accounts.	App.	Amount.	Total.
Amounts brought forward	....	$17,940 18	$6,654,851 11
RAILROAD AND WAREHOUSE COMMISSIONERS—*Contin'd.*			
J. W. Yantis, Secretary— Cash paid for freight, expenses attending National Convention of Railroad Commissioners, office supplies, etc	1893	64 45	
R. N. Dodds— Office supplies furnished	"	2 00	
Evening Telegram— Subscription paid	"	5 20	
J. B. Hudson, for E. L. Harden— Freight and drayage on railroad maps	"	8 35	
Fannie Conner— Services as extra clerk	"	15 00	
Rand, McNally & Co.— Binding, mounting and furnishing 24,000 railroad maps	"	1,892 00	
Rockwell & Rupel Co.— Supplies furnished office	"	3 00	
Illinois State Journal— Subscription paid	"	4 95	
Illinois State Register— Subscription paid	"	5 20	
Adams Express Co.— Express charges paid	"	54 40	
American Express Co.— Express charges paid	"	52 80	
United States Express Co.— Express charges paid	"	54 20	
Western Union Telegraph Co.— Telegraphic services rendered	"	114 80	
Postal Telegraph-Cable Co.— Telegraphic services rendered	"	20 84	
Central Union Telephone Co.— Rental of telephone, etc	"	48 30	
John M. Striffler— Ice furnished office	"	30 25	
T. M. M. Jones— Printing and furnishing letter heads, printing and lithographing	"	52 50	
W. H. Sammons— Repairing bells and changing wires in office	"	1 50	
M. K. Weems & Co.— Laundried towel supplies furnished	"	5 70	
E. L. Harden & Co.— Freight and drayage paid on railroad maps	"	5 40	
McCord & Stewart— Office and typewriter supplies	"	4 85	
W. F. Downs— Freight and drayage paid on railroad maps	"	9 00	
George W. Chatterton— Repairing clock in office	"	1 50	
J. B. Hudson— Freight and drayage paid on railroad maps	"	8 45	
National Railway Publication Co.— Subscription paid	"	5 00	
George Perry— Cleaning carpets and scrubbing office floors	"	13 00	
Hibbard, Spencer, Bartlett & Co.— Cash advanced J. J. Wait, for assistance on revised schedule of rates	"	86 37	
J. J. Wait— Clerical services rendered	"	332 39	
Emma Lord— Clerical services rendered	"	10 00	
Edward F. Hartmann— Printing and binding 5,000 schedules	"	640 75	
W. S. Cantrell— Salary as Commissioner $3,500 00 Expenses as Commissioner 405 00	1895	3,905 00	
George W. Fithian— Salary as Commissioner	"	3,208 32	
Amounts carried forward	....	$28,605 65	$6,654,851 11

Statement 3—Continued.

Accounts.		App.	Amount.	Total.
Amounts brought forward		....	$28,605 65	$6,654,851 11
RAILROAD AND WAREHOUSE COMMISSIONERS—*Contin'd.*				
Thomas Gahan—				
Salary as Commissioner	$3,500 00	1895		
Expenses as Commissioner	200 00			
			3,700 00	
J. W. Yantis—				
Salary as Secretary	$1,500 00	"		
Expenses as Secretary	441 20			
			1,941 20	
David R. Levy—				
Salary as Assistant Secretary	$1,875 00	"		
Expenses as Assistant Secretary	222 00			
			2,097 00	
R. P. Morgan & Son— Salary as civil engineers		"	3,750 00	
James Miller— Salary as janitor		"	720 00	
J. W. Yantis, Secretary— Expenses to Washington on official business		"	40 00	
David R. Levy, Assistant Secretary— Expenses to Washington on official business		"	40 00	
J. W. Yantis, Secretary— Postage paid on schedules		"	150 00	
J. W. Yantis, Secretary— Postage furnished office		"	300 00	
J. W. Yantis, Secretary— Freight, drayage, etc., paid		"	52 10	
National Railway Publishing Co.— Subscription paid		"	5 00	
Illinois State Register— Subscription paid		"	5 20	
Springfield News— Subscription paid		"	2 08	
Illinois State Journal— Subscription paid		"	6 50	
Morning Monitor— Subscription paid		"	1 30	
Frank Simmons— Daily papers, etc., furnished		"	45 00	
Wyckoff, Seamans & Benedict— Typewriter supplies furnished		"	4 25	
H. J. Hamlin— Attorney's fees, case of People v. C. & A. R. R., in Appellate Court		"	200 00	
H. J. Hamlin— Attorney's fees, certiorari cases in Circuit Court, Cook county		"	150 00	
W. S. Cantrell, for H. J. Hamlin— Legal services rendered in Appellate and Supreme Courts		"	250 00	
J. B. Mann— Attorney's fees, certiorari cases in Circuit Court, Cook County		"	150 00	
W. S. Cantrell, for J. B. Mann— Legal services rendered in Appellate and Supreme Courts		"	250 00	
A. W. O'Hara— Legal services rendered in case of People vs. St. L., A. & T. H. R. R. Co		"	150 00	
Minnie Levy— Services rendered as extra clerk		"	139 00	
Minnie Levy— Copying evidence, etc., elevator cases, Circuit Court, Cook county, writ of certiorari		"	150 00	
Sallie Melroy— Clerical services rendered civil engineers		"	24 00	
Miss M. L. Smith— Copying files, Appellate Court, 8 cases, Board of Trade vs. Geo. A. Seavens, et al		"	49 50	
E. A. Snively, Clerk, Supreme Court— Copy of opinion in case, mandamus		"	10 00	
Chicago Legal News Co.— One statute furnished		"	4 00	
Amounts carried forward		....	$42,991 78	$6,654,851 11

Statement 3—Continued.

Accounts.	App.	Amount.	Total.
Amounts brought forward	....	$42,991 78	$6,654,851 11
RAILROAD AND WAREHOUSE COMMISSIONERS—*Contin'd.*			
Adams Express Co.— Express charges paid	1895	31 57	
American Express Co.— Express charges paid	"	42 42	
United States Express Co.— Express charges paid	"	32 89	
Central Union Telephone Co.— Rental of telephone, etc	"	48 00	
Western Union Telegraph Co.— Telegraphic services rendered	"	93 83	
Postal Telegraph Cable Co.— Telegraphic services rendered	"	6 17	
M. L. Weems & Co.— Towel supplies furnished, laundered	"	9 50	
John M. Striffler— Ice furnished office	"	37 75	
R. N. Dodds— Office supplies furnished	"	1 25	
Hellweg & Hopkins— Plumbing, etc., for office	"	7 35	
Edward F. Hartman— Printing schedules, supplements and circulars	"	82 35	
O. W. Richardson & Co.— 69¾ yds. carpet and lining	"	109 13	
Barkley & Lax— Furniture furnished	"	329 75	
Chicago Carpet Co.— Furniture furnished	"	53 00	
A. M. Brownlee— Printing letterheads and envelopes	"	16 00	
Rand, McNally & Co.— 13,830 railroad maps furnished	"	1,200 00	
George A. Schilling— Water cooler furnished	"	5 00	
George W. Harnett— Glass for door furnished	"	6 50	
Springfield Directory Co.— City directory furnished	"	4 00	
Anna M. Gale— Clerical services rendered	"	10 00	
Illinois Central Railroad Co.— Inspection car and supplies furnished, making inspection of other roads	"	104 48	
Standard Printing Co.— Letterheads and envelopes furnished	"	40 00	
			45,262 72
To amount paid from appropriation of 1893....$21,492 33			
" " " 1895.... 23,770 39			
REPAIRS OF ROOF AND STONE WORK OF CAPITOL BUILDING.			
George Perry, 1 day's work on roof, Capitol Bldg.	1893	2 00	
Link Hudson, 1 " " "	"	2 00	
Chas. Hoffman, 1 " " "	"	2 00	
Martin Henley, 1 " " "	"	2 00	
J. W. Parks, 1 " " "	"	2 00	
Henry Lynch, 1 " " "	"	2 00	
Pete Babbitt, 1 " " "	"	2 00	
Chas. Bedell, 1 " " "	"	2 00	
Mike White, 1 " " "	"	2 00	
Fred Raymond, 1 " " "	"	2 00	
George Hubbard, 1 " " "	"	2 00	
Wm. A. Grady, 3 " " "	"	6 00	
W. J. Colgan, 3 " " "	"	6 00	
G. H. Butler, 1 " " "	"	2 00	
W. P. Ford, 1 " " "	"	2 00	
Evan Jones, 1 " " "	"	2 00	
Peter Vredenburgh— Lumber, etc., furnished for repairs of roof, etc	"	53 02	
Henson Robinson Co.— Labor and material furnished for repairs, etc	"	320 38	
Amounts carried forward	....	$413 40	$6,700,113 83

Statement 3—Continued.

Accounts.	App.	Amount.	Total.
Amounts brought forward	....	$413 40	$6,700,113 83
REPAIRS OF ROOF AND STONE WORK OF CAPITOL BUILDING—*Continued.*			
Sommer & Pierik— Field glasses furnished Secretary of State	1893	16 50	
Henson Robinson Co— Labor and material furnished for repairs, etc	"	180 80	
Chas. Hoffman— 23 days' work, painting on roof, etc	"	46 00	
Schoettker & Gehring— 200 Club cigars furnished firemen	"	12 00	
Bev. Wiltshire, et. al.— Salaries of watchmen and janitors, as per monthly pay-rolls of W. H. Hinrichsen, Sec'y of State	"	120 67	
			789 37
REPORTER AND REPORTS OF SUPREME COURT.			
Mrs. N. L. Freeman, Executrix of the Estate of N. L. Freeman, deceased— Salary of N. L. Freeman, Supreme Court Reporter, in full to August 23, 1894, date of decease	1893	$383 33	
Tranquilla Freeman— Services and expenses in completing the work of the office of Supreme Court Reporter, August 23 to October 24, 1894	1895	1,000 00	
Mrs. N. L. Freeman, Executrix, etc.— 398 copies of 149th Volume	1893	895 50	
398 " 150th "	"	895 50	
398 " 151st "	"	895 50	
Isaac N. Phillips— Salary as Reporter	"	4,133 33	
Isaac N. Phillips— Salary as Reporter	1895	6,000 00	
Jas. D. Stacy— Salary as porter and messenger	"	840 00	
Isaac N. Phillips, Reporter— 398 copies of 152d Volume	1893	895 50	
398 " 153d "	"	895 50	
398 " 154th "	"	895 50	
398 " 155th "	"	895 50	
398 " 156th "	1895	895 50	
398 " 157th "	"	895 50	
398 " 158th "	"	895 50	
398 " 159th "	"	895 50	
398 " 160th "	"	895 50	
398 " 161st "	"	895 50	
Callaghan & Co.— Vols. 1 to 109, both inclusive, Supreme Court Reports of Illinois, furnished Cumberland county, under joint resolution of 39th General Assembly	"	220 00	
W. R. Freeman— Illinois Reports, Supreme Court, etc., furnished	"	67 25	
			24,285 41
To amount paid from appropriation of 1893....$10,785 16 " " " 1895.... 13,500 25			
STATE BOARD OF AGRICULTURE AND AGRICULTURAL SOCIETIES.			
John W. Bunn, Treasurer— Appropriations of $100.00 each, per annum, for fairs held in 1892 and 1893, viz.: Brown County Agricultural Society, 1893	1893	$100 00	
DeWitt County Agricultural Society, 1893	"	100 00	
Edgar County Agricultural Society, 1893	"	100 00	
Effingham County Agricultural Board, 1893	"	100 00	
Johnson County Agricultural Association, 1893	"	100 00	
Knox County Agricultural Board, 1893	"	100 00	
Marion County Agricultural Board, 1893	"	100 00	
McDonough County Agricultural Fair Association, 1893	"	100 00	
Menard County Agricultural Society, 1892 and 1893	"	200 00	
Amounts carried forward	....	$1,100 00	$6,725,188 61

Statement 3—Continued.

Accounts.	App.	Amount.	Total.
Amount brought forward	....	$1,100 00	$6,725,188 61
STATE BOARD OF AGRICULTURE AND AGRICULTURAL SOCIETIES—*Continued.*			
Mercer County Agricultural Board, 1893	1893	100 00	
Morgan County Agricultural Association, 1893	"	100 00	
Vermilion County Agricultural Fair, 1893	"	100 00	
Schuyler County Agricultural Board, 1893	"	100 00	
Southern Illinois Fair Association, Anna, 1893	"	100 00	
Moultrie County Agricultural Board, 1893	"	100 00	
John W. Bunn, Treasurer—			
Appropriations, viz.:			
Encouragement of exhibit at State Fair	1895	10,000 00	
Salary of Secretary	"	5,000 00	
Clerk hire	"	4,400 00	
Salary of curator	"	1,600 00	
Salary of porter	"	1,440 00	
Agricultural Museum	"	600 00	
Live stock and agricultural statistics	"	1,200 00	
Office expenses, furniture, postage, etc	"	2,400 00	
Machinery Hall	"	30,495 00	
Stables for horses and cattle	"	31,112 00	
Sheep and swine building	"	9,985 00	
Buildings for farm and orchard products	"	40,000 00	
Improvement of grounds	"	908 00	
John W. Bunn, Treasurer—			
Appropriations of $100 each, per annum, for fairs held in 1894 and 1895, viz.:			
Adams County Agricultural Society, 1894 and 1895	"	200 00	
Brown " " " " "	"	200 00	
Bureau County Agricultural Board, 1894	"	100 00	
Carroll County Agricultural Board, 1894 and 1895	"	200 00	
Champaign County—Homer fair, 1894 and 1895	"	200 00	
Champaign County Agricultural Board 1894 and 1895	"	200 00	
Champaign County North Agricultural Association, Rantoul, 1894	"	100 00	
Christian County—Pana Union Agricultural Board, 1894	"	100 00	
Coles County Agricultural Society, 1894 and 1895	"	200 00	
DeKalb County Agricultural Society, 1894 and 1895	"	200 00	
DeWitt County—Farmer City Union Agricultural Board, 1894 and 1895	"	200 00	
DeWitt County Agricultural and Mechanical Association, 1895	"	100 00	
Douglas County—Eastern Illinois Agricultural Association, 1894 and 1895	"	200 00	
DuPage County Agricultural Society, 1894 and 1895	"	200 00	
Edgar County Agricultural Association, 1894 and 1895	"	200 00	
Edwards County Agricultural Society, 1894 and 1895	"	200 00	
Effingham County Agricultural Board, 1894 and 1895	"	200 00	
Franklin County Agricultural Society, 1894 and 1895	"	200 00	
Fulton County—Avon District Agricultural Association, 1894 and 1895	"	200 00	
Gallatin County Agricultural Association, 1894	"	100 00	
Greene County Agricultural Board, 1894 and 1895	"	200 00	
Hamilton County Agricultural Board, 1894	"	100 00	
Hancock County Agricultural Society, 1894 and 1895	"	200 00	
Hancock County—LaHarpe District Agricultural Fair, 1894 and 1895	"	200 00	
Hardin County Agricultural Board, 1894	"	100 00	
Henry County Agricultural Board, 1894 and 1895	"	200 00	
Henry County—Kewanee District Agricultural Board, 1894 and 1895	"	200 00	
Iroquois County Agricultural Board, 1894 and 1895	"	200 00	
Jasper County Agricultural Board, 1894 and 1895	"	200 00	
Jersey County Agricultural Board, 1895	"	100 00	
JoDaviess County Agricultural Society, 1894 and 1895	"	200 00	
JoDaviess County—Union Agricultural Society, Warren, 1894 and 1895	"	200 00	
Amounts carried forward	....	$146,340 00	$6,725,188 61

Statement 3—Continued.

Accounts.	App.	Amount.	Total.
Amounts brought forward	....	$146,340 00	$6,725,188 61
STATE BOARD OF AGRICULTURE AND AGRICULTURAL SOCIETIES—*Continued.*			
Johnson County Agricultural Association, 1894 and 1895	"	200 00	
Kankakee County—Kankakee Fair Association, 1894 and 1895	"	200 00	
Kendall County Fair Association, 1894 and 1895	"	200 00	
Lake County Agricultural Society, 1894	"	100 00	
Livingston County—Fairbury Union Agricultural Board, 1895	"	100 00	
Logan County—Atlanta Union Cent. Agricultural Society, 1894 and 1895	"	200 00	
Macon County Agricultural Association, 1894 and 1895	"	200 00	
Marion County Agricultural Board, 1894	"	100 00	
Marion County—The Centralia Fair Association, 1895	"	100 00	
McDonough County Agricultural Association, 1894 and 1895	"	200 00	
McDonough County—Bushnell Agricultural Society, 1894 and 1895	"	200 00	
McHenry County Agricultural Society, 1894 and and 1895	"	200 00	
McLean County—Rock Creek Agricultural Association, Danvers, 1894	"	100 00	
McLean County—Fair Association, Saybrook, 1894 and 1895	"	200 00	
McLean County—The LeRoy Fair and Agricultural Association, 1895	"	100 00	
Menard County Agricultural Society, 1894 and 1895	"	200 00	
Mercer County Agricultural Board, 1894 and 1895	"	200 00	
Morgan County Agricultural Association, 1894 and 1895	"	200 00	
Moultrie County Agricultural Board, 1894 and 1895	"	200 00	
Ogle County—Agricultural and Mechanical Association of Rochelle, 1894 and 1895	"	200 00	
Peoria County Grange Agricultural Fair, Dunlap, 1894 and 1895	"	200 00	
Peoria County—Elmwood Fair Agricultural Association, Elmwood, 1894 and 1895	"	200 00	
Piatt County Agricultural Society, 1894 and 1895	"	200 00	
Pike County—Illinois Valley Agricultural Fair Association, 1894 and 1895	"	200 00	
Pope County Agricultural Association, 1894	"	100 00	
Rock Island County Agricultural Association, 1894 and 1895	"	200 00	
Saline County—El Dorado District Fair Association, 1894	"	100 00	
Schuyler County Agricultural Board, 1895	"	100 00	
Shelby County Agricultural Board, 1894 and 1895	"	200 00	
Stark County—Central Agricultural Society, 1894 and 1895	"	200 00	
Stephenson County—Northern Illinois Agricultural Association, 1894 and 1895	"	200 00	
Tazewell County Agricultural Board, 1894 and 1895	"	200 00	
Tazewell County—Pomona Fair Agricultural Association, Mackinaw, 1894 and 1895	"	200 00	
Union County—Southern Illinois Fair Association, Anna, 1894 and 1895	"	200 00	
Union County Agricultural Society, 1894 and 1895	"	200 00	
Vermilion County Agricultural and Mechanical Association, Catlin, 1894 and 1895	"	200 00	
Vermilion County—Hoopeston District Agricultural Society, 1894 and 1895	"	200 00	
Vermilion County—Indianola Agricultural Fair, 1894 and 1895	"	200 00	
Warren County Agricultural Board, 1894 and 1895	"	200 00	
White County Agricultural Board, 1894 and 1895	"	200 00	
White County—Grayville District Agricultural Fair Association, 1894	"	100 00	
Whiteside County Central Agricultural Society, 1894 and 1895	"	200 00	
Williamson County Agricultural Board, 1894	"	100 00	
Amounts carried forward	....	$153,840 00	$6,725,188 61

Statement 3—Continued.

Accounts.	App.	Amount.	Total.
Amounts brought forward	....	$153,840 00	$6,725,188 61
STATE BOARD OF EQUALIZATION—*Continued.*			
Winnebago County Agricultural Society, 1894 and 1895	1895	200 00	
Woodford County—El Paso District Agricultural Board, 1894 and 1895	"	200 00	
			154,240 00
To amount paid from appropriation of 1893.... $1,600 00			
" " " 1895....152,640 00			
STATE BOARD OF ARBITRATION.			
Anthony Thornton— Salary as member	1895	$1,375 00	
Charles J. Riefler— Salary as member	"	1,750 00	
W. P. Rend— Salary as member	"	1,375 00	
James Malcolm— Salary as Secretary	"	1,350 00	
			5,850 00
STATE BOARD OF EQUALIZATION.			
Pay of members for session of 1894	1893	$7,161 40	
Pay of office and employès for session of 1894, in full	"	822 00	
Pay of committee clerks for session of 1894, in full	"	680 00	
Pay for incidental expenses for session of 1894, in full	"	26 09	
Pay for incidental expenses for session of 1895, in part	"	35 96	
Pay of members for session of 1895, in part	"	241 15	
Pay of members for session of 1895, in part	1895	5,894 85	
Pay of officers and employès for session of 1895	"	1,010 00	
Pay of committee clerks for session of 1895	"	1,056 00	
Pay for incidental expenses for session of 1895, in full	"	36 45	
Pay of members for session of 1896, in part	"	4,200 00	
Pay of officers and employès for session of 1896, in part	"	455 00	
Pay of committee clerks for session of 1896, in part	"	636 00	
Pay for incidental expenses for session of 1896, in part	"	40 56	
			22,295 46
To amount paid from appropriation of 1893.... $8,966 60			
" " " 1895.... 13,328 86			
STATE BOARD OF HEALTH.			
J. W. Scott, M. D.— Salary as Secretary	1893	$2,250 00	
J. W. Scott, M. D.— Traveling expenses as Secretary in connection with official duties	"	349 59	
J. W. Scott, M. D.— Amounts paid, as Secretary for incidental office expenses, viz.:			
Postage	"	440 00	
Telegrams	"	137 12	
Telephone rental, etc	"	48 45	
Express charges	"	247 21	
Janitor and laundry	"	57 75	
Ice	"	27 50	
Incidentals	"	2 20	
J. W. Scott, M. D.— Amounts paid as Secretary, viz.:			
Salaries of clerks	"	3,112 59	
Salary of janitor	"	127 41	
Amounts paid Members of Board for traveling expenses in connection with their official duties, viz.:			
Julius Kohl, M. D	"	73 40	
John A. Vincent, M. D	"	67 75	
B. M. Griffith, M. D	"	57 46	
Wm. E. Quine, M. D	"	16 95	
George Thilo, M. D	"	16 25	
Amounts carried forward	....	$7,031 63	$6,907,574 07

Statement 3—Continued.

Accounts.	App.	Amount.	Total.
Amounts brought forward	....	$7,031 63	$6,907,574 07
STATE BOARD OF HEALTH—*Continued.*			
Fred. A. Treacy—			
Traveling expenses as chief clerk, in connection with official duties	1893	96 35	
J. W. Scott, M. D.—			
Salary as secretary	1895	3,750 00	
Salaries of clerks	"	3,700 00	
Salary of stenographer	"	900 00	
Salary of janitor	"	750 00	
Amounts paid members of Board for traveling expenses in connection with their official duties, viz.:			
J. W. Scott, M. D., Secretary	"	541 88	
F. A. Treacy, Chief Clerk	"	143 70	
B. M. Griffith, M. D	"	67 04	
Julius Kohl, M. D	"	121 35	
John A. Vincent, M. D	"	131 30	
Wm. E. Quine, M. D	"	18 55	
Oscar O. Baines, M. D	"	19 55	
Sarah Hackett Stevenson, M. D	"	14 05	
Daniel K. Brower, M. D	"	24 50	
G. K. Shafer, M. D	"	17 16	
J. W. Scott, M. D.—			
Amounts paid as secretary for incidental office expenses, viz.:			
Postage	"	483 00	
Telephone rental, etc	"	48 00	
Telegrams	"	151 32	
Express charges	"	224 03	
Janitor and laundry	"	66 60	
Ice	"	25 00	
Incidentals	"	12 80	
			18,337 81
To amount paid from appropriation of 1893.... $7,127 98			
" " " 1895.... 11,209 83			
STATE BOARD OF EXAMINERS FOR MINE INSPECTORS AND MINE MANAGERS.			
Bethune Dishon—			
Per diem as examiner $96 00	1893		
Expenses " 79 90	"		
		175 90	
J. M. Browning—			
Per diem as examiner $33 00	"		
Expenses " 62 40	"		
		95 40	
Patrick Meehan—			
Per diem as examiner $54 00	"		
Expenses " 83 70	"		
		137 70	
William McDonald—			
Per diem as examiner $60 00	"		
Expenses " 88 00	"		
		148 00	
J. E. Craine—			
Per diem as examiner $174 00	"		
Expenses " 116 35	"		
		290 35	
Geo. A. Schilling, Secretary—			
Services rendered by Bureau of Labor Statistics, postage paid on reports, etc	"	201 97	
Bethune Dishon—			
Per diem as examiner $132 00	1895		
Expenses " 103 00	"		
		235 00	
J. M. Browning—			
Per diem as examiner $93 00	"		
Expenses " 70 34	"		
		163 34	
Amounts carried forward	....	$1,447 66	$6,925,911 88

Statement 3—Continued.

Accounts.		App.	Amount.	Total.
Amounts brought forward			$1,447 66	$6,925,911 88
STATE BOARD OF HEALTH—*Continued.*				
William McDonald—				
Per diem as examiner	$171 00	1895		
Expenses ″	158 75	″		
			329 75	
J. E. Craine—				
Per diem as examiner	$150 00	″		
Expenses ″	116 00	″		
			266 00	
L. A. Graham—				
Per diem as examiner	$201 00	″		
Expenses ″	146 67	″		
			347 67	
Louis F. Lumaghi—				
Per diem as examiner	$105 00	″		
Expenses ″	131 37	″		
			236 37	
Geo. A. Schilling, Secretary Bureau of Labor Statistics—				
Services rendered board of examiners		″	52 12	
Charles E. Crum—				
Services rendered board as janitor		″	10 25	
				2,689 82
To amount paid from appropriation of 1893	$1,049 32			
″ ″ 1895	1,640 50			
STATE BOARD OF LIVE STOCK COMMISSIONERS AND STATE VETERINARIAN.				
J. H. Paddock—				
Per diem as commissioner	$850 00			
Expenses as commissioner	336 75			
		1893	$1,186 75	
C. W. Piatt—				
Per diem as commissioner	$430 00			
Expenses as commmissioner	264 35			
		″	694 35	
C. D. Bartlett—				
Per diem as commissioner	$1,185 00			
Expenses as commissioner	794 85			
		″	1,979 85	
M. R. Trumbower—				
Per diem as State Veterinarian	$1,528 00			
Expenses as State Veterinarian	716 42			
		″	2,244 42	
W. E. McGarth—				
Salary as Assistant State Veterinarian	$800 00			
Expenses as Assistant State Veterinarian	200 00			
		″	1,000 00	
Joseph Hughes—				
Per diem as Assistant State Veterinarian		″	39 00	
A. H. Baker—				
Per diem as Assistant State Veterinarian	$23 00			
Expenses as Assistant State Veterinarian	60			
			23 60	
H. G. Hoover—				
Per diem as Assistant State Veterinarian	$48 00			
Expenses as Assistant State Veterinarian	22 09			
		″	70 09	
J. F. Ryan—				
Per diem as Assistant State Veterinarian		″	6 00	
W. J. Layman—				
Per diem as Assistant State Veterinarian		″	5 50	
B. A. Pierce—				
Per diem as Assistant State Veterinarian		″	23 00	
O. J. McGurty—				
Per diem as Assistant State Veterinarian	$70 00			
Expenses as Assistant State Veterinarian	27 00			
		″	97 00	
Amounts carried foward			7,369 56	6,928,601 70

Statement 3—Continued.

Accounts.		App.	Amount.	Total.
Amounts brought forward		....	$7,369 56	$6,928,601 70
STATE BOARD OF LIVE STOCK COMMISSIONERS AND STATE VETERINARIAN—*Continued.*				
B. F. Swingley—				
Per diem as Assistant State Veterinarian	$8 00			
Expenses as Assistant State Veterinarian	2 72	1893	10 72	
A. M. Brownlee—				
Salary as Secretary of Board	$1,350 00			
Expenses as Secretary of Board	236 78	"	$1,586 78	
Walter Bretz— Services rendered as janitor		"	40 00	
Annie Ritter— Services rendered as typewriter		"	6 90	
Silas Palmer—				
Office rent furnished Board at Union Stock Yards, Chicago	$105 00			
Glass furnished Board at Union Stock Yards, Chicago	1 50	"	106 50	
Charles J. McDowell—				
Salary as State Agent at Union Stock Yards, Chicago	600 00			
Expenses as State Agent at Union Stock Yards, Chicago	210 00	"	810 00	
Frank B. Seimer—				
Salary as State Agent at Union Stock Yards, Chicago	$600 00			
Expenses as State Agent at Union Stock Yard, Chicago	124 75	"	724 75	
Charles H. Brownell—				
Salary as State Agent at Union Stock Yards, Chicago	$390 00			
Expenses as State Agent at Union Stock Yards, Chicago	12 00	"	402 00	
Daniel Collar— Salary at State Agent at Union Stock Yards, Chicago		"	300 00	
Adams Express Co.— Express charges paid		"	50	
American Express Co.— Express charges paid		"	6 95	
United States Express Co.— Express charges paid		"	4 30	
R. M. Ridgely, P. M.— Postage furnished Board		"	25 00	
A. M. Brownlee— Postage furnished Board		"	40 00	
Western Union Telegraph Co.— Telegraphic services rendered		"	23 62	
David Oliphant— Blank books furnished W. E. Macgarth, State Agent		"	8 00	
C. D. Bartlett— Court costs advanced in case of Wall vs. Nash and Bartlett		"	11 00	
E. H. Schloeman— Horse furnished C. H. Brownell, State Agent		"	27 00	
David R. Levy— Stenographic work on annual report and typewriting		"	37 00	
H. J. Hamlin— Legal services and expenses incurred		"	301 00	
Miller & Starr— Legal services and expenses incurred		"	46 90	
C. D. Bartlett— Cash paid for carriages to convey Senate Committee 39th General Assembly to Union Stock Yards		"	18 00	
E. H. Schloeman— Bill rendered and horse hire furnished		"	16 00	
Amount carried forward		....	$11,922 48	$6,928,601 70

Statement 3—Continued.

Accounts.	App.	Amount.	Total.
Amounts brought forward	....	$11,922 48	$6,928,601 70
STATE BOARD OF LIVE STOCK COMMISSIONERS AND SATE VETERINARIAN—*Continued.*			
Amounts paid as damages for animals diseased or exposed to contagion, slaughtered, for property necessarily destroyed, and for expenses of disinfection of premises, viz.:			
Markel Brothers— 1 cow slaughtered and tanked, account tuberculosis—experiment	1893	15 00	
W. B. Ayers— 1 horse slaughtered, account glanders	"	30 00	
Wm. M. Elliott— 1 mare slaughtered, account glanders	"	10 00	
Hiram H. Smith— 2 mares and 1 mule slaughtered, account glanders	"	43 32	
Joseph Starnes— 3 horses and 1 mare slaughtered, account glanders	"	48 00	
Silas Correll— 1 horse slaughtered, account glanders	"	12 00	
C. D. Bartlett— Balance on heifer slaughtered as diseased animal	"	11 03	
Emanuel Finkenbender— 3 horses slaughtered, account glanders	"	40 00	
David Baker— 1 mare slaughtered, account glanders	"	25 00	
Jacob Koehler— 1 horse slaughtered, account glanders	"	20 00	
William Heller— 3 horses slaughtered, account glanders	"	45 00	
Jane Ginn— 1 mare slaughtered, account glanders	"	30 00	
Joseph Schlitz Brewing Co.— 1 horse slaughtered, account glanders	"	50 00	
Minnie L. Johnson— 1 mare slaughtered, account glanders	"	50 00	
John A. Coleman— 1 mare slaughtered, account glanders	"	25 00	
William Root— 1 horse slaughtered, account glanders	"	50 00	
Martin Brown— 2 horses slaughtered, account glanders	"	50 00	
E. K. Townson— 2 horses slaughtered, account glanders	"	50 00	
A. L. Suddeth— 1 mare slaughtered, account glanders	"	25 00	
D. A. Taylor— 2 mares slaughtered, account glanders	"	50 00	
Wm. P. Ballard— 1 horse slaughtered, account glanders	"	20 00	
Wolf Walper— 1 horse slaughtered, account glanders	"	25 00	
Mrs. Hud. Alsop— 1 horse slaughtered, account glanders	"	10 00	
H. Hutchcraft— 1 horse slaughtered, account glanders	"	20 00	
Richard Doyle— 1 horse slaughtered, account glanders	"	30 00	
Turner, Springer & Co.— 1 horse slaughtered, account glanders	"	25 00	
W. T. Alsop— 1 mare slaughtered, account glanders	"	30 00	
Lewis Bush— 2 mules slaughtered, account glanders	"	40 00	
John Finnegan— 1 horse slaughtered, account glanders	"	100 00	
William P. Ballard— 3 horses slaughtered, account glanders	"	60 00	
Elisha Cardiff— 3 horses slaughtered, disinfection and buildings burned, account glanders	"	125 00	
Melchior Brothers— 1 horse slaughtered, account glanders	"	25 00	
Amounts carried forward	....	$13,111 83	$6,928,601 70

Statement 3—Continued.

Accounts.		App.	Amount.	Total.
Amounts brought forward			$13,111 83	$6,928,601 70
STATE BOARD OF LIVE STOCK COMMISSIONERS AND STATE VETERINARIANS—*Continued.*				
J. Thomas Little: 3 horses slaughtered and disinfection of premises, account glanders		1893	40 00	
William Griffin—2 horses slaughtered, account glanders		"	100 00	
Mike Ryan—5 horses slaughtered, account glanders		"	130 00	
George Powell—Burning barns and disinfecting premises, account tuberculosis		"	200 00	
Cooke Brewing Co.—1 horse slaughtered, account glanders		"	35 00	
M. R. Trumbower—Disinfectants furnished, inspecting horses of Chicago Street Car Stables, etc		"	34 75	
Myers & Eihelman—211 pounds carbolated lime furnished, and cartage		"	8 94	
Joseph Williamson—1 horse slaughtered, account glanders		"	12 50	
Noble R. Galliger—1 horse slaughtered, disinfection, feed burned, account glanders		"	28 00	
Joseph Hughes—Examining, quarantining and destroying horses in Chicago		"	16 00	
A. M. Brownlee—Salary as Secretary	$450 00			
Expenses as Secretary	125 40	1895	575 40	
Geo. M. LeCrone—Salary as Secretary	$1,800 00			
Expenses as Secretary	251 50	"	2,051 50	
H. F. Thayer—Salary as Clerk	$350 00			
Expenses as Clerk	20 00	"	370 00	
W. E. Savage—Services as typewriter, etc		"	71 50	
Zellie L. Matthews—Services as typewriter, etc		"	196 85	
Walter Bretz—Services as janitor		"	10 00	
M. V. Hardesty—Salary as janitor		"	420 00	
W. E. Savage—Salary as janitor		"	68 00	
Richard Egan—Salary as janitor		"	412 00	
D. R. Levy—Services as stenographer, etc		"	5 80	
W. E. Savage—Services, mailing reports, etc		"	52 00	
J. H. Paddock—Per diem as commissioner	$2,345 00			
Expenses as commissioner	740 55	"	3,085 55	
C. W. Piatt—Per diem as commissioner	$1,415 00			
Expenses as commissioner	910 50	"	2,325 50	
C. D. Bartlett—Per diem as commissioner	$2,260 00			
Expenses as commissioner	2,717 70	"	4,977 70	
M. R. Trumbower—Per diem as State Veterinarian	$3,182 00			
Expenses " "	1,615 99	"	4,797 99	
Amounts carried forward			$33,136 81	$6,928,601 70

Statement 3—Continued.

Accounts.		App.	Amount.	Total.
Amounts brought forward		....	$33,136 81	$6,928,601 70
STATE BOARD OF LIVE STOCK COMMISSIONERS AND STATE VETERINARIAN—*Continued.*				
W. E. McGarth—				
Per diem as Assistant State Veterinarian	$2,450 00			
Expenses " "	72 45	1895	2,522 45	
L. C. Tiffany—				
Per diem as Assistant State Veterinarian	$383 00			
Expenses " "	234 43	"	617 43	
O. J. McGurty—				
Per diem as Assistant State Veterinarian	$124 00			
Expenses " "	111 76	"	235 76	
B. F. Swingley—				
Per diem as Assistant State Veterinarian	$24 00			
Expenses " "	7 84	"	31 84	
Joseph Hughes—				
Per diem as Assistant State Veterinarian	$188 00			
Expenses " "	3 00	"	191 00	
F. N. Rowan—				
Per diem as Assistant State Veterinarian	$28 00			
Expenses " "	10 55	"	38 55	
John Scott—				
Per diem as Assistant State Veterinarian	$48 00			
Expenses " "	13 40	"	61 40	
Thomas H. Hope—				
Per diem as Assistant State Veterinarian	$16 00			
Expenses " "	4 40	"	20 40	
Frank Bales—				
Per diem as Assistant State Veterinarian	$20 00			
Expenses " "	12 75	"	32 75	
J. F. Reid—				
Per diem as Assistant State Veterinarian	$20 00			
Expenses " "	19 75	"	39 75	
John Casewell—				
Per diem as Assistant State Veterinarian		"	16 00	
A. G. Alverson—				
Per diem as Assistant State Veterinarian	$24 00			
Expenses " "	14 75	"	38 75	
James Addison—				
Per diem as Assistant State Veterinarian	$24 00			
Expenses " "	15 00	"	39 00	
W. J. Lawson—				
Per diem as Assistant State Veterinarian	$22 00			
Expenses " "	13 49	"	35 49	
J. F. Ryan—				
Per diem as Assistant State Veterinarian	$45 00			
Expenses " "	11 85	"	56 85	
J. F. Pease—				
Per diam as Assistant State Veterinarian	$74 00			
Expenses " "	19 90	"	93 90	
B. A. Pierce—				
Per diem as Assistant State Veterinarian	$256 00			
Expenses " "	10 30	"	266 30	
L. F. Brown—				
Per diem as Assistant State Veterinarian	$24 00			
Expenses " "	13 76	"	37 76	
Amounts carried forward		....	$37,512 19	$6,928,601 70

Statement 3—Continued.

Accounts.		App.	Amount.	Total.
Amounts brought forward		....	$37,512 19	$6,928,601 70
STATE BOARD OF LIVE STOCK COMMISSIONERS AND STATE VETERINARIAN—*Continued.*				
Matthew Wilson—				
Per diem as Assistant State Veterinarian.	$24 00			
Expenses " "	12 50	1895	36 50	
Charles W. Johnson—				
Per diem as Assistant State Veterinarian.	$24 00			
Expenses " "	4 70	"	28 70	
S. V. Rumsey—				
Per diem as Assistant State Veterinarian.	$24 00			
Expenses " "	13 00	"	37 00	
John C. Stewart—				
Per diem as Assistant State Veterinarian.	$13 00			
Expenses " "	7 00	"	20 00	
H. G. Hoover—				
Per diem as Assistant State Veterinarian.	$160 00			
Assistant " "	64 02	"	224 02	
A. H. Baker—				
Per diem as Assistant State Veterinarian.	$164 00			
Expenses " "	13 11	"	177 11	
J. D. Nighbert—				
Per diem as Assistant State Veterinarian.	$4 00			
Expenses " "	1 50	"	5 50	
John Armstrong—				
Per diem as Assistant State Veterinarian		"	10 00	
R. C. Mylne—				
Per diem as Assistant State Veterinarian.	$33 00			
Expenses " "	6 75	"	39 75	
C. F. Behner—				
Per diem as Assistant State Veterinarian.	$28 00			
Expenses " "	23 15	"	51 15	
Charles H. Brownell—				
Salary as State Agent, Union Stock Yards	$48 00			
Expenses " "	2 00	"	50 00	
Daniel Collar—				
Salary as State Agent, Union Stock Yards	$1,275 00			
Expenses " "	5 00	"	1,280 00	
Charles J. McDowell—				
Salary as State Agent, Union Stock Yards	$1,600 00			
Expenses " "	138 00	"	1,738 00	
F. B. Seimer—				
Salary as State Agent, Union Stock Yards	$1,381 00			
Expenses " "	67 70	"	1,448 70	
L. W. Link—				
Salary as State Agent, Nat'l Stock Yards.	$1,525 00			
Expenses " "	58 70	"	1,583 70	
Charles J. Flick—				
Salary as State Agent, Union Stock Yards		"	75 00	
Peter Boyd—				
Salary as State Agent, Union Stock Yards		"	900 00	
J. J. Naughton—				
Salary as State Agent, Union Stock Yards	$596 00			
Expenses " "	265 15	"	861 15	
Amounts carried forward		....	$46,078 47	$6,928,601 70

Statement 3—Continued.

Accounts.	App.	Amount.	Total.
Amounts brought forward	......	$46,078 47	$6,928,001 70
STATE BOARD OF LIVE STOCK COMMISSIONERS AND STATE VETERINARIAN—*Continued.*			
Erwin W. Shultz— Salary as State Agent, Union Stock Yards $146 00 Expenses " " 36 45	1895	182 45	
Emmet L. Dolsen— Salary as State Agent, Union Stock Yards $148 00 Expenses " " 36 47	"	184 47	
Donn Piatt— Salary as State Agent, Union Stock Yards $146 00 Expenses " " 55 89	"	201 89	
Edward Grace— Office rent for Board in Chicago	"	50 00	
Silas Palmer— Office rent for Board in Chicago, etc	"	271 00	
R. M. Ridgely, P. M.— Postage furnished Board	"	188 60	
A. M. Brownlee— Postage furnished Board	"	30 00	
Evening Telegram— Subscription to daily	"	5 70	
Illinois State Register— Subscription to daily	"	10 40	
Illinois State Journal— Subscription to daily	"	13 00	
C. D. Bartlett— Rings for tags, telegraphing, and amount paid Dr. Herring, Assistant State Veterinarian	"	14 00	
Springfield Wire Screen Co.— Screens furnished for door, transom and windows	"	32 00	
M. K. Weems & Co.— Towel supplies furnished office	"	14 50	
Western Union Telegraph Co.— Telegraphic services rendered	"	40 90	
Central Union Telephone Co.— Rental of telephone, etc., furnished	"	32 56	
Adams Express Co.— Express charges on packages	"	17 03	
American Express Co.— Express charges on packages	"	45 42	
United States Express Co.— Express charges on packages	"	34 78	
M. R. Trumbower— Money advanced in payment for telegrams	"	4 95	
A. M. Brownlee— Per diem as Special Agent, etc $30 00 Expenses as Special Agent, etc 15 00	"	45 00	
A. M. Brownlee— Cash paid Barkley & Lax for furniture	"	15 00	
Mallory, Son & Zimmerman— Transportation furnished	"	4 97	
H. W. Rokker— One 100 page med. ledger furnished	"	9 00	
M. R. Trumbower— Material purchased for examination of cattle	"	11 34	
Sharp & Smith— Needles, etc., furnished at Union Stock Yards	"	11 75	
Amounts carried forward	......	$17,549 18	$6,928,001 70

Statement 3—Continued.

Accounts.	App.	Amount.	Total.
Amounts brought forward	....	$47,549 18	$6,928,601 70
STATE BOARD OF LIVE STOCK COMMISSIONERS AND STATE VETERINARIANS—*Continued.*			
Arthur Loewy, Superintendent— Amount paid for cow destroyed, belonging to the Illinois Northern Hospital for the Insane, account tuberculosis	1895	40 00	
Robert Stevenson & Co.— Sulphuric Acid furnished Board	"	4 09	
Hausman & Dunn— German thermometers, Hicks thermometers, globes, mailing, etc	"	41 18	
B. H. Ferguson— Slop pail furnished office	"	1 50	
Hibbard, Spencer, Bartlett & Co.— 8⅓ doz. perfect hog rings	"	6 67	
Geo. M. LeCrone— Money advanced for blanks for Union Stock Yards	"	3 50	
R. F. Kinsella— Painting office, etc	"	7 00	
Geo. M. LeCrone— Stationery furnished	"	5 00	
E. H. Schloeman— Livery furnished Board	"	3 00	
Pasteur Anthrax Vaccine Co.— 6 vials, 10 c. c. Mallein solution furnished	"	8 88	
Red Cross Hygienic Co.— 10 gal. carbonyl for disinfecting	"	12 50	
Geo. V. Mechler— Tags and printing, blank reports for veterinarians	"	35 75	
Richard Egan— Expenses as State agent	"	47 45	
Dr. E. H. Herring— Aiding State Veterinarian in investigation of cattle diseases in Brown Co	"	8 00	
Chas. O. Brockway— Hog rings furnished	"	8 87	
Charles V. Lodge— Bull furnished Deaf and Dumb Institute to replace bull killed by mistake, etc	"	83 95	
Amounts paid as damages for animals, diseased or exposed to contagion, slaughtered, for property necessarily destroyed, for disinfection of premises, etc., viz.:			
Steven Todd— Damages for 1 horse slaughtered, account glanders	"	15 00	
John S. Collins— Damages for 2 horses slaughtered on account glanders	"	15 00	
H. Bronkana— Damages for 3 horses slaughtered, disinfected and stable burned on account glanders	"	105 00	
H. C. Richards— Damages for 2 horses slaughtered and barn burned on account glanders	"	275 00	
George James Bestall— Damages for 1 horse slaughtered, account glanders	"	20 00	
Fred Schoen— Damages for 3 horses slaughtered, on account glanders	"	75 00	
Meyers & Eshellman— Disinfectants furnished Board	"	6 84	
J. W. Kessler— Damages for 1 horse slaughtered and disinfection, account glanders	"	44 00	
N. W. Kish— Damages for 2 horses slaughtered, account glanders	"	50 00	
Amounts carried forward	....	$48,535 36	$6,928,601 70

Statement 3—Continued.

Accounts.	App.	Amount.	Total.
Amounts brought forward	....	$48,535 36	$6,928,601 70
STATE BOARD OF LIVE STOCK COMMISSIONERS AND STATE VETERINARIAN—*Continued.*			
Clayton Ryan—Damages for 7 horses slaughtered, account glanders	1895	210 00	
Nick Deckinga—Damages for 2 horses slaughtered, account glanders	"	66 66	
Frank Reddington—Damages for 1 horse slaughtered, account glanders	"	30 00	
David Grant—Damages for 1 horse and 2 mules slaughtered, account glanders	"	100 00	
John Jones—Damages for 1 horse slaughtered, account glanders	"	35 00	
Marion Judd—Barn burned, account glanders	"	15 00	
Orlando Martin—Damages for 1 horse slaughtered, account glanders	"	20 00	
Kohl & Macklin—Damages for 2 horses slaughtered, account glanders	"	30 00	
David Grant—Damages for 4 mules slaughtered, account glanders	"	133 33	
Anthony Meyers—Damages for 2 mules slaughtered, account glanders	"	30 00	
Sylvester Bradley—Damages for 5 horses slaughtered, account glanders	"	125 00	
E. T. Zeigle—Damages for 1 horse slaughtered, account glanders	"	10 00	
J. Howell Jones—Damages for 4 horses slaughtered, account glanders	"	78 33	
Mrs. George Smith—Damages for 1 mare slaughterer, account glanders	"	20 00	
A. W. Sharp—Damages for 2 horses slaughtered, account glanders	"	15 00	
H. J. Morrey—Damages for 1 horse slaughtered, account glanders	"	10 00	
Jos. J. Brown—Damages for 1 horse slaughtered, account glanders and disinfection of premises	"	15 00	
John Cahill—Damages for 1 horse slaughtered, account glanders	"	15 00	
Thomas E. Ash—Damages for 1 horse slaughtered, account glanders	"	15 00	
Mrs. J. B. Young—Damages for 2 horses slaughtered, and disinfection, account glanders	"	35 00	
E. O. Black—Damages for 1 horse slaughtered, account glanders	"	10 00	
Wm. Achterhof—Damages for 1 mare slaughtered, account glanders	"	25 00	
G. L. Klein—Damages for 1 horse slaughtered, account glanders	"	25 00	
Amounts carried forward	....	$49,603 68	$6,928,601 70

Statement 3—Continued.

Accounts.	App.	Amount.	Total.
Amounts brought forward	....	$49,603 68	$6,928,601 70
STATE BOARD OF LIVE STOCK COMMISSIONERS AND STATE VETERNIARIAN—*Continued.*			
Turner, Springer & Co.— Damages for 1 horse slaughtered, account glanders	1895	25 00	
Joseph Seitz— Damages for 1 horse slaughtered, account glanders	"	40 00	
H. S. Tobey— Damages for 1 horse slaughtered, account glanders	"	50 00	
H. C. Ingwersen— Damages for 1 horse slaughtered, account glanders	"	25 00	
Bony Crosby— Damages for 1 horse slaughtered. account glanders	"	10 00	
John Gates— Damages for 1 mule slaughtered, account glanders	"	20 00	
Duncan McKitchen— Damages for 3 horses slaughtered and disinfection, account of glanders	"	35 00	
Wm. Moench Baking Co.— Damages for 1 horse slaughtered, account glanders	"	25 00	
Gottfried Brewing Co.— Damages for 49 horses slaughtered, account glanders	"	855 16	
R. Dunning— Damages for 1 horse slaughtered, account glanders	"	2 50	
Mike O'Brien— Damages for 1 horse slaughtered, account glanders	"	15 00	
John McIntire— Damages for 3 horses slaughtered, account glanders	"	18 33	
J. Hamil Jones— Damages for 1 horse slaughtered, account glanders	"	25 00	
Carl Hanson, use of B. A. Pierce— Damages for 7 horses slaughtered, account glanders	"	45 00	
J. H. Ripley— Damages for 1 horse slaughtered, account glanders	"	3 35	
John Wheeler— Damages for 2 horses slaughtered, account glanders	"	55 00	
John Dallman— Damages for 2 horses slaughtered, account glanders	"	27 00	
P. F. Lavin— Damages for 1 horse slaughtered, account glanders	"	50 00	
W. R. Forbes— Damages for 1 horse slaughtered, account glanders	"	33 33	
David Scott— Damages for 1 horse slaughtered, account glanders	"	5 00	
Carl Hansen— Damages for 1 horse slaughtered, account glanders	"	10 00	
Mrs. Charles F. Stanck— Damages for 2 horses slaughtered, account glanders	"	20 00	
John Peterson— Damages for 2 horses slaughtered, account glanders	"	30 00	
Amounts carried forward	....	$51,028 35	$6,928,601 70

Statement 3—Continued.

Accounts.	App.	Amount.	Total.
Amounts brought forward	....	$51,028 35	$6,928,601 70
STATE BOARD OF LIVE STOCK COMMISSIONERS AND STATE VETERINARIAN—*Continued.*			
John Ripley—Damages for 1 horse slaughtered, account glanders	1895	15 00	
Wm. Granky—Damages for 4 horses slaughtered and burning barn, account glanders	"	49 00	
John S. Collins—Damages for 1 horse slaughtered, account glanders	"	15 00	
John Higgins—Damages for 1 horse slaughtered, account glanders	"	20 00	
Franklin Brillhart—Damages for 1 horse slaughtered, account glanders	"	25 00	
Robert Givins—Damages for 1 horse slaughtered, account glanders	"	25 00	
P. Foley—Damages for 1 horse slaughtered, account glanders	"	5 00	
C. B. Kinney—Damages for 1 horse slaughtered, account glanders	"	41 66	
W. J. Hutton—Damages for 5 horses slaughtered, account glanders	"	115 00	
J. Shafiro—Damages for 1 horse slaughtered, account glanders	"	27 50	
George Agnew—Damages for 1 horse slaughtered, account glanders	"	20 00	
James J. Bennett—Damages for 3 horses slaughtered, account glanders	"	60 00	
Frank Drull—Damages for 1 horse slaughtered, account glandars	"	15 00	
David Alberts—Damages for 1 mule slaughtered, account glanders	"	15 00	
A. L. Lentgert—Damages for 1 horse slaughtered, account glanders	"	10 00	
John Maskell—Damages for 1 horse slaughtered, account glanders	"	12 50	
George Spitz—Damages for 1 horse slaughtered, account glanders	"	20 00	
The Royal Oil Co.—Damages for 1 horse slaughtered, account glanders	"	15 00	
Jacob Wyes—Damages for 3 horses slaughtered, account glanders	"	40 00	
Wm. J. Hutton—Damages for 1 horse slaughtered, account glanders	"	20 00	
Wm. Wright—Damages for 4 horses slaughtered, and disinfection, account glanders	"	90 00	
Standard Oil Co.—Damages for 1 horse slaughtered, account glanders	"	20 00	
George Prior—Damages for 1 horse slaughtered, account glanders	"	10 00	
The Chicago City Railway Co.—Damages for 5 horses slaughtered, account glanders	"	25 00	
Amounts carried forward	....	$51,739 01	$6,928,601 70

Statement 3—Continued.

Accounts.	App.	Amounts.	Total.
Amounts brought forward	....	$51,739 01	$6,928,601 70
STATE BOARD OF LIVE STOCK COMMISSIONERS AND STATE VETERINARIAN—*Continued.*			
Dr. A. H. Stephanie— Damages for 1 horse slaughtered, account glanders	1895	50 00	
M. N. Sammons— Damages for 1 horse slaughtered, account glanders	"	10 00	
Jacob Kircher— Damages for 6 horses slaughtered, account glanders	"	95 00	
C. F. Kinnally— Damages for 3 horses slaughtered and disinfection, account glanders	"	75 00	
H. Berkman— Damages for 2 horses slaughtered, and disinfection, account glanders	"	50 00	
Edward Huber— Damages for 2 horses slaughtered, account glanders	"	15 00	
W. H. Gericke— Damages for 1 horse slaughtered, account glanders	"	25 00	
Peter Streif— Damages for 2 horses slaughtered, account glanders	"	20 00	
Thomas Carrabine— Damages for 1 horse slaughtered, account glanders	"	25 00	
August Maierhoper— Damages for 1 horse slaughtered, account glanders	"	33 33	
E. Paschke & Co.— Damages for 1 horse slaughtered, account glanders	"	33 33	
Wm. Voege— Damages for 2 horses slaughtered, account glanders	"	35 00	
M. J. Lyons— Damages for 1 horse slaughtered, and disinfection, account glanders	"	7 50	
Hanson & Mathison— Damages for 2 horses slaughtered, account glanders	"	2 50	
Aaron Berkson— Damages for 1 horse slaughtered, account glanders	"	25 00	
J. Hofflein— Damages for 1 horse slaughtered, account glanders	"	15 00	
To amount paid from appropriation of 1893.. $13,717 02 " " " " 1895.. 38,538 65			52,255 67
STATE HISTORICAL LIBRARY AND NATURAL HISTORY MUSEUM.			
Wm. F. E. Gurley— Salary as curator ... $1,875 00 Expenses as curator ... 354 75	1893	2,229 75	
Geo. Walter Murray— Salary as assistant curator	"	750 00	
Patrick J. Kelly— Salary as janitor	"	525 00	
Wm. F. E. Gurley— Salary as curator ... $3,125 00 Expenses as curator ... 746 62	1895	3,871 62	
Geo. Walter Murray— Salary as assistant curator	"	1,250 00	
Amounts carried forward	....	$8,626 37	$6,980,857 37

Statement 3—Continued.

Accounts.	App.	Amount.	Total.
Amounts brought forward	....	$8,626 37	$6,980,857 37
STATE HISTORICAL LIBRARY AND NATURAL HISTORY MUSEUM—*Continued.*			
Patrick J. Kelly—			
Salary as janitor	1895	875 00	
			9,501 37
To amount paid from appropriation of 1893.. $3,504 75			
" " " 1895.. 5,996 62			
STATE LIBRARY.			
S. T. Hinrichsen—			
Salary as assistant librarian	1893	$750 01	
Books purchased, freight charges, etc	"	1,290 38	
S. T. Hinrichsen—			
Salary as assistant librarian	1895	1,250 00	
Books purchased, freight charges, etc	"	1,337 36	
McCoskey & Holcomb—			
Part payment for wiring State House for electric lighting	"	200 00	
			4,827 75
To amount paid from appropriation of 1893.... $2,040 39			
" " " 1895.... 2,787 36			
STORAGE ROOMS, SECRETARY OF STATE, FITTING UP, ETC.			
McCoskey & Holcomb—			
Part payment for wiring State House for electric lighting	1893	$95 41	95 41
STORAGE ROOMS, SECRETARY OF STATE, FURNISHING, ETC.			
McCoskey & Holcomb—			
Part payment for wiring State House for electric lighting	1893	283 95	283 95
SALARIES OF STATE OFFICERS.			
Governor, for salary	1893	7,500 00	
" "	1895	6,000 00	
			13,500 00
Lieutenant Governor, for salary	1893	$1,000 00	
" " incidental expenses	"	50 00	
" " salary	1895	1,000 00	
" " incidental expenses	"	50 00	
			2,100 00
Secretary of State, for salary	1893	$4,375 00	
" " "	1895	2,625 00	
			7,000 00
Auditor of Public Accounts, for salary	1893	$3,500 00	
" " " "	1895	3,791 68	
			7,291 68
State Treasurer, for salary	1893	$3,500 00	
" "	1895	5,833 33	
			9,333 33
Attorney General, for salary	1893	$5,250 00	
" "	1895	2,625 00	
			7,875 00
Adjutant General, for salary	1893	$3,000 00	
" "	1895	3,750 00	
			6,750 00
Amount carried forward			$7,049,415 86

Statement 3—Continued.

Accounts.	App.	Amount.	Total.
Amount brought forward	....	....	$7,049,415 86
SALARIES OF STATE OFFICERS—*Continued.*			
Insurance Superintendent, for salary	1893	$3,500 00	
" "	1895	3,500 00	
			$7,000 00
State Entomologist, for salary	1893	$2,000 00	
" "	1895	2,000 00	
			4,000 00
State Agent at Peoria, to prevent cruelty to animals, for salary	1893	$900 00	
State Agent at Peoria, to prevent cruelty to animals, for salary	1895	1,500 00	
State Agent at National Stock Yards, East St. Louis, to prevent cruelty to animals	1893	1,200 00	
State Agent at National Stock Yards, East St. Louis, to prevent cruelty to animals	1895	1,200 00	
State Agent at Union Stock Yards, Chicago, to prevent cruelty to animals	1893	1,500 00	
State Agent at Union Stock Yards, Chicago, to prevent cruelty to animals	1895	900 00	
			7,200 00
SALARIES—JUDICIARY.			
Judge of Supreme Court, First District, for salary	1893	$5,000 00	
" " " "	1895	5,416 68	
Stenographer to Supreme Judge, First District, for salary	"	1,000 00	
			11,416 68
Judge of Supreme Court, Second District, for salary	1893	$5,000 00	
" " " "	1895	5,416 68	
Stenographer to Supreme Judge, Second District, for salary	"	1,000 00	
			11,416 68
Judge of Supreme Court, Third District, for salary	1893	$5,000 00	
" " " "	1895	5,000 00	
Stenographer to Supreme Judge, Third District, for salary	"	1,250 00	
			11,250 00
Judge of Supreme Court, Fourth District, for salary	1893	$5,000 00	
" " " "	1895	5,000 00	
Stenographer to Supreme Judge, Fourth District for salary	"	1,250 00	
			11,250 00
Judge of Supreme Court, Fifth District, for salary	1893	$5,000 00	
" " " "	1895	5,000 00	
Stenographer to Supreme Judge, Fifth District, for salary	"	1,000 00	
			11,000 00
Judge of Supreme Court, Sixth District, for salary	1893	$5,000 00	
" " " "	1895	3,958 35	
Stenographer to Supreme Judge, Sixth District, for salary	"	750 00	
			9,708 35
Judge of Supreme Court, Seventh District, for salary	1893	$5,000 00	
" " " "	1895	5,000 00	
Stenographer to Supreme Judge, Seventh District, for salary	"	1,000 00	
			11,000 00
JUDGES OF THE SUPERIOR COURT OF COOK COUNTY.			
Joseph E. Gary—For salary	1893	$3,500 00	
"	1895	4,375 00	
Amounts carried forward	....	....	$7,144,657 57

Statement 3—Continued.

Accounts.	App.	Amount.	Total.
Amounts brought forward			$7,144,657 57
JUDGES OF THE SUPERIOR COURT OF COOK COUNTY—*Continued.*			
Theodore Brentano—			
For salary	1893	3,500 00	
" "	1895	3,500 00	
Henry M. Shepard—			
For salary	1893	3,500 00	
" "	1895	3,500 00	
Henry V. Freeman—			
For salary	1893	2,625 00	
" "	1895	3,500 00	
James Goggin—			
For salary	1893	4,375 00	
" "	1895	3,500 00	
Arthur H. Chetlain—			
For salary	1893	4,375 00	
" "	1895	2,625 00	
Jonas Hutchison—			
For salary	1893	3,500 00	
" "	1895	3,500 00	
Philip Stein—			
For salary	1893	3,500 00	
" "	1895	3,500 00	
W. G. Ewing—			
For salary	1893	2,625 00	
" "	1895	3,500 00	
N. C. Sears—			
For salary	1893	3,500 00	
" "	1895	3,500 00	
George F. Blanke—			
For salary	1893	2,893 50	
Farlin Q. Ball—			
For salary	1895	2,187 50	
John Barton Payne—			
For salary	1893	4,375 00	
" "	1895	3,500 00	
			82,956 00
JUDGES OF THE CIRCUIT COURT OF COOK COUNTY.			
Edward F. Dunne—			
For salary	1893	$2,625 00	
" "	1895	3,500 00	
M. F. Tuley—			
For salary	1893	3,500 00	
" "	1895	3,500 00	
R. S. Tuthill—			
For salary	1893	3,500 00	
" "	1895	3,500 00	
Edmund W. Burke—			
For salary	1893	4,375 00	
" "	1895	3,500 00	
S. P. McConnell—			
For salary	1893	77 75	
Chas. G. Neely—			
For salary	1893	797 00	
" "	1895	4,375 00	
Thos. G. Windes—			
For salary	1893	3,500 00	
" "	1895	2,625 00	
A. N. Waterman—			
For salary	1893	2,625 00	
" "	1895	4,375 00	
R. W. Clifford—			
For salary	1893	4,375 00	
" "	1895	2,625 00	
Frank Baker—			
For salary	1893	4,375 00	
" "	1895	3,500 00	
Amounts carried forward			$7,227,613 57

Statement 3—Continued.

Accounts.	App.	Amount.	Total.
Amount brought forward			$7,227,613 57
JUDGES OF THE CIRCUIT COURT OF COOK COUNTY—*Cont.*			
Francis Adams—			
For salary	1893	$3,500 00	
"	1895	3,500 00	
O. H. Horton—			
For salary	1893	3,500 00	
"	1895	3,500 00	
John Gibbons—			
For salary	1893	3,500 00	
"	1895	2,625 00	
Abner Smith—			
For salary	1893	3,500 00	
"	1895	4,375 00	
Elbridge Hanecy—			
For salary	1893	3,500 00	
"	1895	3,500 00	
			96,249 75
JUDGES OF JUDICIAL CIRCUITS.			
Judges of the First Circuit, for salary	1893	$11,375 00	
"	1895	9,625 00	
Judges of the Second Circuit, "	1893	10,500 00	
"	1895	11,375 00	
Judges of the Third Circuit, "	1893	10,500 00	
"	1895	10,500 00	
Judges of the Fourth Circuit, "	1893	9,625 00	
"	1895	10,500 00	
Judges of the Fifth Circuit, "	1893	10,791 68	
"	1895	10,500 01	
Judges of the Sixth Circuit, "	1893	12,250 00	
"	1895	10,500 00	
Judges of the Seventh Circuit, "	1893	10,500 00	
"	1895	10,500 00	
Judges of the Eighth Circuit, "	1893	9,625 00	
"	1895	10,500 00	
Judges of the Ninth Circuit, "	1893	11,375 00	
"	1895	10,500 00	
Judges of the Tenth Circuit, "	1893	9,868 05	
"	1895	11,375 00	
Judges of the Eleventh Circuit, "	1893	11,375 00	
"	1895	9,625 00	
Judges of the Twelfth Circuit, "	1893	10,500 00	
"	1895	9,625 00	
Judges of the Thirteenth Circuit, "	1893	11,375 00	
"	1895	10,354 18	
			275,138 92
STATE'S ATTORNEYS.			
State's Attorney of Adams county for salary	1893	$400 00	
" Alexander " "	"	500 00	
" Bond " "	"	400 00	
" Boone " "	"	400 00	
" Brown " "	"	400 00	
" Bureau " "	"	500 00	
" Calhoun " "	"	400 00	
" Carroll " "	"	500 00	
" Cass " "	"	500 00	
" Champaign " "	"	300 00	
" Christian " "	"	400 00	
" Clark " "	"	400 00	
" Clay " "	"	400 00	
" Clinton " "	"	400 00	
" Coles " "	"	400 00	
" Cook " "	"	400 00	
" Crawford " "	"	300 00	
" Cumberland " "	"	400 00	
" DeKalb " "	"	500 00	
" DeWitt " "	"	300 00	
" Douglas " "	"	400 00	
" DuPage " "		400 00	
Amounts carried forward		$9,000 00	$7,599,002 24

Statement 3—Continued.

ACCOUNTS.				App.	Amount.	Total.
Amounts brought forward					$9,000 00	$7,599,002 24
[STATE'S ATTORNEYS—*Continued.*						
State's Attorney of	Edgar	county for	salary	1893	400 00	
"	Edwards	"	"	"	400 00	
"	Effingham	"	"	"	400 00	
"	Fayette	"	"	"	400 00	
"	Ford	"	"	"	400 00	
"	Franklin	"	"	"	400 00	
"	Fulton	"	"	"	400 00	
"	Gallatin	"	"	"	400 00	
"	Greene	"	"	"	400 00	
"	Grundy	"	"	"	400 00	
"	Hamilton	"	"	"	400 00	
"	Hancock	"	"	"	400 00	
"	Hardin	"	"	"	400 00	
"	Henderson	"	"	"	400 00	
"	Henry	"	"	"	400 00	
"	Iroquois	"	"	"	400 00	
"	Jackson	"	"	"	400 00	
"	Jasper	"	"	"	400 00	
"	Jefferson	"	"	"	400 00	
"	Jersey	"	"	"	400 00	
"	JoDaviess	"	"	"	400 00	
"	Johnson	"	"	"	400 00	
"	Kane	"	"	"	400 00	
"	Kankakee	"	"	"	500 00	
"	Kendall	"	"	"	400 00	
"	Knox	"	"	"	400 00	
"	Lake	"	"	"	400 00	
"	LaSalle	"	"	"	400 00	
"	Lawrence	"	"	"	400 00	
"	Lee	"	"	"	400 00	
"	Livingston	"	"	"	400 00	
"	Logan	"	"	"	400 00	
"	Macon	"	"	"	400 00	
"	Macoupin	"	"	"	500 00	
"	Madison	"	"	"	300 00	
"	Marion	"	"	"	400 00	
"	Marshall	"	"	"	400 00	
"	Mason	"	"	"	300 00	
"	Massac	"	"	"	500 00	
"	McDonough	"	"	"	400 00	
"	McHenry	"	"	"	400 00	
"	McLean	"	"	"	400 00	
"	Menard	"	"	"	300 00	
"	Mercer	"	"	"	400 00	
"	Monroe	"	"	"	500 00	
"	Montgomery	"	"	"	400 00	
"	Morgan	"	"	"	300 00	
"	Moultrie	"	"	"	400 00	
"	Ogle	"	"	"	400 00	
"	Peoria	"	"	"	400 00	
"	Perry	"	"	"	400 00	
"	Piatt	"	"	"	400 00	
"	Pike	"	"	"	400 00	
"	Pope	"	"	"	500 00	
"	Pulaski	"	"	"	500 00	
"	Putnam	"	"	"	400 00	
"	Randolph	"	"	"	400 00	
"	Richland	"	"	"	400 00	
"	Rock Island	"	"	"	400 00	
"	Saline	"	"	"	400 00	
"	Sangamon	"	"	"	400 00	
"	Schuyler	"	"	"	500 00	
"	Scott	"	"	"	400 00	
"	Shelby	"	"	"	400 00	
"	Stark	"	"	"	400 00	
"	St. Clair	"	"	"	400 00	
"	Stephenson	"	"	"	400 00	
"	Tazewell	"	"	"	400 00	
"	Union	"	"	"	400 00	
"	Vermilion	"	"	"	400 00	
"	Wabash	"	"	"	400 00	
"	Warren	"	"	"	400 00	
Amounts carried forward					$38,100 00	$7,599,002 24

Statement 3—Continued.

Accounts.	App.	Amount.	Total.
Amounts brought forward	....	$38,100 00	$7,599,002 24
STATE'S ATTORNEYS—*Continued.*			
State's Attorney of Washington county for salary....	1893	400 00	
" Wayne " "	"	400 00	
" White " "	"	400 00	
" Whiteside " "	"	400 00	
" Will " "	"	500 00	
" Williamson " "	"	400 00	
" Winnebago " "	"	300 00	
" Woodford " "	"	400 00	
" Adams " "	1895	500 00	
" Alexander " "	"	400 00	
" Bond " "	"	400 00	
" Boone " "	"	400 00	
" Brown " "	"	500 00	
" Bureau " "	"	200 00	
" Calhoun " "	"	400 00	
" Carroll " "	"	400 00	
" Cass " "	"	300 00	
" Champaign " "	"	500 00	
" Christian " "	"	500 00	
" Clark " "	"	400 00	
" Clay " "	"	400 00	
" Clinton " "	"	400 00	
" Coles " "	"	300 00	
" Cook " "	"	300 00	
" Crawford " "	"	400 00	
" Cumberland " "	"	400 00	
" DeKalb " "	"	400 00	
" DeWitt " "	"	400 00	
" Douglas " "	"	400 00	
" DuPage " "	"	400 00	
" Edgar " "	"	400 00	
" Edwards " "	"	400 00	
" Effingham " "	"	400 00	
" Fayette " "	"	400 00	
" Ford " "	"	400 00	
" Franklin " "	"	400 00	
" Fulton " "	"	400 00	
" Gallatin " "	"	400 00	
" Greene " "	"	400 00	
" Grundy " "	"	300 00	
" Hamilton " "	"	400 00	
" Hancock " "	"	400 00	
" Hardin " "	"	400 00	
" Henderson " "	"	400 00	
" Henry " "	"	400 00	
" Iroquois " "	"	400 00	
" Jackson " "	"	400 00	
" Jasper " "	"	500 00	
" Jefferson " "	"	400 00	
" Jersey " "	"	400 00	
" Jo Daviess " "	"	400 00	
" Johnson " "	"	400 00	
" Kane " "	"	400 00	
" Kankakee " "	"	300 00	
" Kendall " "	"	500 00	
" Knox " "	"	400 00	
" Lake " "	"	400 00	
" La Salle " "	"	500 00	
" Lawrence " "	"	400 00	
" Lee " "	"	300 00	
" Livingston " "	"	400 00	
" Logan " "	"	400 00	
" Macon " "	"	400 00	
" Macoupin " "	"	400 00	
" Madison " "	"	500 00	
" Marion " "	"	400 00	
" Marshall " "	"	400 00	
" Mason " "	"	206 60	
" Massac " "	"	300 00	
" McDonough " "	"	400 00	
" McHenry " "	"	500 00	
" McLean " "	"	400 00	
Amounts carried forward	....	$67,206 60	$7,599,002 24

Statement 3—Continued.

Accounts.		App.	Amount.	Total.
Amounts brought forward			$67,206 60	$7,599,002 2
STATE'S ATTORNEYS—*Continued.*				
State's Attorney of Menard county for salary		1895	400 00	
" Mercer " "		"	500 00	
" Monroe " "		"	300 00	
" Montgomery " "		"	500 00	
" Morgan " "		"	500 00	
" Moultrie " "		"	500 00	
" Ogle " "		"	500 00	
" Peoria " "		"	300 00	
" Perry " "		"	400 00	
" Piatt " "		"	500 00	
" Pike " "		"	400 00	
" Pope " "		"	300 00	
" Pulaski " "		"	400 00	
" Putnam " "		"	300 00	
" Randolph " "		"	400 00	
" Richland " "		"	400 00	
" Rock Island " "		"	400 00	
" Saline " "		"	400 00	
" Sangamon " "		"	400 00	
" Schuyler " "		"	400 00	
" Scott " "		"	400 00	
" Shelby " "		"	400 00	
" Stark " "		"	400 00	
" St. Clair " "		"	400 00	
" Stephenson " "		"	500 00	
" Tazewell " "		"	400 00	
" Union " "		"	300 00	
" Vermilion " "		"	300 00	
" Wabash " "		"	400 00	
" Warren " "		"	400 00	
" Washington " "		"	400 00	
" Wayne " "		"	400 00	
" White " "		"	400 00	
" Whiteside " "		"	300 00	
" Will " "		"	400 00	
" Williamson " "		"	300 00	
" Winnebago " "		"	400 00	
" Woodford " "		"	400 00	
				81,806 60
WORLD'S COLUMBIAN EXPOSITION.				
Amount paid on account of Illinois Board of World's Fair Commissioners, viz.:				
LaFayette Funk—				
Per diem as commissioner	$30 00			
Expenses "	60			
		1893	$30 60	
David Gore—				
Per diem as commissioner		"	20 00	
J. W. Judy—				
Per diem as commissioner		"	30 00	
J. Irving Pearce—				
Per diem as commissioner	$35 00			
Expenses "	39 00			
		"	74 00	
E. C. Pace—				
Per diem as commissioner	$45 00			
Expenses "	4 50			
		"	49 50	
Wm. Stewart—				
Per diem as commissioner	$40 00			
Expenses "	6 70			
		"	46 70	
John Virgin—				
Per diem as commissioner	$25 00			
Expenses "	75			
		"	25 75	
Amounts carried forward			$276 55	$7,680,808 84

Statement 3—Continued.

Accounts.	App.	Amount.	Total.
Amounts brought forward	....	$276 55	$7,680,808 84
WORLD'S COLUMBIAN EXPOSITION—*Continued.*			
Amount paid on account of Illinois Board of World's Fair Commissioners, viz.:			
B. Pullen—			
Per diem as commissioner $35 00			
Expenses " 7 75	1893	$42 75	
J. K. Dickirson—			
Per diem as commissioner $95 00			
Expenses " 8 45	"	103 45	
J. Harley Bradley—			
Per diem as commissioner $35 00			
Expenses " 70	"	35 70	
E. E. Chester—			
Per diem as commissioner $20 00			
Expenses " 10 00	"	30 00	
E. B. David—			
Per diem as commissioner $40 00			
Expenses " 5 50	"	45 50	
W. H. Fulkerson—			
Per diem as commissioner	"	30 00	
James M. Washburn—			
Per diem as commissioner $60 00			
Expenses " 58 02	"	118 02	
D. W. Vittum—			
Per diem as commissioner $20 00			
Expenses " 2 00	"	22 00	
W. D. Stryker—			
Per diem as commissioner $20 00			
Expenses " 3 50	"	23 50	
A. B. Hostetter—			
Per diem as commissioner $25 00			
Expenses " 8 75	"	33 75	
B. F. Wyman—			
Per diem as commissioner $25 00			
Expenses " 8 19	"	33 19	
S. W. Johns—			
Per diem as commissioner $20 00			
Expenses " 1 25	"	21 25	
Samuel Dysart—			
Per diem as commissioner $75 00			
Expenses " 25 65	"	100 65	
W. C. Garrard—			
Salary as Secretary	"	100 00	
W. C. Garrard, Secretary—			
Amount advanced to prepay freight, drayage, postage and express charges on Final Report, World's Fair Commissioners	"	268 14	
John W. Bunn, Treasurer—			
Amount paid for services of Charles K. Worthen, and transportation	"	51 40	
Nate B. Reed—			
Per diem as clerk and accountant $45 00			
Expenses " " 17 25	"	62 25	
Josua Lindahl—			
Typewriting on final report of commissioners	"	10 75	
E. E. McCoy—			
Services rendered as clerk	"	20 00	
Amounts carried forward	....	$1,428 85	$7,680,808 84

Statement 3—Continued.

Accounts.	App.	Amount.	Total.
Amounts brought forward	....	$1,428 85	$7,680,808 84
WORLD'S COLUMBIAN EXPOSITION—*Continued.*			
Amounts paid on account of Illinois Board of World's Fair Commissioners, viz:			
Helen Blakeslee— Services as stenographer and typewriter..........	1893	40 00	
C. P. Gardner— Use of typewriter..........	"	26 00	
W. R. Kirk— Express charges paid on school exhibit..........	"	2 90	
J. A. Udden— Drawing and retouching cross-section of the State of Illinois, mounting and packing..........	"	8 50	
Wm. Jenkins— Services, compiling final report of commission, balance in full	"	288 98	
A. Zeese & Sons— Zinc etchings, drawing and engraving shell and bowl, and section of oil wells; also 55 cuts for archæological section of final report of commissioners	"	27 25	
Springer and DuBois— Reading proof on final reports of commissioners	"	20 00	
Halliday & Kessberger— One 5x7 negative and 2 prints of cross-section of State of Illinois use in final report of commission..........	"	1 00	
Western Photo Engraving Co.— Three 6x4 half-tone cuts, including one drawing....	"	25 50	
Patrick Higgins— Hauling boxes to railroad depot on contract..........	"	10 00	
C. L. Justice— 15 days' services, counting and packing reports of commissioners, as also further labor, packing and shipping..........	"	79 50	
Otto Redeker— Making 402 boxes for shipping final reports of commission..........	"	139 56	
H. W. Rokker— Printing 20,000 copies final report of Illinois Board of World's Fair Commissioners..........	"	6,961 72	
J. H. Gambrell— Hauling final reports of commission	"	2 80	
O. H. Jewell Filter Co.— Disconnecting and hauling filters from Illinois State Building..........	"	21 00	
Associated Express Co.— Transportation furnished on account of W. D. Stryker, commissioner..........	"	1 95	
Sherman House, Chicago— Board, etc., furnished members of the Illinois Board World's Fair Commission..........	"	43 25	
Leland Hotel, Springfield— Board, etc., furnished members of the Illinois Board World's Fair Commission..........	"	209 25	
St. Nicholas Hotel, Springfield— Board, etc., furnished members of the Illinois Board World's Fair Commission..........	"	45 75	
State Board of Agriculture: Amount advanced for postage to the Illinois Board World's Fair Commissioners, for two years.......	"	25 00	
Amounts paid on account of Woman's Exposition Board, viz.:			
Marcia Louise Gould— Per diem as member of Board.......... $135 00; Expenses " 100 31	"	235 31	
Mary Callahan— Per diem as member of Board.......... $165 00; Expenses " 49 51	"	214 51	
Francine E. Patton— Per diem as member of Board..........	"	50 00	
Amounts carried forward	....	$9,908 58	$7,680,808 84

Statement 3—Continued.

Accounts.	App.	Amount.	Total.
Amounts brought forward	....	$9,908 58	$7,680,808 84
WORLD'S COLUMBIAN EXPOSITION—*Continued.*			
Alice Bradford Wiles—			
Per diem as member of Board $55 00			
Expenses " " 56 72	1893	111 72	
Isabella Laning Candee—			
Per diem as member of Board $140 00			
Expenses " " 80 23	"	220 23	
Frances L. Gilbert—			
Per diem as member of Board $75 00			
Expenses " " 16 25	"	91 25	
Frances Welles Shepard—			
Per diem as member of Board $60 00			
Expenses " " 13 25	"	73 25	
Marcia Louise Gould—			
Amount paid for rebinding report and for livery furnished by N. B. Wiggins at unveiling of statue "Illinois."	"	10 00	
Mary Callahan—			
Amount paid for postage on final reports	"	25 00	
Julia M. Bracken—			
Amount paid for work on statue "Illinois," as per agreement $922 50			
Traveling expenses, etc., incurred to and from Springfield 12 45			
Expenses incurred attending the unveiling of statue "Illinois." 20 00	"	954 95	
The Winslow Brothers Co.—			
Work on statue "Illinois," under contract with Julia M. Bracken	"	262 50	
Charles McBride—			
Personal services and expenses attending unveiling of statue "Illinois."	"	22 66	
The Culver Stone Co.—			
Stone and iron column furnished for support of Statue "Illinois."	"	408 39	
Edward F. Hartmann—			
Printing 100 programs for unveiling of statue "Illinois."	"	2 25	
Watch Factory Band—			
Music furnished at unveiling of statue "Illinois."	"	78 00	
W. H. Hinrichsen—			
Amount paid for drayage on statue "Illinois."	"	2 00	
Anna Brophy—			
Clerical services rendered Board $10 00			
Amount paid for key, express, porter and postage 21 50	"	31 50	
Grace Lincoln Hall—			
Typewritten copy of Final Report of Board	"	9 33	
Porter Printing Co.—			
Printing reports, furnishing envelopes, etc.	"	106 30	
A. B. Dick & Co.—			
1 quire No. 31 —— stencil paper furnished	"	1 75	
Francine E. Patton—			
Postage and express charges paid	"	14 05	
W. B. Conkey Co.—			
1,600 certificates furnished Board $183 50			
Compiling, printing and binding Special Report to Governor 42 00	"	225 50	
			12,550 21
Amounts carried forward	....	....	$7,693,368 0

Statement 3—Continued.

Accounts.	Services.	Expenses.	App.	Amount.	Total.
Amounts brought forward			....	....	$7,693,368 05
SPECIAL STATE FUNDS.					
SCHOOL FUND.					
Superintendent of Public Instruction—					
For salary........................			1893	$4,083 32	
For clerk hire........................			"	3,100 00	
For janitor, porter, etc			"	700 00	
For refurnishing office and library........................			"	83 10	
For office expenses, including stationery, postage, express charges, papers, traveling expenses, etc..			"	1,166 59	
County Superintendents of Schools, for services and expenses, as follows:					
Counties.	Services.	Expenses.			
County Supt. of Adams........	$1,252 00	$132 00	1893	1,384 00	
" Alexander	776 00	86 00	"	862 00	
" Bond.........	1,268 00	131 00	"	1,399 00	
" Boone.........	768 00	96 00	"	864 00	
" Brown	1,120 00	117 00	"	1,237 00	
" Bureau	1,248 00	151 00	"	1,399 00	
" Calhoun	808 00	104 00	"	912 00	
" Carroll........	1,204 00	125 00	"	1,329 00	
" Cass	1,064 00	48 00	"	1,112 00	
" Champaign...	1,248 00	41 00	"	1,289 00	
" Christian.....	1,232 00	91 00	"	1,323 00	
" Clark	1,284 00	166 00	"	1,450 00	
" Clay	980 00	86 00	"	1,066 00	
" Clinton	824 00	113 00	"	937 00	
" Coles	1,256 00	176 00	"	1,432 00	
" Cook	1,252 00	89 00	"	1,341 00	
" Crawford	1,236 00	113 00	"	1,349 00	
" Cumberland..	1,134 00	142 00	"	1,276 00	
" DeKalb	1,276 00	202 00	"	1,478 00	
" DeWitt	1,148 00	53 00	"	1,201 00	
" Douglas	1,264 00	135 00	"	1,399 00	
" DuPage	1,224 00	139 00	"	1,363 00	
" Edgar	1,240 00	48 00	"	1,288 00	
" Edwards	864 00	101 00	"	965 00	
" Effingham....	1,024 00	125 00	"	1,149 00	
" Fayette	1,220 00	158 00	"	1,378 00	
" Ford	1,152 00	72 00	"	1,224 00	
" Franklin......	1,252 00	147 00	"	1,399 00	
" Fulton	1,248 00	64 00	"	1,312 00	
" Gallatin	900 00	36 00	"	936 00	
" Greene	956 00	96 00	"	1,052 00	
" Grundy........	1,240 00	208 00	"	1,448 00	
" Hamilton.....	1,104 00	96 00	"	1,200 00	
" Hancock......	1,248 00	99 00	"	1,347 00	
" Hardin	468 00	46 00	"	514 00	
" Henderson ...	868 00	123 00	"	991 00	
" Henry	1,232 00	135 00	"	1,367 00	
" Iroquois......	1,216 00	103 00	"	1,319 00	
" Jackson	1,212 00	116 00	"	1,328 00	
" Jasper	1,088 00	101 00	"	1,189 00	
" Jefferson	1,024 00	98 00	"	1,122 00	
" Jersey	992 00	133 00	"	1,125 00	
" JoDaviess	1,160 00	134 00	"	1,294 00	
" Johnson	932 00	96 00	"	1,028 00	
" Kane	1,232 00	126 00	"	1,358 00	
" Kankakee	....	....	"	....	
" Kendall	1,160 00	172 00	"	1,332 00	
" Knox	1,280 00	151 00	"	1,431 00	
" Lake..........	1,248 00	147 00	"	1,395 00	
" LaSalle	1,256 00	86 00	"	1,342 00	
" Lawrence.....	976 00	121 00	"	1,097 00	
" Lee	1,264 00	199 00	"	1,463 00	
" Livingston ...	1,240 00	71 00	"	1,311 00	
" Logan	1,240 00	133 00	"	1,373 00	
" Macon	924 00	131 00	"	1,055 00	
" Macoupin.....	1,228 00	78 00	"	1,306 00	
" Madison	1,248 00	124 00	"	1,372 00	
" Marion........	1,248 00	146 00	"	1,394 00	
" Marshall......	1,344 00	156 00	"	1,500 00	
Amounts carried forward			....	$81,239 01	$7,693,368 05

Statement 3—Continued.

ACCOUNTS.	Services.	Expenses.	App.	Amount.	Total.
Amounts brought forward			....	$81,239 01	$7,693,368 05
SPECIAL STATE FUNDS—*Continued.*					
SCHOOL FUND.					
Counties.	Services.	Expenses.			
County Supt. of Mason	$1,244 00	$98 00	1893	1,342 00	
" Massac	780 00	93 00	"	873 00	
" McDonough	1,232 00	63 00	"	1,295 00	
" McHenry	1,252 00	205 00	"	1,457 00	
" McLean	1,228 00	122 00	"	1,350 00	
" Menard	896 00	101 00	"	997 00	
" Mercer	1,204 00	137 00	"	1,341 00	
" Monroe	1,160 00	120 00	"	1,280 00	
" Montgomery	1,248 00	141 00	"	1,389 00	
" Morgan	1,292 00	140 00	"	1,432 00	
" Moultrie	1,028 00	99 00	"	1,127 00	
" Ogle	1,244 00	116 00	"	1,360 00	
" Peoria	1,228 00	92 00	"	1,320 00	
" Perry	940 00	75 00	"	1,015 00	
" Piatt	1,196 00	119 00	"	1,315 00	
" Pike	1,244 00	71 00	"	1,315 00	
" Pope	708 00	90 00	"	798 00	
" Pulaski	952 00	108 00	"	1,060 00	
" Putnam	664 00	73 00	"	737 00	
" Randolph	1,164 00	64 25	"	1,228 25	
" Richland	688 00	78 00	"	766 00	
" Rock Island	1,252 00	60 00	"	1,312 00	
" Saline	984 00	55 00	"	1,039 00	
" Sangamon	1,252 00	178 00	"	1,430 00	
" Schuyler	964 00	90 00	"	1,054 00	
" Scott	849 00	142 00	"	991 00	
" Shelby	1,248 00	129 00	"	1,377 00	
" Stark	1,012 00	151 00	"	1,163 00	
" St. Clair	820 00	101 00	"	921 00	
" Stephenson	1,288 00	192 00	"	1,480 00	
" Tazewell	1,132 00	101 00	"	1,233 00	
" Union	1,040 00	76 00	"	1,116 00	
" Vermilion	1,228 00	48 00	"	1,276 00	
" Wabash	764 00	100 00	"	864 00	
" Warren	1,240 00	51 00	"	1,291 00	
" Washington	1,164 00	108 00	"	1,272 00	
" Wayne	1,248 00	131 00	"	1,379 00	
" White	1,180 00	46 00	"	1,226 00	
" Whiteside	1,244 00	103 00	"	1,347 00	
" Will	1,212 00	200 00	"	1,412 00	
" Williamson	1,108 00	88 00	"	1,196 00	
" Winnebago	1,248 00	141 00	"	1,389 00	
" Woodford	1,268 00	136 00	"	1,404 00	
Amount of "school tax fund orders" for the year 1894, paid to counties			1895	874,620 00	
Amount of "school tax fund orders" for the year 1895, paid to counties			"	875,581 00	
Amount of "school tax fund interest orders" for the year 1894, paid to counties			"	56,937 31	
Amount of "school tax fund interest orders" for the year 1895, paid to counties			"	56,937 31	
Superintendent of Public Instruction—					
For salary			"	3,791 68	
For clerk hire			"	3,000 00	
For stenographer, typewriter, etc			"	1,250 00	
For janitor, porter, etc			"	875 00	
For office expenses, including stationery, postage, express charges, papers, traveling expenses, etc.			"	2,104 03	
County superintendents of schools, for services and expenses as follows:					
Counties.	Services.	Expenses.			
County Supt. of Adams	$1,252 00	$125 00	"	1,377 00	
" Alexander	724 00	92 00	"	816 00	
" Bond	1,236 00	146 00	"	1,382 00	
" Boone	820 00	108 00	"	928 00	
" Brown	1,184 00	133 00	"	1,317 00	
" Bureau	1,248 00	158 00	"	1,406 00	
" Calhoun	732 00	78 00	"	810 00	
" Carroll	1,244 00	122 00	"	1,366 00	
Amounts carried forward			....	$2,017,706 59	$7,693,368 05

Statement 3—Continued.

Accounts.		Services.	Expenses.	App.	Amount.	Total.
Amounts brought forward					$2,017,706 59	$7,693,368 05
SPECIAL STATE FUNDS—*Continued.*						
SCHOOL FUND.						
	Counties.	Services.	Expenses.			
County Supt. of	Cass	$952 00	$172 00	1895	1,124 00	
"	Champaign	1,248 00	49 00	"	1,297 00	
"	Christian	1,248 00	81 00	"	1,329 00	
"	Clark	1,224 00	175 00	"	1,399 00	
"	Clay	1,076 00	75 00	"	1,151 00	
"	Clinton	724 00	91 00	"	815 00	
"	Coles	1,248 00	186 00	"	1,434 00	
"	Cook	1,252 00	121 00	"	1,373 00	
"	Crawford	1,248 00	103 00	"	1,351 00	
"	Cumberland	1,180 00	152 00	"	1,332 00	
"	DeKalb	1,172 00	187 00	"	1,359 00	
"	DeWitt	1,240 00	77 00	"	1,317 00	
"	Douglas	1,248 00	143 00	"	1,391 00	
"	DuPage	1,228 00	151 00	"	1,379 00	
"	Edgar	1,252 00	80 00	"	1,332 00	
"	Edwards	796 00	94 00	"	890 00	
"	Effingham	1,040 00	131 00	"	1,171 00	
"	Fayette	1,256 00	158 00	"	1,414 00	
"	Ford	1,152 00	73 00	"	1,225 00	
"	Franklin	1,252 00	181 00	"	1,433 00	
"	Fulton	1,248 00	84 00	"	1,332 00	
"	Gallatin	968 00	49 00	"	1,017 00	
"	Greene	1,008 00	102 00	"	1,110 00	
"	Grundy	1,232 00	225 00	"	1,457 00	
"	Hamilton	1,026 00	114 00	"	1,140 00	
"	Hancock	1,248 00	95 00	"	1,343 00	
"	Hardin	552 00	69 00	"	621 00	
"	Henderson	900 00	128 00	"	1,028 00	
"	Henry	1,240 00	143 00	"	1,383 00	
"	Iroquois	1,020 00	108 00	"	1,128 00	
"	Jackson	1,264 00	168 00	"	1,432 00	
"	Jasper	1,240 00	102 00	"	1,342 00	
"	Jefferson	1,464 00	121 00	"	1,585 00	
"	Jersey	920 00	105 00	"	1,025 00	
"	JoDaviess	1,240 00	113 00	"	1,353 00	
"	Johnson	824 00	104 00	"	928 00	
"	Kane	1,176 00	89 00	"	1,265 00	
"	Kankakee	....	....	....	....	
"	Kendall	1,080 00	151 00	"	1,231 00	
"	Knox	1,252 00	148 00	"	1,400 00	
"	Lake	1,252 00	144 00	"	1,396 00	
"	LaSalle	1,240 00	97 00	"	1,337 00	
"	Lawrence	1,124 00	136 00	"	1,260 00	
"	Lee	1,256 00	207 00	"	1,463 00	
"	Livingston	1,248 00	54 00	"	1,302 00	
"	Logan	1,248 00	156 00	"	1,404 00	
"	Macon	1,560 00	171 00	"	1,731 00	
"	Macoupin	1,252 00	84 00	"	1,336 00	
"	Madison	1,248 00	147 00	"	1,395 00	
"	Marion	1,248 00	147 00	"	1,395 00	
"	Marshall	1,256 00	204 00	"	1,460 00	
"	Mason	1,248 00	159 00	"	1,407 00	
"	Massac	500 00	75 00	"	575 00	
"	McDonough	1,232 00	113 00	"	1,345 00	
"	McHenry	1,252 00	212 00	"	1,464 00	
"	LcLean	1,260 00	112 00	"	1,372 00	
"	Menard	880 00	89 00	"	969 00	
"	Mercer	1,244 00	146 00	"	1,390 00	
"	Monroe	1,054 00	83 00	"	1,137 00	
"	Montgomery	1,252 00	188 00	"	1,440 00	
"	Morgan	1,272 00	121 00	"	1,393 00	
"	Moultrie	1,084 00	101 00	"	1,185 00	
"	Ogle	1,248 00	121 00	"	1,369 00	
"	Peoria	1,252 00	111 00	"	1,363 00	
"	Perry	960 00	81 00	"	1,041 00	
"	Piatt	1,244 00	136 00	"	1,380 00	
"	Pike	1,276 00	66 00	"	1,342 00	
"	Pope	780 00	91 00	"	871 00	
"	Pulaski	764 00	111 00	"	875 00	
"	Putman	700 00	90 00	"	790 00	
Amounts carried forward					$2,104,529 59	$7,693,368 05

Statement 3—Continued.

Accounts.			App.	Amount.	Total.
Amounts brought forward			....	$2,104,529 59	$7,693,368 05
SPECIAL STATE FUNDS—*Continued.*					
SCHOOL FUNDS.					
County Supt. of Randolph	$1,236 00	$91 00	1895	$1,327 00	
" Richland	1,176 00	137 00	"	1,313 00	
" Rock Island	1,256 00	86 00	"	1,342 00	
" Saline	1,056 00	96 00	"	1,152 00	
" Sangamon	1,252 00	173 00	"	1,425 00	
" Schuyler	1,040 00	101 00	"	1,141 00	
" Scott	732 00	97 00	"	829 00	
" Shelby	1,240 00	156 00	"	1,396 00	
" Stark	1,004 00	151 00	"	1,155 00	
" St. Clair	1,544 00	154 00	"	1,698 00	
" Stephenson	1,260 00	212 00	"	1,472 00	
" Tazewell	1,284 00	210 00	"	1,494 00	
" Union	972 00	74 00	"	1,046 00	
" Vermilion	1,248 00	60 00	"	1,308 00	
" Wabash	828 00	100 00	"	928 00	
" Warren	1,244 00	43 00	"	1,287 00	
" Washington	1,176 00	123 00	"	1,299 00	
" Wayne	1,228 00	114 00	"	1,342 00	
" White	1,012 00	42 00	"	1,054 00	
" Whiteside	1,256 00	88 00	"	1,344 00	
" Will	1,248 00	205 00	"	1,453 00	
" Williamson	1,052 00	91 00	"	1,143 00	
" Winnebago	1,252 00	113 00	"	1,365 00	
" Woodford	1,248 00	154 00	"	1,402 00	$2,135,244 59
UNKNOWN AND MINOR HEIRS' FUND.					
T. B. Stelle, Attorney, Etc.—For amount in State treasury received from W. A. McElvain, master-in-chancery, upon order of Circuit Court of Hamilton county, being amount due one William M. Cook, now deceased, and payable to his heirs at law, Rebecca, Mary R., Henry, Martha and Frank Cook			....	$53 71	$53 71
					$9,828,666 35

Statement 3—Continued.

DISBURSEMENTS ON ACCOUNT OF REGISTERED BONDS OF COUNTIES, TOWNSHIPS, CITIES AND TOWNS, AND SPECIAL DRAINAGE DISTRICTS.

County.	Bond Fund.	For what paid.	Amount.	Total.
	Amount brought forward			$9,828,666 35
Adams	County of Adams	Int., princ., etc.	$1,219 65	
"	City of Quincy	"	161,515 24	
"	" " Sinking Fund	"	107,981 92	
Alexander	County of Alexander	"	25,670 63	
"	City of Cairo	"	59,472 40	
Bureau	Tp. of Ohio	"	8,341 88	
"	" Walnut	"	5,807 87	
"	Village of Buda	"	1,139 05	
Bureau and Whiteside	Green River Special Drain. Dist.	"	8,182 36	
Cass	City of Beardstown	"	19,768 08	
"	Hager Slough Sp'l Drain. Dist.	"	2,727 61	
Cass and Morgan	New Pankey Pond Sp'l Dr'n. Dist	"	913 61	
Champaign	Tp. of Champaign	"	11,661 32	
"	" St. Joseph	"	4,828 49	
"	" Urbana	"	9,156 95	
"	City of Urbana	"	1,678 70	
"	Big Slough Special Drain. Dist.	"	3,614 03	
"	Wild Cat Special Drain. Dist	"	3,030 07	
Christian	Tp. of Johnson	"	1,630 19	
"	" Pana	"	17,147 89	
Clark	County of Clark	"	6,487 53	
"	" " Sinking Funk	"	30,000 00	
"	Tp. of Marshall	"	4,238 54	
"	" " Sinking Fund	"	12,000 00	
"	" Westfield	"	2,432 39	
"	" York	"	978 21	
"	" " Sinking Fund	"	5,000 00	
Clay	" Harter	"	2,304 54	
"	" Louisville	"	5,006 51	
Coles	" Charleston	"	9,151 77	
"	" Mattoon	"	10,706 37	
"	" Seven Hickory	"	7,156 52	
"	" " Sink'g F'd.	"	3,000 00	
"	City of Mattoon	"	6,677 38	
Cook	Inc. Town of Cicero	"	8,444 45	
Crawford	County of Crawford	"	12,121 05	
"	Tp. of Hutsonville	"	1,535 09	
"	" Robinson	"	3,033 10	
Cumberland	" Sumpter	"	2,908 92	
DeWitt	County of DeWitt	"	20,148 79	
"	Tp. of Barnett	"	7,302 60	
"	" Clintonia	"	2,135 13	
"	" Creek	"	4,625 82	
"	" Nixon	"	19 32	
"	" Santa Anna	"	13,883 13	
DeWitt, Macon and Logan	North Branch Lake Fork Special Drainage District	"	14,407 26	
Douglas	County of Douglas	"	10,942 92	
"	Tp. of Camargo	"	6,568 62	
"	" Garrett	"	4,449 63	
"	" Newman	"	4,991 01	
"	" Tuscola	"	2,424 46	
Edgar	" Kansas	"	4,284 47	
"	" Paris	"	987 93	
"	" " Sinking Fund	"	7,000 00	
"	" Ross	"	5,981 81	
"	" Shiloh	"	1,454 48	
"	" Young America	"	3,793 94	
Edwards and White	Inc. Town of Grayville	"	1,641 02	
Effingham	Tp. of Douglas	"	6,669 44	
"	" Liberty	"	187 76	
"	" Liberty Sinking Funk	"	2,000 00	
"	" Mason	"	2,433 52	
"	" Summitt	"	942 75	
"	" West	"	2,550 47	
	Amounts carried forward		$720,496 59	$9,828,666 35

Statement 3—Continued.

County.	Bond Fund.	For what paid.	Amount.	Total.
	Amounts brought forward		$720,496 59	$9,828,666 35
Fayette	Tp. of Bear Grove	Int., princ., etc.	$5,798 77	
“	“ Vandalia	“	12,018 76	
Ford	County of Ford	“	17,685 29	
“	Tp. of Drummer	“	10,381 18	
“	“ Lyman	“	3,257 05	
“	“ Peach Orchard	“	5,935 52	
Ford, Iroquois and Livinston	Vermilion Special Drainage District	“	7,318 33	
Fulton	Tp. of Astoria	“	693 45	
Gallatin	County of Gallatin	“	27,220 51	
“	“ Sinking Fund	“	1,490 00	
“	City of Shawneetown	“	4,613 39	
Greene	“ Whitehall	“	1,739 59	
Hancock	County of Hancock	“	25,658 21	
“	City of Warsaw	“	9,077 66	
Henry	Tp. of Western	“	2,255 59	
Iroquois	“ Douglas	“	1,575 55	
“	“ Martinton	“	2,892 09	
“	“ Sheldon	“	6,079 02	
“	City of Watseka	“	2,375 31	
“	Spl. Drain. Dist. No. 1 of Onarga, Douglas and Danforth Tps	“	6,059 59	
“	Union Drain. Dist. No. 2 of Ashkum and Danforth Tps	“	195 97	
“	Milks Grove Special Drain. Dist.	“	9,607 67	
Jackson	City of Murphysboro	“	970 87	
“	Big Lake Special Drainage Dist.	“	6,669 59	
Jasper	County of Jasper	“	13,491 66	
“	Tp. of Fox	“	1,791 94	
“	“ St. Marie	“	3,566 06	
“	“ Wade	“	2,848 25	
“	“ Willow Hill	“	82 36	
Jefferson	County of Jefferson	“	16,517 05	
“	Tp. of Mt. Vernon	“	1,211 99	
Jersey	School District No. 8, T. 7, R. 12	“	2,553 35	
Jersey and Macoupin	Inc. Town of Brighton	“	2,245 64	
Jo Daviess	City of Galena	“	14,035 40	
Johnson	County of Johnson	“	17	
Kankakee	County of Kankakee	“	5,351 46	
“	Tp. of Aroma	“	7,393 67	
“	“ Ganeer	“	24,255 17	
“	“ Momence	“	4,358 50	
“	“ Pembrooke	“	545 48	
“	“ Pilot	“	2,555 60	
Knox	“ Rio	“	1,397 82	
LaSalle	Inc. Town of Marseilles	“	282 76	
“	Drain. Dist. No. 2 T'wn of Wallace	“	980 00	
Lee	Tp. of Amboy	“	22,251 21	
“	“ Hamilton	“	1,095 92	
“	“ Wyoming	“	10,648 87	
Livingston	“ Amity	“	5,594 55	
“	“ Eppard's Point	“	1,813 53	
“	“ Indian Grove	“	2,537 59	
“	“ Owego	“	185 96	
“	“ Pontiac	“	14,403 77	
“	“ Reading	“	3,996 09	
Logan	County of Logan	“	13,330 03	
“	Tp. of Ætna	“	4,623 04	
“	“ “ Sinking Fund	“	203 05	
“	“ Atlanta	“	4,061 70	
“	“ East Lincoln	“	9,922 14	
“	“ “ Sinking F'd.	“	10,000 00	
“	“ Mt. Pulaski	“	4,383 03	
“	“ Oran	“	4,927 07	
“	“ West Lincoln	“	14,845 02	
“	City of Lincoln	“	5,353 12	
“	School Dist. No. 5, T. 18, R. 2	“	970 91	
Macon	County of Macon	“	37,212 26	
“	Tp. of Decatur	“	8,983 22	
“	City of Decatur	“	2,333 02	
	Amounts carried forward		$1,181,204 9[illegible]	$9,828,666 35

Statement—Continued.

County.	Bond Fund.	For What Paid.	Amount.	Total.
	Amounts brought forward	....	$1,181,204 98	$9,828,666 35
Macoupin	County of Macoupin	Int., princ., etc.	$245,031 78	
"	Inc. Town of Virden..............	"	1,638 76	
Madison	City of Edwardsville	"	7,089 55	
Mason	County of Mason..................	"	17,767 16	
"	Tp. of Havana	"	460 50	
"	" Mason City	"	602 42	
"	Central Special Drainage Dist...	"	43,528 84	
"	Mason & Menard Spl. Drain. Dist	"	1,567 88	
Mason and Tazewell	Mason & Tazewell Special Drainage District.....................	"	52,081 85	
McDonough...	Tp. of Bushnell..................	"	7,208 24	
McLean.......	" Bloomington	"	46,024 50	
"	Village of Saybrook	"	2,312 60	
Mercer........	Tp. of Keithsburg	"	6,707 97	
"	City of New Boston...............	"	1,119 73	
"	" " Sink'g Fund.	"	2,010 80	
Monroe	County of Monroe.................	"	9,284 97	
Montgomery..	City of Litchfield...............	"	3,141 85	
Morgan	County of Morgan	"	8,124 05	
"	City of Jacksonville	"	23,979 67	
"	City of Waverly..................	"	37,886 93	
"	City of Waverly Sinking Fund ..	"	1,010 00	
Moultrie	County of Moultrie...............	"	92,843 66	
"	Tp. of Lowe	"	139 14	
"	" Lowe Sinking Fund	"	2,084 09	
"	" Sullivan	"	7,394 19	
Ogle	" Forreston	"	3,729 65	
"	" Mt. Morris................	"	12,871 21	
"	" Oregon....................	"	11,269 48	
"	" Pine Rock	"	4,927 97	
"	City of Polo.....................	"	606 28	
Peoria	Tp. of Brimfield	"	14,858 08	
"	" Elmwood	"	15,127 26	
"	" Peoria....................	"	9,901 42	
Piatt	" Bement....................	"	14,137 76	
"	" Blue Ridge	"	10,221 41	
"	" Goose Creek	"	7,005 03	
"	" Sangamon	"	7,555 31	
"	" Unity......................	"	1,062 81	
Pike	County of Pike...................	"	61,144 78	
"	Pittsfield School District.........	"	7,347 14	
Pulaski	County of Pulaski	"	7,920 64	
"	City of Mound City	"	2,004 80	
Randolph.....	County of Randolph	"	929 19	
Richland	County of Richland...............	"	39,700 30	
Saline	County of Saline	"	20,884 40	
Sangamon....	County of Sangamon	"	43,788 75	
"	Tp. of Capital	"	5,833 41	
"	" Cartwright	"	5,735 70	
"	" Springfield	"	1,227 20	
"	" Talkington	"	4,004 04	
"	City of Springfield..............	"	93,049 70	
Schuyler	County of Schuyler...............	"	5,664 81	
Shelby	Tp. of Dry Point.................	"	2,908 71	
"	" Okaw	"	762 63	
"	" Prairie....................	"	12,201 58	
"	" Richland..................	"	27,916 78	
"	" Shelbyville	"	3,029 49	
"	" Todd's Point	"	449 29	
"	" Windsor	"	7,958 55	
"	City of Windsor..................	"	3,878 62	
Stark	Tp. of Essex	"	10,423 47	
"	" Goshen	"	5,163 41	
"	" Osceola	"	11,055 75	
"	" Penn	"	6,902 23	
"	" Toulon	"	8,383 15	
"	Village of Wyoming...............	"	984 99	
St. Clair	City of East St. Louis	"	67,905 07	
"	Tp. of Centreville Station........	"	44,400 07	
"	Village of Brooklyn..............	"	1 20	
Tazewell	County of Tazewell...............	"	15,963 97	
"	Tp. of Delavan	"	8,605 98	
"	" Little Mackinaw	"	10,594 16	
"	" Mackinaw	"	3,862 65	
"	" Tremont...................		878 38	
	Amounts carried forward	....	$2,468,493 77	$9,828,666 35

Statement 3—Continued.

County.	Bond Fund.	For What Paid.	Amount.	Total.
	Amounts brought forward		$2,468,493 77	$9,828,666 35
Tazewell	City of Pekin	Int., prin., etc.	89,567 76	
Vermilion	Tp. of Butler	"	4,500 39	
"	" Danville	"	29,219 70	
"	" Elwood	"	4,223 15	
"	" Grant	"	12,171 43	
"	" Ross	"	5,544 75	
Wabash	County of Wabash	"	13,988 91	
"	City of Mt. Carmel	"	4,936 39	
Warren	Tp. of Monmouth	"	5,696 80	
"	" Roseville	"	5,110 90	
"	" Spring Grove	"	5,957 17	
"	" Swan	"	970 06	
Washington	County of Washington	"	35,551 15	
Wayne	County of Wayne	"	10,351 99	
"	Tp. of Big Mound	"	243 37	
"	" Jasper	"	283 38	
"	" Lamard	"	303 59	
White	County of White	"	18,193 46	
"	Village of Enfield	"	1,333 51	
Whiteside	Tp. of Coloma	"	6,329 55	
Williamson	County of Williamson	"	12,668 16	
Woodford	Tp. of Olio	"	5,447 52	
				2,741,086 86
Grand total of warrants issued from Oct. 1, 1894, to Sept. 30, 1896, inclusive				$12,569,753 21

No. 4.

Recapitulation of warrants drawn on the State Treasury from October 1, 1894, to September 30, 1896, inclusive.

To What Accounts Charged.	Amount.
Appropriations—special	$17,060 45
Canal Commissioners	12,345 00
Commission of Claims	2,781 00
" to mark position of Illinois Troops at Chicamauga, monuments, etc.	24,142 01
Commissioners of Labor Statistics	20,738 47
" Public Charities	10,200 64
Contingent fund of Governor	4,083 77
Conveying convicts to Penitentiary	38,348 50
" from and to Penitentiary on writ of habeas corpus, to be used as witnesses	431 00
Conveying convicts to Reformatory	37,142 15
" from and to Reformatory on writ of habeas corpus, to be used as witnesses	762 60
Conveying Juvenile Female Offenders to State Home	1,401 30
Costs and expenses of State suits	1,399 09
Cotton States and International Exposition	14,995 00
Court—Appellate—1st District	22,080 52
" " 2d "	3,759 42
" " 3d "	2,250 15
" " 4th "	2,612 31
" Supreme—Central Grand Division	4,885 35
" " Northern "	6,482 06
" " Southern "	5,056 31
Executive Mansion	6,754 42
Factory and Workshop Inspectors	26,963 68
Farmers' County Institutes	4,711 92
Fire apparatus for State Capitol Building	27 00
Fish Commissioners	21,958 50
Flags for dome of State Capitol Building	392 40
Fugitives from Justice—apprehension and delivery	14,538 84
" " rewards for arrest and conviction	600 00
General Assembly	375,256 69
Heating and lighting	44,460 55
Illinois Dairyman's Association	2,000 00
Illinois State Historical Society	3,461 81
" Horticultural Society	6,000 00
" National Guard	711,479 86
" Asylum for Feeble-Minded Children	179,146 97
" " Incurable Insane	65,000 00
" " Insane Criminals	85,057 79
" Charitable Eye and Ear Infirmary	62,456 07
" Home for Juvenile Female Offenders	116,033 07
" " Soldiers' Orphans'	125,661 17
" " " and Sailors'	324,481 89
" " " Widows'	12,500 00
" Hospital for Insane—Central	364,328 01
" " " Eastern	675,690 84
" " " Northern	329,448 55
" " " Southern	454,397 50
" " " Western	28,822 26
" Industrial home for the Blind	37,000 00
" Institution for the Education of the Blind	125,629 40
" " " Deaf and Dumb	249,782 36
" Normal School—Eastern	33,160 00
Amount carried forward	$4,720,158 65

Statement 4—Continued.

To What Accounts Charged.	Amount.
Amount brought forward	$4,720,158 65
Illinois State Normal University—Normal	114,370 17
" " School—Northern	30,000 00
" " University—Southern	74,534 42
" Penitentiary—Joliet	180,975 28
" " Southern	200,730 81
" Reformatory—Pontiac	381,378 50
" University—Champaign	489,800 00
Incidental expenses	39,667 29
Joint Commission on Statutory Revision	12,370 00
Laborers, janitors, watchmen and policemen of the State House	12,787 23
Lincoln Homestead Trustees	1,913 12
" Monument Commissioners	7,068 01
Mine Inspectors	27,011 92
Money refunded—revenue	111 67
Office of Governor	15,973 91
" Secretary of State	55,914 77
" Auditor of Public Accounts	24,883 97
" State Treasurer	23,493 03
" Attorney General	28,839 67
" Adjutant General	16,916 86
" Insurance Superintendent	59,856 63
Paving and curbing around Capitol Grounds and Executive Mansion	7,941 29
Printer Expert	77,167 00
Printing paper and stationery	41,821 76
Public Printing	51,618 14
Public binding	27,547 01
Railroad and Warehouse Commissioners	45,262 72
Repairs of roof and stonework of Capitol Building	789 37
Reporter and reports of Supreme Court	24,285 41
State Board of Agriculture and Agricultural Societies	154,240 00
State Board of Arbitration	5,850 00
State Board of Equalization	22,295 46
State Board of Health	18,337 81
State Board of Examiners for Mine Inspectors and Mine Managers	2,689 82
State Board of Live Stock Commissioners and State Veterinarian	52,255 67
State Historical Library and Natural History Museum	9,501 37
State Library	4,827 75
Storage room of Secretary of State—fitting up, etc	95 41
" " " —furnishing, etc	283 95
Salaries, Governor	13,500 00
" Lieutenant Governor and incidental expenses	2,100 00
" Secretary of State	7,000 00
" Auditor of Public Accounts	7,291 68
" State Treasurer	9,333 33
" Attorney General	7,875 00
" Adjutant General	6,750 00
" Insurance Superintendent	7,000 00
" State Entomologist	4,000 00
" State Agents to prevent cruelty to animals	7,200 00
" Judge Supreme Court, 1st District	10,416 68
" Stenographer " " "	1,000 00
" Judge " 2d District	10,416 68
" Stenographer " "	1,000 00
" Judge " 3d District	10,000 00
" Stenographer " "	1,250 00
" Judge " 4th District	10,000 00
" Stenographer " "	1,250 00
" Judge " 5th District	10,000 00
" Stenographer " "	1,000 00
" Judge " 6th District	8,958 35
" Stenographer " "	750 00
" Judge " 7th District	10,000 00
" Stenographer " "	1,000 00
" Judges Superior Court, Cook county (13 judges)	82,956 00
" " Circuit " " (15 ")	96,249 75
" " 1st Judicial Circuit	21,000 00
" " 2d "	21,875 00
" " 3d "	21,000 00
" " 4th "	20,125 00
" " 5th "	21,291 69
" " 6th "	22,750 00
" " 7th "	21,000 00
Amount carried forward	~~$7,472,905 01~~

Statement 4—Continued.

To What Accounts Charged.	Amounts.
Amount brought forward	$7,472,905 01
Salaries, Judges 8th Judicial Circuit	$20,125 00
" " 9th "	21,875 00
" " 10th "	21,243 05
" " 11th "	21,000 00
" " 12th "	20,125 00
" " 13th "	21,729 18
" State's Attorney, Adams County	900 00
" " Alexander "	900 00
" " Bond "	800 00
" " Boone "	800 00
" " Brown "	900 00
" " Bureau "	700 00
" " Calhoun "	800 00
" " Carroll "	900 00
" " Cass "	800 00
" " Champaign "	800 00
" " Christian "	900 00
" " Clark "	800 00
" " Clay "	800 00
" " Clinton "	800 00
" " Coles "	700 00
" " Cook "	700 00
" " Crawford "	700 00
" " Cumberland "	800 00
" " DeKalb "	900 00
" " DeWitt "	700 00
" " Douglas "	800 00
" " DuPage "	800 00
" " Edgar "	800 00
" " Edwards "	800 00
" " Effingham "	800 00
" " Fayette "	800 00
" " Ford "	800 00
" " Franklin "	800 00
" " Fulton "	800 00
" " Gallatin "	800 00
" " Greene "	800 00
" " Grundy "	700 00
" " Hamilton "	800 00
" " Hancock "	800 00
" " Hardin "	800 00
" " Henderson "	800 00
" " Henry "	800 00
" " Iroquois "	800 00
" " Jackson "	800 00
" " Jasper "	900 00
" " Jefferson "	800 00
" " Jersey "	800 00
" " Jo Daviess "	800 00
" " Johnson "	800 00
" " Kane "	800 00
" " Kankakee "	800 00
" " Kendall "	900 00
" " Knox "	800 00
" " Lake "	800 00
" " LaSalle "	900 00
" " Lawrence "	800 00
" " Lee "	700 00
" " Livingston "	800 00
" " Logan "	800 00
" " Macon "	800 00
" " Macoupin "	900 00
" " Madison "	800 00
" " Marion "	800 00
" " Marshall "	800 00
" " Mason "	506 60
" " Massac "	800 00
" " McDonough "	800 00
" " McHenry "	900 00
" " McLean "	800 00
" " Menard "	700 00
" " Mercer "	900 00
Amount carried forward	$7,651,908 84

Statement 4—Concluded.

To What Accounts Charged.			Amount.
Amount brought forward			$7,651,908 84
Salaries, State's Attorney, Monroe County			800 00
" " Montgomery "			900 00
" " Morgan "			800 00
" " Moultrie "			900 00
" " Ogle "			900 00
" " Peoria "			700 00
" " Perry "			800 00
" " Piatt "			900 00
" " Pike "			800 00
" " Pope "			800 00
" " Pulaski "			900 00
" " Putnam "			700 00
" " Randolph "			800 00
" " Richland "			800 00
" " Rock Island "			800 00
" " Saline "			800 00
" " Sangamon "			800 00
" " Schuyler "			900 00
" " Scott "			800 00
" " Shelby "			800 00
" " Stark "			800 00
" " St. Clair "			800 00
" " Stephenson "			900 00
" " Tazewell "			800 00
" " Union "			700 00
" " Vermilion "			700 00
" " Wabash "			800 00
" " Warren "			800 00
" " Washington "			800 00
" " Wayne "			800 00
" " White "			800 00
" " Whiteside "			700 00
" " Will "			900 00
" " Williamson "			700 00
" " Winnebago "			700 00
" " Woodford "			800 00
			$7,680,808 84
WORLD'S COLUMBIAN EXPOSITION.			
Illinois Board of World's Fair Commissioners			9,408 76
Illinois Woman's Exposition Board			3,150 45
Total Revenue Fund Warrants issued			$7,693,368 05
SPECIAL STATE FUNDS.			
State School Fund		$2,135,244 59	
Unknown and Minor Heirs' Fund		53 71	
			2,135,298 30
Local Bond Fund, as per detailed statement			2,741,086 86
Total Warrants drawn during two years ending September 30, 1896			$12,569,753 21

No. 5.

Balance of Appropriations made by the Thirty-Eighth General Assembly unexpended October 1, 1894, the Amount of Warrants since drawn thereon, and the Unexpended Balance which lapsed into the State Treasury, September 30, 1895.

Appropriations.	Balance unexpended October 1, 1894.	Warrants drawn since.	Amount lapsed into State Treasury September 30, 1895.
Australian ballot law publication	$457 00		$457 00
Commission to mark position of Illinois troops at Chicamauga, etc	394 97	$394 97	
Commissioners of Labor Statistics—			
Salary as Secretary	1,875 00	1,875 00	
Incidental expenses, clerical services, etc	4,854 15	4,854 15	
Commissioners of Public Charities—			
Salary of Secretary, clerk hire, incidental expenses, etc	2,699 64	2,699 64	
Contingent Fund of Governor	3,122 98	887 59	2,235 39
Conveying convicts to and from penitentiary	7,772 70	7,772 70	
Conveying convicts to and from reformatory	1 45	1 45	
Costs and expenses of State suits	629 34	628 04	1 30
Court—Appellate—1st District—			
Incidental expenses	1,330 43	1,330 43	
Librarian's salary	416 68	416 68	
Rent of court room	6,666 67	6,666 67	
Purchase of law books	1,014 60	1,014 60	
Court—Appellate—2d District—			
Incidental expenses	1,472 73	1,472 39	34
Salary of janitor	400 00	400 00	
Court—Appellate—3d District—			
Incidental expenses	1,072 60	736 52	336 08
Salary of janitor	400 00	400 00	
Court—Appellate—4th District—			
Incidental expenses	922 95	922 95	
Salary of janitor	400 00	400 00	
Court—Supreme—Central Grand Division—			
Incidental expenses	920 44	839 80	80 64
Salary of librarian	1,000 00	1,000 00	
Salary of janitor	333 34	333 34	
Court—Supreme—Northern Grand Division—			
Incidental expenses	3,128 69	3,088 43	40 26
Salary of librarian	500 00	500 00	
Salary of janitor	400 00	400 00	
Law books and binding	78	78	
Repairs on Court House	81 18	81 00	18
Court—Supreme—Southern Grand Division—			
Incidental expenses	1,135 96	1,135 96	
Salary of librarian	500 00	500 00	
Salary as janitor	400 00	400 00	
Executive Mansion and Grounds—			
Care, heating, lighting, etc	1,983 61	1,983 61	
Factory and Workshop Inspectors—			
Salary of Inspectors	8,707 66	4,937 48	3,770 18
Expenses of Inspectors	2,497 90	2,497 90	
Fish Commissioners—			
General expenditures	7,789 52	7,789 52	
Personal and traveling expenses, Commissioners, etc	2,179 84	2,179 84	

Statement 5—Continued.

APPROPRIATIONS.	Balance unexpended October 1, 1894.	Warrants drawn since.	Amount lapsed into State Treasury September 30, 1895.
Fugitives from justice—			
Apprehension and delivery	$9,537 52	$7,171 54	$2,365 98
Rewards for arrest, conviction, etc	2,800 00	200 00	2,600 00
General Assembly—			
Copying laws, journals, etc	490 00	350 00	140 00
Distributing laws, journals, etc	380 00	380 00	
Expressage and postage on laws, journals, etc	811 12	811 12	
Committee expenses, 39th General Assembly	1,000 00	1,000 00	
Pay of emploés, 38th General Assembly (emergency)	140 00		140 00
Heating and Lighting State House—			
Fuel, pay of engineers, fireman, etc., account heating	10,997 49	10,997 49	
Gas, pay of electrician, incidental expenses, etc., account lighting	3,413 84	3,413 84	
Illinois State Historical Society—			
Salary of librarian	500 00	500 00	
Maintenance of library	1,619 07	1,437 45	181 62
Illinois State Horticultural Society	2,000 00	2,000 00	
Illinois State National Guard—			
Ordinary expenses	83,590 12	83,590 12	
Illinois State Asylum for Feeble-Minded Children—			
Ordinary expenses	63,750 00	63,750 00	
Repairs and improvements	2,000 00	2,000 00	
Maintenance of library	200 00	200 00	
Illinois State Asylum for Insane Criminals—			
Ordinary expenses	22,500 00	22,500 00	
Repairs and improvements	750 82	750 82	
Maintenance of library	208 60	73 59	135 01
Water supply	592 36	592 36	
Electric lighting	1,193 37	979 85	213 52
Furniture and repairs	3,649 90	3,649 90	
Plumbing, sewerage and excavating	2 83		2 83
Building road to Asylum	300 00	300 00	
Surgical instruments and apparatus	246 65	44 00	202 65
Illinois State Charitable Eye and Ear Infirmary—			
Ordinary expenses	22,500 00	22,500 00	
Repairs and improvements	927 79	927 79	
Maintenance of library	100 00	100 00	
Raising north wing of building, iron staircases, etc	2 55		2 55
Illinois State Home for Juvenile Female Offenders—			
Buildings, grounds, maintenance, etc	67,748 00	66,884 28	863 72
Ordinary expenses	32,000 00	32,000 00	
Illinois State Home for Soldiers' Orphans—			
Ordinary expenses	54,000 00	54,000 00	
Repairs and improvements	1,162 83	1,162 83	
Maintenance of library	481 58	481 58	
Illinois State Home for Soldiers and Sailors—			
Ordinary expenses	101,250 00	101,250 00	
Repairs and improvements	5,000 00	5,000 00	
Maintenance of library	549 13	549 13	
Improvement of grounds	3,467 75	3,467 75	
Roads, walks and stone gutters	2,000 00	2,000 00	
Painting	1,877 03	1,877 03	
Illinois State Hospital for Insane—Central—			
Ordinary expenses	133,200 00	133,200 00	
Repairs and improvements	4,134 76	4,134 76	
Maintenance of library	343 25	343 25	

Statement 5—Continued.

APPROPRIATIONS.	Balance unexpended October 1, 1894.	Warrants drawn since.	Amount lapsed into State Treasury, September 30, 1895.
Illinois State Hospital for Insane—Eastern—			
Ordinary expenses	$222,000 00	$222,000 00	.....
Repairs and improvements	6,806 07	6,806 07	.....
Maintenance of library	347 78	347 78	.....
Painting	2,767 78	2,767 78	.....
Furniture and fixtures	2,744 28	2,744 28	.....
Pipe covering	83 26	83 26	.....
Improvents of water supply	58 41	58 41	.....
Furnances, changin hot water tanks, laundry, etc	4,280 53	4,280 53	.....
Roads, walks, improvements of grounds and additional stock	874 22	874 22	.....
Illinois State Hospital for Insane—Northern—			
Ordinary expenses	111,000 00	111,000 00	.....
Repairs and improvements	4,910 54	4,910 54	.....
Improvement of of grounds	486 67	486 67	.....
Purchase of cows, etc	998 00	998 00	.....
Purchase of gas machine for laundry, etc	700 00	700 00	.....
Erection of amusent hall and gymnasium, etc	1 57	.....	$1 57
Replacing wires for electric lighting	1 47	.....	1 47
Addition to main and annex kitchens, etc	44 11	42 00	2 11
Construction of iron porches	1,500 00	1,500 00	.....
Illinois State Hospital for Insane—Southern—			
Ordinary expenses	99,900 00	99,900 00	.....
Repairs and improvements	5,055 65	5,055 65	.....
Maintenance of library	464 14	464 14	.....
Laying water pipe	988 02	984 22	3 80
New roads and improvement of grounds	949 00	949 00	.....
Covering steam pipes, additional machinery, etc	396 92	396 92	.....
Erection of cottage for consumptive, etc	7,985 00	7,985 00	.....
Painting	815 26	815 26	.....
Refurnishing center buildging	22 97	22 50	47
Additional stock and implements for farm	393 65	393 65	.....
Illinois State Institution for the Education of the Blind—			
Ordinary expenses	33,750 00	33,750 00	.....
Repairs and improvements	1,466 62	1,466 62	.....
Maintenance of library	564 09	564 09	.....
Erection of workshop, etc	1,042 07	1,042 07	.....
Brick paving in yard	68 44	68 44	.....
Illinois State Institution for the Deaf and Dumb—			
Ordinary expenses	75,000 00	75,000 00	.....
Repairs and improvents	3,290 76	3,290 76	.....
Maintenance of library	256 84	256 84	.....
New radiators and coiled steam fittings	551 55	551 55	.....
Wood carving	364 94	364 94	.....
Illinois State Normal University—Normal—			
Ordinary expenses	23,620 17	23,620 17	.....
Illinois State Normal University—Southern—			
Ordinary expenses	21,457 50	21,457 50	.....
Illinois State Penitentiary—Joliet—			
Maintenance of library	1,000 00	975 28	24 72
Illinois State Penitentiary—Southern—			
Ordinary expenses	70,000 00	70,000 00	.....
Maintenance of library	700 00	280 81	419 19
Building slaughter house	500 00	.....	500 00
Illinois State Reformatory—Pontiac—			
Ordinary expenses	58,750 00	58,750 00	.....
Barn for horses	1,000 00	1,000 00	.....
Illinois State University—Champaign—			
Payment of taxes	765 96	.....	765 96
Incidental expenses—			
Incidental expenses of Secretary of State	6,849 16	6,849 16	.....
Incidental expenses 38th G. A. or Secretary of State	13 53	.....	13 53
Laborers, janitors, watchmen and policemen of State House	4,380 58	4,380 58	.....

Statement 5—Continued.

Appropriations.	Balance unexpended October 1, 1894.	Warrants drawn since.	Amount lapsed into State Treasury September 30, 1895.
Lincoln Homestead Trustees—			
Salary of custodian	$833 34	$833 34	
Repairs on homestead	227 30	173 88	$53 42
Mine Inspectors—			
Traveling expenses	305 65	305 65	
Office of Governor—			
Private secretary, stenographer, etc	4,500 01	4,500 01	
Porter	525 01	525 01	
Incidental expenses	564 27	564 27	
Office of Lieutenant Governor—			
Incidental expenses	50 00	50 00	
Office of Secretary of State—			
Clerk hire	9,103 78	9,103 78	
Stenographers, etc	750 01	750 01	
Porter and messenger	1,168 10	1,168 10	
Office expenses	2,416 88	2 416 88	
Indexing records	2,258 84	2,258 84	
Care of document library	495 03	495 03	
Enforcing anti-trust law	4,384 70	4,384 70	
Office of Auditor of Public Accounts—			
Clerk hire	5,736 67	5,736 67	
Stenographer, etc	749 70	749 70	
Porter and messenger	1,049 40	1,049 40	
Office expenses	967 52	967 52	
Office of State Treasurer—			
Clerk hire	3,000 00	3,000 00	
Stenographer	562 50	562 50	
Messenger and clerk	600 00	600 00	
Watchmen	2,400 00	2,400 00	
Incidental expenses	1,224 80	1,224 80	
Office of Attorney General—			
Assistant	1,875 01	1,875 01	
Second assistant	1,350 00	1,350 00	
Stenographer	1,050 02	1,050 02	
Porter and messenger	525 01	525 01	
Incidental expenses	2,009 71	2,009 71	
Office of Adjutant General—			
Clerk hire	2,500 00	2,500 00	
Ordnance Sergeant, custodian of Memorial Hall, janitor, etc	2,573 81	2,573 81	
Incidental expenses	1,099 10	934 40	164 70
Office of Superintendent of Public Instruction—			
Clerk hire	3,100 00	3,100 00	
Janitor, porter and messenger	700 00	700 00	
Refurnishing office and library	125 99	83 10	42 89
Office expenses, etc	1,166 59	1,166 59	
Office of Insurance Superintendent—			
Clerk hire	11,541 70	11,541 70	
Incidental expenses	354 66	354 66	
Postage	3,837 00	3,837 00	
Expenses attending annual convention of insurance commissioners	145 72	145 72	
Legal expenses	7,962 50	7,955 59	6 91
Examinations and investigations	6,209 83	6,209 83	
Expenses attending World's Fair Auxiliary Congress	100 00		100 00
Printing paper and stationery	17,486 13	17,486 13	
Public printing	14,682 76	14,682 76	
Public binding	14,704 64	14,704 64	
Railroad and Warehouse Commissioners—			
Salary of Civil Engineers	2,250 00	2,250 00	
Office expenses and salary of Secretary	4,899 15	3,498 00	1,401 15
Suits and investigations	3,194 90	3,194 90	
Printing and publishing schedules	2,000 00	740 75	1,259 25
Printing and publishing railroad maps	2,400 00	1,892 00	508 00
Book cases	500 00		500 00
Repairs of roof and stone work of Capitol Building	789 37	789 37	
State Board of Equalization—			
Expenses	8,966 60	8,966 60	

Statement 5—Concluded.

Appropriations.	Balance unexpended October 1, 1894	Warrants drawn since.	Amount lapsed into State Treasury September 30, 1895.
State Board of Examiners for Mine Inspectors and Managers—			
Per diem and expenses	$1,049 32	$1,049 32	....
State Board of Health—			
Salary of Secretary	2,250 00	2,250 00	....
Salary of Assistant Secretary and clerks	3,112 59	3,112 59	....
Office expenses and janitor	1,765 39	1,765 39	....
Contingent fund for preventing and suppressing epidemics, etc	10,000 00	....	$10,000 00
State Board of Live Stock Commissioners and State Veterinarian—			
Per diem and expenses	11,568 60	11,567 48	1 12
Damages for animals slaughtered, property destroyed and disinfecting premises	23,695 19	1,794 54	21,900 65
State Historical Library and Natural History Museum—			
Salary of Curator	1,875 00	1,875 00	....
Salary of Assistant Curator	750 00	750 00	....
Salary of janitor	525 00	525 00	....
Expenses of Curator	354 75	354 75	....
State Library—			
Salary of Assistant Librarian	750 01	750 01	....
Purchase of books and incidental expenses	1,290 38	1,290 38	....
Storage Rooms, Secretary of State—			
Fitting up, etc	95 41	95 41	....
Furnishing, etc	283 95	283 95	....
World's Columbian Exposition—			
Illinois Board of World's Fair Commissioners	82,417 21	9,408 76	73,008 45
Display of dairyman's products	6,863 16	....	6,863 16
Display of manufactured clay products	439 39	....	439 39
Display of apiary products	26 15	....	26 15
Illinois Woman's Exposition Board	4,158 27	3,150 45	1,007 82
Pay of officers and members of the 39th General Assembly and salaries of State officers (estimated)	627,037 80	627,037 80	....
State School Fund—			
For distribution, including payment to County Superintendents of Schools for services and expenses (sum necessary)	135,611 34	135,611 34	....
Interest on State school fund	125 38	....	125 38
State Board of Agriculture and Agricultural Societies—			
County and other agricultural societies holding fairs ($100 each per annum)	8,300 00	8,300 00	....
Supreme Court Reports—			
Purchase of same (sum necessary)	6,268 50	6,268 50	....
Totals	$2,587,435 18	$2,454,524 67	$132,910 51

No. 6.

Appropriations made by the Thirty-Ninth General Assembly, the Amounts of Warrants Drawn thereon, and the Unexpended Balance.

Appropriations.	Amount.	Warrants drawn.	Unexpend'd balance.
Appellate Court—First District—			
Incidental expenses	$3,000 00	$1,616 73	$1,383 27
Librarian	1,000 00	583 32	416 68
Rent of court rooms, fuel and light	15,000 00	8,333 33	6,666 67
Purchase of law books	2,000 00	1,159 26	840 74
Rebinding law books	1,000 00	959 50	40 50
Appellate Court—Second District—			
Incidental expenses	3,000 00	1,487 03	1,512 97
Janitor	800 00	400 00	400 00
Appellate Court—Third District—			
Incidental expenses	2,000 00	713 63	1,286 37
Janitor	800 00	400 00	400 00
Appellate Court—Fourth District—			
Incidental expenses	2,000 00	989 36	1,010 64
Janitor	800 00	300 00	500 00
Blind—Institution for the Education of—			
Ordinary expenses	104,000 00	65,000 00	39,000 00
Repairs and improvements	2,000 00	1,966 94	33 06
Library for inmates	800 00	265 89	434 11
Repairs to organ	500 00	500 00	....
Gymnasium and drill hall	10,000 00	9,905 35	94 65
Piano and musical instruments	1,000 00	1,000 00	....
New boilers	3,000 00	3,000 00	....
Changing steam fittings and plumbing	2,000 00	2,000 00	....
Relaying floors, changing stairways, etc	5,000 00	5,000 00	....
Blind—Industrial Home for—			
Working capital	10,000 00	10,000 00	....
Completion of dormitory	7,000 00	7,000 00	....
Running expenses	20,000 00	20,000 00	....
Board of Live Stock Commissioners and State Veterinarian—			
Salary of Secretary	3,600 00	2,100 00	1,500 00
Salary of janitor	1,440 00	900 00	540 00
Damages, animals destroyed, property destroyed, etc	20,000 00	12,042 24	7,957 76
Incidental expenses, Secretary and Commissioners	4,000 00	3,067 00	933 00
Salaries of agents at stock yards	12,000 00	6,548 00	5,452 00
Salaries of State Veterinarian and assistants, and expenses	10,600 00	6,711 22	3,888 78
Incidental office expenses	2,400 00	1,150 19	1,249 81
Commission to mark position of Illinois troops at Chicamauga—			
Purchase of monuments and expenses of Commission	65,400 00	23,747 04	41,652 96
Commissioners of Lador Statistics—			
Salary of Secretary	5,000 00	3,125 00	1,875 00
Incidental expenses, clerical services, etc.	15,000 00	11,873 80	4,126 20
Commissioners of Public Charities—			
Salary of Secretary	6,000 00	4,000 00	2,000 00
Clerk hire, incidental expenses, etc	8,000 00	4,852 24	3,147 76
Contingent fund of Governor	4,000 00	3,300 18	699 82
Conveying convicts to and from penitentiary	40,000 00	23,506 80	16,493 20

Statement 6—Continued.

Appropriations.	Amount.	Warrants drawn.	Unexpend'd balance.
Conveying convicts to and from penitentiary (emergency)	$7,500 00	$7,500 00	....
Conveying convicts to and from reformatory	30,000 00	20,201 95	$9,798 05
Conveying convicts to and from reformatory (emergency)	20,000 00	20,000 00	....
Conveying juvenile female offenders to State Home	2,000 00	401 30	1,598 70
Conveying juvenile female offenders to State Home (emergency)	1,000 00	1,000 00	....
Costs and expenses of State suits	1,000 00	771 05	228 95
Cotton States and International Exposition at Atlanta, Ga	15,000 00	14,995 00	5 00
Deaf and Dumb—Institution for Education of—			
Ordinary expenses	200,000 00	125,000 00	75,000 00
Repairs and improvements	8,000 00	7,911 10	88 90
Library	1,000 00	541 08	458 92
Improvement of trade school and purchase of printing press	2,000 00	1,366 09	633 91
Cottage for boys and furnishing same	20,000 00	20,000 00	....
Otological laboratory	1,600 00	200 00	1,400 00
Water supply	8,000 00	8,000 00	....
Improvement of bathing facilities and plumbing	5,000 00	5,000 00	....
Boilers and repairs	2,000 00	2,000 00	....
Ice house	300 00	300 00	....
Eye and Ear Infirmary—Illinois Charitable—			
Ordinary expenses	52,000 00	32,500 00	19,500 00
Repairs and improvements	4,000 00	2,665 71	1,334 29
Library	200 00	55 82	144 18
Furniture, clothing and bedding	2,500 00	1,507 33	992 67
Instruments and apparatus	1,000 00	663 31	336 69
Reconstruction of annex	1,000 00	1,000 00	....
Household expenses	1,000 00	536 11	463 89
Executive Mansion and Grounds—			
Care, heating, lighting, etc	6,000 00	4,770 81	1,229 19
Factories and Workshops—Inspectors of—			
Salaries of Inspectors	20,000 00	....	20,000 00
Expenses of Inspectors	8,000 00	5,084 19	2,915 81
Feeble-Minded Children—Asylum for—			
Ordinary expenses	160,000 00	100,000 00	60,000 00
Repairs and improvements	4,000 00	2,000 00	2,000 00
Library for inmates	400 00	196 97	203 03
School house	10,000 00	10,000 00	....
New boiler	1,000 00	1,000 00	....
Fire apparatus—			
For State Capitol building	6,000 00	27 00	5,973 00
Fish Commissioners—			
Expenses, general	15,000 00	9,694 44	5,305 56
Personal and traveling expenses of commissioners and assistants in enforcing fishway laws	5,000 00	2,294 70	2,705 30
Flags for dome of Capitol	600 00	392 40	207 60
Fugitives from Justice—			
Apprehension and delivery of	16,000 00	7,367 30	8,632 70
Rewards for arrest	3,000 00	400 00	2,600 00
General Assembly—			
Pay of employés for 39th General Assembly (emergency)	115,000 00	114,359 50	640 50
Copying laws, journals, etc	600 00	81 50	518 50
Distributing laws, journals, etc	500 00	135 00	365 00
Expressage and postage on laws, journals, etc	2,400 00	2,264 68	135 32
Committee expenses, 39th General Assembly, appropriated by 38th General Assemly	1,000 00	1,000 00	....
Committee expenses 39th General Assembly (emergency)	10,000 00	9,295 89	704 11
Committee expenses, 40th General Assembly, appropriated by 39th General Assembly	1,000 00	....	1,000 00
Heating and Lighting State House—			
Heating, fuel, pay of engineers, firemen, etc	30,000 00	22,944 82	7,055 18
Lighting State House, pay of electrician and incidental expenses thereof	8,000 00	7,104 40	895 60

Statement 6—Continued.

Appropriations.	Amount.	Warrants drawn.	Unexpend'd balance.
Hospital for the Insane—Northern—			
Ordinary expenses	$300,000 00	$187,500 00	$112,500 00
Repairs and improvements	12,000 00	8,005 79	3,994 21
Library for inmates	1,000 00	547 03	452 97
Improvement of grounds	2,000 00	1,315 36	684 64
Cows	2,000 00	1,964 54	35 46
Construction of passageway	1,500 00	....	1,500 00
Inside and outside painting	3,000 00	1,979 92	1,020 08
Concrete walks	1,500 00	1,500 00	....
New boilers	6,000 00	5,999 32	68
New apparatus for laundry	500 00	499 38	62
Repairs to oven and purchase of dough mixer	500 00	500 00	....
Hospital for the Insane—Southern—			
Ordinary expenses	250,000 00	156,250 00	93,750 00
Repairs and improvements	8,000 00	3,706 26	4,293 74
Library for inmates	400 00	29 75	370 25
Painting	1,000 00	456 94	543 06
Rebuilding south dormitory and administration building	171,970 00	171,970 00	....
Reservoir and improvement of water supply	3,000 00	3,000 00	....
Hot water tank and pumps	5,000 00	421 06	4,578 94
Improvement of roads	1,500 00	49 68	1,450 32
Repairs to sidewalk	500 00	....	500 00
Reshingling barn and cottage	500 00	....	500 00
Furniture and equipment of new building	20,000 00	1,942 31	18,057 69
Hospital for the Insane—Eastern—			
Ordinary expenses	616,000 00	385,000 00	231,000 00
Repairs and improvements	30,000 00	14,192 95	15,807 05
Library for inmates	1,000 00	217 02	782 98
Painting	10,000 00	6,297 13	3,702 87
Furniture and fixtures	10,000 00	7,140 97	2,859 03
Reconstruction and improvement, heating and power plant	4,000 00	3,969 09	30 91
Reconstruction and improvement of plumbing	3,000 00	2,154 67	845 33
Material and work repairing slate roof	3,000 00	2,239 85	760 15
Addition for dining-room	1,000 00	983 92	16 08
Dairy house, material and work, repairing barn	2,500 00	2,470 73	29 27
Equipment and support of pathological laboratory	5,000 00	2,401 28	2,598 72
Cement walks	1,500 00	1,472 20	27 80
Additional live stock	2,000 00	1,956 50	43 50
Refitting basement for dining-rooms	5,000 00	4,485 89	514 11
Roads and improvements of grounds	2,000 00	746 31	1,253 69
Hospital for the Insane—Western—			
Purchase and location of side and construction of fire-proof building, etc	100,000 00	28,822 26	71,177 74
Hospital for the Insane—Central.			
Ordinary expenses	330,000 00	206,250 00	123,750 00
Repairs and Improvements	12,000 00	6,000 00	6,000 00
Library for inmates	800 00	800 00	....
Painting	4,000 00	2,000 00	2,000 00
Rebuilding old reservoir	5,000 00	5,000 00	....
New engine for electric light plant	4,000 00	4,000 00	....
New boilers	3,000 00	3,000 00	....
Coverting old amusement hall into wards, etc	2,000 00	....	2,000 00
Incurable Insane—Asylum for—			
Purchase of grounds, erection of building, etc	65,000 00	65,000 00	....
Insane Criminals—Asylum for—			
Ordinary expenses	52,000 00	32,500 00	19,500 00
Repairs and improvements	3,000 00	1,936 37	1,063 63
Library for inmates	500 00	44 00	456 00
Water supply	1,200 00	600 00	600 00
Electric lighting	1,000 00	400 00	600 00
Addition to building	20,000 00	20,000 00	....
Furnishing addition to building	3,000 00	686 90	2,313 10
Illinois National Guard—			
Expenses while in actual service, emergency	254,721 94	254,721 94	....
Uniforming and equiping, emergency	62,000 00	62,000 00	....
Ordinary expenses, emergency, to July 1, 1895	30,000 00	30,000 00	....
Ordinary expenses	360,000 00	281,167 80	78,832 20
Illinois State Dairyman's Association	2,000 00	2,000 00	....
Illinois State Historical Society—			
Salary of Librarian	1,200 00	750 00	450 00
Maintenance of library	3,200 00	1,974 36	1,225 64

Statement 6—Continued.

Appropriations.	Amount.	Warrants drawn.	Unexpend'd balance.
Illinois Horticultural Society	$8,000 00	$4,000 00	$4,000 00
Incidental expenses of Secretary of State in care of state house and grounds	25,000 00	20,818 13	4,181 87
Incidental expenses of 39th General Assembly and Secretary of State (emergency)	12,000 00	12,000 00	....
Interest on State school fund	114,000 00	113,874 62	125 38
Laborers, janitors, policemen and watchmen	12,000 00	8,406 65	3,593 35
Lincoln Homestead Trustees—			
Salary of custodian	1,200 00	700 00	500 00
Repairs at homestead	300 00	205 90	94 10
Lincoln Mouument Commissioners—			
Salary of custodian	2,000 00	1,098 55	901 45
Erection of building for custodian	2,500 00	2,500 00	....
Contingent fund for preserving, beautifying and repairing grounds, etc	30,000 00	3,469 46	26,530 54
Mine Inspectors' expenses	2,986 27	2,986 27	....
Expenses to July 1, 1895	1,000 00	1,000 00	....
Normal University at Normal—			
Ordinary expenses	70,000 00	43,750 00	26,250 00
Renewing heating plant and equiping main building	7,000 00	7,000 00	....
Erecting building for physical training, etc., heating and equiping	40,000 00	40,000 00	....
Normal University, Eastern—			
For erection of building, making improvements, furniture, etc	50,000 00	33,160 00	16,840 00
Normal University, Northern—			
For erection of building, making improvements, furniture, etc	50,000 00	30,000 00	20,000 00
Normal University, Southern—			
Ordinary expenses	57,220 00	35,762 50	21,457 50
Library, museum, etc	40,000 00	17,314 42	22,685 58
Officers—			
Governor—			
Private secretary and clerk hire	12,000 00	7,500 00	4,500 00
Incidental expenses	3,000 00	2,009 62	990 38
Porter	1,400 00	875 00	525 00
Lieutenant Governor—			
Office expenses	100 00	50 00	50 00
Secretary of State—			
Clerk hire	39,480 00	24,674 93	14,805 07
Office expenses	6,000 00	4,522 50	1,477 50
Extra clerk hire	3,000 00	1,890 00	1,110 00
Stenographer and typewriter	4,000 00	2,500 00	1,500 00
Porter and messenger	2,800 00	1,750 00	1,050 00
Auditor of Public Accounts—			
Office expenses	3,000 00	2,475 68	524 32
Porter and messenger	2,800 00	1,750 00	1,050 00
Stenographer and typewriter	2,000 00	1,250 00	750 00
Clerk hire	15,000 00	9,375 00	5,625 00
Extra clerk hire	3,000 00	1,530 00	1,470 00
State Treasurer—			
Clerk hire	1,500 00	9,375 00	5,625 00
Watchman	6,400 00	4,000 00	2,400 00
Messenger and clerk	1,600 00	1,000 00	600 00
Office expenses	2,000 00	1,330 73	669 27
Attorney General—			
Assistant	5,000 00	3,125 00	1,875 00
Second assistant	3,600 00	2,250 00	1,350 00
Stenographer	2,800 00	1,750 00	1,050 00
Porter and messenger	1,400 00	875 00	525 00
Incidental expenses	4,000 00	2,745 25	1,254 75
Legal expenses in relation to Building, Loan and Homstead Associations	6,000 00	3,901 67	2,098 33
Legal expenses in relation to insurance laws	12,000 00	7,383 00	4,617 00
Adjutant General—			
Clerk hire	7,500 00	4,687 50	2,812 50
Custodian of memorial hall	1,400 00	875 00	525 00
Stenographer	2,000 00	1,250 00	750 00
Acting assistant quarter master general	2,400 00	1,500 00	900 00
Sergeant-at-arms	1,200 00	750 00	450 00
Incidental expenses	2,000 00	1,096 15	903 85
Messenger	1,200 00	750 00	450 00

Statement 6—Continued.

Appropriations.	Amount.	Warrants drawn.	Unexpend'd balance.
Officers—*Continued*—			
Superintendent of Public Instruction—			
Assistant superintendent and clerk hire	$4,800 00	$3,000 00	$1,800 00
Office expenses	3,000 00	2,104 03	895 97
Janitor, porter and messenger	1,400 00	875 00	525 00
Stenographer	2,000 00	1,250 00	750 00
Insurance Superintendent—			
Clerk hire	30,000 00	18,352 04	11,647 96
Office expenses	6,000 00	3,667 45	2,332 55
Furnishing office	5,000 00	4,492 55	507 45
Expenses attending annual convention of insurance associations	250 00	250 00	....
Printing blank forms, etc., Farmers' Mutual Insurance Co.	1,000 00	1,000 00	....
Stenographer	2,400 00	1,400 00	1,000 00
Porter and messenger	1,400 00	875 00	525 00
Examinations and investigations	2,000 00	955 09	1,044 91
Paving street in front of State arsenal in Springfield.	288 60	288 60	....
Paving and curbing streets around State House and Executive Mansion grounds	8,000 00	7,941 29	58 71
Pay of officers and members of the 40th General Assembly and salaries of State officers (estimated)	892,000 00	376,222 69	515,777 31
Penitentiary—Joliet—			
Contingent expenses	100,000 00	50,000 00	50,000 00
Painting, relaying floors, etc	50,000 00	25,000 00	25,000 00
Artesian well	5,000 00	5,000 00	....
New hospital building fixtures, furniture, etc	25,000 00	25,000 00	....
Construction of building and walls for female convicts	75,000 00	75,000 00	....
Penitentiary—Southern—			
Ordinary expenses	100,000 00	80,000 00	20,000 00
Contingent expenses	10,000 00	10,000 00	....
Repairs and furnishings	5,000 00	5,000 00	....
Pump and fixtures	1,500 00	1,500 00	....
Maintaining library	500 00	250 00	250 00
Knitting machine and fixtures	2,500 00	2,500 00	....
Dust extracter and heater for pearl button factory	1,700 00	1,700 00	....
Material and construction of additional brick kilns	15,000 00	15,000 00	....
Material and construction of tramway and clay sheds	2,000 00	2,000 00	....
Material and construction of stone wall around prison	15,000 00	10,000 00	5,000 00
Excavating and removing useless stone and earth from penitentiary yard	2,500 00	2,500 00	....
Printing paper and stationery	26,000 00	24,335 63	1,664 37
Public printing	50,000 00	36,935 38	13,064 62
Public binding	16,000 00	13,233 74	2,766 26
Railroad and Warehouse Commissioners—			
Salary of civil engineer	6,000 00	3,750 00	2,250 00
Office expenses, including salary of secretary	8,000 00	3,236 01	4,763 99
Suits and investigations	8,000 00	4,687 18	3,312 82
Printing and publishing schedules	1,000 00	250 00	750 00
Printing and publishing railroad maps	2,400 00	1,200 00	1,200 00
Purchase of book cases, files and furniture	500 00	438 88	61 12
Reporter and Reports of Supreme Court—			
Completing work of office of Supreme Court reporter	1,000 00	1,000 00	....
Porter and messenger	1,440 00	840 00	600 00
School fund—for distribution, including payments to county superintendents for services and expenses (sum necessary)	2,000,000 00	1,885,821 34	114,178 66
Soldiers' Orphans' Home—			
Ordinary expenses	105,000 00	65,625 00	39,375 00
Repairs and improvements	2,000 00	1,956 51	43 49
Library for inmates	600 00	158 90	441 10
Painting	1,000 00	507 20	492 80
Building and furnishing addition to school house	1,800 00	1,769 15	30 85
Soldiers' and Sailors' Home—			
Ordinary expenses	299,000 00	186,875 00	112,125 00
Repairs and improvements	5,000 00	4,181 50	818 50
Library for inmates	500 00	200 38	299 62
Improvement of grounds	1,000 00	421 71	578 29
Painting	1,000 00	344 39	655 61

Statement 6—Continued.

Appropriations.	Amount.	Warrants drawn.	Unexpend'd balance.
Soldiers' and Sailors' Home—*Continued.*			
Storage house for vegetables	$1,500 00	$315 00	$1,185 00
Reconstruction of water closets	2,500 00	....	2,500 00
Cottage annex to hospital	18,000 00	18,000 00	....
Soldiers', Widows' Home—			
Purchase of site and building, fitting, furnishing and maintaining	20,000 00	12,500 00	7,500 00
State Board of Agriculture—			
Encouragement of exhibit	10,000 00	10,000 00	....
Salary of secretary	5,000 00	5,000 00	....
Clerk hire	4,400 00	4,400 00	....
Salary of curator	1,600 00	1,600 00	....
Porter	1,440 00	1,440 00	....
Agricultural museum	600 00	600 00	....
Live stock and agricultural statistics	1,200 00	1,200 00	....
Office expenses, etc	2,400 00	2,400 00	....
Grand stand	35,000 00	35,000 00	....
Machinery hall	75,000 00	75,000 00	....
Stables for horses and cattle	50,000 00	50,000 00	....
Sheep and swine building	18,000 00	18,000 00	....
Building for farm and orchard products	40,000 00	40,000 00	....
Improvement of grounds	7,000 00	7,000 00	....
County and other agricultural societies ($100 each per annum)	6,800 00	6,800 00	....
State Board of Equalization—			
Expenses	16,000 00	15,999 87	13
State Board of Examiners for Mine Inspectors and Mine Managers—	3,000 00	1,640 50	1,359 50
State Board of Health			
Salary of secretary	6,000 00	3,750 00	2,250 00
Salary of assistant secretary and clerk hire	5,900 00	3,700 00	2,200 00
Office expenses and sanitary inspection, including services of janitor	4,000 00	2,453 18	1,546 82
Contingent fund for preventing and suppressing epidemics, etc	10,000 00	....	10,000 00
Stenographer	1,440 00	900 00	540 00
Incidental expenses	660 00	406 65	253 35
State Historical Library and Natural History Museum—			
Salary of curator	5,000 00	3,125 00	1,875 00
Salary of assistant curator	2,000 00	1,250 00	750 00
Salary of janitor	1,400 00	875 00	525 00
Contingent, traveling and necessary expenses of curator	1,000 00	746 62	253 38
State Library—			
Salary of assistant librarian	2,000 00	1,250 00	750 00
Purchase of books and incidental expenses	3,000 00	1,537 36	1,462 64
State Laboratory of Natural History and State Entomologist—			
Field work, office and incidental expenses	3,000 00	3,000 00	....
Improvement of library	2,000 00	2,000 00	....
Salaries and assistants	7,300 00	7,300 00	....
Publication of bulletins	1,000 00	1,000 00	....
Report of State Entomologist—illustration of biennial	500 00	500 00	....
Expenses of experimental investigation of diseases of insects	3,000 00	3,000 00	....
One-half expenses Illinois Biological Station	3,000 00	3,000 00	....
State Reformatory—			
Ordinary expenses from February 15, to July 1, 1895, (emergency)	56,128 50	56,128 50	....
Ordinary expenses	260,000 00	146,750 00	113,250 00
Repairs and improvements	8,000 00	7,000 00	1,000 00
Library for inmates	1,000 00	500 00	500 00
Discharge and parole of prisoners	27,500 00	16,250 00	11,250 00
School books, maps and charts	1,500 00	1,500 00	....
Team, wagons and farm implements	1,500 00	1,500 00	....
Stand pipe and connections	5,000 00	2,500 00	2,500 00
Addition to new cell house	100,000 00	55,000 00	45,000 00
Completion of power house, etc	7,000 00	7,000 00	....
Water tube boiler and furnace	4,500 00	4,500 00	....
Maintenance and repairs, electric light service	3,000 00	500 00	2,500 00
Additional beds, bedding, furniture, etc	3,000 00	1,500 00	1,500 00
Equipment and maintenance of trade schools	15,000 00	6,000 00	9,000 00

Statement 6—Continued.

Appropriations.	Amount.	Warrants drawn.	Unexpended balance.
State Reformatory—*Continued.*			
Material to be used in trade instruction	$10,000 00	$3,000 00	$7,000 00
Additional cooking, bakery and laundry machinery	2,500 00	2,000 00	500 00
Additional engine, dynamo and arc light service	10,000 00	10,000 00	....
State Home for Juvenile Female Offenders—			
Ordinary expenses	30,000 00	15,000 00	15,000 00
Horses and carriage	350 00	213 00	137 00
Farm implements	100 00	22 00	78 00
Furnishing building	500 00	337 90	162 10
Library	400 00	215 73	184 27
Stable and other improvements	1,000 00	1,000 00	....
Improvementof grounds	500 00	360 16	139 84
Statutory Revision Commission	12,370 00	12,370 00	....
Supreme Court—Northern Grand Division—			
Incidental expenses	4,500 00	1,313 08	3,186 92
Librarian	1,000 00	500 00	500 00
Janitor	800 00	400 00	400 00
Purchase of law books and binding	500 00	198 77	301 23
Supreme Court—Central Grand Division—			
Incidental expenses	3,500 00	1,245 55	2,254 45
Librarian	2,000 00	1,000 00	1,000 00
Janitor	800 00	466 66	333 34
Supreme Court—Southern Grand Division—			
Incidental expenses	3,500 00	2,120 35	1,379 65
Librarian	1,000 00	500 00	500 00
Janitor	800 00	400 00	400 00
Supreme Court Reports—purchase of same (sum necessary)	5,660 25	5,660 25	....
University of Illinois—			
Payment of taxes	3,200 00	3,200 00	....
Salaries, maintenance and repairs, ordinary expenses	180,000 00	180,000 00	....
Library	6,000 00	6,000 00	....
Material for shop practice	3,000 00	3,000 00	....
Increase of scientific cabinets and collections	2,000 00	2,000 00	....
Completing, fitting and furnishing engineering hall	5,000 00	5,000 00	....
Extending equipment of college engineering, etc.	30,000 00	30,000 00	....
Improvement in chemical laboratory	5,000 00	5,000 00	....
Laboratory for vegetable physiology	2,000 00	2,000 00	....
Equipment and material for fire protection	2,000 00	2,000 00	....
Building for biological experiment station	2,500 00	2,500 00	....
One-half operating expenses of said station	3,000 00	3,000 00	....
Erection of library building for art, industrial and zoölogical collections	150,000 00	150,000 00	....
Astronomical observatory and equipment	15,000 00	15,000 00	....
Paving streets and laying walks	9,300 00	9,300 00	....
Propagation of pure vaccine virus	3,000 00	3,000 00	....
Addition to apparatus and appliances	6,000 00	6,000 00	....
Special Appropriations—			
To Samuel Warren for physical injuries received in February, 1895, while stopping a runway elevator in State Capitol, containing three children unattended	3,000 00	3,000 00	....
To Mark Clark for physical injuries inflicted by an explosion or blowing out of a steam valve in the Institution for the Blind at Jacksonville	1,000 00	1,000 00	....
To John Scanlon for physical injuries received as member Co. H, 7th Regiment, Illinois National Guard, by falling down elevator shaft at armory in Chicago awarded by Commission of Claims	750 00	750 00	....
To William E. Henry for loss of a part of foot and other serious and permanent injuries received while in discharge of duties as Corporal, Co. A, 3d Regiment, Illinois National Guard	2,500 00	2,500 00	....
To J. A. Cowlin for injuries received while in actual service as member of Co. G, 2d Regiment, Illinois National Guard, at World's Fair, Chicago, August 24, 1893	2,500 00	2,500 00	....
To C. P. Johnson for salary due as former Secretary of the State Board of Live Stock Commissioners, in full	200 00	200 00	....

Statement 6—Concluded.

Appropriations.	Amount.	Warrants drawn.	Unexpended balance.
State Appropriations—*Continued:*			
To Patrick R. Bannon amount in full for damages and costs awarded by Commission of Claims on account of real estate and other property overflowed by waters of dam, etc	$2,258 85	$2,258 85	....
To E. B. Whennan (E. B. Sherman) for services rendered in taking testimony in case of People, etc., v. Illinois Central R. R. Co., as directed by the Supreme Court of the United States	387 20	387 20	....
To John R. O'Conner for services rendered taking testimony as stenographer, in the case of the People of the State of Illinois v. Elizabeth Cooling, et al	800 00	800 00	....
To C. C. Walker (C. E. Walker) for services rendered taking testimony as stenographer, in the case of the People of the State of Illinois v. Continental Investment and Loan Company	600 00	600 00	....
To Charles Mills Rogers (George Mills Rogers) taking testimony as master in chancery, case of the People of the State of Illinois v. Elizabeth Cooling, et al	450 00	450 00	....
To Thomas Taylor, Jr., for services taking testimony as master in chancery, in case of the People of the State of Illinois v. Continental Investment and Loan Company	600 00	600 00	....
To Edward L. Merritt balance due as member 38th General Assembly, for services rendered under joint resolution	25 40	25 40	....
To Joseph W. Drury balance due as member 38th General Assembly, for services rendered under joint resolution	25 40	25 40	....
To Mary, Hiram, Ada, William, Darwin and Marquis McLaughlin, amount heretofore found to be due from the State of Illinois, by the Commission of Claims, at its session of A. D., 1892	400 00	400 00	....
To Greeley-Carlson Company, for survey of the inner break-water, between Oak and Pearson streets, Chicago, making plat showing same, also shore lines of 1883 and 1888, calculations, etc	75 00	75 00	....
Monument to be erected to the memory of Thomas Ford, late Governor of the State of Illinois	1,200 00	1,200 00	....
Memorial stone to the Key Monument Association, to the memory of Francis Scott Key, author of the Star Spangled Banner	300 00	....	$300 00
To E. P. Summers, for lumber furnished by him to State Reformatory at Pontiac	183 00	....	183 00
To Lovejoy Monument Association, for the purpose of erecting in the city of Alton, a suitable monument to the memory of Elijah P. Lovejoy	25,000 00	....	25,000 00
Totals	$10,055,800 41	$7,432,301 13	$2,623,499 28

No. 7—*Statement of Warrants outstanding October 1, 1894, and September 30, 1896.*

Amount of warrants outstanding October 1, 1894	$41,562 45
Amount of warrants issued from October 1, 1894, to September 30, 1896	12,569,753 21
Total	$12,611,315 66
Amount of warrants returned to Auditor's office, cancelled, to October 1, 1896	12,555,709 03
Amount of warrants outstanding September 30, 1896	$55,606 63

No. 8—*Statement of the Condition of the School, College and Seminary Funds, on the first day of October, 1896.*

Amount of surplus revenue credited to School Fund	$335,592 32	
Amount of three per cent. fund credited to School Fund	613,362 96	
		$948,955 28
Amount of three per cent. credited to College Fund		156,613 32
Amount of Seminary Fund		59,838 72
Total School, College and Seminary funds		$1,165,407 32
Paid two years' interest at six per cent. on the above funds, as follows—		
To the Normal University at Normal		$12,987 12
To the Southern Normal University		12,987 12
Distributed to counties, as per table		113,874 62
Total		$139,848 86

No. 9.

Statement of State Treasurer's Accounts with the Different State Funds, from October 1, 1894, to September 30, 1896, inclusive.

Dr. STATE TREASURER, IN ACCOUNT WITH THE STATE OF ILLINOIS. **Cr.**

Funds.	Amount in Treasury Oct. 1, 1894.	Amount received from Oct. 1, 1894, to Sept. 30, 1896, inclusive.	Total.	Funds.	Amount of warrants cancelled from Oct. 1, 1894, to Sept. 30, 1896, inclusive.	Balance in Treasury Oct. 1, 1896.	Total.
Revenue	$1,293,173 44	$6,746,067 62	$8,039,241 06	Revenue	$7,675,511 54	$363,729 52	$8,039,241 06
State School	144,794 04	2,009,011 89	2,153,805 93	State School	2,135,251 90	18,554 03	2,153,805 93
Unknown and Minor Heirs	11,334 24	....	11,334 24	Unknown and Minor Heirs	53 71	11,280 53	11,334 24
Total State Funds	$1,449,301 72	$8,755,079 51	$10,204,381 23	Total State Funds	$9,810,817 15	$393,564 08	$10,204,381 23

No. 10.

Statement showing the amount of Interest on School Fund and the amount of School Tax Fund distributed to the several counties in the State, for the years 1894 and 1895; the amount deducted from School Tax Fund for said years on account of Warrants issued to County Superintendents for services and expenses; also the number of Children in each county under the age of twenty-one years, according to the United States Census of 1890, on which said distributions were made.

Counties.	1894.						1895.					
	Number of children 1890.	Interest.	Tax.			Total tax and interest.	Number of children 1890.	Interest.	Tax.			Total tax and interest.
			Amt. paid Co. Supt. for services and expenses.	Amt. paid Co. Supt. for distribution.	Total.				Amt. paid Co. Supt. for services and expenses.	Amt. paid Co. Supt. for distribution.	Total.	
Adams	27,851	$883 97	$1,381 00	$14,144 23	$15,525 23	$16,409 20	27,851	$883 97	$1,364 00	$14,161 23	$15,525 23	$16,409 20
Alexander	7,785	247 09	1,101 00	3,238 66	4,339 66	4,586 75	7,785	247 09	788 00	3,551 66	4,339 66	4,586 75
Bond	7,564	240 08	1,308 00	2,908 46	4,216 46	4,456 54	7,564	240 08	1,402 00	2,814 46	4,216 46	4,456 54
Boone	4,962	157 49	910 00	1,856 01	2,766 01	2,923 50	4,962	157 49	937 00	1,829 01	2,766 01	2,923 50
Brown	5,906	187 45	1,207 00	2,085 23	3,292 23	3,479 68	5,906	187 45	1,252 00	2,040 23	3,292 23	3,479 68
Bureau	16,170	513 22	1,632 00	7,381 78	9,013 78	9,527 00	16,170	513 22	1,401 00	7,612 78	9,013 78	9,527 00
Calhoun	4,023	127 69	811 00	1,431 57	2,242 57	2,370 26	4,023	127 69	644 00	1,598 57	2,242 57	2,370 26
Carroll	8,148	258 61	1,346 00	3,196 01	4,542 01	4,800 62	8,148	258 61	1,349 00	3,193 01	4,542 01	4,800 62
Cass	7,648	242 74	1,137 00	3,126 29	4,263 29	4,506 03	7,648	242 74	1,130 00	3,133 29	4,263 29	4,506 03
Champaign	20,471	649 73	1,270 00	10,141 33	11,411 33	12,061 06	20,471	649 73	1,299 00	10,112 33	11,411 33	12,061 06
Christian	15,142	480 59	1,311 00	7,129 74	8,440 74	8,921 33	15,142	480 59	1,350 00	7,090 74	8,440 74	8,921 33
Clark	10,963	347 95	1,394 00	4,717 20	6,111 20	6,459 15	10,963	347 95	1,431 00	4,680 20	6,111 20	6,459 15
Clay	8,860	281 21	1,230 00	3,708 90	4,938 90	5,220 11	8,860	281 21	1,051 00	3,887 90	4,938 90	5,220 11
Clinton	9,201	292 03	900 00	4,228 99	5,128 99	5,421 02	9,201	292 03	900 00	4,228 99	5,128 99	5,421 02
Coles	14,704	466 69	1,424 00	6,772 58	8,196 58	8,663 27	14,704	466 69	1,434 00	6,762 58	8,196 58	8,663 27
Cook	523,030	16,600 45	1,323 00	290,234 32	291,557 32	308,157 77	523,030	16,600 45	1,356 00	290,201 32	291,557 32	308,157 77
Crawford	9,052	287 31	877 00	4,168 93	5,045 93	5,333 24	9,052	287 31	1,753 00	3,292 93	5,045 93	5,333 24
Cumberland	8,086	256 65	1,327 00	3,180 45	4,507 45	4,764 10	8,086	256 65	1,337 00	3,170 45	4,507 45	4,764 10
DeKalb	11,736	372 49	1,418 00	5,124 10	6,542 10	6,914 59	11,736	372 49	1,441 00	5,101 10	6,542 10	6,914 59
DeWitt	8,091	256 80	1,147 00	3,363 23	4,510 23	4,767 03	8,091	256 80	1,312 00	3,198 23	4,510 23	4,767 03
Douglas	8,681	275 53	1,283 00	3,556 12	4,839 12	5,114 65	8,681	275 53	1,402 00	3,437 12	4,839 12	5,114 65
DuPage	10,413	330 50	1,334 00	4,470 61	5,804 61	6,135 11	10,413	330 50	1,035 00	4,769 61	5,804 61	6,135 11
Edgar	12,872	408 54	1,328 00	5,847 35	7,175 35	7,583 89	12,872	408 54	1,311 00	5,864 35	7,175 35	7,583 89
Edwards	4,941	156 83	845 00	1,909 30	2,754 30	2,911 13	4,941	156 83	973 00	1,781 30	2,754 30	2,911 13
Effingham	10,205	323 90	1,110 00	4,578 66	5,688 66	6,012 56	10,205	323 90	1,130 00	4,558 66	5,688 66	6,012 56

No. 10—Continued.

Counties.	1894. Number of children 1890.	1894. Interest.	1894. Tax. Amt. paid Co. Supt. for services and expenses.	1894. Tax. Amt. paid Co. Supt. for distribution.	1894. Tax. Total.	1894. Total tax and interest.	1895. Number of children 1890.	1895. Interest.	1895. Tax. Amt. paid Co. Supt. for services and expenses.	1895. Tax. Amt. paid Co. Supt. for distribution.	1895. Tax. Total.	1895. Total tax and interest.
Fayette	12,574	$399 09	$1,385 00	$5,624 23	$7,009 23	$7,408 32	12,574	$399 09	$1,405 00	$5,604 23	$7,009 23	$7,408 32
Ford	8,540	271 06	1,590 00	3,170 53	4,760 53	5,031 59	8,540	271 06	1,212 00	3,548 53	4,760 53	5,031 59
Franklin	9,673	307 02	1,370 00	4,022 10	5,392 10	5,699 12	9,673	307 02	1,412 00	3,980 10	5,392 10	5,699 12
Fulton	20,373	646 62	1,334 00	10,022 70	11,356 70	12,003 32	20,373	646 62	1,312 00	10,044 70	11,356 70	12,003 32
Gallatin	8,116	257 59	915 00	3,609 17	4,524 17	4,781 76	8,116	257 59	958 00	3,566 17	4,524 17	4,781 76
Greene	11,622	368 88	966 00	5,512 55	6,478 55	6,847 43	11,622	368 88	1,123 00	5,355 55	6,478 55	6,847 43
Grundy	10,388	329 71	1,459 00	4,331 67	5,790 67	6,120 38	10,388	329 71	1,451 00	4,339 67	5,790 67	6,120 38
Hamilton	10,011	317 74	1,075 00	4,505 52	5,580 52	5,898 26	10,011	317 74	1,150 00	4,430 52	5,580 52	5,898 26
Hancock	14,416	457 55	1,372 00	6,664 04	8,036 04	8,493 59	14,416	457 55	1,408 00	6,628 04	8,036 04	8,493 59
Hardin	4,072	129 25	630 00	1,639 89	2,269 89	2,399 14	4,072	129 25	624 00	1,645 89	2,269 89	2,399 14
Henderson	4,632	147 02	685 00	1,897 05	2,582 05	2,729 07	4,632	147 02	1,081 00	1,501 05	2,582 05	2,729 07
Henry	15,261	484 37	1,334 00	7,173 07	8,507 07	8,991 44	15,261	484 37	900 00	7,607 07	8,507 07	8,991 44
Iroquois	17,508	555 69	1,308 00	8,451 64	9,759 64	10,315 33	17,508	555 69	1,356 00	8,403 64	9,759 64	10,315 33
Jackson	14,797	469 65	1,283 00	6,965 42	8,248 42	8,718 07	14,797	469 65	1,367 00	6,881 42	8,248 42	8,718 07
Jasper	10,043	318 76	1,005 00	4,593 36	5,598 36	5,917 12	10,043	318 76	1,320 00	4,278 36	5,598 36	5,917 12
Jefferson	12,159	385 91	1,380 00	5,397 90	6,777 90	7,163 81	12,159	385 91	760 00	6,017 90	6,777 90	7,163 81
Jersey	7,017	222 71	1,083 00	2,828 55	3,911 55	4,134 26	7,017	222 71	1,133 00	2,778 55	3,911 55	4,134 26
JoDaviess	11,542	366 33	1,197 00	5,236 96	6,433 96	6,800 29	11,542	366 33	1,317 00	5,116 96	6,433 96	6,800 29
Johnson	8,577	272 23	955 00	3,826 15	4,781 15	5,053 38	8,577	272 23	995 00	3,786 15	4,781 15	5,053 38
Kane	27,629	876 92	1,369 00	14,032 48	15,401 48	16,278 40	27,629	876 92	1,356 00	14,045 48	15,401 48	16,278 40
Kankakee	13,174	418 13	....	7,343 70	7,343 70	7,761 83	13,174	418 13	....	7,343 70	7,343 70	7,761 83
Kendall	5,351	169 84	1,309 00	1,673 85	2,982 85	3,152 69	5,351	169 84	1,326 00	1,656 85	2,982 85	3,152 69
Knox	16,693	529 82	1,394 00	7,911 33	9,305 33	9,835 15	16,693	529 82	1,398 00	7,907 33	9,305 33	9,835 15
Lake	10,459	331 96	1,594 00	4,236 25	5,830 25	6,162 21	10,459	331 96	1,397 00	4,433 25	5,830 25	6,162 21
LaSalle	38,250	1,214 02	1,334 00	19,988 04	21,322 04	22,536 06	38,250	1,214 02	1,314 00	20,008 04	21,322 04	22,536 06
Lawrence	7,654	242 93	1,125 00	3,141 63	4,266 63	4,509 56	7,654	242 93	1,178 00	3,088 63	4,266 63	4,509 56
Lee	11,770	373 57	1,351 00	5,210 05	6,561 05	6,934 62	11,770	373 57	1,588 00	4,973 05	6,561 05	6,934 62
Livingston	19,020	603 68	1,285 00	9,317 49	10,602 49	11,206 17	19,020	603 68	1,311 00	9,291 49	10,602 49	11,206 17
Logan	12,472	395 85	1,385 00	5,567 38	6,952 38	7,348 23	12,472	395 85	1,383 00	5,569 38	6,952 38	7,348 23
Macon	17,636	559 75	1,421 00	8,409 99	9,830 99	10,390 74	17,636	559 75	994 00	8,836 99	9,830 99	10,390 74
Macoupin	19,824	629 19	1,714 00	9,336 67	11,050 67	11,679 86	19,824	629 19	1,366 00	9,684 67	11,050 67	11,679 86
Madison	25,260	801 73	1,422 00	12,658 91	14,080 91	14,882 64	25,260	801 73	1,363 00	12,717 91	14,080 91	14,882 64
Marion	12,228	388 10	1,281 00	5,535 36	6,816 36	7,204 46	12,228	388 10	1,494 00	5,322 36	6,816 36	7,204 46
Marshall	6,078	192 91	1,288 00	2,100 11	3,388 11	3,581 02	6,078	192 91	1,438 00	1,950 11	3,388 11	3,581 02
Mason	7,874	249 91	1,315 00	3,074 27	4,389 27	4,639 18	7,874	249 91	1,414 00	2,975 27	4,389 27	4,639 18

Massac	5,908	187 51	818 00	2,475 35	3,293 35	3,480 86	5,908	187 51	803 00	2,490 35	3,293 35	3,480 86
McDonough	12,723	403 82	1,318 00	5,774 29	7,092 29	7,496 11	12,723	403 82	1,309 00	5,783 29	7,092 29	7,496 11
McHenry	11,595	368 01	1,475 00	4,988 50	6,463 50	6,831 51	11,595	368 01	1,464 00	4,999 50	6,463 50	6,831 51
McLean	28,954	918 97	1,353 00	14,787 08	16,140 08	17,059 05	28,954	918 97	1,378 00	14,762 08	16,140 08	17,059 05
Menard	6,279	199 29	954 00	2,546 15	3,500 15	3,699 44	6,279	199 29	996 00	2,504 15	3,500 15	3,699 44
Mercer	8,653	274 64	1,300 00	3,523 52	4,823 52	5,098 16	8,653	274 64	1,382 00	3,441 52	4,823 52	5,098 16
Monroe	6,832	216 84	1,306 00	2,502 42	3,808 42	4,025 26	6,832	216 84	1,310 00	2,498 42	3,808 42	4,025 26
Montgomery	14,878	472 21	1,303 00	6,990 57	8,293 57	8,765 78	14,878	472 21	1,424 00	6,869 57	8,295 57	8,765 78
Morgan	14,517	460 76	1,384 00	6,708 34	8,092 34	8,553 10	14,517	460 76	1,426 00	6,666 34	8,092 34	8,553 10
Moultrie	7,323	232 42	1,037 00	3,045 12	4,082 12	4,314 54	7,323	232 42	1,146 00	2,936 12	4,082 12	4,314 54
Ogle	12,860	408 16	1,352 00	5,816 66	7,168 66	7,576 82	12,860	408 16	1,367 00	5,801 66	7,168 66	7,576 82
Peoria	30,439	966 10	1,236 00	15,731 88	16,967 88	17,933 98	30,439	966 10	1,324 00	15,643 88	16,967 88	17,933 98
Perry	9,203	292 09	1,226 00	3,904 11	5,130 11	5,422 20	9,203	292 09	993 00	4,137 11	5,130 11	5,422 20
Piatt	8,366	265 53	1,262 00	3,401 53	4,663 53	4,929 06	8,366	265 53	1,366 00	3,297 53	4,663 53	4,929 06
Pike	14,911	473 26	1,332 00	6,979 97	8,311 97	8,785 23	14,911	473 26	1,343 00	6,968 97	8,311 97	8,785 23
Pope	8,082	256 51	850 00	3,655 22	4,505 22	4,761 73	8,082	256 51	902 00	3,603 22	4,505 22	4,761 73
Pulaski	6,053	192 12	1,275 00	2,099 17	3,374 17	3,566 29	6,053	192 12	1,139 00	2,235 17	3,374 17	3,566 29
Putnam	2,119	67 25	918 00	263 21	1,181 21	1,248 46	2,119	67 25	761 00	420 21	1,181 21	1,248 46
Randolph	12,627	400 77	1,187 00	5,851 78	7,038 78	7,439 55	12,627	400 77	1,306 00	5,732 78	7,038 78	7,439 55
Richland	7,721	245 06	438 00	3,865 98	4,303 98	4,549 04	7,721	245 06	766 00	3,537 98	4,303 98	4,549 04
Rock Island	19,474	618 09	1,359 00	9,496 56	10,855 56	11,473 65	19,474	618 09	1,343 00	9,512 56	10,855 56	11,473 65
Saline	10,770	341 83	1,072 00	4,931 61	6,003 61	6,345 44	10,770	341 83	1,140 00	4,863 61	6,003 61	6,345 44
Sangamon	28,196	894 91	1,428 00	14,289 55	15,717 55	16,612 46	28,198	894 91	1,422 00	11,295 55	15,717 55	16,612 46
Schuyler	7,933	251 79	1,037 00	3,385 16	4,422 16	4,673 95	7,933	251 79	1,072 00	3,350 16	4,422 16	4,673 95
Scott	4,923	156 25	1,087 00	1,657 27	2,744 27	2,900 52	4,933	156 25	1,023 00	1,721 27	2,744 27	2,900 52
Shelby	15,959	506 52	1,428 00	7,468 16	8,896 16	9,402 68	15,959	506 52	1,377 00	7,519 16	8,896 16	9,402 68
Stark	4,616	146 51	1,156 00	1,417 13	2,573 13	2,719 64	4,616	146 51	1,157 00	1,416 13	2,573 13	2,719 64
St. Clair	32,977	1,046 66	1,405 00	16,977 66	18,382 66	19,429 32	32,977	1,046 66	1,248 00	17,134 66	18,382 66	19,429 32
Stephenson	14,303	453 96	1,388 00	6,585 05	7,973 05	8,427 01	14,303	453 96	1,485 00	6,488 05	7,973 05	8,427 01
Tazewell	14,263	452 69	1,487 00	6,463 75	7,950 75	8,493 44	14,263	452 69	1,204 00	6,746 75	7,950 75	8,403 44
Union	11,555	366 74	1,136 00	5,305 20	6,441 20	6,807 94	11,555	366 74	1,014 00	5,427 20	6,441 20	6,807 94
Vermilion	24,275	770 46	1,292 00	12,239 83	13,531 83	14,302 29	24,275	770 46	1,295 00	12,236 83	13,531 83	14,302 29
Wabash	6,137	194 78	875 00	2,546 00	3,421 00	3,615 78	6,137	194 78	891 00	2,530 00	3,421 00	3.615 78
Warren	9,432	299 36	1,343 00	3,914 76	5,257 76	5,557 12	9,432	299 36	1,278 00	3,979 76	5,257 76	5,557 12
Washington	10,488	332 88	1,317 00	4,529 42	5,846 42	6,179 30	10,488	332 88	1,296 00	4,550 42	5,846 42	6,179 30
Wayne	13,228	419 84	1,761 00	5,612 80	7,373 80	7,793 64	13,228	419 84	1,371 00	6,002 80	7,373 80	7,793 64
White	13,449	426 86	1,167 00	6,329 99	7,496 99	7,923 85	13,449	426 86	1,266 00	6,230 99	7,496 99	7,923 85
Whiteside	14,064	446 38	1,334 00	6,505 82	7,839 82	8,286 20	14,064	446 38	1,360 00	6,479 82	7,839 82	8,286 20
Will	28,882	916 69	1,765 00	14,334 95	16,099 95	17,016 64	29,882	916 69	1,094 00	15,005 95	16,099 95	17,016 64
Williamson	12,465	395 63	1,159 00	5,789 47	6,948 47	7,344 10	12,465	395 63	901 00	6,047 47	6,948 47	7,344 10
Winnebago	16,704	530 17	1,369 00	7,942 46	9,311 46	9,841 63	16,704	530 17	1,424 00	7,887 46	9,311 46	9,841 63
Woodford	10,585	335 96	1,424 00	4,476 49	5,900 49	6,236 45	10,585	335 96	1,467 00	4,433 49	5,900 49	6,236 45
Total	1,793,919	$56,937 31	$125,380 00	$874,620 00	$1,000,000 00	$1,056,937 31	1,793,919	$56,937 31	$124,419 00	$875,581 00	$1,000,000 00	$1,056,937 31

No. 11.

Statement of the aggregate amount of State Taxes charged on the tax books for the year 1894, (including back taxes) the amount of abatements, commissions, etc., and the net amount collected, and amount paid State Treasurer.

Counties.	Amount charged.	Abatements.			Net amount collected and paid State Treasurer.
		Ordinary abatements, including errors, insolvencies, forfeitures, commissions, etc.	Enjoined from collection on property of railroads and other corporations..........	Total.	
Adams	$37,736 23	$1,449 01	$34 31	$1,483 32	$36,252 91
Alexander	7,704 21	404 92	109 14	514 06	7,190 15
Bond	9,030 92	944 62	....	944 62	8,086 30
Boone	10,612 80	473 45	....	473 45	10,139 35
Brown	6,328 08	261 42	....	261 42	6,066 66
Bureau	31,044 92	981 15	....	981 15	30,063 77
Calhoun	4,015 80	240 93	....	240 93	3,774 87
Carroll	14,267 95	580 91	....	580 91	13,687 04
Cass	10,752 55	430 78	....	430 78	10,321 77
Champaign	30,490 04	1,182 48	....	1,182 48	29,307 56
Christian	25,908 19	947 77	3,702 95	4,650 72	21,257 47
Clark	8,657 60	365 82	....	365 82	8,291 78
Clay	5,737 04	242 89	....	242 89	5,494 15
Clinton	10,356 67	610 84	....	610 84	9,745 83
Coles	16,335 93	647 52	....	647 52	15,688 41
Cook	861,014 90	33,072 04	....	33,072 04	827,942 86
Crawford	5,655 43	270 69	....	270 69	5,384 74
Cumberland	5,343 46	246 80	....	246 80	5,096 66
DeKalb	24,134 75	846 89	....	846 89	23,287 86
DeWitt	11,271 79	411 77	....	411 77	10,860 02
Douglas	12,821 66	487 14	....	487 14	12,334 52
DuPage	19,364 44	777 46	....	777 46	18,586 98
Edgar	18,711 04	680 12	....	680 12	18,030 92
Edwards	4,718 65	211 53	....	211 53	4,507 12
Effingham	8,889 64	387 21	....	387 21	8,502 43
Fayette	10,362 99	406 05	....	406 05	9,956 94
Ford	10,203 35	396 89	....	396 89	9,806 46
Franklin	4,151 26	356 80	....	356 80	3,794 46
Fulton	28,039 14	1,255 66	....	1,255 66	26,783 48
Gallatin	4,890 91	268 29	....	268 29	4,622 62
Greene	17,583 25	888 69	1,069 91	1,958 60	15,624 65
Grundy	14,010 12	858 54	....	858 54	13,151 58
Hamilton	5,079 00	255 74	....	255 74	4,823 26
Hancock	25,418 41	958 31	1,634 17	2,592 48	22,825 93
Hardin	1,766 34	153 40	....	153 40	1,612 94
Henderson	9,141 51	384 49	....	384 49	8,757 02
Henry	29,299 42	939 43	....	939 43	28,359 99
Iroquois	25,849 92	802 08	....	802 08	25,047 84
Jackson	8,833 52	725 37	....	725 37	8,108 15
Jasper	5,425 78	253 19	....	253 19	5,172 59
Jefferson	7,624 99	665 36	....	665 36	6,959 63
Jersey	10,516 01	423 61	....	423 61	10,092 40
Jo Daviess	12,742 26	521 10	....	521 10	12,221 16
Johnson	5,849 26	418 00	849 43	1,267 43	4,581 83
Kane	44,919 79	1,478 15	11 13	1,489 28	43,430 51
Kankakee	15,794 69	598 86	....	598 86	15,195 83
Kendall	11,946 93	480 44	....	480 44	11,466 49
Knox	32,889 42	1,034 28	....	1,034 28	31,855 14
Lake	22,956 88	889 21	....	889 21	22,067 67
LaSalle	51,954 32	1,934 14	....	1,934 14	50,020 18
Lawrence	5,831 05	284 74	....	284 74	5,546 31
Lee	21,034 24	674 08	....	674 08	20,360 16
Livingston	31,608 46	995 41	....	995 41	30,613 05
Logan	24,082 85	2,636 78	....	2,636 78	21,446 07
Macon	27,880 80	1,151 67	....	1,151 67	26,729 13
Macoupin	31,633 28	2,087 63	2,519 66	4,607 29	27,025 99
Madison	43,592 58	2,047 34	4,144 60	6,191 94	37,400 64
Marion	12,171 40	533 47	....	533 47	11,637 93
Marshall	12,571 28	486 79	....	486 79	12,084 49

Statement 11—Concluded.

Counties.	Amount charged.	Abatements.			Net amount collected and paid State Treasurer.
		Ordinary abatements, including errors, insolvencies, forfeitures, commissions, etc.	Enjoined from collection on property of railroads and other corporations.	Total.	
Mason	$20,325 11	$9,552 62	.....	$9,552 62	$10,772 49
Massac	4,994 77	293 10	.....	293 10	4,701 67
McDonough	21,302 02	671 49	.....	671 49	20,630 53
McHenry	20,095 03	802 06	.....	802 06	19,292 97
McLean	54,354 49	1,652 66	.....	1,652 66	52,701 83
Menard	10,708 15	338 66	.....	338 66	10,369 49
Mercer	16,201 09	896 32	.....	896 32	15,304 77
Monroe	8,397 04	654 32	.....	654 32	7,742 72
Montgomery	20,242 61	803 33	.....	803 33	19,439 28
Morgan	24,910 98	688 08	.....	688 08	24,222 90
Moultrie	9,538 38	362 22	.....	362 22	9,176 16
Ogle	25,786 98	832 06	.....	832 06	24,954 92
Peoria	45,546 05	1,355 35	$46 50	1,401 85	44,144 20
Perry	6,661 17	382 14	.....	382 14	6,279 03
Piatt	14,260 05	524 44	443 34	967 78	13,292 27
Pike	22,288 17	2,242 24	97 03	2,339 27	19,948 90
Pope	4,869 61	1,675 65	.....	1,675 65	3,193 96
Pulaski	2,835 35	354 39	.....	354 39	2,480 96
Putnam	4.118 53	189 83	.....	189 83	3,928 70
Randolph	13,676 53	2,379 44	.....	2,379 44	11,297 09
Richland	6.285 69	295 75	.....	295 75	5,989 94
Rock Island	21,533 59	900 21	.....	990 21	20,543 38
Saline	4,543 84	277 58	.....	277 58	4,266 26
Sangamon	44,262 05	1,627 76	.....	1,627 76	42,634 29
Schuyler	9,201 07	479 31	.....	479 31	8,721 76
Scott	7,897 57	248 12	.....	248 12	7.649 45
Shelby	18,636 09	593 22	145 97	739 19	17,896 90
Stark	11,016 62	390 18	1,055 03	1,445 21	9,571 41
St. Clair	45,884 60	3,666 41	855 27	4,521 68	41,362 92
Stephenson	24,089 10	815 37	.....	815 37	23,273 73
Tazewell	24.872 48	861 16	267 63	1,128 79	23,743 69
Union	6,170 63	298 69	.....	298 69	5,871 94
Vermilion	34,138 94	1,106 47	.....	1,106 47	33,032 47
Wabash	5,241 20	191 68	524 43	716 11	4,525 09
Warren	19,744 28	753 71	.....	753 71	18,990 57
Washington	11,289 72	470 96	.....	470 96	10,818 76
Wayne	6,392 18	306 03	.....	306 03	6,086 10
White	8,579 96	489 41	.....	489 41	8,090 55
Whiteside	24,634 09	843 44	.....	843 44	23,790 65
Will	46,082 84	1,840 33	.....	1,840 33	44,242 51
Williamson	6.283 46	255 97	.....	255 97	6.027 49
Winnebago	34,491 87	1,071 8	.....	1,071 88	33.419 99
Woodford	15,956 82	971 02	.....	971 02	14,985 80
Total	$2,616,900 85	$120,895 21	$17,510 50	$138,405 71	$2.478,495 14

No. 12.

Statement of the aggregate amount of State taxes charged on the tax books for the year 1895 (including back taxes), the amount of abatements, commissions, etc., and the net amount collected and paid State Treasurer.

Counties.	Amount charged.	Abatements.			Net amount collected and paid State Treasurer.
		Ordinary abatements, including errors, insolvencies, forfeitures, commissions, etc.	Enjoined from collection on property of railroads and other corporations	Total.	
Adams	$63,195 39	$2,097 51	....	$2,097 51	$61,097 88
Alexander	13,322 36	676 66	$109 14	785 80	12,536 56
Bond	14,824 20	926 33	....	926 33	13,897 87
Boone	18,124 06	713 19	....	713 19	17,410 87
Brown	10,594 62	413 52	....	413 52	10,181 10
Bureau	53,310 42	1,572 75	....	1,572 75	51,737 67
Calhoun	6,278 48	319 44	....	319 44	5,959 04
Carroll	24,469 66	954 50	....	954 50	23,515 16
Cass	18,417 60	827 86	....	827 86	17,589 74
Champaign	50,421 48	1,786 89	....	1,786 89	48,634 59
Christian	41,959 24	1,380 75	3,702 95	5,083 70	36,875 54
Clark	15,832 00	615 35	....	615 35	15,216 65
Clay	9,548 98	398 81	....	398 81	9,150 17
Clinton	17,906 93	1,197 73	....	1,197 73	16,709 20
Coles	26,570 06	1,024 67	....	1,024 67	25,545 39
Cook	1,413,649 59	55,930 58	....	55,930 58	1,357,719 01
Crawford	10,579 13	445 98	....	445 98	10,133 15
Cumberland	9,142 60	387 53	....	387 53	8,755 07
DeKalb	42,879 15	1,391 85	....	1,391 85	41,487 30
DeWitt	20,598 21	836 88	....	836 88	19,761 33
Douglas	21,957 27	851 52	....	851 52	21,105 75
DuPage	33,004 34	1,241 58	....	1,241 58	31,762 76
Edgar	31,605 19	986 65	....	986 65	30,618 54
Edwards	8,041 71	317 38	....	317 38	7,724 33
Effingham	15,110 49	577 13	....	577 13	14,533 36
Fayette	17,210 81	667 34	....	667 34	16,543 47
Ford	17,188 44	642 49	....	642 49	16,545 95
Franklin	7,090 48	385 75	....	385 75	6,704 73
Fulton	47,219 76	1,687 44	....	1,687 44	45,532 32
Gallatin	8,427 05	387 51	....	387 51	8,039 54
Greene	28,687 34	1,353 95	....	1,353 95	27,333 39
Grundy	25,058 48	1,262 81	....	1,262 81	23,795 67
Hamilton	8,251 50	377 32	....	377 32	7,874 18
Hancock	42,950 14	1,962 90	1,634 17	3,597 07	39,353 07
Hardin	2,840 13	187 74	....	187 74	2,652 39
Henderson	15,236 44	646 51	....	646 51	14,589 93
Henry	49,749 57	1,525 03	....	1,525 03	48,224 54
Iroquois	44,443 20	1,366 92	....	1,366 92	43,076 28
Jackson	15,127 78	727 04	....	727 04	14,400 74
Jasper	9,849 65	421 10	....	421 10	9,428 55
Jefferson	13,137 95	872 15	....	872 15	12,265 80
Jersey	19,670 09	725 48	....	725 48	18,944 61
Jo Daviess	22,404 68	832 30	....	832 30	21,572 38
Johnson	10,089 16	655 70	849 43	1,505 13	8,584 03
Kane	74,281 03	2,370 10	11 13	2,381 23	71,899 80
Kankakee	27,888 72	1,039 79	....	1,039 79	26,848 93
Kendall	17,840 55	701 65	....	701 65	17,138 90
Knox	56,821 76	1,860 19	....	1,860 19	54,961 57
Lake	39,403 90	1,431 35	....	1,431 35	37,972 55
LaSalle	87,311 15	3,036 88	....	3,036 88	84,274 27
Lawrence	10,679 46	474 08	....	474 08	10,205 38
Lee	36,058 20	1,122 07	....	1,122 07	34,936 13
Livingston	55,306 37	1,664 27	....	1,664 27	53,642 10
Logan	39,516 45	2,619 42	....	2,619 42	36,897 03
Macon	48,336 35	1,773 08	....	1,773 08	46,563 27
Macoupin	51,369 11	2,760 16	2,519 66	5,279 82	46,089 29
Madison	70,433 77	2,751 95	4,144 60	6,896 55	63,537 22
Marion	20,901 32	845 77	....	845 77	20,055 55
Marshall	21,176 48	806 39	....	806 39	20,370 09

Statement 12—Concluded.

Counties.	Amount charged.	Abatements. Ordidary abatements, including errors, insolvencies, forfeitures, commissions, etc.	Abatements. Enjoined from collection on property of railroads and other corporations	Abatements. Total.	Net amount collected and paid State Treasurer.
Mason	$20,373 84	$1,132 00	....	$1,132 00	$19,241 84
Massac	8,305 22	359 83	....	359 83	7,945 39
McDonough	36,047 73	1,104 97	....	1,104 97	34,942 76
McHenry	31,195 25	1,195 68	....	1,195 68	29,999 57
McLean	94,414 16	2,952 45	....	2,952 45	91,461 71
Menard	18,230 03	566 89	....	566 89	17,663 14
Mercer	28,339 52	1,387 57	....	1,387 57	26,951 95
Monroe	14,205 63	535 62	....	535 62	13,670 01
Montgonery	34,899 78	1,155 10	....	1,155 10	33,744 68
Morgan	43,139 89	1,077 11	....	1,077 11	42,062 78
Moultrie	16,506 88	605 55	....	605 55	15,901 33
Ogle	43,378 93	1,445 34	....	1,445 34	41,933 59
Peoria	77,207 00	2,697 35	....	2,697 35	74,509 65
Perry	12,268 69	640 89	....	640 89	11,627 80
Piatt	24,165 47	864 99	443 34	1,308 33	22,857 14
Pike	34,989 74	3,336 17	....	3,336 17	31,653 57
Pope	6,344 84	580 22	....	580 22	5,764 62
Pulaski	5,483 24	444 79	....	444 79	5,038 45
Putnam	7,349 79	299 03	....	299 03	7,040 76
Randolph	22,747 02	2,857 58	....	2,857 58	19,889 44
Richland	9,508 77	398 56	....	398 56	9,110 21
Rock Island	35,283 80	1,373 50	....	1,373 50	33,910 30
Saline	8,522 77	466 77	....	466 77	8,066 00
Sangamon	76,929 81	2,304 48	....	2,304 48	74,625 33
Schuyler	15,384 80	586 11	....	586 11	14,798 69
Scott	13,792 13	526 66	....	526 66	13,265 47
Shelby	32,418 46	1,078 94	145 97	1,224 91	31,193 55
Stark	18,954 16	664 12	1,055 03	1,719 15	17,235 01
St. Clair	80,351 82	7,268 97	....	7,268 97	73,082 85
Stephenson	42,101 78	1,390 64	....	1,390 64	40,711 14
Tazewell	41,218 24	1,374 17	....	1,374 17	39,844 07
Union	10,650 38	484 73	....	484 73	10,165 65
Vermilion	64,203 22	2,012 18	....	2,012 18	62,191 04
Wabash	8,337 52	377 96	524 43	902 39	7,435 13
Warren	33,736 33	1,216 75	....	1,216 75	32,519 58
Washington	18,375 99	719 06	....	719 06	17,656 93
Wayne	10,810 93	490 09	....	490 09	10,320 84
White	13,972 63	685 24	....	685 24	13,287 39
Whiteside	38,935 00	1,275 82	....	1,275 82	37,659 18
Will	74,890 76	2,405 86	....	2,405 86	72,484 90
Williamson	10,885 01	473 86	....	473 86	10,411 15
Winnebago	57,755 23	1,816 64	....	1,816 64	55,938 59
Woodford	28,274 17	1,192 83	....	1,192 83	27,081 34
Total	$4,378,186 79	$175,640 74	$15,139 85	$190,780 59	$4,187,406 20

No. 13.

Statement showing the aggregate amount of School Fund Tax charged on the tax books of 1894 (including back taxes), the amount deducted for abatements, commissions, etc., the net amount collected, the amount paid to each County, etc.

Counties.	Amount charged.	Amount of abatements, commissions, etc.	Net amount collected.	Amount paid county.	Amount received from county over amount paid.	Amount paid county over amount received.
Adams	$15,216 23	$598 14	$14,618 09	$15,525 23	....	$907 14
Alexander	3,106 54	207 30	2,899 24	4,339 66	....	1,440 42
Bond	3,641 51	380 90	3,260 61	4,216 46	....	955 85
Boone	4,279 35	190 91	4,088 44	2,766 01	$1,322 43	....
Brown	2,551 65	105 41	2,446 24	3,292 23	....	845 99
Bureau	12,518 11	395 63	12,122 48	9,013 78	3,108 70	....
Calhoun	1,619 28	97 15	1,522 13	2,242 57	....	720 44
Carroll	5,753 19	234 22	5,518 97	4,542 01	976 96	....
Cass	4,335 70	173 69	4,162 01	4,263 29	....	101 28
Champaign	12,294 37	476 80	11,817 57	11,411 33	406 24	....
Christian	10,446 85	1,875 29	8,571 56	8,440 74	130 82	....
Clark	3,490 97	147 52	3,343 45	6,111 20	....	2,767 75
Clay	2,313 32	97 93	2,215 39	4,938 90	....	2,723 51
Clinton	4,176 07	246 30	3,929 77	5,128 99	....	1,199 22
Coles	6,587 06	261 10	6,325 96	8,196 58	....	1,870 62
Cook	347,183 43	13,335 53	333,847 90	291,557 32	42,290 58	....
Crawford	2,280 42	109 16	2,171 26	5,045 93	....	2,874 67
Cumberland	2,154 61	99 51	2,055 10	4,507 45	....	2,452 35
DeKalb	9,731 75	341 49	9,390 26	6,542 10	2,848 16	....
DeWitt	4,543 07	164 26	4,378 81	4,510 23	....	131 42
Douglas	5,170 02	196 42	4,973 60	4,839 12	134 48	....
DuPage	7,808 23	313 48	7,494 75	5,804 61	1,690 14	....
Edgar	7,544 77	274 24	7,270 53	7,175 35	95 18	....
Edwards	1,902 68	85 30	1,817 38	2,754 30	....	936 92
Effingham	3,584 52	156 12	3,428 40	5,688 66	....	2,260 26
Fayette	4,178 63	163 75	4,014 88	7,009 23	....	2,994 35
Ford	4,114 26	160 05	3,954 21	4,760 53	....	806 32
Franklin	1,673 89	143 86	1,530 03	5,392 10	....	3,862 07
Fulton	11,306 09	506 31	10,799 78	11,356 70	....	556 92
Gallatin	1,972 14	108 35	1,863 79	4,524 17	....	2,660 38
Greene	7,090 02	789 75	6 300 27	6,478 55	....	178 28
Grundy	5,649 24	346 19	5,303 05	5,790 67	....	487 62
Hamilton	2,047 99	103 13	1,944 86	5,580 52	....	3,635 66
Hancock	10,249 36	1,045 36	9,204 00	8,036 04	1,167 96	....
Hardin	712 22	61 85	650 37	2,269 89	....	1,619 52
Henderson	3,686 09	155 03	3,531 06	2,582 05	949 01	....
Henry	11,814 29	378 81	11,435 48	8,507 07	2,928 41	....
Iroquois	10,423 34	323 40	10,099 94	9,759 64	340 30	....
Jackson	3,561 87	292 46	3,269 41	8,248 42	....	4,979 01
Jasper	2,187 81	102 10	2,085 71	5,598 36	....	3,512 65
Jefferson	3,074 59	268 30	2,806 29	6,777 90	....	3,971 61
Jersey	4,240 33	170 83	4,069 50	3,911 55	157 95	....
JoDaviess	5,138 00	210 12	4,927 88	6,433 96	....	1,506 08
Johnson	2,358 57	511 06	1,847 51	4,781 15	....	2,933 64
Kane	18,112 80	600 51	17,512 29	15,401 48	2,110 81	....
Kankakee	6,368 83	241 41	6,127 42	7,343 70	....	1,216 28
Kendall	4,817 31	193 73	4,623 58	2,982 85	1,640 73	....
Knox	13,261 86	417 04	12,844 82	9,305 33	3,539 49	....
Lake	9,256 81	358 56	8,898 25	5,830 25	3,068 00	....
LaSalle	20,949 33	779 92	20,169 41	21,322 04	....	1,152 63
Lawrence	2,351 23	114 76	2,236 47	4,266 63	....	2,030 16
Lee	8,481 55	271 81	8,209 74	6,561 05	1,648 69	....
Livingsnon	12,745 52	401 55	12,343 97	10,602 49	1,741 48	....
Logan	9,710 83	1,063 23	8,647 60	6,952 38	1,695 22	....
Macon	11,242 25	464 37	10,777 88	9,830 99	946 89	....
Macoupin	12,755 36	1,857 78	10,897 58	11,050 67	....	153 09
Madison	17,577 64	2,496 73	15,080 91	14,080 91	1,000 00	....
Marion	4,907 85	215 15	4,692 70	6,816 36	....	2,123 66
Marshall	5,069 05	196 28	4,872 77	3,388 11	1,484 66	....
Mason	8,195 60	3,851 85	4,343 75	4,389 27	....	45 52
Massac	2,014 06	118 22	1,895 84	3,293 35	....	1,397 51
McDonough	8,589 54	270 78	8,318 76	7,092 29	1,226 47	....
McHenry	8,102 83	323 40	7,779 43	6,463 50	1,315 93	....
McLean	21,917 13	666 41	21,250 72	16,140 08	5,110 64	....

Statement 13—Concluded.

COUNTIES.	Amount charged.	Amount of abatements, commissions, etc.	Net amount collected.	Amount paid county.	Amount received from county over amount paid.	Amount paid county over amount received.
Menard	$4,317 76	$136 52	$4,181 24	$3,500 15	$681 09	....
Mercer	6,532 69	361 42	6,171 27	4,823 52	1,347 75	....
Monroe	3,385 91	263 86	3,122 05	3,808 42	....	$686 37
Montgomery	8,162 33	323 92	7,838 41	8,293 57	....	455 16
Morgan	10,044 75	277 46	9,767 29	8,092 34	1,674 95	....
Moultrie	3,846 13	146 06	3,700 07	4,082 12	....	382 05
Ogle	10,397 97	335 50	10,062 47	7,168 66	2,893 81	....
Peoria	18,365 34	565 25	17,800 09	16,967 88	832 21	....
Perry	2,685 93	154 07	2,531 86	5,130 11	....	2,598 25
Piatt	5,750 03	390 25	5,359 78	4,663 53	696 25	....
Pike	8,987 17	943 26	8,043 91	8,311 97	....	268 06
Pope	1,963 55	675 66	1,287 89	4,505 22	....	3,217 33
Pulaski	1,143 28	142 89	1,000 39	3,374 17	....	2,373 78
Putnam	1,660 70	76 55	1,584 15	1,181 21	402 94	....
Randolph	5,514 73	959 46	4,555 27	7,038 78	....	2,483 51
Richland	2,534 55	119 26	2,415 29	4,303 98	....	1,888 69
Rock Island	8,682 90	399 29	8,283 61	10,855 56	....	2,571 95
Saline	1,832 20	111 94	1,720 26	6,003 61	....	4,283 35
Sangamon	17,847 60	656 35	17,191 25	15,717 55	1,473 70	....
Schuyler	3,710 11	193 27	3,516 84	4,422 16	....	905 32
Scott	3,184 50	100 05	3,084 45	2,744 27	340 18	....
Shelby	7,514 56	298 07	7,216 49	8,896 16	....	1,679 67
Stark	4,442 18	582 74	3,859 44	2,573 13	1,286 31	....
St. Clair	18,501 85	1,823 25	16,678 60	18,382 66	....	1,704 06
Stephenson	9,713 32	328 74	9,384 58	7,973 05	1,411 53	....
Tazewell	10,029 23	455 16	9,574 07	7,950 75	1,623 32	....
Union	2,488 16	120 45	2,367 71	6,441 20	....	4,073 49
Vermilion	13,765 71	446 17	13,319 54	13,531 83	....	212 29
Wabash	2,113 38	288 76	1,824 62	3,421 00	....	1,596 38
Warren	7,961 40	303 91	7,657 49	5,257 76	2,299 73	....
Washington	4,552 30	189 90	4,362 40	5,846 42	....	1,484 02
Wayne	2,577 48	123 41	2,454 07	7,373 80	....	4,919 73
White	3,459 65	197 34	3,262 31	7,496 99	....	4,234 68
Whiteside	9,933 10	340 11	9,592 99	7,839 82	1,753 17	....
Will	18,581 79	742 08	17,839 71	16,099 95	1,739 76	....
Williamson	2,533 65	103 21	2,430 44	6,948 47	....	4,518 03
Winnebago	13,908 01	432 21	13,475 80	9,311 46	4,164 34	....
Woodford	6,434 20	391 54	6,042 66	5,900 49	142 17	....
Total	$1,055,199 91	$55,807 34	$999,392 57	$1,000,000 00	$109,839 54	$110,446 97

No. 14.

Statement showing the aggregate amount of School Fund Tax charged on the tax books of 1895 (including back taxes), the amount deducted for abatements, commissions, etc., the net amount collected, the amount paid to each County, etc.

Counties.	Amount charged.	Amount of abatements, commissions, etc.	Net amount collected.	Amount paid county.	Amount received from county over amount paid.	Amount paid county over amount received.
Adams	$15,798 83	$524 37	$15,274 46	$15,525 23		$250 76
Alexander	3,330 59	196 45	3,134 14	4,339 66		1,205 52
Bond	3,706 04	231 58	3,474 46	4,216 46		742 00
Boone	4,531 01	178 30	4,352 71	2,766 01	$1,586 70	
Brown	2,648 65	103 38	2,545 27	3,292 23		746 96
Bureau	13,327 61	393 20	12,934 41	9,013 78	3,920 63	
Calhoun	1,569 62	79 87	1,489 75	2,242 57		752 82
Carroll	6,117 41	238 62	5,878 79	4,542 01	1,336 78	
Cass	4,601 40	206 97	4,397 43	4,263 29	134 14	
Champaign	12,605 36	446 72	12,158 64	11,411 33	747 31	
Christian	10,489 81	1,270 93	9,218 88	8,440 74	778 14	
Clark	3,959 00	154 84	3,804 16	6,111 20		2,307 04
Clay	2,387 24	99 70	2,287 54	4,938 90		2,651 36
Clinton	4,476 74	299 45	4,177 29	5,128 99		951 70
Coles	6,642 52	256 18	6,386 34	8,196 58		1,810 24
Cook	353,412 39	13,982 64	339,429 75	291,557 32	47,872 43	
Crawford	2,644 78	111 50	2,533 28	5,045 93		2,512 65
Cumberland	2,285 65	96 89	2,188 76	4,507 45		2,318 69
DeKalb	10,719 79	347 97	10,371 82	6,542 10	3,829 72	
DeWitt	5,149 54	209 21	4,940 33	4,510 23	430 10	
Douglas	5,489 32	212 89	5,276 43	4,839 12	437 31	
DuPage	8,251 09	310 40	7,940 69	5,804 61	2,136 08	
Edgar	7,901 29	246 66	7,654 63	7,175 35	479 28	
Edwards	2,010 42	79 35	1,931 07	2,754 30		823 23
Effingham	3,777 62	144 29	3,633 33	5,688 66		2,055 33
Fayette	4,302 70	166 84	4,135 86	7,009 23		2,873 37
Ford	4,297 11	160 63	4,136 48	4,760 53		624 05
Franklin	1,772 62	96 44	1,676 18	5,392 10		3,715 92
Fulton	11,804 93	421 85	11,383 08	11,356 70	26 38	
Gallatin	2,106 76	96 88	2,009 88	4,524 17		2,514 29
Greene	7,171 83	338 48	6,833 35	6,478 55	154 80	
Grundy	6,264 62	315 71	5,948 91	5,790 67	158 24	
Hamilton	2,062 88	94 34	1,968 54	5,580 52		3,611 98
Hancock	10,737 53	899 27	9,838 26	8,036 04	1,802 22	
Hardin	710 02	46 93	663 09	2,269 89		1,606 80
Henderson	3,809 11	161 63	3,647 48	2,582 05	1,065 43	
Henry	12,437 40	381 27	12,056 13	8,507 07	3,549 06	
Iroquois	11,110 80	341 74	10,769 06	9,759 64	1,009 42	
Jackson	3,781 95	181 77	3,600 18	8,248 42		4,648 24
Jasper	2,462 41	105 28	2,357 13	5,598 36		3,241 23
Jefferson	3,284 49	218 04	3,066 45	6,777 90		3,711 45
Jersey	4,917 55	181 40	4,736 15	3,911 55	824 60	
JoDaviess	5,601 17	208 08	5,393 09	6,433 96		1,040 87
Johnson	2,522 29	376 29	2,146 00	4,781 15		2,635 15
Kane	18,570 25	595 30	17,974 95	15,401 48	2,573 47	
Kankakee	6,972 18	259 96	6,712 22	7,343 70		631 48
Kendall	4,460 14	175 42	4,284 72	2,982 85	1,301 87	
Knox	14,205 44	465 05	13,740 39	9,305 33	4,435 06	
Lake	9,850 98	357 85	9,493 13	5,830 25	3,662 88	
LaSalle	21,827 78	759 22	21,068 56	21,322 04		253 48
Lawrence	2,669 86	118 52	2,551 34	4,266 63		1,715 29
Lee	9,014 55	280 52	8,734 03	6,561 05	2,172 98	
Livingston	13,826 59	416 07	13,410 52	10,602 49	2,808 03	
Logan	9,879 11	654 85	9,224 26	6,952 38	2,271 88	
Macon	12,084 08	443 27	11,640 81	9,830 99	1,809 82	
Macoupin	12,842 28	1,319 96	11,522 32	11,050 67	471 65	
Madison	17,608 44	1,724 14	15,884 30	14,080 91	1,803 39	
Marion	5,225 33	211 45	5,013 88	6,816 36		1,802 48
Marshall	5,294 12	201 60	5,092 52	3,388 11	1,704 41	
Mason	5,093 45	283 00	4,810 45	4,389 27	421 18	
Massac	2,076 30	89 96	1,986 34	3,293 35		1,307 01
McDonough	9,011 93	276 25	8,735 68	7,092 29	1,643 39	
McHenry	7,798 81	298 93	7,499 88	6,463 50	1,036 38	

Statement 14—Concluded.

Counties.	Amount charged.	Amount of abatements, commissions, etc.	Net amount collected.	Amount paid county.	Amount received from county over amount paid.	Amount paid county over amount received.
McLean	$23,603 54	$738 12	$22,865 42	$16,140 08	$6,725 34	....
Menard	4,557 51	141 73	4,415 78	3,500 15	915 63	....
Mercer	7,084 88	346 90	6,737 98	4,823 52	1,914 46	....
Monroe	3,551 41	133 92	3,417 49	3,808 42	....	390 93
Montgomery	8,724 94	288 78	8,436 16	8,293 57	142 59	....
Morgan	10,784 98	269 29	10,515 69	8,092 34	2,423 35	....
Moultrie	4,126 72	151 39	3,975 33	4,082 12	....	106 79
Ogle	10,844 73	361 34	10,483 39	7,168 66	3,314 73	....
Peoria	19,301 75	674 34	18,627 41	16,967 88	1,659 53	....
Perry	3,067 18	160 23	2,906 95	5,130 11	....	2,223 16
Piatt	6,041 37	327 09	5,714 28	4,663 53	1,050 75	....
Pike	8,747 43	834 04	7,913 39	8,311 97	....	398 58
Pope	1,586 21	145 06	1,441 15	4,505 22	....	3,064 07
Pulaski	1,370 80	111 19	1,259 61	3,374 17	....	2,114 56
Putnam	1,837 45	74 77	1,762 68	1,181 21	581 47	....
Randolph	5,686 75	714 40	4,972 35	7,038 78	....	2,066 43
Richland	2,377 19	99 65	2,277 54	4,303 98	....	2,026 44
Rock Island	8,820 94	343 37	8,477 57	10,855 56	....	2,377 99
Saline	2,130 69	116 69	2,014 00	6,003 61	....	3,989 61
Sangamon	19,232 46	576 14	18,656 32	15,717 55	2,938 77	....
Schuyler	3,846 20	146 54	3,699 66	4,422 16	....	722 50
Scott	3,448 03	131 67	3,316 36	2,744 27	572 09	....
Shelby	8,104 61	306 22	7,798 39	8,896 16	....	1,097 77
Stark	4,738 54	429 79	4,308 75	2,573 13	1,735 62	....
St. Clair	20,087 95	1,817 24	18,270 71	18,382 66	....	111 95
Stephenson	10,525 44	347 66	10,177 78	7,973 05	2,204 73	....
Tazewell	10,304 56	343 55	9,961 01	7,950 75	2,010 26	....
Union	2,662 59	121 18	2,541 41	6,441 20	....	3,899 79
Vermilion	16,050 80	503 04	15,547 76	13,531 83	2,015 93	....
Wabash	2,084 38	225 60	1,858 78	3,421 00	....	1,562 22
Warren	8,434 08	304 20	8,129 88	5,257 76	2,872 12	....
Washington	4,593 98	179 75	4,414 23	5,846 42	....	1,432 19
Wayne	2,702 73	122 53	2,580 20	7,373 80	....	4,793 60
White	3,493 16	171 32	3,321 84	7,496 99	....	4,175 15
Whiteside	9,733 49	318 70	9,414 79	7,839 82	1,574 97	....
Will	18,722 69	601 47	18,121 22	16,099 95	2,021 27	....
Williamson	2,721 25	118 47	2,602 78	6,948 47	....	4,345 69
Winnebago	14,438 80	454 15	13,984 65	9,311 46	4,673 19	....
Woodford	7,068 54	298 20	6,770 34	5,900 49	869 85	....
Totals	$1,094,547 26	$47,696 27	$1,046,850 99	$1,000,000 00	$142,611 81	$95,960 81

No. 15.

Statement of the amount of State, County, City, Town, School District and other local Taxes charged on the tax books of 1894, including back taxes.

COUNTIES.	State Tax.	County Tax.	City Tax	District and City School Taxes.	Amount of all other Taxes.	Registered Bond Fund Tax.	Total Taxes.
Adams	$87,736 23	$72,427 09	$84,475 07	$133,048 78	$232,933 23	$142,392 41	$703,012 81
Alexander	7,707 11	18,603 15	38,014 70	40,380 03	3,287 48	45,305 58	153,298 05
Bond	9,023 33	10,677 82	7,633 67	33,873 17	16,515 09	....	77,723 08
Boone	10,612 80	11,196 08	15,846 45	40,110 78	22,330 55	....	100,096 66
Brown	6,318 23	13,277 55	5,376 65	25,841 97	13,878 20	....	64,692 60
Bureau	31,044 57	75,144 98	32,842 72	108,514 00	82,729 76	13,101 33	343,377 36
Calhoun	4,015 80	9,591 78	....	10,916 98	5,385 10	....	29,909 66
Carroll	14,267 95	18,425 75	20,324 18	62,690 80	23,944 13	....	139,652 81
Cass	10,716 95	17,312 00	15,075 01	58,180 55	11,205 21	11,739 10	124,228 82
Champaign	30,490 04	73,331 19	55,219 74	144,033 73	85,838 44	14,457 26	403,370 40
Christian	25,906 87	50,320 87	23,280 88	93,735 40	63,418 62	11,182 35	267,844 99
Clark	8,657 60	20,940 37	13,569 30	44,731 51	24,700 00	20,165 03	132,763 81
Clay	5,737 04	13,780 58	5,901 59	30,769 13	16,361 51	2,179 46	74,729 31
Clinton	10,356 67	19,898 69	4,931 80	27,811 12	21,914 47	....	84,912 75
Coles	16,335 93	39,333 49	34,164 49	89,056 19	12,464 27	17,709 10	239,063 47
Cook	860,259 94	2,123,400 55	6,094,728 84	6,506,363 25	3,710,856 40	....	19,295,608 98
Crawford	5,651 40	15,355 37	6,557 29	39,429 60	18,685 16	11,946 67	97,625 49
Cumberland	5,343 46	17,271 90	4,722 84	30,509 84	19,237 99	1,528 35	78,614 38
DeKalb	24,134 75	27,969 15	39,887 50	97,629 32	54,773 07	....	244,393 79
DeWitt	11,270 18	27,269 60	13,241 67	60,113 69	31,097 39	34,888 86	177,881 39
Douglas	12,820 57	26,865 88	15,780 39	56,164 18	41,329 19	9,981 42	162,941 63
DuPage	19,364 44	18,754 28	30,422 51	93,022 85	64,650 81	....	226,214 89
Edgar	18,711 04	45,275 07	24,642 70	77,143 89	67,396 90	5,312 38	238,481 98
Edwards	4,718 65	10,043 27	5,482 11	20,165 10	5,393 72	304 11	46,106 96
Effingham	8,889 64	7,455 89	7,343 99	34,831 90	23,224 69	11,422 26	93,168 37
Fayette	10,362 99	25,092 12	7,681 92	44,079 26	26,847 19	7,270 99	121,334 47
Ford	10,203 35	16,449 80	16,284 97	52,568 62	34,944 28	22,418 14	152,869 16
Franklin	4,150 69	9,796 48	2,316 13	21,954 00	17,695 27	....	55,912 57
Fulton	28,039 14	64,786 04	57,411 45	128,004 78	53,909 70	....	332,151 11
Gallatin	4,890 91	9,476 92	5,149 46	27,687 23	35,658 47	16,248 64	99,111 63
Greene	17,583 25	32,085 43	18,020 19	63,688 63	31,197 00	1,546 72	164,121 22
Grundy	14,010 12	33,132 53	13,949 96	58,345 09	35,043 80	....	154,481 50
Hamilton	5,042 08	12,137 14	4,421 02	22,450 70	13,725 29	....	57,776 23
Hancock	25,418 41	27,087 71	30,918 55	84,429 46	56,725 47	19,576 74	244,156 34
Hardin	1,766 34	4,269 83	503 34	7,010 49	3,664 42	....	17,214 42
Henderson	9,084 34	17,581 09	3,478 51	37,573 46	12,774 23	....	80,491 63
Henry	29,288 63	35,919 54	35,881 42	115,973 02	58,592 73	1,121 86	276,777 20

Iroquois	25,849 14	39,147 12	5,959 54	108,270 19	74,203 94	16,049 57	269,479 50
Jackson	8,833 27	31,676 29	17,917 91	50,637 92	32,635 90	3,155 83	144,857 12
Jasper	5,425 78	13,037 35	3,136 88	27,777 83	18,675 67	14,676 36	82,729 87
Jefferson	7,624 99	18,961 27	10,936 94	41,870 82	21,315 19	8,570 80	109,280 01
Jersey	10,516 01	22,983 37	6,651 29	30,973 41	22,829 57	1,450 29	95,403 94
Jo Daviess	12,742 26	26,215 06	27,786 73	48,073 47	34,479 02	9,167 26	158,463 80
Johnson	5,849 26	11,830 85	4,463 26	21,963 90	13,070 69	1,295 12	58,473 08
Kane	44,919 79	86,940 94	170,556 31	248,488 99	123,392 71	....	674,298 74
Kankakee	15,794 69	35,678 30	26,125 50	84,188 04	58,169 36	10,342 13	230,298 02
Kendall	11,946 93	10,792 41	5,444 23	39,857 90	34,584 08	....	102,625 55
Knox	32,889 42	52,990 94	147,670 24	80,946 92	44,404 96	1,156 39	360,058 87
Lake	22,956 88	54,690 01	77,500 55	67,577 23	43,523 19	....	266,337 86
LaSalle	51,954 32	125,209 92	105,193 34	252,202 74	141,374 50	139 84	676,074 66
Lawrence	5,831 05	18,674 26	2,233 72	34,437 21	20,818 33	....	81,994 57
Lee	21,034 24	39,344 78	24,398 18	83,263 74	60,331 38	14,490 05	242,862 37
Livingston	31,608 46	76,943 47	34,178 33	135,884 74	63,053 22	15,577 08	357,245 30
Logan	24,082 85	45,975 72	59,404 70	70,524 65	43,158 53	36,974 98	280,121 43
Macon	27,880 80	67,151 35	70,454 01	120,341 61	62,504 51	32,057 31	389,389 59
Macoupin	31,633 28	37,201 19	24,715 56	91,164 10	63,898 83	148,080 82	396,693 78
Madison	43,502 58	94,783 64	55,848 52	125,329 34	70,314 90	4,181 69	394,050 67
Marion	12,168 23	29,159 57	17,914 12	52,822 55	25,803 63	....	137,868 10
Marshall	12,571 28	19,478 01	13,031 29	52,797 44	28,223 87	....	126,101 89
Mason	20,320 93	70,997 63	13,128 85	57,139 11	32,481 74	52,762 59	246,830 85
Massac	4,994 77	12,829 37	11,332 57	20,271 50	5,868 46	....	55,296 67
McDonough	21,302 02	35,050 57	52,611 02	59,717 53	36,662 33	5,078 99	210,422 46
McHenry	20,095 03	10,360 71	16,458 30	83,288 58	57,059 05	....	187,261 67
McLean	54,298 35	56,051 72	132,814 27	205,096 63	78,641 94	24,873 87	551,776 78
Menard	10,708 15	25,913 74	8,884 03	45,843 88	12,825 51	....	104,175 31
Mercer	16,199 51	39,343 43	14,528 30	61,644 68	36,094 34	7,548 55	175,358 81
Monroe	8,385 54	17,492 20	59 91	28,089 38	10,983 32	10,610 83	75,621 18
Montgomery	20,242 61	28,673 62	22,413 47	81,787 93	40,432 36	4,085 56	197,635 55
Morgan	24,910 98	60,268 48	43,613 28	94,819 13	28,173 49	21,316 93	273,102 29
Moultrie	9,538 30	12,313 74	7,374 78	42,696 51	20,951 39	45,944 07	138,818 79
Ogle	25,786 98	50,726 64	22,768 74	95,788 49	68,127 40	19,544 58	282,742 83
Peoria	45,546 05	110,260 64	234,339 98	237,885 55	150,836 78	17,699 65	796,568 65
Perry	6,661 17	15,883 82	10,990 46	33,645 63	7,887 49	....	75,068 57
Piatt	14,259 47	18,671 55	12,038 03	68,715 10	33,984 29	18,732 50	166,400 94
Pike	22,288 17	47,969 13	9,358 87	73,314 71	41,340 38	69,494 05	263,765 31
Pope	4,869 61	11,207 82	935 14	18,904 28	8,533 13	....	44,449 98
Pulaski	2,835 35	10,410 02	2,716 67	21,738 60	5,716 50	5,568 95	48,986 09
Putnam	4,118 53	8,086 37	230 72	16,085 83	9,572 31	....	38,093 76
Randolph	13,668 32	30,109 77	16,321 05	54,946 39	17,839 49	1,076 43	133,961 45
Richland	6,285 69	15,156 53	9,286 40	29,754 97	42,139 36	7,496 73	110,119 68
Rock Island	21,524 32	72,710 12	117,191 34	187,273 32	29,244 73	....	427,943 83
Saline	4,543 84	11,044 48	5,536 81	28,042 05	14,154 60	2,198 60	65,520 38
Sangamon	44,262 05	106,808 44	122,184 83	188,423 02	76,558 18	77,629 38	615,865 90
Schuyler	9,200 53	17,713 85	7,803 80	38,252 23	21,318 29	4,172 79	98,461 49
Scott	7,897 57	19,099 04	7,451 59	28,910 83	8,443 12	....	71,802 15
Shelby	18,636 09	44,742 70	24,857 24	74,715 73	47,631 36	42,999 21	253,582 33
Stark	11,016 62	9,920 16	8,417 54	40,748 56	23,680 43	23,146 07	116,929 38
St. Clair	45,837 86	77,995 28	200,977 24	215,498 59	72,060 14	57,502 19	669,871 30
Stephenson	24,089 10	41,098 98	40,899 47	88,199 40	61,975 18	....	256,262 13

Statement 15—Concluded.

Counties.	State Tax.	County Tax.	City Tax.	District and City School Taxes.	Amount of all other Taxes.	Registered Bond Fund Tax.	Total Taxes.
Tazewell	$24,869 39	$59,763 69	$61,393 70	$74,788 31	$54,583 33	$31,394 53	$306,792 95
Union	6,113 23	15,240 02	12,541 23	33,048 48	8,549 81	....	75,492 77
Vermilion	34,138 94	82,394 40	71,160 21	161,364 83	77,073 23	29,110 69	455,242 30
Wabash	5,241 20	11,979 86	6,482 62	24,632 16	7,704 67	11,984 14	68,024 65
Warren	19,743 85	47,715 12	24,818 76	77,047 93	57,893 19	14,746 38	241,965 23
Washington	11,289 72	14,556 48	2,845 38	30,453 85	22,073 53	27,646 20	108,865 16
Wayne	6,391 82	15,475 10	5,123 68	35,018 46	55,295 55	8,704 95	126,009 56
White	8,567 58	20,617 78	8,352 60	49,575 04	31,146 33	11,167 30	129,426 63
Whiteside	24,632 85	45,894 93	42,063 29	103,865 28	72,476 92	6,044 20	294,977 47
Will	46,082 84	81,981 17	100,919 53	211,005 73	154,916 69	....	594,905 96
Williamson	6,270 50	15,022 04	5,241 13	27,879 94	12,189 42	8,242 07	74,845 10
Winnebago	34,491 87	36,714 46	92,529 46	130,222 03	66,716 11	....	360,673 93
Woodford	15,953 08	28,261 21	24,282 78	59,833 13	29,002 32	3,432 58	160,765 10
Total	$2,615,747 33	$5,595,129 61	$9,342,373 23	$13,841,200 55	$7,935,933 40	$1,411,119 84	$40,741,503 96

No. 16.

Statement of the amount of State, County, City, Town, School, District and other local Taxes, charged on the tax books of 1895, including back taxes.

COUNTIES.	State Tax.	County Tax.	City Tax.	District and City School Taxes.	Amount of all other Taxes.	Registered Bond Fund Tax.	Total Tax.
Adams	$63,175 09	$84,782 41	$91,164 74	$135,203 24	$109,997 39	$137,391 98	$621,714 85
Alexander	13,284 52	19,248 74	37,810 97	40,143 76	3,782 81	46,902 97	161,173 77
Bond	14,784 79	14,238 27	7,044 24	32,939 59	20,812 86	....	89,819 75
Boone	18,124 06	14,987 24	16,025 33	43,792 16	22,571 26	....	115,500 05
Brown	10,594 62	14,475 42	5,290 49	25,763 90	12,995 23	....	69,119 66
Bureau	53,310 42	51,311 41	36,715 13	109,792 26	83,680 28	9,256 44	344,065 94
Calhoun	6,278 48	9,100 97	....	10,964 03	4,993 72	....	31,337 20
Carroll	24,469 66	22,121 43	23,690 25	61,882 25	27,841 63	....	160,005 22
Cass	18,404 21	17,706 18	18,546 61	53,571 49	11,635 84	11,523 51	131,387 84
Champaign	50,421 48	72,641 92	76,149 50	150,387 31	81,839 50	45,397 15	476,836 86
Christian	41,959 24	35,977 95	27,569 95	102,425 17	59,651 98	9,826 20	277,410 49
Clark	15,832 00	22,823 86	13,110 10	45,368 73	28,123 95	12,168 23	137,426 87
Clay	9,548 98	13,689 34	9,562 75	35,494 85	17,304 27	2,443 24	88,043 43
Clinton	17,906 79	22,121 80	5,260 05	28,951 29	23,345 38	....	97,585 31
Coles	26,554 81	38,314 42	32,895 22	91,391 62	41,680 02	19,354 75	250,190 84
Cook	1,413,494 39	2,154,906 11	6,278,836 48	8,252,733 43	6,314,010 32	2,761 06	24,416,741 79
Crawford	10,579 13	15,268 83	1,127 92	40,105 33	19,851 55	9,019 68	95,952 44
Cumberland	9,142 60	17,597 43	5,235 49	31,379 50	18,747 49	1,487 80	83,590 31
DeKalb	42,831 95	28,831 79	39,015 70	100,388 02	56,911 85	....	267,979 31
DeWitt	20,595 72	29,669 04	17,794 26	60,340 30	34,531 78	16,739 06	179,670 16
Douglas	21,957 27	25,291 74	19,211 93	65,922 75	40,345 80	9,842 58	182,572 07
DuPage	33,002 59	22,190 69	35,845 53	93,784 05	63,978 54	....	248,801 40
Edgar	31,586 85	45,574 46	34,521 20	85,296 04	67,479 89	13,917 31	278,375 75
Edwards	8,041 71	10,052 47	5,582 45	21,074 40	5,483 65	174 70	50,409 38
Effingham	15,110 49	18,306 95	8,460 09	35,746 23	22,053 83	11,879 43	111,557 02
Fayette	17,210 81	24,924 70	8,558 06	44,357 42	26,464 94	....	121,515 93
Ford	17,188 44	24,778 54	19,893 37	54,160 20	37,577 83	20,757 85	174,356 23
Franklin	7,085 84	10,190 14	2,918 13	22,538 00	25,514 27	....	68,246 38
Fulton	47,124 93	64,333 10	59,228 74	132,156 36	58,922 25	....	361,765 38
Gallatin	8,427 05	9,741 05	5,645 54	29,121 75	34,310 91	15,914 33	103,160 63
Greene	28,687 34	37,709 30	23,633 66	59,713 39	31,318 00	810 78	181,872 47
Grundy	25,058 48	35,644 70	11,652 53	61,547 26	38,477 13	....	172,380 10
Hamilton	8,251 50	10,435 18	4,463 21	19,605 23	11,697 77	....	54,452 89
Hancock	42,934 99	27,313 45	35,795 43	90,829 39	53,379 74	18,241 47	268,494 47
Hardin	2,840 13	4,099 83	333 66	8,600 53	4,608 21	....	20,482 36
Henderson	15,183 71	17,499 33	4,602 66	37,993 92	13,446 25	....	88,725 87
Henry	49,716 54	47,854 41	33,849 21	125,981 76	62,765 79	3,395 44	323,563 15

Statement 15—Concluded.

COUNTIES.	State Tax.	County Tax.	City Tax.	District and City School Taxes.	Amount of all other Taxes.	Registered Bond Fund Tax.	Total Tax.
Iroquois	$44,439 80	$51,257 47	$18,339 72	$110,442 08	$71,197 26	$14,176 48	$309,852 81
Jackson	15,114 68	33,395 94	15,628 70	63,031 53	33,741 50	4,179 66	165,092 01
Jasper	9,849 65	14,181 77	2,510 23	28,225 02	18,505 30	15,906 12	89,178 09
Jefferson	13,137 48	19,768 90	11,695 74	44,198 69	20,687 11	9,547 30	119,035 22
Jersey	19,670 09	28,359 95	7,287 02	33,276 87	26,189 68	1,378 39	116,162 00
Jo Daviess	22,391 22	25,997 86	27,731 93	50,639 26	38,037 76	8,533 21	173,331 24
Johnson	10,089 16	13,170 46	4,711 69	22,241 73	23,035 37	128 18	73,376 59
Kane	74,281 03	102,865 64	175,342 50	255,021 79	105,842 72	....	713,353 68
Kankakee	27,888 72	40,224 12	23,545 17	84,375 00	59,634 74	9,917 34	245,585 09
Kendall	17,840 55	10,297 23	4,727 24	39,076 03	29,362 11	....	101,303 16
Knox	56,781 66	58,954 97	172,261 94	85,551 60	46,420 59	1,094 13	421,064 89
Lake	39,403 90	42,422 63	59,207 56	100,919 15	44,393 41	....	286,346 65
LaSalle	87,289 37	126,255 08	110,680 40	255,677 89	124,087 02	143 37	704,133 13
Lawrence	10,679 46	20,528 20	3,389 50	34,457 20	22,850 48	....	91,904 84
Lee	36,057 41	39,520 10	30,006 11	83,628 62	56,688 94	17,838 64	263,739 82
Livingston	55,306 37	79,686 77	33,360 16	139,538 15	62,624 10	12,332 50	382,848 05
Logan	39,514 11	45,179 95	27,621 49	73,693 37	80,212 96	31,856 00	301,077 88
Macon	48,300 26	69,602 64	72,844 50	157,177 41	64,887 08	27,125 26	439,937 15
Macoupin	51,369 11	42,513 98	24,940 98	97,446 05	65,550 83	131,211 51	416,032 46
Madison	70,433 77	89,337 57	65,704 64	122,533 35	77,578 36	2,747 52	428,335 21
Marion	20,901 32	30,070 24	18,843 14	54,673 20	26,215 72	....	150,703 62
Marshall	21,176 48	21,172 88	14,457 48	56,038 22	24,175 98	....	137,021 04
Mason	19,418 73	25,037 25	14,190 78	53,126 11	31,368 23	53,312 66	196,453 76
Massac	8,305 22	12,768 77	11,335 00	21,579 09	5,560 69	....	59,548 77
McDonough	36,047 73	30,046 82	49,293 34	61,878 26	29,407 57	5,005 04	211,678 76
McHenry	31,194 24	25,532 28	17,357 52	86,037 91	56,076 45	....	216,198 40
McLean	94,293 08	63,516 24	140,357 81	237,487 23	86,211 60	25,187 73	647,053 69
Menard	18,230 03	26,306 78	11,923 31	46,931 05	13,180 56	....	116,571 73
Mercer	28,333 52	37,745 92	15,180 27	61,505 74	32,979 68	6,947 99	182,696 12
Monroe	14,107 89	17,629 82	1,529 68	27,402 03	10,972 98	5,178 11	76,820 51
Montgomery	34,888 97	28,886 47	22,417 97	80,180 85	39,555 93	4,107 72	210,037 91
Morgan	43,106 14	62,164 74	37,746 13	95,057 12	29,265 28	19,221 16	286,560 57
Moultrie	16,506 88	13,346 94	8,010 32	44,127 23	20,044 60	52,697 47	154,733 44
Ogle	43,378 93	50,088 48	23,706 12	92,597 91	65,607 62	15,465 73	290,844 79
Peoria	77,159 32	111,336 28	251,266 87	314,778 74	172,501 23	24,392 42	951,434 86
Perry	12,268 69	16,274 17	11,139 87	36,040 42	8,086 74	....	83,809 89
Piatt	24,165 47	22,771 64	13,424 34	68,604 62	48,140 18	20,148 34	197,254 59
Pike	34,979 49	49,430 15	16,778 88	81,762 83	44,499 68	5,535 78	232,986 81
Pope	6,273 09	9,100 67	919 09	14,488 88	6,201 78	....	36,983 51
Pulaski	5,483 24	13,705 80	....	22,284 39	8,118 66	5,344 27	54,936 36
Putnam	7,349 79	9,893 17	554 06	17,393 40	10,145 96	....	45,336 38

Randolph	22,742 10	33,830 59	17,845 34	54,896 15	18,947 55	1,088 45	149,350 18
Richland	9,508 77	13,700 97	9,718 80	27,034 59	28,637 94	6,593 99	95,195 06
Rock Island	35,170 64	71,202 82	124,624 55	186,811 88	33,116 80	....	450,920 69
Saline	8,522 77	12,239 48	6,251 98	30,983 33	15,751 97	2,120 93	75,870 46
Sangamon	76,919 95	111,163 68	121,379 64	191,244 55	75,684 25	81,976 82	658,368 89
Schuyler	15,384 80	18,970 12	9,666 13	42,092 30	20,087 12	1,555 35	107,755 82
Scott	13,792 13	19,891 56	7,999 97	29,190 05	9,233 98	....	80,107 69
Shelby	32,418 46	46,511 02	24,585 64	74,074 84	50,041 76	29,520 93	257,152 65
Stark	18,954 16	19,192 48	8,314 77	42,103 17	25,612 35	17,985 36	132,162 29
St. Clair	80,351 82	103,290 34	177,115 95	213,846 22	71,580 86	64,057 97	710,243 16.
Stephenson	42,099 80	41,280 39	40,141 98	95,595 06	64,288 38	....	283,405 61
Tazewell	41,217 43	59,436 87	58,496 20	77,842 57	53,783 42	29,997 75	320,774 24
Union	10,647 84	15,387 63	13,676 14	35,593 79	9,153 92	....	84,459 32
Vermilion	64,198 83	92,507 41	73,747 87	181,038 82	97,511 73	26,376 68	535,381 34
Wabash	7,813 09	11,239 35	8,691 48	26,955 30	18,065 66	10,932 32	83,697 20
Warren	33,736 33	48,664 19	34,711 66	79,394 26	4,657 54	3,054 73	248,218 71
Washington	18,375 99	14,135 71	2,626 62	30,946 28	20,853 06	16,964 68	103,902 34
Wayne	10,809 89	15,570 76	5,191 56	37,200 95	57,284 18	5,417 60	131,474 94
White	13,968 28	20,214 66	13,001 94	59,464 07	31,094 96	10,070 38	147,814 29
Whiteside	38,934 89	35,942 76	44,326 10	106,970 81	73,002 83	839 14	300,016 53
Will	74,890 76	79,158 37	107,765 70	215,668 09	151,380 50	....	628,863 42
Williamson	10,853 69	15,642 88	6,409 16	30,094 50	12,989 44	12,511 99	88,501 66
Winnebago	57,755 23	46,659 86	133,405 44	149,669 85	68,584 69	....	456,075 07
Woodford	28,273 08	33,751 88	17,275 02	60,951 49	31,153 43	2,103 95	173,568 85
Total	$4,375,551 40	$5,745,687 12	$9,695,979 32	$15,976,235 85	$10,474,390 67	$1,279,035 01	$47,546,879 37

No. 17.

Statement showing the per cent. of State Tax on real property forfeited to the State, and on personal property delinquent in the several Counties for the years 1894 and 1895, both exclusive of back taxes.

Counties.	1894	1895	Counties.	1894	1895
Adams	0.31	0.29	Livingston	0.10	0.08
Alexander	0.83	1.27	Logan	0.50	0.34
Bond	0.88	0.45	Macon	0.65	0.89
Boone	0.32	0.09	Macoupin	0.85	0.51
Brown	0.26	0.17	Madison	0.18	0.13
Bureau	0.31	0.12	Marion	0.58	0.43
Calhoun	0.21	0.21	Marshall	0.12	0.25
Carroll	0.90	0.18	Mason	1.05	0.45
Cass	0.91	1.41	Massac	1.19	0.60
Champaign	0.22	0.21	McDonough	0.12	0.14
Christian	0.29	0.28	McHenry	0.18	0.17
Clark	0.22	0.19	McLean	0.22	0.34
Clay	0.19	0.21	Menard	0.30	0.24
Clinton	1.57	1.72	Mercer	0.11	0.26
Coles	0.38	0.61	Monroe	1.04	0.98
Cook	1.64	1.71	Montgomery	0.71	0.33
Crawford	0.44	0.34	Morgan	0.44	0.39
Cumberland	0.46	0.41	Moultrie	0.17	0.18
DeKalb	0.16	0.12	Ogle	0.06	0.21
DeWitt	0.08	0.22	Peoria	0.17	0.32
Douglas	0.11	0.42	Perry	1.03	1.88
DuPage	0.27	0.17	Piatt	0.14	0.13
Edgar	0.64	0.22	Pike	0.63	2.10
Edwards	0.56	0.44	Pope	2.07	4.22
Effingham	0.64	0.30	Pulaski	5.83	3.56
Fayette	0.29	0.34	Putnam	0.01	0.02
Ford	0.14	0.14	Randolph	1.61	1.42
Franklin	0.62	0.88	Richland	0.61	0.34
Fulton	0.40	0.33	Rock Island	1.35	0.84
Gallatin	0.44	0.42	Saline	1.07	1.35
Greene	0.16	0.11	Sangamon	0.34	0.33
Grundy	0.22	0.14	Schuyler	0.22	0.19
Hamilton	0.46	0.47	Scott	0.42	0.64
Hancock	0.17	0.26	Shelby	0.17	0.32
Hardin	0.61	0.86	Stark	0.08	0.11
Henderson	0.94	1.10	St. Clair	1.12	1.13
Henry	0.19	0.16	Stephenson	0.10	0.21
Iroquois	0.10	0.16	Tazewell	0.15	0.15
Jackson	0.91	0.96	Union	0.60	0.65
Jasper	0.54	0.57	Vermilion	0.35	0.37
Jefferson	0.67	0.45	Wabash	0.15	1.07
Jersey	0.18	0.11	Warren	0.08	0.11
Jo Daviess	0.29	0.31	Washington	0.30	0.23
Johnson	1.22	1.52	Wayne	0.63	0.63
Kane	0.38	0.36	White	0.73	0.87
Kankakee	0.11	0.22	Whiteside	0.12	0.19
Kendall	0.09	0.16	Will	0.11	0.15
Knox	0.27	0.49	Williamson	0.61	1.10
Lake	0.11	0.06	Winnebago	0.30	0.40
LaSalle	0.27	0.29	Woodford	0.24	0.09
Lawrence	0.38	0.52			
Lee	0.13	0.09	State average	0.52	0.53

No. 18.

Statement showing the per cent. of total amount of State Tax collected for the years 1874 to 1895, inclusive, paid by each of the various Counties.

Counties.	1874	1875	1876	1877	1878	1879	1880	1881	1882	1883	1884
Adams	2.57	2.49	2.42	2.38	2.18	2.22	2.20	2.12	2.00	1.97	1.95
Alexander	0.24	0.19	0.19	0.19	0.27	0.22	0.22	0.22	0.23	0.23	0.25
Bond	0.39	0.40	0.37	0.36	0.33	0.40	0.35	0.38	0.46	0.39	0.42
Boone	0.43	0.47	0.45	0.50	0.57	0.56	0.59	0.56	0.54	0.53	0.49
Brown	0.32	0.34	0.32	0.33	0.31	0.31	0.32	0.34	0.31	0.28	0.29
Bureau	1.37	1.57	1.43	1.70	1.44	1.45	1.50	1.52	1.47	1.50	1.49
Calhoun	0.09	0.10	0.10	0.11	0.11	0.12	0.12	0.12	0.11	0.11	0.11
Carroll	0.53	0.56	0.53	0.54	0.54	0.56	0.58	0.62	0.64	0.65	0.64
Cass	0.51	0.58	0.54	0.56	0.51	0.49	0.50	0.48	0.49	0.50	0.51
Champaign	1.53	1.56	1.54	1.70	1.56	1.48	1.52	1.48	1.45	1.49	1.50
Christian	1.01	1.06	1.13	1.13	1.08	1.09	1.12	1.12	1.11	0.97	1.03
Clark	0.43	0.42	0.35	0.35	0.36	0.49	0.40	0.39	0.47	0.40	0.41
Clay	0.32	0.33	0.32	0.32	0.36	0.46	0.38	0.34	0.34	0.32	0.29
Clinton	0.39	0.45	0.42	0.43	0.47	0.54	0.46	0.47	0.48	0.47	0.48
Coles	0.83	0.85	0.79	0.83	0.81	0.81	0.79	0.77	0.89	0.83	0.83
Cook	25.05	19.76	22.83	20.53	21.91	21.09	20.63	19.86	19.93	21.12	21.92
Crawford	0.28	0.27	0.29	0.28	0.25	0.31	0.30	0.28	0.26	0.30	0.30
Cumberland	0.23	0.22	0.22	0.20	0.19	0.29	0.26	0.28	0.32	0.25	0.27
DeKalb	1.04	1.10	1.10	1.11	1.05	1.01	1.06	1.15	1.11	1.12	1.06
DeWitt	0.61	0.64	0.60	0.66	0.69	0.62	0.70	0.65	0.62	0.58	0.57
Douglas	0.57	0.57	0.50	0.59	0.63	0.60	0.59	0.58	0.59	0.60	0.59
DuPage	0.68	0.73	0.70	0.74	0.80	0.80	0.82	0.82	0.77	0.74	0.71
Edgar	0.86	0.83	0.80	0.80	0.93	0.94	0.90	0.94	0.97	0.95	0.94
Edwards	0.22	0.24	0.23	0.23	0.22	0.22	0.23	0.25	0.23	0.23	0.22
Effingham	0.38	0.36	0.35	0.28	0.33	0.47	0.38	0.36	0.37	0.36	0.34
Fayette	0.59	0.63	0.63	0.40	0.55	0.50	0.52	0.50	0.54	0.53	0.52
Ford	0.48	0.65	0.58	0.54	0.51	0.50	0.50	0.51	0.47	0.48	0.47
Franklin	0.15	0.13	0.13	0.15	0.14	0.10	0.16	0.17	0.19	0.20	0.19
Fulton	1.27	1.50	1.49	1.54	1.43	1.41	1.48	1.41	1.34	1.32	1.30
Gallatin	0.16	0.19	0.18	0.17	0.19	0.21	0.20	0.19	0.21	0.20	0.19
Greene	0.67	0.84	0.74	0.84	0.72	0.71	0.74	0.82	0.85	0.81	0.80
Grundy	0.61	0.67	0.66	0.70	0.67	0.64	0.69	0.66	0.67	0.66	0.67
Hamilton	0.15	0.16	0.16	0.15	0.15	0.24	0.18	0.19	.019	0.21	0.22
Hancock	1.08	1.21	1.25	1.29	1.20	1.18	1.23	1.23	1.20	1.16	1.21
Hardin	0.05	0.06	0.06	0.05	0.07	0.06	0.07	0.08	0.08	0.09	0.08
Henderson	0.42	0.46	0.41	0.47	0.39	0.38	0.40	0.39	0.38	0.38	0.38
Henry	1.30	1.32	1.38	1.42	1.36	0.93	1.35	1.50	1.48	1.49	1.45
Iroquois	1.03	1.28	1.33	1.20	1.28	1.62	1.21	1.27	1.29	1.25	1.23
Jackson	0.43	0.41	0.32	0.26	0.27	0.33	0.33	0.32	0.35	0.35	0.33

Counties.	1885	1886	1887	1888	1889	1890	1891	1892	1893	1894	1895
Adams	1.80	1.69	1.69	1.70	1.70	1.65	1.56	1.55	1.57	1.47	1.44
Alexander	0.23	0.25	0.30	0.27	0.26	0.26	0.25	0.25	0.24	0.29	0.30
Bond	0.39	0.39	0.37	0.38	0.38	0.37	0.34	0.34	0.34	0.33	0.33
Boone	0.50	0.48	0.48	0.46	0.44	0.41	0.40	0.40	0.42	0.41	0.42
Brown	0.28	0.27	0.26	0.26	0.28	0.27	0.24	0.24	0.25	0.24	0.24
Bureau	1.47	1.38	1.39	1.38	1.39	1.34	1.25	1.25	1.20	1.21	1.23
Calhoun	0.15	0.09	0.12	0.10	0.09	0.10	0.13	0.14	0.16	0.15	0.14
Carroll	0.62	0.61	0.64	0.63	0.62	0.61	0.57	0.57	0.57	0.55	0.56
Cass	0.50	0.47	0.46	0.46	0.45	0.43	0.40	0.44	0.45	0.42	0.42
Champaign	1.43	1.34	1.34	1.32	1.31	1.26	1.19	1.22	1.20	1.18	1.16
Christian	1.05	1.00	0.97	0.96	0.90	0.95	0.82	0.89	0.84	0.86	0.88
Clark	0.42	0.40	0.38	0.37	0.38	0.37	0.33	0.33	0.35	0.33	0.37
Clay	0.28	0.26	0.26	0.26	0.28	0.24	0.22	0.23	0.21	0.22	0.22
Clinton	0.47	0.43	0.42	0.41	0.43	0.41	0.34	0.38	0.39	0.39	0.40
Coles	0.82	0.78	0.77	0.74	0.73	0.70	0.63	0.68	0.66	0.63	0.61
Cook	22.77	25.56	25.87	26.90	27.86	29.81	34.49	32.64	31.90	33.40	32.40
Crawford	0.32	0.28	0.27	0.28	0.25	0.25	0.22	0.22	0.23	0.22	0.24
Cumberland	0.21	0.24	0.32	0.22	0.22	0.21	0.20	0.19	0.22	0.21	0.21
DeKalb	1.06	1.03	1.04	1.04	1.03	1.01	0.95	0.96	0.95	0.94	0.99
DeWitt	0.59	0.62	0.56	0.56	0.54	0.52	0.47	0.48	0.44	0.44	0.47
Douglas	0.57	0.62	0.54	0.54	0.54	0.52	0.50	0.52	0.53	0.49	0.50
DuPage	0.69	0.66	0.68	0.68	0.68	0.67	0.64	0.69	0.68	0.75	0.76
Edgar	0.90	0.99	0.86	0.83	0.80	0.77	0.74	0.76	0.76	0.73	0.73
Edwards	0.25	0.23	0.22	0.21	0.20	0.19	0.19	0.20	0.18	0.19	0.19
Effingham	0.37	0.40	0.39	0.40	0.39	0.38	0.34	0.38	0.34	0.34	0.34
Fayette	0.55	0.55	0.53	0.59	0.50	0.51	0.42	0.42	0.41	0.40	0.40
Ford	0.47	0.45	0.45	0.45	0.45	0.45	0.40	0.41	0.42	0.38	0.40
Franklin	0.20	0.19	0.17	0.18	0.16	0.16	0.14	0.17	0.17	0.15	0.16
Fulton	1.29	1.21	1.28	1.16	1.15	1.18	1.06	1.07	1.10	1.08	1.09
Gallatin	0.19	0.18	0.19	0.17	0.18	0.16	0.17	0.19	0.20	0.19	0.19
Greene	0.80	0.73	0.72	0.72	0.72	0.70	0.64	0.65	0.63	0.63	0.65
Grundy	0.66	0.62	0.62	0.61	0.62	0.62	0.58	0.62	0.56	0.53	0.57
Hamilton	0.21	0.25	0.21	0.23	0.21	0.19	0.18	0.20	0.21	0.19	0.19
Hancock	1.12	1.09	1.08	1.07	1.05	1.00	0.94	0.98	0.94	0.92	0.94
Hardin	0.08	0.08	0.10	0.08	0.07	0.06	0.07	0.06	0.10	0.06	0.06
Henderson	0.38	0.37	0.37	0.39	0.38	0.37	0.34	0.37	0.37	0.36	0.35
Henry	1.38	1.30	1.28	1.27	1.25	1.22	1.13	1.18	1.16	1.14	1.15
Iroquois	1.20	1.12	1.13	1.14	1.10	1.09	1.02	1.09	1.05	1.01	1.03
Jackson	0.34	0.32	0.39	0.37	0.37	0.36	0.34	0.34	0.33	0.33	0.34

Statement 18—Concluded.

Counties.	1874	1875	1876	1877	1878	1879	1880	1881	1882	1883	1884	1885	1886	1887	1888	1889	1890	1891	1892	1893	1894	1895
Jasper	0.25	0.22	0.23	0.26	0.23	0.32	0.33	0.30	0.31	0.30	0.28	0.28	0.31	0.26	0.27	0.24	0.22	0.19	0.19	0.20	0.20	0.22
Jefferson	0.29	0.28	0.27	0.19	0.24	0.34	0.29	0.30	0.33	0.32	0.33	0.34	0.33	0.30	0.33	0.33	0.29	0.28	0.29	0.32	0.28	0.30
Jersey	0.52	0.58	0.58	0.59	0.56	0.57	0.57	0.54	0.54	0.53	0.52	0.58	0.48	0.46	0.45	0.45	0.43	0.41	0.40	0.42	0.41	0.45
JoDaviess	0.54	0.56	0.55	0.56	0.54	0.55	0.58	0.60	0.63	0.62	0.64	0.60	0.58	0.60	0.61	0.57	0.55	0.50	0.51	0.52	0.49	0.51
Johnson	0.14	0.10	0.12	0.10	0.69	0.16	0.14	0.13	0.14	0.14	0.15	0.14	0.15	0.14	0.16	0.17	0.17	0.15	0.15	0.18	0.19	0.25
Kane	1.67	1.75	1.69	1.70	1.56	1.55	1.60	1.68	1.63	1.67	1.66	1.69	1.65	1.68	1.68	1.70	1.69	1.61	1.68	1.67	1.74	1.72
Kankakee	0.60	0.67	0.63	0.70	0.63	0.64	0.66	0.72	0.67	0.74	0.74	0.70	0.68	0.69	0.64	0.65	0.66	0.62	0.63	0.62	0.61	0.64
Kendall	0.53	0.61	0.56	0.67	0.59	0.55	0.56	0.54	0.53	0.52	0.51	0.51	0.48	0.48	0.47	0.46	0.45	0.42	0.43	0.39	0.46	0.49
Knox	1.38	1.56	1.47	1.76	1.59	1.54	1.59	1.73	1.68	1.62	1.63	1.59	1.49	1.49	1.43	1.42	1.35	1.22	1.31	1.30	1.29	1.31
Lake	0.64	0.71	0.64	0.73	0.75	0.70	0.68	0.73	0.73	0.71	0.72	0.73	0.68	0.67	0.67	0.69	0.69	0.67	0.74	0.84	0.88	0.90
LaSalle	2.54	2.81	2.54	2.63	2.45	2.37	2.48	2.48	2.44	2.38	2.31	2.34	2.30	2.28	2.31	2.28	2.21	2.07	2.10	2.09	2.02	2.01
Lawrence	0.25	0.23	0.23	0.25	0.26	0.31	0.26	0.25	0.26	0.27	0.25	0.25	0.24	0.24	0.23	0.23	0.24	0.21	0.19	0.22	0.22	0.24
Lee	1.03	1.09	1.02	1.23	1.09	1.05	1.12	1.08	1.06	1.06	1.03	0.98	0.94	0.96	0.93	0.93	0.90	0.85	0.86	0.84	0.82	0.83
Livingston	1.36	1.54	1.46	1.45	1.49	1.34	1.46	1.46	1.49	1.45	1.41	1.38	1.29	1.34	1.38	1.34	1.32	1.23	1.29	1.20	1.23	1.28
Logan	1.15	1.30	1.22	1.31	1.20	1.19	1.23	1.19	1.15	1.11	1.08	1.08	1.08	1.04	1.05	1.02	0.97	0.89	0.88	0.88	0.87	0.88
Macon	1.28	1.41	1.24	1.21	1.16	1.12	1.15	1.19	1.19	1.15	1.18	1.10	1.21	1.13	1.19	1.10	1.09	1.04	1.13	1.60	1.08	1.11
Macoupin	1.02	1.09	1.11	1.33	1.36	1.46	1.40	1.40	1.46	1.49	1.42	1.42	1.35	1.29	1.20	1.24	1.20	1.11	1.14	1.10	1.09	1.10
Madison	1.63	1.72	1.67	1.49	1.92	1.91	1.85	1.84	1.87	1.74	1.68	1.66	1.62	1.57	1.53	1.53	1.47	1.35	1.44	1.44	1.51	1.50
Marion	0.57	0.59	0.60	0.54	0.54	0.59	0.57	0.49	0.49	0.50	0.48	0.50	0.48	0.46	0.46	0.45	0.47	0.44	0.43	0.43	0.47	0.48
Marshall	0.60	0.66	0.58	0.73	0.62	0.59	0.62	0.63	0.63	0.60	0.58	0.56	0.52	0.53	0.53	0.54	0.53	0.48	0.51	0.49	0.49	0.49
Mason	0.53	0.60	0.60	0.62	0.50	0.51	0.56	0.59	0.55	0.54	0.53	0.48	0.47	0.47	0.40	0.41	0.45	0.41	0.38	0.42	0.44	0.46
Massac	0.11	0.10	0.11	0.10	0.12	0.12	0.12	0.13	0.15	0.15	0.16	0.16	0.15	0.17	0.15	0.16	0.14	0.13	0.14	0.19	0.19	0.19
McDonough	0.89	1.08	1.10	1.16	1.10	1.03	1.09	1.12	1.11	1.09	1.08	1.10	1.01	0.99	0.97	0.94	0.88	0.79	0.81	0.83	0.83	0.83
McHenry	0.91	0.82	0.82	0.98	0.96	0.93	0.98	0.97	0.98	0.96	0.98	0.93	0.87	0.85	0.85	0.84	0.81	0.74	0.75	0.75	0.78	0.70
McLean	2.53	2.86	2.49	2.62	2.62	2.63	2.57	2.49	2.46	2.43	2.42	2.47	2.35	2.40	2.31	2.39	2.27	2.12	2.16	2.15	2.13	2.16
Menard	0.49	0.58	0.54	0.63	0.57	0.54	0.55	0.51	0.52	0.50	0.50	0.50	0.49	0.46	0.46	0.48	0.46	0.42	0.44	0.40	0.42	0.42
Mercer	0.75	0.81	0.77	0.86	0.78	0.76	0.80	0.84	0.83	0.80	0.79	0.80	0.76	0.75	0.73	0.73	0.71	0.64	0.65	0.50	0.62	0.64
Monroe	0.62	0.27	0.26	0.30	0.30	0.34	0.35	0.35	0.33	0.37	0.36	0.34	0.33	0.34	0.33	0.33	0.32	0.31	0.32	0.32	0.31	0.33
Montgomery	0.92	0.96	0.91	0.86	0.86	0.99	0.85	0.99	1.01	1.01	0.98	0.98	0.98	0.96	0.96	0.95	0.89	0.79	0.81	0.85	0.78	0.80
Morgan	1.30	1.34	1.36	1.26	1.14	1.10	1.14	1.15	1.12	1.14	1.12	1.19	1.13	1.09	1.10	1.10	1.04	0.96	1.01	0.95	0.98	1.04
Moultrie	0.40	0.44	0.44	0.43	0.46	0.45	0.44	0.45	0.43	0.39	0.38	0.39	0.47	0.50	0.42	0.42	0.39	0.35	0.35	0.38	0.37	0.38
Ogle	1.08	1.16	1.19	1.24	1.17	1.17	1.20	1.34	1.32	1.29	1.26	1.21	1.15	1.17	1.19	1.16	1.11	1.03	1.04	1.04	1.07	1.00
Peoria	1.56	1.58	1.62	1.68	1.64	1.66	1.74	1.76	1.76	1.83	1.82	1.83	1.70	1.71	1.75	1.77	1.87	1.89	1.99	2.01	1.77	1.78
Perry	0.28	0.32	0.27	0.31	0.26	0.28	0.58	0.28	0.31	0.28	0.28	0.29	0.28	0.26	0.27	0.26	0.25	0.24	0.25	0.30	0.25	0.28
Piatt	0.55	0.58	0.53	0.65	0.66	0.66	0.67	0.66	0.70	0.65	0.64	0.63	0.59	0.61	0.63	0.60	0.59	0.56	0.52	0.56	0.53	0.55
Pike	0.99	1.04	1.04	1.10	1.08	1.12	1.12	1.09	1.12	1.06	1.05	1.04	0.99	0.96	0.88	0.90	0.87	0.79	0.79	0.78	0.81	0.75
Pope	0.13	0.13	0.13	0.13	0.12	0.13	0.15	0.16	0.15	0.15	0.15	0.15	0.16	0.13	0.15	0.14	0.13	0.11	0.11	0.12	0.13	0.13
Pulaski	0.08	0.05	0.05	0.06	0.08	0.08	0.07	0.10	0.10	0.09	0.11	0.09	0.10	0.10	0.10	0.09	0.10	0.10	0.10	0.12	0.10	0.12
Putnam	0.23	0.25	0.24	0.25	0.24	0.23	0.24	0.23	0.23	0.22	0.22	0.19	0.20	0.20	0.19	0.19	0.18	0.17	0.17	0.17	0.16	0.17
Randolph	0.43	0.51	0.52	0.49	0.53	0.55	0.55	0.64	0.62	0.57	0.53	0.54	0.53	0.48	0.60	0.54	0.50	0.45	0.46	0.45	0.45	0.47
Richland	0.28	0.31	0.30	0.25	0.31	0.27	0.26	0.27	0.27	0.27	0.25	0.27	0.26	0.26	0.25	0.23	0.22	0.20	0.22	0.24	0.24	0.22

Rock Island	0.93	0.95	0.95	0.90	0.88	0.90	0.97	0.91	0.97	0.94	0.93	0.96	0.95	0.95	0.95	0.90	0.87	0.82	0.80	0.86	0.83	0.80
Saline	0.16	0.13	0.13	0.13	0.12	0.19	0.26	0.19	0.22	0.21	0.20	0.23	0.21	0.21	0.20	0.21	0.20	0.19	0.18	0.18	0.17	0.19
Sangamon	2.18	2.21	2.15	2.14	2.56	2.15	2.10	2.17	2.10	2.14	2.14	2.17	2.06	2.05	2.04	2.03	1.90	1.73	1.69	1.76	1.72	1.78
Schuyler	0.43	0.49	0.36	0.50	0.47	0.45	0.47	0.49	0.48	0.48	0.47	0.46	0.43	0.43	0.42	0.39	0.38	0.30	0.28	0.37	0.35	0.35
Scott	0.34	0.35	0.35	0.35	0.34	0.33	0.35	0.36	0.37	0.34	0.35	0.35	0.33	0.34	0.34	0.34	0.32	0.31	0.31	0.33	0.31	0.32
Shelby	0.89	0.86	0.92	0.93	0.93	0.98	1.00	0.94	0.91	0.89	0.86	0.94	0.90	0.86	0.77	0.81	0.77	0.72	0.68	0.76	0.72	0.74
Stark	0.40	0.51	0.51	0.56	0.49	0.47	0.49	0.53	0.53	0.53	0.52	0.49	0.46	0.46	0.45	0.44	0.43	0.39	0.41	0.41	0.39	0.41
St. Clair	1.97	2.05	2.02	1.84	1.98	2.35	2.00	2.15	2.17	2.18	2.25	2.04	1.97	2.18	2.07	1.93	1.90	1.78	1.92	1.86	1.67	1.75
Stephenson	0.96	1.00	0.92	0.94	0.95	0.95	0.90	1.02	1.03	1.04	1.02	0.99	0.94	0.96	0.97	1.00	0.97	0.90	0.91	0.93	0.94	0.97
Tazewell	1.20	1.38	1.34	1.32	1.20	1.33	1.24	1.24	1.21	1.23	1.20	1.12	1.15	1.17	1.02	1.04	1.03	0.93	0.93	0.96	0.96	0.95
Union	0.24	0.25	0.23	0.20	0.20	0.19	0.20	0.20	0.22	0.25	0.25	0.24	0.22	0.23	0.24	0.22	0.22	0.20	0.21	0.24	0.25	0.24
Vermilion	1.57	1.54	1.52	1.53	1.65	1.66	1.56	1.56	1.56	1.54	1.54	1.56	1.53	1.49	1.45	1.39	1.35	1.29	1.32	1.30	1.33	1.48
Wabash	0.22	0.21	0.22	0.19	0.19	0.22	0.23	0.26	0.23	0.22	0.22	0.23	0.22	0.22	0.21	0.20	0.20	0.19	0.21	0.22	0.18	0.18
Warren	0.80	0.94	0.85	0.99	0.92	0.92	0.95	0.96	0.93	0.93	0.90	0.94	0.88	0.89	0.90	0.89	0.84	0.77	0.71	0.76	0.77	0.78
Washington	0.39	0.41	0.42	0.46	0.44	0.57	0.52	0.55	0.58	0.59	0.57	0.49	0.46	0.45	0,45	0.39	0.43	0.38	0.38	0.41	0.44	0.42
Wayne	0.35	0.33	0.30	0.30	0.34	0.45	0.35	0.33	0.35	0.33	0.29	0.40	0.41	0.36	0.38	0.35	0.33	0.31	0.33	0.28	0.25	0.25
White	0.30	0.27	0.30	0.27	0.37	0.37	0.34	0.35	0.38	9.37	0.39	0.35	0.34	0.32	0.33	0.34	0.33	0.35	0.32	0.35	0.32	0.32
Whiteside	0.98	1.11	1.06	1.19	1.07	1.06	1.11	1.16	1.13	1.13	1.12	1.08	1.02	1.01	1.01	0.99	0.96	0.91	0.94	0.88	0.96	0.90
Will	1.80	1.96	1.80	1.64	1.55	1.57	1.60	1.63	1.62	1.59	1.58	1.62	1.54	1.57	1.62	1.65	1.56	1.61	1.68	1.75	1.79	1.73
Williamson	0.20	0.22	0.17	0.18	0.16	0.22	0.20	0.19	0.20	0.24	0.25	0.25	0.21	0.24	0.23	0.23	0.22	0.22	0.23	0.25	0.24	0.25
Winnebago	0.93	1.14	1.08	1.10	1.10	1.07	1.10	1.16	1.16	1.21	1.25	1.24	1.23	1.24	1.19	1.21	1.23	1.26	1.41	1.45	1.35	1.34
Woodford	0.75	0.82	0.86	0.90	0.87	0.84	0.90	0.88	0.95	0.88	0.84	0.83	0.78	0.76	0.78	0.72	0.71	0.66	0.68	0.68	0.61	0.65
Total	100.00	100.00	100.00	100.00	100.00	100.00	100.00	100.00	100.00	100.00	100.00	100.00	100.00	100.00	100.00	100.00	100.00	100.00	100.00	100.00	100.00	100.00

No. 19.

Statement Showing the Average Rate of Taxation in the several Counties for the years 1888 to 1895, inclusive. Compiled from the returns received from the various County Clerks, of the total amount of all taxes charged upon the tax books for said years, including back taxes.

Counties.	Av. rate on the $100 for the year 1888.....	Av. rate on the $100 for the year 1889.....	Av. rate on the $100 for the year 1890.....	Av. rate on the $100 for the year 1891.....	Av. rate on the $100 for the year 1892.....	Av. rate on the $100 for the year 1893.....	Av. rate on the $100 for the year 1894.....	Av. rate on the $100 for the year 1895.....
Adams..........	$4 21	$3 99	$4 83	$4 18	$4 28	$4 52	$5 83	$5 14
Blexander.......	5 72	5 86	5 86	6 22	6 84	5 98	6 29	6 38
Bond............	2 53	2 39	1 93	2 77	2 67	2 61	2 95	3 21
Boone...........	1 98	2 30	2 26	2 55	2 64	2 76	2 86	3 31
Brown...........	3 04	2 79	2 72	3 14	2 91	2 88	3 18	3 40
Bureau..........	2 62	2 61	2 73	2 88	2 82	3 08	3 43	3 36
Calhoun.........	2 86	3 05	2 79	2 30	2 33	2 18	2 36	2 64
Carroll	2 72	2 52	2 54	2 86	2 82	2 91	3 04	3 42
Cass............	3 29	3 51	3 40	3 50	3 87	3 78	3 58	3 71
Champaign......	3 62	3 55	3 47	3 95	3 77	3 93	4 15	4 93
Christian........	4 12	3 21	3 01	3 51	3 22	3 41	3 80	3 80
Clark...........	4 82	4 01	3 23	4 13	4 50	5 03	4 76	4 49
Clay............	4 65	4 17	4 47	4 12	3 60	4 03	4 08	4 77
Clinton.........	2 48	2 23	2 11	2 47	2 72	2 52	2 56	2 87
Coles	3 71	3 84	3 88	4 34	4 27	4 41	4 59	4 91
Cook............	5 54	5 60	6 30	5 93	6 95	6 92	6 99	9 01
Crawford........	3 95	3 86	3 93	4 55	4 97	4 90	5 41	4 72
Cumberland.....	3 69	3 66	3 86	3 77	4 15	4 16	4 56	4 77
DeKalb..........	2 59	2 64	2 62	2 79	2 91	2 88	3 14	3 25
DeWitt	3 94	3 85	3 99	4 58	4 20	4 60	4 86	4 54
Douglas.........	3 09	3 19	3 27	3 71	3 93	3 76	3 94	4 33
DuPage..........	2 77	2 79	3 11	3 49	3 31	3 56	3 62	3 92
Edgar...........	3 59	3 58	3 50	3 72	4 72	4 66	3 95	4 58
Edwards.........	2 36	2 33	2 44	2 85	2 13	3 04	3 03	3 20
Effingham.......	2 94	2 94	2 87	3 35	3 17	3 39	3 25	3 84
Fayette..........	2 45	2 64	2 47	2 80	3 19	3 29	3 61	3 67
Ford............	3 63	3 68	4 02	4 63	4 73	4 52	4 65	5 28
Franklin.........	3 18	2 97	3 19	3 49	4 39	5 38	4 27	5 01
Fulton...........	3 19	3 34	3 00	3 19	3 36	3 55	3 72	3 89
Gallatin.........	6 25	4 55	4 81	4 78	4 91	5 05	6 28	6 37
Greene	2 51	2 79	2 81	3 21	3 14	3 00	3 14	3 34
Grundy..........	2 91	2 81	2 76	2 91	3 06	3 27	3 50	3 63
Hamilton........	2 72	2 66	3 03	4 20	3 98	3 10	3 58	3 45
Hancock.........	2 62	2 64	2 70	2 87	2 89	3 14	3 16	3 40
Hardin	2 87	3 22	3 46	3 22	3 35	2 76	3 09	3 77
Henderson......	2 26	3 25	2 21	2 17	2 31	2 43	2 75	3 05
Henry...........	2 51	2 43	2 45	2 68	2 62	2 83	2 93	3 38
Iroquois	2 83	2 75	2 88	3 01	3 20	3 17	3 25	3 64
Jackson.........	3 90	4 09	4 22	4 55	4 79	5 01	5 26	5 73
Jasper..........	4 01	4 23	4 56	4 54	4 76	4 98	4 77	4 73
Jefferson........	3 41	3 55	3 84	4 18	4 31	4 11	4 65	4 87
Jersey...........	2 51	2 37	2 74	2 44	2 53	2 80	2 82	3 08
Jo Daviess......	3 17	3 27	3 41	3 59	3 48	3 77	3 87	4 03
Johnson	5 41	5 28	5 14	5 03	5 07	3 88	3 73	4 24
Kane............	3 64	3 87	4 17	4 57	4 38	4 68	4 67	4 99
Kankakee........	4 21	4 09	4 25	4 33	4 06	4 56	4 52	4 58
Kendall..........	2 55	2 25	2 55	2 74	3 12	3 22	2 66	2 93
Knox	2 63	2 53	2 79	3 18	3 10	3 42	3 40	3 86
Lake............	2 94	3 20	3 27	3 33	3 41	3 06	3 61	3 78
LaSalle..........	3 37	3 74	3 71	3 71	3 76	3 84	4 08	4 22
Lawrence........	3 37	3 99	3 51	4 01	4 84	4 31	4 48	4 47
Lee	4 73	3 10	3 04	3 32	3 21	3 43	3 59	3 81
Livingston......	2 73	2 62	2 76	2 84	2 73	2 49	3 51	3 61
Logan...........	3 25	3 20	3 05	3 64	3 64	3 82	3 92	4 12
Macon...........	3 22	3 18	3 62	3 91	3 98	4 34	4 37	4 75
Macoupin........	3 81	3 68	3 08	4 28	3 71	4 24	4 45	4 54
Madison.........	2 86	2 82	3 02	3 23	3 07	3 34	3 17	3 41
Marion	2 95	2 75	2 78	3 06	3 04	3 33	3 54	3 76
Marshall.........	2 59	2 65	2 57	3 09	2 62	2 99	3 12	3 37
Mason...........	6 30	6 91	7 02	7 69	8 03	7 98	6 72	5 39
Massac	4 23	3 74	4 08	4 11	4 09	3 41	3 45	3 72
McDonough.....	2 62	2 77	2 82	3 09	2 93	2 89	3 06	3 06

Statement 19—Concluded.

COUNTIES.	Av. rate on the $100 the year 1888.....	Av. rate on the $100 for the year 1889.....	Av. rate on the $100 for the year 1890.....	Av. rate on the $100 for the year 1891.....	Av. rate on the $100 for the year 1892.....	Av. rate on the $100 for the year 1893.....	Av. rate on the $100 for the year 1894.....	Av. rate on the $100 for the year 1895.....
McHenry........	$2 56	$2 46	$2 44	$2 52	$2 84	$2 85	$2 89	$3 61
McLean..........	3 02	2 81	2 98	3 12	3 17	2 92	3 16	3 58
Menard..........	2 61	2 53	2 68	2 88	2 86	2 37	3 02	3 33
Mercer	2 53	2 49	2 58	2 70	2 96	3 39	3 42	3 39
Monroe..........	2 71	2 59	2 41	2 52	2 63	2 79	2 92	2 81
Montgomery	2 50	2 69	2 73	2 71	2 58	2 77	3 08	3 14
Morgan..........	3 06	2 95	2 84	3 14	3 02	3 39	3 43	3 46
Moultrie.........	3 90	3 38	3 57	4 67	4 53	4 11	4 51	4 89
Ogle.............	2 58	2 54	2 78	2 94	3 03	3 60	3 41	3 48
Peoria...........	4 80	4 47	4 48	4 81	4 76	4 74	5 24	6 41
Perry............	2 74	3 03	2 99	3 25	3 33	3 18	3 48	3 58
Piatt.............	3 28	3 61	3 39	3 78	3 54	3 72	3 80	4 33
Pike..............	2 66	2 95	3 32	2 81	3 03	3 18	4 23	3 67
Pope.............	3 57	3 59	3 58	4 02	4 26	4 32	3 91	3 08
Pulaski..........	6 12	5 51	5 49	5 50	5 82	4 79	5 44	5 25
Putnam..........	2 75	3 34	3 32	2 76	2 52	2 96	2 88	3 21
Randolph........	2 78	2 88	3 03	3 56	3 48	3 37	3 57	3 78
Richland	3 95	4 56	4 92	6 26	5 89	4 94	5 46	5 23
Rock Island.....	4 66	5 13	5 11	5 38	5 90	5 78	6 21	6 69
Saline	3 94	4 06	4 34	4 05	4 85	4 01	4 46	4 65
Sangamon.......	3 47	3 25	3 75	4 20	4 22	4 19	4 34	4 47
Schuyler	2 91	2 58	2 81	3 66	4 49	2 75	3 37	3 68
Scott.............	2 65	2 33	2 34	2 49	2 70	2 66	2 82	3 02
Shelby...........	3 29	3 02	3 32	3 31	3 79	3 44	4 25	4 11
Stark	3 56	3 06	3 15	3 04	3 54	3 38	3 64	3 84
St. Clair.........	3 67	3 42	3 71	3 89	3 63	4 07	4 75	4 74
Stephenson......	2 69	2 83	2 76	3 11	3 06	3 07	3 31	3 51
Tazewell	3 35	3 29	3 35	3 64	3 73	3 61	3 86	4 07
Union............	3 74	3 72	3 85	4 18	4 14	3 72	3 94	4 13
Vermilion.......	3 60	3 68	3 91	3 96	4 17	4 33	4 15	4 36
Wabash.........	3 65	4 00	4 14	4 35	4 01	4 17	4 47	5 57
Warren..........	3 20	3 79	3 36	3 36	3 16	3 61	3 80	3 82
Washington.....	2 60	3 08	2 94	3 17	2 99	2 58	2 98	2 94
Wayne...........	3 47	3 61	3 62	6 50	5 48	5 43	6 12	6 34
White............	5 02	4 89	4 30	4 45	4 80	4 52	4 73	5 52
Whiteside.......	3 02	2 88	3 02	3 14	3 35	3 68	3 74	4 02
Will..............	3 47	3 24	3 34	3 72	3 07	3 83	4 13	4 39
Williamson......	3 71	3 55	3 52	3 72	3 54	3 69	3 72	4 25
Winnebago......	2 87	3 08	3 12	3 06	3 13	3 55	3 25	4 11
Woodford.......	2 69	2 47	2 56	2 79	2 74	2 72	3 21	3 22
State average.	$3 38	$3 34	$3 40	$3 67	$3 73	$3 74	$3 92	$4 15

No 20.

STATEMENT OF PROPERTY ASSESSED *for the year 1895, in the several counties in the State of Illinois, as returned to the Auditor's office.*

DISTRICTS.	COUNTIES.	HORSES.			CATTLE.			MULES AND ASSES.		
		No.	Value.	Av.	No.	Value.	Av.	No.	Value.	Av.
1, 2, 3, 4	Cook	34,392	$654,553	$19 03	30,209	$205,036	$6 78	213	$2,537	$11 91
5	Boone	6,291	86,596	13 76	17,171	142,820	8 32	13	145	11 16
	DeKalb	18,039	207,157	11 48	36,417	243,701	6 69	138	1,414	10 25
	Kane	13,551	213,510	15 75	42,221	306,415	7 21	129	1,692	13 11
	Lake	7,549	144,370	19 14	20,418	176,097	8 62	34	494	14 53
	McHenry	13,627	213,337	15 66	50,274	399,373	7 95	42	675	16 07
6	Carroll	11,743	113,463	9 67	26,874	161,640	6 01	146	1,637	11 21
	JoDaviess	9,345	139,747	14 96	32,332	204,975	6 34	135	1,994	14 77
	Ogle	20,632	264,788	12 83	39,566	263,222	6 65	95	1,187	12 49
	Stephenson	11,251	246,031	21 86	34,526	223,210	6 46	136	2,693	19 80
	Winnebago	12,944	216,163	16 70	28,457	175,780	6 17	122	2,001	16 40
7	Bureau	22,167	301,467	13 60	35,004	234,374	6 70	615	6,866	11 16
	Henry	18,864	257,063	13 63	37,875	202,361	5 34	452	6,248	13 82
	Lee	14,983	187,790	12 53	27,618	163,946	5 94	195	2,169	11 12
	Putnam	3,608	58,407	16 19	5,059	42,111	8 32	83	1,395	16 81
	Whiteside	14,433	194,558	13 48	30,731	192,990	6 28	322	2,767	8 59
8	DuPage	7,070	102,849	14 55	20,106	139,715	6 95	73	920	12 60
	Grundy	9,805	130,387	13 29	10,837	63,460	5 85	272	3,571	13 12
	Kendall	8,518	131,807	15 47	13,316	108,392	8 14	71	1,015	14 29
	LaSalle	28,225	422,178	14 96	32,503	248,822	7 65	566	8,845	15 63
	Will	18,294	178,496	9 75	28,098	176,930	6 29	186	1,810	9 73
9	Ford	9,510	149,881	15 76	9,491	45,381	4 77	508	6,820	13 43
	Iroquois	26,670	347,837	13 04	26,678	203,110	7 61	794	10,015	12 61
	Kankakee	7,853	119,839	15 26	11,220	77,704	6 93	137	2,033	11 81
	Livingston	27,690	231,812	8 73	23,461	122,549	5 22	1,018	9,167	9 00
	Marshall	8,002	101,485	12 68	8,968	56,002	6 24	169	2,495	14 76
	Woodford	12,548	173,551	13 83	13,383	88,169	6 59	316	4,416	13 98
10	Fulton	22,172	206,138	9 29	28,836	147,047	5 10	571	4,841	8 47
	Knox	20,295	312,238	15 38	27,734	216,832	7 82	443	5,883	13 28
	Peoria	15,579	237,512	15 25	25,631	181,398	7 07	417	5,649	13 54
	Stark	9,033	87,983	9 74	9,899	58,587	5 91	135	1,360	10 07
11	Hancock	21,603	220,644	10 21	28,291	184,005	6 51	1,092	12,027	11 01
	Henderson	8,424	102,735	12 19	10,206	97,645	9 57	216	2,850	13 19
	McDonough	16,281	191,877	11 79	22,130	162,783	7 36	464	5,495	11 83
	Mercer	15,818	146,138	9 24	27,751	141,917	5 12	502	5,108	10 17
	Rock Island	10,185	108,789	10 68	16,199	80,516	4 97	220	2,454	11 16
	Schuyler	9,372	139,883	14 93	12,834	90,116	7 02	285	4,413	15 48
	Warren	13,309	121,720	9 15	16,655	104,379	6 27	303	2,457	8 11
12	Adams	14,520	222,276	15 31	19,246	128,387	6 67	1,798	26,850	14 93
	Brown	5,431	73,281	13 49	6,963	49,881	7 16	273	3,881	14 21
	Calhoun	3,139	37,090	11 82	2,991	22,678	7 58	661	7,710	11 66
	Cass	6,076	83,073	13 67	9,013	83,443	9 26	497	6,746	13 59
	Greene	10,294	117,260	11 39	17,793	124,715	7 01	1,089	12,678	11 64
	Jersey	6,200	79,188	12 77	7,292	51,736	7 10	436	5,258	12 04
	Pike	13,813	147,534	10 68	19,213	103,332	5 38	1,702	17,940	10 54
	Scott	5,601	76,231	13 61	8,240	72,220	8 76	414	5,370	12 97
13	Christian	17,517	170,584	9 70	18,830	134,571	7 15	2,203	22,129	10 04
	Mason	6,424	95,935	14 93	5,450	37,094	6 81	1,281	17,321	13 52
	Menard	5,644	112,305	19 93	9,430	112,010	11 87	410	8,190	19 97
	Morgan	9,602	152,983	15 93	17,825	223,776	12 55	775	11,000	14 19
	Sangamon	22,513	284,534	12 64	25,905	224,458	8 67	2,250	27,545	12 24
	Tazewell	13,598	179,235	13 18	17,124	111,381	6 50	692	9,686	13 99

Statement 20—Continued.

Districts.	Counties.	Horses.			Cattle.			Mules and Asses.		
		No.	Value.	Av.	No.	Value.	Av.	No.	Value.	Av.
14	DeWitt	9,981	$96,110	$9 63	9,073	$66,563	$7 34	552	$5,301	$9 60
	Logan	14,139	225,906	15 91	11,594	78,837	6 80	1,161	18,491	15 92
	Macon	16,363	212,049	12 95	12,456	94,953	7 62	1,554	19,936	12 83
	McLean	31,312	308,872	9 54	31,872	200,371	6 29	1,517	14,924	9 84
	Piatt	11,268	95,581	8 48	10,788	52,925	4 90	1,091	9,356	8 58
15	Champaign	24,007	318,725	13 28	20,318	150,601	7 41	1,680	23,265	13 84
	Coles	12,065	164,497	13 63	13,619	96,314	7 08	961	12,635	13 15
	Douglas	12,121	110,960	9 16	10,653	60,639	5 69	1,012	8,812	8 71
	Edgar	14,021	188,317	13 43	18,167	129,176	7 11	835	10,872	13 02
	Vermilion	22,958	285,018	12 41	25,383	186,708	7 36	1,175	14,031	11 94
16	Clay	8,686	70,558	8 12	7,990	37,137	4 65	833	6,431	7 72
	Clark	7,872	94,897	12 18	9,558	39,585	4 14	452	5,301	11 50
	Crawford	8,571	85,522	9 98	8,641	37,361	4 33	428	4,150	9 70
	Cumberland	7,441	71,417	9 60	7,641	36,084	4 71	795	7,313	9 20
	Edwards	5,350	91,194	17 05	5,589	42,222	7 55	795	14,641	18 42
	Jasper	9,140	84,173	9 21	9,148	32,414	3 54	597	5,705	9 55
	Lawrence	6,885	74,203	10 78	7,102	40,957	5 76	714	7,598	10 64
	Richland	4,795	74,186	15 48	5,247	27,003	5 15	320	4,796	14 99
	Wayne	8,556	104,210	12 18	10,991	51,156	4 65	1,323	15,821	11 95
	Wabash	3,862	50,992	13 20	4,608	21,966	4 77	740	10,229	13 82
17	Effingham	7,062	86,603	12 26	7,751	53,090	6 85	554	6,569	11 85
	Fayette	15,303	102,018	6 67	11,976	65,204	5 45	1,073	7,420	6 92
	Macoupin	17,646	162,117	9 19	21,791	147,841	6 78	1,539	13,014	8 46
	Montgomery	16,932	173,629	10 25	16,605	102,192	6 16	1,741	16,684	9 58
	Moultrie	8,029	80,644	10 04	6,698	38,795	5 79	619	5,936	9 58
	Shelby	19,505	201,963	10 35	19,142	124,474	6 50	1,427	13,634	9 55
18	Bond	7,829	66,728	8 52	7,668	54,223	7 07	765	6,465	8 45
	Madison	10,191	200,809	19 77	12,967	102,380	7 89	2,904	74,323	25 59
	Monroe	3,407	62,379	18 31	4,422	26,257	5 94	2,229	47,906	21 49
	St. Clair	10,174	133,389	13 11	11,921	51,692	4 33	4,269	56,469	13 22
	Washington	7,118	95,207	13 37	9,787	61,650	6 29	1,665	21,675	13 02
19	Clinton	5,999	89,087	14 85	7,152	50,794	7 10	1,153	21,304	18 50
	Franklin	6,618	70,382	10 63	6,135	33,950	5 53	1,949	18,558	9 52
	Gallatin	3,626	53,827	14 84	4,140	21,796	5 26	1,172	25,769	21 99
	Hamilton	7,702	90,207	11 71	7,015	31,149	4 44	1,422	16,034	11 27
	Hardin	1,875	58,391	31 14	2,726	23,898	8 77	866	26,533	30 64
	Jefferson	9,393	88,399	9 41	9,316	47,300	5 08	2,047	17,862	8 67
	Marion	10,331	117,036	11 33	9,009	60,012	6 66	1,461	16,065	10 99
	Saline	5,527	78,516	14 21	5,669	27,992	4 93	2,080	29,859	14 36
	White	8,294	89,733	10 82	9,840	40,576	4 12	2,874	30,252	10 53
20	Alexander	1,835	28,895	15 75	2,403	13,161	5 48	1,157	18,990	16 41
	Jackson	5,938	110,402	18 59	8,358	50,679	6 06	2,485	44,115	17 75
	Johnson	4,793	87,793	18 32	5,502	40,464	7 35	2,022	40,512	20 04
	Massac	2,321	44,533	19 18	3,321	20,428	6 15	1,642	33,574	20 45
	Perry	4,443	82,418	18 55	5,633	53,946	9 57	1,044	18,151	17 45
	Pope	4,470	108,559	24 10	5,278	37,552	7 11	1,877	43,742	23 31
	Pulaski	3,331	41,023	12 31	2,779	17,925	6 45	1,672	20,150	12 05
	Randolph	8,201	100,442	12 24	12,158	61,276	5 04	2,030	26,285	12 95
	Union	6,000	101,457	16 91	6,031	31,662	5 25	2,461	45,473	18 48
	Williamson	6,037	104,081	17 24	5,830	53,563	9 19	2,585	44,022	17 03
	Grand agg.	1,169,360	$15,014,342	$12 84	1,593,755	$10,642,105	$6 68	97,428	$1,348,815	$13 84

Statement 20—Continued.

Districts....	Counties.	Sheep.			Hogs.			Steam Engines, including Boilers.		
		No.	Value.	Av.	No.	Value.	Av.	No.	Value.	Av.
1, 2, 3, 4	Cook	1,134	$1,069	$0 94	7,788	$8,729	$1 12	566	$116,656	$206 11
5	Boone	3,772	3,799	1 01	9,112	14,671	1 61	43	3,072	71 44
	DeKalb	8,152	8,800	1 08	30,239	46,890	1 55	93	13,530	145 48
	Kane	9,173	9,420	1 02	13,448	22,481	1 67	250	40,630	162 52
	Lake	11,416	9,294	81	6,167	9,949	1 61	71	22,471	316 50
	McHenry	7,970	4,013	50	17,820	22,136	1 24	66	6,325	95 83
6	Carroll	11,295	8,714	77	28,126	43,426	1 54	34	4,190	123 24
	JoDaviess	10,368	10,640	1 03	22,410	40,951	1 83	52	4,266	82 04
	Ogle	8,073	10,306	1 27	35,990	63,871	1 77	97	7,959	82 05
	Stephenson	11,936	11,934	1 00	29,981	42,081	1 40	99	13,155	132 87
	Winnebago	7,436	7,212	97	17,005	25,927	1 52	76	12,725	167 43
7	Bureau	9,142	9,687	1 06	42,517	73,217	1 72	148	16,920	114 32
	Henry	9,455	9,814	1 03	46,784	78,101	1 66	56	5,012	89 50
	Lee	2,447	2,431	99	20,966	30,738	1 47	89	6,588	75 14
	Putnam	2,126	2,119	99	6,565	11,681	1 78	18	1,570	87 22
	Whiteside	4,702	3,953	85	25,109	48,196	1 92	74	7,945	107 34
8	DuPage	1,243	1,259	1 01	7,993	10,262	1 28	97	8,815	90 87
	Grundy	2,180	2,176	1 00	10,199	11,904	1 16	114	13,761	120 71
	Kendall	4,873	4,873	1 00	11,361	26,346	2 32	52	4,200	80 77
	LaSalle	9,596	9,840	1 02	30,800	59,095	1 91	302	52,730	174 60
	Will	3,344	3,300	98	12,986	15,391	1 19	269	100,171	372 38
9	Ford	1,986	1,272	64	13,617	20,640	1 52	81	5,920	73 09
	Iroquois	4,443	4,553	1 02	31,614	45,612	1 44	191	15,479	81 05
	Kankakee	1,370	1,039	76	6,375	12,558	1 97	56	5,340	95 37
	Livingston	4,086	2,184	53	26,844	35,923	1 34	205	17,739	86 53
	Marshall	4,383	4,203	95	15,184	21,012	1 38	77	8,548	111 01
	Woodford	2,291	2,137	93	17,535	28,530	1 63	125	9,998	79 98
10	Fulton	14,162	9,602	68	63,781	78,570	1 23	156	11,498	73 70
	Knox	5,849	5,916	1 01	30,239	46,269	1 53	112	16,495	147 28
	Peoria	4,767	4,203	88	18,831	31,014	1 63	244	20,027	82 08
	Stark	6,348	6,166	97	18,250	25,592	1 40	58	3,236	55 79
11	Hancock	4,335	4,124	95	43,514	61,542	1 41	107	6,407	59 80
	Henderson	2,053	2,075	1 01	19,035	44,125	2 32	21	1,930	91 90
	McDonough ...	3,126	3,171	1 01	43,881	75,553	1 72	93	9,342	100 45
	Mercer	4,757	3,578	75	39,033	60,692	1 55	80	7,925	99 06
	Rock Island	2,234	2,086	93	17,947	22,603	1 26	112	32,575	290 85
	Schuyler	3,129	3,164	1 01	30,534	42,126	1 38	88	6,598	74 97
	Warren	2,873	2,291	80	34,226	51,055	1 49	70	5,032	71 88
12	Adams	7,374	6,175	84	41,618	44,662	1 07	203	30,714	151 30
	Brown	5,239	5,261	1 00	17,578	25,231	1 43	42	1,750	41 67
	Calhoun	1,079	979	91	9,046	12,390	1 37	13	2,780	213 85
	Cass	1,918	1,654	86	15,701	24,661	1 57	33	4,266	129 27
	Greene	7,576	5,992	79	28,986	38,962	1 34	56	4,597	82 08
	Jersey	3,177	3,182	1 00	16,047	21,065	1 31	45	5,701	126 70
	Pike	13,031	8,202	55	38,821	44,617	1 15	84	5,300	63 10
	Scott	2,509	2,623	1 04	14,790	32,898	2 22	33	1,721	52 15
13	Christian	8,761	7,912	90	29,766	39,315	1 32	1 49	11,780	79 20
	Mason	165	165	1 00	11,117	22,717	2 04	64	3,794	59 28
	Menard	3,552	4,530	1 27	15,402	52,295	3 39	42	5,845	139 17
	Morgan	6,985	9,181	1 31	25,655	68,144	2 66	40	8,915	222 88
	Sangamon	9,492	8,464	89	39,318	70,960	1 81	275	41,804	152 01
	Tazewell	5,694	5,109	89	17,529	25,527	1 46	167	17,953	107 50
14	DeWitt	6,546	4,923	75	16,461	21,645	1 31	56	2,356	42 05
	Logan	3,955	3,957	1 00	21,280	30,565	1 43	114	9,699	85 07
	Macon	3,542	3,431	97	17,979	31,413	1 75	218	34,483	158 18
	McLean	18,215	9,844	54	46,062	72,149	1 57	257	19,408	75 52
	Piatt	1,865	883	48	13,815	14,280	1 04	67	4,806	71 73

Statement 20—Continued.

Districts....	Counties.	Sheep.			Hogs.			Steam Engines, including Boilers.		
		No.	Value.	Av.	No.	Valve.	Av.	No.	Value.	Av.
15	Champaign	5,310	$4,134	$0 78	25,376	$34,886	$1 37	207	$15,113	$73 01
	Coles	8,117	6,217	77	26,591	32,826	1 23	92	7,704	80 48
	Douglas........	5,330	3,823	72	18,025	19,601	1 08	144	8,415	58 43
	Edgar	14,061	10,319	73	23,140	28,846	1 25	95	3,280	34 53
	Vermilion......	14,908	13,328	89	30,359	48,715	1 60	167	14,128	84 60
16	Clay	8,541	4,486	53	14,497	12,799	88	71	4,099	57 73
	Clark	12,167	6,097	50	19,483	17,665	91	60	2,819	46 98
	Crawford	14,458	9,898	69	19,126	16,551	87	53	4,139	78 09
	Cumberland ...	3,340	1,859	56	14,903	15,084	1 01	51	2,150	42 16
	Edwards	7,778	8,144	1 05	10,296	19,116	1 86	48	3,993	83 19
	Jasper	9,118	4,564	50	16,102	12,770	79	76	3,763	49 51
	Lawrence	7,277	4,957	68	12,949	13,356	1 03	45	3,880	86 22
	Richland.......	7,416	7,412	1 00	9,482	7,559	80	49	4,239	86 71
	Wayne	15,107	9,915	66	16,290	13,951	86	76	6,276	82 58
	Wabash	3,671	2,405	66	8,920	9,402	1 05	57	4,689	82 26
17	Effingham	4,495	4,516	1 00	8,859	8,660	98	74	3,908	52 81
	Fayette	10,402	7,903	76	18,378	18,451	1 00	118	8,760	74 24
	Macoupin	18,701	19,370	1 04	37,380	49,694	1 33	156	16,808	107 74
	Montgomery...	15,117	8,700	58	29,393	41,791	1 42	155	13,105	84 55
	Moultrie	2,599	2,529	97	10,673	16,062	1 50	60	2,638	43 97
	Shelby	17,225	15,281	89	34,284	51,147	1 49	136	8,503	62 52
18	Bond	6,983	6,594	94	10,031	12,652	1 26	65	3,204	49 29
	Madison	5,542	5,311	96	21,698	34,938	1 61	192	56,495	294 24
	Monroe.........	1,674	1,433	86	12,197	13,300	1 09	91	10,905	119 78
	St. Clair........	1,881	1,470	78	19,810	17,421	88	375	102,295	272 74
	Washington ...	3,011	2,996	1.00	9,212	9,248	1 00	92	6,751	73 38
19	Clinton	4,631	4,470	96	7,776	9,207	1 18	79	4,838	61 24
	Franklin	3,649	2,669	73	12,625	11,845	94	30	2,491	83 03
	Gallatin	1,446	1,194	82	8,325	8,633	1 03	51	4,515	88 53
	Hamilton	6,362	4,752	75	17,743	14,172	80	43	3,421	79 56
	Hardin.........	1,328	1,629	1 23	7,761	10,041	1 29	20	3,855	192 75
	Jefferson.......	6,684	4,109	61	18,223	13,271	73	37	3,848	104 00
	Marion	6,982	6,907	99	11,780	11,493	98	63	4,194	66 57
	Saline	3,178	2,798	88	14,389	14,532	1 01	62	5,689	93 37
	White	4,968	4,189	85	30,027	21,561	71	74	4,231	57 31
20	Alexander	447	447	1 00	5,947	5,628	95	56	6,480	115 71
	Jackson	2,691	2,694	1 00	19,682	19,800	1 00	128	21,333	166 66
	Johnson........	4,214	4,932	1 17	14,427	17,562	1 22	65	9,789	150 60
	Massac	935	915	1 00	9,389	9,705	1 03	51	8,351	163 74
	Perry	2,679	2,786	1 05	6,333	11,982	1 89	81	4,705	58 09
	Pope	5,065	5,720	1 11	15,406	17,196	1 11	31	4,155	143 03
	Pulaski	855	861	1 00	4,700	6,703	1 43	29	6,323	218 03
	Randolph	4,518	3,104	69	18,138	16,961	93	147	13,410	91 23
	Union	2,558	2,378	93	17,534	16,840	90	83	10,211	123 02
	Williamson	3,599	4,515	1 25	14,486	21,003	1 45	54	12,236	226 59
	Grand Agg.	615,718	$523,614	$0 85	2072,922	$2,937,581	$1 42	10,489	$1,320,286	$125 87

Statement 20—Continued.

District.	Counties.	Fire and Burglar-proof Safes.			Billiard, Pigeon-hole, etc., Tables.			Carriages and Wagons.		
		No.	Value.	Av.	No.	Value.	Av.	No.	Value.	Av.
1, 2, 3, 4	Cook	481	$15,178	$31 56	217	$6,304	$29 05	23,325	$512,354	$23 25
5	Boone	72	1,093	15 18	11	450	40 91	2,684	18,683	6 96
	DeKalb	138	3,438	24 91	32	655	20 47	5,502	55,851	10 15
	Lake	486	8,812	18 13	76	1,740	22 89	8,036	79,183	9 85
	Kane	50	733	14 66	12	173	14 42	3,900	31,951	8 19
	McHenry	113	3,173	28 08	27	550	20 37	5,788	48,123	8 31
6	Carroll	119	1,942	16 32	30	526	17 53	3,849	24,670	6 41
	Jo Daviess	137	2,931	21 39	4	45	11 25	3,569	27,470	7 70
	Ogle	156	3,583	22 96	23	265	11 52	6,519	46,718	7 32
	Stephenson	178	4,655	26 15	26	700	26 92	5,197	43,061	8 29
	Winnebago	119	3,196	26 85	384	4,235	11 03	5,232	54,982	10 51
7	Bureau	124	2,535	20 44	34	631	18 56	6,634	51,279	7 73
	Henry	105	2,388	22 74	47	1,175	25 00	6,509	56,471	8 67
	Lee	134	2,353	17 56	17	245	14 41	5,408	40,698	7 53
	Putnum	6	290	48 33	2	15	7 50	706	6,420	9 09
	Whiteside	119	1,883	15 82	45	1,030	22 89	5,269	37,592	7 13
8	DuPage	48	1,525	31 73	29	560	19 65	3,340	37,309	11 18
	Grundy	119	1,575	13 23	27	273	10 11	3,179	20,826	6 55
	Kendall	30	490	16 33	7	115	16 43	2,518	23,306	9 26
	LaSalle	425	7,087	16 67	99	1,560	15 75	9,556	87,148	9 12
	Will	309	3,547	11 45	60	885	14 75	7,559	53,347	7 06
9	Ford	113	2,598	22 99	12	250	20 84	3,445	24,484	7 11
	Iroquois	132	2,802	21 23	19	518	27 30	8,640	56,174	6 50
	Kankakee	106	1,408	13 28	30	575	19 16	2,699	24,846	9 21
	Livingston	201	2,899	14 42	59	1,035	17 54	8,977	46,396	5 17
	Marshall	86	1,101	12 80	14	202	14 43	2,918	21,447	7 35
	Woodford	109	1,912	17 54	14	170	12 14	4,756	31,177	6 56
10	Fulton	192	2,910	15 15	17	365	21 47	7,154	43,801	6 12
	Knox	157	5,910	37 79	45	1,204	26 76	4,797	49,298	10 27
	Peoria	365	7,326	20 07	51	1,075	21 08	6,213	63,653	10 25
	Stark	58	939	16 19	11	143	13 00	2,621	16,085	6 15
11	Hancock	102	2,437	23 89	14	296	21 14	6,803	40,739	5 99
	Henderson	28	750	26 80	1	10	10 00	1,820	14,880	8 18
	McDonough	58	1,703	29 36	7	83	11 86	5,338	35,875	6 72
	Mercer	91	2,024	22 24	26	325	12 50	3,784	23,361	6 17
	Rock Island	154	2,385	15 49	48	1,090	22 71	3,691	37,192	10 08
	Schuyler	25	414	16 58	......	......	......	3,070	23,515	7 66
	Warren	29	1,112	38 34	23	490	21 30	3,505	22,920	6 54
12	Adams	293	6,026	20 57	31	605	19 52	6,662	70,007	10 51
	Brown	13	229	17 61	1	25	25 00	2,052	14,123	6 88
	Calhoun	12	185	15 42	7	135	19 29	911	6,109	6 71
	Cass	99	1,855	18 74	13	132	10 15	2,096	15,895	7 58
	Greene	55	1,310	23 82	14	165	11 79	2,962	23,427	7 91
	Jersey	59	952	16 14	14	256	18 29	2,356	18,266	7 76
	Pike	68	1,489	21 90	13	280	21 54	4,733	27,046	5 71
	Scott	38	1,423	37 46	3	125	41 67	2,272	18,213	8 01
13	Christian	147	2,321	15 79	10	228	22 80	5,485	33,519	6 11
	Mason	79	1,248	15 79	10	125	12 50	2,292	12,900	5 63
	Menard	59	1,795	30 42	10	189	18 90	1,800	21,830	12 12
	Morgan	70	7,591	108 44	20	865	43 25	3,026	45,801	15 14
	Sangamon	268	5,595	20 85	24	618	25 75	8,351	68,995	8 26
	Tazewell	214	3,630	16 96	21	379	18 05	5,478	41,077	7 49
14	DeWitt	56	600	10 71	12	235	19 58	3,155	17,504	5 54
	Logan	111	2,891	26 04	34	669	19 85	4,753	35,070	7 38
	Macon	208	6,553	31 50	36	750	20 84	6,036	48,895	8 90
	McLean	312	5,611	17 98	44	543	12 34	11,778	64,246	5 46
	Piatt	41	565	12 84	......	......	......	3,992	19,682	4 93

Statement 20—Continued.

District.	Counties.	Fire and Burglar-proof Safes.			Billiard, Pigeon-hole, etc., Tables.			Carriages and Wagons.		
		No.	Value.	Av.	No.	Value.	Av.	No.	Value.	Av.
15	Champaign	187	$3,065	$16 23	41	$925	$22 56	8,958	60,548	$6 76
	Coles	82	993	12 11	29	436	15 04	4,888	29,367	6 01
	Douglas	126	1,403	11 13	10	189	18 90	4,723	23,939	5 06
	Edgar	80	1,517	18 96	13	345	26 54	4,769	33,039	6 90
	Vermilion	175	3,594	20 54	29	695	23 96	9,148	59,662	6 52
16	Clay	34	549	16 15	3	40	13 33	3,999	13,914	3 48
	Clark	56	955	17 05	5	50	10 00	3,317	14,161	4 26
	Crawford	34	498	14 65	....	....	......	3,072	17,021	5 54
	Cumberland	33	857	25 97	1	10	10 00	2,792	13,169	4 71
	Edwards	28	1,040	37 14	....	....	......	2,269	18,814	8 34
	Jasper	6	85	14 16	3	30	10 00	3,222	12,683	3 97
	Lawrence	30	649	21 63	2	10	5 00	2,559	13,164	5 14
	Richland	25	647	25 88	3	75	25 00	1,983	15,054	7 60
	Wayne	57	993	17 42	....	....	......	3,303	19,295	5 84
	Wabash	22	450	20 46	11	240	21 82	1,690	11,183	6 62
17	Effingham	53	1,748	32 98	23	325	14 12	2,854	18,488	6 48
	Fayette	73	1,071	14 67	8	68	8 50	5,025	26,744	5 32
	Macoupin	170	3,043	17 90	35	603	17 23	5,777	32,780	5 62
	Montgomery	126	2,091	16 59	10	109	10 90	5,580	32,851	5 89
	Moultrie	37	529	14 30	8	160	20 00	2,251	11,160	4 95
	Shelby	41	998	24 34	8	125	15 63	6,618	42,976	6 49
18	Bond	33	510	15 45	5	90	18 00	2,378	15,152	6 37
	Madison	226	8,839	39 11	38	640	16 84	5,957	55,421	9 30
	Monroe	15	373	24 86	19	261	13 74	2,373	17,092	7 20
	St. Clair	283	5,408	19 11	46	409	8 89	6,304	54,476	8 64
	Washington	41	630	15 36	3	25	8 33	3,430	19,125	5 57
19	Clinton	44	570	13 00	23	320	14 00	2,744	16,867	6 15
	Franklin	15	511	34 06	....	....	......	2,368	13,330	5 63
	Gallatin	38	640	16 85	7	100	14 28	1,489	10,375	6 90
	Hamilton	29	456	15 72	....	....	......	2,535	11,376	4 49
	Hardin	19	587	30 89	3	110	36 66	878	9,813	11 18
	Jefferson	46	1,639	35 63	9	75	8 33	3,163	17,253	5 44
	Marion	74	1,302	17 69	18	251	13 94	4,076	23,375	5 73
	Saline	30	1,268	42 26	....	....	......	2,293	18,858	8 22
	White	118	1,368	11 59	25	274	10 96	3,789	19,132	5 05
20	Alexander	147	2,923	19 88	32	736	23 00	1,292	10,891	8 43
	Jackson	71	1,061	14 95	7	115	16 43	3,140	19,548	6 23
	Johnson	27	974	36 07	....	....	......	2,135	17,453	8 17
	Massac	43	1,207	28 07	6	90	15 00	1,632	14,586	8 94
	Perry	63	1,425	22 62	19	315	16 58	2,002	17,474	8 73
	Pope	40	922	23 05	6	165	27 50	1,803	19,766	10 96
	Pulaski	37	427	11 54	8	131	16 38	1,355	7,814	5 77
	Randolph	96	1,868	19 46	11	125	11 37	4,660	25,271	5 42
	Union	99	1,921	19 44	5	65	13 00	3,844	26,223	6 82
	Williamson	38	1,300	34 21	5	105	21 00	2,515	24,946	9 92
	Grand Agg.	10,826	$229,810	21 22	2,454	$45,115	$18 38	$441,652	$3,571,500	$8 09

Statement 20—Continued.

Districts.	Counties.	Watches and Clocks.			Sewing and Knitting Machines.			Pianos.		
		No.	Value.	Av.	No.	Value.	Av.	No.	Value.	Av.
1 2 3 4	Cook	6,342	$19,865	$3 13	4,326	$18,646	$4 31	11,679	$338,023	$28 94
5	Boone	1,885	2,894	1 54	971	4,319	4 46	143	4,280	29 93
	DeKalb	5,088	8,614	1 69	3,153	12,608	4 00	424	15,691	37 01
	Kane	9,158	25,934	2 82	5,222	20,136	3 85	1,903	54,718	28 75
	Lake	1,721	4,968	2 89	1,234	4,862	3 94	435	11,948	27 47
	McHenry	3,563	6,235	1 76	2,215	10,460	4 72	364	14,128	38 81
6	Carroll	4,512	7,723	1 71	2,269	9,574	4 24	261	7,990	30 61
	Jo Daviess	3,578	5,220	1 46	2,363	7,711	3 26	256	5,897	23 04
	Ogle	5,330	10,501	1 97	3,291	13,674	4 16	450	12,528	27 84
	Stephenson	3,757	7,202	1 91	2,458	10,426	4 24	355	11,038	31 09
	Winnebago	924	6,231	6 74	1,838	8,923	4 85	809	31,428	38 84
7	Bureau	5,176	10,938	2 11	3,455	11,673	3 38	503	14,344	28 51
	Henry	3,793	9,212	2 42	3,242	16,071	4 95	484	16,853	34 82
	Lee	4,689	9,360	2 00	2,811	10,239	3 64	482	13,862	28 75
	Putnam	35	185	5 29	202	1,010	5 00	40	875	21 87
	Whiteside	3,796	6,650	1 75	2,726	10,964	4 02	482	12,140	25 19
8	DuPage	926	5,391	5 82	1,343	6,660	4 96	578	18,135	31 37
	Grundy	2,555	3,628	1 42	1,791	5,228	2 92	196	4,257	21 72
	Kendall	136	946	6 95	551	2,877	5 22	143	3,709	25 93
	LaSalle	6,497	16,816	2 59	4,501	21,974	4 88	1,130	31,718	28 06
	Will	4,814	9,413	1 96	3,908	15,792	4 04	938	18,879	20 12
9	Ford	3,001	4,215	1 41	2,133	6,548	3 07	210	4,727	22 51
	Iroquois	7,480	11,288	1 51	4,392	13,463	3 07	377	9,857	26 15
	Kankakee	811	2,850	3 51	1,045	5,133	4 91	283	7,248	25 61
	Livingston	7,269	10,432	1 43	4,524	12,890	2 85	421	11,240	26 70
	Marshall	2,755	4,093	1 48	1,603	6,332	3 95	294	7,457	25 36
	Woodford	4,399	6,251	1 42	2,545	9,299	3 65	274	6,763	24 61
10	Fulton	7,728	11,260	1 45	5,177	18,347	3 54	579	11,946	20 63
	Knox	938	5,795	6 17	294	1,587	5 40	810	26,377	32 56
	Peoria	3,658	12,584	3 44	3,033	14,406	4 75	967	28,277	29 24
	Stark	2,504	4,123	1 65	1,288	4,612	3 58	172	6,186	35 97
11	Hancock	7,013	10,666	1 53	4,024	13,791	3 42	429	11,141	25 97
	Henderson	592	3,615	6 11	757	4,365	5 77	111	3,685	33 20
	McDonough	5,293	9,095	1 72	2,965	11,762	3 97	353	10,388	29 42
	Mercer	2,573	5,943	2 31	1,986	7,212	3 64	267	7,415	27 77
	Rock Island	754	5,178	6 87	2,622	12,365	4 72	806	24,063	29 85
	Schuyler	3,035	4,408	1 45	1,796	6,647	3 70	130	3,859	29 68
	Warren	1,475	4,131	2 80	1,242	5,812	4 68	251	7,628	30 39
12	Adams	5,378	10,794	2 01	4,634	23,123	4 99	776	25,779	33 23
	Brown	1,999	2,517	1 26	1,176	3,418	2 91	89	2,896	32 31
	Calhoun	639	1,490	2 39	431	2,042	4 74	30	1,590	53 00
	Cass	1,640	4,177	2 55	1,190	6,583	5 53	269	7,151	26 58
	Greene	751	4,673	6 22	1,278	7,282	5 69	261	7,505	28 75
	Jersey	1,350	3,340	2 48	943	4,056	4 30	175	5,462	30 64
	Pike	3,737	6,853	1 99	2,580	8,086	3 13	335	8,773	26 19
	Scott	1,548	3,677	2 37	1,008	4,862	4 82	167	4,600	27 54
13	Christian	3,805	6,145	1 61	2,545	9,757	3 83	363	7,581	20 88
	Macon	1,857	2,879	1 55	1,487	6,138	4 12	198	8,512	42 99
	Menard	713	4,985	6 99	1,133	7,515	6 63	170	7,235	42 56
	Morgan	1,995	10,340	5 18	1,453	10,168	6 70	335	23,792	71 02
	Sangamon	6,252	17,353	2 78	4,155	27,050	5 93	1,237	38,145	30 84
	Tazewell	5,027	10,445	2 08	3,316	10,974	3 31	419	12,956	30 92
14	DeWitt	2,518	5,341	2 12	1,718	5,659	3 29	228	2,957	12 97
	Logan	3,043	6,229	2 05	2,224	8,706	3 91	366	9,162	25 03
	Macon	4,299	13,934	3 24	4,078	19,900	4 88	754	23,630	32 67
	McLean	8,930	16,641	1 86	5,743	17,718	3 09	1,185	27,887	23 62
	Piatt	919	1,456	1 59	1,388	5,175	3 73	206	4,791	23 26

Statement—Continued.

Districts.	Counties.	Watches and Clocks.			Sewing and Knitting Machines.			Pianos.		
		No.	Value.	Av.	No.	Value.	Av.	No.	Value.	Av.
15	Champaign....	6,607	$10,421	$1 58	4,297	$15,931	$3 71	617	$18,575	$30 11
	Coles..........	5,020	8,256	1 64	2,873	10,652	3 71	386	9,157	23 20
	Douglas........	4,295	6,862	1 59	2,399	6,774	2 82	273	7,888	28 89
	Edgar..........	3,931	5,059	1 29	2,483	9,137	3 68	347	8,954	25 80
	Vermilion......	7,503	13,774	1 83	4,102	16,940	4 13	766	17,696	23 12
16	Clay...........	3,110	4,225	1 36	1,848	5,888	3 19	112	3,052	27 22
	Clark..........	3,090	3,609	1 16	1,930	4,800	2 49	121	2,174	17 97
	Crawford	2,793	3,434	1 23	1,803	4,482	2 48	93	3,199	34 40
	Cumberland....	2,746	3,189	1 16	1,683	5,349	3 18	81	1,619	19 99
	Edwards.......	2,019	3,544	1 76	1,280	6,709	5 25	82	2,561	31 23
	Jasper.........	2,345	2,515	1 07	1,639	4,281	2 55	52	936	18 00
	Lawrence	2,512	3,200	1 27	1,560	4,415	2 83	69	1,988	28 81
	Richland.......	2,375	2,477	1 04	1,315	5,163	3 93	107	3,200	29 90
	Wayne.........	3,255	3,881	1 19	2,033	6,524	3 21	82	1,239	15 11
	Wabash........	1,824	2,775	1 52	1,111	3,923	3 53	111	3,610	32 52
17	Effingham.....	3,126	4,090	1 31	2,031	7,503	3 69	116	4,140	36 55
	Fayette........	4,502	6,297	1 40	2,596	7,885	3 04	114	2,520	22 10
	Macoupin......	6,258	8,442	1 35	4,247	12,470	2 94	500	9,048	18 09
	Montgomery...	5,144	5,723	1 11	3,157	10,723	3 40	364	8,238	22 62
	Moultrie	1,840	1,902	1 03	1,499	3,092	2 06	80	1,953	24 41
	Shelby........	5,199	7,347	1 41	3,317	11,459	3 45	216	5,839	27 50
18	Bond..........	731	2,042	2 79	1,233	5,965	4 83	109	2,980	27 34
	Madison.......	3,044	12,380	4 06	2,573	14,388	5 59	650	28,188	43 37
	Monroe	1,706	2,693	1 56	1,254	5,151	4 11	69	1,827	26 48
	St. Clair.......	1,338	4,069	3 04	1,762	5,768	3 27	387	10,468	27 05
	Washington ...	2,837	3,251	1 14	1,764	4,521	2 56	102	2,127	20 85
19	Clinton.........	2,557	3,168	1 25	1,753	4,721	2 70	141	3,643	25 84
	Franklin.......	2,139	2,573	1 20	1,480	5,017	3 36	53	2,078	39 21
	Gallatin	406	1,870	4 60	824	4,165	5 05	77	2,085	27 08
	Hamilton	2,408	2,818	1 17	1,453	3,966	2 73	77	2,221	28 84
	Hardin	792	2,078	2 62	532	3,975	7 47	19	1,614	84 85
	Jefferson	3,000	3,951	1 31	2,121	8,837	4 16	153	4,393	28 71
	Marion........	4,158	6,158	1 48	2,442	9,670	3 96	315	9,680	30 23
	Saline.........	2,190	3,326	1 51	1,583	6,417	4 05	91	3,377	37 11
	White.........	3,862	4,981	1 29	3,021	7,319	2 42	251	4,091	16 29
20	Alexander......	1,144	4,126	3 61	944	4,752	5 04	296	8,027	27 13
	Jackson	3,753	6,185	1 65	2,346	9,276	3 95	229	6,424	28 05
	Johnson	2,503	4,841	1 93	1,483	7,976	5 39	45	3,260	72 44
	Massac........	1,849	3,156	1 71	1,088	5,686	5 23	120	7,907	65 89
	Perry..........	2,349	3,795	1 62	1,716	7,266	4 23	180	4,905	27 25
	Pope...........	1,943	3,822	1 97	1,179	8,360	7 09	35	2,770	79 14
	Pulaski........	1,121	2,188	1 95	984	4,042	4 11	114	3,092	27 12
	Randolph	3,990	5,927	1 49	2,387	8,151	3 42	234	6,002	25 65
	Union	3,818	5,514	1 44	2,356	7,886	3 35	202	7,358	36 43
	Williamson....	2,661	4,710	1 77	1,999	11,608	5 81	65	2,978	45 82
	Grand Agg.	331,755	$637,766	$1 92	227,556	$895,593	$3 94	45,055	$1,310,183	$29 08

Statement 20—Continued.

Districts	Counties.	Melodeons and Organs.			Franchises.			Annuities and Royalties.		
		No.	Value.	Av.	No.	Value.	Av.	No.	Value.	Av.
1 2 3 4	Cook	537	$4,295	$8 00	3	$5,560	$1,853 33	1	$1,000	$1,000 00
5	Boone	404	3,061	7 58						
	DeKalb	1,024	8,854	8 65						
	Kane	1,135	9,681	8 53	1	433	433 00			
	Lake	394	3,338	8 47						
	McHenry	622	6,669	10 72						
6	Carroll	815	6,343	7 78						
	Jo Daviess	639	5,306	8 31						
	Ogle	1,160	9,828	8 47						
	Stephenson	932	7,972	8 55				1	50	50 00
	Winnebago	644	6,513	10 11	1	10	10 00			
7	Bureau	1,017	9,737	9 58				1	66	66 00
	Henry	1,215	11,371	9 36	1	50	50 00			
	Lee	835	6,588	7 88	1	275	275 00			
	Putnam	79	765	9 73						
	Whiteside	1,038	7,095	6 83						
8	DuPage	271	3,019	11 14						
	Grundy	471	3,354	7 12						
	Kendall	231	2,532	10 96						
	LaSalle	1,312	12,020	9 16	1	2,510	2,510 00			
	Will	854	6,273	7 35	2	35	17 50			
9	Ford	651	4,190	6 44						
	Iroquois	1,303	9,001	6 91	1	778	778 00			
	Kankakee	397	3,425	8 63						
	Livingston	1,567	9,474	6 05				1	175	175 00
	Marshall	462	3,586	7 76						
	Woodford	799	7,169	8 97	1	1,500	1,500 00			
10	Fulton	1,762	13,850	7 86						
	Knox	719	7,564	10 52						
	Peoria	971	9,148	9 42						
	Stark	559	4,478	8 01						
11	Hancock	1,568	10,906	6 98						
	Henderson	337	4,050	12 02						
	McDonough	1,325	11,326	8 55	1	2,846	2,846 00	1	700	700 00
	Mercer	854	6,678	7 82				1	67	67 00
	Rock Island	749	6,348	8 48				1	5	5 00
	Schuyler	651	6,010	9 23						
	Warren	534	3,873	7 25						
12	Adams	1,234	11,380	9 22	1	10	10 00			
	Brown	384	3,418	8 90						
	Calhoun	72	1,245	17 29						
	Cass	229	2,185	9 54						
	Greene	456	4,624	10 12	1	1,450	1,450 00			
	Jersey	173	1,988	11 49						
	Pike	845	7,042	8 33						
	Scott	262	2,312	8 82						
13	Christian	962	7,833	8 14	1	5	5 00	1	388	388 00
	Mason	571	4,637	8 12	1	1,307	1,307 00			
	Menard	369	5,650	15 32						
	Morgan	465	6,232	13 40						
	Sangamon	1,152	11,565	10 04	14	2,500	178 57	3	1,800	600 00
	Tazewell	918	8,567	9 33				1	10	10 00
14	DeWitt	615	3,864	6 28						
	Logan	558	4,685	8 38				1	200	200 00
	Macon	1,270	10,312	8 12						
	McLean	2,029	13,094	6 45						
	Piatt	747	5,122	6 86						

Statement 20—Continued.

Districts....	Counties.	Melodeons and Organs.			Franchises.			Annuities and Royalties.		
		No.	Value.	Av.	No.	Value.	Av.	No.	Value.	Av.
15	Champaign....	1,581	$13,712	$8 79	1	$1,000	$1,000 00	1	$600	$600 00
	Coles..........	964	7,351	7 63	1	50	50 00	......	....	....
	Douglas........	832	5,672	6 82	......	....	....	......	....	....
	Edgar..........	806	6,141	7 62	......	....	....	......	....	....
	Vermilion......	1,467	11,978	8 16	2	1,000	500 00	......	....	....
16	Clay............	508	3,874	7 63	......	....	....	......	....	....
	Clark...........	540	3,288	6 09	1	505	505 00	......	....	....
	Crawford.......	520	3,949	7 60	......	....	....	......	....	....
	Cumberland...	451	3,545	7 86	......	....	....	......	....	....
	Edwards.......	413	5,011	12 13	1	497	497 00	......	....	....
	Jasper.........	476	3,631	7 63	......	....	....	......	....	....
	Lawrence......	422	3,831	9 08	......	....	....	......	....	....
	Richland.......	391	3,929	10 05	......	....	....	......	....	....
	Wayne.........	471	3,556	7 55	......	....	....	......	....	....
	Wabash........	292	2,382	8 16	1	9,000	9,000 00	......	....	....
17	Effingham.....	463	4,891	10 64	......	....	....	......	....	....
	Fayette.........	558	4,772	8 55	......	....	....	1	10	10 00
	Macoupin......	1,237	7,729	6 24	1	100	100 00	......	....	....
	Montgomery...	997	7,729	7 75	1	1	1 00	......	....	....
	Moultrie........	447	3,240	7 03	......	....	....	......	....	....
	Shelby.........	925	8,127	8 79	......	....	....	......	....	....
18	Bond............	414	3,603	8 70	......	....	....	......	....	....
	Madison........	352	3,998	11 36	1	1,150	1,150 00	......	....	....
	Monroe........	26	220	8 46	......	....	....	......	....	....
	St. Clair........	166	1,401	8 44	1	25	25 00	1	700	700 00
	Washington....	317	2,540	8 27	......	....	....	1	1	1 00
19	Clinton.........	252	2,257	9 00	......	....	....	......	....	....
	Franklin........	319	2,527	7 92	......	....	....	......	....	....
	Gallatin........	307	2,918	9 50	1	50	50 00	......	....	....
	Hamilton.......	381	3,074	8 07	......	....	....	......	....	....
	Hardin.........	122	3,466	28 41	1	35	35 00	......	....	....
	Jefferson......	745	5,838	7 83	......	....	....	......	....	....
	Marion.........	658	6,894	10 47	1	214	214 00	......	....	....
	Saline..........	517	5,260	10 17	......	....	....	......	....	....
	White..........	652	5,060	7 76	......	....	....	......	....	....
20	Alexander......	123	1,397	11 33	......	....	....	......	....	....
	Jackson........	495	4,693	9 48	......	....	....	......	....	....
	Johnson........	373	5,907	15 84	......	....	....	......	....	....
	Massac.........	318	5,981	18 81	......	....	....	......	....	....
	Perry...........	341	3,380	9 91	......	....	....	1	15	15 00
	Pope...........	261	5,584	21 39	2	420	210 00	......	....	....
	Pulaski.........	199	2,133	10 72	......	....	....	......	....	....
	Randolph......	243	2,748	11 29	2	1,010	505 00	......	....	....
	Union..........	552	6,784	12 29	3	35	11 67	......	....	....
	Williamson....	496	7,704	15 53	......	....	....	......	....	....
	Grand agg..	67,538	$585,150	$8 63	52	$34,361	$660 79	18	$5,787	$321 50

Statement 20—Continued.

Districts....	Counties.	Patent Rights.			Steamboats, Sailing Vessels, Etc.			Total value of enumerated property.	Merchandise.
		No.	Value.	Av.	No.	Value.	Av.		
1 2 3 4	Cook	1	$220	$220 00	240	$66,780	$278 25	$2,006,805	$13,214,260
5	Boone							285,883	47,000
	DeKalb							627,203	161,064
	Kane				52	292	5 61	795,077	373,991
	Lake				115	2,520	21 91	423,168	90,400
	McHenry				1	150	150 00	735,347	154,418
6	Carroll							301,838	83,215
	Jo Daviess							457,153	107,034
	Ogle				2	250	125 00	708,680	131,472
	Stephenson							624,208	178,206
	Winnebago				6	1,425	237 50	556,751	348,814
7	Bureau				8	1,000	125 00	744,734	163,674
	Henry							672,190	225,703
	Lee				2	50	25 00	477,332	135,595
	Putnam				26	625	24 04	127,468	9,265
	Whiteside				2	2,150	1,075 00	529,913	152,009
8	DuPage							336,419	70,280
	Grundy	1	15	15 00	1	300	300 00	264,715	78,969
	Kendall							310,608	43,640
	La Salle				10	1,098	109 80	983,441	393,213
	Will				20	3,300	165 00	587,560	291,488
9	Ford							276,926	75,764
	Iroquois	1	100	100 00	1	25	25 00	730,612	185,887
	Kankakee				52	350	6 73	264,348	78,903
	Livingston				1	70	70 00	513,985	162,063
	Marshall				3	435	145 00	238,308	67,505
	Woodford							371,042	93,978
10	Fulton							560,175	182,076
	Knox	1	20	20 00	1	50	50 00	701,438	246,569
	Peoria		7,050	2,350 00	23	2,315	100 65	625,637	559,899
	Stark							219,490	53,819
11	Hancock				2	525	262 50	579,250	170,988
	Henderson							282,715	35,180
	McDonough							531,999	159,761
	Mercer				2	20	10 00	418,403	93,362
	Rock Island				34	13,380	393 53	351,029	217,367
	Schuyler				9	70	7 78	331,223	45,323
	Warren							332,900	71,484
12	Adams	1	1	1 00	12	906	75 50	607,695	402,881
	Brown							185,911	52,400
	Calhoun				31	1,645	53 06	98,068	43,720
	Cass				1	170	170 00	241,991	72,311
	Greene				1	15	15 00	354,655	96,170
	Jersey				10	2,010	201 00	202,460	47,157
	Pike				16	110	6 87	386,624	85,538
	Scott							226,275	63,809
13	Christian	1	25	25 00				454,093	129,864
	Mason				1	200	200 00	214,972	50,436
	Menard							344,365	76,340
	Morgan	1	100	100 00	1	100	100 00	578,988	231,059
	Sangamon	1	25	25 00	1	25	25 00	831,436	359,764
	Tazewell				9	505	56 11	437,434	182,139
14	DeWitt	1	14	14 00	1	10	10 00	233,082	66,793
	Logan							435,067	125,376
	Macon				1	250	250 00	520,489	342,460
	McLean	1	12	12 00	7	18	2 57	771,338	320,491
	Piatt							214,622	57,910

Statement 20—Continued.

Districts....	Counties.	Patent Rights.			Steamboats, Sailing Vessels, Etc.			Total value of enumerated property.	Merchandise.
		No.	Value.	Av.	No.	Value.	Av.		
15	Champaign							$671,501	$198,054
	Coles							386,155	151,666
	Douglas	1	$20	$20 00				264,997	70,724
	Edgar	1	10	10 00				435,012	101,377
	Vermilion							687,267	261,477
16	Clay				5	$5	$1 00	167,057	53,581
	Clark	1	25	25 00				195,931	44,638
	Crawford				4	65	16 25	190,269	40,852
	Cumberland							161,645	27,104
	Edwards							217,486	42,922
	Jasper							167,550	28,802
	Lawrence				1	15	15 00	172,223	26,087
	Richland							155,740	34,700
	Wayne							236,817	37,599
	Wabash				4	415	103 75	133,661	27,845
17	Effingham							204,531	68,703
	Fayette							259,123	64,859
	Macoupin							483,059	130,109
	Montgomery	1	60	60 00				423,626	136,348
	Moultrie	1	8	8 00				168,648	39,521
	Shelby							491,873	119,807
18	Bond							180,208	58,822
	Madison				10	13,550	1,355 00	612,810	241,326
	Monroe							189,798	44,132
	St. Clair	1	300	300 00	10	78,312	7,831 00	524,072	271,480
	Washington				1	20	20 00	229,767	63,347
19	Clinton							211,246	42,972
	Franklin							165,931	31,484
	Gallatin				4	490	122 50	138,427	41,503
	Hamilton							183,646	28,899
	Hardin				26	352	13 54	146,377	37,610
	Jefferson	1	5	5 00				216,760	49,658
	Marion							273,251	107,340
	Saline	1	5	5 00				197,897	156,828
	White				2	50	25 00	232,817	70,457
20	Alexander				6	22,927	3,821 17	129,380	132,775
	Jackson							296,325	97,008
	Johnson							241,463	44,400
	Massac				3	2,474	824 67	158,593	53,656
	Perry				1	75	75 00	212,638	56,234
	Pope				11	2,138	194 36	260,871	40,901
	Pulaski				5	1,075	215 00	113,887	34,789
	Randolph	1	7	7 00	14	1,379	98 50	273,966	91,741
	Union	1	5	5 00	4	21	5 25	263,833	65,578
	Williamson							292,771	64,291
	Grand Agg	23	$8,012	$349 00	816	$226,507	$277 58	$39,336,542	$25,394,259

Statement 20—Continued.

Districts.	Counties.	Material and manufactured articles.	Man'f'ers' tools, implements and machinery.	Agricult'l tools, implements and machinery.	Gold and silver plate and plated ware.	Diamonds and jewelry.	Moneys of bank, banker, broker, etc.	Credits of bank, banker, broker, etc.
1, 2, 3, 4	Cook	$768,580	$1,272,549	$62,500	$15,368	$12,054	$44,800	$12,225
5	Boone	12,035	8,388	20,860	....	....	....	....
	DeKalb	15,185	23,942	40,551	760	245	15,964	300
	Kane	206,456	235,783	36,732	1,142	4,207	36,285	3,405
	Lake	22,015	41,036	19,297	625	250	10,825	550
	McHenry	6,509	11,703	44,644	70	265	24,476	2,140
6	Carroll	1,296	4,271	22,510	203	115	38,822	1,775
	JoDaviess	4,819	8,850	22,878	449	70	53,289	4,820
	Ogle	1,438	5,718	48,543	150	380	47,322	14,389
	Stephenson	17,065	27,484	51,608	75	245	18,174	5,485
	Winnebago	164,447	127,170	38,757	3,225	3,140	40,478	99,610
7	Bureau	1,034	6,532	40,404	408	272	25,591	241,985
	Henry	13,450	19,339	62,768	273	....	36,303	8,747
	Lee	1,638	8,159	26,975	....	1,043	7,980	2,300
	Putnam	40	375	6,455	....	....	14,125	1,795
	Whiteside	21,202	15,056	29,384	....	....	16,027	8,418
8	DuPage	1,395	8,610	35,363	615	850	1,775	....
	Grundy	8,040	13,680	17,091	85	143	9,156	45,061
	Kendall	2,860	4,764	25,363	15	....	2,300	8,666
	LaSalle	65,162	36,856	68,917	1,462	782	98,582	9,789
	Will	78,625	182,693	45,220	976	1,818	21,965	21,995
9	Ford	1,685	5,909	28,223	42	70	10,750	125
	Iroquois	1,736	11,827	66,135	280	328	31,135	32,910
	Kankakee	5,189	8,954	17,199	295	250	10,125	17,045
	Livingston	6,928	6,022	62,241	108	437	41,887	46,370
	Marshall	1,335	2,960	19,148	17	367	4,184	575
	Woodford	1,858	3,757	38,420	45	20	14,281	20,015
10	Fulton	11,321	11,925	41,678	....	20	35,528	62,181
	Knox	11,420	18,480	37,430	235	1,675	41,078	65,700
	Peoria	47,725	38,120	37,465	2,070	4,205	322,406	5,750
	Stark	320	1,768	15,193	....	....	15,450	3,115
11	Hancock	5,579	5,911	31,189	175	1,233	134,726	16,054
	Henderson	710	720	15,940	45	5	16,195	36,825
	McDonough	10,559	5,501	30,554	206	554	111,235	47,820
	Mercer	1,616	4,829	23,835	31	158	21,738	20,193
	Rock Island	172,207	98,866	14,635	455	895	17,750	27,300
	Schuyler	928	1,791	17,263	63	....	29,928	52,680
	Warren	7,185	4,946	21,696	82	107	14,155	15,010
12	Adams	110,427	75,502	37,267	2,500	3,155	18,256	25,676
	Brown	945	1,885	13,191	7	....	84,385	285
	Calhoun	3,840	3,800	9,137	....	....	3,973	....
	Cass	660	1,635	19,350	25	20	11,932	14,688
	Greene	1,630	2,625	21,783	90	....	15,425	35,534
	Jersey	1,455	3,580	18,155	208	45	5,833	5,115
	Pike	3,354	5,112	30,342	....	....	29,155	47,290
	Scott	369	1,032	15,758	134	....	19,500	....
13	Christian	9,681	12,527	30,831	95	73	80,084	33,124
	Mason	1,740	3,556	14,917	65	35	21,116	11,834
	Menard	1,120	6,045	24,065	....	95	26,235	215
	Morgan	....	2,695	38,152	298	866	69,700	700
	Sangamon	26,461	42,336	39,879	2,504	3,163	174,576	23,000
	Tazewell	15,615	10,387	38,521	492	640	98,398	14,877
14	DeWitt	179	2,445	15,033	52	195	75,943	21,800
	Logan	1,945	2,715	40,280	315	255	51,329	10,781
	Macon	35,020	46,069	33,708	1,243	1,980	51,906	29,221
	McLean	7,835	16,670	54,268	879	1,653	71,454	76,768
	Piatt	558	3,687	27,391	25	35	27,266	10,213

Statement 20—Continued.

Districts.	Counties.	Material and manufactured articles.	Man'f'ers' tools, implements and machinery.	Agricult'l tools, implements and machinery.	Gold and silver plate and plated ware.	Diamonds and jewelry.	Moneys of bank, banker, broker, etc,	Credits of bank, banker, broker, etc.
15	Champaign....	$8,012	$9,766	$54,828	$2,383	$2,690	$57,101	$12,921
	Coles..........	4,287	8,881	22,928	748	544	36,921	12,529
	Douglas.......	2,715	4,698	30,009	425	422	32,200	23,506
	Edgar..........	1.078	5,819	25,823	128	197	25,627	13,101
	Vermilion.....	1,535	12,445	40,250	292	1,541	90,571	32,599
16	Clay...........	619	2,990	12,064	54	20	19,072	1,389
	Clark..........	1,611	2,842	11,193	59	....	3,230	3,579
	Crawford......	898	4,940	15,051	....	50	11,410	471
	Cumberland...	760	2,222	12,955	....	100	4,591	4,490
	Edwards	1,105	5,316	16,553	71	180	13,004	10,50
	Jasper.........	576	1,714	15,437	2	3	2,005	2,73
	Lawrence......	995	1,325	13,415	35	....	6,803	1,538
	Richland	157	3,668	10,097	9	....	542	21,850
	Wayne.........	562	2,549	15,551	10	5	3,989	4,337
	Wabash........	4,595	3,550	13,577	300	....	11,145	11,118
17	Effingham.....	1,592	6,359	18,400	139	25	10,648	3,237
	Fayette........	1,382	6,116	29,122	305	181	35,988	17,521
	Macoupin......	1,559	6,303	26,465	197	209	48,216	16,874
	Montgomery .	1,631	12,603	34.893	87	397	23,488	17,668
	Moultrie.......	390	2,296	11,197	25	....	13,557	5,453
	Shelby.........	3,227	4.168	40,518	122	64	7,030	12,089
18	Bond..........	1,408	4,093	15,938	25	....	18,187	3,405
	Madison.......	52,280	65,768	64,452	770	605	25,430	1,545
	Monroe........	6,858	3,714	24,925	252	....	....	8,330
	St. Clair.......	50,831	107,570	43,800	125	765	69,990	27,760
	Washington...	3,951	2,841	24,839	20	10	16,505	5,635
19	Clinton........	3,383	4,142	20,455	190	645	5,414	....
	Franklin.......	423	3.113	14,145	20	....	4,148	640
	Gallatin.......	1,341	4.348	12,067	....	50	1,430	....
	Hamilton......	32	3,389	11,683	37	271	4,796	5,776
	Hardin	1,225	5,263	12,732	16	....	285	530
	Jefferson......	3,355	9,344	14,641	35	45	18,434	2,046
	Marion	2,062	3,463	17,786	226	99	28,740	9,130
	Saline.........	1,137	8,261	13,278	6	65	11,013	25,325
	White..........	111	3,735	18,728	28	20	11,919	5,743
20	Alexander.....	4,725	4,369	6,317	400	272	925	....
	Jackson	5,071	23,337	23,593	204	84	3,004	1,152
	Johnson	4,038	8,640	22,939	208	50	8,330	23,637
	Massac	7,974	15,901	15,075	100	125	5,642	4,950
	Perry..........	990	2,289	18,671	13	15	3,433	1,860
	Pope...........	678	3,811	23,706	140	30	8,102	14,277
	Pulaski........	10,623	8,461	7,846	43	180	2,007	6,775
	Randolph......	12,512	12,753	32,453	295	128	8,135	7,009
	Union..........	5,514	7,378	23,339	184	135	16,991	13,111
	Williamson....	2,170	18,625	23,257	85	15	4,368	2,219
	Grand agg.	$2,146,304	$2,984,725	$2,784,083	$47,805	$58,650	$3,107,622	$1,724,611

Statement 20—Continued.

Districts	Counties.	Moneys of other than banker, etc.	Credits of other than banker, etc.	Bonds and stocks.	Shares of capital stock of companies not of this State.	Pawnbrokers' property.	Property of corporations not before enumerated.	Bridge property.
1 2 3 4	Cook	$1,459,384	$67,660	$6,283,440	$40,725	$1,475	$755,734	$2,125
5	Boone	215,816					1,300	
	DeKalb	134,439	172,378	7,924			4,216	
	Kane	119,792	340,494	33,267		110	4,825	
	Lake	40,745	52,845	15,990			22,241	
	McHenry	68,952	177,290				638	
6	Carroll	143,905	94,703				3,990	
	JoDaviess	135,636	176,469	4,030	$250		11,110	
	Ogle	172,064	297,154	72	2,420		10,745	
	Stephenson	178,842	233,823	2,323	100		116,750	
	Winnebago	110,799	805,804	6,295	225		1,630	
7	Bureau	155,321	55,216	1,902	250		12,444	
	Henry	56,819	464,440	21,166	170		1,035	
	Lee	47,014	156,661	1,545	83			$150
	Putman	11,310	6,140	400			10,335	
	Whiteside	25,918	210,866	340			15,195	25,000
8	DuPage	16,541	135,255	4,609	2,754		7,686	
	Grundy	65,085	19,737	533			2,100	
	Kendall	107,320	103,372				9,200	100
	LaSalle	231,322	245,082	400			46,671	1,000
	Will	92,204	111,089	14,063	925	650	41,680	500
9	Ford	7,185	24,365	2,381			2,247	
	Iroquois	161,858	148,880	27,656	14,449		6,498	
	Kankakee	17,425	20,487	23,763	550		24,673	
	Livingston	102,783	101 041	5,202	75		9,500	
	Marshall	46,711	65,530				525	2,500
	Woodford	90,860	80,486	690	905		7,526	40
10	Fulton	158,278	253,980	107,878			2,486	
	Knox	218,197	275,674	500	2,200		9,369	
	Peoria	105,092	125,264	11,175	800		26,052	
	Stark	91,174	70,785	250				
11	Hancock	132,893	166,464	8,834	7,829		4,371	
	Henderson	35,180	99,265		380			
	McDonough	113,472	177,283	14,676	2,273		8,271	20
	Mercer	34,936	241,505	7,029	265		1,344	
	Rock Island	49,838	43,701	4,100	5,829	50	10,485	6,000
	Schuyler	87,062	52,372	300	74		40	
	Warren	14,685	349,752	1,030	15		4,193	25
12	Adams	116,619	175,208	3,410	6,213		280,713	
	Brown	20,997	16,786	50	291		450	
	Calhoun	6,388	216,076	500				
	Cass	81,195	26,152	4,943	23		25	20
	Greene	41,890	170,920	6,210	29,910		40	
	Jersey	37,245	2,080	19,015	200		1,600	
	Pike	131,947	91,696	125			1,798	
	Scott	261,679	14,713				100	
13	Christian	62,298	57,305	2,260	54,287		12,843	
	Mason	1,885	1,564	3,592			3,436	
	Menard	68,160	210,305	6,985			1,705	
	Morgan	37,223	380,426	3,235			8,999	
	Sangamon	134,695	64,000	41,625	1,548	575	34,025	15
	Tazewell	158,533	135,092	2,884	221		20,826	15
14	DeWitt	18,838	74,153	1,885	3,248		1,000	
	Logan	61,165	71,874	650			6,471	
	Macon	87,848	160,105	2,166			35,128	
	McLean	224,915	485,779	217,596	15,183		21,249	
	Piatt	40,001	10,193	6,173	845		578	

Statement 20—Continued.

Districts...	Counties.	Moneys of other than banker, etc.	Credits of other than banker, etc.	Bonds and stocks.	Shares of capital stock of companies not of this State.	Pawnbrokers' property.	Property of corporations not before enumerated.	Bridge property.
15	Champaign	$25,314	$57,741	$3,854	$33,179	....	$10,222	....
	Coles	43,292	39,718	19,667	1,645	....	$8,874	....
	Edgar	28,007	43,380	18,244	9,722	....	44	....
	Douglas	37,786	140,872	958	13,431	....	33,478	....
	Vermilion	147,118	91,939	15,246	23,712	....	65,892	....
16	Clay	20,947	30,145	12,710	4,947	....	1,434	....
	Clark	17,419	18,355	....	....	....	3,898	....
	Crawford	7,729	33,428	2,177	1,176	....	1,202	....
	Cumberland	12,955	8,445	3,466	....	....	40	....
	Edwards	41,006	76,678	13,462	391	....	....	....
	Jasper	16,554	5,520	887	2,386	....	923	$75
	Lawrence	15,914	10,930	4,273	581	....	39	....
	Richland	5,730	34,599	683	....	....	760	....
	Wayne	8,515	31,100	20	7,760	....	325	....
	Wabash	2,172	18,497	649	3,386	....	23	....
17	Effingham	25,876	2,350	....	5,383	....	205	....
	Fayette	53,737	44,769	5,554	3,260	....	1,155	....
	Macoupin	64,219	93,250	4,775	3,904	....	13,950	....
	Montgomery	118,521	93,975	33,447	6,010	....	6,814	....
	Moultrie	27,427	12,563	5,495	5,687	....	1,744	....
	Shelby	71,582	110,023	38,403	5,698	....	5,242	....
18	Bond	6,488	84,115	11,065	530	$16	....	10
	Madison	429,820	66,320	24,650	1,121	....	67,535	40,000
	Monroe	186,350	6,820	1,394	1,933	....	100	....
	St. Clair	544,619	10,935	24,990	1,642	50	24,353	105
	Washington	77,607	83,237	8,459	9	....	866	....
19	Clinton	12,861	101,356	7,991	17	....	100	....
	Franklin	12,375	6,110	692	....	....	....	....
	Gallatin	6,381	550	....	1,757	....	149	....
	Hamilton	15,083	42,610	4,971	....	....	....	....
	Hardin	3,287	14,829	....	....	....	....	....
	Jefferson	18,907	20,832	370	266	....	25	....
	Marion	39,559	64,343	20,411	13,470	....	13,199	....
	Saline	5,526	6,956	....	636	....	....	....
	White	20,418	41,769	666	....	....	1,300	....
20	Alexander	1,600	....	....	225	....	22,557	....
	Jackson	10,096	43,669	10,655	607	....	5,900	....
	Johnson	20,620	28,477	....	....	....	588	3
	Massac	22,679	29,067	160	1,750	....	8,415	....
	Perry	10,795	1,240	11,349	567	....	4,333	....
	Pope	17,377	12,354	11,112	....	....	2,699	....
	Pulaski	1,777	8,078	7,249	290	....	....	....
	Randolph	157,887	40,538	4,485	1,065	....	1,779	....
	Union	90,134	22,562	12,434	500	....	6,056	....
	Williamson	22,503	16,991	200	525	....	1,876	....
	Grand Agg.	$9,176,947	$10,342,774	$7,284,331	$354,683	$2,926	$1,946,185	$77,703

Statement 20—Continued.

Districts.	Counties.	Property of saloons and eating houses.	Household and office furniture.	Investments in real estate and improvements thereon.	Grain of all kinds.	Shares of stock of State and National banks.	All other property.
1, 2, 3, 4	Cook	$87,130	$2,974,111	$6,235	$4,115	$278,802	$66,344
5	Boone	225	36,274		5,495	69,000	7,216
	DeKalb	1,190	123,297	5,837	53,749	33,572	16,095
	Kane	10,653	283,585	2,935	8,753	246,360	44,943
	Lake	2,225	92,575	990	5		4,104
	McHenry	1,981	93,511	1,190	1,124	20,000	29,481
6	Carroll	977	56,987	50	13,406	47.300	11,803
	JoDaviess	1,675	62,440	770		8,440	6,395
	Ogle	630	104,064	1,440	102,187	39,399	21,449
	Stephenson	2,426	110,356	2,755	19,549	170,000	15,992
	Winnebago	6,568	204,988	9,000	15,463		75,010
7	Bureau	2,164	94,521	3,186	132,567	142,021	21,761
	Henry	1,866	141,088	186	167,043	193,432	37,711
	Lee	2,043	98,919	960	30,984	60,000	23,587
	Putnam	60	9,295		26,544		3,224
	Whiteside	2,350	113,430	210	23,382	91,678	23,708
8	DuPage	605	130,887	3,325	100		13,272
	Grundy	1,680	40,576	1,000	38,962	51,464	34,281
	Kendall	175	42,751	585	45,985		3,888
	LaSalle	8,415	189,208	3,260	249,303	154,662	88,467
	Will	4,933	149,194	15,600	2,157	155.865	91,495
9	Ford	330	44,099		66,538		24,751
	Iroquois	2,266	98,608	8,345	263,189	10,165	33,000
	Kankakee	3,030	45,887	1,871	7,203	1,250	28,534
	Livingston	1,827	106,593	5,698	303,133	43,500	37,765
	Marshall	2,465	46,695		41,309	56,000	10,604
	Woodford	2,030	66,697	5,531	110,571	10,000	5,448
10	Fulton	758	123,478		36,713		15,846
	Knox	3,630	183,668	1,260	100,035	126,740	30,522
	Peoria	14,995	209,675	4,965	91,539		346,459
	Stark	98	30,184	2,085	65,809		8,240
11	Hancock	690	92,769	35	54,215	350	11,883
	Henderson		34,715				449
	McDonough	808	84,645		70,759	23,248	18,468
	Mercer	500	64,751		567	87,204	28,771
	Rock Island	5,210	167,508	2,870	11,106	208,000	61,327
	Schuyler	75	37,954	125	8,604		3,441
	Warren	145	58,403	500	74.354	98,825	5,382
12	Adams	9,365	268,782	7,715	7,452		23,423
	Brown	1,915	31,790	25	4,145		7,489
	Calhoun	145	12,945		7,855		930
	Cass	1,285	42,142	2,222	25,842	36,035	4,437
	Greene	1,010	54,687	2,495	15,170		5,115
	Jersey	645	39,352		9,996		27,456
	Pike	223	83,946		15,378		6,534
	Scott	530	33,644		22,066		765
13	Christian	3,735	74,587	2,466	97,960	21,280	26,599
	Mason	420	33,955	2,240	27,370		5,809
	Menard	1,040	60,520	3,100	44,950	17,500	3,802
	Morgan	9,005	100,131		74,852	90,000	53,973
	Sangamon	8,697	253,114	5,055	199,624	296,420	43,050
	Tazewell	3,547	116,288	450	102,322	20,246	16,939
14	Dewitt	2,322	42,319	2,237	107,831		5,042
	Logan	1,620	80,953	725	153,947	77,300	45,534
	Macon	7,821	223,942	10,462	242,478	35,225	33,983
	McLean	2,806	194,135	6,097	417,356		33,612
	Piatt	130	50,892		114,436	80	5,683

Statement 20—Continued.

Districts.	Counties.	Property of saloons and eating houses.	House-hold and office furniture.	Invest-ments in real estate and improve-ments thereon.	Grain of all kinds.	Shares of stock of State and National banks.	All other property.
15	Champaign	$1,354	$140,728	$1,765	$316,139	$36,066	$18,500
	Coles	6,035	84,826	3,012	64,457	134,307	24,545
	Douglas	315	65,216	260	96,548	26,600	31,202
	Edgar	100	62,572	1,326	129,437	64,080	5,075
	Vermilion	10,404	160,933	5,575	210,244	91,664	18,092
16	Clay	62	33,430	266	1,458	....	3,593
	Clark	473	35,419	....	10,376	....	2,062
	Crawford	100	35,755	....	6,255	1,614	....
	Cumberland	74	30,090	90	7,132	....	1,397
	Edwards	50	27,693	....	2,440	....	681
	Jasper	303	27,527	80	1,679	....	1,586
	Lawrence	250	30,369	....	2,350	....	3,354
	Richland	2,070	27,312	650	233	....	639
	Wayne	150	29,184	2,448	1,184	....	1,915
	Wabash	1,450	44,586	250	3,003	....	5,670
17	Effingham	659	43,596	90	2,457	....	3,675
	Fayette	1,089	49,143	1,319	6,503	....	12,849
	Macoupin	2,378	81,714	562	15,128	7,566	36,419
	Montgomery	3,365	80,376	....	25,678	55,151	18,590
	Moultrie	605	25,254	....	66,766	1,537	6,231
	Shelby	275	86,815	388	101,223	21,000	13,316
18	Bond	210	33,802	5	2,504	4,925	....
	Madison	13,392	167,084	2,750	12,811	33,839	105,000
	Monroe	1,335	33,487	....	8,302	8,334	3,981
	St. Clair	4,754	80,554	5,435	9,747	34,880	142,530
	Washington	815	42,894	90	3,497	....	9,779
19	Clinton	925	43,888	1,180	6,341	....	3,089
	Franklin	235	28,525	255	711	....	558
	Gallatin	270	29,750	....	4,192	19,322	1,290
	Hamilton	....	22,474	173	351	5	595
	Hardin	1,180	22,946	800	2,190	....	145
	Jefferson	93	38,470	223	1,828	....	4,870
	Marion	996	65,361	1,315	2,494	62,080	3,999
	Saline	....	41,713	....	4,503	26,598	9,224
	White	800	42,669	....	11,921	7,680	3,621
20	Alexander	3,366	67,708	60	9,270	55,020	4,845
	Jackson	3,035	59,975	....	1,871	24,233	19,176
	Johnson	....	58,143	560	1,577	7,474	....
	Massac	1,665	53,834	2,794	262	24,500	3,028
	Perry	793	45,622	1,570	160	80	9,152
	Pope	540	46,160	202	4,881	....	3,485
	Pulaski	1,334	25,949	....	790	....	4,443
	Randolph	1,026	61,781	334	6,956	10,011	10,939
	Union	106	60,770	756	2,894	....	5,183
	Williamson	2,555	51,524	3,210	2,600	15,000	1,180
	Grand aggregate	$306,070	$10,874,131	$177,881	$5,110,890	$3,794,629	$2,220,779

Statement 20—Continued.

Districts.	Counties.	Total value of unenumerated property.	Total value of personal property.
1, 2, 3, 4	Cook	$27,420,616	$29,436,421
5	Boone	423,609	709,492
	DeKalb	810,708	1,437,911
	Kane	1,993,718	2,788,795
	Lake	416,718	839,886
	McHenry	638,392	1,373 739
6	Carroll	525,328	917,166
	JoDaviess	609,424	1,066,577
	Ogle	1,001,036	1,709,716
	Stephenson	1,151,258	1,775,466
	Winnebago	2,061,423	2,618,174
7	Bureau	1,101,253	1,845,987
	Henry	1,451,539	2,123,729
	Lee	605,636	1,082,968
	Putnam	99,363	226,831
	Whiteside	774,173	1,304,086
8	DuPage	433,922	770,341
	Grundy	427,643	692,358
	Kendall	400,984	711,592
	LaSalle	1,892,553	2,875,994
	Will	1,325,135	1,912,704
9	Ford	294,464	571,390
	Iroquois	1,105,152	1,835,764
	Kankakee	312,633	576,981
	Livingston	1,043,173	1,557,158
	Marshall	368,430	606,828
	Woodford	553,158	924,260
10	Fulton	1,044,141	1,604,316
	Knox	1,374,382	2,075,820
	Peoria	1,953,656	2,579,293
	Stark	358,290	577,780
11	Hancock	846,188	1,425,438
	Henderson	275,609	538,324
	McDonough	880,113	1,412,112
	Mercer	632,625	1,051,028
	Rock Island	1,125,499	1,476,528
	Schuyler	338,023	669,246
	Warren	741,974	1,074,874
12	Adams	1,574,564	2,182,259
	Brown	237,036	422,947
	Calhoun	309,309	407,377
	Cass	344,942	586,933
	Greene	500,704	855,359
	Jersey	219,137	421,597
	Pike	532,438	919,062
	Scott	434,099	660,374
13	Christian	711,899	1,165,992
	Mason	183,970	398,942
	Menard	552,181	896,547
	Morgan	1,101,314	1,680,302
	Sangamon	1,754,126	2,585,562
	Tazewell	938,432	1,375,866
14	DeWitt	441,215	674,297
	Logan	733,232	1,168,299
	Macon	1,380,765	1,901,254
	McLean	2,168,746	2,940,084
	Piatt	356,096	570,718

Statement 20—Continued.

Districts.	Counties.	Total value of unenumerated property.	Total value of personal property.
15	Champaign	$990,617	$1,662,118
	Coles	668,882	1,055,037
	Douglas	484,237	749,234
	Edgar	662,265	1,097,277
	Vermilion	1,281,529	1,968,796
16	Clay	198,781	365,838
	Clark	155,154	351,085
	Crawford	163,108	353,377
	Cumberland	115,911	277,556
	Edwards	252,059	469,545
	Jasper	108,794	276,344
	Lawrence	118,258	290,481
	Richland	143,699	299,439
	Wayne	150,203	387,020
	Wabash	151,816	285,477
17	Effingham	193,394	397,925
	Fayette	334,852	593,975
	Macoupin	553,767	1,036,856
	Montgomery	669,042	1,092,668
	Moultrie	225,748	394,396
	Shelby	640,990	1,132,863
18	Bond	245,548	425,756
	Madison	1,416,498	2,029,308
	Monroe	340,247	530,045
	St. Clair	1,456,915	1,980,987
	Washington	344,401	574,168
19	Clinton	254,949	466,195
	Franklin	103,434	269,365
	Gallatin	124,400	262,827
	Hamilton	141,145	324,791
	Hardin	103,038	249,415
	Jefferson	183,442	400,202
	Marion	456,083	729,334
	Saline	311,069	508,966
	White	241,585	474,402
20	Alexander	314,434	443,814
	Jackson	332,670	628,995
	Johnson	229,384	470,847
	Massac	251,577	410,170
	Perry	169,166	381,804
	Pope	190,455	451,326
	Pulaski	120,634	234,521
	Randolph	461,827	735,793
	Union	333,625	597,458
	Williamson	233,194	525,965
	Grand aggregate	$89,918,003	$129,254,545

Statement 20—Continued.

Districts	Counties.	Real Estate—Lands. Improved Lands. Number of acres.	Improved Lands. Value.	Improved Lands. Average value per acre.	Unimproved Lands. Number of acres.	Unimproved Lands. Value.	Unimproved Lands. Average value per acre.	Total Lands. Number of acres.	Total Lands. Value.	Total Lands. Average value per acre.
1, 2, 3, 4	Cook	353,784	$6,316,942	$17 85	90,381	$6,264,034	$69 31	444,165	$12,580,976	$28 33
5	Boone	177,442	1,895,743	10 68	....	....	....	177,442	1,895,743	10 68
	DeKalb	394,428	4,665,187	11 83	....	....	....	394,428	4,665,187	11 83
	Kane	316,256	4,584,029	14 49	1,534	8,000	5 22	317,790	4,592,029	14 45
	Lake	262,768	3,628,778	13 81	15,448	117,195	7 59	278,216	3,745,973	13 46
	McHenry	382,745	3,508,284	9 17	....	....	....	382,745	3,508,284	9 17
6	Carroll	249,438	2,279,694	9 13	38,572	88,336	2 29	288,010	2,368,030	8 22
	Jo Daviess	243,011	2,050,196	8 44	137,558	447,655	3 25	380,569	2,497,851	6 56
	Ogle	438,770	4,572,452	10 42	40,450	216,173	5 34	479,220	4,788,625	9 99
	Stephenson	340,264	5,085,903	14 94	13,694	149,047	10 88	353,958	5,234,950	14 79
	Winnebago	310,559	4,496,331	14 47	8,383	62,981	7 51	318,942	4,559,312	14 29
7	Bureau	480,830	6,783,765	14 11	66,868	350,861	5 25	547,698	7,134,626	13 03
	Henry	481,634	6,069,304	12 60	32,900	143,838	4 37	514,534	6,213,142	12 08
	Lee	456,110	4,968,459	10 89	3,769	42,431	11 26	459,879	5,010,890	10 89
	Putnam	87,671	1,087,675	12 41	18,357	28,681	1 56	106,028	1,116,356	10 53
	Whiteside	356,583	3,991,638	11 19	75,684	358,247	4 73	432,267	4,349,885	10 06
8	DuPage	159,330	3,226,169	20 25	42,260	522,500	12 36	201,590	3,748,669	18 59
	Grundy	260,746	2,495,280	9 47	6,836	54,012	7 90	267,582	2,549,292	9 53
	Kendall	202,102	2,648,469	13 20	....	....	....	202,102	2,648,469	13 20
	LaSalle	632,039	9,841,260	15 57	76,817	614,127	7 99	708,856	10,455,387	14 75
	Will	501,779	6,480,089	12 91	19,676	171,659	8 72	521,455	6,651,748	12 76
9	Ford	301,773	2,503,385	8 29	2,755	13,553	4 92	304,528	2,516,938	8 27
	Iroquois	679,199	6,401,654	9 43	24,084	109,307	4 54	703,283	6,510,961	9 26
	Kankakee	358,649	2,825,390	7 87	60,208	277,106	4 60	418,857	3,102,496	7 41
	Livingston	653,463	6,414,678	9 82	2,374	15,233	6 41	655,837	6,429,911	9 80
	Marshall	193,609	2,719,498	14 04	53,125	218,029	4 10	246,734	2,937,527	11 92
	Woodford	281,968	4,479,461	15 89	54,731	218,096	3 99	336,699	4,697,557	13 95

10	Fulton	341,503	4,091,655	11 98	206,310	659,439	3 20	547,813	4,751,094	8 67
	Knox	434,290	4,953,803	11 41	12,295	76,954	6 26	446,585	5,030,757	11 26
	Peoria	345,586	5,718,652	16 55	34,258	139,805	4 08	379,844	5,858,457	15 42
	Stark	176,670	2,356,379	13 34	4,130	24,940	6 04	180,800	2,381,319	13 17
11	Hancock	414,281	4,720,232	11 39	71,661	316,347	4 41	485,942	5,036,579	10 36
	Henderson	167,941	1,653,315	9 84	66,157	195,090	2 95	234,098	1,848,405	7 90
	McDonough	334,692	3,960,068	11 83	28,380	93,869	3 66	363,072	4,053,937	11 17
	Mercer	317,903	2,961,513	9 32	30,309	67,047	2 21	348,212	3,028,560	8 70
	Rock Island	212,782	2,188,806	10 20	51,472	269,691	5 24	264,254	2,458,497	9 31
	Schuyler	249,468	1,619,070	6 45	25,682	45,152	1 76	275,150	1,664,222	6 05
	Warren	331,882	3,722,785	11 22	7,161	48,885	6 82	339,043	3,771,670	11 12
12	Adams	398,143	5,387,318	13 53	129,817	482,105	3 71	527,960	5,869,423	11 12
	Brown	123,031	1,108,465	9 01	66,418	146,577	2 21	189,449	1,255,042	6 62
	Calhoun	61,943	859,765	13 88	102,640	103,545	1 01	164,583	963,310	5 85
	Cass	163,854	2,235,182	13 64	75,352	171,443	2 28	239,206	2,406,625	10 06
	Greene	309,571	3,044,456	9 83	32,840	66,933	2 04	342,411	3,111,389	9 09
	Jersey	145,154	1,784,213	12 29	84,939	159,132	1 87	230,093	1,943,345	8 45
	Pike	345,725	3,117,234	9 02	164,392	405,780	2 47	510,117	3,523,014	6 91
	Scott	126,697	1,515,574	11 96	32,972	132,086	4 01	159,669	1,647,660	10 31
13	Christian	409,376	4,494,455	10 98	38,335	238,225	6 21	447,711	4,732,680	10 57
	Mason	238,981	2,218,784	9 28	108,804	154,629	1 43	347,785	2,373,413	6 82
	Menard	180,146	2,685,635	14 91	18,690	76,050	4 07	198,836	2,761,685	13 89
	Morgan	316,280	6,359,854	20 11	36,901	201,090	5 45	353,181	6,560,944	18 57
	Sangamon	538,784	8,907,845	16 53	9,550	74,405	7 79	548,334	8,982,250	16 38
	Tazewell	325,547	4,290,996	13 17	82,891	359,204	4 33	408,438	4,650,200	11 38
14	DeWitt	230,376	2,429,664	10 55	20,122	122,281	6 08	250,498	2,551,945	10 18
	Logan	348,995	4,632,602	13 28	39,888	290,856	6 54	388,883	4,893,458	12 58
	Macon	360,195	5,564,225	15 45	5,917	43,608	7 37	366,112	5,607,833	15 32
	McLean	737,510	10,168,515	13 79	653	6,104	9 34	738,163	10,174,619	13 78
	Piatt	258,899	2,951,199	11 40	16,390	155,921	9 52	275,289	3,107,120	11 29
15	Champaign	605,914	6,708,775	11 07	18,937	141,877	7 49	624,851	6,850,652	10 96
	Coles	290,185	3,146,646	10 84	30,538	131,030	4 26	320,723	3,277,676	10 22
	Douglas	260,270	2,726,840	10 48	1,851	11,182	9 71	262,121	2,738,022	10 45
	Edgar	379,607	3,693,600	9 73	12,436	64,089	5 15	392,043	3,757,689	9 58
	Vermilion	551,308	6,675,858	12 11	13,470	94,706	7 03	564,778	6,770,564	11 99
16	Clay	208,164	908,846	4 37	78,549	129,792	1 65	286,713	1,038,638	3 62
	Clark	211,206	883,229	4 13	105,692	195,388	1 84	316,898	1,078,617	3 40
	Crawford	205,802	1,001,492	4 87	67,053	146,569	2 19	272,855	1,148,061	4 21
	Cumberland	173,311	704,188	4 06	43,984	82,789	1 88	217,295	786,977	3 62
	Edwards	109,932	710,563	6 50	30,173	112,400	3 73	140,105	822,963	5 87
	Jasper	236,715	945,217	3 99	72,403	125,729	1 73	309,118	1,070,946	3 46
	Lawrence	160,195	754,416	4 71	69,673	130,954	1 88	229,868	885,370	3 85
	Richland	174,514	948,697	5 44	48,994	160,123	3 27	223,508	1,108,820	4 96
	Wayne	276,440	882,743	3 19	171,024	328,822	1 92	447,464	1,211,565	2 74
	Wabash	106,685	864,949	8 11	30,849	135,383	4 39	137,534	1,000,332	7 42

Statement 20—Continued.

Districts	Counties.	Real Estate—Lands. Improved Lands. Number of acres.	Value.	Average value per acre.	Unimproved Lands. Number of acres.	Value.	Average value per acre.	Total Lands. Number of acres.	Value.	Average value per acre.
17	Effingham	215,363	$1,218,734	$5 66	78,386	$210,147	$2 68	293,749	$1,428,881	$4 86
	Fayette	290,812	1,543,888	5 31	134,739	261,295	1 19	425,551	1,805,183	4 24
	Macoupin	425,033	4,169,282	9 81	112,609	376,125	3 34	537,642	4,545,407	8 49
	Montgomery	383,875	3,538,075	9 21	58,466	200,994	3 43	442,341	3,739,069	8 45
	Moultrie	215,797	1,932,227	8 95	....	....	....	215,797	1,932,227	8 95
	Shelby	443,122	3,816,249	8 61	40,056	144,495	3 61	483,178	3,960,744	8 20
18	Bond	206,889	1,631,305	7 88	32,153	98,780	3 07	239,042	1,730,085	7 26
	Madison	363,373	6,074,293	16 71	79,712	498,175	6 26	443,085	6,572,468	14 83
	Monroe	134,850	1,457,541	10 81	104,557	240,999	2 30	239,407	1,698,540	7 09
	St. Clair	309,417	6,326,801	20 45	102,553	850,808	8 29	411,970	7,177,609	17 42
	Washington	247,772	1,934,891	7 81	102,215	218,918	2 14	349,987	2,153,809	6 15
19	Clinton	207,332	1,668,395	8 05	98,502	189,988	1 93	305,834	1,858,383	6 08
	Franklin	164,058	497,833	3 03	93,387	120,922	1 29	257,445	618,755	2 40
	Gallatin	116,033	375,096	3 23	86,625	103,788	1 19	202,658	478,884	2 36
	Hamilton	179,765	521,636	2 90	94,149	172,482	1 83	273,914	694,118	2 53
	Hardin	53,415	299,214	5 60	56,058	132,268	2 36	109,473	431,482	3 94
	Jefferson	227,834	751,119	3 29	127,517	240,956	1 88	355,351	992,075	2 79
	Marion	248,514	1,600,916	6 45	103,728	249,085	2 40	352,242	1,850,001	5 25
	Saline	136,212	572,470	4 20	101,919	198,347	1 94	238,131	770,817	3 11
	White	240,192	798,713	3 33	72,208	104,190	1 44	312,400	902,903	2 89
20	Alexander	35,374	387,031	10 94	86,733	193,562	2 23	122,107	580,593	4 75
	Jackson	160,723	988,567	6 15	183,492	270,085	1 47	344,215	1,258,652	3 66
	Johnson	100,073	699,279	6 98	112,516	203,748	1 81	212,589	903,027	4 24
	Massac	66,224	476,639	7 20	72,669	188,450	2 59	138,893	665,089	4 79
	Perry	149,256	1,009,427	6 76	114,836	230,183	2 00	264,092	1,239,610	4 69
	Pope	100,120	325,390	3 25	131,877	214,637	1 63	231,997	540,027	2 33
	Pulaski	54,010	374,390	6 93	76,194	183,740	2 41	130,204	558,130	4 29
	Randolph	217,472	1,776,131	8 17	136,317	300,901	2 21	353,789	2,077,032	5 87
	Union	126,430	858,495	6 79	107,509	164,115	1 53	233,939	1,022,610	4 37
	Williamson	179,429	961,677	5 36	91,721	204,440	2 23	271,150	1,166,117	4 30
	Grand aggregate	28,452,172	$307,863,735	$10 82	6,080,819	$24,545,750	$4 04	34,532,991	$332,409,485	$9 63

Statement 20—Continued.

Districts.	Counties.	Real Estate—Town and City Lots: Improved Town and City Lots: Number of lots.	Value.	Average value per lot.	Unimproved Town and City Lots: Number of lots.	Value.	Average value per lot.	Total Town and City Lots: Number of lots.	Value.	Average value per lot.	Total value of personal property, lands and lots.
1, 2, 3, 4	Cook	198,477	$138,829,729	$699 47	512,987	$30,422,692	$59 30	711,464	$169,252,421	$237 89	$211,269,818
5	Boone	2,700	536,110	198 56	9	210	23 33	2,709	536,320	197 97	3,141,555
	DeKalb	5,895	1,498,098	254 09	1,339	33,169	24 77	7,234	1,531,267	211 67	7,634,365
	Kane	12,000	5,587,178	465 60	16,751	743,614	44 39	28,751	6,330,792	220 20	13,711,616
	Lake	10,044	1,905,045	189 67	15,571	481,411	30 92	25,615	2,386,456	93 17	6,972,315
	McHenry	4,504	833,123	184 97	2,158	45,441	21 05	6,662	878,564	131 88	5,760,587
6	Carroll	2,513	525,160	208 97	1,320	26,462	20 04	3,833	551,622	143 91	3,836,818
	Jo Daviess	3,967	449,929	113 16	3,980	36,740	9 23	7,947	486,669	61 24	4,051,097
	Ogle	6,063	714,804	117 89	2,993	35,213	11 77	9,056	750,017	82 82	7,248,358
	Stephenson	6,701	1,734,988	258 91	2,418	70,879	29 31	9,119	1,805,867	198 03	8,816,283
	Winnebago	11,381	4,783,874	420 34	10,259	441,771	43 06	21,640	5,225,645	241 48	12,403 131
7	Bureau	7,271	1,118,721	153 86	2,523	63,029	24 98	9,794	1,181,750	120 66	10,162,363
	Henry	7,965	1,476,931	185 43	1,524	27,896	18 30	9,489	1,504,827	158 62	9,841,698
	Lee	5,931	1,256,058	211 77	154	2,601	16 89	6,085	1,258,659	207 01	7,352,517
	Putnam	944	63,000	66 74	301	1,725	5 73	1,245	64,725	51 99	1,407,912
	Whiteside	4,283	1,620,390	378 33	2,662	89,591	33 65	6,945	1,709,981	246 22	7,363,952
8	DuPage	4,556	1,231,067	270 21	17,990	413,371	22 97	22,546	1,644,438	72 94	6,163,448
	Grundy	4,785	581,702	121 59	3,459	29,196	8 44	8,244	610,898	74 05	3,852,548
	Kendall	2,790	278,316	99 75	....	....	....	2,790	278,316	99 75	3,638,377
	LaSalle	13,941	3,306,559	237 18	13,809	303,407	21 97	27,750	3,609,966	130 09	16,941,347
	Will	17,155	3,778,704	220 26	5,308	64,787	12 25	22,463	3,848,491	171 13	12,407,943
9	Ford	2,549	422,243	165 65	2,500	37,518	15 01	5,049	459,761	91 06	3,548,089
	Iroquois	6,758	576,342	85 44	3,546	34,614	9 73	10,304	610,856	59 29	8,957,581
	Kankakee	4,925	812,117	164 89	6,595	87,298	13 24	11,520	899,415	78 08	4,578,892
	Livingston	6,249	928,266	148 52	5,274	67,611	12 82	11,523	995,877	86 42	8,982,946
	Marshall	3,032	433,846	143 09	2,359	40,109	17 00	5,391	473,955	87 91	4,018,310
	Woodford	4,398	557,646	126 79	2,539	32,177	12 67	6,937	589,823	85 03	6,211,580

Statement 20—Continued.

Districts.	Counties.	REAL ESTATE—TOWN AND CITY LOTS. Improved Town and City Lots. Number of lots.	Value.	Average value per lot.	Unimproved Town and City Lots. Number of lot.	Value.	Average value per lot.	Total Town and City Lots. Number of lots.	Value.	Average value per lot.	Total value of personal property, lands and lots.
10	Fulton	7,923	$17,279,875	$161 54	1,949	$28,016	$14 37	9,872	$1,307,891	$132 48	$7,663,301
	Knox	10,324	2,398,791	232 35	3,860	113,815	29 49	14,184	2,512,606	177 14	9,619,183
	Peoria	10,698	7,042,844	658 33	10,247	909,646	88 77	20,945	7,952,490	379 68	16,390,240
	Stark	2,051	284,412	138 67	57	285	5 00	2,108	284,697	135 05	3,243,796
11	Hancock	8,902	871,336	97 88	1,653	15,882	9 61	10,555	887,218	84 06	7,349,235
	Henderson	1,057	134,633	127 37	4,332	26,386	6 09	5,389	161,019	29 88	2,567,748
	McDonough	5,839	967,131	165 63	556	4,434	7 97	6,395	971,565	151 93	6,437,614
	Mercer	5,156	401,289	77 83	1,492	10,343	6 93	6,648	411,632	61 92	4,491,220
	Rock Island	8,793	3,156,759	357 87	3,635	188,309	51 80	12,428	3,345,068	267 99	7,280,093
	Schuyler	1,736	232,271	133 80	212	998	4 71	1,948	233,269	119 75	2,566,737
	Warren	4,484	775,272	172 85	147	4,510	30 68	4,631	779,782	168 38	5,626,326
12	Adams	9,426	4,577,613	485 64	2,781	159,914	57 50	12,207	4,737,527	388 11	12,789,209
	Brown	1,013	188,891	186 47	588	9,285	15 79	1,601	198,176	123 78	1,876,165
	Calhoun	356	34,135	95 88	....	....	....	356	34,135	95 88	1,404,822
	Cass	2,357	594,796	252 35	3,248	74,722	23 01	5,605	669,518	119 45	3,663,076
	Greene	3,336	597,098	178 97	1,182	24,783	20 97	4,518	621,881	137 65	4,588,629
	Jersey	2,543	500,176	196 69	2,108	26,569	12 60	4,651	526,745	113 25	2,891,687
	Pike	3,465	421,476	121 64	2,210	26,449	11 97	5,675	447,925	78 93	4,890,001
	Scott	1,134	218,286	192 49	1,260	17,616	13 98	2,394	235,902	98 53	2,543,936
13	Christian	6,007	1,003,056	166 95	2,904	53,495	18 42	8,911	1,056,551	118 57	6,955,223
	Mason	2,816	388,636	138 01	1,831	29,555	16 12	4,647	418,191	89 98	3,190,546
	Menard	2,612	499,755	189 03	211	3,590	17 01	2,823	497,345	176 18	4,155,577
	Morgan	4,285	2,618,400	611 06	2,250	135,205	60 09	7,535	2,753,605	365 44	10,994,851
	Sangamon	11,008	4,803,174	436 34	7,805	456,188	57 17	18,813	5,259,362	279 56	16,827,174
	Tazewell	4,581	769,935	168 07	4,635	80,478	17 36	9,216	850,413	92 27	6,876,479
14	DeWitt	3,939	384,885	97 71	556	9,110	16 38	4,495	393,995	87 65	3,620,237
	Logan	5,509	788,167	143 07	2,825	53,699	19 01	8,334	841,866	101 02	6,903,623
	Macon	7,679	2,523,346	328 60	4,334	143,157	33 03	12,013	2,666,503	221 97	10,175,590
	McLean	11,287	3,304,569	291 00	4,736	127,441	26 06	16,023	3,432,010	214 19	16,546,713
	Piatt	3,996	408,559	102 24	633	8,346	13 18	4,629	416,905	90 01	4,094,743

15	Champaign	5,835	1,362,092	233 44	4,898	149,674	30 56	10,733	1,511,766	140 85	10,024,536
	Coles	4,343	936,536	215 64	3,057	73,798	24 14	7,400	1,010,334	136 53	5,343,047
	Douglas	3,832	480,807	125 47	98	917	9 36	3,930	481,724	122 58	3,968,980
	Edgar	3,816	619,317	162 29	2,024	44,769	22 11	5,840	664,086	113 73	5,519,052
	Vermilion	7,581	2,370,979	312 75	6,470	152,247	23 53	14,051	2,523,226	179 57	11,262,586
16	Clay	2,250	207,271	92 12	912	5,871	6 43	3,162	213,142	67 41	1,617,618
	Clark	2,037	219,740	107 87	1,500	18,122	12 08	3,537	237,862	67 25	1,667,564
	Crawford	2,880	191,732	66 57	804	4,622	5 75	3,684	196,354	53 30	1,697,792
	Cumberland	1,461	88,386	60 50	776	5,744	7 40	2,237	94,130	42 92	1,158,663
	Edwards	1,100	148,481	134 98	1,038	15,915	15 33	2,138	164,396	76 89	1,456,904
	Jasper	1,065	88,078	82 70	1,012	12,072	11 92	2,077	100,150	48 21	1,447,440
	Lawrence	1,103	113,126	102 56	1,257	8,780	6 98	2,360	121,906	51 66	1,297,757
	Richland	1,337	202,765	151 65	1,224	19,162	15 66	2,561	221,927	86 65	1,630,186
	Wayne	1,454	166,730	114 73	1,107	11,221	10 14	2,561	177,951	69 45	1,776,536
	Wabash	1,397	284,667	203 77	1,499	28,426	18 96	2,896	313,093	108 11	1,598,902
17	Effingham	3,470	407,911	117 55	1,410	27,039	19 18	4,880	434,950	89 13	2,261,756
	Fayette	3,305	313,373	94 81	2,593	46,603	17 97	5,898	359,976	61 03	2,759,134
	Macoupin	7,430	905,688	121 90	3,033	33,451	11 03	10,463	939,139	90 14	6,521,402
	Montgonery	5,805	716,023	123 34	3,669	38,567	10 51	9,474	754,590	79 64	5,586,327
	Moultrie	2,965	174,668	58 91	350	2,001	5 72	3,315	176,669	53 29	2,503,292
	Shelby	4,325	678,892	156 97	1,977	33,217	16 80	6,302	712,109	113 00	5,805,716
18	Bond	1,864	243,083	130 40	1,357	12,000	8 85	3,221	255,083	79 19	2,410,924
	Madison	8,211	2,773,671	337 80	12,501	565,782	45 26	20,712	3,339,453	161 23	11,941,229
	Monroe	945	256,870	271 82	993	18,575	18 69	1,938	275,445	142 13	2,504,030
	St. Clair	9,223	2,957,598	320 67	30,697	764,492	24 90	39,920	3,722,090	93 24	12,880,686
	Washington	2,064	254,828	123 46	3,141	17,360	5 53	5,205	272,188	52 29	3,000,165
19	Clinton	2,334	313,473	134 30	2,249	21,018	9 35	4,583	334,491	72 98	2,659,069
	Franklin	657	84,730	128 96	739	8,341	11 29	1,396	93,071	66 67	981,191
	Gallatin	1,239	137,840	111 24	1,642	12,749	7 76	2,881	150,589	52 27	892,300
	Hamilton	762	141,371	185 53	1,087	16,497	15 18	1,849	157,868	85 38	1,176,777
	Hardin	269	72,835	270 76	235	3,482	14 82	504	56,317	151 42	757,214
	Jefferson	2,213	223,786	101 12	2,435	32,046	13 16	4,648	225,832	55 04	1,648,109
	Marion	3,589	803,957	224 00	3,081	47,086	15 28	6,670	851,043	127 59	3,430,378
	Saline	1,242	166,312	133 90	1,109	13,609	12 27	2,351	177,921	76 53	1,459,704
	White	2,051	226,843	110 60	2,168	16,883	7 79	4,219	243,726	57 76	1,621,031
20	Alexander	3,134	1,124,849	358 92	4,318	165,296	38 28	7,452	1,290,145	173 13	2,314,552
	Jackson	3,059	530,985	173 58	2,297	54,992	23 94	5,356	585,977	100 95	2,473,624
	Johnson	680	133,895	196 90	968	13,663	14 11	1,648	147,558	89 54	1,521,432
	Massac	1,284	406,755	316 78	762	23,725	31 14	2,046	430,480	210 40	1,505,739
	Perry	1,932	312,536	161 77	1,678	25,072	14 95	3,610	337,608	93 52	1,959,022
	Pope	545	116,085	213 00	448	9,517	21 24	993	125,602	126 49	1,116,955
	Pulaski	1,162	137,290	118 15	1,857	27,806	14 97	3,019	165,096	54 69	957,747
	Randolph	3,569	473,053	132 54	3,877	43,720	11 27	7,446	516,773	69 40	3,329,598
	Union	1,558	246,868	158 45	1,157	12,153	10 50	2,715	259,021	95 40	1,879,089
	Williamson	1,294	202,663	156 62	1,385	18,654	13 47	2,679	221,317	82 61	1,913,399
	Total aggregate	639,760	$241,022,950	$376 74	$37,454	$39,051,394	$46 63	$1,478,214	$280,074,344	189 47	$741,738,374

Statement 20—Continued.

Districts.	Counties.	RAILROAD PROPERTY ASSESSED IN COUNTIES.								
		Class C—Personal Property	Class D—Lands.			Class D—Lots.			Total value of railroad property assessed in county.	Total value of all property assessed in county.
		Value.	Number of acres.	Value.	Av. val. per acre.	Number of lots.	Value.	Av. val. per lot.		
1, 2, 3, 4	Cook	$293,215	392	$72,458	$184 84	818	$844,395	$1,032 27	$1,210,068	$212,479,886
5	Boone	860	150	1,130	7 54	....	....	....	1,990	3,143,545
	DeKalb	1,208	....	....	....	....	1,305	....	2,513	7,636,878
	Kane	117,813	88	3,057	34 74	13	1,250	96 15	122,120	13,839,736
	Lake	1,270	452	8,115	17 96	89	3,790	42 58	13,175	6,985,490
	McHenry	3,230	54	536	9 93	....	....	....	3,766	5,764,353
6	Carroll	5,225	....	....	....	....	150	....	5,375	3,842,193
	Jo Daviess	770	189	1,157	6 12	3	30	8 00	1,957	4,053,054
	Ogle	1,630	53	736	17 04	....	180	....	2,546	7,250,904
	Stephenson	3,670	92	1,177	12 97	....	....	....	4,847	8,821,130
	Winnebago	2,017	113	1,658	14 67	26	5,640	216 92	9,315	12,412,446
7	Bureau	4,154	206	2,185	10 60	3	205	68 34	6,544	10,168,907
	Henry	2,001	54	2,910	53 89	8	485	60 63	5,396	9,847,094
	Lee	2,290	21	450	21 43	....	....	....	2,740	7,355,257
	Putnam	113	....	....	....	....	....	....	113	1,408,025
	Whiteside	100,475	248	1,971	7 95	2	65	32 50	102,511	7,466,463
8	DuPage	2,050	811	17,965	21 15	1	50	50 00	20,065	6,183,513
	Grundy	1,069	....	....	....	....	....	....	1,069	3,853,617
	Kendall	323	....	....	....	....	....	....	323	3,638,700
	LaSalle	5,486	48	1,240	25 84	....	....	....	6,726	16,948,073
	Will	23,568	436	24,831	56 95	40	3,370	84 25	51,769	12,459,712
9	Ford	570	7	70	10 00	9	160	16 67	800	3,548,889
	Iroquois	872	25	365	14 60	20	680	34 00	1,917	8,959,498
	Kankakee	1,543	379	5,729	15 12	....	....	....	7,272	4,586,164
	Livingston	1,851	55	451	8 20	25	1,260	50 40	3,562	8,986,508
	Marshall	....	119	900	7 56	....	....	....	900	4,019,210
	Woodford	700	11	227	20 00	13	595	45 77	1,522	5,213,102

Dist.	County									
10	Fulton	3,217	20	510	25 50				3,727	7,667,028
	Knox	25,214	51	4,800	94 12				30,014	9,649,197
	Peoria	10,167	25	286	11 44	49	6,030	123 06	16,483	16,406,723
	Stark	485				4	50	12 50	535	3,244,331
11	Hancock	1,231							1,231	7,350,466
	Henderson	720							720	2,568,468
	McDonough	1,038	10	135	13 50	1	5	5 00	1,178	6,438,792
	Mercer	1,009							1,009	4,492,229
	Rock Island	4,278		480			6,660		11,418	7,291,511
	Schuyler	797	303	303	1 00				1,100	2,567,837
	Warren	1,083							1,083	5,627,409
12	Adams	4,421	56	750	13 39	14	10,135	723 93	15,306	12,804,515
	Brown	120							120	1,876,285
	Calhoun									1,404,822
	Cass	3,442							3,442	3,666,518
	Greene	1,202							1,202	4,589,831
	Jersey	170	6	500	83 33				670	2,892,357
	Pike	3,157	208	1,370	6 59				4,527	4,894,528
	Scott									2,543,936
13	Christian	8,800	11	220	22 00	13	870	66 92	9,899	6,965,122
	Mason	550	9	360	40 00		1,250		2,160	3,192,706
	Menard	230							230	4,155,807
	Morgan	610	12	120	10 00				730	10,995,581
	Sangamon	12,085				92	6,750	73 37	18,835	16,846,009
	Tazewell	832	97	1,362	13 01	1	25	25 00	2,219	6,878,698
14	DeWitt	1,932	67	1,195	17 83	9	480	53 33	3,607	3,623,844
	Logan	590							590	6,904,213
	Macon	3,735				5	225	45 00	3,960	10,179,550
	McLean	77,780							77,780	16,624,493
	Piatt									4,094,743
15	Champaign	4,273	14	550	39 28	6	250	41,67	5,073	10,029,609
	Coles	43,380		2,495			500		46,375	5,389,422
	Douglas	4,605							4,605	3,973,586
	Edgar	623				13	519	39 92	1,142	5,520,194
	Vermilion	12,896	10	250	25 00	65	335	5 15	13,481	11,276,067
16	Clay	755							755	1,618,373
	Clark	153	10	180	18 00	11	315	28 64	648	1,668,212
	Crawford	77							77	1,697,869
	Cumberland									1,158,663
	Edwards	80							80	1,456,984
	Jasper									1,447,440
	Lawrence	148	40	88	2 20		136		372	1,298,129
	Richland	260	69	700	10 14	13	540	41 54	1,500	1,631,686
	Wayne									1,776,536
	Wabash	177							177	1,599,079

Statement 20—Continued.

DISTRICTS	COUNTIES.	RAILROAD PROPERTY ASSESSED IN COUNTIES. Class C—Personal Property								
		Class C—Personal Property	Class D—Lands.			Class D—Lots.			Total value of railroad property assessed in county.	Total value of all property assessed in county.
		Value.	Number of acres.	Value.	Av. val. per acre.	Number of lots.	Value.	Av. val. per lot.		
17	Effingham	$3,265							$3,265	$2,265,021
	Fayette	105				1	$100	$100 00	205	2,759,339
	Macoupin	1,076	89	$895	$10 06	5	587	117 40	2,558	6,523,960
	Montgomery	495							495	5,586,822
	Moultrie	300	1	20	20 00	1	75	75 00	395	2,503,687
	Shelby	5,685							5,685	5,811,401
18	Bond	1,650	24	320	13 33	1	15	15 00	1,985	2,412,909
	Madison	1,572	113	1,720	13 03	3	175	58 33	3,467	11,944,696
	Monroe		7	200	48 57				200	2,504,230
	St. Clair	15,740	1,588	158,404	99 75	485	14,055	29 00	188,199	13,068,885
	Washington	1,070	6	33	5 50		165		1,268	3,001,433
19	Clinton	555					2,017		2,572	2,661,641
	Franklin	115							115	981,306
	Gallatin	310				53	2,795	52 74	3,105	895,405
	Hamilton	260							260	1,177,037
	Hardin									757,214
	Jefferson	225							225	1,648,334
	Marion	240		886			100		1,226	3,431,604
	Saline									1,459,704
	White	620							620	1,621,651
20	Alexander									2,314,552
	Jackson	4,425							4,425	2,478,049
	Johnson									1,521,432
	Massac									1,505,739
	Perry	440	58	600	10 04	2	5	2 50	1,045	1,960,067
	Pope									1,116,955
	Pulaski	815							815	958,562
	Randolph	125					200		325	3,329,923
	Union	40							40	1,879,129
	Williamson	223		50		1	50		323	1,913,722
	Grand Aggregate	$853,655	6,907	$ 20,100	47 67	1,918	$919,024	$477 70	$2,101,779	$743,840,153

No. 21.

Statement of rates per cent. of addition to or deduction from the assessed value of each class of property in each county in the State, for the year 1896, as determined by the State Board of Equalization.

Counties.	Personal Property.		Lands.		Lots.	
	Add.	Ded.	Add.	Ded.	Add.	Ded.
Adams		13		11		13
Alexander	5					5
Bond	10			2		
Boone		21	10			15
Brown	1				1	
Bureau		15		14		16
Calhoun		16		15		16
Carroll	2		2		1	
Cass		12		12		12
Champaign		11		11		11
Christian		10				5
Clark	10		87			
Clay	3			6		
Clinton			18			
Coles		17		17		17
Cook	19		20		17	
Crawford	18		11			
Cumberland	12		30			
DeKalb		22	1			11
DeWitt						2
Douglas		3		4		3
DuPage		13		14		13
Edgar		3		2		3
Edwards		10		3		
Effingham			8			
Fayette			8			
Ford		21		20		20
Franklin	15		40			10
Fulton	8		7		8	
Gallatin	10		113			
Greene	6		7		6	
Grundy		1		1		
Hamilton	10		30			15
Hancock		4		8		
Hardin		45		15		50
Henderson		12		11		12
Henry		15		14		14
Iroquois		16		16		10
Jackson						
Jasper	25		16			
Jefferson	10		33			
Jersey			26			
Jo Daviess		7		7		8
Johnson						
Kane		7		7		7
Kankakee		3		3		4
Kendall		16		15		15
Knox	1				1	
Lake		32		7	5	
LaSalle		12		13		13
Lawrence	20		58			

Statement 21—Concluded.

Counties.	Personal Property.		Lands.		Lots.	
	Add.	Ded.	Add.	Ded.	Add.	Ded.
Lee		16		15		16
Livingston		1				
Logan						22
Macon				17		22
Macoupin	29		30			
Madison		10		15		10
Marion	15		16			10
Marshall		13		13		14
Mason						
Massac		5				
McDonough		1		2		
McHenry		21	2			35
McLean						3
Menard		25		25		10
Mercer		5	15			
Monroe		10	6			
Montgomery			10			
Morgan		40		25		40
Moultrie		14	14			
Ogle						
Peoria		20		19		20
Perry						
Piatt				3		6
Pike	14		14		14	
Pope			15			
Pulaski						
Putnam		5		4		5
Randolph			10			
Richland	3			1		
Rock Island		7		8		30
Saline	10		2			10
Sangamon		20		20		20
Schuyler		4	14			
Scott		5		5		6
Shelby		4		5		
Stark		4		3		4
St. Clair				9		5
Stephenson		17		17		17
Tazewell		10				
Union						
Vermilion		5		4		5
Wabash		2		24		10
Warren		2	5			
Washington	10		10			
Wayne	5			1		
White	5		73			
Whiteside		13		13		13
Will		1		2		2
Williamson						
Winnebago		18		18		18
Woodford		20		21		20

No. 22.

Statement Showing the assessed value of Railroad Property in each County in the State of Illinois, for the year A. D. 1895.

County—Railroad.	Main Track, Including Right of Way and Improvements Thereon.				Second Main Track.			Side or Turnout Track.			Rolling Stock.	Total assessment by the State Board of Equalization...	Equalized value of railroad property assessed by local assessors..........	Equalized value of railroad property in county..........
	Miles	Feet........	Assess'd value excluding buildings.	Value of buildings on right of way.	Miles	Feet........	Assess'd value.	Miles	Feet........	Assess'd value.	Assess'd value.			
Adams:														
Chicago, Burlington & Quincy..........	74	766	$467,114	$9,464	......	......	....	16	2,964	$41,403	$88,153	$606,134	$10,185	$616,319
Quincy, Omaha & Kansas City	......	......	....	9,350	......	......	....	......	5,204	13,942	....	13,292	....	13,292
same (C., B. & Q.)......................	2	4,435	....	....	......	......	....	......	......	....	884	884	....	884
Wabash	21	646	95,050	3,944	......	......	....	2	273	5,129	31,984	136,107	3,145	139,252
same (C., B. & Q.)......................	21	......	....	....	......	......	....	......	......	....	31,799	31,799	....	31,799
Total	119	567	$562,164	$22,758	......	......	....	19	3,161	$50,474	$152,820	$788,216	$13,330	$801,546
Alexander:														
Cairo, Vincennes & Chicago	6	2,651	19,506	6,150	......	......	....	11	3,551	23,345	4,734	53,735	....	53,735
Chicago & Texas..........................	6	83	9,023	700	......	......	....	1	1,470	1,278	3,866	14,867	....	14,867
Mobile & Ohio.............................	27	1,775	109,344	2,700	......	......	....	12	3,687	31,746	30,494	174,284	....	174,284
Total	39	4,509	137,873	$9,550	......	......	....	25	3,428	$56,369	$39,094	$242,886	....	$242,886
Bond:														
Jacksonville, Louisville & St. Louis....	27	1,979	71,174	1,500	......	......	....	1	2,605	2,987	10,866	86,527	1,693	88,220
same (C., G. & D.)	4	156	10,475	....	......	......	....	......	2,100	795	1,600	12,870	11	12,881
Terre Haute & Indianapolis............	22	2,771	141,906	2,760	......	......	....	5	474	12,724	65,961	223,351	424	223,775
Toledo, St. Louis & Kansas City.......	8	1,690	33,280	375	......	......	....	1	250	2,618	11,121	47,394	16	47,410
Total	62	1,316	$256,835	$4,635	......	......	....	8	149	$19,124	$89,548	$370,142	$2,144	$372,286
Boone:														
Chicago, Madison & Northern..........	6	1,275	31,207	1,020	......	......	....	......	4,038	1,912	2,203	36,342	47	36,389
Chicago & Northwestern................	37	3,229	216,266	2,720	......	......	....	15	4,038	39,412	49,209	307,607	1,847	309,454
same (Nor. Ill.).............	7	4,141	....	....	......	......	....	......	......	....	10,185	10,185	....	10,185
Northern Illinois.........................	7	4,141	19,461	495	......	......	....	......	3,295	1,560	....	21,516	28	21,544
Total	59	2,226	$266,934	$4,235	......	......	....	17	811	$42,884	$61,597	$375,650	$1,922	$377,572

Statement 22—Continued.

County—Railroad.	Main Track, Including Right of Way and Improvements Thereon.				Second Main Track.			Side or Turnout Track.			Rolling Stock.	Total assessment by the State Board of Equalization...	Equalized value of railroad property assessed by local assessors..........	Equalized value of railroad property in county..........
	Miles......	Feet........	Assess'd value excluding buildings.	Value of buildings on right of way.	Miles......	Feet........	Assess'd value.	Miles......	Feet........	Assess'd value.	Assess'd value.			
Brown:														
Wabash....................................	23	3,370	$106,372	$3,175	....	....	....	1	4,370	$4,569	$35,794	$149,910	$121	$150,031
Bureau:														
Chicago, Burlington & Quincy..........	72	4,260	458,683	4,229	40	3,337	$142,212	12	2,463	31,166	86,562	722,852	2,048	724,900
same (I. V. N.)........................	30	546	....	....	....	....	....	....	....	....	35,791	35,791	....	35,791
Chicago & Northwestern (Nor. Ill.).....	6	215	....	....	....	....	....	....	....	....	7,903	7,903	187	8,090
Chicago, Rock Island & Pacific..........	40	2,786	344,485	9,375	40	2,786	141,847	7	1,522	18,221	46,353	560,281	2,827	563,108
same (Peo. Br.)........................	4	2,550	38,105	....	....	....	....	1	3,232	4,030	5,127	47,262	....	47,262
DePue, Ladd & Eastern..................	3	1,760	6,667	....	....	....	....	....	2,000	379	20	7,066	30	7,096
Illinois Valley & Northern.............	30	546	90,310	2,163	....	....	....	3	4,029	9,408	....	101,881	490	102,371
LaSalle & Bureau Co....................	1	1,715	3,975	....	....	....	....	....	1,880	890	....	4,865	....	4,865
Northern Illinois......................	6	215	15,102	803	....	....	....	11	3,160	28,996	....	44,901	....	44,901
Total..................................	194	4,033	$957,327	$16,570	81	843	$284,059	37	2,446	$93,070	$181,756	$1,532,802	$5,582	$1,538,384
Carroll:														
Chicago, Burlington & Northern.........	48	4,285	244,657	6,675	....	....	....	10	1,407	25,666	86,494	362,892	1,488	364,380
Chicago, Milwaukee & St. Paul..........	47	462	200,122	32,213	21	3,155	75,591	21	3,524	54,169	52,365	414,460	3,994	418,454
Total..................................	95	4,747	$444,179	$38,888	21	3,155	$75,591	31	4,931	$79,835	$138,859	$777,352	$5,482	$782,834
Cass:														
Baltimore & Ohio Southwestern..........	25	4,169	77,369	1,280	....	....	....	6	483	15,229	44,689	138,567	207	138,774
Chicago & Alton........................	2	2,248	15,282	220	....	....	....	....	3,561	1,686	5,054	22,242	44	22,286
Chicago, Peoria & St. Louis............	15	453	42,240	894	....	....	....	2	78	4,029	25,504	72,667	26	72,693
St. Louis, Rock Island & Chicago.......	10	4,507	43,414	14,468	....	....	....	8	878	20,416	7,498	85,796	2,752	88,548
Total..................................	54	817	$178,305	$16,862	....	....	....	16	5,000	$41,360	$82,745	$319,272	$3,029	$322,301

Champaign:														
Chicago & Eastern Illinois	8	745	30,936	970					4,613	1,747	20,091	53,744	65	53,809
Chicago, Havana & Western	12	910	36,517	513				1	3,083	3,168	2,760	42,958	80	43,038
Chicago & Springfield		1,500	881								173	1,054		1,054
Peoria & Eastern	29	648	116,491	8,558				10	2,270	26,075	31,255	182,379	3,666	186,045
Rantoul	28	1,229	50,819	3,106				3	2,608	3,494	3,990	61,409	374	61,783
Wabash	28	2,503	128,131	6,269				5	4,068	14,426	43,116	191,942	241	192,183
same (C. P.)	6	1,947	28,659	1,288				1	1,904	3,402	9,644	42,993	35	43,028
same (C. & S. E.)	11	3,617	52,583	1,300				1	1,753	3,330	17,694	74,907	53	74,960
Total	124	2,539	$445,017	$22,004				24	4,459	$55,642	$128,723	$651,386	$4,514	$655,900
Christian:														
Baltimore & Ohio Southwestern	30	4,577	92,601	9,205				5	1,576	13,246	53,437	168,539	6,109	174,648
Cleveland, Cin., Chicago & St. Louis	10	5,153	55,977	920				2	4,018	6,903	23,075	86,875	751	87,626
Wabash	31	163	139,639	6,175				6	3,257	16,542	46,988	209,344	2,114	211,458
Total	72	4,613	$288,217	$16,300				14	3,571	$36,691	$123,550	$464,758	$8,974	$473,732
Clark:														
Cairo, Vincennes & Chicago	20	4,370	62,483	555				1	3,993	$3,512	$15,164	$81,714	$105	$81,819
Chicago & Ohio River	14	4,157	26,617	50					3,698	700	1,295	28,662	455	29,117
Terre Haute & Indianapolis	29	696	183,530	2,186				4	4,646	12,200	85,309	283,225	260	283,485
Terre Haute & Peoria		3,750	1,776								483	2,259		2,259
same (T., H. & I.)		3,268									421	421		421
Total	66	401	$274,406	$2,791				7	1,777	$16,412	$102,672	$396,281	$820	$397,101
Clay:														
Baltimore & Ohio Southwestern	48	3,589	146,039	2,060				6	2,585	16,224	84,353	248,676	778	249,454
Clinton:														
Baltimore & Ohio Southwestern	30	3,540	92,011	2,420				5	5,073	14,902	53,146	162,479	375	162,854
Centralia & Chester	2	3,636	6,722								651	7,373		7,373
Jacksonville, Louisville & St. Louis	15	2,060	40,015	450					1,782	675	6,109	47,249	2,027	49,276
Louisville, Evansville & St. Louis Con.	31	2,263	110,060	3,100				1	4,093	4,438	43,636	161,174	60	161,234
Louisville & Nashville	3	4,775	15,617	1,000					4,101	1,942	4,008	22,567	110	22,677
Total	84	434	$264,365	$6,970				8	4,489	$21,957	$107,550	$400,842	$2,572	$403,414
Coles:														
Chicago & Ohio River	1	5,207	3,575								174	3,749		3,749
Cleveland, Cincin., Chicago & St. Louis	27	4,796	142,332	17,855				13	4,986	34,860	58,674	253,721	26,295	280,016
Peoria, Decatur & Exansville	16	1,285	40,608	4,560				6	1,811	12,686	22,865	80,719	10,641	91,360
Terre Haute & Peoria	5	1,316	13,123	220					3,440	1,303	3,573	18,219	796	19,015
Toledo, St. Louis & Kansas City	31	4,699	127,560	2,625				5	2,573	13,718	42,628	186,531	759	187,290
Total	83	1,463	$327,198	$25,260				26	2,250	$62,567	$127,914	$542,939	$38,491	$581,430

Statement 22—Continued.

County—Railroad.	Main Track, including Right of Way and Improvements Thereon.				Second Main Track.			Side or Turnout Track.			Rolling Stock.	Total assessment by the State Board of Equalization...	Equalized value of railroad property assessed by local assessor..........	Equalized value of railroad property in county..........
	Miles	Feet........	Assess'd value, excluding buildings.	Value of buildings on right of way.	Miles	Feet........	Assess'd value.	Miles	Feet........	Assess'd value.	Assess'd value.			
Crawford:														
Cairo, Vincennes & Chicago..........	24	944	$72,536	$735				3	676	$6,256	$17,601	$97,128	$91	$97,219
Indiana & Illinois Southern..........	21		31,500	900				1		1,000	4,265	37,665		37,665
Total..........	45	944	$104,036	$1,635				4	676	$7,256	$21,866	$134,793	$91	$134,884
Cumberland:														
Chicago & Ohio River..........	7	520	12,777						810	154	621	13,552		13,552
Peoria, Decatur & Evansville..........	17	2,651	43,755	425				1	763	2,289	24,636	71,105		71,105
Terre Haute & Indianapolis..........	20	4,145	130,946	1,065				2	2,164	6,025	60,866	198,902		198,902
Toledo, St. Louis & Kansas City..........	7	3,590	30,720	188					4,698	2,225	10,266	43,399		43,399
Total..........	53	346	$218,198	$1,678				4	3,155	$10,693	$96,389	$326,958		$326,958
Cook:														
Baltimore, Ohio & Chicago..........	5	4,821	53,218	34,640	5	4,588	$29,345	19	1,635	57,929	9,524	184,656	$4,169	188,825
same (C., R. I. & P.)..........	6	1,848									10,228	10,228		10,228
same (C. & N. P.)..........	3	3,696									5,958	5,958		5,958
Baltimore & Ohio Connecting..........	2	940	19,602		2	940	10,890					30,492	12,578	43,070
Belt Railway Co. of Chicago..........	20	3,125	308,878	11,400	13	1,973	53,495	50	4,015	126,901	122,040	622,714	5,740	628,454
Blue Island..........	3	4,461	15,380	3,600				1	4,148	4,464	4,100	27,544	438	27,982
Calumet & Blue Island..........											362,400	362,400		362,400
Calumet River..........	4	2,312	26,627									26,627	416	27,043
Chicago & Alton..........	25	3,233	161,358	32,870	25	3,232	89,642	29	883	72,918	53,364	410,152	9,570	419,722
Chicago, Burlington & Quincy..........	15	468	95,058	37,933	15	468	52,810	118	3,503	296,659	17,939	500,399	318,623	819,022
Chicago & Calumet Terminal..........	25	1,593	151,810	9,600				7	3,834	19,315	52,021	232,746	36	232,782
Chicago & Eastern Illinois..........	11	4,539	45,067	10,410	11	4,615	35,622	27	116	54,044	29,270	174,413	5,757	180,170
same (C. & W. I.)..........	16	1,056									39,983	39,983		39,983
Chicago & Erie (C. & W. I.)..........	19	5,227									43,141	43,141	6,810	49,951
Chicago & Grand Trunk..........	21	5,075	658,835	30,135	16	2,860	82,708	12	1,484	42,984	55,249	869,911	33,992	903,903
same (G. T. Jc.)..........	3	4,630									9,753	9,753		9,753
same (C. & W. I.)..........	4	4,631									12,270	12,270		12,270
Chicago & Great Western..........	5	3,021	32,318	2,500				1	52	2,525	7,100	44,443	18	44,461
same (C. & N. P.)..........	10	950									12,970	12,970		12,970
Chicago & Illinois Southern..........		2,200	1,637						500	189		1,856		1,856

Chicago & Indiana State Line	3	755	26,715		2	3,458	10,620	1	1,426	3,810		41,145		41,145
Chicago, Madison & Northern	16	1,155	81,094	4,950	6	578	21,383	14	1,053	35,499	5,725	148,651	18,112	166,763
Chicago, Milwaukee & St. Paul	57	1,971	243,836	87,704	47	1,049	165,196	105	2,898	263,872	63,804	824,412	106,438	930,850
same (C., St. L. & P.)	2	1,941									2,633	2,633		2,633
same (P., Ft. W. & C.)		2,604									548	548		548
Chicago & Northern Pacific	42	1,106	949,713	195,690	24	3,480	123,295	55	1,003	137,975	107,160	1,513,833	3,151	1,516,984
same (Wis. Cen.)	4	2,590									11,400	11,400		11,400
Chicago & Northwestern	68	5,066	396,517	184,960	68	1,066	238,707	156	558	300,264	90,223	1,300,671	125,224	1,425,895
same (Junc.)	6	3,757									8,781	8,781	4,138	12,919
Chicago, Rock Island & Pacific	31	5,034	271,604	183,313	31	922	109,111	114	3,460	286,638	36,546	887,212	307,459	1,194,671
Chicago, Santa Fé & California	17	4,956	95,075	31,405				47	2,766	118,810	21,492	266,782	104,200	370,982
Chicago & South Side Rapid Transit	8	2,951	171,178	13,200				1	2,640	3,750	136,120	324,248	2,618	326,866
Chicago & Union Transfer	15	1,819	92,067	348	18	4,954	56,815		581	275	100	149,605	1,309	150,914
Chicago & Western Indiana	26	4,082	803,193	195,075	26	4,082	132,540	70	28	210,016	8,960	1,349,784	78,818	1,428,602
Elgin, Joliet & Eastern	26	3,432	119,925	4,950				10	2,495	26,181	57,661	208,717	10,705	219,422
Englewood Connecting	2	1,858	23,519						5,027	3,332		26,851		26,851
Grand Trunk Junction	3	4,630	155,076	61,000	3	4,640	19,414	21	2,368	85,794		321,284		321,284
Junction	6	3,757	20,135	518	6	3,757	16,779	1	2,718	3,787		41,219		41,219
Lake Shore & Michigan Southern	7	3,215	456,534	148,211	7	3,215	38,045	67	2,461	269,864	26,072	938,726	20,066	958,792
same (C., R. I. & P.)	6	2,317									22,062	22,062		22,062
Lake Street Elevated	6	2,027	63,839	16,600				1	2,717	3,029	80,800	164,268		164,268
Louisv., New Albany & Chi. (C. & W. I.)	19	4,540									29,382	29,382		29,382
Michigan Central	6	1,555	62,945	26,720				11	631	38,918	9,851	138,434	22,033	160,467
Michigan Central (J. & Nor. Ind.)	13	3,172	136,007	2,400				1	4,554	6,519	21,285	166,211	155	166,366
same (Ill. Cen.)	14										21,910	21,910		21,910
New York, Chicago & St. Louis	9	5,101	249,152	65,724				19	1,624	67,577	44,414	426,876	15,841	442,708
same (L. S. & M. S.)	8	4,720									39,636	39,636		39,636
Pittsburgh, Cincinnati, Chicago & St. L	27	5,230	1,119,621	54,863	18	4,673	75,540	53	1,456	186,465	77,684	1,514,173	51,121	1,565,294
same (Eng. Conn.)	2	1,858									6,527	6,527		6,527
Pittsburgh, Ft. Wayne & Chicago	13	5,125	837,983	248,450	13	3,283	68,109	66	2,050	232,359	68,786	1,455,687	113,418	1,569,105
same (S. C. & S.)	10	1,320									50,467	50,467		50,467
South Chicago	4	4,016	28,564	8,820	4	2,740	18,076	3	75	7,536	15,000	77,996	3,048	81,044
South Chicago & Southern	10	863	50,820	1,650				2	4,412	9,925		62,395	900	63,295
The Metropolitan West Side Elevated	8	4,330	176,402	28,000				12	2,030	30,961		235,363	893	236,256
Union Stock Yards & Transit	8	3,775	435,748	55,585	8	3,128	85,924	88	3,768	354,855	66,910	999,022	3,877	1,002,899
Wisconsin Central	20	985	100,933	8,324				6	3,548	16,680	31,624	157,561	2,493	160,054
same (C. & N. P.)	10	4,723									17,067	17,067		17.067
Wabash (C. & S.)	21	1,014	95,364	4,925				16	3,708	41,756	32,089	174,134	29,654	203,788
same (C. & W. I.)	7	3,696									11,659	11,659		11,659
Totals	790	632	$8,833,377	$1,806,473	380	341	$1,534,066	219	3,025	$3,514,375	$2,071,688	$17,759,970	$1,423,818	$19.183,797
DEKALB:														
Chicago, Burlington & Quincy	9	4,095	61,586	681	5	2,008	18,891	3	52	7,525	11,622	100,305	76	100,381
Chicago Great Western	18	655	105,119	3,900				3	2,948	8,896	23,092	141,007	23	141,030
Chicago & Iowa	18	2,936	92,780	1,980				3	943	7,947	13,945	116,652	44	116,696
Chicago, Madison & Northern	14	537	70,508	3,720				2	2,650	6,254	4,978	85,460	195	85,655
Chicago, Milwaukee & St. Paul	18	919	77,240	7,181	12	4,492	44,978	5	393	12,686	20,211	162,296	1,430	163,726

Statement 22—Continued.

County—Railroad.	Main Track, Including Right of Way and Improvements Thereon.				Second Main Track.			Side or Turnout Track.			Rolling Stock.	Total assessment by the State Board of Equalization...	Equalized value of railroad property assessed by local assessors..........	Equalized value of railroad property in county..........
	Miles........	Feet........	Assess'd value excluding buildings.	Value of buildings on right of way.	Miles........	Feet........	Assess'd value.	Miles........	Feet........	Assess'd value.	Assess'd value.			
DeKalb—*Concluded.*														
Chicago & Northwestern	17	2,640	$100,625	$1,990	**17**	2,640	$61,250	8	4,428	$22,097	$22,896	**$208,858**	**$152**	**$209,010**
same (Nor. Ill.)	38	4,976									50,950	**50,950**		**50,950**
same (S. & C.)	4	3,366									6,067	**6,067**		**6,067**
Northern Illinois	38	4,976	97,356	1,748				5	4,414	14,590		**113,694**	**47**	**113,741**
Sycamore & Cortland	4	3,366	13,912	1,070					4,004	1,896		**16,878**	**136**	**17,014**
Total	183	2,066	$619,126	$22,270	**35**	3,950	$125,119	32	3,992	$81,891	$153,761	**$1,002,167**	**$2,103**	**$1,004,270**
DeWitt:														
Chicago, Havana & Western	24	4,530	74,574	1,656				1	3,860	3,462	5,637	**85,329**	**170**	**85,499**
Chicago & Springfield	32	4,034	101,568	10,460				8	1,752	20,830	19,972	**152,830**	**3,375**	**156,205**
Peoria & Eastern	4	3,922	18,971	150				1	1,939	3,418	5,091	**27,630**	**22**	**27,652**
Terre Haute & Peoria	18	3,175	46,503	460				1	2,340	2,887	12,660	**62,510**	**30**	**62,540**
Total	80	5,101	$241,616	$12,726				12	4,611	$30,597	$43,360	**$328,299**	**$3,597**	**$331,896**
Douglas:														
Chicago & Eastern Illinois	24	751	91,740	2,865				3	4,339	7,644	59,585	**161,834**	**2,968**	**164 802**
Indiana, Decatur & Western	27	4,752	111,600	2,400				3	949	7,949	28,784	**150,733**	**1,188**	**151,921**
Terre Haute & Peoria	22	4,064	56,924	640				2	4,410	5,671	15,497	**78,732**	**311**	**79,043**
Toledo, St. Louis & Kansas City		3,221	2,440								815	**3,255**		**3,255**
Total	75	2,228	$262,704	$5,905				9	4,418	$21,261	$104,681	**$394,554**	**$4,467**	**$399,021**
DuPage:														
Chicago, Burlington & Quincy	21	3,517	136,496	2,380	**18**	1,218	$63,807	12	479	30,227	25,759	**258,669**	**2,150**	**260,819**
Chicago Great Western	17	3,916	102,902	3,800				3	1,210	8,073	22,604	**137,379**		**137,379**
Chicago, Madison & Northern	19	124	95,117	5,310				5	5,136	14,932	6,716	**122,075**		**122,075**
Chicago, Milwaukee & St. Paul	12	1,138	51,916	2,725		4,709	3,181	3	3,578	9,194	13,585	**80,601**		**80,601**
Chicago & Northwestern	25	396	144,181	6,070	**18**	2,255	64,495	11	4,694	29,723	32,807	**277,276**	**15,083**	**292,359**
Chicago, Santa Fé & California	4	4,622	25,840	20					2,320	1,008	5,841	**32,799**		**32,799**
Elgin, Joliet & Eastern	18	4,092	84,488	5,563				5	1,575	13,246	40,622	**143,919**	**43**	**143,962**
Total	119	1,965	$640,940	$25,868	**37**	2,992	$131,483	42	3,152	$106,493	$147,934	**$1,052,718**	**$17,276**	**$1,069,994**

Edgar:														
Cairo, Vincennes & Chicago	29	3,265	88,855	685	......	......	....	3	4,055	7,536	21,564	118,640	740	119,380
Chicago & Ohio River	27	2,997	49,622	500	......	......	....	1	3,940	1,747	2,413	54,281	....	54,281
Cleveland, Cincinna'i, Chicago & St. L.	25	1,481	128,930	3,525	......	......	....	5	5,129	14,928	53,149	200,532	....	200,532
Indiana, Decatur & Western	21	2,323	85,760	700	......	......	....	2	1,759	5,833	22,120	114,413	11	114,424
Terre Haute & Peoria	25	4,724	64,737	830	......	......	....	3	5,127	7,942	17,623	91,132	316	91,448
Toledo, St. Louis & Kansas City	19	4,487	79,399	1,238	......	......	....	1	2,561	3,713	26,533	110,883	40	110,923
Total	149	3,437	$497,303	$7,478	......	......	....	19	1,451	$41,698	$143,402	$689,881	$1,107	$690,988
Edwards:														
Cairo, Vincennes & Chicago	3	3,765	11,139	....	......	......	....	......	2,323	880	2,703	14,722	....	14,722
Louisville, Evansville & St. Louis Con.	9	3,967	34,130	1,250	......	......	....	1	262	2,624	13,539	51,543	27	51,570
Peoria, Decatur & Evansville	22	1,653	55,783	350	......	......	....	1	3,052	3,156	31,408	90,697	45	90,742
Total	35	4,105	$101,052	$1,600	......	......	....	3	357	$6,660	$47,650	$156,962	$72	$157,034
Effingham:														
Baltimore & Ohio Southwestern	22	1,957	67,112	815	......	......	....	2	1,729	5,819	38,764	112,510	....	112,510
Chicago, Paducah & Memphis	3	5,050	9,891	300	......	......	....	......	1,000	379	860	11,430	....	11,430
Indiana & Illinois Southern	11	......	16,500	....	......	......	....	......	300	57	2,234	18,791	....	18,791
Terre Haute & Indianapolis	25	2,078	159,979	5,603	......	......	....	9	81	22,538	74,362	262,482	3,185	265,667
Wabash (C. & P.)	19	909	86,275	1,619	......	......	....	......	4,058	1,921	29,031	118,846	80	118,926
Total	81	4,714	$339,757	$8,337	......	......	....	12	1,888	$30,714	$145,251	$524,059	$3,265	$527,324
Fayette:														
Baltimore & Ohio Southwestern	1	1,726	3,981	75	......	......	....	......	310	147	2,299	6,502	....	6,502
Chicago, Paducah & Memphis	16	3,820	41,809	1,900	......	......	....	1	2,284	2,865	3,636	50,210	....	50,210
Terre Haute & Indianapolis	25	4,332	162,669	1,763	......	......	....	4	1,276	10,604	75,612	250,648	165	250,813
Toledo, St. Louis & Kansas City	16	3,960	67,000	825	......	......	....	......	4,727	2,238	22,390	92,453	40	92,493
Total	60	3,278	$275,459	$4,563	......	......	....	6	3,317	$15,854	$103,937	$399,813	$205	$400,018
Ford:														
Chicago & Springfield	25	3,303	79,439	1,685	......	......	....	2	1,847	5,874	15,621	102,619	118	102,737
Kankakee & Southwestern	5	2,513	15,333	1,150	......	......	....	......	4,231	1,603	3,609	21,695	48	21,743
Lake Erie & Western	28	3,151	142,984	3,570	......	......	....	5	1,254	13,094	49,556	209,204	367	209,571
Toledo, Peoria & Western	6	99	24,075	445	......	......	....	......	3,062	1,450	5,424	31,394	18	31,412
Wabash (C. & P.)	15	2,503	69,633	**2,881**	......	......	....	3	920	7,936	23,431	103,881	83	103,964
Total	81	1,009	$331,464	**$9,731**	......	......	....	12	754	$29,957	$97,641	$468,793	$634	$469,427
Franklin:														
Belleville & Eldorado	27	420	54,159	**1,900**	......	......	....	1	3,479	2,986	13,000	72,054	132	72,186
Chicago, Paducah & Memphis	18	2,382	46,128	**800**	......	......	....	......	5,200	1,970	4,012	52,910	....	52,910
Total	45	2,802	$100,287	**$2,700**	......	......	....	2	3,399	$4,956	$17,021	$124,964	$132	$125,096

Statement 22—Continued.

County—Railroad.	Main Track, Including Right of Way and Improvements Thereon.				Second Main Track.			Side or Turnout Track.			Rolling Stock.	Total assessment by the State Board of Equalization	Equalized value of railroad property assessed by local assessors	Equalized value of railroad property in county
	Miles	Feet	Assess'd value excluding buildings.	Value of buildings on right of way.	Miles	Feet	Assess'd value.	Miles	Feet	Assess'd value.	Assess'd value.			
Fulton:														
Chicago, Burlington & Quincy	51	2,656	$324,469	$2,628				6	1,195	$15,566	$61,233	$403,896	$1,373	$405,269
Chicago, Havana & Western		2,573	1,462								110	1,572	321	1,893
Fulton County Narrow Gauge	41	3,875	62,601	1,300				1	3,763	857	9,416	74,174	144	74,318
Illinois Western	2	3,190	7,813					1	4,498	3,704		11,517		11,517
Iowa Central	12	5,074	38,853	1,155				3	3,331	7,262	12,190	59,490	490	59,980
St. Louis, Rock Island & Chicago	16	3,313	66,510	1,126				3	1,794	8,349	11,487	87,472	911	88,383
Toledo, Peoria & Western	33	2,105	133,595	2,155				5	4,845	14,794	30,098	180,642	781	181,423
Total	159	1,666	$635,333	$8,364				22	3,586	$50,532	$124,534	$818,763	$4,020	$822,783
Gallatin:														
Baltimore & Ohio Southwestern	16	3,902	50 217	670				4	2,835	11,342	29,006	91,235	304	91,539
same (L. & N.)	2	3,456									4,600	4,600		4,600
Cairo, Vincennes & Chicago		1,168	664								161	825		825
Louisville & Nashville	10	5,098	43,862	1,370				1	435	2,706	11,256	59,194	2,832	62,026
same (B. & O. S. W.)	2	3,459									2,725	2,725		2,725
Total	33	1,243	$94,743	$2,040				5	3,270	$14,048	$47,748	$158,579	$3,136	$161,715
Greene:														
Chicago & Alton	39	675	246,505	14,595				9	2,151	23,519	81,524	366,143	1,007	367,150
Litchfield, Carrollton & Western	25	4,731	46,613	825				1	4,588	1,869	3,840	53,147	32	53,179
St. Louis, Rock Island & Chicago	23	4,399	95,333	1,410				3	390	7,685	16,465	120,893	235	121,128
Total	88	4,525	$388,451	$16,830				14	1,849	$33,073	$101,829	$540,183	$1,274	$541,457
Grundy:														
Chicago & Alton	18	1,723	115,456	1,930	8	2,776	$29,840	5	35	12,517	38,183	197,926	99	198,025
same (C. & Ill. R.)	1	3,665	10,673					4	4,331	12,050	3,530	26,253	49	26,302
Chicago, Rock Island & Pacific	20	1,147	171,846	1,250	20	1,147	70,760	3	3,505	9,160	23,123	276,139	148	276,287
Chicago, Santa Fé & California	20	964	106,968	1,275				4	342	10,162	24,181	142,586	558	143,144
Clev., Cin., Chi. & St. Louis (K. & S.)	20	679									42,318	42,318		42,318
Elgin, Joliet & Eastern	19	3,795	88,734	9,488				12	864	30,409	42,664	171,295	173	171,468
Kankakee & Seneca	20	679	50,322	1,250				4	3,114	9,180		60,752	31	60,783
Total	120	2,092	$543,999	$15,193	28	3,923	$100,600	34	1,631	$83,478	$173,999	$917,269	$1,058	$918,327

HAMILTON:														
Louisville & Nashville	36	3,680	146,788	2,530				2	2,049	5,970	37,668	192,956	286	193,242
HANCOCK:														
Chicago, Burlington & Quincy	41	1,576	260,181	1,536				3	2,993	8,917	49,101	319,735	432	320,167
Chicago, Santa Fé & California	7	330	37,431	1,270				3	3,105	8,970	8,462	56,133	400	56,533
Toledo, Peoria & Western	41	2,501	165,895	2,470				4	1,689	10,800	37,357	216,540	187	216,727
Wabash	22	909	99,775	4,006				1	3,090	3,963	33,574	141,318	163	141,481
same (T., P. & W.)	7	5									10,601	10,601		10,601
Total	119	41	$563,282	$9,282				13	317	$32,650	$139,113	$744,327	$1,182	$745,509
HENDERSON:														
Chicago, Burlington & Quincy	32	2,890	205,048	1,750	18	175	$63,116	6	3,394	17,607	38,696	325,217	258	325,475
Chicago, Santa Fé & California	22	3,213	118,821	3,560				4	1,234	10,584	26,860	159,825	284	160,109
Iowa Central		4,320	2,455								769	3,224		3,224
St. Louis, Rock Island & Chicago	14	4,112	59,115	320					2,222	1,052	10,210	70,697	92	70,789
Toledo, Peoria & Western	4	3,108	18,354						1,607	761	4,125	23,250		23,250
same (C., B. & Q.)	8	564									7,306	7,306		7,306
Total	83	1,367	$403,793	$5,630	18	175	$63,116	11	3,177	$29,004	$87,976	$589,519	$634	$590,153
HENRY:														
Chicago, Burlington & Quincy	35	1,364	222,128	2,931	14	3,281	51,175	7	5,072	19,902	41,919	338,055	843	338,898
Chicago, Rock Island & Pacific	27	3,710	235,473	3,250	27	3,710	96,959	5	4,132	14,456	31,685	381,823	3,147	384,970
Rock Island & Peoria	31	3,625	180,614	8,250				3	2,624	8,742	31,621	229,227	454	229,681
St. Louis, Rock Island & Chicago	27	907	108,687	876				3	4,837	9,790	18,771	138,124	177	138,301
Total	121	4,326	$746,902	$15,307	42	1,711	$148,134	21	825	$52,890	$123,996	$1,087,229	$4,621	$1,091,850
IROQUOIS:														
Chicago & Eastern Illinois	47	2,341	180,285	4,225	36	1,334	108,758	7	3,342	15,266	117,093	425,627	1,315	426,942
Chicago & Springfield	9	1,926	29,031	1,125				1	2,724	3,790	5,708	39,654	67	39,721
Cincinnati, Lafayette & Chicago	20	2,595	102,457	395				4	2,692	11,275		114,127	42	114,169
Cleve., Cin., Chi. & St. L. (C., L., F. C.)	20	2,595									43,081	43,081		43,081
Toledo, Peoria & Western	31	2,480	125,879	2,530				4	3,407	11,613	28,360	168,382	227	168,609
Total	129	1,377	$437,652	$8,275	36	1,334	$108,758	18	1,605	$41,944	$194,242	$790,871	$1,651	$792,522
JACKSON:														
Chicago & Texas	31	2,020	47,074	600				8	2,459	8,466	20,167	76,307	1,525	77,832
Mobile & Ohio	34	1,411	137,069	11,900				10	4,878	27,310	38,226	214,505	2,800	217,305
St. Louis Southern	24	4,213	94,232	1,200				3	356	7,669	26,554	129,655	100	129,755
Total	90	2,364	$278,375	$13,700				22	2,413	$43,445	$84,947	$420,467	$4,425	$424,892
JASPER:														
Chicago & Ohio Riter	23	70	41,424	170				1	535	1,101	2,015	44,710		44,710
Indiana & Illinois Southern	24		36,000						3,000	568	4,875	41,443		41,443
Peoria, Decatur & Evansville	23	3,105	58,970	675				1	4,973	3,884	33,203	96,732		96,732
Motal	70	3,175	$136,394	$845				3	3,228	$5,553	$40,093	$182,885		$182,885

Statement 22—Continued.

County—Railroad.	Main Track, including Right of Way and Improvements thereon.				Second Main Track.			Side or Turnout Track.			Rolling Stock.	Total assessment by the State Board of Equalization.	Equalized value of railroad property assessed by local assessors	Equalized value of railroad property in county
	Miles	Feet	Assess'd value excluding buildings.	Value of buildings on right of way.	Miles	Feet	Assess'd value.	Miles	Feet	Assess'd value.	Assess'd value.			
Jefferson:														
Chicago, Paducah & Memphis	24	2,310	$61,094	$800					4,700	$1,780	$5,313	$68,987		$68,987
Louisville, Evansville & St. Louis Con.	26	1,447	91,959	3,130				2	3,791	6,795	36,479	138,363	$110	138,473
Louisville & Nashville	26	4,827	107,657	3,150				3	3,150	8,992	27,526	147,325	138	147,463
Louisville & St. Louis	10	3,790	21,435	250					3,815	722	68	22,475		22,475
Wabash, Chester & Western	17	1,816	39,023	1,700				1	1,782	2,675	5,776	49,174		49,174
Total	105	3,630	$321,168	$9,030				9	1,398	$20,964	$75,162	$426,324	$248	$426,572
Jersey:														
Chicago & Alton	16	4,660	106,348	1,060				1	1,574	3,245	35,171	145,824	705	146,529
St. Louis, Chicago & St. Paul	33	914	82,933	1,401				1	2,024	1,383	46,759	132,476	45	132,521
St. Louis, Rock Island & Chicago	5	3,746	22,838	90					1,947	922	3,944	27,794	50	27,844
Total	55	4,030	$212,119	$2,551				3	265	$5,550	$85,874	$306,094	$800	$306,894
JoDaviess:														
Chicago, Burlington & Northern	22	1,158	111,078	4,500				4	574	10,272	39,366	165,216	1,631	166,850
same (Ill. Cen.)	13	1,617									23,579	23,579		23,579
same (D. & D. Bdg.)		880									295	295		295
Chicago Great Western	30	661	174,726	5,500				3	826	7,808	28,383	226,500	65	226,565
same (C., B. & Q.)	1	4,488									2,357	2,357		2,357
same (Ill. Cen.)	13	1,214									16,856	16,856		16,856
same (D. & D. Bdg.)		898									217	217		217
Chicago, Milwaukee & St. Paul	1	49	4,289	25					915	433	1,122	5,869	28	5,897
Chicago & Northwestern	10	1,571	59,211	200				1	2,119	3,503	13,473	76,387	93	76,480
Total	92	1,956	$349,304	$10,225				8	4,434	$22,099	$135,648	$517,276	$1,820	$519,096
Johnson:														
Cairo, Vincennes & Chicago	28	1,396	84,793	1,185				3	368	6,139	20,578	112,695		112,695
Chicago, St. Louis & Paducah	22	308	72,793	2,900				1	2,839	3,844	20,420	99,957		99,957
Total	50	1,704	$157,586	$4,085				4	3,207	$9,983	$40,998	$212,652		$212,652

Kane:														
Chicago, Burlington & Quincy	24	3,608	155,505	45,738	6	849	21,563	30	1,807	75,856	29,347	328,009	105,493	433,502
Chicago Great Western	18	1,918	106,507	4,000				3	3,952	9,372	23,397	143,276	483	143,759
Chicago & Iowa	14	1,643	71,556	520				1	1,817	3,360	10,755	86,191	131	86,322
Chicago, Madison & Northern	18	4,310	94,110	4,860				3	4,424	9,595	6,644	115,209	760	115,969
Chicago, Milwaukee & St. Paul	19	2,814	83,015	7,206				8	362	20,171	21,722	132,114	1,157	133,271
Chicago & Northwestern	56	2,612	324,845	6,085	17	3,071	61,535	27	2,157	68,521	73,914	534,900	4,895	539,795
Elgin, Joliet & Eastern	4	205	18,175	3,213				1	3,595	4,202	8,739	34,329	652	34,901
Total	156	1,300	$853,713	$71,622	23	3,920	$83,098	76	2,274	$191,077	$174,518	$1,374,028	$113,571	$1,487,599
Kankakee:														
Chicago & Eastern Illinois	32	110	121,679	6,915	19	3,812	59,166	21	2,342	42,887	79,029	309,676	4,494	314,170
Cincinnati, Lafayette & Chicago	12	2,588	62,451	3,060				17	1,166	43,052		108,563	443	109,006
Cleve., Cin., Chi. & St. L. (C., L. F. & C.)	12	2,588									26,259	26,259		26,259
same (K. & S.)	20	3,021									43,250	43,250	29	43,279
Indiana, Illinois & Iowa	38	3,485	154,640	18,732				11	4,824	29,784	22,746	225,902	1,884	227,786
Kankakee & Seneca	20	3,021	51,430	950				1	1,760	2,667		55,047		55,047
Kankakee & Southwestern	29	84	81,245	2,900				3	1,342	6,508	19,121	109,774	126	109,900
Wabash (C. & S.)	8	4,160	39,545	1,450				1	3,459	4,138	13,307	58,440	78	58,518
Total	174	3,217	$510,990	$34,007	19	3,812	$59,166	56	4,333	$129,036	$203,712	$936,911	$7,054	$943,965
Kendall:														
Chicago, Burlington & Quincy	33	2,545	210,937	1,777	14	2,033	50,348	6	1,982	15,938	39,808	318,808	254	319,062
Elgin, Joliet & Eastern	3	2,922	15,990	413					1,846	874	7,688	24,965	17	24,982
Total	37	187	$226,927	$2,190	14	2,033	$50,348	6	3,828	$16,812	$47,496	$343,773	$271	$344,044
Knox:														
Chicago, Burlington & Quincy	71	1,798	449,445	24,715	25	3,794	90,015	48	3,640	121,724	84,819	770,718	28,420	799,138
same (G. & R.)	12	1,010									14,495	14,495		14,495
Chicago, Santa Fé & California	25	651	133,153	9,590				7	622	17,795	30,100	190,638	986	191,624
Fulton County Narrow Gauge	17	2,989	26,349	830					3,223	305	3,964	31,448	107	31,555
Galesburg, Etherley & Eastern	11	3,089	46,340	1,500					2,700	1,278	1,020	50,138		50,138
Galesburg & Rio	12	1,010	48,765	378				1	30	2,514		51,657	88	51,745
Iowa Central	15	4,943	47,808	428					4,650	1,761	14,988	64,985	110	65,095
Rock Island & Peoria	2	201	11,617								2,034	13,651	7	13,658
St. Louis, Rock Island & Chicago	5	1,854	21,415	270					1,376	652	3,697	26,024	548	26,572
Total	173	1,705	$784,882	$37,711	25	3,794	$90,015	59	401	$146,029	$155,117	$1,213,754	$30,266	$1,244,020
Lake:														
Chicago, Milwaukee & St. Paul	27	2,047	116,398	6,238	24	2,047	85,357	6	1,180	15,559	30,457	254,009	1,656	255,665
Chicago & Northwestern	28	3,684	165,012	4,420	24	3,456	86,291	16	4,096	41,939	37,546	335,208	444	335,652
Elgin, Joliet & Eastern	23	5,078	107,828	10,950				8	4,092	21,938	51,845	192,561	8,610	201,171
Wisconsin Central	25	2,529	127,395	7,824				9	4,893	24,817	39,915	199,951	1,681	201,632
Waukegan & Mississippi Valley											8,950	8,950		8,950
Total	105	2,778	$516,633	$29,432	49	223	$171,648	41	3,701	$104,253	$168,713	$990,679	$12,391	$1,003,070

Statement 22—Continued.

County—Railroad.	Main Track, Including Right of Way and Improvements Thereon.				Second Main Track.			Side or Turnout Track.			Rolling Stock.	Total assessment by State Board of Equalization......	Equalized value of railroad property assessed by local assessors..........	Equalized value of railroad property in county..........
	Miles	Feet........	Assess'd value excluding buildings.	Value of buildings on right of way.	Miles	Feet........	Assess'd value.	Miles	Feet........	Assess'd value.	Assess'd value.			
LaSalle:														
Chicago & Alton..........	12	1,036	$76,908	$885	......	......	....	1	2,483	$3,675	$25,435	$106,903	$374	$107,277
Chicago, Burlington & Quincy..........	80	4,926	509,878	8,736	25	3,102	$89,556	23	3,356	59,089	96,223	763,482	2,674	766,156
same (I., V. & N.)..........	28	978	....	....	......	......	....	......	......	....	33,510	33,510	....	33,510
Chicago & Northwestern (Nor. Ill.)..........	21	2,037	....	....	......	......	....	......	......	....	27,980	27,980	....	27,980
Chicago, Rock Island & Pacific..........	31	2,557	267,616	10,563	31	2,557	110,195	21	4,040	54,413	36,010	478,797	1,366	480,163
Chicago, Santa Fé & California..........	25	3,067	135,579	4,695	......	......	....	12	225	30,107	30,648	201,029	681	201,710
Cleveland, Cin., Chi. & St. L. (K. & S.).	1	1,981	....	....	......	......	....	......	......	....	2,891	2,891	....	2,891
Illinois Valley & Northern..........	28	978	84,556	3,100	......	......	....	6	449	15,212	....	102,868	264	103,132
Kankakee & Seneca..........	1	1,981	3,438	....	......	......	....	......	2,586	979	....	4,417	....	4,417
LaSalle & Bureau County..........	5	122	15,069	....	......	......	....	......	970	459	....	15,528	209	15,737
Northern Illinois..........	21	2,037	53,464	915	......	......	....	2	3,479	6,647	....	61,026	163	61,189
Wabash (C. & P.)..........	1	657	5,060	1,338	......	......	....	1	3,074	3,956	1,703	12,057	176	12,233
Total..........	258	1,297	$1,151,568	$30,232	57	379	$199,751	69	4,822	$174,537	$254,400	$1,810,488	$5,907	$1,816,395
Lawrence:														
Baltimore & Ohio Southwestern..........	21	2,396	64,361	890	......	......	....	2	797	5,377	37,175	107,803	120	107,923
Cairo, Vincennes & Chicago..........	21	2,700	64,534	490	......	......	....	2	5,043	5,910	15,661	86,595	333	86,928
Total..........	42	5,096	$128,895	$1,380	......	......	....	5	560	$11,287	$52,836	$194,398	$453	$194,851
Lee:														
Chicago, Burlington & Quincy..........	42	4,741	270,257	919	......	......	....	3	907	7,929	51,002	330,107	803	330,910
Chicago & Iowa..........	8	4,589	44,346	340	......	......	....	......	3,643	1,725	6,665	53,076	63	53,139
Chicago & Northwestern..........	26	677	150,237	2,665	26	677	91,449	12	2,931	31,388	34,185	309,924	1,440	311,364
Total..........	77	4,727	$164,840	$3,924	26	677	$91,449	16	2,201	$41,042	$91,852	$693,107	$2,306	$695,413
Livingston:														
Chicago & Alton..........	51	3,843	325,885	7,695	29	2,440	103,117	5	4,691	14,721	167,776	559,194	1,799	560,993
Chicago, Santa Fe & California..........	13	5,002	73,921	990	......	......	....	5	3,179	14,005	16,710	105,626	296	105,922
Indiana, Illinois & Iowa..........	30	98	120,074	4,538	......	......	....	4	5,227	12,475	17,661	154,748	75	154,823
Kankakee & Southwestern..........	61	5,113	173,511	13,800	......	......	....	5	667	10,253	40,836	238,400	296	238,696
Toledo, Peoria & Western..........	18	574	72,435	1,370	......	......	....	4	3,670	11,738	16,319	101,862	67	101,929

Wabash (C. & P.)	33	1,976	150,184	3,425				2	3,139	6,486	50,536	210,631	535	211,166
same (C. & S.)	32	458	141,390	13,219				8	2,029	20,961	48,586	227,156	475	227,631
same (T., P. & W.)	5										7,571	7,571		7,571
Total	246	1,224	$1,060,400	$45,037	29	2,440	$103,117	37	1,482	$90,639	$305,995	$1,605,188	$3,543	$1,608,731
LOGAN:														
Chicago & Alton	28	2,880	179,836	3,305				4	4,928	12,333	59,475	254,949	250	255,199
Chicago, Havana & Western	24	2,950	73,676	2,550				2	3,812	5,444	5,569	87,239	150	87,389
Chicago & Springfield	17	163	52,796	1,350				1	4,769	4,758	10,381	69,285	110	69,395
Peoria, Decatur & Evansville	33	1,401	83,163	550				4	3,488	9,321	46,825	139,859	70	139,929
Terre Haute & Peoria	11	3,095	28,965	170					3,261	1,235	7,885	38,255	10	38,265
Total	114	5,209	$418,436	$7,925				14	4,418	$33,091	$130,135	$589,587	$590	$590,177
MACON:														
Chicago, Havana & Western	16	170	48,097	1,344				1	3,589	3,360	3,635	56,436	110	56,546
Indiana, Decatur & Western	11	2,008	45,521	400				1	4,327	4,549	11,741	62,211	10	62,221
Peoria, Decatur & Evansville	16	3,303	41,564	150				1	3,557	3,347	23,403	68,464	171	68,635
same (T. H. & P.)	7	2,657									10,562	10,562		10,562
Terre Haute & Peoria	14	808	35,383	736				2	547	4,207	9,632	49,958	95	50,053
same (Ill. Cen.)	15	2,214									10,494	10,494		10,494
Wabash	40	1,810	181,543	29,594				24	356	60,169	61,088	332,394	3,524	335,918
Total	121	2,410	$352,108	$32,224				31	1,816	$75,632	$130,555	$590,519	$3,910	$594,429
MACOUPIN:														
Chicago & Alton	40	3,607	256,304	3,035				10	1,945	25,921	84,764	370,024	1,510	371,534
Chicago, Peoria & St. Louis	8	2,949	23,964	625				2	3,257	5,234	14,468	44,291	26	44,317
Cleveland, Cincinnati, Chicago & St. L.	20	3,612	105,489	1,125				5	500	12,737	43,486	162,837	155	162,992
Jacksonville, Louisville & St. Louis	18	2,770	48,165	1,125				2	1,707	4,647	7,353	61,290	38	61,328
Litchfield, Carrollton & Western	21	4,868	44,866	500				1	503	1,095	3,695	50,150	576	50,726
St. Louis & Chicago								1	3,143	3,190		3,190		3,190
St. Louis, Chicago & St. Paul	28	1,655	70,784	1,696				1	5,191	1,983	39,910	114,373	129	114,502
St. Louis & Peoria	5	3,900	17,216	1,650					800	152	2,370	21,388	258	21,646
St. Louis, Rock Island & Chicago	13	2,568	53,946	406				2	3,528	6,670	9,317	70,339	344	70,683
Wabash	8	3,639	39,101	2,488				4	187	10,089	13,157	64,835	103	64,938
Total	169	3,168	$659,829	$12,650				31	4,921	$71,718	$218,520	$962,717	$3,139	$965,856
MADISON:														
Chicago & Alton	39	1,786	247,831	9,165	1	2,258	$4,997	15	4,827	39,785	81,962	383,740	1,785	385,525
Chicago, Peoria & St. Louis	32	2,813	91,092	963				3	4,463	7,691	54,996	154,742	564	155,306
Cleveland, Cincinnati, Chicago & St. L.	33	378	168,665	1,985				12	2,649	31,254	69,529	271,443	189	271,622
Madison, Illinois & St. Louis	4	1,584	64,500	2,200				5	5,115	20,891	6,717	94,308		94,308
St. Louis, Chicago & St. Paul	22	2,890	56,368	1,290				5	1,740	5,339	31,782	94,770		91,770
St. Louis & Eastern	12	1,643	36,934	2,575				5	3,575	11,354	72,160	123,023		123,023
St. Louis & Peoria	7		21,000								2,890	23,890		23,890

Statement 22—Continued.

County—Railroad.	Main Track, Including Right of Way and Improvements Thereon.				Second Main Track.			Side or Turnout Track.			Rolling Stock.	Total assessment by the State Board of Equalization...	Equalized value of railroad property assessed by local assessors..........	Equalized value of railroad property in county..........
	Miles.......	Feet.......	Assess'd value exclud-ing build-ings.	Value of build-ings on right of way.	Miles.......	Feet.......	Assess'd value.	Miles.......	Feet.......	Assess'd value.	Assess'd value.			
Madison—*Continued.*														
St. Louis, Rock Island & Chicago.......	8	4,727	$35,581	$60	......	....	....	1	876	$2,915	$6,145	$44,701	$61	$44,762
same (I. & St. L.).......	17	153	....	....	......	....	....	......	...	....	11,764	11,764	....	11,764
Terre Haute & Indianapolis.......	24	3,000	154,780	3,098	......	....	....	11	421	27,700	71,945	257,523	63	257,586
Toledo, St. Louis & Kansas City.......	37	1,901	149,440	9,038	......	....	....	9	2,634	23,747	49,939	232,164	108	232,272
Wabash.......	40	5,242	184,468	6,430	......	....	....	8	2,478	21,173	62,072	274,163	265	274,428
Total.......	279	4,997	$1,210,659	$36,824	1	2,258	$4,997	79	2,378	$191,840	$521,901	$1,966,221	$3,035	$1,969,256
Marion:														
Baltimore & Ohio Southwestern.......	24	766	72,435	1,175	......	....	....	5	2,059	13,475	41,839	128,924	270	129,194
Centralia & Chester.......	1	1,960	3,428	150	......	....	....	......	3,202	1,213	332	5,123	....	5,123
Chicago, Paducah & Memphis.......	25	3,620	64,214	1,400	......	....	....	1	1,770	2,670	5,584	73,868	....	73,868
Jacksonville, Louisville & St. Louis.......	2	4,666	7,498	100	......	....	....	......	2,330	883	1,145	9,626	242	9,868
Louisville, Evansville & St. Louis Con.......	......	3,701	2,453	....	......	....	....	......	1,617	766	973	4,192	90	4,282
same (L. & St. L.).......	7	2,569	....	....	......	....	....	......	..	....	10,395	10,395	....	10,395
Louisville & St. Louis.......	5	3,957	11,499	50	......	....	....	......	215	41	37	11,627	792	12,419
Total.......	68	119	$161,527	$2,875	......	....	....	8	633	$19,048	$60,305	$243,755	$1,394	$245,149
Marshall:														
Chicago & Alton.......	28	5,238	182,650	2,300	......	....	....	2	1,721	5,819	60,406	251,175	....	251,175
Chi., Rock Island & Pacific (Peo. Br.).......	13	3,689	116,439	1,875	......	....	....	1	1,015	2,981	15,668	136,963	783	137,746
Chicago, Santa Fé & California.......	23	20	121,920	3,870	......	....	....	9	4,237	24,506	27,561	177,857	....	177,857
Total.......	65	3,667	$421,009	$8,045	......	....	....	13	1,693	$33,306	$103,635	$565,995	$783	$566,778
Mason:														
Chicago & Alton.......	12	4,370	80,814	1,170	......	....	....	2	3,138	6,486	26,727	115,197	150	115,347
Chicago, Havana & Western.......	25	4,304	77,445	3,669	......	....	....	2	1,852	4,701	5,854	91,669	930	92,599
Chicago, Peoria & St. Louis.......	49	3,748	139,188	3,969	......	....	....	7	3,694	15,399	84,034	242,590	1,080	243,670
Total.......	88	1,862	$297,447	$8,808	......	....	....	12	3,404	$26,586	$116,615	$449,456	$2,160	$451,616
Massac:														
Chicago, St. Louis & Paducah.......	19	3,693	65,008	3,400	......	....	....	4	2,730	11,293	18,236	97,937	....	97,937

McDonough:														
Chicago, Burlington & Quincy	34	1,720	216,252	2,864				8	2,670	21,264	40,811	281,191	805	281,996
St. Louis, Rock Island & Chicago	19	2,779	78,105	420				2	1,186	5,562	13,489	97,576	137	97,713
Toledo, Peoria & Western	27	3,876	110,936	1,92[illegible]				2	5,072	7,401	24,994	145,251	223	145,474
Total	81	3,095	$405,293	$5,204				13	3,648	$34,227	$79,294	$524,018	$1,165	$525,183
McHenry:														
Chicago & Northwestern	96	1,653	$553,800	$9,460				23	1,562	$58,240	$126,010	$747,510	$3,099	$750,609
McLean:														
Chicago & Alton	56	5,205	359,011	72,560	25	357	$87,737	24	1,054	60,499	118,731	698,538	76,830	775,368
Chicago & Springfield	10	4,808	33,823	775				1	332	2,681	6,651	43,930	50	43,980
Kankakee & Southwestern	29	1,113	81,790	4,125				3	727	6,275	19,249	111,439	180	111,619
Lake Erie & Western	42	1,021	210,967	8,820				6	415	15,197	73,118	308,102	300	308,402
Peoria & Eastern	37	151	148,114	2,588				7	971	17,960	39,740	208,402	130	208,532
Rantoul	16	4,188	30,228	1,150				1	630	1,119	2,374	34,871	140	35,011
Toledo, Peoria & Western	21	348	84,264	1,620				2	2,899	6,372	18,984	111,240	110	111,350
Wabash (C. & P.)	2	2,952	11,516	963					4,235	2,005	3,875	18,359	40	18,399
Total	216	3,946	$959,713	$92,601	25	357	$87,737	46	753	$112,108	$282,722	$1,534,881	$77,780	$1,612,661
Menard:														
Chicago & Alton	23	1,040	146,141	1,250				3	2,000	8,447	48,331	204,169	142	204,311
Chicago, Peoria & St. Louis	21	2,371	60,057	1,394				4	4,638	9,757	36,260	107,468	30	107,498
Total	44	3,411	$206,198	$2,644				8	1,358	$18,204	$84,591	$311,637	$172	$311,809
Mercer:														
Chicago, Burlington & Quincy	36	973	227,961	1,788				4	1,397	10,661	43,020	283,430	423	283,853
Iowa Central	10	1,144	30,650	4,343				3	1,664	6,630	9,609	51,232	342	51,574
Rock Island & Peoria	14	3,295	83,357	3,900				3	3,243	9,036	14,594	110,887	71	110,958
St. Louis, Rock Island & Chicago	8	4,567	35,460	150					2,799	1,325	6,124	43,059	123	43,182
Total	69	4,699	$377,428	$10,181				11	3,823	$27,652	$73,347	$488,608	$959	$489,567
Monroe:														
Mobile & Ohio	27	417	108,316	4,750				4	3,919	11,856	30,208	155,130	212	155,342
Montgomery:														
Chicago, Peoria & St. Louis	4	520	11,476								6,928	18,404	10	18,414
Cleveland, Cincinnati, Chicago & St. L.	34	1,353	174,707	2,945				10	2,743	26,299	72,018	275,969	210	276,179
Jacksonville, Louisville & St. Louis	20	2,709	53,334	1,075					5,111	1,936	8,143	64,488	30	64,518
Litchfield, Carrollton & Western		4,445	1,515						765	145	125	1,785	10	1,795
St. Louis & Chicago	25	3,570	64,190	715				5	4,528	11,715	12,414	89,034	40	89,074
Toledo, St. Louis & Kansas City	15	2,904	62,200	938				2	510	5,241	20,786	89,165	45	89,210
Wabash	20	383	90,326	4,588				5	3,065	13,951	30,394	139,259	150	139,409
Total	121	44	$457,748	$10,261				25	882	$59,287	$150,808	$678,104	$495	$678,599

Statement 22—Continued.

County—Railroad.	Main Track, including Right of Way and Improvements Thereon.				Second Main Track.			Side or Turnout Track.			Rolling Stock.	Total assessment by the State Board of Equalization...	Equalized value of railroad property assessed by local assessors..........	Equalized value of railroad property in county..........
	Miles	Feet........	Assess'd value excluding buildings.	Value of buildings on right of way.	Miles.......	Feet........	Assess'd value.	Miles.......	Feet........	Assess'd value.	Assess'd value,			
Morgan:														
Chicago & Alton	28	2,352	$179,206	$2,430				3	3,687	$9,245	59,267	$250,148	$210	$250,358
Chicago, Peoria & St. Louis	9	4,446	27,558	10,800				4	595	8,225	16,638	63,221	12	63,233
Jacksonville, Louisville & St. Louis	19	198	49,498	400				1	3,363	3,274	7,557	60,729	18	60,747
St. Louis, Chicago & St. Paul	6	367	15,174	213					2,890	547	8,555	24,489		24,489
St. Louis, Rock Island & Chicago	9	2,696	38,042	330				1	180	2,585	6,570	47,527	57	47,584
Wabash	30	521	135,444	13,531				7	2,487	18,677	45,576	213,228	159	213,387
Total	103	20	$444,922	$27,704				18	2,642	$42,553	$144,163	$659,342	$456	$659,798
Moultrie:														
Chicago & Eastern Illinois	17	4,103	67,553	1,350				1	4,624	3,751	43,875	116,529	95	116,624
Cleveland, Cincinnati, Chicago & St. L.	4	1,153	21,514	90					3,657	1,732	8,869	32,205	26	32,231
Peoria, Decatur & Evansville	22	4,307	57,039	425				3	1,584	6,600	32,116	96,180	137	96,317
Terre Haute & Peoria	15	3,878	39,336	422				1	2,807	3,063	10,709	53,530	26	53,556
Wabash (C. & P.)	22	3,133	101,670	1,356				1	1,538	3,228	34,211	140,465	72	140,537
Total	83	734	$287,112	$3,643				8	3,650	$18,374	$129,780	$438,909	$356	$439,265
Ogle:														
Chicago, Burlington & Northern	18	3,327	93,151	1,770				3	318	7,651	33,012	135,584	840	136,424
same (C. & Ill. R.)		1,365									458	458		458
Chicago Great Western	28	97	162,507	20,300				3	4,599	9,677	35,699	228,183	456	228,639
Chicago & Iowa	36	865	180,819	7,468				7	1,471	18,197	27,177	233,661	255	233,916
same (C., R. & N.)	14	4,698	74,444					1	630	2,798	11,189	88,431		88,431
Chicago, Milwaukee & St. Paul	39	3,596	168,645	10,925	7	5,101	$27,881	7	4,696	19,724	44,129	271,304	905	272,209
same (C., R. & N.)	3	2,769									3,920	3,920		3,920
Chicago & Northwestern	11	1,777	65,185	690	11	1,777	39,678	4	1,289	10,610	14,832	130,995	90	131,085
Total	152	2,649	$744,751	$41,153	19	1,598	$67,559	27	2,443	$68,657	$170,416	$1,002,536	$2,546	$1,095,082

PEORIA:														
Chicago, Burlington & Quincy	44	4,780	282,903	4,249				14	128	35,061	53,389	375,602	698	376,298
Chicago, Rock Island & Pacific (Peo. Br.)	22	1,423	189,291	9,125				10	1,360	25,644	25,471	249,531	1,760	251,291
Chicago, Santa Fé & California	28	1,061	149,465	13,265				15	3,530	39,171	33,787	235,688	2,389	238,077
Iowa Central	19	3,183	58,808	1,163				5	4,088	11,549	18,437	89,957	288	90,245
Peoria & Pekin Union	10	447	181,524	31,550	2	374	8,283	33	2,597	83,730	40,041	345,128	1,696	346,824
Rock Island & Peoria	27	1,767	155,807	2,460				10	382	25,181	27,278	210,726	5,577	216,303
Toledo, Peoria & Western	12	403	48,305	4,515				2	3,233	6,531	10,883	70,234	784	71,018
same (P. & P. U.)	8										7,210	7,210		7,210
Total	172	2,504	$1,066,103	$66,327	2	374	$8,283	91	4,758	$226,867	$216,496	$1,584,076	$13,190	$1,597,266
PERRY:														
Belleville & Eldorado	5	2,510	10,951	500					4,461	1,521	2,630	15,602	50	15,652
Centralia & Chester	1	4,920	4,829								468	5,297		5,297
Mobile & Ohio	2	3,062	10,320								2,878	13,198		13,198
St. Louis, Alton & Terre Haute	22	3,880	122,768	700				4	3,151	11,492	90,743	225,703	720	226,423
St. Louis Southern	8	2,673	32,324	625				1	4,303	4,537	9,109	46,595	120	46,715
Wabash, Chester & Western	26	4,780	60,538	150				1	1,773	2,671	8,960	72,319	155	72,474
Total	68	705	$241,730	$1,975				8	3,128	$20,221	$114,788	$378,714	$1,045	$379,759
PIATT:														
Chicago, Havana & Western	28	1,661	84,944	1,931				2	3,754	5,422	6,420	98,717		98,717
Indiana, Decatur & Western	15	211	60,160	700				1	2,387	3,630	15,517	80,007		80,007
Peoria & Eastern	8	1,210	32,917	150				1	1,171	3,054	8,831	44,952		44,952
Wabash	15	2,373	69,523	4,275				5	1,627	13,270	23,394	110,462		110,462
same (C. & P.)	35	751	158,140	5,788				4	4,217	11,997	53,213	229,138		229,138
Total	102	926	$405,684	$12,844				15	2,596	$37,373	$107,375	$563,276		$563,276
PIKE:														
Chicago & Alton	23	5,073	150,953	2,383				5	688	12,826	49,923	216,085	$4,453	220,538
Chicago, Burlington & Quincy	29	2,405	185,570	431				1	2,457	3,663	35,020	224,684	229	224,913
Wabash	1	1,584	5,850								1,969	7,819	479	8,298
same (Han. Bdg.)	1	4,146	8,034	275					1,440	682	2,703	11,694		11,694
same (H. & N.)	45	501	202,930	7,381				7	1,568	18,242	68,284	296,837		296,837
Total	101	3,149	$553,337	$10,470				14	873	$35,413	$157,899	$757,119	$5,161	$762,280
PULASKI:														
Cairo, Vincennes & Chicago	19	4,487	59,549	775				2	3,368	5,276	14,452	80,052	775	80,827
Mound City	2	4,520	2,285						220	17	20	2,322	40	2,362
Total	22	3,727	$61,834	$775				2	3,588	$5,293	$14,472	$82,374	$815	$83,189
PUTNAM:														
Chicago, Rock Island & Pacific (Peo. Br.)	6	1,436	53,312	250					2,442	1,156	7,173	61,891	107	61,998

Statement 22—Continued.

County—Railroad.	Main Track, including Right of Way and Improvements Thereon.				Second Main Track.			Side or Turnout Track.			Rolling Stock.	Total assessment by the State Board of Equalizations..	Equalized value of railroad property assessed by local assessors..........	Equalized value of railroad property in county..........
	Miles.......	Feet........	Assess'd value excluding buildings.	Value of buildings on right of way.	Miles.......	Feet........	Assess'd value.	Miles.......	Feet........	Assess'd value.	Assess'd value.			
Randolph:														
Centralia & Chester	27	1,259	68,096	1,275	......	......	....	2	4,863	5,842	6,595	81,808	....	81,808
Mobile & Ohio	31	1,027	124,778	2,450	......	......	....	6	3,979	16,884	34,799	178,911	....	178,911
St. Louis, Alton & Terre Haute	6	2,130	34,578	400	......	......	....	1	1,370	3,148	25,558	63,684	125	63,809
Wabash, Chester & Western	19	422	42,930	950	......	......	....	3	3,304	7,252	6,354	57,486	200	57,686
Total	83	4,838	$270,382	5,075	......	......	....	14	2,956	$33,126	$73,306	$381,889	$325	$382,214
Richland:														
Baltimore & Ohio Southwestern	20	2,916	61,657	1,650	......	......	....	3	908	7,930	35,613	106,850	378	107,228
Chicago & Ohio River	1	826	2,081	150	......	......	....	......	2,538	481	101	2,813	716	3,529
Peoria, Decatur & Evansville	20	352	50,167	400	......	......	....	1	4,176	3,582	28,246	82,395	407	82,802
Total	41	4,094	$113,905	$2,200	......	......	....	5	2,342	$11,993	65,960	$192,058	$1,501	$193,559
Rock Island:														
Chicago, Milwaukee & St. Paul	22	285	93,729	3,231	......	......	....	5	680	12,822	24,526	134,308	363	134,671
same (C., R. I. & P.)	6	3,848	....	....	......	......	....	......	......	....	7,483	7,483	....	7,483
Chicago, Rock Island & Pacific	11	1,390	95,738	19,625	11	1,031	$39,184	23	479	57,727	12,882	225,156	5,825	230,981
Rock Island & Peoria	25	5,137	148,046	16,950	......	......	....	8	3,746	21,774	25,919	212,689	2,212	214,901
St. Louis, Rock Island & Chicago	26	189	104,143	6,236	......	......	....	14	2,949	36,396	17,986	164,761	683	165,444
Total	92	289	$411,656	$46,042	11	1,031	$39,184	51	2,574	$128,719	$88,796	$744,397	$9,083	$753,480
Saline:														
Belleville & Eldorado	16	4,340	33,644	500	......	......	....	......	2,688	916	8,081	43,141	....	43,141
Cairo, Vincennes & Chicago	28	2,336	85,327	680	......	......	....	4	1,857	8,704	20,708	115,419	....	115,419
Louisville & Nashville	12	4,273	51,237	200	......	......	....	......	3,184	1,507	13,148	66,093	....	66,093
Total	58	389	$170,208	$1,380	......	......	....	5	2,449	$11,128	$41,937	$224,653	....	$224,653

Sangamon:														
Baltimore & Ohio Southwestern	34	2,905	103,651	1,570				6	4,257	17,016	59,869	182,106	160	182,266
same (Ill. Cent.)		3,077									1,010	1,010		1,010
Chicago & Alton	34	2,721	217,447	3,360				8	1,996	20,945	71,913	313,665	680	314,345
Chicago, Peoria & St. Louis	10	1,351	28,716	544				2	1,770	4,671	17,337	51,268	2,008	53,276
Chicago & Springfield	15	2,608	48,031	3,180				5	4,165	14,472	9,444	75,127	920	76,047
Jacksonville, Louisville & St. Louis	8	3,079	22,316	100					1,221	462	3,407	26,285		26,285
Pawnee	9		9,000	250					2,300	238	1,520	10,988		10,988
St. Louis & Chicago	18	4,506	47,134	535				2	4,458	5,689	9,116	62,474	744	63,218
St. Louis, Chicago & St. Paul	20	4,206	51,991	2,289				4	4,005	4,759	29,314	88,353		88,353
Wabash	44	2,562	200,184	52,094				20	59	50,028	67,360	369,666	10,556	380,222
Total	197	615	$728,470	$63,922				51	3,111	$118,260	$270,290	$1,180,942	$15,068	$1,196,010
Schuyler:														
Chicago, Burlington & Quincy	11	2,060	71,558	838					5,148	2,438	13,542	88,576	465	89,041
St. Louis, Rock Island & Chicago	13	2,946	54,232	370				1	2,946	3,895	9,366	67,863	645	68,508
Total	24	5,006	$125,990	$1,208				2	2,814	$6,333	$22,908	$156,439	$1,110	$157,549
Scott:														
Chicago & Alton	3	4,274	24,000	220					2,833	1,341	7,937	33,498		33,498
St. Louis, Rock Island & Chicago	18	2,541	73,925	770				2	2,617	6,239	12,767	93,701		93,701
Wabash	10	2,229	46,900	5,600				3	3,623	9,215	15,782	77,497		77,497
same (H. & N.)	4	2,665	20,271	875							6,821	27,967		27,967
Total	37	1,149	$165,096	$7,465				6	3,793	$16,795	$43,307	$232,663		$232,663
Shelby:														
Baltimore & Ohio Southwestern	17	3,866	53,197	250				1	2,507	3,687	30,727	87,861	240	88,101
Chicago & Eastern Illinois	11	4,985	45,388	1,150				2	2,595	4,983	29,479	81,000	1,182	82,182
Cleveland, Cincinnati, Chicago & St. L's	26	2,122	134,650	1,915				2	4,114	6,948	55,507	199,020	2,030	201,050
Toledo, St. Louis & Kansas City	30	2,534	121,920	1,913				2	3,625	6,716	40,743	171,292	1,224	172,516
Wabash (C. & P.)	18	2,800	83,463	919				1	1,237	3,086	28,085	115,553	782	116,335
Total	105	557	$438,618	$6,147				10	3,518	$25,420	$184,541	$654,726	$5,458	$660,184
Stark:														
Chicago, Burlington & Quincy	20	4,802	131,837	1,088				1	4,624	4,689	21,880	162,494	168	162,662
Rock Island & Peoria	19	469	108,806	4,800				2	3,967	6,878	19,049	139,533	346	139,879
Total	40	81	$240,643	$5,888				4	3,311	$11,567	$43,920	$302,027	$514	$302,541
Stephenson:														
Chicago Great-Western	28	4,140	166,948	3,850				3	4,586	9,671	36,674	217,143	726	217,869
Chicago, Madison & Northern	39	3,817	198,615	22,320				8	2,487	21,177	14,022	256,134	1,035	257,169
Chicago, Milwaukee & St. Paul	23	5,179	101,919	12,763				7	1,418	18,172	26,609	159,523	1,079	160,602
Chicago & Northwestern	11	4,266	67,896	2,910				2	2,201	6,042	15,449	92,297	1,183	93,480
Total	104	1,562	$535,378	$41,843				22	132	$55,062	$92,814	$725,097	$4,023	$729,120

Statement 22—Continued.

County—Railroad.	Main Track, Including Right of Way and Improvements Thereon.				Second Main Track.			Side or Turnout Track.			Rolling Stock.	Total assessment by the State Board of Equalization....	Equalized value of railroad property assessed by local assessors..........	Equalized value of railroad property in county..........
	Miles.......	Feet.......	Assess'd value exclud-ing build-ings.	Value of build-ings on right of way.	Miles.......	Feet.......	Assess'd value.	Miles.......	Feet'.......	Assess'd value.	Assess'd value.			
St. Clair:														
Baltimore & Ohio Southwestern........	27	1,978	82,124	7,200				14	4,486	37,124	47,435	173,883	61,724	235,607
Belleville & Carondelet..................	16	4,795	42,270	700				2	3,676	5,392	12,240	60,602	2,001	62,603
Chicago & Alton........................	1	2,330	9,080	3,300	1	2,330	$5,045	3	5,073	9,902	3,003	30,330	400	30,730
Chicago, Peoria & St. Louis	1	2,233	3,984	1,000					3,203	1,213	2,405	8,602	10	8,612
Cleveland, Cincinnati, Chicago & St. L.	2	1,006	11,259	3,205				8	644	20,305	4,641	39,410	28,114	67,524
East St. Louis & Carondelet	9	391	45,370					8	3,728	21,762	16,040	83,172		83,172
East St. Louis Connecting..............	6	3,532	106,703	3,000				20	5,105	167,776	24,500	301,979		301,979
Louisville, Evansville & St. Louis Con.	30	2,687	106,781	22,750				20	2,434	51,152	42,359	223,042	40,434	263,476
same (E. St. L. & C.).....................		1,056									278	278		278
Louisville & Nashville..................	35	1,565	141,186	7,970				14	3,428	36,623	36,231	222,010	5,084	227,094
Madison, Illinois & St. Louis (V. & C.).	3	1,136	48,227	150				3	4,585	13,539	5,023	66,939	11,959	78,898
Mobile & Ohio...........................	16	415	64,314	3,150				9	2,848	23,848	17,936	109,248	4,946	114,194
St. Louis, Alton & Terre Haute	40	3,895	219,984	8,665				25	1,780	63,343	162,599	454,591	5,102	459,693
St. Louis, Belleville & Southern........	13		32,500	725				1	3,620	3,371	6,440	43,036	100	43,136
St. Louis, Rock Island & Chicago.......		5,079	3,848	4,036				5	3,392	14,106	665	22,655	435	23,090
same (I. & St. L.)........................		3,168									414	414		414
Terminal R. R. of East St. Louis	1	500	27,367	1,875				10	4,480	108,485	26,480	164,207	1,100	165,307
Terre Haute & Indianapolis.............	10	4,780	68,704	8,415				15	1,270	38,101	31,935	147,155	10,606	157,761
Toledo, St. Louis & Kansas City........	2	370	8,280	2,430				2	2,770	6,312	2,767	19,789	975	20,764
Wabash	2	816	9,696	14,106				10	4,592	27,174	3,263	54,239	250	54,489
Total	221	4,862	$1,031,677	$92,677	1	2,330	$5,045	180	3,034	$649,528	$446,654	$2,225,581	$173,240	$2,398,821
Tazewell:														
Chicago & Alton.........................	24	795	152,149	2,315				2	3,906	6,849	50,318	211,631	681	212,312
Chicago, Peoria & St. Louis	11	935	31,296	2,056				3	3,912	7,482	18,895	59,729	9	59,738
Chicago, Santa Fé & California	21	912	112,215	1,575				2	4,597	7,177	25,367	146,334	1,190	147,524
Lake Erie & Western	16	244	80,231	3,300				2	1,131	5,536	27,807	116,874	36	116,910
Peoria, Decatur & Evansville...........	20	5,116	52,423	720				4	3,829	9,450	29,516	92,109	41	92,150
Peoria & Eastern.........................	21	856	84,649	413				10	384	25,182	22,711	132,955	60	133,015
Peoria & Pekin Union	8	299	145,019	450				7	4,906	19,823	31,989	197,281		197,281
Terre Haute & Peoria....................	28	2,711	71,284	528				2	2,368	4,897	19,406	96,115	61	96,176
same (T. P. & W.).........................	5	1,122									3,547	3,547		3,547
Toledo, Peoria & Western	15	4,010	63,038	1,080				1	5,173	4,949	14,202	83,269	58	83,327
Total	172	1,160	$792,304	$12,437				38	3,806	$91,345	$243,758	$1,139,844	$2,136	$1,141,980

UNION:														
Chicago & Texas	17	267	25,576	200	......	.....	....	1	120	1,023	10,957	37,755	40	37,706
Mobile & Ohio	22	174	88,132	2,700	......	.....	....	2	2,315	6,110	24,579	121,521	....	121,521
Total	39	441	$113,708	$2,900	......	.....	....	3	2,465	$7,133	$35,536	$159,277	$40	$159,317
VERMILION:														
Cairo, Vincennes & Chicago	15	1,330	45,756	310	......	.....	....	2	331	4,125	11,104	61,295	52	61,347
Chicago & Eastern Illinois	95	3,729	363,684	48,595	25	2,554	$76,451	50	4,724	101,790	236,209	826,729	11,489	838,218
Chicago & Ohio River	2	2,742	4,535	75	......	.....	....	.....	1,795	340	221	5,171	129	5,300
Lake Erie & Western	21	5,055	109,787	10,005	......	.....	....	6	3,887	16,840	38,050	174,682	172	174,854
Peoria & Eastern	22	972	88,736	638	......	.....	....	6	2,363	16,119	23,808	129,301	171	129,472
Rantoul	21	958	38,126	1,863	......	.....	....	1	822	1,156	2,994	44,139	98	44,237
Toledo, St. Louis & Kansas City	8	4,910	35,720	450	......	.....	....	1	1,461	3,192	11,937	51,299	....	51,299
Wabash	25	4,472	116,311	15,550	......	.....	....	18	685	45,324	39,135	216,320	698	217,018
Total	213	3,048	$802,655	$77,486	25	2,554	$76,451	87	226	$188,886	$363,458	$1,508,936	$12,809	$1,521,745
WABASH:														
Cairo, Vincennes & Chicago	25	363	75,207	3,895	......	.....	....	6	45	12,017	18,251	109,370	105	109,475
Louisville, Evansville & St. Louis Con.	12	3,304	44,190	720	......	.....	....	1	954	2,952	17,530	65,392	68	65,460
Total	37	3,667	$119,397	$4,615	......	.....	....	7	999	$14,969	$35,781	$174,762	$173	$174,935
WARREN:														
Chicago Burlington & Quincy	20	4,617	131,509	1,190	19	1,457	$67,466	6	3,351	16,587	24,818	241,570	147	241,717
Chicago, Santa Fé & California	20	1,495	107,501	3,665	......	.....	....	4	4,009	11,898	24,301	147,365	608	147,973
Iowa Central	29	663	87,377	1,605	......	.....	....	3	1,207	6,457	27,393	122,832	41	122,873
St. Louis, Rock Island & Chicago	34	2,030	137,538	1,630	......	.....	....	5	1,457	13,190	23,754	176,112	265	176,377
Total	104	3,525	$463,925	$8,090	19	1,457	$67,466	19	4,744	$48,132	$100,266	$687,879	$1,061	$688,940
WASHINGTON:														
Centralia & Chester	27	4,065	69,425	750	......	.....	....	2	1,214	4,460	6,724	81,359	110	81,469
Louisville & Nashville	28	2,968	114,248	2,960	......	.....	....	2	2,201	6,085	29,318	152,611	1,268	153,879
Total	56	1,753	$183,673	$3,710	......	.....	....	4	3,505	$10,545	$36,042	$233,970	$1,378	$235,348
WAYNE:														
Baltimore & Ohio Southwestern	25	1,829	76,039	1,015	......	.....	....	2	650	5,308	43,921	126,283	....	126,283
Louisville, Evansville & St. Louis Con.	30	2,549	106,690	1,600	......	.....	....	2	726	5,344	42,323	155,957		155,957
Total	55	4,378	$182,729	$2,615	......	.....	....	4	1,376	$10,652	$86,244	$282,240	....	$282,240
WHITE:														
Baltimore & Ohio Southwestern	24	3,579	74,033	610	......	.....	....	2	1,382	5,654	42,762	123,059	$126	123,185
Cairo, Vincennes & Chicago	32	4,789	88,721	1,040	......	.....	....	2	3,362	5,274	23,958	128,993	315	129,308
Louisville & Nashville	21	968	81,732	1,470	......	.....	....	2	2,587	6,224	21,744	114,170	194	114,364
same (C., V. & C.)	......	1,890	....	....	......	.....	....	.....	.....	....	350	350	....	350
Peoria, Decatur & Evansville	2	930	5,440	175	......	.....	....	.....	3,994	1,513	3,063	10,191	16	10,207
Total	81	1,594	$262,926	$3,295	......	.....	....	8	765	$18,665	$91,877	$376,763	$651	$377,414

Statement 22—Concluded.

County—Railroad.	Main Track, Including Right of Way and Improvements Thereon.				Second Main Track.			Side or Turnout Track.			Rolling Stock.	Total assessment by the State Board of Equalization...	Equalized value of railroad property assessed by local assessors..........	Equalized value of railroad property in county..........
	Miles	Feet........	Assess'd value excluding buildings.	Value of buildings on right of way.	Miles	Feet........	Assess'd value.	Miles	Feet........	Assess'd value.	Assess'd value.			
Whiteside:														
Chicago, Burlington & Northern........	5	435	$25,412	....	......	......	....	......	1,610	$762	$9,006	$35,180	....	$35,180
same (C., B. & Q.)........	......	3,520									1,181	1,181	....	1,181
Chicago, Burlington & Quincy........	41	1,248	259,789	$3,936	......	......	....	10	2,130	26,008	49,027	338,760	$129	338,889
Chicago, Milwaukee & St. Paul........	13	4,926	59,215	925	......	......	....	1	1,885	3,392	15,495	79,027	57	79,084
Chicago & Northwestern........	31	1,742	180,147	3,450	31	1,742	$109,654	13	3,892	34,343	40,990	368,584	88,999	457,583
St. Louis, Rock Island Chicago........	22	85	88,064	520	......	......	....	2	99	5,047	15,209	108,840	....	108,840
same (C. & N. W.)........	5	1,441	....	....	......	......	....	......	......	....	3,643	3,643	....	3,643
Total........	119	2,837	$612,627	$8,831	31	1,742	$109,654	27	4,336	$69,552	$134,551	$935,215	$89,185	$1,024,400
Will:														
Calumet & Blue Island........	......	......	....	....	......	......	....	......	......	....	17,800	17,800	742	18,542
Chicago & Alton........	32	4,953	207,510	8,940	11	517	38,843	26	2,262	66,071	68,627	389,991	9,632	399,623
same (C. & Ill. R.)........	17	1,859	100,318	....	......	......	....	2	1,670	5,790	36,153	151,261	....	151,261
Chicago & Eastern Illinois........	11	5,161	45,514	2,870	11	5,161	35,993	1	4,311	3,633	29,561	117,511	619	118,130
Chicago, Rock Island & Pacific........	24	3,993	210,428	5,750	24	3,993	86,617	19	2,501	48,681	28,315	379,824	4,544	384,368
Chicago, Santa Fé & California........	28	5,251	153,671	6,215	......	......	....	12	2,228	31,528	34,738	226,152	8,967	235,119
Elgin, Joliet & Eastern........	50	1,907	226,625	26,788	......	......	....	32	559	80,265	108,964	442,642	21,639	464,281
Michigan Central (J. & N. Ind.)........	14	5,208	149,864	15,600	......	......	....	3	3,639	12,912	23,454	101,830	2,672	204,502
Wabash (C. & S.)........	29	4	130,503	8,063	......	......	....	6	450	15,213	43,914	197,693	2,154	199,847
Total........	210	1,936	$1,233,433	$74,226	47	4,391	$161,423	104	2,780	$264,096	$391,526	$2,124,704	$50,969	$2,175,673
Williamson:														
Cairo, Vincennes & Chicago........	1	4,612	5,621	....	......	......	....	......	1,617	613	1,364	7,598	....	7,598
Chicago, Paducah & Memphis........	8	4,272	22,022	600	......	......	....	2	3,340	5,265	1,915	29,802	....	29,802
Chicago, St. Louis & Paducah........	11	4,688	39,230	1,100	......	......	....	......	4,207	1,992	11,004	53,326	113	53,439
St. Louis Southern........	13	3,630	52,012	500	......	......	....	2	4,661	7,207	14,657	74,376	210	74,586
Total........	36	1,362	$118,885	$2,200	......	......	....	6	3,265	$15,077	$28,940	$165,102	$323	$165,425

WINNEBAGO:														
Chicago & Iowa	8	3,283	43,109	5,104				6	2,037	15,964	6,479	70,656	2,644	73,300
Chicago, Madison & Northern	25	4,564	129,322	14,670				13	3,206	34,018	9,130	187,140	1,333	188,473
Chicago, Milwaukee & St Paul	35	55	148,794	7,000				12	3,777	31,788	38,935	226,517	1,684	228,201
same (C., R. & N.)	8	3,170									9,564	9,564		9,564
Chicago & Northwestern	45	963	259,799	7,865				12	786	30,372	59,114	357,150	1,978	359,128
Total	123	1,475	$581,024	$34,639				44	4,526	$112,142	$123,222	$851,027	$7,639	$858,666
WOODFORD:														
Chicago & Alton	13	893	82,965	1,300				1	937	2,943	27,438	114,646	140	114,786
Chicago, Santa Fé & California	20	3,500	109,513	870				2	2,916	6,381	24,756	141,520	943	142,463
Kankakee & Southwestern	5	1,686	14,894	275							3,505	18,674	16	18,690
Lake Erie & Western	9	4,257	49,031	1,680					4,922	2,330	16,993	70,034	16	70,050
Toledo, Peoria & Western	18	1,634	73,238	1,625				2	1,843	5,873	16,500	97,236	100	97,336
Total	67	1,410	$329,641	$5,750				7	58	$17,527	$89,192	$442,110	$1,215	$443,325
*Grand aggregate	10,280	3,816	48,907,541	3,410,078	1,111	994	$4,047,317	3,431	2,701	9,032,148	13,922,301	79,319,385	2,245,913	81,565.238

* The aggregate mileage of main track embraces the mileage of leased track on which rolling stock assessment only is distributed.

No. 23.

Table showing the Assessment of Railroad Property for the year A. D. 1895.

Number	Name of Company.	Aggregate Assessment by the State Board of Equalization. Main Track.	Second Main Track.	Side or Turnout Track.	Buildings on Right of Way.	Rolling Stock.	Total Assessment	Equalized value of railroad property assessed by local assessors	Aggregate Equalized value of railroad property	Number
1	Baltimore & Ohio & Chicago	$53,218	$29,345	$57,929	$34,646	$25,710	$200,842	$4,169	$205,011	1
2	Baltimore & Ohio Connecting	19,602	10,890				30,492	12,578	43,070	2
3	Baltimore & Ohio Southwestern	1,116,827		172,480	30,885	650,695	1,970,887	70,791	2,041,678	3
4	Belleville & Carondelet	42,270		5,392	700	12,240	60,602	2,001	62,603	4
5	Belleville & Eldorado	98,754		5,423	2,900	23,720	130,797	182	130,979	5
6	Belt Railway Company of Chicago	308,878	53,495	126,901	11,400	122,040	622,714	5,740	628,454	6
7	Blue Island	15,380		4,464	3,600	4,100	27,544	438	27,982	7
8	Cairo, Vincennes & Chicago	774,691		89,587	16,500	188,003	1,068,781	2,516	1,071,297	8
9	Calumet & Blue Island					380,200	380,200	742	380,942	9
10	Calumet River	26,627					26,627	416	27,043	10
11	Centralia & Chester	152,500		11,515	2,175	14,770	180,960	110	181,070	11
12	Chicago & Alton	3,643,630	359,221	439,539	176,288	1,205,012	5,823,684	110,510	5,934,194	12
13	Chicago, Burlington & Northern	473,698		44,351	12,945	193,391	724,385	3,962	728,347	13
14	Chicago, Burlington & Quincy	5,334,364	710,950	868,879	161,801	1,090,486	8,166,489	476,694	8,643,183	14
15	Chicago & Calumet Terminal	151,810		19,315	9,600	52,021	232,746	36	232,782	15
16	Chicago & Eastern Illinois	991,846	315,930	235,745	79,350	684,175	2,307,046	27,984	2,335,030	16
17	Chicago & Erie					43,141	43,141	6,810	49,951	17
18	Chicago & Grand Trunk	658,835	82,708	42,984	30,135	77,272	891,934	33,992	925,926	18
19	Chicago Great Western	851,027		56,105	43,850	219,349	1,170,331	1,771	1,172,102	19
20	Chicago, Havana & Western	396,715		25,557	11,663	29,985	463,920	1,761	465,681	20
21	Chicago & Illinois Southern	1,667		189			1,856		1,856	21
22	Chicago & Indiana State Line	26,715	10,620	3,810			41,145		41,145	22
23	Chicago & Iowa	507,054		49,991	15,412	76,210	648,667	3,137	651,804	23
24	Chicago, Madison & Northern	699,973	21,383	123,387	56,850	49,418	951,011	21,482	972,493	24
25	Chicago, Milwaukee & St. Paul	1,349,118	402,184	461,982	178,136	377,168	2,768,588	118,791	2,887,379	25
26	Chicago & Northern Pacific	949,713	123,295	137,975	195,690	168,560	1,525,233	3,151	1,528,384	26
27	Chicago & Northwestern	2,683,721	753,059	766,454	233,485	722,514	5,159,233	249,015	5,408,248	27
28	Chicago & Ohio River	110,631		4,522	945	6,840	152,938	1,300	154,238	28
29	Chicago, Paducah & Memphis	245,158		14,929	5,800	21,320	287,207		287,207	29
30	Chicago, Peoria & St. Louis	459,571		63,701	22,245	277,465	822,982	3,775	826,757	30
31	Chicago, Rock Island & Pacific	1,994,337	654,703	523,110	244,376	268,353	3,684,879	327,966	4,012,845	31
32	Chicago, Santa Fé & California	1,481,073		332,192	82,265	334,804	2,230,334	121,502	2,351,836	32
33	Chicago, St. Louis & Paducah	177,031		17,129	7,400	49,660	251,220	113	251,333	33
34	Chicago & South Side Rapid Transit	171,178		3,750	13,200	136,120	324,248	2,618	326,866	34
35	Chicago & Springfield	315,569		52,405	18,575	67,950	484,499	4,640	489,139	35

36	Chicago & Texas	81,673	....	10,767	1,500	34,990	128,930	1,565	130,495	36
37	Chicago Union Transfer	92,067	56,815	275	348	100	149,605	1,309	150,914	37
38	Chicago & Western Indiana	803,193	132,540	210,016	195,075	8,960	1,349,784	78,818	1,428,602	38
39	Cincinnati, Lafayette & Chicago	164,908	....	54,327	3,455	....	222,690	....	222,690	39
40	Cleveland, Cincinnati, Chicago & St. Lo'is	943,523	....	155,966	33,565	546,747	1,679,801	58,375	1,738,176	40
41	DePue, Ladd & Eastern	6,667	....	379	....	20	7,066	30	7,096	42
42	East St. Louis & Carondelet	45,370	....	21,762	....	16,040	83,172	....	83,172	42
43	East St. Louis Connecting	106,703	....	167,776	3,000	24,500	301,979	....	301,979	43
44	Elgin, Joliet & Eastern	661,765	....	177,115	61,365	318,183	1,218,428	41,839	1,260,267	44
45	Englewood Connecting	23,519	....	3,332	....	....	26,851	....	26,851	45
46	Fulton County Narrow Guage	88,950	....	1,162	2,130	13,380	105,622	251	105,873	46
47	Galesburg, Etherley & Eastern	46,340	....	1,278	1,500	1,020	50,138	....	50,138	47
48	Galesburg & Rio	48,765	....	2,514	378	....	51,657	88	51,745	48
49	Grand Trunk Junction	155,076	19,414	85,794	61,000	....	321,284	....	321,284	49
50	Illinois Valley & Northern	174,866	....	24,620	5,263	....	204,749	754	205,503	50
51	Illinois Western	7,813	....	3,704	....	....	11,517	....	11,517	51
52	Indiana, Decatur & Western	303,041	....	21,961	4,200	78,162	407,364	1,209	408,573	52
53	Indiana, Illinois & Iowa	274,714	....	42,259	23,270	40,407	380,650	1,959	382,609	53
54	Indiana & Illinois Southern	84,000	....	1,625	900	11,374	97,899	....	97,899	54
55	Iowa Central	265,981	....	33,659	8,694	83,386	391,720	1,271	392,991	55
56	Jacksonville, Louisville & St. Louis	302,475	....	15,659	4,750	46,180	369,064	4,059	373,123	56
57	Junction	20,135	16,779	3,787	518	....	41,219	....	41,219	57
58	Kankakee & Seneca	105,190	....	12,826	2,200	....	120,216	....	120,216	58
59	Kankakee & Southwestern	366,773	....	24,639	22,250	86,320	499,982	666	500,648	59
60	Lake Erie & Western	593,000	....	52,997	27,375	205,524	878,896	891	879,787	60
61	Lake Shore & Michigan Southern	456,534	38,045	269,864	148,211	48,134	960,788	20,066	980,854	61
62	LaSalle & Bureau County	19,044	....	1,349	....	....	20,393	209	20,602	62
63	Lake Street Elevated	63,839	....	3,029	16,600	80,800	164,268	....	164,268	63
64	Litchfield, Carrollton & Western	92,988	....	3,109	1,325	7,660	105,082	618	105,700	64
65	Louisville, Evansville & St. Louis Con.	496,203	....	74,071	32,550	207,512	810,336	40,789	851,125	65
66	Louisville & Nashville	705,327	....	70,050	20,650	183,974	980,001	9,912	989,913	66
67	Louisville, New Albany & Chicago	....	....	....	....	29,382	29,382	....	29,382	67
68	Louisville & St. Louis	32,934	....	763	300	105	34,102	792	34,894	68
69	Madison, Illinois & St. Louis	112,727	....	34,430	2,350	11,740	161,247	11,959	173,206	69
70	Michigan Central	348,816	....	58,349	44,720	76,500	528,385	24,860	553,245	70
71	Mobile & Ohio	642,273	....	117,754	27,650	179,120	966,797	7,958	974,755	71
72	Mound City	2,285	....	17	....	20	2,322	40	2,362	72
73	New York, Chicago & St. Louis	249,152	....	67,577	65,724	84,050	466,503	15,841	482,344	73
74	Northern Illinois	185,383	....	51,793	3,961	....	241,137	164	241,301	74
75	Pawnee	9,000	....	218	250	1,520	10,988	....	10,988	75
76	Peoria, Decatur & Evansville	488,912	....	55,828	8,430	285,843	839,013	11,528	850,541	76
77	Peoria & Eastern	489,878	....	91,808	12,497	131,436	725,619	3,989	729,608	77
78	Peoria & Pekin Union	326,543	8,283	103,553	32,000	72,030	542,409	1,696	544,105	78
79	Pittsburgh, Cincinnati, Chicago & St. L.	1,119,621	75,540	186,465	54,863	84,211	1,520,700	51,121	1,571,821	79
80	Pittsburgh, Ft. Wayne & Chicago	837,983	68,109	232,359	248,450	119,253	1,506,154	113,418	1,619,572	80
81	Quincy, Omaha & Kansas City	....	....	3,942	9,350	884	14,176	....	14,176	81
82	Rantoul	119,173	....	5,769	6,119	9,358	140,419	612	141,031	82
83	Rock Island & Peoria	688,247	....	71,611	36,390	120,465	916,713	8,667	925,380	83
84	St. Louis, Alton & Terre Haute	377,330	....	77,983	9,765	278,900	743,978	5,947	749,925	84
85	St. Louis, Belleville & Southern	32,500	....	3,371	725	6,440	43,036	100	43,136	85
86	St. Louis & Chicago	111,324	....	20,594	1,250	21,530	154,698	784	155,482	86
87	St. Louis, Chicago & St. Paul	277,250	....	14,002	6,889	156,320	454,461	174	454,635	87

Statement 23—Concluded.

Number	Name of Company.	Aggregate Assessment by the State Board of Equalization.					Total Assessment	Equalized value of railroad property assessed by local assessors	Aggregate Equalized value of railroad property	Number
		Main Track.	Second Main Track.	Side or Turnout Track.	Buildings on Right of Way.	Rolling Stock.				
88	St. Louis & Eastern	$36,934	....	$11,354	$2,575	$72,160	$123,023	....	$123,023	88
89	St. Louis & Peoria	38,216	....	152	1,650	5,260	45,278	$258	45,536	89
90	St. Louis, Rock Island & Chicago	1,120,186	....	146,796	33,488	209,285	1,509,755	7,515	1,517,270	90
91	St. Louis Southern	178,568	....	19,413	2,325	50,320	250,626	430	251,056	91
92	South Chicago	28,564	18,076	7,536	8,820	15,000	77,996	3,048	81,044	92
93	South Chicago & Southern	50,820	....	9,925	1,650	....	62,395	900	63,295	93
94	Sycamore & Cortland	13,912	....	1,896	1,070	....	16,878	47	16,925	94
95	Terminal R. R. of East St. Louis	27,357	....	108,485	1,875	26,480	164,207	1,100	165,307	95
96	Terre Haute & Indianapolis	1,002,514	....	129,892	24,890	465,990	1,623,286	14,703	1,637,989	96
97	Terre Haute & Peoria	358,031	....	31,205	4,006	111,930	505,172	1,645	506,817	97
98	The Metropolitan West Side Elevated	176,402	....	30,961	28,000	....	235,363	893	236,256	98
99	Toledo, Peoria & Western	920,014	....	82,282	19,730	221,790	1,243,816	2,555	1,246,371	99
100	Toledo, St. Louis & Kansas City	717,959	....	69,720	20,020	239,925	1,047,624	3,207	1,050,831	100
101	Union Stock Yards & Transit	435,748	85,924	354,855	55,585	66,910	999,022	3,877	1,002,899	101
102	Wabash, Chester & Western	142,491	....	12,598	2,800	21,090	178,979	355	179,334	102
103	Wisconsin Central	228,328	....	41,497	16,148	88,606	374,579	4,174	378,753	103
104	Waukegan & Mississippi Valley	....	....	....	....	8,950	8,950	....	8,950	104
105	Wabash	3,036,533	....	462,038	228,910	1,083,403	4,810,884	56,185	4,867,069	105
	Totals	$48,907,541	$4,047,317	$9,032,148	$3,410,078	$13,922,301	$79,319,385	$2,245,913	$81,565,298	

No. 24.

Assessment made by the State Board of Equalization upon the Capital Stock of Companies and Associations incorporated under the laws of the State, other than Railway Companies, for the year 1895, being the equalized value of Capital Stock over the equalized value of Tangible Property of such Corporations assessed by local assessors.

Number	Name of Company.	County.	Location.	Amount of capital stock paid up, as reported by company	Equalized value of tangible property assessed by local assessors	Net assessment of capital stock, being excess of equalized value of capital stock and debt over tangible property assessed by local assessors	Total amount assessed, being net assessment of capital stock by the board, and equalized value of tangible property assessed by local assessors	Number
1	Quincy Gas Light and Coke Company	Adams	Quincy	$300,000	$27,914	$10,086	$38,000	1
2	Quincy Horse Railway and Carrying Company	"	"	160,000	21,033	13,967	35,000	2
3	Thomson-Houston Electric Light and Power Company	"	"	100,000	10,092	4,908	15,000	3
4	Andrew Lohr Bottling Company	Alexander	Cairo	50,000	2,063	1,437	3,500	4
5	Cairo City Ferry Company	"	"	28,000	....	500	500	5
6	Cairo City Gas Company	"	"	100,000	14,199	3,801	18,000	6
7	Cairo Electric Light and Power Company	"	"	25,000	4,522	478	5,000	7
8	Cairo Electric Railway Company	"	"	75,000	2,158	5,842	8,000	8
9	Cairo Transfer Company	"	"	100,000	15,000	10,000	25,000	9
10	Cairo Water Company	"	"	200,000	25,797	4,203	30,000	10
11	Delta Electric Company	"	"	30,000	4,691	309	5,000	11
12	Halliday and Phillips Wharfboat Company	"	"	10,000	4,656	344	5,000	12
13	Sorento Prospecting and Mining Company	Bond	Sorento	*	....	6,000	6,000	13
14	Belvidere Electric Light Company	Boone	Belvidere	27,200	986	3,014	4,000	14
15	Princeton Electric Light and Power Company	Bureau	Princeton	12,000	1,159	2,341	3,500	15
16	Mount Corroll Electric Light Company	Carroll	Mt. Carroll	11,400	1,525	975	2,500	16
17	Savanna Electric Light and Power Company	"	Savanna	15,000	2,033	767	2,800	17
18	Urbana and Champaign Electric Street Railway Company	Champaign	Champaign	50,000	12,740	3,260	16,000	18
19	Christian County Abstract Rating and Guarantee Company	Christian	Taylorville	3,820	270	1,230	1,500	19
20	Christian County Implement Company	"	Taylorville	10,000	1,000	1,000	2,000	20
21	Citizens' Gas Light and Fuel Company	"	"	11,000	635	1,865	2,500	21
22	Consumers' Electric Light Company	"	Pana	4,000	900	600	1,500	22
23	Pana Modern Electric Light, Power and Street Railway Co.	"	"	25,000	3,885	4,115	8,000	23
24	Taylorville Electric Company	"	Taylorville	22,000	2,485	2,542	5,000	24
25	Clay County Telephone Company	Clay	Sailor Springs	500	....	200	200	25

Statement 24—Continued.

Number	Name of Company.	County.	Location.	Amount of capital stock paid up, as reported by company	Equalized value of tangible property assessed by local assessors	Net assessment of capital stock, being excess of equalized value of capital stock and debt over tangible property assessed by local assessors	Total amount assessed, being net assessment of capital stock by the board, and equalized value of tangible property assessed by local assessors	Number
26	Louisville Improvement Company	Clay	Louisville	*		$200	$200	26
27	Mattoon Clear Water Company	Coles	Mattoon	$50,000	$1,245	10,755	12,000	27
28	Mattoon Gas Light and Coke Company	"	"	50,000	2,822	1,178	4,000	28
29	Acme Cement Plaster Company	Cook	Chicago	800,000	32,025	2,975	35,000	29
30	Adams and Lewis Auction Company	"	"	*		500	500	30
31	Ætna Fuel Company	"	"	*		1,000	1,000	31
32	American Security Company	"	"	*		10,000	10,000	32
33	Atlantic and Western Telephone Company	"	"	50,000		5,000	5,000	33
34	American Telephone and Telegraph Company	"	"	100,000	35,762		35,762	34
35	Archer Electric Light Company	"	"	*		500	500	35
36	Auditorium Hotel Company	"	"	500,000	35,700	9,300	45,000	36
37	Baker Electric Company	"	"	*		12,000	12,000	37
38	Board of Trade Telegraph Company	"	"	75,000	16,105	6,895	23,000	38
39	California Company	"	"	*		5,000	5,000	39
40	Calumet Elevator Company	"	"	200,000	18,546	6,454	25,000	40
41	Calumet Electric Street Railway Company	"	"	*		75,000	75,000	41
42	Calumet Gas Company	"	"	668,000	15,719	4,281	20,000	42
43	Central Union Telephone Company	"	"	6,005,300	1,554,393		1,554,393	43
44	Chamber of Commerce Safety Vault Company	"	"	1,000,000	255,060		255,060	44
45	Chicago City Railway Company	"	"	9,000,000	664,070	685,930	1,350,000	45
46	Chicago Deposit Vault Company	"	"	*		40,000	40,000	46
47	Chicago Dock Company	"	"	*		264,000	264,000	47
48	Chicago Dock and Canal Company	"	"	825,600	257,131		257,131	48
49	Chicago Edison Company	"	"	4,400,000	261,658		261,658	49
50	Chicago Gas Light and Coke Company	"	"	4,984,200	554,307	120,693	675,000	50
51	Chicago Insurance Company	"	"	100,000	95	4,905	5,000	51
52	Chicago Long Distance Telephone Co	"	"	*		50,000	50,000	52
53	Chicago Mortgage Loan Company	"	"	2,500	1,190		1,190	53
54	Chicago Opera House Company	"	"	350,000	215,806		215,806	54
55	Chicago and Pacific Elevator Company	"	"	20,000	9,336		9,336	55
56	Chicago Steamship Company	"	"	*		10,000	10,000	56
57	Chicago Telephone Company	"	"	3,796,200	197,155	312,845	510,000	57
58	Chicago Towing Company	"	"	*		6,000	6,000	58

No.	Name						Total	No.
59	Chicago Wharfing and Storage Company	"	"	250,000	28,845	1,500	30,343	59
60	Chippewa Springs Water Company	"	"	*		1,000	1,000	60
61	Cicero and Proviso Street Railway Company	"	"		43,047		43,047	61
62	Cicero Water, Gas and Electric Light Company	"	"	228,650	18,965		18,963	62
63	Commercial Safe Deposit Company	"	"	120,000		5,000	5,000	63
64	Consumers' Gas Company	"	"	3,000,000	250,004		250,004	64
65	Consolidated Electric Company	"	"	50,000	595	1,405	2,000	65
66	Edgar French Company	"	"	15,000		1,000	1,000	66
67	Englewood Electric Light Company	"	"	90,000	1,190	810	2,000	67
68	Fair, The	"	"	*		50,000	50,000	68
69	Fidelity Mortgage Loan Company	"	"	2,500	1,785		1,785	69
70	Fidelity Safe Deposit Company	"	"	500,000	59,275	725	60,000	70
71	Fireman's Insurance Company—Geo. L. Harding, President	"	"	250,000	85,524	15,000	100,524	71
72	G. H. Hammond Company	"	"	40,000		4,000	4,000	72
73	Green's Dredging Company	"	"	80,000		5,000	5,000	73
74	Grand Crossing and Windsor Park Railway Company	"	"	*		5,000	5,000	74
75	Hanrahan Refrigerator Car Company	"	"	500,000		2,500	2,500	75
76	Harrison International Telephone Company	"	"	40,000,000	595	6,905	7,500	76
77	Harvey Transit Company	"	"	*		35,000	35,000	77
78	Home Safety Deposit Vault Company	"	"	*		3,000	3,000	78
79	Hyde Park Gas Company	"	"	300,000	38,485	11,515	50,000	79
80	Illinois Vault Company	"	"	*		20,000	20,000	80
81	Lake Gas Company	"	"	800,000	46,130	8,870	55,000	81
82	Lackawana Live Stock Transportation Company	"	"	*		20,000	20,000	82
83	Lemont Electric Light and Power Company	"	Lemont	13,000		500	500	83
84	Merchants' Arc Light and Power Company	"	Chicago	34,800	595	2,405	3,000	84
85	Merchants' Safe Deposit Company	"	"	50,000		5,000	5,000	85
86	Merchants' Transfer Company	"	"	10,000	595	405	1,000	86
87	Mississippi River Railroad and Toll Bridge Company	"	"	1,000,000	167,500	12,500	180,000	87
88	Mississippi River Bridge Company	"	"	*		5,000	5,000	88
89	Montgomery Ward and Company	"	"	*		30,000	30,000	89
90	National Elevator and Dock Company	"	"	500,000	40,031	49,969	90,000	90
91	National Panorama Company	"	"	*		1,000	1,000	91
92	National Safe Deposit Company	"	"	500,000	110,448		110,448	92
93	North Chicago Street Railroad Company	"	"	5,499,500	287,964	229,036	517,000	93
94	Northwestern Gas Light Company	"	"	*		1,000	1,000	94
95	Pacific Grain and Stock Exchange	"	"	*		25,000	25,000	95
96	People's Gas Light and Coke Company	"	"	4,000,000	215,886	34,114	250,000	96
97	Pitkin and Brooks Company	"	"	*		7,000	7,000	97
98	Pullman's Palace Car Company	"	"	35,430,600	989,351	697,439	1,686,790	98
99	Railroad Wrecking and Salvage Company	"	"	*		9,000	9,000	99
100	Siegel, Cooper and Company	"	"	*		30,000	30,000	100
101	Sibley Elevator Company	"	"	*		250	250	101
102	South Chicago City Railway Company	"	"	1,200,000	7,636	7,364	15,000	102
103	Spaulding and Company	"	"	*		10,000	10,000	103
104	Standard Light and Heat Company	"	"	*		5,000	5,000	104
105	Standard Tiffany Refrigerator Car Company	"	"	*		20,000	20,000	105
106	Sterling Company	"	"	*		10,000	10,000	106
107	Street's Stable Car Line	"	"	*		85,000	85,000	107
108	Street's Western Stable Car Line	"	"	4,611,700	11,980	48,020	60,000	108
109	Takamine Ferment Company	"	"	10,000,000		10,000	10,000	109
110	Title Guarantee and Trust Company	"	"	1,600,000	19,040	55,960	75,000	110

Statement 24—Continued.

Number	Name of Company.	County.	Location.	Amount of capital stock paid up, as reported by company	Equalized value of tangible property assess'd by local assessors	Net assessment of capital stock, being excess of equalized value of capital stock and debt over tangible property assessed by local assessors	Total amount assessed, being net assessment of capital stock by the board, and equalized value of tangible property assessed by local assessors	Number
111	Traders' Insurance Company	Cook	Chicago	$500,000	$89,250	$20,750	$110,000	111
112	United States Transfer Company	"	"	*	....	30,000	30,000	112
113	Western Bank Note and Engraving Company	"	"	450,000	72,740	3,500	76,240	113
114	West Chicago Street Railroad Company	"	"	13,189,000	1,028,635	115,365	1,444,000	114
115	Western Finance Company	"	"	*	....	120,000	120,000	115
116	Sycamore Electric Light Company	DeKalb	Sycamore	*	....	1,500	1,500	116
117	DeKalb Electric Light Company	"	DeKalb	*	....	2,500	2,500	117
118	Clinton Electric Light, Heat and Power Company	DeWitt	Clinton	15,000	4,900	100	5,000	118
119	Paris Gas Light and Coke Company	Edgar	Paris	21,000	2,910	2,090	5,000	119
120	Vandalia Light and Fuel Company	Fayette	Vandalia	*	....	1,000	1,000	120
121	Lewistown Water Company	Fulton	Lewistown	15,000	....	3,000	3,000	121
122	Morris Gas Company	Grundy	Morris	40,000	1,416	584	2,000	122
123	Dallas Transportation Company	Hancock	Dallas City	8,000	6,240	760	7,000	123
124	F. M. King Company	"	Augusta	15,000	....	500	500	124
125	Keokuk and Hamilton Bridge Company	"	Keokuk, Ia	1,000,000	207,000	1,000	208,000	125
126	Geneseo Electric Light Company	Henry	Geneseo	20,000	1,347	2,653	4,000	126
127	Kewanee Electric Light and Motor Company	"	Kewanee	20,000	3,207	....	3,207	127
128	Kewanee Gas Light and Coke Company	"	"	40,000	3,351	1,649	5,000	128
129	Milford Electric Light and Power Company	Iroquois	Milford	8,000	858	642	1,500	129
130	Carbondale Electric Company	Jackson	Carbondale	5,000	1,500	500	2,000	130
131	Murphysboro Street Railway Company	"	Murphysboro	11,000	450	50	500	131
132	Murphysboro Water Works, Electric and Gas Light Co	"	"	15,000	10,000	....	10,000	132
133	Mt. Vernon Electric Light Company	Jefferson	Mt. Vernon	15,000	2,060	940	3,000	133
134	Mt. Vernon Water Works Company	"	"	18,000	1,760	1,240	3,000	134
135	Dunlieth and Dubuque Bridge Company	JoDaviess	Dubuque, Ia	1,000,000	....	5,000	5,000	135
136	Galena Water Company	"	Galena	65,000	1,021	979	2,000	136
137	Aurora Gas Light Company	Kane	Aurora	300,000	29,411	4,589	34,000	137
138	Aurora Street Railway Company	"	"	300,000	33,485	3,515	37,000	138
139	C. H. Woodruff Company	"	Elgin	60,000	6,524	1,476	8,000	139
140	Elgin American Gas Company	"	"	100,000	3,000	9,000	12,000	140
141	Elgin City Railway Company	"	"	100,000	15,000	7,696	23,000	141
142	Geo. W. Ludlow Company	"	"	150,000	8,235	1,765	10,000	142

No.	Company	County	City						No.
143	Kankakee Electric Railway Company	Kankakee	Kankakee		50,000	5,210	790	6,000	143
144	North Kankakee Electric Light and Railway Company	"	"		32,600	582		582	144
145	Galesburg Electric Motor and Power Company	Knox	Galesburg		210,000	8,363	1,637	10,000	145
146	Galesburg Gas and Electric Light Company	"	"		200,000	23,594	6,406	30,000	146
147	Wauconda Telegraph and Telephone Company	Lake	Wauconda		1,000		500	500	147
148	City Electric Railway Company	LaSalle	Peru	*			5,000	5,000	148
149	Illinois Valley Electric Light and Power Company	"	Ottawa	†			2,500	2,500	149
150	Marquette Heating and Lighting Company	"	LaSalle		1,638	176	1,024	1,200	150
151	Marseilles Land and Water Company	"	Marseilles		500,000	14,886	4,114	19,000	151
152	Mendota Electric Light Company	"	Mendota		10,000	1,517	1,483	3,000	152
153	Ottawa Electric Street Railway Company	"	Ottawa		100,000		1,000	1,000	153
154	Ottawa Gas Light and Coke Company	"	"		45,000	4,574	5,426	19,000	154
155	Ottawa Hydraulic Company	"	"		18,000	800	4,200	5,000	155
156	Streator Gas Light Company	"	Streator	*			2,240	2,240	156
157	Streator Railway Company	"	"		250,000	9,620	2,380	12,000	157
158	Dixon Power and Lighting Company	Lee	Dixon		100,000	8,400	6,600	15,000	158
159	Dixon Water Company	"	"		60,000	11,088	2,912	14,000	159
160	Fairbury Electric Light, Heat and Power Company	Livingston	Fairbury			842	1,158	2,000	160
161	Leslie E. Keeley Company	"	Dwight		25,000	36,154		36,154	161
162	Pontiac Light, Heat and Power Company	"	Pontiac		20,000	2,985	15	3,000	162
163	Pontiac Water, Light and Power Company	"	"		40,000	4,980	5,020	10,000	163
164	Lincoln Electric Street Railway Company	Logan	Lincoln		65,000	5,746	2,254	8,000	164
165	Lincoln Gas and Electric Light Company	"	"	*			8,000	8,000	165
166	Lincoln Water, Light and Power Company	"	"		250,000	11,514	486	12,000	166
167	Citizens' Mutual Telephone Company	Macon	Decatur	*			3,000	3,000	167
168	City Electric Railway Company	"	"		81,580	10,018	24,982	35,000	168
169	Decatur Gas Light and Coke Company	"	"		100,000	32,725	3,275	36,000	169
170	Decatur Union Elevator Company	"	"		20,000	1,995	2,005	4,000	170
171	Lime & Scraggs Dry Goods and Carpet Company	"	"		100,000	17,280	2,720	20,000	171
172	Maroa Electric Light Company	"	Maroa		12,000	1,463	1,037	2,500	172
173	Municipal Electric Company	"	Decatur		25 000	2,680	1,320	4,000	173
174	Young Bros. & Maris Company	"	"		125,000	15,330	4,670	20,000	174
175	Carlinville Water Company	Macoupin	Carlinville		75,000	4,198	12,052	16,250	175
176	Alton Electric Street Railroad Company	Madison	Alton		100,000	11,700	4,300	16,000	176
177	Alton Gas and Electric Light Company	"	"		60,000	12,600	2,400	15,000	177
178	Alton Improvement Association	"	"		25,000	4,550	1,450	6,000	178
179	Alton and Upper Alton Horse Railway and Carrying Co	"	"		42,000	4,253	4,217	8,500	179
180	Madison County Ferry Company	"	Venice			24,980	20,020	45,000	180
181	St. Louis Merchants Bridge Company	"	"		1,500,000	160,000	40,000	200,000	181
182	Centralia and Central City Railway Company	Marion	Centralia		8,150	364	1,436	1,800	182
183	Centralia Light and Power Company	"	"		31,000	3,031	3,969	7,000	183
184	Bloomington City Railway Company	McLean	Bloomington			8,461	11,539	20,000	184
185	Bloomington Electric Light Company	"	"		125,000	3,618		3,618	185
186	Citizens' Gas Light and Heating Company	"	"		250,000	12,401	12,599	25,000	186
187	Normal Electric Light and Power Company	"	Normal		12,500	2,044	456	2,500	187
188	Safe Deposit Company	"	Bloomington		10,000	1,525	1,475	3,000	188
189	Keithsburg Bridge Company	Mercer	Keithsburg		600,000	24,500	5,500	30,000	189
190	Hillsboro Electric Light and Power Company	Montgomery	Hillsboro		18,000	1,300	1,200	2,500	190
191	Litchfield Electric Light and Power Company	"	Litchfield		15,000	2,500	5,500	8,000	191
192	Litchfield Car and Machine Company	"	"		200,000	3,341		3,341	192

Statement 24—Continued.

Number	Name of Company.	County.	Location.	Amount of capital stock paid up, as reported by company	Equalized value of tangible property assess'd by local assessors	Net assessment of capital stock, being excess of equalized value of capital stock and debt over tangible property assesssed by local assessors	Total amount assessed, being net assessment of capital stock by the board, and equalized value of tangible property assessed by local assessors	Number
193	Litchfield Light, Heat and Power Company	Montgomery	Litchfield	$50,000	$300	$7,700	$8,000	193
194	Litchfield Water Supply Company	"	"	20,000	7,416		7,416	194
195	Nokomis Electric Light and Power Company	"	Nokomis	8,500		2,000	2,000	195
196	Prairie Heights Water Company	"	Hillsboro	5,000	20	980	1,000	196
197	Eagle Electric Company	Monroe	Columbia	7,000	900	1,100	2,000	197
198	Jacksonville Gas Light and Coke Company	Morgan	Jacksonville	127,000	6,222	18,778	25,000	198
199	Jacksonville Railroad Company	"	"	33,350		2,000	2,000	199
200	Central Railway Company	Peoria	Peoria	600,000	42,604	17,396	60,000	200
201	Distilling and Cattle Feeding Company	"	"	*		15,000	15,000	201
202	Elmwood Electric Light Company	"	Elmwood	*		600	600	202
203	German Fire Insurance Company	"	Peoria	200,000	400	6,100	6,500	203
204	Peoria Gas Light and Coke Company	"	"	175,000	48,800	16,200	65,000	204
205	Peoria General Electric Company	"	"	150,000	16,220	15,780	52,000	205
206	Peoria Water Company	"	"	1,000,000	48,168	12,832	61,000	206
207	Title Guaranty Abstract and Trust Company	"	"	22,500		3,000	3,000	207
208	DuQuoin Light, Heat and Power Company	Perry	DuQuoin	50,000	325	1,675	2,000	208
209	Pinckneyville Electric Light Company	"	Pinckneyville	2,250	700	100	800	209
210	Pittsfield Electric Company	Pike	Naperville	20,000	5,138		5,138	210
211	Chester Light, Water and Ice Company	Randolph	Chester	35,000	5,782	1,218	7,000	211
212	Sparta Natural Gas and Oil Company	"	Sparta	15,000	1,515	485	2,000	212
213	Olney Edison Electric Company	Richland	Olney	*		8,000	8,000	213
214	Moline Central Steel Railway Company	Rock Island	Moline	20,000	3,297	703	4,000	214
215	People's Power Company	"	Rock Island	300,000	10,897	11,103	22,000	215
216	Rock Island and Davenport Ferry Company	"	"	60,000	1,116	3,384	4,500	216
217	American Aluminum Company	St. Clair	East St. Louis	1,000,000	5,820	14,180	20,000	217
218	Belleville Electric Light and Power Company	"	Belleville	*		12,000	12,000	218
219	Belleville Gas Light and Coke Company	"	"			10,000	10,000	219
220	Blendville Mining and Milling Company	"	East St. Louis	*		12,000	12,000	220
221	Carpenter Electric Power and Light Company	"	"			3,000	3,000	221

222	Citizens' Electric Light and Power Company	"	"	25,000	4,951	1,200	6,250	222
223	City Water Company	"	"	....	30,360	59,610	90,000	223
224	East St. Louis Belt S. D. and E. Railway Company	"	"	*	....	50,000	50,000	224
225	East St. Louis Dock and Warehouse Company	"	"	*	....	20,000	20,000	225
226	East St. Louis Electric Street Railroad Company	"	"	150,000	19,064	20,936	40,000	226
227	Evans Snider Buell Company	"	Nat. Stock Y'ds	50,000	3,450	550	4,000	227
228	Mascoutah Electric Light Company	"	Mascoutah	5,000	485	515	1,000	228
229	Mississippi and Bonne Terre Transportation Company	"	East St. Louis	*	....	8,000	8,000	229
230	St. Louis National Stock Yards Company	"	"	1,250,000	112,410	153,590	266,000	230
231	North and South Rolling Stock Company	"	"	*	....	3,000	3,000	231
232	Wiggins' Ferry Company	"	"	1,000,000	477,575	122,425	600,000	232
233	Capital Electric Company	Sangamon	Springfield	*	....	10,000	10,000	233
234	Springfield Consolidated Railway Company	"	"	750,000	27,116	17,884	45,000	234
235	Springfield Electric Light and Power Company	"	"	50,000	6,000	4,000	10,000	235
236	Springfield Gas Light Company	"	"	75,000	25,636	4,364	30,000	236
237	The Abstract and Title Guarantee Company	"	"	*	....	500	500	237
238	Rushville Electric Light Company	Schuyler	Rushville	12,500	672	2,328	3,000	238
239	E. B. Hillman & Co. Electric Light Company	Stark	Wyoming	*	....	1,300	1,300	239
240	Toulon Light and Power Company	"	Toulon	10,000	2,016	484	2,500	240
241	Freeport Light and Fuel Company	Stephenson	Freeport	....	6,117	1,883	8,000	241
242	Freeport Water Company	"	"	150,000	12,824	5,176	18,000	242
243	Freeport Street Railway Company	"	"	*	....	5,000	5,000	243
244	German Insurance Company	"	"	200,000	81,040	33,960	115,000	244
245	Pekin Electric Light and Power Company	Tazewell	Pekin	15,000	2,893	1,107	4,000	245
246	Pekin Gas Light Company	"	"	66,920	5,317	683	6,000	546
247	Pekin Water Works Company	"	"	100,000	16,000	4,000	20,000	247
248	Danville Gas, Electric Light and Street Railway Company	Vermilion	Danville	250,000	26,261	8,739	35,000	248
249	Danville Water Company	"	"	200,000	19,920	25,080	45,000	246
250	Edison Illuminating Company	Warran	Monmouth	10,000	8,278	1,022	9,300	250
251	Monmouth Gas Company	"	"	30,000	9,880	1,120	11,000	251
252	Washington Mineral Springs Company	Washington	Okawville	40,000	2,451	3,549	6,000	252
253	Southern Illinois Improvement Company	Wayne	Fairfield	300,000	46,662	....	46,662	253
254	Fulton Electric Light and Power Company	Whiteside	Fulton	20,000	1,914	1,586	3,500	254
255	Morrison Electric Light and Power Company	"	Morrison	20,000	....	3,000	3,000	255
256	Sterling Gas and Electric Light Company	"	Sterling	39,000	5,422	1,578	7,000	256
257	Sterling Water Company	"	"	....	16,704	3,296	20,000	257
258	Economy Light and Power Company	Will	Joliet	400,000	50,391	4,609	55,000	258
259	Joliet Gas Light Company	"	"	100,000	12,361	7,639	20,000	259
260	Joliet Street Railway Company	"	"	300,000	49,978	10,022	60,000	260
261	Union Elevator Company	"	"	66,500	11,760	1,240	13,000	261
262	Wilmington Electric Light and Power Company	"	Wilmington	21,000	986	2,014	3,000	262
263	Ingalls' Park Company	"	Joliet	150,000	17,884	2,116	20,000	263
264	Electric Light, Street Railroad and Power Company	Williamson	Creel Springs	*	....	500	500	264
265	Hope Electric Light and Power Company	"	Carterville	8,800	1,235	265	1,500	265
266	Marion Electric Light and Street Railway Company	"	Marion	20,000	1,300	200	2,500	266

Statement 24—Concluded.

Number	Name of Company.	County.	Location.	Amount of capital stock paid up, as reported by company	Equalized value of tangible property assessed by local assessors	Net assessment of capital stock, being excess of equalized value of capital stock and debt over tangible property assessed by local assessors	Total amount assessed being net assessment of capital stock by the board, and equalized value of tangible property assessed by local assessor	Number
267	Forest City Electric Light and Power Company	Winnebago	Rockford	$80,000	$11,193	$8,807	$20,000	267
268	Forest City Insurance Company	"	"	*	....	1,000	1,000	268
269	Holland Ferguson Company	"	"	50,000	82	4,918	5,000	269
270	Rockford City Railway Company	"	"	36,000	8,717	9,283	18,000	270
271	Rockford Electric Power Company	"	"	53,000	6,888	6,112	13,000	271
272	Rockford Gas Light and Coke Company	"	"	300,000	22,337	7,663	30,000	272
273	Rockford Insurance Company	"	"	200,000	47,336	32,664	80,000	273
274	West End Street Railway Company	"	"	57,000	6,478	5,522	12,000	274
	Totals			$179,177,258	$10,192,779	$4,782,509	$14,975,288	

* Company failed to make complete return.

No. 25.

Statement of the Equalized Assessment of all Taxable Property in the State of Illinois for the year 1895, as Equalized or Assessed by the State Board of Equalization, showing the valuation of the several classes of property in each County.

Counties.	Assessed in Counties by Local Assessors.						Assessed by State Board of Equalization.		
	Assessed value of lands, lots and personal property, including railroad property, assessed by local assessors.	Average rate per cent. of addition or reduction.		Net amount added.	Net amount deducted.	Equalized value of property assessed by local assessors.	Equalized value of railroad track, rolling stock, and improvements on right of way.	Equalized value of capital stock of corporations other than railroads	Total equalized value of property assessed for year 1895.
		Add.	Ded.						
Adams	$12,804,515		12		$1,547,186	$11,257,329	$788,216	$28,961	$12,074,506
Alexander	2,314,552		2		43,316	2,272,236	242,886	26,914	2,542,036
Bond	2,412,909			$8,133		2,421,042	370,142	6,000	2,797,184
Boone	3,143,545		1		39,935	3,103,610	375,650	3,014	3,482,274
Brown	1,876,285			6,212		1,882,497	149,910		2,032,407
Bureau	10,168,907		14		1,465,786	8,703,121	1,532,802	2,341	10,238,264
Calhoun	1,404,822		15		215,139	1,189,683			1,189,683
Carroll	3,842,193	2		71,328		3,913,521	777,352	1,742	4,692,615
Cass	3,666,518		12		439,982	3,226,536	319,272		3,545,808
Champaign	10,029,609		11		1,103,258	8,926,351	651,386	3,260	9,580,997
Christian	6,965,122		2		170,352	6,794,770	464,758	11,352	7,270,880
Clark	1,668,212	58		973,678		2,641,890	396,281		3,038,171
Clay	1,618,373		3		51,320	1,567,053	248,676	400	1,816,129
Clinton	2,661,641	13		334,509		2,996,150	400,842		3,396,992
Coles	5,389,422		17		916,202	4,473,220	542,939	11,933	5,028,092
Cook	212,479,886	17		37,095,777		249,575,663	17,759,979	3,512,085	270,847,727
Crawford	1,697,869	11		189,909		1,887,778	134,793		2,022,571
Cumberland	1,158,663	23		269,400		1,428,063	326,958		1,755,021
DeKalb	7,636,878		6		438,537	7,198,341	1,002,167	4,000	8,204,508
DeWitt	3,623,844				5,889	3,617,955	328,299	100	3,946,354
Douglas	3,973,585		4		146,588	3,826,997	394,554		4,221,551
DuPage	6,183,513		14		841,524	5,341,989	1,052,718	2,090	6,396,797
Edgar	5,520,194		2		128,030	5,392,164	689,881		6,082,045
Edwards	1,456,984		5		71,652	1,385,332	156,962		1,542,294
Effingham	2,265,021	5		114,310		2,379,331	524,059		2,903,390

Statement 25—Concluded.

Counties.	Assessed in Counties by Local Assessors.						Assessed by State Board of Equalization.		Total equalized value of property assessed for year 1895.
	Assessed value of lands, lots and personal property, including railroad property, assessed by local assessors.	Average rate per cent. of addition or deduction.		Net amount added.	Net amount deducted.	Equalized value of property assessed by local assessors.	Equalized value of railroad track, rolling stock, and improvements on right of way.	Equalized value of capital stock of corporations other than railroads.	
		Add.	Ded.						
Fayette	$2,759,339	5		$144,415		$2,903,754	$399,813	$1,000	$3,304,567
Ford	3,548,889		29		$715,498	2,833,391	468,793		3,302,184
Franklin	981,306	29		278,617		1,259,923	124,964		1,384,887
Fulton	7,667,028	7		565,846		8,232,874	818,763	3,000	9,054,637
Gallatin	895,405	63		567,453		1,462,858	158,579		1,621,437
Greene	4,589,831	7		306,504		4,896,335	540,183		5,436,518
Grundy	3,853,617		1		32,428	3,821,189	917,269	584	4,739,042
Hamilton	1,177,037	18		217,060		1,394,097	192,956		1,587,053
Hancock	7,350,466		3		208,164	7,142,302	744,327	2,260	7,888,889
Hardin	757,214		28		215,118	542,096			542,096
Henderson	2,568,468		11		289,732	2,278,736	589,519		2,868,255
Henry	9,847,094		14		1,399,850	8,447,244	1,087,229	4,302	9,538,775
Iroquois	8,959,498		16		1,396,828	7,562,670	790,871	642	8,354,183
Jackson	2,478,049					2,478,049	420,467	550	2,899,066
Jasper	1,447,440	17		240,437		1,687,877	182,885		1,870,762
Jefferson	1,648,334	23		367,428		2,015,762	426,324	2,180	2,444,266
Jersey	2,892,357	17		505,400		3,397,757	306,094		3,703,851
JoDaviess	4,053,054		7		288,581	3,764,473	517,276	5,979	4,287,728
Johnson	1,521,432					1,521,432	212,652		1,734,084
Kane	13,833,736		7		968,362	12,865,374	1,374,028	28,041	14,267,443
Kankakee	4,586,164		3		146,579	4,439,585	936,911	790	5,377,286
Kendall	3,638,700		15		552,924	3,085,776	343,773		3,429,549
Knox	9,649,197			46,136		9,695,333	1,213,754	8,043	10,917,130
Lake	6,985,490		6		412,443	6,573,047	990,679	500	7,564,226
LaSalle	16,948,073		13		2,174,434	14,773,639	1,810,488	29,367	16,613,494
Lawrence	1,298,129	44		571,693		1,869,822	194,398		2,064,220
Lee	7,355,257		15		1,126,728	6,228,529	693,107	9,512	6,931,148
Livingston	8,986,508				15,591	8,970,917	1,605,188	6,193	10,582,298
Logan	6,904,213		3		185,211	6,719,002	589,587	10,740	7,319,329
Macon	10,179,550		15		1,540,013	8,639,537	590,519	43,009	9,273,065
Macoupin	6,523,960	26		1,664,891		8,188,851	962,717	12,052	9,163,620
Madison	11,944,696		13		1,523,178	10,421,518	1,966,221	72,417	12,460,156

Marion	3,431,604	9		320,464		3,752,068	243,755	5,405	4,001,228
Marshall	4,019,210		13		527,238	3,491,972	565,995		4,057,967
Mason	3,192,706					3,192,706	449,456		3,642,162
Massac	1,505,739		1		20,509	1,485,230	97,937		1,583,167
McDonough	6,438,792		1		95,213	6,343,579	524,018		6,867,597
McHenry	5,764,353		9		526,483	5,237,870	747,510		5,985,380
McLean	16,624,493		1		103,960	16,520,533	1,534,881	26,069	18,081,483
Menard	4,155,807		23		964,351	3,191,456	311,637		3,503,093
Mercer	4,492,229	9		401,683		4,893,912	488,608	5,500	5,388,020
Monroe	2,504,230	2		48,919		2,553,149	155,130	1,100	2,709,379
Montgomery	5,586,822	7		373,907		5,960,729	678,104	17,380	6,656,213
Morgan	10,995,581		31		3,414,073	7,581,508	659,342	20,778	8,261,628
Moultrie	2,503,687	9		215,258		2,718,945	438,909		3,157,854
Ogle	7,250,904					7,250,904	1,092,536		8,343,440
Peoria	16,406,723		20		3,222,757	13,183,966	1,584,076	86,908	14,854,950
Perry	1,960,067					1,960,067	378,714	1,775	2,340,556
Piatt	4,094,743		3		124,227	3,970,516	563,276		4,533,792
Pike	4,894,528	14		685,235		5,579,763	757,119		6,336,882
Pope	1,116,955	7		81,004		1,197,959			1,197,959
Pulaski	958,562					958,562	82,374		1,040,936
Putnam	1,408,025		4		59,238	1,348,787	61,891		1,410,678
Randolph	3,329,923	5		207,703		3,537,626	381,889	1,703	3,921,218
Richland	1,631,686				2,104	1,629,582	192,058	8,000	1,829,640
Rock Island	7,291,511		18		1,305,892	5,985,619	744,397	15,190	6,745,206
Saline	1,459,704	3		48,972		1,508,676	224,653		1,733,329
Sangamon	16,846,009		20		3,369,201	13,476,808	1,180,942	36,748	14,694,498
Schuyler	2,567,837	8		206,231		2,774,068	156,439	2,328	2,932,835
Scott	2,543,936		5		129,556	2,414,380	232,663		2,647,043
Shelby	5,811,401		4		243,579	5,567,822	654,726		6,222,548
Stark	3,244,331		3		105,960	3,138,371	302,027	1,784	3,442,182
St. Clair	13,068,885		6		847,049	12,221,836	2,225,581	491,135	14,938,552
Stephenson	8,821,130		17		1,499,592	7,321,538	725,097	46,019	8,092,654
Tazewell	6,878,698		2		137,670	6,741,028	1,139,844	5,790	7,886,662
Union	1,879,129					1,879,129	159,277		2,038,406
Vermilion	11,276,067		4		496,096	10,779,971	1,508,936	33,819	12,322,726
Wabash	1,599,079		17		277,103	1,321,976	174,762		1,496,738
Warren	5,627,409	3		167,065		5,794,474	687,879	2,142	6,484,495
Washington	3,001,433	9		272,908		3,274,341	233,970	3,548	3,511,860
Wayne	1,776,536			7,235		1,783,771	282,240		2,066,011
White	1,621,651	42		682,219		2,303,870	376,763		2,680,633
Whiteside	7,466,463		13		970,640	6,495,823	935,215	9,460	7,440,498
Will	12,459,712		2		229,832	12,229,880	2,124,704	27,640	14,382,224
Williamson	1,913,722					1,913,722	165,102	965	2,079,789
Winnebago	12,412,446		18		2,234,239	10,178,207	851,027	75,969	11,105,203
Woodford	6,213,102		21		1,289,599	4,923,503	442,110		5,365,613
Total	$743,840,153			$48,257,939	$43,011,519	$749,086,573	$79,319,385	$4,782,509	$833,188,467

No 26.

STATEMENT OF PROPERTY ASSESSED *for the year 1896, in the several counties in the State of Illinois, as returned to the Auditor's office.*

Districts....	Counties.	Horses.			Cattle.			Mules and Asses.		
		No.	Value.	Av.	No.	Value.	Av.	No.	Value.	Av.
1 2 3 4	Cook	34,091	$621,331	$18 23	29,205	$207,711	$7 11	136	$1,450	$10 66
5	Boone	6,066	80,858	13 33	17,950	150,255	8 38	6	72	12 00
	DeKalb	16,881	179,449	10 63	36,913	245,573	6 65	139	1,344	9 66
	Kane	13,125	192,820	14 69	41,822	308,585	7 38	114	1,522	13 35
	Lake	7,624	102,506	13 44	20,872	152,271	7 29	29	324	11 17
	McHenry	12,847	202,241	15 75	52,746	421,108	7 98	34	512	15 06
6	Carroll	11,277	88,414	7 84	27,267	150,924	5 53	145	1,226	8 45
	JoDaviess	8,966	118,525	13 22	29,656	187,550	6 32	116	1,494	12 88
	Ogle	19,512	223,842	11 47	36,901	249,906	6 77	96	960	10 00
	Stephenson	10,482	194,363	18 54	31,576	213,583	6 76	126	2,160	17 14
	Winnebago	11,894	144,234	12 13	26,969	157,042	5 82	147	1,602	10 90
7	Bureau	20,722	255,190	12 31	34,296	221,533	6 46	548	5,699	10 40
	Henry	18,210	239,987	13 18	37,468	196,697	5 25	479	6,236	13 02
	Lee	14,315	155,587	10 86	.27,060	152,344	5 63	209	2,059	9 85
	Putnam	3,152	49,830	15 81	4,677	34,934	7 47	54	730	13 52
	Whiteside	13,541	159,753	11 79	28,343	185,970	6 56	264	2,886	10 93
8	DuPage	6,984	80,191	11 47	19.532	116,768	5 97	51	524	10 27
	Grundy	9,110	86,664	9 51	10,337	57,394	5 55	256	2,507	9 79
	Kendall	8,011	114,184	14 25	12,923	87,334	6 75	62	801	12 92
	LaSalle	26,705	306,017	11 45	31,379	235,945	7 52	588	8,102	13 78
	Will	17,987	176,292	9 24	27,722	175,615	6 34	155	1,353	8 73
9	Ford	8,872	127,269	14 35	8,692	41,490	4 77	541	6,633	12 26
	Iroquois	24,701	311,152	12 59	26,391	152,219	5 77	833	9,519	11 46
	Kankakee	8,530	92,918	10 90	10,868	72,132	6 64	151	1,655	10 96
	Livingston	25,767	145,949	5 66	22,711	118,753	5 23	995	5,513	5 54
	Marshall	7,782	97,210	12 49	8,934	51,624	5 78	187	2,050	10 96
	Woodford	12,015	154,578	12 87	12,749	83,978	6 59	309	3,719	12 03
10	Fulton	19,693	156,565	7 95	27,710	137,271	4 95	560	4,161	7 43
	Knox	19,180	292,904	15 27	26,711	203,655	7 62	461	5,932	12 86
	Peoria	15,014	209,171	13 93	28,364	205,999	7 26	393	4,764	12 12
	Stark	8,452	79,268	9 38	9,476	48,972	5 17	156	1,504	9 64
11	Hancock	19,065	179,534	9 42	23,918	193,300	8 08	1,078	10,329	9 58
	Henderson	7,770	92,790	11 94	9,837	86,195	8 77	196	2,530	12 91
	McDonough	14,877	156,808	10 54	24,847	175,102	7 05	576	5,286	9 18
	Mercer	15,077	132,740	8 80	22,582	127,229	5 63	612	5,570	9 10
	Rock Island	9,585	91,319	9 53	15,831	91,466	5 77	219	2,128	9 71
	Schuyler	8,651	109,725	12 68	13,656	96,342	7 06	371	4,554	12 28
	Warren	12,291	110,846	9 02	16,799	90,085	5 36	305	2,506	8 22
12	Adams	14,430	201,111	13 91	20,094	119.662	5 98	1,716	22,504	13 12
	Brown	4,965	59,613	12 00	7,733	56,127	7 26	280	3,326	11 88
	Calhoun	3,304	38,305	11 59	3,349	24,860	7 43	703	7,760	11 04
	Cass	5,869	57,147	9 74	8,793	70,502	8 01	506	5,528	10 92
	Greene	10,324	101,915	9 87	19,017	125,935	6 62	1,022	9,845	9 63
	Jersey	5,934	71,960	12 12	6,797	45,834	6 74	363	4,166	11 48
	Pike	13,445	124,386	9 25	20,734	103,819	5 00	1,591	13,927	8 75
	Scott	5,429	61,505	11 33	7,651	64,359	8 41	382	4,662	12 20
13	Christian	15,479	128.620	8 30	15,793	105,455	6 67	2,027	16,880	8 32
	Mason	6,339	77,994	12 30	5,192	34,081	6 56	1,264	13,515	10 69
	Menard	4,882	92,690	18 98	8,607	98,255	11 41	417	7,645	18 33
	Morgan	8,586	138,614	16 14	14,853	183,098	12 32	581	8,976	15 44
	Sangamon	21,250	250,329	11 78	24,720	203,046	8 21	2,071	25,052	12 10
	Tazewell	14,516	126,146	8 69	18,046	110,318	6 11	673	7,011	10 42

Statement 26—Continued.

Districts.	Counties.	Horses.			Cattle.			Mules and Asses.		
		No.	Value.	Av.	No.	Value.	Av.	No.	Value.	Av.
14	DeWitt	9,382	$77,904	$8 30	8,625	$56,939	$6 60	514	$4,187	$8 15
	Logan	13,862	182,047	13 14	11,899	80,101	6 73	1,268	19,058	15 03
	Macon	14,850	186,359	12 54	12,128	95,209	7 85	1,427	17,312	12 13
	McLean	29,989	248,010	8 27	31,727	181,095	5 71	1,651	13,376	8 10
	Piatt	10,521	85,138	8 09	11,245	49,366	4 39	1,106	8,422	7 62
15	Champaign	23,364	270,018	11 56	19,369	132,858	6 86	1,772	20,057	11 32
	Coles	11,404	123,572	10 84	10,718	79,740	7 45	799	8,201	10 26
	Douglas	11,859	82,399	6 95	10,306	54,312	5 27	946	6,887	7 28
	Edgar	13,978	116,541	8 34	17,473	108,874	6 23	917	7,304	7 97
	Vermilion	22,494	208,314	9 27	22,796	151,579	6 65	1,280	10,645	8 32
16	Clay	8,514	72,703	8 54	8,582	46,537	5 42	782	6,660	8 52
	Clark	6,917	82,482	11 92	8,603	34,029	3 96	373	4,386	11 76
	Crawford	7,549	76,197	10 09	7,737	38,495	4 98	394	3,635	9 23
	Cumberland	6,990	58,955	8 43	6,310	30,125	4 77	734	5,665	7 72
	Edwards	4,778	72,820	15 24	5,605	39,236	7 00	843	12,652	15 01
	Jasper	8,826	93,896	10 64	8,862	52,649	5 95	583	5,559	9 54
	Lawrence	5,334	61,712	11 57	6,101	31,862	5 22	585	6,182	10 57
	Richland	5,044	62,056	12 30	5,287	26,858	5 08	309	3,755	12 15
	Wayne	8,859	92,545	10 45	11,020	50,935	4 62	1,541	13,921	9 03
	Wabash	3,920	40,147	10 24	4,464	19,064	4 27	726	7,991	11 01
17	Effingham	6,700	56,824	8 48	6,981	44,130	6 32	507	4,187	8 26
	Fayette	13,201	92,833	7 04	11,871	63,594	5 35	931	6,266	6 73
	Macoupin	15,749	149,770	9 51	21,337	140,331	6 58	1,423	12,641	8 88
	Montgomery	15,179	134,975	8 89	14,917	94,387	6 33	1,671	15,172	9 08
	Moultrie	7,438	58,239	7 83	6,594	32,549	4 94	529	3,763	7 11
	Shelby	18,211	168,898	9 28	17,320	109,956	6 35	1,308	11,263	8 61
18	Bond	7,656	58,359	7 62	8,252	53,747	6 51	809	6,440	7 96
	Madison	10,628	159,011	14 96	13,598	91,976	6 76	3,250	57,248	17 61
	Monroe	3,242	58,019	17 89	4,159	28,265	6 79	2,236	43,057	19 25
	St. Clair	10,024	115,963	11 50	11,273	48,462	4 30	3,696	42,466	11 49
	Washington	6,962	80,393	11 64	9,323	55,405	5 94	1,500	19,177	12 78
19	Clinton	6,228	64,594	10 37	7,095	45,194	6 37	1,049	14,443	13 76
	Franklin	6,535	61,027	9 34	6,389	32,465	5 08	1,938	17,773	9 17
	Gallatin	3,387	47,186	13 93	3,463	17,340	5 01	1,593	22,150	13 90
	Hamilton	7,424	71,566	9 64	6,854	35,184	5 13	1,372	12,554	9 15
	Hardin	2,059	53,185	25 83	2,903	22,386	7 71	915	24,991	27 31
	Jefferson	9,257	79,895	8 63	8,958	47,765	5 33	1,796	15,409	8 58
	Marion	10,271	85,752	8 35	9,403	56,829	6 04	1,307	11,341	8 68
	Saline	5,861	64,801	11 05	6,145	27,418	4 46	2,039	22,137	10 85
	White	8,377	70,604	8 43	9,763	38,878	3 98	2,687	24,896	9 27
20	Alexander	1,911	27,569	14 43	1,957	12,508	6 39	1,175	18,923	16 10
	Jackson	5,955	98,458	16 53	8,125	46,287	5 70	2,347	38,404	16 36
	Johnson	4,469	79,737	17 84	4,995	35,024	7 01	1,830	37,731	20 62
	Massac	2,396	42,625	17 79	3,613	21,834	6 04	1,618	30,922	19 11
	Perry	4,088	77,241	18 92	5,197	50,305	9 68	835	15,610	18 69
	Pope	4,478	99,848	22 30	5,066	38,087	7 52	1,695	38,714	22 84
	Pulaski	2,887	35,748	12 38	2 897	17,156	5 92	1,514	16,339	10 79
	Randolph	7,692	91,741	11 93	11,300	59,874	5 30	1,836	23,101	12 58
	Union	6,030	82,168	13 63	5,673	31,965	5 64	2,486	37,216	14 98
	Williamson	5,794	95,619	16 50	5,928	47,466	8 01	2,331	39,895	17 11
	Grand agg.	1,112,094	$12,599,782	$11 33	1,547,156	$10,036,926	$6 49	94,066	$1,142,860	$12 15

Statement 26—Continued.

Districts.	Counties.	Sheep.			Hogs.			Steam Engines, including Boilers.		
		No.	Value.	Av.	No.	Value.	Av.	No.	Value.	Av.
1, 2, 3, 4	Cook	889	$883	$0 99	7,868	$8,794	$1 12	521	$120,855	$231 97
5	Boone	3,282	3,281	1 00	9,157	14,653	1 60	29	2,710	93 45
	DeKalb	4,699	5,126	1 09	25,310	43,505	1 72	102	15,210	149 11
	Kane	4,667	4,785	1 03	13,919	19,105	1 37	220	38,363	174 38
	Lake	9,973	6,665	67	6,048	7,907	1 30	102	23,526	230 64
	McHenry	6,328	3,209	51	16,192	23,370	1 45	70	6,535	93 36
6	Carroll	6,725	5,073	75	29,165	36,329	1 25	52	4,114	80 66
	JoDaviess	8,148	7,934	98	20,352	33,556	1 65	52	3,773	72 56
	Ogle	5,577	5,308	95	31,749	51,298	1 61	100	8,874	88 74
	Stephenson	7,451	7,451	1 00	26,571	39,571	1 48	97	13,038	134 41
	Winnebago	6,084	5,687	93	16,054	24,943	1 55	69	12,283	178 01
7	Bureau	7,694	7,792	1 01	30,826	49,975	1 62	159	15,358	96 59
	Henry	9,770	9,963	1 02	33,601	57,288	1 70	77	7,671	99 62
	Lee	2,046	2,061	1 00	18,434	24,088	1 31	81	6,488	80 09
	Putnam	1,905	1,915	1 01	4,903	7,451	1 52	19	1,435	75 53
	Whiteside	3,836	3,305	86	23,911	40,934	1 71	78	8,772	112 46
8	DuPage	1,819	1,395	77	7,844	7,861	1 00	85	6,386	75 12
	Grundy	3,504	3,830	1 09	6,019	7,486	1 22	109	11,367	104 21
	Kendall	3,695	3,695	1 00	11,274	20,243	1 79	62	4,600	74 19
	LaSalle	8,119	8,161	1 00	26,321	40,844	1 55	311	45,411	146 01
	Will	2,677	2,685	1 00	12,548	15,249	1 22	231	101,149	437 87
9	Ford	1,644	1,174	71	9,810	15,718	1 60	79	5,320	67 34
	Iroquois	4,109	4,151	1 01	23,743	35,691	1 50	195	15,348	78 71
	Kankakee	1,190	932	78	6,657	11,426	1 72	73	4,345	59 52
	Livingston	3,159	1,611	51	18,558	16,688	90	203	16,006	78 89
	Marshall	4,152	3,532	85	9,430	10,980	1 16	73	8,456	115 84
	Woodford	1,751	1,541	88	11,701	18,925	1 62	114	9,074	79 95
10	Fulton	11,088	6,032	54	42,913	45,724	1 07	154	11,269	73 18
	Knox	5,127	5,159	1 00	30,700	45,687	1 48	114	18,210	159 73
	Peoria	5,209	4,184	80	15,706	23,770	1 50	217	18,755	86 45
	Stark	6,740	4,799	71	10,674	12,682	1 19	52	3,132	60 23
11	Hancock	4,580	3,605	79	35,627	50,728	1 42	128	10,033	78 38
	Henderson	2,007	2,030	1 01	17,251	28,635	1 66	23	1,850	80 44
	McDonough	3,456	2,490	72	38,239	54,131	1 42	104	9,424	90 61
	Mercer	4,147	3,095	75	38,629	44,619	1 16	58	6,806	117 34
	Rock Island	2,121	1,270	60	17,534	20,997	1 19	133	36,367	273 43
	Schuyler	3,024	2,932	97	24,363	29,006	1 19	80	6,071	75 89
	Warren	2,375	1,679	70	26,131	34,404	1 32	59	4,380	74 24
12	Adams	7,127	5,546	78	38,794	38,542	99	206	30,826	149 64
	Brown	4,805	4,802	1 00	13,745	19,251	1 40	33	2,035	61 66
	Calhoun	940	850	91	8,382	10,916	1 30	16	2,510	156 88
	Cass	1,526	1,138	74	12,721	17,515	1 37	40	4,125	103 12
	Greene	6,989	4,746	69	25,698	29,631	1 15	58	4,035	69 57
	Jersey	2,949	2,616	89	10,930	13,548	1 24	43	5,105	118 72
	Pike	14,440	7,424	51	35,973	35,909	1 00	92	5,782	62 85
	Scott	2,249	2,333	1 04	14,110	24,801	1 08	33	2,567	77 79
13	Christian	7,441	5,205	69	25,783	27,258	1 05	118	8,981	76 18
	Mason	183	155	85	9,828	13,214	1 34	76	3,588	47 20
	Menard	2,918	4,030	1 38	11,162	38,325	3 44	41	4,915	119 87
	Morgan	5,841	7,133	1 22	21,128	46,107	2 15	40	8,755	218 88
	Sangamon	8,902	8,442	95	36,385	57,951	1 59	308	41,550	134 90
	Tazewell	4,991	4,462	81	14,667	18,533	1 27	199	17,677	88 83
14	DeWitt	6,430	5,012	78	12,965	16,221	1 25	52	2,145	41 25
	Logan	3,407	3,375	99	17,614	28,213	1 61	109	10,644	97 65
	Macon	2,842	2,696	94	15,121	23,209	1 53	209	30,395	145 43
	McLean	17,350	9,248	53	35,630	39,190	1 10	270	22,535	83 46
	Piatt	1,914	686	36	10,690	8,068	75	85	4,414	51 93

Statement 26—Continued.

Districts....	Counties.	Sheep.			Hogs.			Steam Engines, including Boilers.		
		No.	Value.	Av.	No.	Valve.	Av.	No.	Value.	Av.
15	Champaign	4,256	$3,140	$0 74	19,053	$21,749	$1 14	228	$15,044	$65 98
	Coles	5,393	4,988	92	17,585	18,167	1 03	130	6,893	53 03
	Douglas........	4,245	2,166	51	13,792	11,977	87	146	7,634	52 29
	Edgar	10,336	5,531	54	22,938	27,411	1 11	113	4,805	42 52
	Vermilion......	13,252	9,969	75	28,366	33,232	1 17	158	12,423	78 63
16	Clay	7,295	4,439	61	16,984	13,816	81	76	4,413	58 07
	Clark..........	9,018	4,512	60	16,414	14,717	90	58	2,543	43 84
	Crawford	11,081	6,816	62	13,854	13,945	1 00	55	3,422	62 22
	Cumberland ...	2,445	1,418	58	12,120	11,377	94	45	1,973	43 84
	Edwards	7,799	7,434	95	10,275	16,726	1 63	43	3,594	83 58
	Jasper	7,578	4,856	64	19,009	15,553	82	75	3,792	50 56
	Lawrence	5,480	3,127	57	11,318	11,465	1 01	45	3,095	68 78
	Richland	6,811	3,419	50	10,902	8,350	76	49	3,916	79 92
	Wayne	12,657	6,772	54	18,633	16,136	87	79	5,259	66 57
	Wabash	2,052	1,752	85	7,064	5,335	75	53	3,150	59 43
17	Effingham	3,263	3,225	99	9,800	8,760	90	62	2,691	43 40
	Fayette	8,917	6,412	72	20,144	17,087	84	121	7,680	63 48
	Macoupin	16,772	17,427	1 04	31,275	41,332	1 32	161	16,177	100 48
	Montgomery...	12,327	7,079	57	28,004	32,664	1 17	154	12,413	80 60
	Moultrie	2,312	2,213	96	8,806	11,733	1 33	54	1,947	36 06
	Shelby	14,119	11,252	80	30,587	35,637	1 17	133	8,956	67 34
18	Bond	6,923	5,136	74	12,064	11,545	95	61	3,125	51 23
	Madison	4,446	3,973	89	18,990	24,032	1 26	223	67,886	303 98
	Monroe.........	1,298	1,103	85	13,142	13,452	1 02	100	12,454	124 54
	St. Clair........	1,653	1,136	69	19,135	15,559	81	344	94,524	274 78
	Washington ...	2,443	2,426	1 00	7,986	8,009	1 00	83	5,486	66 09
19	Clinton	3,622	3,624	1 00	7,081	7,555	1 07	71	3,951	55 64
	Franklin	3,156	2,501	79	14,036	12,660	90	36	2,075	57 64
	Gallatin	937	876	93	6,933	6,780	97	45	3,485	77 44
	Hamilton	4,302	3,980	92	19,239	16,646	86	53	3,550	66 98
	Hardin	1,048	1,076	1 02	8,360	10,081	1 20	19	3,750	187 37
	Jefferson.......	5,396	3,836	71	18,793	14,034	75	32	2,556	79 87
	Marion	6,512	6,127	94	13,838	11,506	83	59	3,942	66 78
	Saline	2,135	1,788	89	16,650	15,392	92	46	3,996	86 87
	White	4,065	2,799	69	22,427	17,911	80	62	3,565	57 50
20	Alexander	422	487	1 15	6,011	5,983	99	67	5,838	87 14
	Jackson	2,625	2,680	1 02	16,696	17,570	1 05	132	20,646	156 41
	Johnson........	3,213	3,559	1 11	14,981	19,622	1 31	50	8,715	174 30
	Massac	862	832	97	11,207	10,798	96	147	7,329	49 86
	Perry	2,007	2,029	1 01	5,360	10,742	2 00	90	5,239	58 21
	Pope	4,192	4,309	1 03	17,015	18,928	1 11	31	3,113	100 42
	Pulaski	599	568	95	5,347	5,781	1 08	16	6,084	380 25
	Randolph	3,753	2,415	64	17,430	15,134	87	147	11,674	79 41
	Union	2,122	1,963	92	18,755	18,384	98	77	8,533	110 82
	Williamson	2,665	3,042	1 14	17,613	18,820	1 06	54	12,887	238 64
	Grand Agg.	515,816	$410,531	$0 80	1,823,155	$2,294,822	$1 26	10,596	$1,291,471	$121 88

Statement 26—Continued.

Districts.	Counties.	Fire and Burglar-proof Safes. No.	Value.	Av.	Billiard, Pigeon-hole, etc., Tables. No.	Value.	Av.	Carriages and Wagons. No.	Value.	Av.
1, 2, 3, 4	Cook	369	$14,255	$38 63	260	$6,340	$24 38	24,485	$539,493	$22 03
5	Boone	66	1,118	16 94	6	120	20 00	2,688	16,796	6 25
	DeKalb	159	3,665	23 05	19	465	24 47	5,671	57,095	10 06
	Kane	481	8,762	18 23	77	1,555	20 19	8,200	81,776	9 97
	Lake	46	622	13 52	11	143	13 00	4,012	32,149	8 01
	McHenry	130	3,100	23 84	34	730	21 47	5,929	47,702	8 05
6	Carroll	120	2,001	16 67	28	462	16 50	3,818	24,975	6 54
	Jo Daviess	127	2,802	22 06	4	35	8 75	3,689	27,333	7 41
	Ogle	159	3,105	19 53	18	205	11 39	6,842	46,208	6 75
	Stephenson	174	5,980	34 37	33	675	20 46	5,025	40,614	8 08
	Winnebago	111	3,193	28 77	23	880	38 27	5,535	53,628	9 69
7	Bureau	141	2,780	19 71	33	707	21 42	6,964	51,549	7 40
	Henry	125	2,851	22 81	49	1,036	21 12	6,605	57,612	8 72
	Lee	126	2,079	16 50	20	330	16 50	5,652	39,683	7 02
	Putnum	4	280	70 00	3	30	10 00	672	6,160	9 17
	Whiteside	118	1,611	13 65	50	995	19 90	5,122	36,283	7 08
8	DuPage	61	1,407	23 06	33	690	20 91	3,469	33,229	9 62
	Grundy	104	1,418	13 63	22	236	10 73	3,049	20,249	6 64
	Kendall	23	648	28 17	8	108	13 50	2,820	23,501	8 33
	LaSalle	404	6,260	15 49	105	1,566	14 91	9,982	89,165	8 93
	Will	282	3,201	11 35	58	842	14 52	8,257	57,575	6 97
9	Ford	106	2,481	23 41	9	200	22 22	3,574	25,427	7 11
	Iroquois	127	3,088	24 31	19	380	20 00	9,110	57,208	6 28
	Kankakee	70	1,056	15 08	27	290	10 74	3,187	25,972	8 15
	Livingston	184	2,587	14 06	47	719	15 30	9,552	47,216	4 94
	Marshall	79	1,219	15 43	17	172	10 12	2,733	20,121	7 36
	Woodford	101	1,598	15 82	12	137	11 42	4,426	29,679	6 71
10	Fulton	214	2,727	12 74	30	510	17 00	7,286	39,167	5 38
	Knox	140	3,039	21 70	38	993	26 14	4,973	49,899	10 03
	Peoria	379	6,959	18 36	42	695	16 55	6,510	71,632	11 00
	Stark	52	959	18 44	13	162	12 46	2,685	16,785	6 21
11	Hancock	124	2,575	20 77	14	241	17 21	7,217	42,685	5 91
	Henderson	18	695	38 61	4	40	10 00	1,616	14,331	8 88
	McDonough	67	2,166	32 33	8	125	15 62	5,810	37,989	6 54
	Mercer	91	2,060	22 64	25	329	13 16	4,079	23,052	5 65
	Rock Island	137	1,911	13 94	47	865	18 40	3,854	35,022	9 09
	Schuyler	22	370	16 82	......	......	......	3,204	21,783	6 80
	Warren	35	1,170	33 43	22	390	17 73	3,308	22,848	6 90
12	Adams	314	6,042	19 24	46	755	16 41	7,227	70,548	9 76
	Brown	12	244	20 33	6	130	21 66	2,113	13,219	6 25
	Calhoun	14	170	12 14	7	85	14 17	932	6,535	7 01
	Cass	96	1,733	18 05	17	191	11 23	2,195	16,785	7 65
	Greene	85	1,213	14 27	10	165	16 50	3,222	24,377	7 57
	Jersey	54	907	16 79	15	202	13 46	2,384	17,926	7 52
	Pike	56	964	17 21	12	175	14 58	4,748	28,113	5 92
	Scott	44	1,651	37 52	2	15	7 50	2,502	17,665	7 06
13	Christian	122	1,984	16 26	11	150	13 64	5,061	28,164	5 56
	Mason	110	2,850	25 90	6	297	49 50	2,399	13,661	5 69
	Menard	59	1,765	29 91	6	150	25 00	1,951	21,225	10 88
	Morgan	69	7,521	109 00	29	1,335	46 04	3,181	46,244	14 67
	Sangamon	307	6,540	21 30	31	770	24 84	8,684	68,482	7 88
	Tazewell	221	2,834	12 82	34	665	19 56	5,770	40,145	6 96
14	DeWitt	64	722	11 28	13	215	16 54	3,164	16,312	5 16
	Logan	104	2,763	26 56	37	589	15 92	4,894	38,304	9 87
	Macon	245	6,413	26 17	34	615	18 09	6,373	53,703	8 42
	McLean	302	5,529	18 31	57	656	11 51	12,387	67,722	5 47
	Piatt	74	1,066	14 41	......	......	......	4,224	21,257	5 03

Statement 26—Continued.

Districts	Counties.	Fire and Burglar-proof Safes.			Billiard, Pigeon-hole, etc., Tables.			Carriages and Wagons.		
		No.	Value.	Av.	No.	Value.	Av.	No.	Value.	Av.
15	Champaign	263	$3,535	$13 44	36	$750	$20 83	9,585	$58,943	$6 15
	Coles	82	849	10 35	19	350	18 42	4,398	25,686	5 84
	Douglas	125	1,556	12 45	3	25	8 33	3,816	22,744	4 72
	Edgar	103	1,693	16 44	16	395	24 69	5,362	34,711	6 47
	Vermilion	216	4,066	18 82	31	665	21 45	9,434	54,135	5 74
16	Clay	25	524	20 96	4	58	14 50	3,861	19,867	5 15
	Clark	55	806	14 65	4	50	12 50	3,070	11,585	3 76
	Crawford	40	565	14 13	6	350	58 33	2,969	15,865	5 34
	Cumberland	39	694	17 79	....	....	......	2,919	13,670	4 68
	Edwards	27	980	36 30	....	....	......	2,335	17,321	7 42
	Jasper	14	221	15 79	....	....	......	3,323	18,049	5 43
	Lawrence	28	430	15 36	....	....	......	2,618	13,748	5 25
	Richland	26	677	26 04	6	120	20 00	1,962	15,732	8 02
	Wayne	58	940	16 21	....	....	......	3,018	19,622	6 50
	Wabash	23	277	12 04	14	176	12 57	1,949	9,651	4 95
17	Effingham	67	892	13 31	24	365	15 21	3,145	17,157	5 46
	Fayette	82	1,206	14 71	13	210	16 15	5,208	25,060	4 82
	Macoupin	169	2,976	17 61	28	538	19 21	6,017	31,717	5 27
	Montgomery	111	2,210	19 91	6	75	12 50	5,532	32,007	5 79
	Moultrie	29	536	18 48	11	200	18 18	2,410	11,599	4 81
	Shelby	75	1,753	23 37	11	170	15 45	6,802	41,397	6 09
18	Bond	26	538	20 69	5	132	26 40	2,395	14,375	6 00
	Madison	226	8,253	36 52	41	666	16 24	6,056	51,708	8 54
	Monroe	27	533	19 74	16	172	10 75	2,450	18,688	7 62
	St. Clair	254	4,976	19 60	42	311	7 40	6,154	52,118	8 47
	Washington	40	561	14 02	8	58	7 25	3,303	17,341	5 25
19	Clinton	42	534	12 71	27	334	12 37	2,752	14,513	5 27
	Franklin	17	499	29 35	....	....	......	2,510	14,118	5 58
	Gallatin	47	853	18 14	7	65	9 28	1,516	9,921	6 54
	Hamilton	36	542	15 06	....	....	......	2,848	13,403	4 71
	Hardin	17	400	23 53	3	130	43 33	905	8,903	9 84
	Jefferson	25	388	15 52	....	....	......	3,156	17,460	5 53
	Marion	66	1,388	21 03	14	210	15 00	4,144	22,981	5 54
	Saline	39	1,400	35 92	2	25	12 50	2,477	17,043	6 88
	White	92	2,086	22 67	13	175	13 46	3,503	17,710	5 06
20	Alexander	136	2,226	16 37	17	560	32 94	1,371	11,148	8 16
	Jackson	70	1,133	16 19	6	60	10 00	3,245	19,797	6 10
	Johnson	23	564	24 52	....	....	......	2,028	18,859	9 30
	Massac	44	819	18 61	10	50	5 00	1,696	15,884	9 37
	Perry	65	1,315	20 23	16	335	20 94	2,074	15,023	7 24
	Pope	31	698	22 52	1	25	25 00	1,811	19,943	11 01
	Pulaski	37	430	11 62	16	116	7 25	1,249	6,112	4 89
	Randolph	97	2,463	25 40	17	141	8 30	4,072	24,525	6 02
	Union	96	1,642	17 10	3	118	39 33	4,143	29,521	7 12
	Williamson	25	752	30 08	5	55	11 00	2,541	22,847	8 99
	Grand Agg.	10,863	$223,087	$20 54	2,141	$39,793	$18 59	454,153	$3,558,135	$7 83

Statement 26—Continued.

Districts	Counties.	Watches and Clocks.			Sewing and Knitting Machines.			Pianos.		
		No.	Value.	Av.	No.	Value.	Av.	No.	Value.	Av.
1, 2, 3, 4	Cook	5,507	$14,787	$2 68	3,797	$16,071	$4 23	12,542	$330,157	$26 32
5	Boone	1,909	2,749	1 44	916	4,004	4 37	141	3,822	27 11
	DeKalb	4,164	8,821	2 12	3,337	13,289	3 98	468	17,445	37 28
	Kane	9,453	26,477	2 89	5,562	20,272	3 64	1,906	54,574	28 63
	Lake	1,830	4,893	2 67	1,295	4,777	3 61	474	12,213	25 77
	McHenry	3,596	5,843	1 63	2,245	10,317	4 59	398	15,047	37 81
6	Carroll	4,442	7,686	1 74	2,301	8,558	3 72	301	9,106	30 25
	Jo Daviess	3,578	4,945	1 38	3,027	7,655	2 53	268	5,707	21 29
	Ogle	5,292	9,584	1 81	3,221	12,977	4 03	488	13,567	27 88
	Stephenson	3,755	7,268	1 93	2,193	9,013	4 11	367	11,460	31 23
	Winnebago	680	5,313	7 81	1,216	6,742	5 55	819	31,307	38 23
7	Bureau	5,376	10,975	2 05	3,439	11,475	3 34	503	13,930	27 69
	Henry	3,741	7,318	1 96	2,931	13,273	4 53	562	18,262	32 49
	Lee	4,524	8,083	1 78	2,716	9,476	3 48	489	14,739	30 15
	Putnam	82	410	5 00	168	840	5 00	42	870	20 71
	Whiteside	3,600	6,533	1 81	2,785	11,089	3 98	515	11,773	22 86
8	DuPage	1,367	4,247	3 10	1,485	6,485	4 36	597	16,459	27 55
	Grundy	2,440	3,210	1 31	1,719	5,157	3 00	219	4,559	20 81
	Kendall	119	847	7 12	222	1,235	5 56	133	3,458	26 00
	LaSalle	7,232	16,721	2 31	4,634	21,336	4 60	1,232	32,868	26 68
	Will	5,137	10,597	2 06	4,248	18,116	4 26	1,119	21,309	19 04
9	Ford	2,964	4,293	1 45	2,148	6,495	3 02	223	4,832	21 67
	Iroquois	7,379	11,959	1 62	4,307	14,179	3 30	443	9,890	22 33
	Kankakee	1,069	3,805	3 55	1,136	5,283	4 65	396	9,940	25 10
	Livingston	7,320	10,308	1 42	4,567	13,227	2 89	469	10,355	22 08
	Marshall	2,543	3,446	1 36	1,574	5,371	3 41	300	7,062	23 54
	Woodford	3,991	5,759	1 44	2,328	8,237	3 54	286	6,706	23 45
10	Fulton	7,481	10,520	1 41	4,882	15,855	3 25	580	12,221	21 07
	Knox	1,037	7,902	7 62	417	1,960	4 70	973	29,466	30 28
	Peoria	3,320	11,289	3 40	2,774	12,927	4 66	1,278	38,934	30 47
	Stark	2,474	3,378	1 36	1,287	4,632	3 60	195	7,098	36 34
11	Hancock	7,096	10,703	1 51	4,073	13,056	3 25	524	13,157	25 11
	Henderson	554	3,305	5 97	737	3,940	5 34	102	3,635	35 63
	McDonough	1,617	9,151	5 66	2,964	11,533	3 90	367	10,644	29 00
	Mercer	2,691	4,796	1 78	2,027	6,449	3 18	293	7,802	26 63
	Rock Island	778	5,294	6 80	2,809	12,990	4 62	780	23,829	30 55
	Schuyler	2,916	4,604	1 58	1,676	6,000	3 58	134	3,719	27 75
	Warren	1,597	4,067	2 51	1,331	5,765	4 33	276	7,475	27 09
12	Adams	5,030	9,989	1 99	4,693	22,612	4 82	829	26,820	32 35
	Brown	2,168	2,699	1 24	1,208	3,653	3 02	102	3,241	30 80
	Calhoun	515	1,346	2 62	371	1,877	5 07	32	1,875	58 59
	Cass	1,479	4,309	2 91	1,144	6,228	5 44	255	7,233	28 36
	Greene	723	4,464	6 17	1,480	7,546	5 10	291	8,030	27 59
	Jersey	1,287	3,325	2 59	956	3,979	4 16	160	5,036	31 48
	Pike	3,688	6,166	1 67	2,653	8,467	3 19	331	7,742	23 39
	Scott	1,836	3,648	1 99	1,064	4,391	4 13	177	4,551	25 71
13	Christian	3,872	5,110	1 32	2,460	7,772	3 16	387	7,744	20 01
	Mason	1,923	3,219	1 67	1,510	5,286	3 50	212	5,455	25 73
	Menard	643	4,295	6 68	1,032	6,925	6 71	189	7,775	41 13
	Morgan	1,967	9,262	4 71	1,527	10,772	7 06	312	23,578	7 56
	Sangamon	6,489	17,574	2 70	4,569	20,466	4 48	1,436	38,886	27 08
	Tazewell	5,167	10,839	2 10	3,256	10,791	3 31	474	13,387	28 24
14	DeWitt	2,479	4,483	1 81	1,685	5,079	3 01	252	3,702	14 69
	Logan	3,354	6,941	2 07	2,244	8,594	3 83	371	9,990	26 92
	Macon	3,910	14,848	3 79	4,157	20,304	4 88	796	20,700	26 01
	McLean	9,034	18,183	2 01	5,870	17,088	2 91	1,336	28,542	21 36
	Piatt	1,851	3,387	1 83	1,598	4,772	2 99	225	4,855	21 58

Statement 26—Continued.

Districts.	Counties.	Watches and Clocks.			Sewing and Knitting Machines.			Pianos.		
		No.	Value.	Av.	No.	Value.	Av.	No.	Value.	Av.
15	Champaign	7,129	$12,376	1 74	4,755	$16,909	$3 56	780	$23,165	29 70
	Coles	3,493	5,526	1 59	2,145	8,268	3 85	403	8,449	20 97
	Douglas	3,726	6,047	1 62	2,226	5,234	2 35	268	7,703	28 74
	Edgar	4,124	5,171	1 25	2,362	7,469	3 16	364	9,625	26 44
	Vermilion	6,657	13,387	2 01	3,828	14,264	3 73	808	17,836	22 07
16	Clay	3,083	4,024	1 31	2,010	5,986	2 80	124	3,176	25 61
	Clark	2,997	3,455	1 15	2,019	4,104	2 03	141	2,281	16 17
	Crawford	2,407	3,159	1 31	1,802	4,471	2 48	104	3,308	31 81
	Cumberland	2,683	3,211	1 20	1,683	4,551	2 70	75	1,243	16 57
	Edwards	2,133	3,639	1 71	1,342	5,779	4 31	89	2,806	31 53
	Jasper	2,466	3,058	1 24	1,783	5,729	3 21	69	1,253	18 16
	Lawrence	2,301	2,847	1 24	1,509	4,056	2 69	82	1,986	24 22
	Richland	2,344	2,401	1 02	1,286	5,055	3 93	109	2,740	25 14
	Wayne	3,135	3,689	1 18	1,839	6,375	3 47	92	1,460	15 87
	Wabash	1,786	2,325	1 30	1,052	3,423	3 25	109	3,109	28 52
17	Effingham	3,194	3,756	1 18	2,122	7,183	3 39	155	5,171	33 36
	Fayette	4,343	5,774	1 33	2,715	7,273	2 68	137	2,760	20 14
	Macoupin	5,921	8,250	1 39	4,012	11,469	2 86	536	10,485	19 56
	Montgomery	5,321	5,939	1 12	3,296	10,442	3 17	382	8,302	21 73
	Moultrie	1,872	1,922	1 03	1,258	3,397	2 70	90	2,119	23 54
	Shelby	5,091	7,278	1 43	3,499	11,986	3 43	241	6,498	26 96
18	Bond	1,039	2,605	2 50	1,263	5,786	4 57	129	4,048	31 37
	Madison	3,092	11,518	3 72	2,564	12,746	4 97	643	27,677	43 04
	Monroe	1,854	2,684	1 44	1,235	4,583	3 71	87	2,108	24 23
	St. Clair	1,222	3,855	3 10	1,587	4,810	3 03	373	9,899	26 54
	Washington	2,828	3,204	1 13	1,805	4,470	2 47	121	2,667	22 04
19	Clinton	2,584	2,998	1 17	1,758	5,104	2 90	126	3,507	27 83
	Franklin	2,006	2,624	1 31	1,586	5,554	3 50	59	2,116	35 86
	Gallatin	384	1,586	4 13	902	4,725	5 23	83	2,180	26 26
	Hamilton	2,741	3,103	1 13	1,608	4,046	2 51	86	2,463	28 64
	Hardin	915	1,762	1 92	563	3,801	6 75	18	1,289	71 61
	Jefferson	2,528	3,162	1 25	1,953	7,198	3 68	106	2,375	22 40
	Marion	4,243	5,942	1 40	2,566	9,361	3 65	294	10,291	35 00
	Saline	2,158	2,885	1 34	1,656	6,184	3 73	100	3,785	37 85
	White	3,410	4,105	1 20	2,363	7,261	3 07	121	2,530	20 90
20	Alexander	1,111	3,628	3 27	1,002	4,676	4 67	294	7,652	26 03
	Jackson	3,502	5,864	1 67	2,297	8,134	3 54	240	6,553	27 30
	Johnson	2,324	4,004	1 72	1,428	7,446	5 21	46	2,948	64 09
	Massac	1,977	3,919	1 98	1,227	6,495	5 29	132	7,602	57 60
	Perry	2,081	3,685	1 77	1,568	5,731	3 65	195	5,610	28 77
	Pope	1,823	3,604	1 97	1,131	7,444	6 59	43	2,342	54 47
	Pulaski	1,027	2,023	1 97	939	3,812	4 06	109	3,033	27 83
	Randolph	3,782	5,761	1 52	2,410	7,907	3 28	244	5,595	22 93
	Union	3,890	4,860	1 25	2,263	8,226	3 63	220	7,308	33 22
	Williamson	2,401	3,535	1 47	1,786	9,633	5 39	72	2,617	36 34
	Grand Agg.	323,174	$616,123	$1 91	225,974	$845,214	$3 74	48,468	$1,332,209	$27 49

Statement 26—Continued.

Districts.	Counties.	Melodeons and Organs.			Franchises.			Annuities and Royalties.		
		No.	Value.	Av.	No.	Value.	Av.	No.	Value.	Av.
1, 2, 3, 4	Cook	485	$3,327	$6 86	1	$200	$200 00			
5	Boone	402	2,755	6 85	1	10	10 00			
	DeKalb	1,055	9,013	8 54						
	Kane	1,230	10,390	8 45						
	Lake	444	3,483	7 85						
	McHenry	602	6,325	10 51						
6	Carroll	834	6,068	7 27						
	Jo Daviess	630	4,880	7 74				1	$400	$400 00
	Ogle	1,184	9,720	8 21						
	Stephenson	954	7,810	8 18						
	Winnebago	439	4,849	11 05						
7	Bureau	1,031	9,793	9 50						
	Henry	1,313	11,896	9 06	1	200	200 00			
	Lee	824	6,078	7 37						
	Putnam	80	725	9 06						
	Whiteside	990	6,235	6 29						
8	DuPage	277	2,547	9 19						
	Grundy	445	3,252	7 30						
	Kendall	113	1,057	9 35						
	LaSalle	1,326	11,876	8 95	1	3,491	3,491 00			
	Will	944	7,134	7 56	1	20	20 00	1	15	15 00
9	Ford	676	4,320	6 39						
	Iroquois	1,314	9,323	7 09	25	1,673	66 92			
	Kankakee	534	4,527	8 48						
	Livingston	1,605	9,880	6 21						
	Marshall	451	3,347	7 42						
	Woodford	797	7,190	9 02	1	1,500	1,500 00	2	350	175 00
10	Fulton	1,819	12,860	7 07						
	Knox	823	7,836	9 52						
	Peoria	1,017	9,551	9 39						
	Stark	568	4,609	8 11						
11	Hancock	1,574	10,619	6 74				1	700	700 00
	Henderson	329	3,615	10 99	1	1,000	1,000 00			
	McDonough	1,431	11,540	8 05	1	166	166 00	1	368	368 00
	Mercer	898	6,227	6 93				1	42	42 00
	Rock Island	741	5,846	7 89						
	Schuyler	675	5,914	8 76						
	Warren	547	4,013	7 33						
12	Adams	1,307	11,939	9 14	1	5	5 00			
	Brown	414	3,530	8 52						
	Calhoun	73	1,257	17 22						
	Cass	237	2,162	9 12						
	Greene	461	4,392	9 53						
	Jersey	167	1,894	11 34						
	Pike	892	6,897	7 69						
	Scott	295	2,259	7 66	1	100	100 00			
13	Christian	917	6,421	7 02				1	510	510 00
	Mason	561	4,211	7 50	1	800	800 00			
	Menard	365	4,930	13 50						
	Morgan	505	6,988	13 84				1	250	250 00
	Sangamon	1,063	9,453	8 90	2	20	10 00	2	900	450 00
	Tazewell	919	7,793	8 48						
14	DeWitt	629	3,690	5 87						
	Logan	626	5,548	8 86				1	200	200 00
	Macon	1,340	10,274	7 66				1	75	75 00
	McLean	2,152	13,901	6 46	1	3,473	3,473 00			
	Piatt	757	5,078	6 71						

Statement 26—Continued.

Districts....	Counties.	Melodeons and Organs.			Franchises.			Annuities and Royalties.		
		No.	Value.	Av.	No.	Value.	Av.	No.	Value.	Av.
15	Champaign....	1,686	$13,048	$7 74	1	$1,000	$1,000 00	......	....	....
	Coles..........	895	6,709	7 50	1	130	130 00	......	....	....
	Douglas........	837	5,696	6 81	......	....	....	......	....	....
	Edgar..........	815	5,218	6 40	1	367	367 00	......	....	....
	Vermilion......	1,542	11,802	7 65	2	1,300	650 00	......	....	....
16	Clay...........	532	4,158	7 82	......	....	....	......	....	....
	Clark..........	586	3,438	5 87	1	500	500 00	......	....	....
	Crawford.......	540	4,038	7 48	......	....	....	......	....	....
	Cumberland...	501	3,253	6 49	......	....	....	......	....	....
	Edwards.......	431	4,899	11 37	......	....	....	1	$205	$205 00
	Jasper.........	613	5,213	8 50	......	....	....	1	10	10 00
	Lawrence......	465	3,967	8 53	......	....	....	......	....	....
	Richland.......	442	4,197	9 50	......	....	....	......	....	....
	Wayne.........	480	4,348	9 06	......	....	....	......	....	....
	Wabash........	277	1,950	7 04	......	....	....	......	....	....
17	Effingham.....	443	4,250	9 59	......	....	....	1	8	8 00
	Fayette........	616	4,871	7 91	1	80	80 00	......	....	....
	Macoupin......	1,295	8,069	6 23	......	....	....	......	....	....
	Montgomery...	1,011	7,602	7 52	......	....	....	......	....	....
	Moultrie........	466	3,158	6 78	......	....	....	......	....	....
	Shelby.........	927	7,364	7 94	......	....	....	......	....	....
18	Bond...........	441	4,017	9 11	......	....	....	......	....	....
	Madison........	380	3,933	10 35	1	10	10 00	......	....	....
	Monroe........	39	291	7 46	......	....	....	......	....	....
	St. Clair........	165	1,294	7 84	1	25	25 00	1	440	440 00
	Washington....	329	2,594	7 88	......	....	....	......	....	....
19	Clinton.........	165	1,929	11 69	......	....	....	......	....	....
	Franklin........	338	2,656	6 84	......	....	....	......	....	....
	Gallatin........	343	3,344	9 75	1	25	25 00	......	....	....
	Hamilton.......	433	2,871	6 63	......	....	....	......	....	....
	Hardin.........	120	3,093	25 77	......	....	....	......	....	....
	Jefferson......	756	5,557	7 35	......	....	....	......	....	....
	Marion.........	719	6,318	8 78	......	....	....	......	....	....
	Saline..........	564	5,904	10 46	......	....	....	......	....	....
	White..........	678	4,372	6 45	1	2,586	2,586 00	......	....	....
20	Alexander......	146	1,441	9 87	......	....	....	......	....	....
	Jackson........	492	4,640	9 43	......	....	....	......	....	....
	Johnson........	403	6,360	15 78	......	....	....	......	....	....
	Massac.........	322	5,510	17 11	......	....	....	......	....	....
	Perry..........	367	3,154	8 59	......	....	....	......	....	....
	Pope...........	292	5,507	18 86	1	50	50 00	......	....	....
	Pulaski.........	197	1,728	8 77	......	....	....	......	....	....
	Randolph......	335	2,469	7 37	2	1,013	506 50	1	5	5 00
	Union..........	665	7,600	11 45	1	100	100 00	23	1,464	63 57
	Williamson....	516	6,072	11 66	......	....	....	......	....	....
	Grand agg..	69,689	$572,949	8 22	54	$19,844	$367 48	41	$5,942	$144 93

Statement 26—Continued.

Districts.	Counties.	Patent Rights.			Steamboats, Sailing Vessels, Etc.			Total value of enumerated property.	Merchandise.
		No.	Value.	Av.	No.	Value.	Av.		
1, 2, 3, 4	Cook				214	$53,570	$250 33	$1,939,224	$10,762,752
5	Boone							283,203	49,895
	DeKalb							600,000	160,606
	Kane							768,986	400,883
	Lake				142	2,499	17 59	353,978	84,999
	McHenry				4	445	111 25	746,484	151,133
6	Carroll							344,936	80,846
	Jo Daviess							406,589	104,278
	Ogle	2	$300	$150 00				635,854	127,099
	Stephenson	1	500	500 00				553,486	169,907
	Winnebago				6	850	141 66	452,553	330,501
7	Bureau				9	208	23 11	656,964	160,015
	Henry							630,240	237,417
	Lee				3	90	30 00	423,185	135,594
	Putnam				9	465	51 67	106,075	8,090
	Whiteside				2	1,615	807 50	477,754	157,006
8	DuPage							278,189	65,571
	Grundy	1	20	20 00	3	180	60 00	207,529	75,969
	Kendall							261,711	43,697
	La Salle				5	450	90 00	828,213	386,608
	Will	1	110	110 00	15	2,790	186 00	594,052	280,735
9	Ford							245,652	74,556
	Iroquois	1	100	100 00	2	40	20 00	635,950	181,539
	Kankakee				87	435	5 00	234,716	92,702
	Livingston				1	50	50 00	398,862	154,708
	Marshall				4	630	157 50	215,220	63,377
	Woodford	1	15	15 00				332,986	86,766
10	Fulton							454,882	171,290
	Knox				1	50	50 00	672,691	254,693
	Peoria				34	2,290	67 36	620,926	642,183
	Stark							187,980	56,228
11	Hancock				6	561	93 50	541,826	155,821
	Henderson							244,651	35,865
	McDonough							486,923	144,844
	Mercer				5	20	4 00	370,836	88,753
	Rock Island				27	14,745	546 11	344,049	235,466
	Schuyler				7	4,167	595 29	295,187	41,810
	Warren							289,628	60,703
12	Adams	1	300	300 00	8	609	76 13	567,810	378,495
	Brown	1	203	203 00				172,073	53,548
	Calhoun				30	1,938	64 60	100,284	46,550
	Cass				2	190	95 00	194,786	66,990
	Greene							326,294	90,772
	Jersey				10	1,808	180 80	178,306	46,449
	Pike				11	86	7 82	349,857	90,946
	Scott				2	155	77 50	194,662	54,204
13	Christian							350,255	116,694
	Mason				3	205	68 33	178,531	48,461
	Menard							292,925	73,235
	Morgan	1	50	50 00				498,683	201,241
	Sangamon	2	10	5 00				749,471	390,708
	Tazewell				1	265	265 00	370,866	144,979
14	DeWitt				1	10	10 00	196,621	62,687
	Logan							396,367	120,280
	Macon							482,202	296,319
	McLean	1	5	5 00	7	21	3 00	668,574	321,775
	Piatt							196,509	57,765

Statement 26—Continued.

Districts....	Counties.	Patent Rights.			Steamboats, Sailing Vessels, Etc.			Total value of enumerated property.	Merchandise.
		No.	Value.	Av.	No.	Value.	Av.		
15	Champaign	1	$150	$150 00	10	$10	$1 00	$592,752	$193,976
	Coles	1	5	5 00				297,533	137,162
	Douglas							214,380	61,846
	Edgar							335,115	103,645
	Vermilion							543,617	241,735
16	Clay				4	4	1 00	186,365	57,102
	Clark				1	35	35 00	168,873	39,221
	Crawford				6	54	9 00	174,320	42,409
	Cumberland	2	30	30 00				136,165	26,566
	Edwards							188,091	37,835
	Jasper							209,838	38,439
	Lawrence				5	132	26 40	144,609	27,823
	Richland							139,276	33,906
	Wayne							222,002	41,107
	Wabash				4	315	78 75	98,665	24,352
17	Effingham							158,599	67,997
	Fayette	1	10	10 00				241,116	65,597
	Macoupin				1	15	15 00	451,197	126,650
	Montgomery							363,267	134,957
	Moultrie							133,375	33,882
	Shelby							422,408	110,375
18	Bond							169,853	57,782
	Madison				13	11,910	916 15	532,477	227,614
	Monroe							185,409	52,973
	St. Clair	1	550	550 00	10	78,312	7,831 12	474,700	260,433
	Washington							201,791	62,530
19	Clinton							168,280	42,910
	Franklin							156,068	35,701
	Gallatin				2	160	80 00	120,676	35,670
	Hamilton							169,908	28,427
	Hardin				15	97	6 46	134,944	34,850
	Jefferson	1	333	333 00				199,968	47,101
	Marion	1	8	8 00				231,996	103,711
	Saline							172,758	50,112
	White	1	13	13 00	1	250	125 00	199,741	61,753
20	Alexander				18	25,835	1,993 05	138,514	124,979
	Jackson				1	1	1 00	270,207	97,677
	Johnson							224,572	39,499
	Massac				6	1,260	210 00	155,879	51,496
	Perry							196,019	55,843
	Pope				8	264	33 00	242,876	38,516
	Pulaski				3	1,097	365 67	100,027	31,483
	Randolph	1	16	16 00	6	1,215	202 50	255,049	86,646
	Union	1	25	25 00	8	32	4 00	241,155	68,148
	Williamson							263,240	51,275
	Grand Agg	24	$2,753	$114 71	784	$222,475	$283 77	$35,214,916	$22,570,714

Statement 26—Continued.

Districts.	Counties.	Material and manufactured articles.	Man'f'ers' tools, implements and machinery.	Agricult'l tools, implements and machinery.	Gold and silver plate and plated ware.	Diamonds and jewelry.	Moneys of bank, banker, broker, etc.	Credits of bank, banker, broker, etc.
1 2 3 4	Cook	$1,543,931	$1,502,721	$62,329	$6,960	$9,719	$44,620	$16,400
5	Boone	14,520	10,703	20,972	....	....	210,478	....
	DeKalb	12,828	24,787	43,647	547	210	32,303	4,015
	Kane	134,363	250,121	36,558	991	4,576	29,980	11,191
	Lake	23,440	43,721	20,172	700	360	900	....
	McHenry	3,127	15,409	44,261	50	190	10,715	27,145
6	Carroll	662	3,266	21,544	58	160	33,329	31,669
	JoDaviess	5,984	7,151	22,760	437	20	58,014	92,103
	Ogle	2,045	5,559	47,772	225	320	28,748	9,856
	Stephenson	20,528	21,857	46,036	80	187	21,464	18,593
	Winnebago	146,156	112,846	38,900	2,865	2,925	54,253	214,664
7	Bureau	371	4,639	40,404	364	69	27,400	7,738
	Henry	14,092	20,054	56,225	53	....	19,404	1,116
	Lee	2,095	6,707	24,872	....	1,025	9,100	3,710
	Putnam	....	550	6,235	....	....	665	130
	Whiteside	19,333	17,369	29,191	....	102	14,275	8,138
8	DuPage	1,625	8,740	30,456	560	385	9,025	500
	Grundy	7,733	11,959	16,972	40	165	4,973	43,261
	Kendall	850	3,988	24,593	26	....	1,888	3,080
	LaSalle	51,406	36,216	72,378	745	841	42,293	62,296
	Will	135,736	147,249	43,235	784	1,495	1,728	10,299
9	Ford	3,755	5,894	25,761	56	65	12,965	2,565
	Iroquois	3,082	11,624	70,531	409	241	43,711	54,558
	Kankakee	8,382	5,466	18,560	520	1,588	7,295	2,740
	Livingston	13,623	5,852	57,519	185	275	20,800	11,474
	Marshall	2,190	2,895	15,906	70	255	2,400	3,360
	Woodford	1,343	3,009	36,454	7	....	24,154	6,821
10	Fulton	7,846	12,398	38,455	100	70	19,954	44,837
	Knox	16,750	21,200	41,779	415	5,267	77,081	49,971
	Peoria	34,479	41,389	41,207	2,215	3,580	314,764	9,856
	Stark	45	1,747	15,232	....	....	10,608	300
11	Hancock	3,744	7,166	31,386	155	218	67,608	45,728
	Henderson	515	1,680	14,970	230	....	30,005	7,445
	McDonough	13,870	7,689	30,477	156	455	114,822	17,308
	Mercer	672	4,504	23,093	66	215	26,259	11,972
	Rock Island	202,025	104,240	14,760	534	1,010	16,749	8,320
	Schuyler	1,169	996	15,756	80	....	15,600	12,767
	Warren	7,065	4,852	22,086	1,692	100	15,249	112,960
12	Adams	102,992	72,818	36,708	2,448	2,645	19,824	30,370
	Brown	621	1,196	11,937	55	....	78,827	3,415
	Calhoun	3,785	3,660	8,800	....	....	6,605	....
	Cass	856	1,893	20,995	35	45	11,703	3,948
	Greene	2,170	2,690	23,818	95	89	55,353	25,283
	Jersey	1,125	5,506	15,404	226	30	13,710	4,965
	Pike	2,972	4,750	25,449	....	....	29,390	47,050
	Scott	218	1,324	14,969	103	10	26,000	....
13	Christian	8,156	6,607	24,676	40	40	58,895	34,770
	Mason	565	1,475	15,239	22	30	15,760	1,123
	Menard	920	3,025	24,620	75	....	8,920	3,840
	Morgan	17,450	1,985	46,068	194	600	67,966	....
	Sangamon	29,406	44,247	41,249	2,485	3,715	96,191	32,348
	Tazewell	12,982	13,089	37,045	504	375	34,751	21,493
14	DeWitt	226	2,563	14,775	22	197	74,669	7,591
	Logan	1,970	4,237	40,317	330	325	13,043	5,978
	Macon	34,355	53,959	32,933	1,260	1,990	15,393	31,519
	McLean	6,309	21,405	52,430	770	1,892	86,496	41,163
	Piatt	1,430	6,774	24,668	36	....	24,142	2,342

Statement 26—Continued.

Districts...	Counties.	Material and manufactured articles.	Man'f'ers' tools, implements and machinery.	Agricult'l tools, implements and machinery.	Gold and silver plate and plated ware.	Diamonds and jewelry.	Moneys of bank, banker, broker, etc,	Credits of bank, banker, broker, etc.
15	Champaign....	$11,774	$12,402	$56,561	$2,081	$2,470	$38,589	$13,269
	Coles	4,472	7,268	21,824	147	265	26,487	20,297
	Douglas........	3,001	4,253	24,002	120	280	6,658	15,474
	Edgar..........	1,968	4,414	27,031	120	195	21,898	12,844
	Vermilion.....	1,698	5,919	34,765	197	1,540	34,430	57,000
16	Clay...........	609	2,690	17,258	27	30	19,530	2,363
	Clark	1,051	3,632	8,911	44	23	5,965	5,074
	Crawford......	1,038	3,546	12,895	....	....	1,090	6,197
	Cumberland...	509	1,880	12,836	12	....	2,605	2,062
	Edwards	393	5,150	14,150	50	139	500	14,812
	Jasper.........	831	1,801	15,566	89	35	11,958	80
	Lawrence......	360	1,484	14,519	31	....	5,420	4,545
	Richland	550	5,274	9,104	14	....	33	22,675
	Wayne.........	90	2,748	15,660	3	5	13,610	9,196
	Wabash........	3,545	4,818	14,336	....	....	10,615	640
17	Effingham.....	1,874	5,029	17,846	70	9,560	....	250
	Fayette........	2,063	7,784	25,258	170	146	18,474	18,262
	Macoupin......	1,520	4,771	25,927	216	141	30,245	8,322
	Montgomery .	3,769	10,980	33,845	107	255	28,063	2,087
	Moultrie.......	927	1,439	11,190	64	....	19,670	10,098
	Shelby.........	2,003	4,005	38,867	122	132	27,741	13,645
18	Bond...........	677	4,597	14,059	32	....	22,999	6,121
	Madison.......	46,284	70,473	56,012	449	590	15,544	12,740
	Monroe........	5,265	4,128	26,290	....	....	209,747	13,435
	St. Clair.......	38,911	79,063	43,437	390	658	75,702	42,045
	Washington...	7,558	4,086	24,650	54	60	17,163	8,294
19	Clinton........	2,192	3,953	19,225	180	355	11,180	650
	Franklin.......	....	1,339	14,072	10	....	2,058	4,438
	Gallatin........	1,085	4,690	10,684	185	10	325	150
	Hamilton.......	450	4,119	12,202	39	284	6,503	6,202
	Hardin	580	3,740	12,265	....	....	800	340
	Jefferson......	3,027	9,367	14,129	46	....	19,679	4,762
	Marion	1,254	2,984	15,857	145	99	20,447	7,739
	Saline..........	198	5,077	12,037	....	56	10,885	11,154
	White..........	928	3,469	16,313	58	20	9,245	10,350
20	Alexander.....	8,929	3,778	5,971	400	232	....	....
	Jackson	1,819	24,738	22,944	181	84	3,477	11,740
	Johnson.......	2,600	7,697	20,909	2	....	1,510	1,625
	Massac	2,913	10,953	17,483	70	114	910	4,654
	Perry..........	1,260	2,647	17,747	60	9	3,410	....
	Pope...........	2,315	2,620	21,112	114	15	15,390	2,147
	Pulaski........	7,021	7,307	5,515	34	133	8,048	232
	Randolph......	14,323	11,729	31,624	249	592	6,508	9,927
	Union..........	4,354	9,415	24,699	88	95	17,645	22,709
	Williamson....	500	7,583	18,848	10	....	18,923	2,460
	Grand agg.	$2,888,335	$3,142,255	$2,705,979	$37,555	$66,693	$3,034,896	$1,689,190

Statement 26—Continued.

Districts.	Counties.	Moneys of other than banker, etc.	Credits of other than banker, etc.	Bonds and stocks.	Shares of capital stock of companies not of this State.	Pawnbrokers' property.	Property of corporations not before enumerated.	Bridge property.
1, 2, 3, 4	Cook	$1,279 057	$83,084	$5,261,550	$3,225	$15,150	$917,495	$100
5	Boone				1,200		400	
	DeKalb	212,115	140,101	3,849			805	
	Kane	179,650	288,564	10,600		50	27,516	
	Lake	54,595	44,313	14,760			1,859	
	McHenry	69,811	153,750	2,370			1,190	
6	Carroll[1]	137,652	82,107				4,629	
	JoDaviess	100,960	85,302	2,080	620		11,495	
	Ogle	219,809	273,879	180	1,523		12,130	
	Stephenson	141,071	267,143		275		112,250	
	Winnebago	87,220	724,461	8,935	20		1,350	
7	Bureau	172,707	232,341	2,715			6,974	
	Henry	1,441	540,743	29,574	25	297	325	
	Lee	33,298	150,511	1,200			1,775	
	Putman	12,730	19,985				254	4,000
	Whiteside	22,292	201,371				4,947	
8	DuPage	25,112	123,450	9,430	2,876		6,465	
	Grundy	69,306	29,912		330		3,600	
	Kendall	69,435	121,596	600			7,050	
	LaSalle	216,154	209,588	400	6,200		42,692	800
	Will	143,135	62,440	5,390	1,100		30,940	1,000
9	Ford	1,600	23,940	2,651	5,000		2,374	
	Iroquois	103,204	147,422	31,331	2,246		10,157	
	Kankakee	13,895	140,615	19,738	294		24,560	
	Livingston	123,381	83,825	6,934	2,550		9,750	
	Marshall	43,842	63,916					2,510
	Woodford	61,348	93,696		225		5,782	
10	Fulton	88,136	348,782	44,933				
	Knox	218,400	247,380	23,260	1,333	25	300	
	Peoria	92,232	136,400	7,050	988	150	29,785	
	Stark	88,856	78,405	250				
11	Hancock	198,257	188,396	4,307			13,323	
	Henderson	42,735	101,170	760				
	McDonough	106,545	297,660	5,373	10,554		4,043	74
	Mercer	59,858	226,647	2,923	22		1,567	
	Rock Island	44,213	50,694	8,275	546		23,315	6,000
	Schuyler	85,155	92,765	335	1,300			
	Warren	63,125	194,613				4,246	20
12	Adams	109,533	149,624	545	5,635	40	272,332	
	Brown	22,368	22,244		101		838	
	Calhoun	12,405	224,218	500				
	Cass	92,430	32,441	450				
	Greene	93,039	90,435	5,240	1,294		3,321	
	Jersey	25,943	6,925	3,337	75		1,400	
	Pike	103,363	122,497				5,307	
	Scott	156,477	100,513					
13	Christian	61,234	32,054	6.679	13,455		17,614	
	Mason	1,133	6,764	863	60		475	
	Menard[2]	61,535	214,850	4.510	350		1,705	
	Morgan	33,867	411,311	2,000	1.500		5,360	
	Sangamon	143;098	114,019	37,725	1,900	615	39,214	
	Tazewell	124,843	136,448	6,705	4,036		19,392	
14	DeWitt	36,977	54,649	1,320	4,804		268	
	Logan	44,538	55,192	250	5,000		7,781	
	Macon	49,330	205,823	2,166			29,900	
	McLean	250,872	472,378	19,104	8,225	3	29,031	
	Piatt	17,338	36,203	8,896	720		2,089	

Statement 26—Continued.

Districts.	Counties.	Moneys of other than banker, etc.	Credits of other than banker, etc.	Bonds and stocks.	Shares of capital stock of companies not of this State.	Pawnbrokers' property.	Property of corporations not before enumerated.	Bridge property.
15	Champaign	$31,572	$78,571	$4,756	$15,922	....	$5,967	....
	Coles	29,803	33,351	12,511	1,015	....	5,896	$800
	Douglas	13,773	62,604	14,845	5,922	$9	1,954	....
	Edgar	36,434	124,467	3,063	518	....	3,704	....
	Vermilion	75,112	132,666	6,738	10,016	....	64,216	....
16	Clay	23,842	36,177	403	5,262	....	1,613	....
	Clark	12,376	12,851	60	35	....	1,890	....
	Crawford	10,533	37,760	1,282	520	....	1,252	....
	Cumberland	2,186	15,623	8,423	....	....	10	....
	Edwards	81,420	37,993	6,011	989	....	320	....
	Jasper	21,265	7,049	3,327	....	....	1,144	....
	Lawrence	8,936	21,195	2,985	893	....	....	....
	Richland	10,001	28,722	1,542	....	....	766	....
	Wayne	13,627	16,194	....	4,592	60	....	....
	Wabash	8,396	16,050	....	....	....	4,621	....
17	Effingham	10,926	24,408	1,845	....	....	1,040	....
	Fayette	72,406	26,659	3,980	2,054	....	1,756	....
	Macoupin	81,472	82,380	16,248	2,911	....	3,552	....
	Montgomery	145,962	52,706	35,534	1,859	....	1,363	....
	Moultrie	11,165	10,992	150	18	....	1,966	....
	Shelby	96,052	54,835	27,730	29,135	....	7,072	....
18	Bond	47,498	51,136	7,324	275	....	3,873	....
	Madison	339,400	87,884	11,085	750	....	74,665	40,045
	Monroe	....	....	1,095	2,566	....	100	....
	St. Clair	334,349	144,712	20,323	1,220	....	33,159	....
	Washington	101,112	46,971	5,174	65	....	866	....
19	Clinton	8,007	112,171	1,600	17	....	100	....
	Franklin	9,569	8,752	....	....	....	....	....
	Gallatin	2,795	495	4,265	....	....	104	....
	Hamilton	21,308	32,094	3,000	....	....	25	....
	Hardin	2,960	6,630	....	....	....	....	....
	Jefferson	10,156	31,149	1,600	....	....	2,450	....
	Marion	62,201	63,274	21,895	1,813	....	11,565	....
	Saline	11,970	27,259	1,385	27,265	....	....	....
	White	11,718	43,113	5,933	15	....	....	....
20	Alexander	2,400	....	....	225	....	11,332	....
	Jackson	5,874	11,242	10,557	607	....	5,625	....
	Johnson	11,074	24,531	7,050	21,000	....	....	....
	Massac	16,102	53,520	120	570	....	11,110	....
	Perry	8,581	1,900	....	....	....	....	....
	Pope	13,958	19,461	2,050	2,410	....	170	....
	Pulaski	4,323	2,163	2,350	8	....	....	....
	Randolph	183,575	16,745	9,586	679	500	6,342	....
	Union	54,687	39,835	13,261	1,200	140	4,997	56
	Williamson	12,650	11,562	....	445	....	20	....
	Grand Agg.	$8,196,180	$10,592,422	$5,888,129	$232,488	$17,039	$2,037,975	$55,405

Statement 26—Continued.

Districts.	Counties.	Property of saloons and eating houses.	Household and office furniture.	Investments in real estate and improvements thereon.	Grain of all kinds.	Shares of stock of State and National banks.	All other property.
1, 2, 3, 4	Cook	$82, 609	$2, 849, 823	$5, 234	$6, 190	$186, 873	$103, 257
5	Boone	680	36, 688	....	8, 456	69, 000	8, 612
	DeKalb	1, 942	128, 864	5, 052	87, 243	17, 000	25, 251
	Kane	10, 224	272, 982	2, 100	9, 860	253, 000	43, 812
	Lake	1, 940	87, 148	1, 065	25	....	21, 415
	McHenry	2, 794	93, 103	1, 850	2, 422	17, 500	26, 157
6	Carroll	870	56, 874	50	13, 798	44, 000	14, 968
	JoDaviess	1, 626	60, 847	1, 015	....	7, 599	6, 444
	Ogle	714	101, 996	2, 068	97, 579	39, 395	33, 047
	Stephenson	2, 997	102, 237	1, 940	16, 801	172, 750	17, 097
	Winnebago	6, 060	196, 035	10, 320	19, 951	....	79, 739
7	Bureau	2, 197	95, 927	1, 067	136, 906	141, 659	27, 487
	Henry	2, 083	147, 425	....	141, 364	226, 458	43, 049
	Lee	1, 718	94, 798	1, 605	41, 146	60, 000	22, 270
	Putnam	60	8, 460	....	25, 670	....	1, 310
	Whiteside	2, 150	104, 733	330	36, 541	91, 680	22, 662
8	DuPage	1, 346	126, 350	3, 905	100	....	6, 572
	Grundy	1, 795	40, 153	1, 863	62, 857	52, 021	28, 203
	Kendall	295	42, 357	775	61, 164	....	13, 300
	LaSalle	7, 834	190, 247	13, 975	255, 090	156, 001	69, 015
	Will	6, 347	145, 117	14, 200	6, 120	147, 287	115, 444
9	Ford	50	44, 760	....	67, 475	....	17, 532
	Iroquois	1, 726	93. 183	10, 249	230, 705	7, 360	38, 046
	Kankakee	2, 102	63, 010	6, 220	5, 047	2, 884	29, 371
	Livingston	1, 655	100, 223	6, 508	319, 573	38, 270	37, 265
	Marshall	2, 570	47, 153	30	46, 426	57, 000	11, 680
	Woodford	1, 164	63, 821	3, 260	93, 867	10, 000	4, 232
10	Fulton	835	117 643	....	43, 476	....	85, 435
	Knox	6, 260	186, 059	3, 020	121, 461	107, 140	53, 709
	Peoria	13, 920	241, 340	6, 595	75, 717	....	205, 223
	Stark	....	31, 335	1, 711	54, 406	....	7, 449
11	Hancock	785	88, 764	3, 749	88, 486	....	20, 949
	Henderson	10	34, 275	1, 025	76, 485	....	3, 269
	McDonough	1, 142	86, 682	....	90, 558	19, 117	17, 295
	Mercer	395	64, 231	215	78, 990	....	27, 117
	Rock Island	5, 540	161, 212	2, 629	6, 822	50, 025	212, 466
	Schuyler	....	34, 172	....	22, 360	....	4, 395
	Warren	382	57, 213	100	60, 835	97, 000	6, 382
12	Adams	8, 118	258, 996	6, 115	35, 067	....	23, 989
	Brown	1, 465	31, 530	20	10, 514	....	2, 714
	Calhoun	145	13, 095	....	23, 575	....	1, 320
	Cass	840	43, 094	1, 895	27, 973	33, 069	5, 360
	Greene	295	54, 690	1, 910	19, 768	75	5, 155
	Jersey	400	39, 196	....	15, 182	500	27, 074
	Pike	16	78, 312	....	33, 941	....	7, 747
	Scott	655	31, 054	20	29, 833	....	275
13	Christian	3, 729	68, 681	1, 770	48, 044	19, 750	17, 528
	Mason	420	34, 447	993	16, 356	....	8, 225
	Menard	1, 200	58, 605	4, 770	61, 750	17, 500	1, 695
	Morgan	7, 275	113, 265	....	76, 624	90, 000	52, 154
	Sangamon	6, 970	249, 142	5, 290	131, 181	423, 094	51, 235
	Tazewell	3, 323	116, 447	1, 055	87, 316	55, 400	21, 633
14	Dewitt	2, 272	41, 141	1, 885	64, 957	8	4, 567
	Logan	2, 130	83, 198	2, 190	150, 493	76, 030	47, 300
	Macon	6, 820	254, 961	6, 120	162, 644	37, 500	17, 374
	McLean	2, 913	200, 927	4, 359	274, 852	180, 000	47, 020
	Piatt	332	52, 196	1, 136	73, 111	4, 100	6, 265

Statement 26—Continued.

Districts.	Counties.	Property of saloons and eating houses.	Household and office furniture.	Investments in real estate and improvements thereon.	Grain of all kinds.	Shares of stock of State and National banks.	All other property.
15	Champaign	$3,095	$156,441	$1,795	$231,274	$38,090	$36,541
	Coles	5,852	78,469	1,885	31,689	136,455	22,892
	Douglas	721	62,268	35	64,788	24,242	30,819
	Edgar	305	61,486	1,578	90,364	76,580	10,531
	Vermilion	10,255	158,016	8,185	130,451	85,010	31,848
16	Clay	185	35,026	2,023	1,330	....	5,916
	Clark	395	32,644	....	4,084	....	2,137
	Crawford	145	34,856	475	6,533	....	1,437
	Cumberland	65	30,805	132	1,291	....	744
	Edwards	....	27,599	15	3,320	....	1,493
	Jasper	195	32,037	64	2,978	....	2,014
	Lawrence	240	31,746	75	6,634	....	4,889
	Richland	1,200	26,510	640	225	....	578
	Wayne	50	29,371	....	1,246	1,702	....
	Wabash	895	37,703	200	5,779	....	8,220
17	Effingham	600	42,175	62	1,901	4,296	....
	Fayette	845	47,459	340	4,208	27,648	7,008
	Macoupin	2,242	81,346	550	9,349	10,794	46,010
	Montgomery	1,662	75,194	2,040	12,066	54,535	13,403
	Moultrie	490	24,113	....	43,125	....	5,114
	Shelby	733	85,039	356	44,512	290	14,092
18	Bond	308	32,581	15	4,032	71	3,421
	Madison	11,903	157,371	2,120	10,294	39,881	110,690
	Monroe	1,108	36,340	30	13,225	8,335	4,634
	St. Clair	4,298	74,385	3,910	7,948	35,000	132,286
	Washington	553	40,666	659	2,477	....	9,186
19	Clinton	890	41,236	1,005	4,302	642	1,716
	Franklin	70	26,917	594	2,056	....	3,228
	Gallatin	145	27,513	....	8,838	10,000	770
	Hamilton	25	23,634	13	2,563	....	290
	Hardin	993	22,303	50	1,240	....	5,840
	Jefferson	1,325	39,928	973	411	....	2,329
	Marion	1,130	59,673	1,040	2,148	71,000	3,666
	Saline	93	40,471	....	6,610	....	2,446
	White	835	38,416	280	14,381	....	2,787
20	Alexander	3,120	72,666	....	3,525	55,000	10,456
	Jackson	3,520	59,093	15	5,060	25,057	6,001
	Johnson	....	45,831	....	4,677	....	4,787
	Massac	1,365	53,274	3,001	2,432	30,000	4,085
	Perry	1,215	44,139	465	997	....	8,189
	Pope	80	42,874	160	10,538	....	12,911
	Pulaski	1,149	25,303	17	778	....	6,295
	Randolph	1,208	59,351	9,502	5,901	800	10,110
	Union	300	62,408	2,078	3,663	4,893	....
	Williamson	820	45,126	25	1,691	92	12,771
	Grand aggregate	$292,758	$10,682,018	$200,345	$4,671,000	$3,748,458	$2,464,166

Statement 26—Continued.

Districts.	Counties.	Total value of unenumerated property.	Total value of personal property.
1, 2, 3, 4	Cook	$24,743,079	$26,682,303
5	Boone	431,604	714,807
	DeKalb	901,165	1,501,165
	Kane	1,967,051	2,736,037
	Lake	401,412	755,390
	McHenry	622,977	1,369,461
6	Carroll	526,482	871,418
	JoDaviess	568,735	975,324
	Ogle	1,003,944	1,639,798
	Stephenson	1,133,214	1,686,700
	Winnebago	2,037,201	2,489,754
7	Bureau	1,060,980	1,717,944
	Henry	1,481,145	2,111,385
	Lee	591,424	1,014,609
	Putnam	88,139	194,214
	Whiteside	735,120	1,212,874
8	DuPage	422,468	700,657
	Grundy	451,112	658,641
	Kendall	394,693	656,404
	LaSalle	1,820,869	2,649,082
	Will	1,299,871	1,893,923
9	Ford	291,014	536,666
	Iroquois	1,041,324	1,677,274
	Kankakee	444,989	679,705
	Livingston	994,370	1,393,232
	Marshall	365,580	580,800
	Woodford	495,949	828,935
10	Fulton	1,024,190	1,479,072
	Knox	1,435,503	2,108,194
	Peoria	1,899,072	2,519,998
	Stark	346,572	531,552
11	Hancock	918,842	1,460,668
	Henderson	350,439	595,090
	McDonough	968,673	1,455,596
	Mercer	617,499	988,335
	Rock Island	1,149,841	1,493,890
	Schuyler	328,660	623,847
	Warren	708,623	998,251
12	Adams	1,516,294	2,084,104
	Brown	241,393	413,466
	Calhoun	344,658	444,942
	Cass	344,017	538,803
	Greene	475,492	801,786
	Jersey	207,447	385,753
	Pike	551,740	901,597
	Scott	415,655	610,317
13	Christian	540,416	890,671
	Mason	152,411	330,942
	Menard	543,105	636,030
	Morgan	1,128,860	1,627,543
	Sangamon	1,843,832	2,593,303
	Tazewell	841,766	1,212,632
14	DeWitt	375,578	572,199
	Logan	660,582	1,056,949
	Macon	1,240,366	1,722,568
	McLean	2,021,924	2,690,498
	Piatt	319,543	516,052

Statement 26—Continued.

Districts.	Counties.	Total value of unenumerated property.	Total value of personal property.
15	Champaign	$935,146	$1,527,898
	Coles	578,540	876,073
	Douglas	397,614	611,964
	Edgar	581,145	916,260
	Vermilion	1,089,797	1,633,414
16	Clay	211,386	397,751
	Clark	130,393	299,266
	Crawford	161,968	336,288
	Cumberland	105,756	241,921
	Edwards	232,189	420,280
	Jasper	138,872	348,710
	Lawrence	131,775	276,384
	Richland	141,740	281,016
	Wayne	149,261	371,263
	Wabash	140,170	238,835
17	Effingham	189,879	348,478
	Fayette	232,117	543,233
	Macoupin	534,646	985,843
	Montgomery	910,387	973,654
	Moultrie	173,403	306,778
	Shelby	556,736	979,144
18	Bond	256,801	426,654
	Madison	1,315,704	1,848,181
	Monroe	379,271	564,680
	St. Clair	1,332,229	1,806,929
	Washington	332,124	533,915
19	Clinton	252,331	420,911
	Franklin	108,804	264,872
	Gallatin	107,719	228,395
	Hamilton	141,178	311,086
	Hardin	92,591	227,535
	Jefferson	188,432	388,400
	Marion	452,241	684,237
	Saline	207,018	379,776
	White	219,614	419,355
20	Alexander	303,013	441,527
	Jackson	295,311	565,518
	Johnson	192,792	417,364
	Massac	264,172	420,051
	Perry	146,462	342,481
	Pope	186,841	429,717
	Pulaski	102,159	202,186
	Randolph	465,897	720,946
	Union	334,671	575,826
	Williamson	184,801	448,041
	Grand agg	$85,214,000	$120,428,916

Statement 26—Continued.

Districts.	Counties.	Real Estate—Lands. Improved Lands. Number of acres.	Improved Lands. Value.	Improved Lands. Average value per acre.	Unimproved Lands. Number of acres.	Unimproved Lands. Value.	Unimproved Lands. Average value per acre.	Total Lands. Number of acres.	Total Lands. Value.	Total Lands. Average value per acre.
1, 2, 3, 4	Cook	351,607	$6,322,336	$17 98	90,875	$5,792,087	$63 74	442,482	$12,114,423	$27 38
5	Boone	177,686	1,905,760	10 73	...	...	...	177,686	1,905,760	10 73
	DeKalb	394,410	4,672,459	11 84	...	...	...	394,410	4,672,459	11 84
	Kane	314,716	4,537,296	14 42	1,624	8,835	5 38	316,340	4,546,131	14 37
	Lake	259,976	3,623,807	13 94	16,911	130,054	7 69	276,887	3,753,861	13 55
	McHenry	380,798	3,509,424	9 22	2,026	10,780	5 32	382,824	3,520,204	9 19
6	Carroll	248,926	2,280,386	9 16	38,237	86,697	2 26	287,163	2,367,083	8 24
	Jo Daviess	242,850	2,071,250	8 53	135,423	436,064	3 22	378,273	2,507,314	6 62
	Ogle	441,314	4,583,708	10 38	37,096	197,054	5 31	478,410	4,780,762	9 99
	Stephenson	341,763	5,103,669	14 93	12,442	131,637	10 59	354,204	5,235,306	14 78
	Winnebago	311,006	4,470,711	14 37	7,963	59,998	7 53	318,970	4,530,709	14 20
7	Bureau	483,449	6,839,060	14 15	63,554	338,965	5 33	547,003	7,178,025	13 12
	Henry	481,055	6,090,967	12 68	33,041	151,536	4 58	514,096	6,242,503	12 14
	Lee	456,972	4,980,039	10 89	2,917	35,531	12 52	459,888	5,015,570	10 91
	Putnam	85,812	1,098,271	12 80	20,220	32,764	1 62	106,033	1,131,035	10 67
	Whiteside	362,476	4,029,505	11 12	70,164	337,210	4 82	432,640	4,366,715	10 09
8	DuPage	158,040	2,660,688	16 83	44,332	460,678	10 39	202,372	3,121,366	15 42
	Grundy	259,648	2,295,264	8 84	6,847	48,437	7 07	266,495	2,343,701	8 79
	Kendall	202,135	2,599,424	12 85	...	...	...	202,135	2,599,424	12 85
	LaSalle	635,917	9,804,507	15 42	74,897	616,985	8 24	710,814	10,421,492	14 66
	Will	503,245	6,365,284	12 65	18,924	169,326	8 95	522,169	6,534,610	12 51
9	Ford	304,524	2,566,545	8 43	65	195	3 00	304,589	2,566,740	8 43
	Iroquois	679,798	6,462,746	9 51	23,479	102,765	4 38	703,277	6,565,511	7 34
	Kankakee	363,026	2,850,057	7 85	56,088	258,379	4 61	419,114	3,108,436	7 41
	Livingston	653,299	6,435,818	9 85	2,481	14,437	5 82	655,780	6,450,255	9 84
	Marshall	194,653	2,705,157	13 89	55,251	218,620	3 95	249,904	2,923,777	11 62
	Woodford	283,156	4,443,107	15 69	53,576	215,890	4 03	336,732	4,658,997	13 84

10	Fulton	342,341	4,080,665	11 92	205,836	654,855	3 18	548,177	4,735,520	8 64
	Knox	435,633	5,009,949	11 50	10,526	56,139	5 34	446,159	5,066,088	11 35
	Peoria	353,011	5,685,401	16 11	30,146	121,483	4 03	383,157	5,806,884	15 16
	Stark	180,822	2,377,046	13 14				180,820	2,377,046	13 14
11	Hancock	418,517	4,710,428	11 02	71,618	309,088	4 32	490,135	5,019,516	10 24
	Henderson	189 855	1,637,350	8 62	58,623	193,580	3 32	248,478	1,830,930	7 41
	McDonough	358,288	4,042,538	11 28				358,248	4,042,538	11 28
	Mercer	319,311	2,985,815	9 34	28,138	60,915	2 16	347,449	3,046,730	8 77
	Rock Island	212,215	2,158,057	16 16	52,042	278,566	5 35	264,255	2,436,623	9 22
	Schuyler	265,788	1,633,537	6 15	9,363	10,932	1 17	275,151	1,644,469	5 98
	Warren	332,509	3,715,643	11 17	6,828	47,265	6 92	339,337	3,762,908	11 09
12	Adams	400,754	5,295,731	13 21	127,591	478,105	3 75	528,345	5,773,836	10 93
	Brown	124,901	1,107,088	8 86	63,596	146,126	2 30	188,497	1,253,214	6 25
	Calhoun	62,387	861,760	13 81	103,068	102,970	1 00	165,455	964,730	5 83
	Cass	172,731	2,290,571	13 26	65,421	162,932	2 49	238,152	2,453,503	10 30
	Greene	313,991	3,069,933	9 78	29,468	62,752	2 13	343,459	3,132,685	9 12
	Jersey	147,042	1,821,503	12 38	84,967	159,709	1 88	232,009	1,981,212	8 54
	Pike	347,862	3,038,608	8 74	161,448	402,018	2 48	509,310	3,440,626	6 75
	Scott	128,605	1,541,367	11 99	29,652	106,190	3 58	158,257	1,647,557	10 41
13	Christian	413,829	4,503,367	10 88	33,570	212,390	6 33	447,399	4,715,757	10 54
	Mason	244,691	2,176,456	8 89	112,712	154,889	1 37	357,403	2,331,345	6 62
	Menard	181,138	2,693,150	14 86	17,678	73,750	4 17	198,816	2,766,900	13 91
	Morgan	321,650	6,306,018	19 61	31,540	275,915	8 75	353,190	6,581,933	18 64
	Sangamon	538,784	8,634,620	16 03	9,550	65.858	6 90	548,334	8,700,478	15 88
	Tazewell	326,807	4,307,200	13 18	82,774	354,400	4 29	409,581	4,661,600	11 38
14	DeWitt	232,124	2,436,923	10 49	19,940	119,771	6 01	252,064	2,556,694	10 14
	Logan	350,943	4,625,243	13 18	36,697	231,764	6 32	387,640	4,857,007	12 53
	Macon	360,034	5,563,475	15 45	5,787	39,779	6 87	365,821	5,603,254	15 32
	McLean	732,464	9,917,830	13 54	562	5,323	9 47	733,026	9,923,153	13 54
	Piatt	273,682	3,103,656	11 34	2,273	14,912	6 56	275,955	3,118,568	11 30
15	Champaign	606,343	6,675,443	11 01	18,169	151,118	8 32	624,512	6,826,561	10 93
	Coles	294,798	3,154,471	10 70	25,490	110,593	4 34	320,288	3,265,064	10 19
	Douglas	260,308	2,755,098	10 58	1,862	10,690	5 74	262,170	2,765,788	10 55
	Edgar	380,933	3,656,238	9 60	11,723	58,575	5 00	392,656	3,714,813	9 46
	Vermilion	553,969	6,704,578	12 10	9,911	84,303	8 51	563,880	6,788,881	12 04
16	Clay	214,052	950,677	4 44	76,304	134,454	1 76	290,356	1,085,131	3 74
	Clark	214,309	870,034	4 06	101,715	184,126	1 81	316,024	1,054,160	3 34
	Crawford	209,780	1,057,963	5 04	62,231	138,950	2 23	272,011	1,196,913	4 40
	Cumberland	176,936	725,104	4 10	42,427	81,040	1 91	219,363	806,144	3 68
	Edwards	111,226	721,083	6 48	28,847	112,110	3 89	140,073	833,193	5 95
	Jasper	236,109	1,012,365	4 29	73,583	156,805	2 13	309,692	1,169,170	3 78
	Lawrence	168,718	780,787	4 63	59,400	116,181	1 96	228,118	896,968	3 93
	Richland	179,260	973,856	5 43	44,003	145,139	3 30	223,263	1,118,995	5 01
	Wayne	289,198	933,969	3 23	157,619	323,234	2 05	446,817	1,257,203	2 81
	Wabash	107,881	838,[illegible]	7 77	29,765	128,373	4 31	137,646	966,462	7 02

Statement 26—Continued.

Districts.	Counties.	Real Estate—Lands. Improved Lands. Number of acres.	Improved Lands. Value.	Improved Lands. Average value per acre.	Unimproved Lands. Number of acres.	Unimproved Lands. Value.	Unimproved Lands. Average value per acre.	Total Lands. Number of acres.	Total Lands. Value.	Total Lands. Average value per acre.
17	Effingham	216,944	$1,061,499	$4 89	77,660	$171,148	$2 20	294,604	$1,232,647	$4 18
	Fayette	318,442	1,519,068	4 77	128,324	291,021	2 27	446,766	1,810,089	4 05
	Macoupin	423,654	4,122,885	9 73	111,719	368,169	3 30	535,373	4,491,054	8 39
	Montgomery	386,032	3,515,977	9 11	56,146	197,597	3 52	442,178	3,713,574	8 40
	Moultrie	214,324	1,913,795	8 93	953	6,672	7 00	215,277	1,920,467	8 93
	Shelby	442,920	3,798,866	8 58	39,423	131,911	3 35	482,343	3,930,777	8 15
18	Bond	207,689	1,634,681	7 87	31,584	96,627	3 06	239,273	1,731,308	7 24
	Madison	363,397	5,465,453	15 04	81,370	462,610	5 68	444,767	5,928,063	13 33
	Monroe	131,823	1,448,920	10 99	105,025	240,470	2 29	236,848	1,689,390	7 13
	St. Clair	311,753	6,206,022	19 91	100,492	797,351	7 93	412,245	7,003,373	16 98
	Washington	250,913	1,943,527	7 74	101,976	213,547	2 09	352,889	2,157,006	6 11
19	Clinton	220,672	1,682,500	7 62	91,613	170,848	1 86	312,285	1,853,348	5 93
	Franklin	158,425	511,659	3 23	95,371	140,547	1 48	253,796	652,206	2 57
	Gallatin	121,154	388,275	3 20	78,940	94,939	1 20	200,094	483,214	2 41
	Hamilton	190,218	544,996	2 86	83,788	157,473	1 89	274,006	702,469	2 56
	Hardin	55,483	306,758	5 53	54,320	115,093	2 10	109,803	421,851	3 84
	Jefferson	231,020	734,982	3 18	127,136	244,364	1 92	358,156	979,346	2 73
	Marion	254,053	1,586,898	6 24	98,962	242,591	2 46	353,015	1,829,489	5 18
	Saline	132,357	643,719	4 86	100,600	173,923	1 73	232,957	817,642	3 48
	White	245,823	791,489	3 22	67,049	92,555	1 38	312,872	884,044	2 82
20	Alexander	35,957	384,931	10 71	86,608	193,885	2 24	122,565	578,816	4 72
	Jackson	170,910	1,049,613	6 14	174,101	294,292	1 69	345,011	1,343,905	3 90
	Johnson	100,146	680,057	6 79	110,745	217,525	1 96	210,891	897,582	4 26
	Massac	78,972	504,901	6 39	68,859	183,103	2 66	147,831	688,004	4 65
	Perry	149,585	1,009,265	6 75	114,798	229,602	2 00	264,383	1,238,867	4 68
	Pope	100,120	320,384	3 20	131,877	207,343	1 57	231,997	527,727	2 27
	Pulaski	76,829	429,042	5 58	53,675	134,205	2 50	130,504	563,247	4 32
	Randolph	220,196	1,775,924	8 07	135,581	279,971	2 06	355,777	2,055,895	5 78
	Union	128,556	894,890	6 96	106,966	166,132	1 55	235,522	1,061,022	3 16
	Williamson	187,315	934,075	4 99	84,043	212,640	2 53	271,358	1,146,715	4 23
	Grand aggregate	28,784,468	$306,252,979	$10 64	5,802,600	$23,221,145	$4 00	34,587,068	$329,474,124	$9 53

Statement 26—Continued.

Districts	Counties.	Real Estate—Town and City Lots: Improved Town and City Lots. Number of lots.	Value.	Average value per lot.	Unimproved Town and City Lots. Number of lots.	Value.	Average value per lot.	Total Town and City Lots. Number of lots.	Value.	Average value per lot.	Total value of personal property, lands and lots.
1, 2, 3, 4	Cook	203,344	$137,666,955	$677 02	515,156	$30,004,389	$58 24	718,500	$167,671,344	$233 36	$206,468,070
5	Boone	2,864	576,128	201 16	7	150	21 43	2,871	576,278	200 72	3,196,845
	DeKalb	6,246	1,578,495	252 72	1,319	32,942	24 97	7,565	1,611,437	213 02	7,785,061
	Kane	12,172	5,676,838	466 38	16,904	762,750	45 12	29,076	6,439,588	221 47	13,721,756
	Lake	4,280	1,819,195	425 05	21,648	671,470	31 01	25,928	2,490,665	96 06	6,999,916
	McHenry	4,407	740,330	168 00	2,260	42,076	18 62	6,667	782,406	117 36	5,672,071
6	Carroll	2,641	545,543	206 64	1,369	27,012	19 73	4,010	572,555	142 78	3,811,056
	Jo Daviess	4,192	461,363	110 05	3,938	35,959	9 12	8,130	497,322	61 10	3,979,960
	Ogle	6,116	727,849	119 01	3,060	35,344	11 55	9,176	763,193	83 17	7,183,753
	Stephenson	7,354	1,797,957	244 49	1,679	29,516	17 58	9,033	1,827,473	202 31	8,749,479
	Winnebago	11,275	4,820,856	427 57	9,955	335,387	33 69	21,230	5,156,243	242 87	12,176,706
7	Bureau	7,334	1,155,048	154 49	2,522	60,089	23 83	9,856	1,215,137	123 28	10,111,106
	Henry	8,111	1,552,408	191 40	1,487	27,144	18 25	9,598	1,579,552	164 57	9,933,440
	Lee	5,851	1,274,215	217 77	221	4,577	20 75	6,072	1,278,792	210 60	7,308,971
	Putnam	944	62,900	66 63	301	1,715	5 70	1,245	64,615	51 90	1,389,864
	Whiteside	4,338	1,673,999	385 89	2,559	66,347	25 92	6,897	1,740,346	252 33	7,319,935
8	DuPage	4,673	1,037,978	222 12	18,835	375,321	19 92	23,508	1,413,299	60 12	5,235,322
	Grundy	3,975	587,127	147 71	2,971	31,963	10 75	6,946	619,090	89 13	3,621,432
	Kendall	2,724	270,789	99 41	....	....	....	2,724	270,789	99 41	3,526,617
	LaSalle	14,114	3,274,544	232 00	14,337	308,014	21 48	28,451	3,582,558	125 92	16,653,132
	Will	17,415	3,434,470	197 21	4,592	51,614	11 24	22,007	3,486,084	158 41	11,914,617
9	Ford	2,659	444,069	167 00	2,617	38,171	14 58	5,276	482,240	91 43	3,585,646
	Iroquois	7,162	766,833	107 07	3,527	50,872	14 42	10,689	817,705	76 49	9,060,490
	Kankakee	5,341	841,603	157 57	6,100	98,397	16 13	11,441	940,000	82 16	4,728,141
	Livingston	5,775	913,582	158 19	5,536	73,959	13 36	11,311	987,541	87 32	8,831,028
	Marshall	3,160	429,170	135 81	1,770	38,697	21 86	4,930	467,867	94 90	3,972,444
	Woodford	4,557	588,742	129 20	2,634	27,932	10 60	7,191	616,674	85 75	6,104,606

Statement 26—Continued.

Districts	Counties.	Real Estate—Town and City Lots.									
		Improved Town and City Lots.			Unimproved Town and City Lots.			Total Town and City Lots.			Total value of personal property, lands and lots.
		Number of lots.	Value.	Average value per lot.	Number of lot.	Value.	Average value per lot.	Number of lots.	Value.	Average value per lot.	
10	Fulton	8,243	$1,307,686	$158 64	2,036	$25,637	$12 59	10,279	$1,333,323	$129 71	$7,547,915
	Knox	11,182	2,520,045	225 36	2,600	101,004	38 84	13,782	2,621,049	190 17	9,795,331
	Peoria	10,787	7,064,389	654 87	12,199	967,592	77 51	22,986	8,031,981	349 43	16,358,863
	Stark	2,052	293,152	142 86	62	335	5 40	2,114	293,487	138 83	3,205,085
11	Hancock	8,691	888,285	102 21	1,609	12,680	7 88	10,300	900,965	87 47	7,381,149
	Henderson	1,209	148,498	122 83	4,353	25,800	5 92	5,562	174,298	31 34	2,600,318
	McDonough	6,402	958,827	149 77				6,402	958,827	149 77	6,456,961
	Mercer	5,508	409,554	74 36	1,572	9,622	6 12	7,080	419,176	59 21	4,454,241
	Rock Island	9,339	3,204,879	343 17	4,001	188,465	47 05	13,340	3,393,344	254 37	7,323,857
	Schuyler	1,783	231,542	129 86	190	1,150	6 05	1,973	232,692	117 94	2,501,008
	Warren	4,804	796,405	165 78	148	3,995	27 00	4,952	800,400	169 70	5,561,559
12	Adams	9,488	4,564,797	481 11	2,903	166,506	57 36	12,391	4,731,303	381 83	12,589,243
	Brown	1,035	191,035	184 57	623	10,061	16 15	1,658	201,096	121 29	1,867,776
	Calhoun	374	37,250	99 60				374	37,250	99 60	1,446,922
	Cass	2,475	613,380	247 83	3,219	76,896	23 88	5,694	690,276	121 23	3,682,582
	Greene	3,327	611,390	183 77	1,157	23,369	20 19	4,484	634,759	141 56	4,569,230
	Jersey	2,658	512,563	192 82	2,035	23,743	11 67	4,693	536,306	114 28	2,903,271
	Pike	3,587	415,714	115 88	2,116	24,656	11 65	5,703	440,370	77 22	4,782,593
	Scott	1,088	225,005	206 80	1,185	15,311	12 92	2,273	240,316	105 73	2,498,190
13	Christian	6,381	1,001,184	156 90	2,607	44,120	16 92	8,988	1,045,304	116 30	6,651,732
	Mason	3,010	400,011	132 92	1,737	32,749	18 85	4,747	432,760	91 15	3,095,047
	Menard	2,695	500,210	185 60	225	3,400	15 11	2,920	503,610	172 47	4,106,540
	Morgan	4,302	2,692,259	625 81	2,261	135,660	60 00	6,563	2,827,919	430 89	11,037,395
	Sangamon	13,419	4,963,868	369 91	8,187	491,659	60 05	21,606	5,455,527	252 50	16,749,308
	Tazewell	4,764	784,490	164 67	4,415	76,439	17 31	9,179	860,929	93 79	6,735,161
14	DeWitt	4,010	410,645	102 41	525	9,853	18 77	4,535	420,498	92 72	3,549,391
	Logan	5,541	830,566	149 89	2,806	52,781	18 81	8,347	883,347	105 83	6,797,303
	Macon	8,051	2,644,333	328 45	4,417	144,418	32 69	12,468	2,788,751	223 68	10,114,573
	McLean	9,804	3,405,950	347 40	5,303	138,905	26 19	15,107	3,544,855	234 65	16,158,506
	Piatt	4,849	421,440	86 91	657	8,796	13 39	5,506	430,236	78 14	4,064,856

15	Champaign	6,371	1,476,055	231 68	4,902	135,861	27 72	11,273	1,611,916	142 99	9,966,375
	Coles	4,419	947,838	214 49	3,167	75,387	23 80	7,586	1,023,225	134 88	5,164,362
	Douglas	3,965	494,730	124 77	150	1,883	12 55	4,115	496,613	120 68	3,874,395
	Edgar	4,058	657,451	162 01	2,040	41,946	20 56	6,098	699,397	114 69	5,330,470
	Vermilion	7,372	2,364,319	320 72	5,776	143,804	24 90	13,148	2,508,123	190 76	10,930,418
16	Clay	2,181	213,936	98 09	869	4,608	5 30	3,050	218,544	71 65	1,701,426
	Clark	2,112	226,447	107 22	1,665	21,667	13 01	3,777	248,114	65 69	1,601,540
	Crawford	2,040	202,213	99 12	784	4,573	5 83	2,824	206,786	73 23	1,749,987
	Cumberland	1,200	90,383	75 32	951	8,842	9 30	2,151	99,225	46 13	1,137,290
	Edwards	1,137	150,299	132 19	1,028	15,809	15 38	2,165	166,108	76 72	1,419,581
	Jasper	1,122	103,188	91 97	1,141	13,953	12 24	2,263	117,141	51 76	1,635,021
	Lawrence	1,221	116,868	95 71	1,246	8,183	6 57	2,467	125,051	50 69	1,298,403
	Richland	1,438	203,207	141 31	1,225	19,069	55 57	2,663	222,276	83 47	1,622,287
	Wayne	1,467	165,642	112 91	1,276	12,510	9 80	2,743	178,152	64 95	1,806,618
	Wabash	1,417	264,354	186 56	792	25,240	31 87	2,209	289,594	131 10	1,494,891
17	Effingham	3,493	413,011	118 24	1,499	25,832	17 23	4,992	438,843	87 89	2,019,968
	Fayette	3,591	327,459	91 19	2,500	36,895	14 76	6,091	364,354	59 81	2,747,676
	Macoupin	7,209	925,579	128 39	3,061	34,941	11 41	10,270	960,520	93 53	6,437,417
	Montgonery	6,030	692,126	114 78	3,380	37,813	11 19	9,410	729,939	77 57	5,417,167
	Moultrie	3,082	189,823	61 59	300	1,869	6 23	3,382	191,692	56 68	2,418,937
	Shelby	4,818	702,530	145 81	1,620	23,208	14 33	6,438	725,738	112 73	5,635,659
18	Bond	1,908	251,324	131 72	1,305	11,838	9 07	3,213	263,162	81 92	2,421,124
	Madison	10,622	2,714,113	255 52	12,790	456,825	35 72	23,412	3,170,938	135 44	10,947,182
	Monroe	984	259,995	264 22	972	17,500	18 00	1,956	277,495	141 87	2,531,565
	St. Clair	9,683	2,801,549	289 33	28,542	832,822	29 18	38,225	3,634,371	95 08	12,444,673
	Washington	2,108	249,727	118 46	3,159	17,758	5 62	5,267	267,485	50 78	2,958,474
19	Clinton	1,994	314,041	157 49	2,215	20,110	9 07	4,209	334,151	79 39	2,608,110
	Franklin	596	83,666	139 37	823	9,218	11 20	1,419	92,284	65 03	1,009,362
	Gallatin	1,263	137,421	108 81	1,587	13,420	8 46	2,850	150,841	52 96	862,450
	Hamilton	755	134,788	178 53	1,099	19,818	18 03	1,854	154,606	83 39	1,168,161
	Hardin	271	71,875	265 22	235	3,986	16 96	506	75,861	149 92	725,247
	Jefferson	2,154	205,145	95 24	2,676	39,945	14 93	4,830	245,090	50 75	1,612,836
	Marion	3,844	809,157	210 49	3,469	43,369	12 50	7,313	852,526	116 58	3,366,252
	Saline	1,375	178,418	129 76	1,091	13,786	12 63	2,466	192,204	77 95	1,380,622
	White	1,667	129,141	77 47	1,805	11,512	6 38	3,472	140,653	40 51	1,444,052
20	Alexander	3,196	1,139,364	356 49	4,278	164,665	38 49	7,474	1,304,029	174 48	2,324,372
	Jackson	3,758	528,820	140 72	3,040	54,827	18 04	6,798	583,647	85 86	2,493,070
	Johnson	656	120,272	183 34	988	18,944	19 17	1,644	139,216	84 68	1,454,162
	Massac	1,676	400,922	239 22	762	22,302	29 27	2,438	423,224	173 59	1,531,279
	Perry	1,907	289,806	151 97	1,684	25,725	15 27	3,591	315,531	87 87	1,896,879
	Pope	545	109,000	200 00	435	7,834	18 01	980	116,834	119 22	1,074,278
	Pulaski	1,162	147,500	126 94	1,857	26,515	14 28	3,019	174,015	57 64	939,448
	Randolph	3,651	477,310	130 73	4,029	39,551	9 82	7,680	516,861	67 30	3,293,702
	Union	1,545	249,469	161 47	1,205	13,546	11 24	2,750	263,015	95 65	1,899,863
	Williamson	1,593	170,882	107 27	1,118	11,172	9 90	2,711	182,054	67 15	1,776,810
	Grand aggregate	652,538	$240,678,901	$368 61	842,988	$38,628,290	$45 79	$1,495,526	$279,307,191	$186 65	$729,210,231

Statement 26—Continued.

Districts	Counties.	Railroad property assessed in counties. Class C—Personal property: Value.	Class D—Lands: Number of acres.	Class D—Lands: Value.	Class D—Lands: Av. val. per acre.	Class D—Lots: Number of lots.	Class D—Lots: Value.	Class D—Lots: Av. val. per lot.	Total value of railroad property assessed in county.	Total value of all property assessed in county.
1, 2, 3, 4	Cook	$201,635	478	$58,344	$122 06	848	$802,643	$946 51	$1,062,622	$207,530,692
5	Boone	960	145	925	6 38				1,885	3,198,730
	DeKalb	1,218					2,205		3,423	7,788,484
	Kane	123,434	88	2,747	31 32	13	1,245	95 77	127,426	13,849,182
	Lake	3,035	455	8,035	17 66	90	5,900	65 55	16,970	7,016,886
	McHenry	3,210	54	536	9 93				3,746	5,675,817
6	Carroll	4,740				2	150	75 00	4,890	3,815,946
	Jo Daviess	770	189	1,250	6 61	3	30	10 00	2,050	3,982,010
	Ogle	1,600		903			13		2,516	7,186,269
	Stephenson	3,615	92	1,176	12 78				4,791	8,754,270
	Winnebago	1,947	104	1,583	15 22	26	5,640	216 86	9,170	12,185,876
7	Bureau	4,189	95	635	6 68	3	205	68 33	5,029	10,116,135
	Henry	2,601	55	2,911	52 93	10	484	48 40	5,996	9,939,436
	Lee	2,290	21	450	21 43				2,740	7,311,711
	Putnam	50							50	1,389,914
	Whiteside	1,124	590	106,150	179,92	4	65	16 25	107,339	7,427,274
8	DuPage	1,860	811	12,215	15 06	1	40	40 00	14,115	5,249,437
	Grundy	2,864							2,864	3,624,296
	Kendall	323							332	3,526,940
	LaSalle	6,790	49	1,240	25 31				8,030	16,661,162
	Will	22,147	439	25,131	57 25	40	3,410	85 25	50,688	11,965,305
9	Ford	570	7	70	10 00	9	160	18 00	800	3,586,446
	Iroquois	783	5	30	6 00				83	9,061,303
	Kankakee	1,543	325	3,481	9 04		2,302		7,326	4,735,467
	Livingston	1,981	55	451	8 20	25	1,260	50 40	3,692	8,834,720
	Marshall		119	900	7 56				900	3,973,344
	Woodford	667	11	227	20 64	13	595	45 77	1,489	6,106,095

10	Fulton	3,070	46	460	10 00				3,530	7,551,445
	Knox	24,739	41	4,700	114 63				29,439	9,824,770
	Peoria	8,652	28	286	10 21	51	6,050	118 63	14,988	16,373,851
	Stark	585				4	50	12 50	635	3,205,720
11	Hancock	1,033							1,033	7,382,182
	Henderson	720							720	2,601,038
	McDonough	1,402	10	135	13 50	3	5	1 66	1,542	6,458,503
	Mercer	584							584	4,454,825
	Rock Island	4,178		480			1,660		6,318	7,330,175
	Schuyler	712	304	303	1 00				1,015	2,502,023
	Warren	1,024				6	60	10 00	1,084	5,562,643
12	Adams	4,555	56	750	13 39	14	10,135	723 93	15,440	12,604,683
	Brown	120							129	1,867,896
	Calhoun									1,446,922
	Cass	3,442							3,442	3,686,024
	Greene	2,484							2,484	4,571,714
	Jersey	250	6	500	83 33	10	60	6 00	810	2,904,081
	Pike	1,361	190	510	2 68				1,871	4,784,464
	Scott									2,498,190
13	Christian	7,709	11	220	20 00	13	720	55 33	8,649	6,660,381
	Mason	550		360			1,000		1,910	3,096,957
	Menard	190							190	4,106,730
	Morgan	670	10	120	12 00	3	300	100 00	1,090	11,038,485
	Sangamon	12,145				77	5,555	72 14	17,700	16,767,008
	Tazewell	799	97	1,512	15 59		115		2,426	6,737,587
14	DeWitt	1,927	116	1,140	9 83	17	10 75	63 24	4,142	3,553,533
	Logan	545							545	6,797,848
	Macon	3,720				5	125	25 00	3,845	10,118,418
	McLean	81,695							81,695	16,240,201
	Piatt									4,064,856
15	Champaign	4,273	14	550	38 95	6	250	41 67	5,073	9,971,448
	Coles	44,290	63	2,135	33 89	2	315	157 50	46,740	5,211,102
	Douglas	4,575							4,575	3,878,970
	Edgar	743		100		14	560	40 00	1,403	5,331,873
	Vermilion	13,163	10	185	19 01	3	280	93 33	13,628	10,944,046
16	Clay	805							805	1,702,231
	Clark	123	5	70	14 00	9	401	44 56	594	1,602,134
	Crawford	77							77	1,740,064
	Cumberland									1,147,290
	Edwards	90							90	1,419,671
	Jasper									1,635,021
	Lawrence	148	40	88	2 20				236	1,298,639
	Richland	260	45	560	12 44	2	250	125 00	1,070	1,623,357
	Wayne	125							125	1,806,743
	Wabash	177							177	1,495,068

Statement 26—Concluded.

Districts.	Counties.	Class C—Personal Property	Class D—Lands.			Class D—Lots.			Total value of railroad property assessed in county.	Total value of all property assessed in county.
		Value.	Number of acres.	Value.	Av. val. per acre.	Number of lots.	Value.	Av. val. per lot.		
17	Effingham	$3,855							$3,855	$2,023,823
	Fayette	90				1	$250	$250 00	340	2,748,016
	Macoupin	906	89	$920	$10 33	5	587	117 40	2,413	6,439,830
	Montgomery	580							580	5,417,747
	Moultrie	295		20		1	75	75 00	390	2,419,327
	Shelby	5,975							5,975	5,641,634
18	Bond	135	32	320	10 00	1	10	10 00	465	2,421,589
	Madison	1,447	44	875	19 88	1	50	50 00	2,372	10,949,554
	Monroe		6	200	33 33				200	2,531,765
	St. Clair	26,840	1,657	189,529	114 38	483	11,205	23 20	227,574	12,672,247
	Washington	1,000	6	35	5 83	8	165	20 63	1,200	2,959,674
19	Clinton	615		2,016					2,631	2,610,741
	Franklin									1,009,362
	Gallatin	2,900				50	2,795	55 90	5,695	868,145
	Hamilton	385							385	1,168,546
	Hardin									725,247
	Jefferson	17	86	568	6 10	52	2,159	41 52	2,744	1,615,580
	Marion	240	2	877	438 50				1,117	3,367,369
	Saline	1,590							1,590	1,391,212
	White	1,640							1,640	1,445,692
20	Alexander									2,324,372
	Jackson	4,425					3,137		7,562	2,500,632
	Johnson									1,454,162
	Massac									1,531,279
	Perry	940	58	600	10 51	2	6	3 00	1,546	1,898,425
	Pope									1,074,278
	Pulaski	795							795	940,243
	Randolph	125		240					365	3,294,067
	Union									1,899,863
	Williamson	300							300	1,777,110
	Grand Aggregate	$688,751	7,259	$440,754	$60 72	1,930	$875,752	$453 76	$2,005,268	$731,215,488

No 27.

Showing the rates per cent. of addition to or deduction from the assessed value of each class of property in each county in the State, for the year 1896, as determined by the State Board of Equalization.

Counties.	Personal Property.		Lands.		Lots.	
	Add.	Ded.	Add.	Ded.	Add.	Ded.
Adams				18		10
Alexander						
Bond		2		3		
Boone		12		3		9
Brown				4		
Bureau		20		19		19
Calhoun				21		
Carroll		3		4		4
Cass	10			28		
Champaign		12		11		12
Christian				5		20
Clark	25		82			
Clay		14		15		
Clinton	10		16			
Coles		11		12		11
Cook	27		35		20	
Crawford	3		4			
Cumberland	20		19			
DeKalb		13		9		12
DeWitt		3		4		3
Douglas		5		3		5
DuPage				4		3
Edgar		3		1		2
Edwards		14		15		14
Effingham	13		13		14	
Fayette			5			
Ford		14		15		14
Franklin	15		16			10
Fulton	3		3		2	
Gallatin	20		95			
Greene	15			2		
Grundy			2			8
Hamilton	10		33			15
Hancock		8		9		
Hardin		25		24		25
Henderson		16		2		
Henry		20		21		21
Iroquois		13		13		13
Jackson						
Jasper	10		6			
Jefferson	10		23		5	
Jersey	15		16			
Jo Daviess		13		12		12
Johnson						
Kane		11		11		10
Kankakee		5		6		6
Kendall		10		15		18
Knox		7		7		8
Lake		14		10		6
LaSalle		18		19		7
Lawrence	28		29			

Statement 27—Concluded.

Counties.	Personal Property.		Lands.		Lots.	
	Add.	Ded.	Add.	Ded.	Add.	Ded.
Lee	.....	18	.....	18	.....	19
Livingston	.....	7	.....	8	.....	7
Logan	.....	.....	.....	5	.....	32
Macon	.....	.....	.....	15	.....	27
Macoupin	22	.....	22	.....	.....	5
Madison	.....	.....	.....	10	.....	.....
Marion	.....	1	19	.....	.....	.....
Marshall	.....	10	.....	10	.....	10
Mason	.....	.....	.....	.....	.....	.....
Massac	5	.....	.....	.....	.....	.....
McDonough	.....	9	.....	9	.....	.....
McHenry	.....	26	.....	12	.....	20
McLean	.....	.....	.....	.....	.....	20
Menard	.....	25	.....	25	.....	20
Mercer	.....	8	8	.....	.....	.....
Monroe	.....	.....	.....	2	.....	.....
Montgomery	5	.....	5	.....	.....	.....
Morgan	.....	50	.....	25	.....	50
Moultrie	6	.....	4	.....	.....	.....
Ogle	.....	4	.....	2	.....	2
Peoria	.....	18	.....	17	.....	18
Perry	.....	.....	.....	.....	.....	.....
Piatt	.....	.....	.....	9	.....	28
Pike	15	.....	8	.....	.....	.....
Pope	.....	.....	.....	.....	.....	.....
Pulaski	.....	.....	.....	.....	.....	.....
Putnam	.....	10	.....	11	.....	10
Randolph	10	.....	10	.....	.....	.....
Richland	.....	3	.....	2	.....	.....
Rock Island	.....	9	.....	9	.....	30
Saline	3	.....	3	.....	.....	10
Sangamon	.....	20	.....	20	.....	20
Schuyler	.....	2	13	.....	5	.....
Scott	.....	.....	.....	15	.....	.....
Shelby	.....	8	.....	9	.....	8
Stark	.....	6	.....	7	.....	6
St. Clair	.....	.....	.....	21	5	.....
Stephenson	.....	20	.....	21	.....	20
Tazewell	.....	20	.....	.....	.....	.....
Union	10	.....	15	.....	.....	.....
Vermilion	.....	11	.....	12	.....	12
Wabash	.....	26	.....	27	.....	10
Warren	.....	.....	.....	5	.....	.....
Washington	13	.....	13	.....	.....	.....
Wayne	7	.....	7	.....	.....	.....
White	10	.....	51	.....	40	.....
Whiteside	.....	17	.....	16	.....	16
Will	.....	1	.....	3	.....	.....
Williamson	4	.....	3	.....	.....	.....
Winnebago	.....	18	.....	19	.....	19
Woodford	.....	10	.....	10	.....	10

No. 28.

Statement showing the proportion of the Total Equalized Assessments of Taxable property in the various Counties for the years ending 1884 to 1895, inclusive, assessed on Real and Personal Property respectively.

County.	1884.		1885.		1886.		1887.		1888.		1889.		1890.		1891.		1892.		1893.		1894.		1895.	
	Per cent. of real property......	Per cent. of personal property	Per cent. of real property......	Per cent. of personal property	Per cent. of real property......	Per cent. of personal property	Per cent. of real property......	Per cent. of personal property	Per cent. of real property......	Per cent. of personal property	Per cent. of real property......	Per cent. of personal property	Per cent. of real property......	Per cent. of personal property	Per cent. of real property......	Per cent. of personal property	Per cent. of real property......	Per cent. of personal property	Per cent. of real property......	Per cent. of personal property	Per cent. of real property......	Per cent. of personal property	Per cent. of real property......	Per cent. of personal property
Adams	78.56	21.44	77.88	22.12	79.97	20.03	80.42	19.58	80.99	19.01	78.49	21.51	79.17	20.83	81.03	18.97	80.48	19.52	80.52	19.48	81.34	18.66	83.02	16.98
Alexander	77.16	22.84	84.95	15.05	83.12	16.88	77.69	22.31	76.89	23.11	79.98	20.02	80.60	19.40	82.45	17.55	80.65	19.35	80.84	19.16	80.61	19.39	79.37	20.63
Bond	81.20	18.80	82.03	17.97	81.91	18.29	81.48	18.52	81.74	18.26	80.90	19.10	81.14	18.86	79.45	20.55	80.48	19.52	80.48	19.52	79.85	20.15	80.63	19.37
Boone	75.23	24.77	72.90	27.10	73.45	26.55	73.65	26.35	74.64	25.36	77.19	22.81	77.49	22.51	75.78	24.22	76.02	23.98	76.04	23.96	75.76	24.24	81.99	18.01
Brown	71.04	28.96	70.67	29.33	71.13	28.87	73.56	26.44	73.36	26.64	72.78	27.22	74.09	25.91	76.11	23.89	74.25	25.75	74.33	25.67	74.55	25.45	77.18	22.82
Bureau	81.78	18.22	80.95	19.05	82.08	17.92	80.59	19.41	81.15	18.85	80.20	19.80	80.21	19.79	79.47	20.53	80.84	19.16	79.87	20.13	80.32	19.68	81.92	18.08
Calhoun	58.86	41.14	61.98	38.02	63.72	36.28	62.93	37.07	70.76	29.24	66.30	33.70	69.70	30.30	76.55	23.45	70.12	29.88	70.14	29.86	64.17	35.83	71.23	28.77
Carroll	78.72	21.28	76.04	23.96	73.57	26.43	79.20	20.80	76.52	23.48	75.71	24.29	75.37	24.63	72.53	27.47	76.72	23.28	76.68	23.32	75.46	24.54	75.97	24.03
Cass	80.65	19.35	82.24	17.76	83.88	16.12	83.74	16.26	82.24	17.76	81.95	18.05	83.17	16.83	83.39	16.61	81.74	18.26	81.55	18.45	82.02	17.98	84.12	15.88
Champaign	81.67	18.33	82.11	17.89	81.49	18.51	80.99	19.01	79.42	20.58	80.28	19.72	81.56	18.44	79.63	20.37	80.45	19.55	80.20	19.80	81.43	18.57	83.52	16.48
Christian	81.39	18.61	82.00	18.00	81.82	18.18	80.54	19.46	82.15	17.85	80.85	19.15	80.54	19.46	80.15	19.85	82.06	17.94	82.11	17.89	82.35	17.65	84.48	15.52
Clark	78.55	21.45	79.11	20.89	80.71	19.29	75.55	24.45	76.67	23.33	80.86	19.14	80.79	19.21	79.17	20.83	80.34	19.66	80.31	19.69	80.74	19.26	85.38	14.62
Clay	72.57	27.43	70.87	29.13	72.01	27.99	74.83	25.17	76.01	23.99	74.55	25.45	73.28	26.72	70.64	29.36	70.91	29.09	71.11	28.89	72.76	27.24	75.93	24.07
Clinton	79.37	20.63	79.81	20.19	80.77	19.23	80.96	19.04	80.21	19.79	81.26	18.74	81.60	18.40	81.73	18.27	81.44	18.56	81.32	18,68	80.62	19.38	84.43	15.57
Coles	75.74	24.26	76.44	23.56	71.31	28.69	72.94	27.06	75.31	24.69	71.79	28.21	74.03	25.97	74.53	25.47	71.91	28.09	72.01	27.99	76.37	23.63	79.79	20.21
Crawford	80.76	19.24	80.75	19.25	81.51	18.49	80.81	19.19	85.99	14.01	80.62	19.38	82.53	17.47	84.91	15.09	82.85	17.15	83.56	16.44	85.29	14.71	79.46	20.54
Cumberland	74.65	25.35	77.32	22.68	75.80	24.20	75.99	24.01	77.63	22.37	75.81	24.19	77.36	22.64	75.82	24.18	71.92	28.08	72.03	27.97	75.26	24.74	77.82	22.18
Cook	74.47	25.53	73.64	26.36	75.62	24.38	73.76	26.24	74.19	25.81	73.73	26.27	74.38	25.62	76.83	23.17	93.71	26.29	73.02	26.98	72.94	27.06	78.21	21.79
DeKalb	74.55	25.45	77.23	22.77	77.03	22.97	77.41	22.59	78.81	21.19	78.49	21.51	78.90	21.10	78.66	21.34	79.09	20.91	79.10	20.90	80.01	19.99	84.47	15.53
DeWitt	78.10	21.90	80.08	19.92	80.96	19.04	79.79	20.21	80.43	19.57	79.34	20.66	79.50	20.50	77.10	22.90	79.09	20.91	70.93	29.07	80.29	19.71	81.31	18.69
Douglas	76.39	23.61	78.55	21.45	78.47	21.53	77.54	22.46	77.18	22.82	77.55	22.45	78.71	21.29	77.01	22.99	75.86	24.14	76.03	23.97	80.58	19.42	81.16	18.84
DuPage	83.23	16.77	82.91	17.09	84.23	15.77	83.85	16.15	84.68	15.32	84.79	15.21	84.62	15.38	84.68	15.32	80.77	19.23	80.87	19.13	85.42	14.58	87.41	12.59
Edgar	79.42	20.58	80.69	19.31	80.11	19.89	79.49	20.51	79.22	20.78	81.09	18.91	78.87	21.13	78.34	21.66	78.34	21.66	78.31	21.69	79.31	20.69	80.57	19.43
Edwards	68.88	31.12	68.53	31.47	69.65	30.35	70.44	29.56	73.03	26.97	71.30	28.70	72.34	27.66	74.15	25.85	72.58	27.42	72.61	27.39	68.42	31.58	69.62	30.38
Effingham	73.72	26.28	77.36	22.64	78.90	21.10	78.92	21.08	78.89	21.11	81.73	18.27	81.19	18.81	81.94	18.06	82.84	17.16	82.85	17.15	83.05	16.95	83.25	16.75
Fayette	70.91	29.09	74.95	25.05	76.65	23.35	75.97	24.03	79.52	20.48	76.59	23.41	80.97	19.03	76.80	23.20	77.20	22.80	77.22	22.78	75.51	24.49	79.68	20.32
Ford	79.61	20.39	79.50	20.50	79.65	20.35	80.05	19.95	80.61	19.39	81.39	18.61	81.71	18.29	80.69	19.31	81.24	18.76	81.31	18.69	82.19	17.81	84.10	15.90
Franklin	70.94	29.06	70.31	29.69	73.21	26.79	75.79	24.21	73.01	26.99	73.76	26.24	74.19	25.81	71.23	28.77	67.62	32.38	66.47	33.53	71.03	28.97	74.86	25.14
Fulton	76.00	24.00	77.29	22.71	77.53	22.47	77.61	22.39	78.18	21.82	78.34	21.66	75.23	24.77	74.40	25.60	74.17	25.83	74.15	25.85	76.12	23.88	78.94	21.06

Statement 28—Concluded.

County.	1884. Per cent of real property	1884. Per cent. of personal property	1885. Per cent. of real property	1885. Per cent. of personal property	1886. Per cent. of real property	1886. Per cent. of personal property	1887. Per cent. of real property	1887. Per cent. of personal property	1888. Per cent. of real property	1888. Per cent. of personal property	1889. Per cent. of real property	1889. Per cent. of personal property
Gallatin	67.43	32.57	68.93	31.07	70.48	29.52	71.27	28.73	71.17	28.83	72.77	27.23
Greene	80.14	19.86	80.84	19.16	81.13	18.87	81.32	18.68	80.97	19.03	80.04	19.96
Grundy	82.39	17.61	80.98	19.02	82.32	17.68	82.47	17.53	82.44	17.56	81.32	18.68
Hamilton	68.72	31.28	68.11	31.89	75.58	24.42	77.15	22.85	72.01	27.99	72.38	27.62
Hancock	76.66	23.31	78.53	21.47	79.96	20.04	77.58	22.42	80.95	19.05	77.92	22.08
Hardin	68.35	31.65	68.89	31.11	74.84	25.16	70.77	29.23	67.97	32.03	69.20	30.80
Henderson	75.58	24.42	75.39	24.61	76.71	23.29	78.22	21.78	78.38	21.62	79.48	20.52
Henry	76.91	23.09	77.45	22.55	79.27	20.73	79.64	20.36	80.89	19.11	80.57	19.43
Iroquois	78.20	21.80	77.60	22.40	79.28	20.72	78.63	21.37	78.54	21.46	76.91	23.09
Jackson	74.76	25.24	75.32	24.68	73.38	26.62	79.49	20.51	77.09	22.91	80.01	19.99
Jasper	72.22	27.78	78.59	21.41	77.84	22.16	74.04	25.96	76.71	23.29	81.69	18.31
Jefferson	68.88	31.12	70.68	29.32	76.31	23.69	75.89	24.11	73.49	26.51	74.80	25.20
Jersey	80.16	19.84	81.39	18.61	83.99	16.01	85.57	14.43	84.20	15.80	84.29	15.71
Jo Daviess	68.84	31.16	69.18	30.82	67.24	32.76	69.83	30.17	73.07	26.93	74.68	25.32
Johnson	68.02	31.98	70.98	29.02	69.67	30.33	66.39	33.61	65.72	34.28	74.33	25.67
Kane	74.55	25.45	74.85	25.15	76.21	23.79	77.08	22.92	77.64	22.36	78.47	21.53
Kankakee	83.54	16.46	82.96	17.04	83.61	16.39	83.11	16.89	83.81	16.19	84.92	15.08
Kendall	78.48	21.52	78.12	21.88	78.57	21.43	78.59	21.41	79.28	20.72	79.50	20.50
Knox	74.15	25.85	74.63	25.37	76.19	23.81	76.27	23.73	74.87	25.13	78.25	21.75
Lake	83.25	16.75	84.60	15.40	85.69	14.31	84.67	15.33	84.86	15.14	85.28	14.72
LaSalle	78.09	21.91	78.04	21.96	78.56	21.44	77.87	22,13	79.11	20.89	80.33	19.67
Lawrence	73.44	26.56	80.61	19.39	74.21	25.79	74.98	25.02	75.78	24.22	75.27	24.73
Lee	82.84	17.16	82.88	17.12	83.49	16.51	83.85	16.15	83.87	16.13	83.15	16.85
Livingston	78.90	21.10	77.80	22.20	80.10	19.90	78.07	21.93	79.07	20.93	77.36	22.64
Logan	81.76	18.24	83.82	16.18	83.11	16.89	82.33	17.67	83.16	16.84	82.33	17.67
Macon	79.82	20.18	80.34	19.66	81.07	18.93	79.88	20.12	80.34	19.76	77.58	22.42
Macoupin	81.35	18.65	82.26	17.74	82.14	17.86	81.04	18.86	80.85	19.15	83.40	16.60
Madison	81.12	18.88	82.55	17.45	82.22	17.78	82.28	17.72	81.10	18.90	80.41	19.59
Marion	69.18	30.82	70.55	29 45	76.44	23.56	77.52	22.48	76.06	23.94	77.52	22.48
Marshall	80.02	19.98	81.66	18.31	82.79	17.21	82.13	17.87	82.93	17.07	80.37	19.63
Mason	84.35	15.65	83.48	16.52	86.00	14.00	85.29	14.71	85.41	14.59	84.73	15.27
Massac	66.64	33.36	65.19	34.81	68.12	31.88	67.46	32.54	68.67	31.33	71.38	28.62
McDonough	74.23	25.77	76.46	23.54	75.11	24.89	76.59	23.41	75.75	24.25	77.19	22.81

County.	1890. Per cent. of real property	1890. Per cent. of personal property	1891. Per cent. of real property	1891. Per cent. of personal property	1892. Per cent. of real property	1892. Per cent. of personal property	1893. Per cent. of real property	1893. Per cent. of personal property	1894. Per cent. of real property	1894. Per cent. of personal property	1895. Per cent. of real property	1895. Per cent. of personal property
Gallatin	78.03	21.97	79.22	20.78	78.21	21.79	77.58	22.42	73.21	26.79	80.14	19.86
Greene	79.04	20.96	79.48	20.52	78.30	21.70	78.26	21.74	79.52	20.48	81.88	18.12
Grundy	80.21	19.79	80.13	19.87	78.28	21.72	78.18	21.82	80.28	19.72	82.30	17.70
Hamilton	72.23	27.77	71.46	18.54	69.47	30.53	70.02	29.98	66,92	33.08	74.89	25.11
Hancock	78.34	21.66	77.07	22.93	77.91	22.09	77.26	22.74	78.75	21.25	80.84	19.16
Hardin	77.92	22.08	65.04	34.96	78.17	21.83	78.12	21.88	62.78	37.22	74.49	25.51
Henderson	80.40	19.60	74.42	25.58	72.68	27.32	72.66	27.34	72.67	27.33	77.00	23.00
Henry	79.78	20.22	78.26	21.76	76.74	23.26	76.77	23.23	77.08	22.92	78.67	21.33
Iroquois	77.39	22.61	79.36	20.64	78.15	21.85	78.20	21.80	78.92	21.08	76.38	23.62
Jackson	77.41	22.59	77.57	22.43	77.02	22.98	76.78	23.22	75.09	24.91	75.79	24.21
Jasper	76.63	23.37	79.27	20.73	75.52	24.48	75.57	24.43	73.32	26.68	79.26	20.74
Jefferson	77.47	22.53	75.39	24.61	71.92	28.08	71.73	28.27	70.78	29.22	78.26	21.74
Jersey	85.33	14.67	87.61	12.39	86.15	13.85	86.05	13.95	83.74	16.26	87.75	12.25
Jo Daviess	69.21	30.79	66.17	33.83	71.73	28.27	71.72	28.28	72.62	27.38	73.73	26.27
Johnson	70.91	29.09	70.12	29.88	64.55	35.45	65.20	34.80	63.83	36.17	68.66	31.34
Kane	77.57	22.43	78.50	21.50	78.23	21.77	70.26	29.74	77.87	22.13	79.13	20.87
Kankakee	83.88	16.12	83.74	16.26	86.44	13.56	86.19	13.81	88.05	11.95	87.53	12.47
Kendall	79.30	20.70	78.04	21.96	75.01	24.99	75.10	24.90	79.02	20.98	80.62	19.38
Knox	75.95	24.05	74.45	25.55	75.92	24.08	76.00	24.00	76.53	23.47	78.26	21.74
Lake	85.07	14.93	86.17	13.83	86.16	13.84	86.36	13.64	87.66	12.34	91.37	8.63
LaSalle	79.23	20.77	80.11	19.89	77.15	22.85	77.19	22.81	81.26	18.74	82.72	17.28
Lawrence	76.43	23.57	75.09	24.91	73.41	26.59	73.36	26.64	77.07	22.93	80.97	19.03
Lee	83.74	16.26	83.69	16.31	83.83	16.17	83.74	16.26	84.21	15.79	85.23	14.77
Livingston	78.51	21.40	77.59	22.41	78.47	21.53	88.21	11.79	77.74	22.26	82.96	17.04
Logan	82.38	17.62	83.21	16.79	79.65	20.35	79.69	20,31	82.88	17.12	82.76	17.24
Macon	78.65	21.35	77.99	22.01	78.72	21.28	78.40	21.60	80.00	20.00	78.15	21.85
Macoupin	83.66	16.34	83.93	16.07	83.76	16.24	83.07	16.93	81.73	18.27	83.65	16.35
Madison	80.23	19.77	82.37	17.63	81.56	18.44	83.07	16.93	81.24	18.76	81.83	18.17
Marion	77.14	22.86	78.09	21.91	76.48	23.52	76.23	23.77	77.80	22.20	77.62	22.38
Marshall	81.26	18.74	82.43	17.57	81.52	18.48	81.33	18.67	84.47	15.53	84.57	15.43
Mason	85.94	14.06	87.65	12.35	85.83	14.17	85,93	14.07	85.48	14.52	87.48	12.52
Massac	68.16	31.84	68.62	31.38	67.29	32.71	67.27	32.73	67.56	32.44	73.58	26.42
McDonough	76.73	23.27	74.16	25.84	74.84	25.16	75.08	24.91	75.91	24.09	77.89	22.11

McHenry	74.72	25.28	75.68	24.32	76.67	23.33	77.07	22.93	76.90	23.10	76.90	23.10	76.32	23.68	75.87	24.13	76.72	23.28	76.64	23.36	77.14	22.86	79.39	20.61
McLean	77.53	22.47	78.35	21.65	78.98	21.02	77.78	22.22	78.77	21.23	78.83	21.17	79.08	20.92	78.29	21.71	80.50	19.50	80.62	19.38	81.33	18.67	82.05	17.95
Menard	77.11	22.89	78.37	21.63	77.45	22.55	79.57	20.43	81.79	18.21	79.05	20.95	81.25	18.75	83.11	16.89	81.96	18.04	81.91	18.09	80.80	19.20	78.93	21.07
Mercer	75.69	24.31	74.29	25.71	76.11	23.89	75.39	24.61	77.93	22.07	76.66	23.24	76.71	23.29	75.65	24.35	74.92	25.08	73.23	26.77	74.87	25.13	79.58	20.42
Monroe	77.68	22.32	74.98	25.02	78.86	21.14	79.50	20.50	80.37	19.63	80.53	19.44	80.17	19.83	78.17	21.83	76.83	23.17	76.84	23.16	78.53	21.47	81.28	18.72
Montgomery	78.69	21.31	79.66	20.34	80.26	19.74	79.27	20.73	79.79	20.21	81.12	18.88	80.34	19.66	78.88	21.12	79.58	20.42	79.70	20.30	80.36	19.64	81.81	18.19
Morgan	81.88	18.12	82.15	17.85	81.62	18.38	82.90	17.10	83.36	16.64	83.30	16.70	86.14	13.86	85.60	14.40	84.43	15.57	84.57	15.43	84.26	15.74	87.14	12.86
Moultrie	78.12	21.88	79.56	20.44	80.43	19.57	81.24	18.76	81.83	18.17	83.81	16.19	81.73	18.27	82.16	17.84	83.83	16.17	83.88	16.12	82.34	17.66	87.58	12.42
Ogle	77.15	22.85	73.85	26.15	74.79	25.21	76.59	23.41	77.96	22.04	75.49	24.51	76.16	23.84	73.41	26.59	72.44	27.56	72.47	27.53	74.22	25.78	76.47	23.53
Peoria	80.71	19.29	80.61	19.39	82.10	17.90	82.57	17.43	82.54	17.46	79.07	10.93	82.84	17.16	83.76	16.24	80.88	19.12	80.89	19.11	83.08	16.91	84.32	15.68
Perry	79.67	20.33	81.16	18.84	81.19	18.81	80.51	19.49	81.37	18.63	82.55	17.45	81.67	18.33	83.47	16.53	81.72	18.28	81.80	18.20	79.52	20.48	80.55	19.45
Piatt	79.44	20.56	79.25	20.75	80.27	19.73	80.08	19.92	81.33	18.67	78.91	21.09	80.48	19.52	79.58	20.42	77.38	22.62	77.27	22.73	82.37	17.63	85.70	14.30
Pike	77.52	22.48	78.54	21.46	78.89	21.11	80.04	19.96	77.57	22.43	77.08	22.92	78.23	21.77	75.41	24.59	77.09	22.91	77.10	22.90	76.70	23.30	81.15	18.85
Pope	56.66	43.34	67.58	32.42	71.91	28.09	62.26	37.74	59.15	40.85	75.12	24.88	73.85	26.15	63.24	36.00	64.46	35.54	64.55	35.45	56.30	43.70	62.33	37.67
Pulaski	73.83	26.17	69.64	30.36	72.52	27.48	72.31	27.69	77.14	22.86	76.98	23.02	75.36	24.64	75.40	24.60	72.93	27.07	72.58	27.42	74.35	25.65	75.64	24.36
Putnam	81.15	18.85	80.92	19.08	80.17	19.83	79.44	20.56	81.36	18.64	82.04	17.96	83.04	16.96	82.79	17.21	83.36	16.64	82.82	17.18	82.94	17.06	84.06	15.94
Randolph	76.28	23.72	78.41	21.59	76.22	23.78	77.84	22.16	78.45	21.55	80.56	19.44	78.80	21.20	77.70	22.30	75.80	24.20	75.65	24.35	74.87	25.13	79.04	20.96
Richland	73.57	26.43	74.51	25.49	73.79	26.21	78.39	21.61	78.64	21.36	74.88	25.12	76.62	23.38	78.67	21.33	80.99	19.01	81.07	18.93	77.71	22.29	80.81	19.19
Rock Island	76.58	23.42	76.60	23.40	75.77	24.23	73.96	26.04	75.39	24.61	73.68	26.32	74.75	25.25	73.24	26.76	71.79	28.21	71.80	28.20	75.70	24.30	77.06	22.94
Saline	72.08	27.92	74.00	26.00	75.52	24.48	73.17	26.83	68.54	31.46	67.54	32.46	72.40	27.60	71.75	28.25	67.15	32.85	65.12	34.88	66.20	33.80	67.83	32.17
Sangamon	77.49	22.51	79.51	20.49	80.34	19.66	78.44	21.56	81.68	18.32	82.71	17.29	79.87	20.13	81.27	18.73	81.68	18.32	81.69	18.30	82.42	17.58	84.67	15.33
Schuyler	74.52	25.48	75.53	24.47	75.07	24.93	76.16	23.84	75.07	24.93	75.77	24.23	75.23	24.77	71.46	28.54	61.80	38.20	61.82	38.18	70.81	29.19	76.79	23.21
Scott	79.96	20.04	77.99	22.01	79.42	20.58	77.83	22.17	75.13	24.87	76.26	23.74	75.51	24.49	71.34	28.66	68.02	31.98	60.30	39.70	73.13	26.87	73.89	26.11
Shelby	76.12	23.88	76.90	23.10	78.01	21.99	78.13	21.87	79.46	20.54	77.13	22.87	76.75	23.25	77.32	22.68	78.55	21.45	78.57	21.43	76.92	23.08	80.39	19.61
Stark	80.28	19.72	80.65	19.35	76.05	23.95	81.48	18.52	82.73	17.27	80.12	19.88	80.56	19.44	80.63	19.37	78.82	21.18	78.79	21.21	80.19	19.81	82.32	17.68
St. Clair	83.59	16.41	82.92	17.08	82.49	17.51	81.75	18.25	80.34	19.66	79.46	20.54	80.97	19.03	80.55	19.45	82.66	17.34	80.83	19.17	79.03	20.97	83.07	16.93
Stephenson	79.54	20.46	71.93	28.07	75.43	24.57	76.18	23.82	81.18	18.82	76.97	23.03	77.04	22.96	75.40	24.60	76.07	23.93	76.09	23.91	80.06	19.94	79.73	20.27
Tazewell	79.49	20.51	79.52	20.48	80.06	19.94	79.52	20.48	80.66	19.34	80.13	19.87	78.13	21.87	78.58	21.42	79.62	20.38	79.01	20.99	77.92	22.08	81.79	18.21
Union	65.47	34.53	67.99	32.01	68.52	31.48	67.22	32.78	68.17	31.83	70.85	29.15	71.63	28.37	67.30	32.70	65.97	34.03	65.76	34.24	65.53	34.47	68.19	31.81
Vermilion	78.44	21.56	80.20	19.80	79.71	20.29	77.87	22.13	79.44	20.56	78.72	21.28	81.02	18.98	78.75	21.25	83.06	16.94	83.11	16.89	83.08	16.91	82.78	17.22
Wabash	80.71	19.29	77.71	22.29	81.84	18.16	81.57	18.43	81.66	18.34	81.06	18.94	80.70	19.30	81.71	18.29	82.29	17.71	80.62	19.38	80.61	19.39	78.91	21.09
Warren	77.59	22.41	78.57	21.43	81.53	18.47	79.71	20.29	80.81	19.19	78.67	21.33	78.57	21.43	74.55	25.45	76.87	23.13	76.85	23.15	79.00	21.00	81.80	18.20
Washington	78.84	21.16	79.96	20.04	80.52	19.48	80.09	19.91	81.58	18.42	79.47	20.53	80.33	19.67	81.06	18.94	80.35	19.65	80.28	19.72	80.13	19.87	80.68	19.32
Wayne	73.16	26.84	75.95	24.05	81.84	18.16	73.28	26.72	76.99	23.01	75.54	24.46	81.52	18.48	77.39	22.61	78.55	21.45	78.62	21.38	76.56	23.44	77.08	22.92
White	72.50	27.50	70.23	29.77	72.15	27.85	71.28	28.72	71.61	28.39	72.08	27.92	73.01	26.99	75.03	24.97	72.10	27.90	72.06	27.94	73.24	26.76	78.52	21.48
Whiteside	79.16	20.84	77.65	22.36	79.91	20.09	79.83	20.17	80.35	19.65	79.67	20.33	79.76	20.24	79.34	20.66	80.03	19.97	80.04	19.96	80.19	19.81	82.29	17.71
Will	80.23	19.77	77.37	22.63	81.19	18.81	80.35	19.65	80.28	19.72	80.62	19.38	80.64	19.36	80.10	19.90	80.38	19.62	80.40	19.60	80.03	19.97	84.17	15.83
Williamson	64.21	35.79	70.59	29.41	71.67	28.33	63.77	36.23	68.97	31.03	77.10	22.90	76.61	23.39	69.12	30.80	71.64	28.36	71.84	28.16	68.32	31.68	72.44	27.56
Winnebago	69.66	30.34	69.89	30.11	70.84	29.16	73.64	26.36	74.66	25.34	73.38	26.62	71.08	28.92	70.13	29.87	76.93	23.07	77.04	22.96	85.67	14.33	78.95	21.05
Woodford	80.33	19.67	81.34	18.66	82.19	17.81	82.11	17.89	83.13	16.97	79.94	20.06	80.57	19.43	82.51	17.49	82.86	17.14	82.86	17.14	81.16	18.84	85.04	14.96
Total	78.51	21.49	79.01	20.99	79.77	20.23	79.30	20.70	79.82	20.18	78.19	21.81	78.46	21.54	79.98	20.02	79.76	20.24	80.87	19.13	82.74	17.26	81.64	18.36

No.

Statement *Showing the Aggregate Equalized Assessment of Tax-*
the Year 1873 and

Number.	Counties.	1873.	1884.	1885.	1886.	1887.	1888.
1	Adams	$32,468,468	$15,746,954	$14,391,422	$13,488,505	$13,462,212	$13,300,907
2	Alexander	3,321,047	2,124,574	1,951,813	1,935,023	2,518,657	2,176,866
3	Bond	5,904,041	3,433,319	3,228,403	3,060,705	3,005,977	2,970,533
4	Boone	6,269,751	4,082,964	4,004,413	3,894,709	3,885,641	3,688,268
5	Brown	4,719,545	2,843,325	2,256,816	2,171,624	2,114,565	2,071,149
6	Bureau	19,219,442	11,921,232	11,789,336	11,042,323	11,053,368	10,895,701
7	Calhoun	1,356,514	889,988	865,651	764,408	953,810	766,420
8	Carroll	7,229,205	5,197,928	4,991,596	4,891,771	5,095,981	5,024,236
9	Cass	7,305,621	4,159,497	4,021,576	3,780,603	3,713,915	3,686,149
10	Champaign	20,921,837	12,118,876	11,393,654	10,726,674	10,811,996	10,317,027
11	Christian	12,817,700	8,140,056	8,321,813	7,894,330	7,722,945	7,502,834
12	Clark	6,074,842	3,425,315	3,277,538	3,156,037	3,052,100	2,953,458
13	Clay	5,379,418	2,445,959	2,319,654	2,092,165	2,105,867	2,024,504
14	Clinton	7,017,753	3,887,008	3,781,493	3,482,391	3,384,644	3,294,701
15	Coles	10,722,911	6,811,196	6,608,335	6,206,698	6,134,947	5,829,228
16	Cook	306,208,660	175,916,389	180,632,077	203,625,833	209,696,456	210,245,184
17	Crawford	3,686,405	2,400,890	2,539,663	2,253,642	2,160,891	2,208,532
18	Cumberland	3,748,680	1,997,089	1,683,980	1,835,083	1,819,845	1,781,025
19	DeKalb	13,960,530	8,639,911	8,439,072	8,250,639	8,347,478	8,173,712
20	DeWitt	7,755,132	4,668,919	4,761,534	4,464,313	4,482,517	4,456,954
21	Douglas	7,003,935	4,791,839	4,637,361	4,354,296	4,350,146	4,292,760
22	DuPage	9,976,127	5,761,946	5,494,559	5,275,961	5,419,755	5,350,377
23	Edgar	10,712,172	7,915,136	7,385,097	6,891,434	6,835,200	6,555,996
24	Edwards	2,992,722	1,885,889	1,934,728	2,810,516	1,760,160	1,674,524
25	Effingham	5,014,241	2,751,315	3,080,512	3,255,247	3,124,607	3,172,680
26	Fayette	7,811,711	4,297,562	4,490,644	4,369,465	4,234,282	4,637,341
27	Ford	7,148,871	3,866,644	3,693,054	3,572,790	3,558,857	3,557,825
28	Franklin	1,961,748	1,593,905	1,601,020	1,539,867	1,391,947	1,344,011
29	Fulton	19,141,214	10,546,933	10,226,446	9,640,383	9,662,436	9,150,238
30	Gallatin	2,820,858	1,617,181	1,579,414	1,443,085	1,541,568	1,373,788
31	Greene	8,758,416	6,526,202	6,306,545	5,863,289	5,759,548	5,701,731
32	Grundy	7,955,405	5,452,395	5,308,809	4,999,028	4,941,536	4,841,830
33	Hamilton	2,809,343	1,702,583	1,689,147	2,000,720	1,715,511	1,831,983
34	Hancock	16,497,180	9,872,912	8,900,135	8,689,371	8,630,481	8,419,063
35	Hardin	1,548,537	669,488	681,483	655,287	777,134	625,403
36	Henderson	6,367,002	3,287,097	3,186,648	2,991,860	2,963,795	3,052,700
37	Henry	17,367,373	11,687,269	10,996,184	10,449,618	10,227,075	9,976,961
38	Iroquois	14,972,570	9,868,208	9,322,510	8,882,615	8,927,120	8,961,135
39	Jackson	6,991,434	2,723,611	2,684,755	2,637,467	3,139,182	2,969,594
40	Jasper	3,463,869	2,269,025	2,227,240	2,488,860	2,120,208	2,089,729
41	Jefferson	4,073,959	2,715,012	2,673,653	2,665,387	2,426,030	2,641,914
42	Jersey	7,816,527	4,231,407	4,124,746	3,817,445	3,681,701	3,576,674
43	JoDaviess	7,507,512	5,124,070	4,789,831	4,665,119	4,817,426	4,614,764
44	Johnson	2,192,328	1,198,003	1,136,864	1,249,288	1,081,330	1,288,530
45	Kane	24,212,811	13,512,812	13,477,683	13,189,671	13,436,427	13,334,353
46	Kankakee	8,487,935	6,001,587	5,701,938	5,445,728	5,485,625	5,037,269
47	Kendall	8,067,393	4,127,263	4,067,743	3,869,948	3,815,268	3,709,858
48	Knox	19,795,440	13,131,427	12,666,700	11,888,163	11,890,606	11,223,192
49	Lake	7,822,019	5,770,536	5,807,765	5,473,118	5,432,466	5,349,125
50	LaSalle	36,464,291	18,735,073	18,782,408	18,024,810	18,197,081	17,883,233
51	Lawrence	3,481,264	2,068,981	2,063,317	1,972,666	1,949,149	1,862,248
52	Lee	13,627,012	8,342,944	7,830,118	7,464,601	7,642,944	7,315,091
53	Livingston	19,316,312	11,386,756	10,839,103	10,481,677	10,680,157	10,859,641
54	Logan	15,667,653	8,756,242	8,611,637	8,284,554	8,268,600	8,208,802
55	Macon	16,510,032	9,628,451	9,282,840	8,940,983	9,017,903	9,435,801
56	Macoupin	14,556,814	11,443,444	11,340,643	10,532,389	10,066,219	9,197,617
57	Madison	24,994,865	13,600,903	13,329,347	12,628,827	12,339,055	11,917,261
58	Marion	7,085,315	3,905,156	4,057,138	3,830,195	3,735,854	3,636,150
59	Marshall	8,090,091	4,738,134	4,478,557	4,207,634	4,223,750	4,167,431
60	Mason	8,623,290	4,366,576	3,864,438	3,878,885	3,799,557	3,112,533
61	Massac	1,581,007	1,343,485	1,301,160	1,182,743	1,319,647	1,226,102
62	McDonough	13,264,705	8,676,667	8,497,559	7,981,218	7,897,727	7,654,171
63	McHenry	11,214,072	7,953,264	7,444,402	6,968,447	6,826,102	6,741,599
64	McLean	36,525,911	19,499,079	19,596,108	18,804,958	18,926,241	18,145,320
65	Menard	6,494,009	4,082,114	3,980,672	3,857,238	3,667,437	3,580,776
66	Mercer	10,045,258	6,399,290	6,502,023	6,074,140	6,064,800	5,798,970
67	Monroe	3,846,140	2,894,122	2,722,529	2,658,940	2,709,361	2,612,847
68	Montgomery	11,439,730	7,947,268	7,902,843	7,542,304	7,537,306	7,474,745
69	Morgan	16,228,653	8,966,711	9,387,097	9,091,020	8,662,886	8,662,698
70	Moultrie	5,758,124	3,109,775	3,209,231	3,303,501	3,182,726	3,297,766
71	Ogle	14,865,413	10,132,227	9,646,372	9,150,846	9,305,641	9,382,162

29.

able Property in the several counties in the State of Illinois, for 1884 to 1896, inclusive.

1889.	1890.	1891.	1892.	1893.	1894.	1895.	1896.	Number.
$13,433,999	$13,326,534	$12,637,023	$12,852,564	$13,167,537	$12,041,285	$12,074,506	$11,881,202	1
2,007,866	2,184,037	2,002,539	2,053,691	2,497,299	2,448,742	2,542,036	2,582,776	2
3,005,434	3,099,368	2,768,280	2,823,807	3,068,655	2,715,670	2,797,184	2,737,584	3
3,566,432	3,359,217	3,295,529	3,412,384	3,560,247	3,422,685	3,482,274	3,384,783	4
2,190,646	2,077,927	1,994,012	2,058,313	2,136,318	2,020,309	2,032,407	1,968,451	5
10,968,421	10,873,995	10,306,528	10,337,358	10,229,220	9,948,530	10,238,264	9,695,433	6
720,045	795,050	1,103,799	1,214,566	1,326,131	1,270,007	1,189,683	1,244,329	7
4,964,768	4,944,182	4,668,937	4,771,310	4,808,930	4,585,239	4,692,615	4,452,484	8
3,553,488	3,534,238	3,265,422	3,388,316	3,598,357	3,459,944	3,545,808	3,375,241	9
10,390,295	10,164,464	9,702,230	10,025,165	10,143,723	9,717,093	9,580,997	9,481,526	10
7,111,359	7,565,817	6,735,277	7,305,770	7,431,802	7,040,657	7,270,880	6,693,139	11
3,039,438	3,029,676	2,776,793	2,761,739	2,982,014	2,795,783	3,038,171	2,948,531	12
2,090,213	1,947,286	1,828,694	1,940,663	1,892,950	1,809,988	1,816,129	1,741,440	13
3,444,336	3,358,710	3,142,820	3,205,502	3,327,302	3,321,144	3,396,992	3,335,262	14
5,706,704	5,682,694	5,190,652	5,599.948	5,578,692	5,128,730	5,028,092	5,137,210	15
219,819,560	240,308,050	282,495,410	270,637,093	272,306,144	275,958,232	270,847,727	272,940,874	16
2,021,575	2,082,303	1,866,327	1,915,401	1,980,439	1,822,476	2,022,571	1,925,624	17
1,794,164	1,728,622	1,621,300	1,619,805	1,810,258	1,722,184	1,755,021	1,867,611	18
8,164,379	8,162,446	7,856,611	7,992,480	8,113,586	7,771,363	8,204,508	8,003,704	19
4,315,827	4,213,325	3,887,844	4,035,247	4,058,279	3,623,324	3,946,354	3,748,252	20
4,296,853	4,122,034	4,167,129	4,370,719	4,428,710	4,122,494	4,221.551	4,137,628	21
5,452,694	5,486,177	5,325,481	5,838,846	5,842,626	6,233,983	6,393,797	6,130,368	22
6,329,978	6,254,441	6,152,606	6,315,795	6,401,579	6,011,051	6,082,045	5,952,163	23
1,570,256	1,523,560	1,550,342	1,694,008	1,542,467	1,512,128	1,542,294	1,358,858	24
3,098,063	3,091,305	2,829,011	3,134,538	2,944,506	2,867,784	2,903,390	2,825,460	25
3,985,728	4,168,617	3,446,016	3,451,330	3,578,323	3,342,222	3,304,567	3,241,868	26
3,547,939	3,681,806	3,316,174	3,434,604	3,555,807	3,285,844	3,302,184	3,500,419	27
1,316,754	1,283,742	1,444,844	1.261,143	1,366,307	1,297,485	1,384,887	1,271,736	28
9,103,033	9,460,240	8,609,801	8,940,201	9,297,639	8,926,904	9,054,637	8,572,591	29
1,510,511	1,324,703	1,457,841	1,513,074	1,698,719	1,577,619	1,621,437	1,532,493	30
5,732,034	5,708,356	5,273,245	5,424,387	5,442,133	5,230,988	5,436,518	5,165,731	31
4,842,513	5,003,181	4,785,447	5,090,312	4,793,929	4,414,908	4,739,042	4,532,925	32
1,621,737	1,557,890	1,465,495	1,582,228	1,722,532	1,593,449	1,587,053	1,596,292	33
8,348,611	8,181,686	7,818,589	8,252,480	8,065,195	7,710,322	7,888,889	7,577,686	34
550,498	484,875	523,034	531,931	833,051	565,896	542,096	548,154	35
3,006,765	2,965,104	2,839,337	3,082,566	3,433,923	2,867,764	2,868,255	3,056,465	36
9,912,888	9,866,211	9,296,559	9,770,847	9,777,073	9,415,627	9,538,745	8,962,211	37
8,687,140	8,779,473	8,326,633	9,032,664	8,755,981	8,286,787	8,354,183	8,600,944	38
2,990,270	2,968,746	2,814,177	2,902,566	2,802,529	2,770,063	2,899,066	2,950,020	39
1,916,187	1,769,048	1,571,373	1,595,238	1,679,738	1,725,885	1,870,762	1,934,702	40
2,352,811	2,380,696	2,305,422	2,443,057	2,669,784	2,349,512	2,444,266	2,302,855	41
3,589,210	3,404,235	3,989,026	3,319,338	3,552,796	3,377,695	3,703,851	3,584,624	42
4,529,088	4,521,901	4,123,107	4,248,429	4,376,463	4,087,679	4,287,728	4,025,807	43
1,359,536	1,429,996	1,271,279	1,280,144	1,505,584	1,549,717	1,734,084	1,654,120	44
13,500,065	13,737,489	13,276,918	13,988,103	14,142,141	14,485,797	14,267,443	13,784,656	45
5,180,632	5,349,935	5,087,621	5,205,791	5,253,694	5,093,979	5,377,286	5,376,218	46
3,724,041	3,687,861	3,467,861	3,569,669	3,311,836	3,852,040	3,429,549	3,360,234	47
11,272,412	10,929,382	10,306,993	10,905,063	10,026,568	10,544,180	10,917,150	10,317,824	48
5,449,788	5,606,156	5,574,234	6,108,799	7,203,666	7,395,592	7,564,226	7,409,726	49
17,978,362	17,820,258	16,968,218	17,344,585	17,566,288	16,572,453	16,613,494	15,799,438	50
1,874,605	1,907,353	1,781,358	1,614,070	1,903,538	1,848,844	2,064,220	1,858,544	51
7,281,076	7,279,261	6,982,995	7,137,091	7,130,081	6,767,168	6,931,148	6,676,593	52
10,662,258	10,661,248	10,691,559	10,658,056	10,306,913	10,193,290	10,582,298	9,751,451	53
8,020,081	7,757,850	7,241,798	7,267,010	7,383,475	7,124,384	7,319,329	6,862,507	54
8,680,625	8,828,326	8,520,738	9,399,489	8,959,799	8,869,941	9,273,065	9,171,789	55
9,720,005	9,672,813	9,068,597	9,436,588	9,268,859	8,908,949	9,163,620	8,566,813	56
12,216,065	11,811,556	10,955,450	12,004,033	12,111,175	12,463,085	12,460,156	12,387,802	57
3,911,181	3,789,514	3,603,724	3,608,102	3,818,715	3,878,917	4,001,228	3,967,167	58
4,322,757	4,266,447	3,960,102	4,211,230	4,117,903	4,038,236	4,057,967	4,140,064	59
3,319,203	3,678,312	3,378,151	3,396,008	3,572,049	3,577,436	3,642,162	3,549,952	60
1,284,570	1,180,479	1,135,342	1,183,478	1,602,772	1,617,871	1,583,167	1,645,046	61
7,417,558	7,111,209	7,488,744	6,722,807	7,185,864	6,828,236	6,867,597	6,490,614	62
6,690,214	6,596,856	6,193,552	6,291,292	6,337,628	6,645,307	5,985,350	5,486,728	63
18,968,352	18,364,209	17,297,556	17,925,201	18,153,296	17,478,743	18,081,483	17,034,029	64
3,770,211	3,724,800	3,457,905	3,635,537	3,316,788	3,450,484	3,503,093	3,418,197	65
5,805,307	5,727,460	5,309,689	5,343,675	5,083,988	5,127,005	5,388,020	5,105,970	66
2,687,124	2,509,191	2,536,366	2,643,574	2,769,095	2,589,217	2,709,379	2,652,478	67
7,421,890	7,211,925	6,452,669	6,856,004	7,168,432	6,585,867	6,656,213	6,383,108	68
8,673,321	8,381,346	7,867,771	8,306,186	8,136,477	7,961,568	8,261,628	7,833,558	69
3,362,556	3,160,309	2,860,483	2,957,545	3,282,198	3,071,258	3,157,854	2,949,409	70
9,175,111	8,930,888	8,491,888	8,632,468	8,702,458	8,302,280	8,343,440	8,103,738	71

Statement 29

Number.	Counties.	1873.	1884.	1885.	1886.	1887.	1888.
72	Peoria	$28,781,251	$14,776,913	$14,636,565	$13,600,799	$13,630,365	$13,783,045
73	Perry	4,721,642	2,251,155	2,381,065	2,207,317	2,114,342	2,164,267
74	Piatt	7,263,382	5,191,901	4,955,054	4,6980632	4,857,658	4,968,183
75	Pike	14,342,458	8,532,001	8,263,078	7,884,610	7,690,990	6,930,970
76	Pope	1,816,842	1,269,102	1,231,257	1,265,380	1,107,584	1,206,145
77	Pulaski	1,479,903	868,993	732,108	737,037	860,537	796,969
78	Putnam	3,301,824	1,778,434	1,698,793	1,595,494	1,592,621	1,533,805
79	Randolph	6,802,954	4,345,471	4,300,252	4,247,727	3,867,098	4,697,020
80	Richland	4,941,681	2,078,567	2,181,612	2,115,088	2,061,932	1,995,725
81	Rock Island	12,577,897	7,573,987	7,711,335	7,502,023	7,586,330	7,500,594
82	Saline	2,482,461	1,695,594	1,836,182	1,796,825	8,710,221	1,614,458
83	Sangamon	30,309,371	17,330,781	17,300,325	16,416,166	16,303,665	16,032,074
84	Schuyler	6,236,180	3,878,406	3,646,521	3,439,917	3,425,744	3,319,153
85	Scott	4,221,045	2,770,066	2,770,054	2,613,069	2,670,969	2,654,063
86	Shelby	11,942,458	6,958,366	7,150,344	7,107,857	6,909,983	5,714,766
87	Stark	6,916,053	4,185,455	3,923,467	3,710,997	3,678,070	3,541,033
88	St. Clair	24,718,956	18,275,842	17,302,793	16,608,670	16,861,567	15,883,514
89	Stephenson	12,786,963	8,269,401	7,806,124	7,467,659	7,697,505	7,656,785
90	Tazewell	16,998,365	9,776,236	8,957,406	8,434,929	8,496,359	8,024,624
91	Union	3,295,876	1,839,579	1,914,568	1,767,316	1,864,126	1,861,100
92	Vermilion	20,454,025	12,326,283	12,389,529	12,001,891	11,827,158	11,414,225
93	Wabash	3,055,243	1,825,505	1,879,778	1,731,185	1,777,894	1,701,122
94	Warren	11,200,391	7,343,621	7,503,573	7,084,065	7,113,300	7,092 596
95	Washington	5,842,970	4,616,103	4,030,850	3,663,327	3,670,912	3,528,464
96	Wayne	4,921,070	2,531,168	3,228,521	3,136,453	2,889,472	3,044,890
97	White	4,668,731	3,150,078	2,866,209	2,769,832	2,629,100	2,647,874
98	Whiteside	15,192,293	8,987,027	8,580,856	8,095,727	7,909,869	7,829,249
99	Will	24,810,823	12,682,573	12,922,122	12,312,906	12,564,784	12,725,902
100	Williamson	2,624,583	1,976,705	1,956,390	1,685,845	1,864,824	1,747,996
101	Winnebago	14,470,412	10,031,893	9,807,433	9,745,594	9,770,632	9,369,872
102	Woodford	10,315,605	6,778,304	6,632,823	6,225,449	6,215,891	5,997,000
	Total	$1,355,401,317	$809,169,803	$798,482,823	$793,563,498	$796,752,888	$784,911,874

—Concluded.

1889.	1890.	1891.	1892.	1893.	1894.	1895.	1896.	Number
$14,071,091	$15,135,316	$15,567,159	$16,570,920	$15,998,895	$14,707,631	$14,854,950	$15,185,577	72
2,051,186	2,034,557	1,949,134	2,086,530	2,510,042	2,143,396	2,340,556	2,270,146	73
4,761,626	4,827,504	4,616,082	4,336,791	4,700,214	4,425,267	4,533,792	4,225,271	74
7,150,026	7,003,701	6,515,995	6,084,447	6,758,551	6,228,923	6,836,882	5,947,796	75
1,133,647	1,087,088	904,553	968,224	1,068,313	1,138,443	1,197,959	1,074,278	76
757,599	797,872	758,963	839,540	1,023,466	879,286	1,040,936	1,017,727	77
1,492,765	1,419,471	2,411,532	1,404,813	1,430,266	1,323,574	1,410,678	1,301,564	78
4,268,698	4,019,425	3,740,926	3,863,540	3,821,507	3,745,084	3,921,218	3,964,185	79
1,873,448	1,766,554	1,682,588	1,818,701	1,923,054	2,008,683	1,829,640	1,799,703	80
7,046,771	7,034,683	6,786,082	6,718,403	7,325,804	6,914,466	6,745,206	6,721,638	81
1,713,156	1,667,892	1,552,572	1,548,888	1,612,018	1,467,417	1,733,329	1,622,901	82
16,074,145	15,350,203	14,119,930	14,162,647	14,824,223	14,183,974	14,694,498	14,706,150	83
3,089,371	3,042,793	2,481,747	2,348,806	3,108,849	2,910,525	2,932,835	2,871,517	84
2,618,614	2,619,603	2,504,476	2,621,428	2,161,950	2,549,161	2,647,043	2,483,884	85
6,402,229	6,220,963	5,842,995	5,646,070	6,559,016	5,929,522	6,222,548	5,793,220	86
3,543,000	3,533,296	3,190,352	3,442,424	3,498,755	3,197,392	3,442,182	3,290,664	87
15,662,284	15,597,841	14,783,224	15,454,552	15,898,992	14,137,727	14,938,552	14,156,702	88
7,902,511	7,850,115	7,414,967	7,571,694	7,848,320	7,720,326	8,092,654	7,748,742	89
8,211,961	8,167,751	7,587,191	7,693,379	8,264,133	7,875,743	7,886,662	7,671,179	90
1,802,746	1,788,028	1,686,966	1,746,350	1,988,746	1,954,040	2,038,406	2,283,026	91
11,013,614	10,856,587	10,558,137	10,830,871	11,002,432	10,872,083	12,322,726	11,172,154	92
1,567,956	1,598,666	1,609,729	1,709,882	1,706,604	1,516,775	1,496,738	1,305,919	93
7,106,199	6,854,014	6,352,470	6,650,035	6,594,681	6,360,952	6,484,495	6,052,449	94
3,104,215	3,534,528	3,122,865	3,219,962	3,453,611	3,636,295	3,511,860	3,542,086	95
2,751,446	3,644,203	2,542,533	2,668,534	2,335,679	2,031,219	2,066,011	2,197,698	96
2,776,812	2,739,013	2,888,383	2,818,127	2,839,035	2,731,584	2,680,633	2,365,523	97
7,834,178	7,708,170	7,482,103	7,783,860	7,488,898	6,542,657	7,440,498	7,166,262	98
13,071,993	12,648,913	13,220,604	14,028,616	16,341,696	14,397,502	14,382,224	13,841,344	99
1,823,362	1,815,831	1,759,175	1,925,201	2,136,610	2,001,769	2,079,789	2,021,630	100
9,560,058	9,958,302	10,316,607	11,626,540	12,248,758	11,110,781	11,105,203	10,810,733	101
5,493,388	5,758,669	5,433,567	5,647,410	5,742,989	4,989,980	5,365,613	5,932,663	102
$792,197,542	$808,892,782	$822,109,429	$831,310,306	$847,191,516	$824,651,628	$833,188,467	$816,679,620	

No. 30.

Statement Showing the assessed value of Railroad Property in each County in the State of Illinois, for the year A. D. 1896.

County—Railroad.	Main Track, Including Right of Way and Improvements Thereon.				Second Main Track.			Side or Turnout Track.			Rolling Stock.	Total assessment by the State Board of Equalization...	Equalized value of railroad property assessed by local assessors..........	Equalized value of railroad property in county..........
	Miles	Feet........	Assess'd value exclud-ing build-ings.	Value of build-ings on right of way.	Miles	Feet........	Assess'd value.	Miles	Feet........	Assess'd value.	Assess'd value.			
Adams:														
Chicago, Burlington & Quincy..........	74	766	$452,285	$9,165				16	3,072	$41,455	$89,563	$502,468	$10,963	$603,431
Quincy, Omaha & Kansas City				7,350					5,204	3,942		11,292		11,292
same (C., B. & Q.)........................	2	4,435									863	863		863
Wabash..	21	646	95,051	3,945				2	273	5,129	32,529	136,654	3,328	139,982
same (C., B. & Q.)........................	21										32,341	32,341		32,341
Total	119	567	$547,336	$20,460				19	3,269	$50,526	$155,296	$773,618	$14,291	$787,909
Alexander:														
Cairo, Vincennes & Chicago	6	2,651	17,555	6,150				11	4,784	23,812	4,729	52,246		52,246
Chicago & Texas.............................	6	83	12,032	700				1	1,470	1,917	3,380	18,029		18,029
Mobile & Ohio................................	27	1,775	109,344	2,650				12	3,687	31,746	29,864	173,604		173,604
Total	39	4,509	138,931	$9,500				25	4,661	$57,475	$37,973	$243,879		$243,879
Bond:														
Jacksonville, Louisville & St. Louis....	27	1,979	71,174	1,200				1	1,792	2,679	13,373	88,426	39	88,465
same (C., G. & S.)	4	152	10,475						2,200	833	1,968	13,276	10	13,286
Terre Haute & Indianapolis.............	22	1,460	140,342	2,311				6	1,080	15,511	67,436	225,600	389	225,989
Toledo, St. Louis & Kansas City.......	8	1,690	29,120	250				1	250	2,095	11,713	43,178	14	43,192
Total	62	1	$251,111	$3,761				9	42	$21,118	$94,490	$370,480	$452	$370,932
Boone:														
Chicago, Madison & Northern...........	6	1,275	31,207	1,020					4,038	1,912	2,203	36,342	53	36,395
Chicago & Northwestern.................	37	3,229	216,266	2,920				16	4,062	41,923	48,764	309,873	1,658	311,531
same (Nor. Ill.)............................	7	4,141									10,092	10,092		10,092
Northern Illinois..........................	7	4,141	19,461	495					3,295	1,248		21,204	31	21,235
Total	59	2,286	$266,934	$4,435				18	835	$45,083	$61,059	$277,511	$1,742	$379,253

Brown:														
Wabash	23	3,370	106,372	3,176				1	4,714	4,732	36,404	150,684	120	150,804
Bureau:														
Chicago, Burlington & Quincy	72	4,260	444,122	4,009	40	3,337	142,212	12	2,463	31,166	87,946	709,545	870	710,415
same (I., V. N.)	30	548									36,363	36,363		36,363
Chicago & Northwestern (Nor. Ill.)	6	215									7,832	7,832	176	8,008
Chicago, Rock Island & Pacific	40	2,786	344,485	9,375	40	2,786	141,847	8	4,806	22,276	46,743	564,726	2,493	567,219
same (Peo. Br.)	4	2,550	38,105					1	3,232	4,030	5,170	47,305		47,305
DePue, Ladd & Eastern	3	1,760	6,667						2,000	379	20	7,066	27	7,093
Illinois Valley & Northern	30	546	90,310	2,064				3	4,029	9,408		101,782	465	102,247
LaSalle & Bureau Co	1	1,715	3,975						1,880	890		4,865		4,865
Northern Illinois	6	215	15,102	803				11	3,160	23,197		39,102		39,102
Total	194	4,033	$942,766	$16,341	81	843	$284,059	39	450	$91,346	$184,074	$1,518,586	$4,031	$1,522,617
Carroll:														
Chicago, Burlington & Northern	48	4,285	244,057	6,675				10	1,184	25,560	86,637	362,929	1,415	364,344
Chicago, Milwaukee & St. Paul	47	462	200,122	32,534	21	3,155	75,591	22	1,581	55,749	52,565	416,561	3,327	419,888
Total	95	4,747	$444,179	$39,209	21	3,155	$75,591	32	2,765	$81,309	$139,202	$779,490	$4,742	$784,232
Cass:														
Baltimore & Ohio Southwestern	25	4,169	77,369	1,280				6	1,273	15,603	46,918	141,170	259	141,429
Chicago & Alton	2	2,248	15,282	220					3,561	1,686	4,954	22,142	55	22,197
Chicago, Peoria & St. Louis	15	453	42,240	821				2	78	4,029	27,102	74,192	32	74,224
St. Louis, Rock Island & Chicago	10	4,507	43,414	13,144				8	878	20,416	7,496	84,470	3,440	87,910
Total	54	817	$178,305	$15,465				17	510	$41,734	$86,470	$321,974	$3,786	$325,760
Champaign:														
Chicago & Eastern Illinois	8	745	30,936	970					4,613	1,747	19,544	53,197	63	53,260
Chicago, Havana & Western	12	910	36,517	513				1	3,083	3,168	2,760	42,958	79	43,037
Chicago & Springfield		1,500	881								173	1,054		1,054
Peoria & Eastern	29	648	101,930	8,447				10	3,674	26,740	28,959	166,076	3,631	169,707
Rantoul	28	1,229	50,819	3,109				3	2,608	3,494	4,127	61,549	370	61,919
Wabash	28	2,503	128,133	6,270				5	4,068	14,426	43,851	192,680	238	192,918
same (C. P.)	6	1,947	28,659	1,288				1	1,904	3,402	9,808	43,157	35	43,192
same (C. & S. E.)	11	3,617	52,583	1,302				1	1,753	3,330	17,996	75,211	53	75,264
Total	124	2,539	$430,458	$21,899				25	583	$56,307	$127,218	$635,882	$4,469	$640,351
Christian:														
Baltimore & Ohio Southwestern	30	4,577	92,601	8,930				5	1,976	13,436	56,155	171,122	5,816	176,938
Cleveland, Cin., Chicago & St. Louis	10	5,153	55,977	920				2	4,018	6,902	23,494	87,293	670	87,963
Wabash	31	163	139,639	6,177				6	3,784	16,792	47,789	210,397	2,008	212,405
Total	72	4,613	$288,217	$16,027				14	4,498	$37,130	$127,438	$468,812	$8,494	$477,306

Statement 30—Continued.

County—Railroad.	Main Track, including Right of Way and Improvements Thereon.				Second Main Track.			Side or Turnout Track.			Rolling Stock.	Total assessment by the State Board of Equalization...	Equalized value of railroad property assessed by local assessor..........	Equalized value of railroad property in county..........
	Miles	Feet........	Assess'd value, excluding buildings.	Value of buildings on right of way.	Miles	Feet........	Assess'd value.	Miles	Feet........	Assess'd value.	Assess'd value.			
Clark:														
Cairo, Vincennes & Chicago	20	4,370	$56,235	$555				1	3,993	$3,513	$15,148	$75,451	$128	$75,579
Peoria, Decatur & Evansville (Chi. Div.)	14	4,157	36,969	230					3,696	1,401	1,620	40,220	393	40,613
Terre Haute & Indianapolis	29	696	183,530	2,079				5	3,014	13,927	88,188	287,724	161	287,885
Terre Haute & Peoria		4,157	1,968						1,917	726	555	3,249		3,249
same (T., H. & I.)		3,268									437	437		437
Total	66	808	$278,702	$2,864				8	2,062	$19,567	$105,948	$407,081	$682	$407,763
Clay:														
Baltimore & Ohio Southwestern	48	3,589	146,039	1,960				8	2,147	21,017	88,561	257,577	692	258,269
Clinton:														
Baltimore & Ohio Southwestern	30	3,540	92,011	2,495				3	908	7,930	55,797	158,233	413	158,646
Centralia & Chester	2	3,636	6,722								603	7,325		7,325
Jacksonville, Louisville & St. Louis	15	2,060	40,014	650					1,782	675	7,518	48,857	2,349	51,206
Louisville, Evansville & St. Louis Con	31	2,263	102,143	1,190				1	4,785	3,812	42,615	149,760	83	149,843
Louisville & Nashville	3	4,775	14,837	713					3,494	1,489	4,325	21,364	171	21,535
Total	84	434	$255,727	$5,048				6	409	$13,906	$110,858	$385,539	$3,016	$388,555
Coles:														
Cleveland, Cincin., Chicago & St. Louis	27	4,796	142,332	18,120				14	128	35,061	59,738	255,251	29,063	284,314
Peoria, Decatur & Evansville	16	1,285	40,609	4,635				6	1,811	12,686	18,902	76,832	11,214	88,046
same (Chi. Div.)	1	5,207	4,966								218	5,184		5,184
Terre Haute & Peoria	5	1,471	13,197	220					3,455	1,309	3,723	18,449	837	19,286
Toledo, St. Louis & Kansas City	31	4,699	111,615	1,750				5	2,573	10,975	44,896	169,236	463	169,699
Total	83	1,618	$312,719	$24,725				26	2,687	$60,031	$127,477	$524,952	$41,577	$566,529
Crawford:														
Cairo, Vincennes & Chicago	24	944	$65,283	$735				3	1,284	6,486	17,586	90,090	79	90,169
Indiana & Illinois Southern	21		31,500	900				1		1,000	4,102	37,502		37,502
Total	45	944	$96,783	$1,635				4	1,284	$7,486	$21,688	$127,592	$79	$127,671

CUMBERLAND:														
Peoria, Decatur & Evansville	17	2,651	43,755	425	......	......	....	1	763	2,289	20,366	66,835	....	66,835
same (Chi. Div.)	7	520	17,746	....	......	......	....	......	810	307	777	18,830	....	18,830
Terre Haute & Indianapolis	20	4,145	130,946	969	......	......	....	3	2,475	8,672	62,921	203,508	....	203,508
Toledo, St. Louis & Kansas City	7	3,590	26,880	125	......	......	....	......	4,698	1,780	10,812	39,597	....	39,597
Total	53	346	$219,327	$1,519	......	......	....	5	3,466	$13,048	$94,876	$328,770	....	$328,770
COOK:														
Baltimore, Ohio & Chicago	5	4,821	53,218	34,640	5	4,588	$23,476	19	1,635	57,929	9,914	179,177	4,442	183,619
same (C., R. I. & P.)	6	1,848	....	....	......	......	....	......	......	....	10,646	10,646	....	10,646
same (C. & N. P.)	3	3,696	....	....	......	......	....	......	......	....	6,204	6,204	....	6,204
Baltimore & Ohio Connecting	2	940	19,602	....	2	940	8,712	......	......	....	....	28,314	4,200	32,514
Belt Railway Co. of Chicago	20	3,125	308,878	8,075	13	1,973	53,495	51	128	127,561	119,310	617,319	484	617,803
Blue Island	3	4,461	15,380	3,600	......	......	....	1	4,148	5,357	4,100	28,437	651	29,088
Calumet River	4	2,312	26,627	....	......	......	....	......	......	....	....	26,627	745	27,372
Chicago & Alton	25	3,233	161,358	31,675	25	3,232	89,642	29	1,336	73,133	52,312	408,120	12,399	420,519
Chicago, Burlington & Quincy	15	468	92,041	37,094	15	468	52,810	120	2,167	301,026	18,226	501,197	332,508	833,705
Chicago & Calumet Terminal	25	1,593	151,810	9,600	......	......	....	7	3,834	23,178	52,021	236,609	38	236,647
Chicago & Eastern Illinois	11	4,539	45,067	10,430	11	4,615	35,622	27	2,455	54,929	28,472	174,520	6,143	180,663
same (C. & W. I.)	16	1,056	....	....	......	......	....	......	......	....	38,892	38,892	....	38,892
Chicago & Erie (C. & W. I.)	19	3,274	....	....	......	......	....	......	......	....	40,908	40,908	4,877	45,785
Chicago & Grand Trunk	21	5,075	439,224	10,970	16	2,861	66,167	12	4,711	38,677	45,099	600,137	20,879	621,016
same (G. T. Jc.)	3	4,630	....	....	......	......	....	......	......	....	7,962	7,962	....	7,962
same (C. & W. I.)	4	4,631	....	....	......	......	....	......	......	....	10,016	10,016	....	10,016
Chicago & Great Western	5	3,021	32,318	2,500	......	......	....	1	52	2,525	6,968	44,311	25	44,336
same (C. & N. P.)	10	950	....	....	......	......	....	......	......	....	12,731	12,731	....	12,731
Chicago & Illinois Southern	......	2,200	1,667	....	......	......	....	......	500	237	....	1,904	....	1,904
Chicago & Indiana State Line	3	759	26,722	....	2	3,457	10,619	1	1,426	3,810	....	41,151	....	41,151
Chi., Lake Shore & East. (B. & O & C.)	1	850	....	....	......	......	....	......	......	....	176	176	....	176
same (C., R. I. & P.)	22	662	....	....	......	......	....	......	......	....	3,349	3,349	....	3,349
same (E., J. & E.)	5	3,894	....	....	......	......	....	......	......	....	869	869	....	869
same (L. S. & M. S.))	3	355	....	....	......	......	....	......	......	....	464	464	....	464
same (S. C. & S.)	9	2,683	....	....	......	......	....	......	......	....	1,439	1,439	....	1,439
same (P., C., C. & St. L.)	21	3,305	....	....	......	......	....	......	......	....	3,274	3,274	....	3,274
Chicago, Madison & Northern	16	1,155	81,094	5,625	6	578	21,383	14	1,053	35,499	5,725	149,326	19,361	168,687
Chicago, Milwaukee & St. Paul	57	937	243,004	83,410	47	1,049	165,196	110	2,250	276,065	63,829	831,504	117,223	948,727
same (C., St. L. & P.)	2	1,941	....	....	......	......	....	......	......	....	2,643	2,643	....	2,643
same (P., Ft. W. & C.)	......	2,620	....	....	......	......	....	......	......	....	554	554	....	554
Chicago & Northern Pacific	42	1,106	1,118,551	195,690	24	3,480	123,296	55	1,003	137,975	107,160	1,682,672	3,376	1,686,048
same (Wis. Cen.)	4	2,580	....	....	......	......	....	......	......	....	11,400	11,400	....	11,400
Chicago & Northwestern	68	5,066	396,517	185,440	68	1,066	238,707	156	3,047	391,443	89,406	1,301,513	126,385	1,427,898
same (Junc.)	6	3,757	....	....	......	......	....	......	......	....	8,702	8,702	4,306	13,008
Chicago, Rock Island & Pacific	31	5,054	271,604	183,189	31	922	109,111	113	5,032	284,883	36,853	885,640	230,830	1,116,470
Chicago, Santa Fé & California	18	794	96,197	30,695	......	......	....	47	2,667	118,478	21,355	266,725	102,998	369,723
Chicago & South Side Rapid Transit	8	2,951	171,178	11,675	......	......	....	10	311	25,147	136,120	344,120	5,080	349,200
Chicago & Union Transfer	15	1,849	122,756	290	18	4,954	56,815	......	581	275	100	180,236	2,032	182,268
Chicago & Western Indiana	26	4,082	803,193	209,145	26	4,082	133,866	69	4,730	209,688	11,600	1,367,492	68,308	1,435,800
Elgin, Joliet & Eastern	26	3,432	119,925	3,960	......	......	....	10	2,495	26,181	57,638	207,704	11,434	219,138
Englewood Connecting	2	1,858	23,519	620	......	......	....	......	5,027	3,332	....	27,471	....	27,471
Grand Trunk Junction	3	4,630	116,307	69,320	3	4,640	19,394	21	2,368	75,070	....	280,091	....	280,091
Hammond & Blue Island	10	508	50,481	....	......	......	....	......	1,850	1,051	....	51,532	....	51,532

Statement 30—Continued.

County—Railroad.	Main Track, Including Right of Way and Improvements Thereon.				Second Main Track.			Side or Turnout Track.			Rolling Stock.	Total assessment by the State Board of Equalization...	Equalized value of railroad property assessed by local assessors..........	Equalized value of railroad property in county..........
	Miles........	Feet........	Assess'd value exclud-ing build-ings.	Value of build-ings on right of way.	Miles........	Feet........	Assess'd value.	Miles........	Feet...	Assess'd value.	Assess'd value.			
Cook—*Concluded*.														
Junction....	6	3,757	$20,135	$518	6	3,757	$16,779	1	2,718	$3,787		$41,219		$41,219
Lake Shore & Michigan Southern.......	7	3,215	456,534	96,750	7	3,215	30,436	66	2,210	199,256	$25,188	808,164	$17,315	825,479
same (C., R. I. & P.)................	6	2,317									21,314	21,314		21,314
Lake Street Elevated..................	6	4,910	69,299	16,650				1	2,717	3,029	80,100	169,078	251	169,332
Louisv., New Albany & Chi. (C. & W. I.)	19	4,541									29,190	29,190		29,190
Michigan Central	6	1,555	50,356	26,720				11	631	33,358	9,410	119,844	22,776	142,620
Michigan Central (J. & Nor. Ind.).......	13	3,172	108,896	2,400				1	4,554	5,588	20,832	137,126	165	137,291
same (Ill. Cen.)......................	14										20,928	20,928		20,928
New York, Chicago & St. Louis..........	9	5,101	199,322	66,124	1	1,946	4,790	19	3,237	68,646	35,165	374,047	15,460	389,507
same (L. S. & M. S.)..................	8	4,720									31,382	31,382		31,382
Pittsburgh, Cincinnati, Chicago & St. L	27	5,230	1,119,621	66,152	18	4,673	94,425	56	1,047	196,694	77,933	1,553,824	59,142	1,613,967
same (Eng. Conn.).....................	2	1,858									6,548	6,548		6,548
Pittsburgh, Ft. Wayne & Chicago.......	13	5,125	838,239	292,439	13	3,283	68,109	67	2,406	236,095	68,180	1,503,062	72,669	1,575,731
same (S. C. & S.)......................	10	1,320									50,023	50,023		50,023
South Chicago..........................	4	4,016	28,564	8,820	4	2,740	18,076	3	75	7,536	15,000	77,996	3,141	81,137
South Chicago & Southern	10	863	81,308	1,650				2	4,679	10,102		93,060	6,473	99,533
The Metropolitan West Side Elevated..	13	3,538	273,402	29,530				20	80	50,038	71,020	423,990	2,223	426,213
Union Stock Yards & Transit	8	3,775	435,748	55,585	8	3,128	85,924	89	605	356,458	66,910	1,000,625	4,016	1,004,641
Wisconsin Central	20	985	121,119	8,324				6	3,548	23,352	32,416	185,211	1,403	186,614
same (C. & N. P.)......................	10	4,723									17,495	17,495		17,495
Wabash (C. & S.).......................	21	1,014	95,364	4,926				16	4,430	42,098	32,637	175,025	14,251	189,276
same (C. & W. I.)	7	3,696									11,858	111,858		11,858
Total......................................	868	2,572	$8,886,055	$1,804,231	381	2,287	$1,526,850	1,247	2,661	$3,509,486	$1,749,466	$17,476,08[illegible]	$1,298,012	$18,774,100
DeKalb:														
Chicago, Burlington & Quincy	9	4,095	59,631	694	5	2,098	18,891	2	5,078	7,404	11,808	98,428	85	98,513
Chicago Great Western..................	18	655	105,119	3,900				3	3,942	9,367	22,665	141,051	26	141,077
same (D. & G. W.)......................	5	4,280									7,267	7,267		7,267
Chicago & Iowa.........................	18	2,936	92,780	1,980				3	943	7,947	13,945	116,652	48	116,700
Chicago, Madison & Northern	14	537	70,508	3,720				2	2,650	6,254	4,978	85,460	217	85,677
Chicago, Milwaukee & St. Paul..........	18	919	77,240	7,226	12	4,492	44,978	5	423	12,700	20,288	162,432	2,240	164,672
Chicago & Northwestern.................	17	2,640	100,625	1,900	17	2,640	61,250	9	907	22,929	22,689	209,483	170	209,653
same (Nor. Ill.)........................	38	4,976									50,489	50,489		50,489

same (S. & C.)	4	3,366									6,012	6,012		6,012
De Kalb & Great Western	5	4,280	11,621	1,400				2	1,256	2,238		15,259	10	15,269
Northern Illinois	38	4,976	97,356	1,748				5	4,414	11,672		110,776	152	110,928
Sycamore & Cortland	4	3,366	13,912	1,070					4,004	1,896		16,878	52	16,930
Total	195	66	$628,792	$23,728	35	3,950	$125,119	35	2,497	$82,407	$160,151	$1,020,178	$3,000	$1,023,187
DEWITT:														
Chicago, Havana & Western	24	4,530	74,574	1,657				1	3,860	3,462	5,636	85,329	238	85,567
Chicago & Springfield	32	4,034	101,568	10,460				8	1,752	20,830	19,972	152,830	3,723	156,553
Peoria & Eastern	4	3,922	16,600	375				1	1,939	3,418	4,716	25,109	21	25,130
Terre Haute & Peoria	18	3,681	46,743	410				1	2,358	2,893	13,188	63,234	24	63,258
Total	81	327	$239,485	$12,902				12	4,629	$30,603	$43,512	$326,502	$4,006	$330,508
DOUGLAS:														
Chicago & Eastern Illinois	24	751	91,740	2,885				3	4,339	7,644	57,959	160,228	2,926	163,154
Indiana, Decatur & Western	27	4,752	111,600	2,300				4	65	10,031	29,879	153,810	1,116	154,926
Terre Haute & Peoria	22	3,650	56,728	610				3	2,421	6,917	16,005	80,260	304	80,564
Toledo, St. Louis & Kansas City		3,221	2,135								859	2,994		2,994
Total	75	1,814	$262,203	$5,795				11	1,545	$24,592	$104,702	$397,292	$4,346	$401,638
DUPAGE:														
Chicago, Burlington & Quincy	21	3,517	132,163	2,258	18	1,218	$63,807	12	271	30,128	26,171	254,527	2,400	256,927
Chicago Great Western	17	3,916	102,902	3,800				3	2,905	8,918	22,187	137,807		137,807
Chicago, Madison & Northern	19	124	95,117	4,635				5	5,136	14,932	6,716	121,400		121,400
Chicago, Milwaukee & St. Paul	12	1,138	51,916	2,413		4,799	3,181	3	3,578	9,194	13,637	80,341		80,341
Chicago & Northwestern	25	396	144,181	6,870	18	2,255	64,495	12	974	30,461	32,510	278,517	11,175	289,692
Chicago, Santa Fè & California	4	4,622	25,840	20					3,585	1,697	5,736	33,293		33,293
Elgin, Joliet & Eastern	18	4,092	84,488	4,450				5	1,575	13,246	40,696	142,790	50	142,840
Total	119	1,965	$636,607	$24,446	37	2,992	$131,483	43	2,274	$108,576	$147,563	$1,048,675	$13,625	$1,062,300
EDGAR:														
Cairo, Vincennes & Chicago	29	3,265	79,971	685				3	4,273	7,619	21,542	109,817	711	110,528
Cleveland, Cincinnati, Chicago & St. L.	25	1,481	128,930	3,045				5	5,129	14,928	54,113	201,016		201,016
Indiana, Decatur & Western	21	2,323	85,760	700				1	4,848	4,796	22,961	114,217	14	114,231
Peoria, Decatur & Evansville (Chi. Div.)	27	2,997	68,919	825				1	3,940	3,492	3,021	76,157	280	76,437
Terre Haute & Peoria	26	4,985	67,360	820				3	5,193	7,967	19,005	95,152	325	95,477
Toledo, St. Louis & Kansas City	19	4,487	69,474	825				1	2,561	2,970	27,945	101,214	39	101,253
Total	150	3,698	$500,414	$6,800				18	4,824	$41,772	$148,587	$697,573	$1,369	$698,942
EDWARDS:														
Cairo, Vincennes & Chicago	3	3,765	10,025						2,323	880	2,700	13,605		13,605
Louisville, Evansville & St. Louis Con.	9	3,963	31,689	420				1	222	2,084	13,221	47,414	34	47,448
Peoria, Decatur & Evansville	22	1,653	55,783	350				1	3,052	3,156	25,965	85,254	43	85,297
Total	35	4,101	$97,497	$770				3	317	$6,120	$41,886	$146,273	$77	$146,350

Statement 30—Continued.

County—Railroad.	Main Track, Including Right of Way and Improvements Thereon.				Second Main Track.			Side or Turnout Track.			Rolling Stock.	Total assessment by the State Board of Equalization...	Equalized value of railroad property assessed by local assessors........	Equalized value of railroad property in county..........
	Miles......	Feet........	Assess'd value excluding buildings.	Value of buildings on right of way.	Miles.......	Feet.......	Assess'd value.	Miles.......	Feet........	Assess'd value.	Assess'd value.			
Effingham:														
Baltimore & Ohio Southwestern	22	1,957	$67,112	$815				2	1,157	$5,539	$10,698	$114,164	$158	$114,322
Chicago, Paducah & Memphis	3	5,050	9,891	270					1,000	379	1,425	11,965		11,965
Indiana & Illinois Southern	11		16,500						300	57	2,149	18,706		181,706
Terre Haute & Indianapolis	25	2,078	159,980	5,200				9	2,733	23,794	76,872	265,846	4,017	269,863
Wabash (C. & P.)	19	909	86,275	1,619					4,058	1,921	29,526	119,341	181	119,522
Total	81	4,714	$339,758	$7,904				12	3,948	$31,690	$150,670	$530,022	$4,356	$534,378
Fayette:														
Baltimore & Ohio Southwestern	1	1,726	3,981	75					310	146	2,414	6,616		6,616
Chicago, Paducah & Memphis	16	3,820	41,809	1,710				1	2,284	2,865	6,023	52,407		52,407
Terre Haute & Indianapolis	25	4,272	162,597	1,734				5	3,857	14,317	78,130	256,778	300	257,078
Toledo, St. Louis & Kansas City	16	3,960	58,625	550					4,727	1,790	23,582	84,547	40	84,587
Total	60	3,218	$267,012	$4,069				8	598	$19,118	$110,149	$400,348	$340	$400,688
Ford:														
Chicago & Springfield	25	3,303	79,439	1,685				2	1,847	5,874	15,620	102,618	129	102,747
Kankakee & Southwestern	5	2,513	15,333	1,150					4,231	1,603	3,776	21,862	52	21,914
Lake Erie & Western	28	3,151	114,357	3,570				5	1,254	13,094	48,354	179,405	395	179,800
Toledo, Peoria & Western	6	99	24,075	445					3,662	1,734	7,323	33,577	21	33,598
Wabash (C. & P.)	15	2,503	69,683	2,882				3	920	7,936	23,831	104,282	90	104,372
Total	81	1,009	$302,867	$9,732				12	1,354	30,241	$98,904	$441,744	687	$142,431
Franklin:														
Belleville & Eldorado	27	420	54,159	1,900				1	3,479	2,986	13,009	72,054		72,054
Chicago, Paducah & Memphis	18	2,382	46,128	720					5,200	1,970	6,646	55,464		55,464
Total	45	2,802	$100,287	$2,620				2	3,399	$4,956	$19,655	$127,518		$127,518

Fulton:														
Chicago, Burlington & Quincy	51	2,656	314,169	2,541				6	4,087	16,935	62,213	395,858	1,347	397,205
Chicago, Havana & Western		2,573	1,462								111	1,573	309	1,882
Fulton County Narrow Gauge	41	3,875	50,081	1,300				1	3,763	857	9,417	61,655	150	61,805
Illinois Western	2	3,190	7,813					1	4,498	4,630		12,443		12,443
Iowa Central	12	5,074	38,883	1,157				3	2,990	7,132	9,326	56,498	469	56,967
St. Louis, Rock Island & Chicago	16	3,313	66,510	934				3	1,794	8,349	11,484	87,277	616	87,893
Toledo, Peoria & Western	33	2,105	133,595	2,155				6	1,574	15,745	40,687	192,132	745	192,877
Total	159	1,666	$612,513	$8,087				23	2,866	$53,648	$133,188	$807,436	$3,636	$811,072
Gallatin:														
Baltimore & Ohio Southwestern	16	3,902	50,217	570				4	3,275	11,551	30,453	92,791	318	93,109
same (L. & N.)	2	3,456									4,829	4,829		4,829
Cairo, Vincennes & Chicago		1,168	597								161	758		758
Louisville & Nashville	10	5,098	41,669	1,028				1	1,487	2,884	12,138	57,719	5,957	63,676
same (B. & O. S. W.)	2	3,459									2,939	2,939		2,939
Total	33	1,243	$92,483	$1,598				5	4,762	$14,435	$50,520	$159,036	$6,275	$165,311
Greene:														
Chicago & Alton	39	675	246,505	12,605				9	612	22,790	79,917	361,817	2,185	364,002
Litchfield, Carrollton & Western	25	4,731	46,613	705				1	4,588	1,869	3,777	52,964	162	53,126
St. Louis, Rock Island & Chicago	23	4,399	95,333	1,192				3	1,611	8,263	16,461	121,249	510	121,759
Total	88	4,525	$388,451	$14,502				14	1,531	$32,922	$100,155	$536,030	$2,857	$538,887
Grundy:														
Chicago & Alton	18	1,723	115,456	1,780	8	2,776	$29,840	5	1,483	13,202	37,431	197,709	150	197,859
same (C. & Ill. R.)	1	3,665	10,672					2	4,199	6,988	3,460	21,120	50	21,170
Chicago, Rock Island & Pacific	20	1,147	171,846	1,750	20	1,147	70,760	3	3,305	9,160	23,317	276,833	150	276,983
Chicago, Santa Fé & California	20	984	106,968	1,235				4	870	10,412	23,746	142,361	1,714	144,075
Clev., Cin., Chi. & St. Louis (K. & S.)	20	679									43,085	43,085		43,085
Elgin, Joliet & Eastern	19	3,795	88,734	7,590				12	864	30,409	42,647	169,380	175	169,555
Kankakee & Seneca	20	679	50,322	1,250				4	3,225	9,222		60,794	625	61,419
Total	120	2,092	$543,998	$13,605	28	3,923	$100,600	32	3,586	$79,393	$173,686	$911,282	$2,864	$914,146
Hamilton:														
Louisville & Nashville	36	3,680	139,449	2,084				2	3,099	5,820	40,621	187,974	424	188,398
Hancock:														
Chicago, Burlington & Quincy	41	1,576	251,921	1,524				3	2,993	8,917	49,886	312,248	413	312,661
Chicago, Santa Fé & California	7	320	37,431	1,275				3	2,806	8,828	8,309	55,843	211	56,054
Toledo, Peoria & Western	41	2,501	165,895	2,645				4	1,689	10,800	50,462	229,802	170	229,972
Wabash	22	909	99,775	4,007				1	3,090	3,963	34,146	141,891	156	142,047
same (T., P. & W.)	7	5									10,782	10,782		10,782
Total	119	41	$555,022	$9,451				13	18	$32,508	$153,585	$750,566	$950	$751,516

Statement 30—Continued.

County—Railroad.	Main Track, including Right of Way and Improvements thereon.				Second Main Track.			Side or Turnout Track.			Rolling Stock.	Total assessment by the State Board of Equalization...	Equalized value of railroad property assessed by local assessors	Equalized value of railroad property in county ....
	Miles.......	Feet.......	Assess'd value excluding buildings.	Value of buildings on right of way.	Miles.......	Feet	Assess'd value.	Miles.......	Feet.......	Assess'd value.	Assess'd value.			
Henderson:														
Chicago, Burlington & Quincy..........	32	2,890	$198,539	$1,633	18	175	$63,116	6	3,394	$16,607	$39,315	$319,210	$246	$319,456
Chicago, Santa Fé & California..........	22	2,213	118,821	3,560	......	......	....	4	2,378	11,126	26,377	159,884	272	160,156
Iowa Central..........	......	4,320	2,455	....	......	......	....	......	......	....	589	3,044	....	3,044
St. Louis, Rock Island & Chicago.......	14	4,112	59,115	300	......	......	....	......	2,222	1,052	10,207	70,674	87	70,761
Toledo, Peoria & Western..........	4	3,108	18,355	....	......	......	....	......	1,607	761	5,583	24,699	....	24,699
same (C., B. & Q.)..........	8	564	....	....	......	......	....	......	......	....	9,864	9,864	....	9,864
Total..........	83	1,367	$397,285	$5,493	18	175	$63,116	11	4,321	$29,546	$91,935	$587,375	$605	$587,980
Henry:														
Chicago, Burlington & Quincy..........	35	1,364	215,076	2,858	14	3,281	51,175	7	5,072	19,902	42,590	331,601	781	332,382
Chicago, Rock Island & Pacific..........	27	3,710	235,473	3,125	27	3,710	96,959	5	4,122	14,451	31,951	381,959	3,396	385,355
Rock Island & Peoria..........	31	3,625	180,613	9,625	......	......	....	3	2,624	8,742	33,374	232,354	420	232,774
St. Louis, Rock Island & Chicago..........	27	907	108,687	766	......	......	....	4	22	10,010	18,766	138,229	166	138,395
Total..........	121	4,326	$739,849	$16,374	42	1,711	$148,134	21	1,280	$53,105	$126,681	$1,084,143	24,763	$1,988,906
Iroquois:														
Chicago & Eastern Illinois..........	47	2,341	180,285	4,415	36	1,334	108,758	7	3,463	15,312	113,899	422,669	372	423,041
Chicago, Lake Shore & East'n (C. & EI.)	36	1,334	....	....	......	......	....	......	......	....	5,488	5,488	....	5,488
Chicago & Springfield	9	1,926	29,031	1,125	......	......	....	1	2,724	3,790	5,708	39,654	70	39,724
Cincinnati, Lafayette & Chicago	20	2,595	102,457	395	......	......	....	5	3,147	13,990	....	116,842	117	116,959
Cleve., Cin., Chi. & St. L. (C., L., F. C.)	20	2,595	....	....	......	......	....	......	......	....	43,862	43,862	....	43,862
Toledo, Peoria & Western	31	2,480	125,879	2,530	......	......	....	4	3,407	11,613	38,290	178,312	148	178,460
Total	165	2,711	$437,652	$8,465	36	1,334	$108,758	19	2,181	$44,705	$207,247	$806,827	$707	$807,533
Jackson:														
Chicago & Texas	36	220	72,083	600	......	......	....	8	3,459	12,983	20,218	105,914	2,047	107,961
Mobile & Ohio..........	34	1,411	137,069	11,900	......	......	....	11	2,090	28,490	37,437	214,896	5,415	220,311
St. Louis Southern..........	25	2,799	91,908	1,200	......	......	....	3	1,481	8,201	26,919	128,228	100	128,328
Total	95	4,430	$301,060	$13,700	......	......	....	23	1,750	$49,674	$84,604	$449,038	$7,562	$456,600

Jasper:														
Indiana & Illinois Southern	24		36,000						3,000	568	4,688	41,256		41,256
Peoria, Decatur & Evansville	23	3,105	58,970	675				1	4,973	3,884	27,448	90,977		90,977
same (Chi. Div.)	23	70	57,533	170				1	535	2,203	2,521	62,427		62,427
Motal	70	3,175	$152,503	$845				3	32,228	$6,655	$34,657	$194,660		$194,660
Jefferson:														
Chicago, Paducah & Memphis	24	2,310	61,094	720					4,700	1,780	8,802	72,396	485	72,881
Louisville, Evansville & St. Louis Con.	26	1,447	85,391	1,070				2	4,667	5,768	35,626	127,855	294	128,149
Louisville & Nashville	26	4,827	102,274	1,989				3	3,150	8,092	29,792	142,147	1,005	143,152
Louisville & St. Louis	10	3,790	21,435	500					3,815	722	59	22,716		22,716
Wabash, Chester & Western	17	1,816	34,688	1,700				1	1,782	2,408	5,806	44,602	1,201	45,803
Total	105	3,630	$304,882	$5,979				9	2,274	$18,770	$80,085	$409,716	$2,985	$412,701
Jersey:														
Chicago & Alton	16	4,650	106,348	1,010				1	1,574	3,245	34,478	145,081	695	145,776
St. Louis, Chicago & St. Paul	33	1,319	83,125	1,401				3	1,773	5,004	43,174	132,704	175	132,879
St. Louis, Rock Island & Chicago	5	3,746	22,838	80					1,947	922	3,943	27,783	58	27,841
Total	55	4,435	$212,311	$2,491				5	14	$9,171	$81,595	$305,568	$928	$306,496
JoDaviess:														
Chicago, Burlington & Northern	22	1,138	111,078	4,500				4	574	10,272	39,431	165,281	1,622	166,903
same (Ill. Cen.)	13	1,617									23,617	23,617		23,617
same (D. & D. Bdg.)		890									296	296		296
Chicago Great Western	30	661	174,726	4,700				3	826	7,891	37,673	224,990	61	225,051
same (C., B. & N.)	1	4,488									2,314	2,314		32,314
same (Ill. Cen.)	13	1,214									16,545	16,545		16,545
same (D. & D. Bdg.)		898									213	213		213
Chicago, Milwaukee & St. Paul	1	49	4,280	25					915	433	1,126	5,873	26	5,899
Chicago & Northwestern	10	1,571	59,211	200				1	2,119	3,503	13,351	76,265	87	76,352
Total	92	1,956	$349,304	$9,425				8	4,434	$22,099	$134,566	$515,394	$1,796	$517,190
Johnson:														
Cairo, Vincennes & Chicago	28	1,396	76,314	1,185				3	368	6,139	20,557	104,195		104,195
Chicago, St. Louis & Paducah	21	5,110	68,100	3,200				1	2,839	3,844	20,619	95,763		95,763
Total	50	1,226	$144,414	$4,385				4	3,207	$9,983	$41,176	$199,958		$199,958

Statement 30—Continued.

County—Railroad.	Main Track, Including Right of Way and Improvements Thereon.				Second Main Track.			Side or Turnout Track.			Rolling Stock.	Total assessment by State Board of Equalization......	Equalized value of railroad property assessed by local assessors..........	Equalized value of railroad property in county..........
	Miles	Feet........	Assess'd value exclud-ing build-ings.	Value of build-ings on right of way.	Miles	Feet........	Assess'd value.	Miles	Feet........	Assess'd value.	Assess'd value.			
Kane:														
Chicago, Burlington & Quincy	24	3,608	$150,568	$45,275	6	849	$21,563	30	4,362	$77,065	$29,816	$324,287	$105,392	$429,679
Chicago Great Western..................	18	1,918	106,507	4,000	......	......	....	5	809	12,883	22,965	146,355	479	146,834
Chicago & Iowa..........................	14	1,643	71,556	520	......	......	....	1	1,817	3,360	10,755	86,191	182	86,373
Chicago, Madison & Northern...........	18	4,346	94,110	4,860	......	......	....	3	4,424	9,595	6,644	115,209	776	115,985
Chicago, Milwaukee & St. Paul..........	19	2,814	83,015	7,475	......	......	....	8	1,171	20,554	21,805	132,849	1,539	134,388
Chicago & Northwestern	57	2,612	324,845	6,085	17	3,071	61,535	28	3,556	71,684	73,248	537,395	4,426	541,821
Elgin, Joliet & Eastern	4	205	18,175	2,570	......	......	....	1	3,595	4,202	8,735	33,682	627	34,309
Total..................................	156	1,300	$848,776	$70,785	23	3,920	$83,098	79	3,894	$199,343	$173,966	$1,375,968	$113,421	$1,489,389
Kankakee:														
Chicago & Eastern Illinois	32	110	121,679	8,635	19	3,812	59,166	21	3,242	43,228	76,873	309,581	4,804	314,385
Chi., Lake Shore & Eastern (C. & E. I.)	21	19	....	....	......	......	....	......	......	....	3,179	3,179	....	3,179
Cincinnati, Lafayette & Chicago........	12	2,588	62,451	3,060	......	......	....	17	1,388	43,157	....	108,668	43	108,711
Cleve., Cin., Chi. & St. L. (C., L. F. & C.)	12	2,588	....	....	......	......	....	......	......	....	26,735	26,735	....	26,735
same (K. & S.)........................	20	3,021	....	....	......	......	....	......	......	....	44,035	44,035	....	44,035
Indiana, Illinois & Iowa.................	38	3,485	127,578	13,707	......	......	....	14	183	35,096	24,591	200,962	100	201,062
Kankakee & Seneca......................	20	3,021	51,430	970	......	......	....	1	1,760	2,667	....	55,067	29	55,096
Kankakee & Southwestern.............	29	84	81,245	2,800	......	......	....	3	1,342	6,508	20,007	110,560	123	110,683
Wabash (C. & S.).......................	8	4,160	39,546	1,450	......	......	....	1	3,459	4,138	13,534	58,668	1,803	60,471
Total..................................	195	3,236	$483,929	$30,622	19	3,812	$59,166	59	814	$134,784	$208,954	$917,455	$6,902	$924,357
Kendall:														
Chicago, Burlington & Quincy..........	33	2,545	204,240	1,634	14	2,033	50,348	6	2,274	16,077	40,444	312,743	272	313,015
Elgin, Joliet & Eastern..................	3	2,922	15,990	330	......	......	....	......	1,846	874	7,685	24,879	19	24,898
Total..................................	37	187	$220,230	$1,964	14	2,033	$50,348	6	4,120	$16,951	$48,129	$337,622	$291	$337,913
Knox:														
Chicago, Burlington & Quincy..........	71	1,798	435,177	24,433	25	3,794	90,015	49	1,748	123,328	86,175	759,128	25,999	785,127
same (G. & R.)........................	12	1,010	....	....	......	......	....	......	......	....	14,726	14,726	....	14,726
Chicago, Santa Fé & California.........	25	651	133,153	9,545	......	......	....	7	622	17,795	29,559	190,052	767	190,819
Fulton County Narrow Gauge...........	17	2,989	21,079	830	......	......	....	......	3,223	305	3,963	26,177	6	26,183
Galesburg, Etherley & Eastern.........	11	3,089	46,340	1,500	......	......	....	......	2,700	1,278	1,020	50,138	....	50,138

Galesburg & Rio	12	1,010	48,765	318				1	641	2,704		51,787	546	52,333
Iowa Central	15	4,943	47,808	428				1	25	2,010	11,467	61,713	9	61,722
Rock Island & Peoria	2	201	11,617								2,147	13,764	6	13,770
St. Louis, Rock Island & Chicago	5	1,854	21,405	216					1,376	652	3,696	25,969	45	26,014
Total	173	1,705	$765,344	$37,270	25	3,794	$90,015	59	5,055	$148,072	$152,753	$1,193,454	$27,378	$1,220,832
LAKE:														
Chicago, Milwaukee & St. Paul	27	2,047	116,398	6,144	24	2,047	85,357	6	1,999	15,947	30,574	254,420	3,310	257,730
Chicago & Northwestern	28	3,684	165,012	4,380	24	3,456	86,291	16	4,096	41,939	37,207	334,829	1,119	335,948
Elgin, Joliet & Eastern	23	5,075	107,828	8,760				8	4,092	21,938	51,824	190,350	9,236	199,586
Waukegan & Mississippi Valley											8,950	8,950		8,950
Wisconsin Central	25	2,529	152,874	7,824				9	4,893	34,743	40,914	236,355	1,722	238,077
Total	105	2,778	$542,112	$27,108	49	223	$171,648	41	4,520	$114,567	$169,469	$1,024,904	$15,387	$1,040,291
LASALLE:														
Chicago & Alton	12	1,096	76,908	690				1	2,483	3,676	24,934	106,208	348	106,556
Chicago, Burlington & Quincy	80	4,926	493,691	7,974	25	3,102	89,556	24	684	60,324	97,762	749,307	348	752,425
same (L. V. & N.)	28	978									34,046	34,046		34,046
Chicago & Northwestern (Nor. Ill.)	21	2,037									27,727	27,727	205	27,932
Chicago, Rock Island & Pacific	31	2,557	267,616	10,563	31	2,557	110,195	22	3,677	56,741	36,312	481,427	1,476	482,903
Chicago, Santa Fé & California	25	3,067	135,579	5,005				12	2,304	31,091	30,097	201,772	738	202,510
Cleveland, Cin., Chi. & St. L. (K. & S.)	1	1,981									2,944	2,944		2,944
Illinois Valley & Northern	28	978	84,556	2,875				6	2,350	16,112		103,543	247	103,790
Indiana, Illinois & Iowa	1	497	3,611	1,160				1	3,105	3,970	696	9,437		9,437
Kankakee & Seneca	1	1,981	3,438						2,586	979		4,417		4,417
LaSalle & Bureau County	5	122	15,069						970	459		15,528	194	15,722
Northern Illinois	21	2,037	53,464	915				2	3,479	5,318		59,697		59,697
Wabash (C. & P.)	1	657	5,060	1,338				1	3,074	3,956	1,732	12,086	246	12,332
Total	259	1,794	$1,128,992	$30,520	57	379	$199,751	73	3,592	$182,626	$256,250	$1,808,139	$6,572	$1,814,711
LAWRENCE:														
Baltimore & Ohio Southwestern	21	2,396	64,361	880				15	740	37,850	39,030	142,121	128	142,249
Cairo, Vincennes & Chicago	21	2,700	58,081	490				2	5,255	5,991	15,646	80,208	175	80,383
Total	42	5,096	$122,442	$1,370				18	715	$43,841	$54,676	$222,329	$303	$222,632
LEE:														
Chicago, Burlington & Quincy	42	4,741	261,677	888				3	907	7,929	51,818	322,312	783	323,095
Chicago & Iowa	8	4,589	44,346	340					3,643	1,725	6,665	53,076	62	53,138
Chicago & Northwestern	26	677	150,237	2,665	26	677	91,449	13	352	32,667	33,875	310,893	1,402	312,295
Total	77	4,727	$456,260	$3,893	26	677	$91,449	16	4,902	$42,321	$92,358	$686,281	$2,247	$688,528

Statement 30—Continued.

County—Railroad.	Main Track, Including Right of Way and Improvements Thereon.				Second Main Track.			Side or Turnout Track.			Rolling Stock.	Total assessment by the State Board of Equalization...	Equalized value of railroad property assessed by local assessors........	Equalized value of railroad property in county..........
	Miles......	Feet......	Assess'd value excluding buildings.	Value of buildings on right of way.	Miles......	Feet......	Assess'd value.	Miles......	Feet......	Assess'd value.	Assess'd value.			
Livingston:														
Chicago & Alton	51	3,843	$325,885	$6,915	29	2,440	$103,117	5	4,789	$14,768	$105,652	$556,337	$1,702	$558,039
Chicago, Santa Fe & California	13	5,002	73,921	1,600				5	3,179	14,005	16,410	105,336	266	105,602
Indiana, Illinois & Iowa	29	5,258	98,986	4,208				5	3,167	14,000	19,080	136,274	70	136,344
Kankakee & Southwestern	61	5,113	173,511	13,600				5	667	10,253	42,728	240,092	298	240,390
Toledo, Peoria & Western	18	574	72,435	1,370				4	3,670	11,738	22,033	107,576	73	107,649
Wabash (C. & P.)	33	1,970	150,184	3,425				2	2,139	6,013	51,398	211,020	536	211,556
same (C. & S.)	32	458	144,391	13,219				8	2,029	20,961	49,415	227,986	484	228,470
same (T., P. & W.)	5										7,700	7,700		7,700
Total	246	1,104	$1,039,313	$43,737	29	2,440	$103,117	37	3,800	$91,738	$314,416	$1,592,321	$3,429	$1,595,750
Logan:														
Chicago & Alton	28	2,880	179,836	3,105				4	4,928	12,333	58,303	253,577	200	253,777
Chicago, Havana & Western	24	2'950	73,676	2,550				2	3,812	5,444	5,569	87,239	150	87,389
Chicago & Springfield	17	163	52,796	1,350				1	4,769	4,758	10,381	69,285	110	69,395
Peoria, Decatur & Evansville	33	1,401	83,163	550				4	3,588	9,359	38,709	131,781	70	131,851
Terre Haute & Peoria	11	3,048	28,943	230					3,248	1,230	8,166	38,569	15	38,584
Total	114	5,162	$418,414	$7,785				14	4,505	$33,124	$121,128	$580,451	$545	$580,996
Macon:														
Chicago, Havana & Western	16	170	48,097	1,344				1	3,589	3,360	3,635	56,436	165	56,601
Indiana, Decatur & Western	11	2,008	45,521	3,400				2	4,397	7,082	12,187	68,190	10	68,200
Peoria, Decatur & Evansville	16	3,203	41,564	450				1	3,557	3,347	19,346	64,707	35	64,742
same (T. H. & P.)	7	2,657									8,731	8,731		8,731
Terre Haute & Peoria	14	1,488	35,705	520				1	3,140	3,189	10,074	49,488	80	49,568
same (Ill. Cen.)	15	2,214									10,876	10,876		10,876
Wabash	40	1,810	181,543	29,594				24	356	60,169	62,130	333,436	3,521	336,957
Total	121	3,090	$352,430	$35,308				31	4,479	$77,147	$126,979	$591,864	$3,811	$595,675
Macoupin:														
Chicago & Alton	40	3,607	256,304	2,825				10	1,945	25,921	83,094	368,144	1,452	369,596
Chicago, Peoria & St. Louis	8	2,949	23,964	670				2	3,724	5,411	15,376	45,421	24	45,445
Cleveland, Cincinnati, Chicago & St. L.	20	3,612	105,489	1,120				5	500	12,737	44,274	163,620	146	163,766

Jacksonville, Louisville & St. Louis	18	2,770	48,164	825				2	1,707	4,647	9,049	62,685	37	62,722
Litchfield, Carrollton & Western	24	4,868	44,860	475				1	503	1,095	3,635	50,065	546	50,611
St. Louis, Chicago & St. Paul	28	1,613	70,764	1,696				2	556	3,158	36,754	112,372	122	112,494
St. Louis & Eastern	5	4,407	16,645	10				1	3,293	3,247	10,436	29,738	36	29,774
St. Louis, Rock Island & Chicago	13	2,568	53,946	344				2	3,528	6,670	9,315	70,275	324	70,599
Wabash	8	3,639	39,101	2,488				4	187	10,089	13,382	65,060	98	65,158
Total	169	3,633	$658,637	$10,453				32	103	$72,975	$225,315	$967,380	$2,785	$970,165
MADISON:														
Chicago & Alton	39	4,092	250,583	8,415	1	2,258	$4,997	15	4,993	39,864	81,239	385,098	1,662	386,760
Chicago, Peoria & St. Louis	32	2,813	91,092	860				3	4,213	7,596	58,447	157,995		157,995
Cleveland, Cincinnati, Chicago & St. L.	33	378	168,665	2,485				12	4,570	32,164	70,789	274,103	210	274,313
Louisville, Evansville & St. Louis Con.		730	449						830	314	188	951		951
Madison, Illinois & St. Louis	4	1,584	86,000	2,200				5	5,115	20,891	6,717	115,808		115,808
St. Louis, Chicago & St. Paul	22	2,890	56,368	1,290				5	1,740	7,994	29,277	94,929		94,929
St. Louis & Eastern	27	557	74,540	790				4	4,444	9,683	48,484	133,497		133,497
St. Louis, Rock Island & Chicago	8	4,727	35,581	60				1	1,740	3,324	6,144	45,109	67	45,176
same (I. & St. L.)	17	153									11,761	11,761		11,761
Terre Haute & Indianapolis	24	3,000	154,780	2,430				9	1,003	22,975	74,374	254,559	55	254,614
Toledo, St. Louis & Kansas City	37	1,901	130,760	6,025				9	2,634	18,998	52,597	208,380	120	208,500
Wabash	40	5,242	184,468	6,450				8	3,267	21,547	63,131	275,596	170	275,766
Total	288	1,667	$1,233,286	$31,005	1	2,258	$4,997	77	2,869	$185,350	$503,148	$1,957,786	$2,284	$1,960,070
MARION:														
Baltimore & Ohio Southwestern	24	766	72,435	1,380				3	4,205	9,491	43,926	127,232	236	127,468
Centralia & Chester	1	1,960	3,428	150					3,202	1,213	308	5,099		5,099
Chicago, Paducah & Memphis	25	3,620	64,214	1,260				1	1,770	2,671	9,251	77,396		77,396
Jacksonville, Louisville & St. Louis	2	4,666	7,498	450					2,330	883	1,409	10,240	236	10,476
Louisville, Evansville & St. Louis Con.		3,701	2,278						1,000	379	951	3,608		3,608
same (L. & St. L.)	7	2,569									10,152	10,152		10,152
Louisville & St. Louis	5	3,957	11,499	100					215	41	31	11,671	810	12,481
Total	68	119	$161,352	$3,340				6	2,162	$14,678	$66,028	$245,398	$1,282	$246,680
MARSHALL:														
Chicago & Alton	28	5,238	182,650	2,200				2	1,721	5,815	59,215	249,880		249,880
Chi., Rock Island & Pacific (Peo. Br.)	13	3,689	116,439	1,875				1	1,029	2,987	15,799	137,100	810	137,910
Chicago, Santa Fé & California	23	20	121,920	3,335				9	4,762	24,755	27,065	177,075		177,075
Total	65	3,667	$421,009	$7,410				13	2,232	$33,557	$102,079	$564,055	$810	$564,865
MASON:														
Chicago & Alton	12	4,370	80,814	1,170				2	3,138	6,486	26,200	114,670	150	114,820
Chicago, Havana & Western	25	4,304	77,445	3,669				2	1,852	4,701	5,854	91,669	680	92,349
Chicago, Peoria & St. Louis	49	3,748	139,188	2,763				7	3,694	15,399	89,306	246,656	1,080	247,736
Total	88	1,862	$297,447	$7,602				12	3,404	$26,586	$121,360	$452,995	$1,910	$454,905
MASSAC:														
Chicago, St. Louis & Paducah	19	1,753	59,929	3,400				4	2,730	11,293	18,142	92,764		92,764

Statement 30—Continued.

County—Railroad.	Main Track, including Right of Way and Improvements Thereon.				Second Main Track.			Side or Turnout Track.			Rolling Stock.	Total assessment by the State Board of Equalization...	Equalized value of railroad property assessed by local assessors..........	Equalized value of railroad property in county..........
	Miles	Feet........	Assess'd value exclud-ing build-ings.	Value of build-ings on right of way.	Miles.......	Feet........	Assess'd value.	Miles.......	Feet........	Assess'd value.	Assess'd value.			
McDonough:														
Chicago, Burlington & Quincy..........	34	1,720	$209,387	$2,864	......	......	....	8	2,769	$21,311	$41,463	$274,975	$1,170	$276,145
St. Louis, Rock Island & Chicago.......	19	2,779	78,105	368	......	......	....	2	1,186	5,562	13,486	97,521	120	97,641
Toledo, Peoria & Western..............	27	3,876	110,936	1,920	......	......	....	3	1,022	7,984	33,745	154,585	114	154,699
Total..............................	81	3,095	$398,428	$5,102	......	......	....	13	4,977	$34,857	$88,694	$527,081	$1,404	$528,485
McHenry:														
Chicago & Northwestern	96	1,653	553,800	9,460	......	......	....	23	1,987	58,441	124,870	746,571	2,847	749,418
McLean:														
Chicago & Alton........................	56	5,205	359,011	74,035	25	357	$87,737	24	1,333	60,631	116,391	697,805	$0,745	778,550
Chicago & Springfield..................	10	4,808	33,823	875	......	......	....	1	382	2,681	6,651	44,030	50	44,080
Kankakee & Southwestern..............	29	1,113	81,790	4,125	......	......	....	3	727	6,275	20,141	112,331	180	112,511
Lake Erie & Western..................	42	1,021	168,773	8,820	......	......	....	6	974	15,461	71,344	264,398	300	264,698
Peoria & Eastern......................	37	151	129,600	2,588	......	......	....	8	5,005	22,370	36,821	191,379	130	191,509
Rantoul................................	16	4,188	30,228	1,213	......	......	....	1	630	1,119	2,455	35,015	140	35,155
Toledo, Peoria & Western..............	21	348	84,263	1,620	......	......	....	2	2,899	6,373	25,632	117,888	110	117,998
Wabash (C. & P.).......................	2	2,952	11,516	963	......	......	....	......	4,235	2,005	3 941	18,425	40	18,465
Total..............................	216	3,946	$899,004	$94,239	25	357	$87,737	48	345	$116,915	$283,376	$1,481,271	$81,695	$1,562,966
Menard:														
Chicago & Alton........................	23	1,040	146,141	1,150	......	......	....	3	2,000	8,447	47,379	203,117	112	203,229
Chicago, Peoria & St. Louis............	21	2,371	60,057	1,505	......	......	....	4	4,638	9,757	38,534	109,853	30	109,883
Total..............................	44	3,411	$206,198	$2,655	......	......	....	8	1,358	$18,204	$85,913	$312,970	$142	$313,112
Mercer:														
Chicago, Burlington & Quincy..........	36	973	220,724	1,675	......	......	....	4	1,379	10,653	43,708	276,760	408	277,168
Iowa Central...........................	10	1,144	30,650	4,343	......	......	....	4	4,984	9,888	7,352	52,233	41	52,274
Rock Island & Peoria..................	14	3,295	83,357	4,550	......	......	....	4	282	10,134	15,403	113,444	52	113,496
St. Louis, Rock Island & Chicago.......	8	4,567	35,460	126	......	......	....	......	2,799	1,325	6,123	43,034	36	43,070
Total..............................	69	4,699	$370,191	$10,694	......	......	....	13	4,164	$32,000	$72,586	$485,471	$537	$186,008

Monroe:														
Mobile & Ohio	27	417	108,316	4,750				4	3,919	11,855	29,584	154,505	196	154,701
Montgomery:														
Chicago, Peoria & St. Louis	4	2,774	12,671						402	152	8,130	20,953	11	20,964
Cleveland, Cincinnati, Chicago & St. L.	34	1,353	174,707	2,645				10	2,743	26,299	73,335	276,976	220	277,196
Jacksonville, Louisville & St. Louis	20	2,709	53,334	975					4,711	1,784	10,020	66,113	42	66,155
Litchfield, Carrollton & Western		4,445	1,515						765	145	123	1,783		1,783
St. Louis & Eastern	25	3,570	70,610	715				5	4,528	11,715	45,927	128,967	131	129,098
Toledo, St. Louis & Kansas City	15	2,904	54,425	625				2	1,304	4,494	21,892	81,436	47	81,483
Wabash	20	383	90,326	4,838				5	3,065	13,951	30,913	140,028	158	140,186
Total	121	2,298	$457,588	$9,798				25	1,678	$58,540	$190,330	$716,256	$609	$716,865
Morgan:														
Chicago & Alton	28	2,352	179,206	2,530				3	3,687	9,246	58,099	249,081	215	249,296
Chicago, Peoria & St. Louis	9	4,446	27,558	9,559				4	490	8,186	17,682	62,985	10	62,995
Jacksonville, Louisville & St. Louis	19	198	49,498	600				3	4,648	7,760	9,300	67,158	170	67,328
St. Louis, Chicago & St. Paul	6	367	15,174	213					2,890	821	7,881	24,089		24,089
St. Louis, Rock Island & Chicago	9	2,696	38,042	288				1	180	2,585	6,569	47,484	48	47,532
Wabash	30	521	135,444	13,531				7	2,487	18,678	46,353	214,006	132	214 138
Total	103	20	$444,922	$26,721				20	3,822	$47,276	$145,884	$664,803	$575	$665,378
Moultrie:														
Chicago & Eastern Illinois	17	4,103	67,553	1,530				2	794	4,301	42,678	116,062	116	116,178
Cleveland, Cincinnati, Chicago & St. L.	4	1,153	21,514	90					3,657	1,731	9,029	32,364	32	32,396
Peoria, Decatur & Evansville	22	4,307	57,039	425				3	1,584	6,609	26,549	90,613	144	90,757
Terre Haute & Peoria	15	4,940	39,839	370				1	3,431	3,300	11,240	54,749	27	54,776
Wabash (C. & P.)	22	3,133	101,670	1,356				1	1,538	3,228	34,795	141,049	90	141,139
Total	83	1,796	$287,615	$3,771				9	444	$19,160	$124,291	$434,837	$409	$435,246
Ogle:														
Chicago, Burlington & Northern	18	3,327	93,151	1,770				3	318	7,651	33,067	135,639	950	136,589
same (C. & Ill. R.)		1,365									459	459		459
Chicago Great Western	28	97	162,507	20,300				3	4,599	9,677	35,038	227,522	429	227,951
Chicago & Iowa	36	865	180,819	7,168				7	1,471	18,197	27,177	233,361	346	233,707
same (C., R. & N.)	14	4,693	74,444					1	1,138	3,038	11,189	88,671		88,671
Chicago, Milwaukee & St. Paul	39	3,596	168,645	10,969	7	5,101	$27,881	8	1,568	20,743	44,297	272,535	610	273,145
same (C., R. & N.)	3	2,769									3,934	3,934	13	3,947
Chicago & Northwestern	11	1,777	65,185	690	11	1,777	39,678	4	1,289	10,610	14,698	130,861	86	130,947
Total	152	2,649	$744,751	$40,897	19	1,598	$67,559	27	5,103	$69,916	$169,859	$1,092,982	$2,434	$1,095,416

Statement 30—Continued.

County—Railroad.	Main Track, including Right of Way and Improvements Thereon.				Second Main Track.			Side or Turnout Track.			Rolling Stock.	Total assessment by the State Board of Equalization	Equalized value of railroad property assessed by local assessors	Equalized value of railroad property in county
	Miles	Feet	Assess'd value excluding buildings.	Value of buildings on right of way.	Miles	Feet	Assess'd value.	Miles	Feet	Assess'd value.	Assess'd value.			
Peoria:														
Chicago, Burlington & Quincy	44	4,780	$273,922	$4,048				14	2,305	$36,092	$54,243	$368,305	$714	$369,019
Chicago, Rock Island & Pacific (Peo. Br.)	22	1,423	189,291	9,125				10	4,683	27,217	25,685	251,318	1,804	253,122
Chicago, Santa Fé & California	28	1,061	149,465	13,515				16	911	40,431	33,180	236,591	1,223	237,814
Iowa Central	19	3,183	58,808	1,163				7	479	14,182	14,105	88,258	294	88,552
Peoria & Pekin Union	10	447	231,948	31,550	2	374	$8,283	34	1,584	85,750	40,486	398,017	1,738	399,755
Rock Island & Peoria	27	1,767	155,808	2,345				10	562	25,266	28,790	212,209	5,716	217,925
Toledo, Peoria & Western	12	403	48,305	4,515				2	3,713	6,758	14,694	74,272	804	75,076
same (P. & P. U.)	8										9,734	9,734		9,734
Total	172	2,504	$1,107,547	$66,261	2	374	$8,283	95	3,677	$235,696	$220,917	$1,638,704	$12,293	$1,650,997
Perry:														
Belleville & Eldorado	5	2,510	10,951	500					4,461	1,521	2,630	15,602	50	15,652
Centralia & Chester	1	4,920	4,829								432	5,262		5,262
Mobile & Ohio	2	3,062	10,320								2,818	13,138		13,138
St. Louis, Alton & Terre Haute	22	3,880	122,768	700				4	3,151	11,492	90,743	225,703	720	226,423
St. Louis Southern	8	2,673	30,623	625				1	4,303	4,538	8,969	44,755	620	45,375
Wabash, Chester & Western	26	4,780	53,810	150				1	1,773	2,404	9,007	65,371	156	65,527
Total	68	705	$233,301	$1,975				8	3,128	$19,955	$114,600	$369,831	$1,546	$371,377
Piatt:														
Chicago, Havana & Western	28	1,661	84,944	1,931				2	3,754	5,422	6,420	98,717		98,717
Indiana, Decatur & Western	15	211	60,160	1,150				1	2,299	3,588	16,107	81,005		81,005
Peoria & Eastern	8	1,210	28,802	150				1	1,667	3,289	8,183	40,424		40,424
Wabash	15	2,373	69,522	4,275				5	1,627	13,270	23,793	110,860		110,860
same (C. & P.)	35	751	158,140	6,288				4	4,217	11,997	54,121	230,546		230,546
Total	102	926	$401,568	$13,794				15	3,004	$37,566	$108,624	$561,552		$561,552
Pike:														
Chicago & Alton	23	5,073	150,953	2,175				5	688	12,826	48,939	214,893	1,528	216,421
Chicago, Burlington & Quincy	29	2,405	179,678	419				1	2,457	3,663	35,580	219,340	231	219,571

Wabash	1	1,584	5,850								2,002	7,852	173	8,025
same (Han. Bdg.)	1	4,146	8,033	275					1,440	681	2,749	11,738		11,738
same (H. & N.)	45	501	202,927	7,384				7	1,568	18,242	69,448	298,001	184	298,185
Total	101	3,149	$547,441	$10,253				14	873	$35,412	$158,718	$751,824	$2,116	$753,940
PULASKI:														
Cairo, Vincennes & Chicago	19	4,487	53,594	775				2	3,647	5,381	14,437	74,187	775	74,962
Mound City	2	4,520	2,856	400					220	21	20	3,297	20	3,317
Total	22	3,727	$56,450	$1,175				2	3,867	$5,402	$14,457	$77,484	$795	$78,279
PUTNAM:														
Chicago, Rock Island & Pacific (Peo. Br.)	6	1,436	53,312	250					2,442	1,156	7,234	61,952	45	61,997
RANDOLPH:														
Centralia & Chester	32	1,444	80,684	1,275				3	3,673	7,391	7,238	96,588		96,588
Mobile & Ohio	31	1,027	124,778	2,450				7	204	17,597	34,080	178,905		178,905
St. Louis, Alton & Terre Haute	6	2,130	34,578	400				1	1,370	3,149	25,558	63,685	182	63,867
Wabash, Chester & Western	19	422	38,160	950				3	3,304	6,526	6,387	52,023	220	52,243
Total	88	5,023	$278,200	$5,075				15	3,271	$34,663	$73,263	$391,201	$402	$391,603
RICHLAND:														
Baltimore & Ohio Southwestern	20	2,916	61,657	1,585				6	2,566	16,215	37,390	116,847	327	117,174
Peoria, Decatur & Evansville	20	352	50,167	900				1	4,176	3,582	23,350	77,999	63	78,062
same (Chi. Div.)	1	826	2,891	350					2,538	961	127	4,329	661	4,990
Total	41	4,094	$114,715	$2,835				8	4,000	$20,758	$60,867	$199,175	$1,051	$200,226
ROCK ISLAND:														
Chicago, Milwaukee & St. Paul	22	285	93,729	3,375				5	680	12,822	24,620	134,546	264	134,810
same (C., R. I. & P.)	6	3,848									7,511	7,511		7,511
Chicago, Rock Island & Pacific	11	1,390	95,738	19,625	11	1,031	$39,184	23	487	57,731	12,990	225,268	2,275	227,543
Rock Island & Peoria	25	5,137	148,046	19,775				8	4,646	22,200	27,356	217,377	2,194	219,571
St. Louis, Rock Island & Chicago	26	189	104,143	5,530				15	781	37,870	17,982	165,525	668	166,193
Total	92	289	$441,656	$48,305	11	1,031	$39,184	52	1,314	$130,623	$99,459	$750,227	$5,401	$755,628
SALINE:														
Belleville & Eldorado	16	4,340	33,644	500					2,598	886	8,081	43,111	319	43,430
Cairo, Vincennes & Chicago	28	2,336	76,795	980				4	1,857	8,703	20,689	107,167	1,010	108,177
Louisville & Nashville	12	4,273	48,675	450					3,184	1,357	14,179	64,661	309	64,970
Total	58	389	$159,114	$1,930				5	2,359	$10,946	$42,949	$214,939	$1,638	$216,577

Statement 30—Continued.

County—Railroad.	Main Track, Including Right of Way and Improvements Thereon.				Second Main Track.			Side or Turnout Track.			Rolling Stock.	Total assessment by the State Board of Equalization...	Equalized value of railroad property assessed by local assessors..........	Equalized value of railroad property in county..........
	Miles.......	Feet.......	Assess'd value excluding buildings.	Value of buildings on right of way.	Miles.......	Feet.......	Assess'd value.	Miles.......	Feet.......	Assess'd value.	Assess'd value.			
Sangamon:														
Baltimore & Ohio Southwestern........	34	2,905	$103,650	$1,520	......	......	....	6	4,175	$16,977	$62,855	$185,002	$160	$185,162
same (Ill. Cent.)........................	......	3,077	....	....	......	......	....	......	......	....	1,060	1,060	....	1,060
Chicago & Alton..........................	34	2,721	217,447	13,070	......	......	....	8	4,245	22,010	70,496	323,023	680	323,703
Chicago, Peoria & St. Louis............	12	1,993	34,657	9,225	......	......	....	5	4,891	11,853	22,237	77,972	1,320	79,292
Chicago & Springfield..................	15	2,608	48,031	6,080	......	......	....	5	4,165	14,472	9,445	78,028	920	78,948
Jacksonville, Louisville & St. Louis....	8	3,079	22,316	100	......	......	....	......	3,495	1,324	4,193	27,933	....	27,933
Pawnee.....................................	9	......	9,000	225	......	......	....	......	2,300	218	2,520	11,963	....	11,963
St. Louis, Chicago & St. Paul...........	20	4,206	51,991	2,280	......	......	....	3	1,449	4,912	27,004	86,187	....	86,187
St. Louis & Eastern......................	18	4,506	51,847	535	......	......	....	2	4,458	5,689	33,723	91,794	524	92,318
Wabash.....................................	44	2,562	200,184	52,094	......	......	....	21	2,591	53,727	68,509	374,514	10,556	385,070
Total.......................................	199	1,257	$739,123	$85,129	......	......	....	56	89	$131,182	$302,042	$1,257,476	$14,160	$1,271,636
Schuyler:														
Chicago, Burlington & Quincy..........	11	2,060	69,480	756	......	......	....	......	5,148	2,438	13,759	86,433	123	86,556
St. Louis, Rock Island & Chicago.......	13	2,946	54,232	292	......	......	....	1	2,946	3,895	9,364	67,783	917	68,700
Total.......................................	24	5,006	$123,712	$1,048	......	......	....	2	2,814	$6,333	$23,123	$154,216	$1,040	$155,256
Scott:														
Chicago & Alton..........................	3	4,274	24,000	220	......	......	....	......	2,833	1,341	7,781	33,342	....	33,342
St. Louis, Rock Island & Chicago.......	18	2,541	73,925	708	......	......	....	2	2,617	6,239	12,764	93,636	....	93,636
Wabash.....................................	10	2,229	46,900	5,600	......	......	....	3	3,623	9,215	16,051	77,766	....	77,766
same (H. & N.)..........................	4	2,665	20,271	875	......	......	....	......	......	....	6,938	28,084	....	28,084
Total.......................................	37	1,149	$165,096	$7,403	......	......	....	6	3,793	$16,795	$43,534	$232,828	....	$232,828
Shelby:														
Baltimore & Ohio Southwestern........	17	3,866	53,197	250	......	......	....	1	2,507	3,687	32,259	89,393	230	89,623
Chicago & Eastern Illinois..............	11	4,985	45,388	1,540	......	......	....	2	2,595	4,983	28,675	80,586	1,490	82,076
Cleveland, Cincinnati, Chicago & St. L's	26	2,122	134,650	1,865	......	......	....	2	4,114	6,948	56,513	199,976	1,854	201,830
Toledo, St. Louis & Kansas City........	30	2,534	106,680	1,275	......	......	....	2	3,625	5,373	42,911	156,239	1,173	157,412
Wabash (C. & P.)........................	18	2,890	83,463	919	......	......	....	1	1,237	3,085	28,564	116,031	750	116,781
Total.......................................	105	557	$423,378	$5,849	......	......	....	10	3,518	$24,076	$188,922	$642,225	$5,497	$647,722

Stark:														
Chicago, Burlington & Quincy	20	4,892	127,652	1,075				1	4,624	4,689	25,278	158,694	235	158,929
Rock Island & Peoria	19	469	108,806	5,600				2	4,913	7,326	20,105	141,837	362	142,199
Total	40	81	$236,458	$6,675				4	4,257	$12,015	$45,383	$300,531	$597	$301,128
St. Clair:														
Baltimore & Ohio Southwestern	27	1,978	82,124	6,605				4	4,764	12,255	49,801	150,785	80,710	231,495
Belleville & Carondelet	16	4,795	42,270	700				2	3,676	5,392	12,240	60,602	2,015	62,617
Chicago & Alton	1	2,330	9,080	3,300	1	2,330	$5,045	3	5,073	9,902	2,944	30,271	100	30,371
Chicago, Peoria & St. Louis	1	2,233	3,984	625				1	1,257	2,476	2,556	9,641	110	9,751
Cleveland, Cincinnati, Chicago & St. L.	2	1,096	11,259	2,555				9	665	22,815	4,725	41,354	24,466	65,820
East St. Louis & Carondelet	9	588	45,557					8	1,903	26,901	16,040	82,498		82,498
East St. Louis Connecting	8	960	130,909	3,000				20	3,030	164,601	27,500	326,010	16,104	342,114
Louisville, Evansville & St. Louis Con.	37	1,234	121,010	8,640				23	2,096	46,794	50,486	226,930	36,724	263,654
same (E. St. L. & C.)		1,056									271	271		271
Louisville & Nashville	35	1,565	134,126	5,730				17	4,343	40,101	39,070	219,027	4,318	223,345
Madison, Illinois & St. Louis (V. & C.)	3	1,136	64,303	150				3	4,585	13,539	5,023	83,015	4,900	87,915
Mobile & Ohio	16	415	64,314	3,150				9	2,848	23,848	17,566	108,878	5,092	113,970
St. Louis, Alton & Terre Haute	40	3,895	219,984	8,665				25	1,780	63,342	162,599	454,590	100	454,690
St. Louis, Belleville & Southern	13	603	32,785	725				1	4,580	3,735	6,440	43,685	535	44,220
St. Louis, Rock Island & Chicago		5,079	3,848	1,076				5	3,392	14,106	664	19,694		19,694
same (I. & St. L.)		3,168									414	414		414
Terminal R. R. of East St. Louis	1	500	27,367	2,500				10	4,480	108,485	33,440	171,792	4,100	175,892
Terre Haute & Indianapolis	10	1,232	64,470	7,268				16	2,582	41,223	30,979	143,940	7,854	151,794
Toledo, St. Louis & Kansas City	2	370	7,245	1,620				2	2,770	5,049	2,914	16,828	955	17,783
Wabash	2	816	9,695	14,106				10	4,592	27,174	3,318	54,293	250	54,543
Total	229	3,369	$10,074,330	$70,415	1	2,330	$5,045	179	336	$625,738	$468,990	$2,244,518	$188,333	$2,432,851
Stephenson:														
Chicago Great Western	28	4,140	166,948	4,650				3	4,586	9,671	35,996	217,265	717	217,982
Chicago, Madison & Northern	39	3,817	198,615	22,320				8	2,487	21,177	14,022	256,134	1,272	257,406
Chicago, Milwaukee & St. Paul	23	5,179	101,919	11,525				7	1,418	18,172	26,771	158,387	752	159,139
Chicago & Northwestern	11	4,266	67,896	2,910				2	2,525	6,196	15,309	92,311	1,080	93,391
Total	104	1,562	$535,378	$41,405				22	456	$55,216	$92,098	$724,097	$3,821	$727,918
Tazewell:														
Chicago & Alton	24	795	152,149	2,365				2	3,906	6,849	49,327	210,690	360	211,050
Chicago, Peoria & St. Louis	11	935	31,296	1,800				3	5,112	7,936	20,080	61,112	7	61,119
Chicago, Santa Fé & California	21	912	112,215	1,710				2	4,597	7,177	24,911	146,013	1,112	147,125
Lake Erie & Western	16	244	64,185	3,300				1	5,105	4,917	27,132	99,534	32	99,566
Peoria, Decatur & Evansville	20	5,116	52,422	720				4	3,829	9,450	24,400	86,992	36	87,028
Peoria & Eastern	21	856	74,067	660				10	3,457	26,637	21,043	122,407	54	122,461
Peoria & Pekin Union	8	299	185,302	450	1	1,301	$4,986	9	1,039	22,992	32,344	246,074	461	246,535
Terre Haute & Peoria	28	4,821	72,283	530				3	18	6,007	20,394	99,214	152	99,366
same (T. P. & W.)	5	528									3,597	3,597		3,597
Toledo, Peoria & Western	15	4,010	63,038	1,080				2	1,752	5,829	19,175	89,122	52	89,174
Total	172	2,676	$806,957	$12,615	1	1,301	$4,986	41	2,415	$97,794	$242,403	$1,164,755	$2,266	$1,167,021

Statement 30—Continued.

County—Railroad.	Main Track, Including Right of Way and Improvements Thereon.				Second Main Track.			Side or Turnout Track.			Rolling Stock.	Total assessment by the State Board of Equalization...	Equalized value of railroad property assessed by local assessors..........	Equalized value of railroad property in county..........
	Miles	Feet........	Assess'd value exclud-ing build-ings.	Value of build-ings on right of way.	Miles	Feet........	Assess'd value.	Miles	Feet........	Assess'd value.	Assess'd value.			
Union;														
Chicago & Texas	17	267	$34,101	$200				1	120	$1,534	$9,579	$45,414		$45,414
Mobile & Ohio	22	174	88,132	2,700				2	2,345	6,110	24,071	121,013		121,013
Total	39	441	$122,233	$2,900				3	2,465	$7,644	$33,650	$166,427		$166,427
Vermilion:														
Cairo, Vincennes & Chicago	15	1,330	41,180	310				2	331	4,125	11,093	56,708	$49	56,757
Chicago & Eastern Illinois	95	3,729	363,684	49,025	25	2,554	$76,451	54	4,287	109,624	229,765	828,549	10,723	839,272
Chi., Lake Shore & Eastern (C. & E. I.)	95	3,729									14,488	14,488		14,488
same (L. E. & W.)	8	363									1,221	1,221		1,221
Lake Erie & Western	21	5,055	87,830	9,780				6	3,887	16,840	37,127	151,577	392	151,969
Peoria, Decat'r & Evansville (Chi. Div.)	2	2,742	6,298	275					1,796	679	276	7,528	62	7,590
Peoria & Eastern	22	972	77,644	1,913				7	2,179	18,531	22,059	120,147	133	120,280
Rantoul	21	958	38,126	1,863				1	822	1,156	3,096	44,241	89	44,330
Toledo, St. Louis & Kansas City	8	4,910	31,255	300				1	1,461	2,553	12,572	46,680	9	46,689
Wabash	25	4,472	116,311	15,550				18	685	45,324	39,806	216,991	667	217,658
Total	317	1,860	$762,328	$79,016	25	2,554	$76,451	91	4,885	$198,832	$371,503	$1,488,130	$12,124	$1,500,254
Wabash:														
Cairo, Vincennes & Chicago	25	363	67,685	3,895				6	363	12,138	18,233	101,951	79	102,030
Louisville, Evansville & St. Louis Con.	12	3,304	41,034	360				1	1,142	2,433	17,120	60,947	52	60,999
Total	37	3,667	$108,719	$4,255				7	1,505	$14,571	$35,353	$162,898	$131	$163,029
Warren:														
Chicago Burlington & Quincy	20	4,617	127,334	1,174	19	1,457	$67,466	6	3,484	16,650	25,215	237,839	239	238,078
Chicago, Santa Fé & California	20	1,495	107,501	3,475				4	4,441	12,103	23,864	146,943	505	147,448
Iowa Central	29	663	87,377	1,605				3	2,258	6,855	20,958	116,795	40	116,835
St. Louis, Rock Island & Chicago	34	2,030	137,538	1,398				5	1,457	13,190	23,748	175,874	300	176,174
Total	104	3,525	$459,750	$7,652	19	1,457	$67,466	20	1,080	$48,798	$93,785	$677,451	$1,084	$678,535

Washington:														
Centralia & Chester	27	4,065	69,425	750				2	1,214	4,460	6,228	80,863		80,863
Louisville & Nashville	28	2,968	108,536	2,070				2	3,518	5,999	31,616	148,221	1,335	149,556
Total	56	1,753	$177,961	$2,820				4	4,732	$10,459	$37,844	$229,084	$1,335	$230,419
Wayne:														
Baltimore & Ohio Southwestern	25	1,829	76,039	915				2	1,000	5,473	46,111	128,538		128,538
Louisville, Evansville & St. Louis Con.	30	2,549	99,069	770				2	647	4,245	41,332	145,416	134	145,550
Total	55	4,378	$175,108	$1,685				4	1,647	$9,718	$87,443	$273,954	$134	$274,088
White:														
Baltimore & Ohio Southwestern	24	3,579	74,034	585				2	1,382	5,654	44,895	125,168	132	125,300
Cairo, Vincennes & Chicago	32	4,789	88,849	1,040				2	3,362	5,273	23,934	119,096	330	119,426
Louisville & Nashville	21	966	80,495	1,290				4	4,869	11,075	23,447	116,307	1,326	117,633
same (C., V. & C.)		1,800									377	377		377
Peoria, Decatur & Evansville	2	930	5,440	175					3,994	1,513	2,532	9,660	16	9,676
Total	81	1,504	$248,818	$3,090				10	3,047	$23,515	$95,185	$370,608	$1,804	$372,412
Whiteside:														
Chicago, Burlington & Northern	5	435	25,412						1,610	762	9,021	35,195	9	35,204
same (C., B. & Q.)		3,520									1,184	1,184		1,184
Chicago, Burlington & Quincy	41	1,248	251,542	3,869				10	2,130	26,008	49,811	331,230	349	331,579
Chicago, Milwaukee & St. Paul	13	4,926	59,215	925				1	1,885	3,392	15,554	79,086	87	79,173
Chicago & Northwestern	31	1,742	180,147	3,450	31	1,742	$109,654	13	4,394	34,581	40,619	368,451	89,539	457,990
St. Louis, Rock Island Chicago	22	85	88,064	432				1	3,569	4,190	15,206	107,892	170	108,062
same (C. & N. W.)	5	1,441									3,642	3,642		3,642
Total	119	2,837	$604,380	$8,676	31	1,742	$109,654	27	3,028	$68,933	$135,037	$926,680	$90,154	$1,016,834
Will:														
Chicago & Alton	32	4,953	207,510	7,020	11	517	38,843	25	5,046	64,889	67,275	385,537	4,912	390,449
same (C. & Ill. R.)	17	1,859	109,318					2	1,777	5,841	35,441	150,600	1,810	152,410
Chicago & Eastern Illinois	11	5,161	45,514	2,870	11	5,161	35,933	1	4,311	3,633	28,755	116,705	619	117,324
Chi., Lake Shore & East'n (C. R. I. & P.)	26	490									3,950	3,950	1,389	5,339
same (C. & E. I.)	11	5,161									1,813	1,813		1,813
Chicago, Rock Island & Pacific	24	3,993	210,428	5,750	24	3,993	86,647	19	207	47,598	28,553	378,976	3,866	382,842
Chicago, Santa Fé & California	28	5,251	153,671	6,520				12	4,629	32,192	34,114	226,497	9,305	235,802
Elgin, Joliet & Eastern	50	1,907	226,625	21,430				32	559	80,265	108,920	437,240	23,615	460,855
Michigan Central (J. & N. Ind.)	14	5,208	119,891	15,600				3	3,639	11,068	22,403	168,962	2,069	171,031
Wabash (C. & S.)	29	4	130,504	8,063				6	450	15,213	44,663	198,443	2,128	200,571
Total	248	2,307	$1,203,461	$67,253	47	4,391	$161,423	103	4,778	$260,699	$375,887	$2,068,723	$49,713	$2,118,436

Statement 30—Concluded.

County—Railroad.	Main Track, Including Right of Way and Improvements Thereon.				Second Main Track.			Side or Turnout Track.			Rolling Stock.	Total assessment by the State Board of Equalization...	Equalized value of railroad property assessed by local assessors..........	Equalized value of railroad property in county..........
	Miles	Feet........	Assess'd value excluding buildings.	Value of buildings on right of way.	Miles	Feet........	Assess'd value.	Miles	Feet........	Assess'd value.	Assess'd value.			
WILLIAMSON:														
Cairo, Vincennes & Chicago............	1	4,612	$5,058	....	.....	.....	....	.....	1,617	$613	$1,362	$7,033	....	$7,033
Chicago, Paducah & Memphis..........	8	4,272	22,022	$540	.....	.....	....	2	3,340	5,265	3,173	31,000	$84	31,084
Chicago, St. Louis & Paducah..........	11	3,240	36,003	1,100	.....	.....	....	.....	4,207	1,992	10,899	49,994	114	50,108
St. Louis Southern......................	13	3,630	49,275	500	.....	.....	....	2	4,661	7,207	14,432	71,414	114	71,528
Chicago & Texas........................	11	370	22,140	600	.....	.....	....	1	70	1,520	6,218	30,478	....	30,478
Total..................................	47	284	$134,498	$2,740	.....	.....	....	7	3,335	$16,597	$36,084	$189,919	$312	$190,231
WINNEBAGO:														
Chicago & Iowa (C. R. & N.)............	8	3,283	43,109	5,044	.....	.....	....	6	1,894	15,897	6,479	70,529	2,614	73,143
Chicago, Madison & Northern..........	25	4,564	129,322	14,370	.....	.....	....	13	3,206	34,018	9,130	186,840	1,370	188,210
Chicago, Milwaukee & St Paul..........	35	55	148,794	7,000	.....	.....	....	12	3,777	31,788	39,083	226,665	1,488	228,153
same (C., R. & N.)......................	8	3,170	....	....	.....	.....	....	.....	.....	....	9,601	9,601	....	9,601
Chicago & Northwestern................	45	963	259,799	7,865	.....	.....	....	12	619	30,293	58,579	356,536	1,975	358,511
Total..................................	123	1,475	$581,024	$34,279	.....	.....	....	44	4,216	$111,996	$122,872	$850,171	$7,447	$857,618
WOODFORD:														
Chicago & Alton.........................	13	893	82,966	1,280	.....	.....	....	1	937	2,944	26,897	114,087	180	114,267
Chicago, Santa Fé & California.........	20	3,500	109,513	950	.....	.....	....	2	2,916	6,381	24,311	141,155	1,011	142,166
Kankakee & Southwestern..............	5	1,686	14,894	575	.....	.....	....	.....	.....	....	3,668	19,137	18	19,155
Lake Erie & Western....................	9	4,257	39,225	1,650	.....	.....	....	.....	4,922	2,331	16,581	59,787	18	59,805
Toledo, Peoria & Western..............	18	1,634	73,238	1,625	.....	.....	....	2	1,843	5,872	22,278	103,013	112	103,125
Total..................................	67	1,410	$319,836	$6,080	.....	.....	....	7	58	$17,528	$93,735	$437,179	$1,339	$438,518
*Grand aggregate......................	10,611	5,114	48,622,626	3,372,022	1,113	4,241	$4,045,087	3,528	4,341	9,160,543	13,796,066	78,996,324	2,141,126	81,137,450

*** The aggregate mileage of main track embraces the mileage of leased track on which rolling stock assessment alone is distributed.**

No. 31.

Table showing the Assessment of Railroad Property for the year A. D. 1896.

Number.	Name of Company.	Aggregate Assessment by the State Board of Equalization.					Total assessment by the State Board of Equalization.	Equalized value of railroad property assessed by local assessors..	Aggregate Equalized value of railroad property ...	Number.
		Main Track.	Second Main Track.	Side or Turnout Track.	Buildings on Right of Way.	Rolling Stock.				
1	Baltimore & Ohio & Chicago	$53,218	$23,476	$57,929	$34,640	$26,764	$196,027	$4,442	$200,469	1
2	Baltimore & Ohio Connecting	19,602	8,712	....	....	....	28,314	4,200	32,514	2
3	Baltimore & Ohio Southwestern	1,116,827	....	182,824	29,845	683,152	2,012,648	89,579	2,102,227	3
4	Belleville & Carondelet	42,270	....	5,392	700	12,240	60,602	2,015	62,617	4
5	Belleville & Eldorado	98,754	....	5,393	2,900	23,720	130,767	369	131,136	5
6	Belt Railway Company of Chicago	308,878	53,495	127,561	8,075	119,310	617,319	454	617,803	6
7	Blue Island	15,380	....	5,357	3,600	4,100	28,437	651	29,088	7
8	Cairo, Vincennes & Chicago	697,222	....	90,673	16,800	187,817	992,512	2,326	994,838	8
9	Calumet River	26,627	....	....	....	....	26,627	745	27,372	9
10	Centralia & Chester	165,088	....	13,064	2,175	14,810	195,137	....	195,137	10
11	Chicago & Alton	3,646,382	359,221	434,833	179,755	1,182,158	5,802,349	111,690	5,914,039	11
12	Chicago, Burlington & Northern	473,698	....	44,245	12,945	193,712	724,600	3,996	728,596	12
13	Chicago, Burlington & Quincy	5,165,019	710,959	879,767	157,900	1,107,925	8,021,570	488,646	8,510,216	13
14	Chicago & Calumet Terminal	151,810	....	23,178	9,600	52,021	236,609	38	236,647	14
15	Chicago & Eastern Illinois	991,846	315,930	245,401	82,300	665,512	2,300,989	27,256	2,328,245	15
16	Chicago & Erie	....	....	....	....	40,908	40,908	4,877	45,785	16
17	Chicago & Grand Trunk	439,224	66,167	38,677	10,970	63,077	618,115	20,879	638,994	17
18	Chicago Great Western	851,027	....	60,932	43,850	222,562	1,178,371	1,737	1,180,108	18
19	Chicago, Havana & Western	396,715	....	25,557	11,664	29,985	463,921	1,621	465,542	19
20	Chicago & Illinois Southern	1,667	....	237	....	....	1,904	....	1,904	20
21	Chicago & Indiana State Line	26,722	10,619	3,810	....	....	41,151	....	41,151	21
22	Chicago & Iowa	507,054	....	50,164	15,052	76,210	648,480	3,252	651,732	22
23	Chicago, Lake Shore & Eastern	....	....	....	....	39,710	39,710	1,389	41,099	23
24	Chicago, Madison & Northern	699,973	21,383	133,387	56,550	49,418	950,711	23,049	973,760	24
25	Chicago, Milwaukee & St. Paul	1,348,286	402,184	477,559	173,021	378,392	2,779,442	130,879	2,910,321	25
26	Chicago & Northern Pacific	1,148,551	123,296	137,975	195,690	118,560	1,694,072	3,376	1,697,448	26
27	Chicago & Northwestern	2,683,721	753,059	776,670	234,925	715,977	5,164,352	246,636	5,410,988	27
28	Chicago, Paducah & Memphis	245,158	....	14,930	5,220	35,320	300,628	569	301,197	28
29	Chicago, Peoria & St. Louis	466,707	....	72,795	27,828	299,450	866,780	1,624	869,404	29
30	Chicago, Rock Island & Pacific	1,994,337	654,703	528,230	244,627	270,607	3,692,504	247,145	3,939,649	30
31	Chicago, Santa Fé & California	1,482,195	....	336,471	81,840	329,034	2,229,540	120,122	2,349,662	31
32	Chicago, St. Louis & Paducah	164,032	....	17,129	7,700	49,660	238,521	114	238,635	32
33	Chicago & South Side Rapid Transit	171,178	....	25,147	11,675	136,120	344,120	5,080	349,200	33
34	Chicago & Springfield	345,569	....	52,405	21,575	67,950	487,499	5,002	492,501	34
35	Chicago & Texas	140,356	....	17,954	2,100	39,425	199,835	2,047	201,882	35

Statement 31—Concluded.

Number	Name of Company.	Aggregate Assessment by the State Board of Equalization. Main Track.	Second Main Track.	Side or Turnout Track.	Buildings on Right of Way.	Rolling Stock.	Total assessment by the State Board of Equalization.	Equalized value of railroad property assessed by local assessors	Aggregate Equalized value of railroad property	Number
36	Chicago Union Transfer	$122,756	$56,815	$275	$290	$100	$180,236	$2,032	$182,268	36
37	Chicago & Western Indiana	803,193	133,866	209,688	209,145	11,600	1,367,492	68,308	1,435,800	37
38	Cincinnati, Lafayette & Chicago	164,908		57,147	3,455		225,510	160	225,670	38
39	Cleveland, Cincinnati, Chicago & St. Lo'is	943,523		159,585	32,845	556,661	1,692,614	57,725	1,750,339	39
40	DeKalb & Great Western	11,621		2,238	1,400		15,259	10	15,239	40
41	DePue, Ladd & Eastern	6,667		379		20	7,066	27	7,093	41
42	East St. Louis & Carondelet	45,557		20,901		16,040	82,498		82,498	42
43	East St. Louis Connecting	130,909		164,601	3,000	27,500	326,010	16,104	342,114	43
44	Elgin, Joliet & Eastern	661,765		177,115	49,090	318,055	1,206,025	45,156	1,251,181	44
45	Englewood Connecting	23,519		3,332	620		27,471		27,471	45
46	Fulton County Narrow Guage	71,160		1,162	2,130	13,380	87,832	156	87,988	46
47	Galesburg, Etherley & Eastern	46,340		1,278	1,500	1,020	50,138		50,138	47
48	Galesburg & Rio	48,765		2,704	318		51,787	546	52,333	48
49	Grand Trunk Junction	116,307	19,394	75,070	69,320		280,091		280,091	49
50	Hammond & Blue Island	50,481		1,051			51,532		51,532	50
51	Illinois Valley & Northern	174,866		25,520	4,939		205,325	712	206,037	51
52	Illinois Western	7,813		4,630			12,443		12,443	52
53	Indiana, Decatur & Western	303,041		25,497	7,550	81,134	417,222	1,140	418,362	53
54	Indiana, Illinois & Iowa	230,175		53,056	19,075	44,367	346,673	170	346,843	54
55	Indiana & Illinois Southern	84,000		1,625	900	10,939	97,464		97,464	55
56	Iowa Central	265,981		40,067	8,696	63,797	378,541	853	379,394	56
57	Jacksonville, Louisville & St. Louis	302,473		20,585	4,800	56,830	384,688	2,883	387,571	57
58	Junction	20,135	16,779	3,787	518		41,219		41,219	58
59	Kankakee & Seneca	105,190		12,868	2,220		120,278	654	120,932	59
60	Kankakee & Southwestern	366,773		24,639	22,250	90,320	503,982	671	504,653	60
61	Lake Erie & Western	474,400		52,643	27,120	200,538	754,701	1,137	755,838	61
62	Lake Shore & Michigan Southern	456,534	30,436	199,256	96,750	46,502	829,478	17,315	846,793	62
63	LaSalle & Bureau County	19,044		1,349			20,393	194	20,587	63
64	Lake Street Elevated	69,299		3,029	16,650	80,100	169,078	254	169,332	64
65	Litchfield, Carrollton & Western	92,988		3,109	1,180	7,535	104,812	708	105,520	65
66	Louisville, Evansville & St. Louis Con.	483,063		65,829	12,450	211,962	773,304	37,321	810,625	66
67	Louisville & Nashville	670,061		76,817	15,354	198,504	960,736	14,845	975,581	67
68	Louisville, New Albany & Chicago					29,190	29,190		29,190	68
69	Louisville & St. Louis	32,934		763	600	90	34,387	810	35,197	69
70	Madison, Illinois & St. Louis	150,303		34,430	2,350	11,740	198,823		198,823	70
71	Michigan Central	279,053		50,014	44,720	73,073	446,860	25,010	471,870	71
72	Mobile & Ohio	642,273		119,646	27,600	175,420	964,939	10,511	975,450	72

No.	Road									No.
73	Mound City	2,856	....	21	400	20	3,297	20	3,317	73
74	New York, Chicago & St. Louis	199,322	4,790	68,646	66,124	66,547	405,429	15,460	420,889	74
75	Northern Illinois	185,383	....	41,435	3,961	....	230,779	183	230,962	75
76	Pawnee	9,000	....	218	225	2,520	11,963	....	11,963	76
77	Peoria, Decatur & Evansville (main line)	488,912	....	55,866	9,305	236,298	790,381	13,017	803,398	77
78	Peoria, Decatur & Evansville (Chi. Div.)	195,322	....	9,043	1,750	8,560	214,675	....	214,675	78
79	Peoria & Eastern	428,643	....	100,985	14,133	121,781	665,542	3,915	669,457	79
80	Peoria & Pekin Union	417,250	13,269	108,742	32,000	72,830	644,091	2,199	646,290	80
81	Pittsburgh, Cincinnati, Chicago & St. L	1,119,621	94,425	196,694	66,152	84,481	1,561,373	59,142	1,620,515	81
82	Pittsburgh, Ft. Wayne & Chicago	838,239	68,109	236,095	292,439	118,203	1,553,085	72,669	1,625,754	82
83	Quincy, Omaha & Kansas City	....	....	3,942	7,350	863	12,155	....	12,155	83
84	Rantoul	119,173	....	5,769	6,185	9,678	140,805	599	141,404	84
85	Rock Island & Peoria	688,247	....	73,668	41,895	127,175	930,985	8,750	939,735	85
86	St. Louis, Alton & Terre Haute	377,330	....	77,983	9,765	278,900	743,978	5,994	749,972	86
87	St. Louis, Belleville & Southern	32,785	....	3,735	725	6,440	43,685	100	43,785	87
88	St. Louis, Chicago & St. Paul	277,422	....	21,889	6,880	144,090	450,281	297	450,578	88
89	St. Louis & Eastern	213,042	....	30,334	2,050	138,570	383,996	691	384,687	89
90	St. Louis, Rock Island & Chicago	1,120,186	....	148,620	27,254	209,235	1,505,295	8,107	1,513,402	90
91	St. Louis Southern	171,806	....	19,946	2,325	50,320	244,397	834	245,231	91
92	South Chicago	28,564	18,076	7,536	8,820	15,000	77,996	3,141	81,137	92
93	South Chicago & Southern	81,308	....	10,102	1,650	....	93,060	6,473	99,533	93
94	Sycamore & Cortland	13,912	....	1,896	1,070	....	16,878	52	16,930	94
95	Terminal R. R. of East St. Louis	27,367	....	108,485	2,500	33,440	171,792	4,100	175,892	95
96	Terre Haute & Indianapolis	996,645	....	140,419	21,991	478,900	1,637,955	14,266	1,652,221	96
97	Terre Haute & Peoria	362,766	....	33,538	3,710	117,260	517,274	274	517,548	97
98	The Metropolitan West Side Elevated	273,402	....	50,038	29,530	71,020	423,990	2,223	426,213	98
99	Toledo, Peoria & Western	920,014	....	85,207	19,905	299,450	1,324,576	2,349	1,326,925	99
100	Toledo, St. Louis & Kansas City	628,214	....	56,077	13,345	252,693	950,329	2,860	953,189	100
101	Union Stock Yards & Transit	435,748	85,924	356,458	55,585	66,910	1,000,625	4,016	1,004,641	101
102	Wabash, Chester & Western	126,658	....	11,338	2,800	21,200	161,996	1,577	163,573	102
103	Waukegan & Mississippi Valley	....	....	....	....	8,950	8,950	....	8,950	103
104	Wisconsin Central	273,993	....	58,095	16,148	90,825	439,061	3,125	442,186	104
105	Wabash	3,036,533	....	466,392	229,673	1,101,884	4,834,482	42,446	4,876,928	105
	Totals	$48,622,626	$4,045,087	$9,160,543	$3,372,002	$13,796,066	$78,996,324	$2,141,126	$81,137,450	

No. 32.

Assessment made by the State Board of Equalization upon the Capital Stock of Companies and Associations incorporated under the laws of the State, other than Railway Companies, for the year 1896, being the equalized value of Capital Stock over the equalized value of Tangible Property of such Corporations assessed by local assessors.

Number	Name of Company.	County.	Location.	Amount of capital stock paid up, as reported by company	Equalized value of tangible property assessed by local assessors	Net assessment of capital stock, being excess of equalized value of capital stock and debt over tangible property assessed by local assessors	Total amount assessed, being net assessment of capital stock by the board, and equalized value of tangible property assessed by local assessors	Number
1	Empire Light and Power Company	Adams	Quincy	$48,000	$6,100	$900	$7,000	1
2	Quincy Gas Light and Coke Company	"	"	300,000	28,075	7,925	36,000	2
3	Quincy Horse Railway and Carrying Company	"	"	160,000	23,755	6,245	30,000	3
4	Thomson-Houston Electric Light and Power Company	"	"	100,000	11,600	1,400	13,000	4
5	Cairo City Ferry Company	Alexander	Cairo	28,500	1,000	500	1,500	5
6	Cairo City Gas Company	"	"			2,000	2,000	6
7	Cairo Electric Light and Power Company	"	"	*		500	500	7
8	Cairo Electric Railway Company	"	"	52,400	1,250	3,750	5,000	8
9	Cairo Transfer Company	"	"	100,000	15,000	1,000	16,000	9
10	Cairo Water Company	"	"	200,000	25,050	4,950	30,000	10
11	Delta Electric Company	"	"	*		500	500	11
12	Egypt Electric Company	"	"		4,175	825	5,000	12
13	Halliday and Phillips Wharfboat Company	"	"	*		500	500	13
14	Sorento Prospecting and Mining Company	Bond	Sorento	*		6,000	6,000	14
15	Belvidere Electric Light Company	Boone	Belvidere	*		3,500	3,500	15
16	Mount Carrol Electric Light Company	Carroll	Mt. Carroll	11,700	576	924	1,500	16
17	Urbana and Champaign Electric Street Railway Company	Champaign	Champaign	50,000		2,500	2,500	17
18	Christian County Abstract Rating and Guarantee Company	Christian	Taylorville		300	1,200	1,500	18
19	Citizens' Gas Light and Fuel Company	"	"	11,000	625	1,375	2,000	19
20	Consumers' Electric Light Company	"	Pana	5,000	1,100	100	1,200	20
21	Pana Modern Electric Light, Power and Street Railway Co.	"	"	25,000	3,300	2,700	6,000	21
22	Taylorville Electric Company	"	Taylorville	22,000	1,425	3,575	5,000	22
23	Clay County Telephone Company	Clay	Sailor Springs	*		200	200	23
24	Mattoon Clear Water Company	Coles	Mattoon	61,580	9,790	2,210	12,000	24
25	Mattoon Gas Light and Coke Company	"	"	50,000	3,160	4,840	8,000	25

26	Acme Cement Plaster Company	Cook	Chicago		800,000		3,000	3,000	26
27	Ætna Fuel Company	"	"	*			2,000	2,000	27
28	American Security Company	"	"	*			10,000	10,000	28
29	American Spirits Manufacturing Company	"	"	*			75,000	75,000	29
30	American Telephone and Telegraph Company	"	"		100,000	45,418		45,418	30
31	Atlantic and Western Telephone Company	"	"	*			5,000	5,000	31
32	Automatic Long Distance Telephone Company	"	"		5,000,000	444	24,556	25,000	32
33	Badts Multiphase Electric Railway Company	"	"		1,000,000		10,000	10,000	33
34	Baker Electric Company	"	"	*			12,000	12,000	34
35	Board of Trade Telegraph Company	"	"	*			10,000	10,000	35
36	California Company	"	"	*			5,000	5,000	36
37	Calumet Elevator Company	"	"			13,470	6,530	20,000	37
38	Calumet Electric Street Railway Company	"	"		500,000	20,077		20,077	38
39	Calumet Gas Company	"	"	*			5,000	5,000	39
40	Central Union Telephone Company	"	"		6,605,300	2,180 345		2,180,345	40
41	Chamber of Commerce Safety Vault Company	"	"		1,000,000	264,480		264,480	41
42	Chicago City Railway Company	"	"		10,000,000	711,183	588,817	1,300,000	42
43	Chicago Dock Company	"	"		500,000	110,724	476	111,200	43
44	Chicago Dock and Canal Company	"	"		825,600	263,890	11,110	275,000	44
45	Chicago Edison Company	"	"		5,000,000	283,132		283,132	45
46	Chicago Elevator Company	"	"	*			22,500	22,500	46
47	Chicago Gas Light and Coke Company	"	"		4,984,200	621,045	28,955	650,000	47
48	Chicago Insurance Company	"	"		100,000		10,000	10,000	48
49	Chicago Long Distance Telephone Co.	"	"	*			50,000	50,000	49
50	Chicago Mortgage Loan Company	"	"		2,500	1,270		1,270	50
51	Chicago Opera House Company	"	"		350,000	221,340		221,340	51
52	Chicago and Pacific Elevator Company	"	"		20,000	9,631		9,631	52
53	Chicago Steamship Company	"	"		100,000		5,000	5,000	53
54	Chicago Telephone Company	"	"		4,069,800	231,016	218,984	450,000	54
55	Chippewa Springs Water Company	"	"				1,000	1,000	55
56	Cicero and Proviso Street Railway Company	"	"		2,500,000	20,584	4,416	25,000	56
57	Cicero Water, Gas and Electric Light Company	"	"		276,100	19,871		19,871	57
58	Consumers' Gas Company	"	"		3,000,000	260,868		260,868	58
59	Congress Hotel Compan.y	"	"	*			10,000	10,000	59
60	Consolidated Produce and Stock Exchange	"	"	*			25,000	25,000	60
61	Eldorado Gold Mining Company	"	"	*			20,000	20,000	61
62	Englewood Electric Light Company	"	"		120,000	1,524	476	2,000	62
63	Evanston Electric Illuminating Company	"	"	*			10,000	10,000	63
64	Equitable Produce and Stock Exchange	"	"	*			25,000	25,000	64
65	Fair, The	"	"	*			50,000	50,000	65
66	Fidelity Mortgage Loan Company	"	"		2,500	190	310	500	66
67	Fidelity Safe Deposit Company	"	"	*			2,000	2,000	67
68	Fireman's Insurance Company—Geo. L. Harding, President	"	"				15,000	15,000	68
69	German Mexican International Oil Company	"	"	*			75,000	75,000	69
70	G. H. Hammond Company	"	"	*			4,000	4,000	70
71	Hanrahan Refrigerator Car Company	"	"	*			25,000	25,000	71
72	Harrison International Telephone Company	"	"	*			20,000	20,000	72
73	Harvey Transit Company	"	"		143,500	5,419		5,419	73
74	Home Safety Deposit Vault Company	"	"	*			3,000	3,000	74
75	Hyde Park Gas Company	"	"		300,000	41,475	8,525	50,000	75
76	Illinois Vault Company	"	"	*			20,000	20,000	76
77	International Coöperative Industrial Association	"	"	*			25,000	25,000	77

Statement 32—Continued.

Number	Name of Company.	County.	Location.	Amount of capital stock paid up, as reported by company	Equalized value of tangible property assessed by local assessors	Net assessment of capital stock, being excess of equalized value of capital stock and debt over tangible property assessed by local assessors	Total amount assessed, being net assessment of capital stock by the board, and equalized value of tangible property assessed by local assessors	Number
78	International Oil Refining and Developing Company	Cook	Chicago	*		$25,000	$25,000	78
79	International Patent Promotion and Manufact'ng Company	"	"	*		50,000	50,000	79
80	Lake Gas Company	"	"	$800,000	$50,650		50,650	80
81	Lackawana Live Stock Transportation Company	"	"	*		20,000	20,000	81
82	Lemont Electric Light and Power Company	"	Lemont	13,000	1,143	857	2,000	82
83	Marquette Safety Deposit Company	"	Chicago	*		10,000	10,000	83
84	Merchants' Arc Light and Power Company	"	"	34,800	635	1,865	2,500	84
85	Merchants' Safe Deposit Company	"	"	50,000		5,000	5,000	85
86	Merchants' Transfer Company	"	"	*		500	500	86
87	Mill Creek Gold Placer Company	"	"	*		10,000	10,000	87
88	Mississippi River Railroad and Toll Bridge Company	"	"	*		15,000	15,000	88
89	Natural Elevator and Dock Company	"	"	500,000	43,890	46,110	90,000	89
90	North Chicago Street Railroad Company	"	"	6,600,000	315,180	184,820	500,000	90
91	Northwestern Gas Light Company	"	"	*		1,000	1,000	91
92	Pacific Grain and Stock Exchange	"	"	*		25,000	25,000	92
93	People's Gas Light and Coke Company	"	"	4,000,000	253,610		253,610	93
94	Pullman's Palace Car Company	"	"	35,430,600	1,130,367	431,588	1,561,955	94
95	Railroad Wrecking and Salvage Company	"	"	*		9,000	9,000	95
96	Rialto, The	"	"	600,000	213,001		213,001	96
97	Sierra Gold Company	"	"	5,000,000		10,000	10,000	97
98	South Chicago City Railway Company	"	"	1,200,000	22,267		22,267	98
99	Standard Light and Heat Company	"	"	*		5,000	5,000	99
100	Standard Tiffany Refrigerator Car Company	"	"	*		20,000	20,000	100
101	Street's Stable Car Line	"	"	*		85,000	85,000	101
102	Street's Western Stable Car Line	"	"	4,611,700	13,340	39,160	52,500	102
103	Takamine Ferment Company	"	"			10,000	10,000	103
104	Title Guarantee and Trust Company	"	"	1,600,000	20,320	49,680	70,000	104
105	Two Republics Mining and Developing Company	"	"	*		35,000	35,000	105
106	Traders' Insurance Company	"	"	76,264	98,372	11,628	110,000	106
107	United States Transfer Company	"	"	*		30,000	30,000	107
108	West Chicago Street Railroad Company	"	"	13,189,000	1,078,698	21,302	1,100,000	108
109	Western Finance Company	"	"	*		120,000	120,000	109
110	DeKalb Electric Light Company	DeKalb	DeKalb	*		3,000	3,000	110

111	Sycamore Electric Light Company	DeKalb	Sycamore	*		1,500	1,500	111
112	Clinton Electric Light, Heat and Power Company	DeWitt	Clinton	15,000	4,098	402	4,500	112
113	Paris Gas Light and Coke Company	Edgar	Paris	21,000	3,125	1,375	4,500	113
114	Effingham Water Works Company	Effingham	Effingham	$100,000	870	4,130	5,000	114
115	Vandalia Light and Fuel Company	Fayette	Vandalia		5,700		5,700	115
116	Lewistown Water Company	Fulton	Lewistown	15,000		3,000	3,000	116
117	Morris Gas Company	Grundy	Morris			500	500	117
118	Dallas Transportation Company	Hancock	Dallas City	8,000	6,164	836	7,000	118
119	F. M. King Company	"	Augusta	15,000		2,000	2,000	119
120	Keokuk and Hamilton Bridge Company	"	Keokuk, Ia.	*		10,000	10,000	120
121	LaHarpe Electric Light and Power Company	"	La Harpe	9,000	1,806	694	2,500	121
122	Western Illinois Telephone Company	"	Augusta	2,500		100	100	122
123	Geneseo Electric Light Company	Henry	Geneseo	*		4,000	4,000	123
124	Kewanee Electric Light and Motor Company	"	Kewanee	20,000	3,014		3,014	124
125	Kewanee Gas Light and Coke Company	"	"	40,000	3,726	774	4,500	125
126	Milford Electric Light and Power Company	Iroquois	Milford	11,000	716	784	1,500	126
127	Carbondale Electric Company	Jackson	Carbondale	5,000	1,700	300	2,000	127
128	Murphysboro Street Railway Company	"	Murphysboro	1,500	450	50	500	128
129	Murphysboro Water Works, Electric and Gas Light Co.	"	"	1,500	12,206		12,206	129
130	Mt. Vernon Electric Light Company	Jefferson	Mt. Vernon	15,000	2,127	373	2,500	130
131	Mt. Vernon Water Works Company	"	"	18,000	1,900	600	2,500	131
132	Dunlieth and Dubuque Bridge Company	JoDaviess	Dubuque, Ia	1,000,000		15,000	15,000	132
133	Galena Water Company	"	Galena		994	1,006	2,000	133
134	Aurora Gas Light Company	Kane	Aurora	300,000	34,051	3,949	38,000	134
135	Aurora Street Railway Company	"	"	300,000	32,163	3,837	36,000	135
136	C. H. Woodruff Company	"	Elgin	*		1,500	1,500	136
137	Elgin American Gas Company	"	"	100,000	9,025	3,975	13,000	137
138	Elgin City Railway Company	"	"	100,000	24,753	5,247	30,000	138
139	Kankakee Electric Railway Company	Kankakee	Kankakee	50,000	3,889	611	4,500	139
140	North Kankakee Electric Light and Railway Company	"	"	32,600	2,807		2,807	140
141	Galesburg Electric Motor and Power Company	Knox	Galesburg	210,000	5,674	3,326	9,000	141
142	Galesburg Gas and Electric Light Company	"	"	200,000	19,781	10,219	30,000	142
143	Wauconda Telegraph and Telephone Company	Lake	Wauconda	1,000		100	100	143
144	City Electric Railway Company	LaSalle	Peru	120,000	3,503	3,497	7,000	144
145	Illinois Valley Electric Light and Power Company	"	Ottawa	*		2,500	2,500	145
146	Marseilles Land and Water Company	"	Marseilles	500,000	13,538	5,462	19,000	146
147	Mendota Light and Heat Company	"	Mendota	25,000	1,177	1,823	3,000	147
148	Ottawa Electric Street Railway Company	"	Ottawa		6,180		6,180	148
149	Ottawa Gas Light and Coke Company	"	"	45,000	4,560	5,440	10,000	149
150	Ottawa Hydraulic Company	"	"	18,000	349	3,651	4,000	150
151	Streator Aqueduct Company	"	Streator	150,000	15,122	9,878	25,000	151
152	Streator Gas Light Company	"	"	100,000	6,810		9,810	152
153	Streator Railway Company	"	"	250,000	4,960	7,040	12,000	153
154	Dixon Power and Lighting Company	Lee	Dixon	100,000	7,730	4,270	12,000	154
155	Dixon Water Company	"	"	60,000	10,773	3,227	14,000	155
156	Fairbury Electric Light, Heat and Power Company	Livingston	Fairbury	12,000	819	1,181	2,000	156
157	Leslie E. Keeley Company	"	Dwight	25,000	33,583		33,583	157
158	Pontiac Light, Heat and Power Company	"	Pontiac	20,000	2,790	210	3,000	158
159	Pontiac Water, Light and Power Company	"	"		2,044	5,956	8,000	159
160	Lincoln Electric Street Railway Company	Logan	Lincoln	65,000	4,471	1,529	6,000	160

Statement 32—Continued.

Number	Name of Company.	County.	Location.	Amount of capital stock paid up, as reported by company	Equalized value of tangible property assess'd by local assessors	Net assessment of capital stock, being excess of equalized value of capital stock and debt over tangible property assessed by local assessors	Total amount assessed, being net assessment of capital stock by the board, and equalized value of tangible property assessed by local assessors	Number
161	Lincoln Gas and Electric Light Company	Logan	Lincoln	*	…	$8,000	$8,000	161
162	Lincoln Water, Light and Power Company	″	″	$250,000	$12,502	…	12,502	162
163	Logan County Electric Light Company	″	″	2,700	400	200	600	163
164	Bachman Bros. and Martin Company	Macon	Decatur	20,000	3,069	931	4,000	164
165	Citizens' Mutual Telephone Company	″	″	60,000	1,050	1,950	3,000	165
166	City Electric Railway Company	″	″	96,280	10,961	14,039	25,000	166
167	Decatur Gas Light and Coke Company	″	″	100,000	26,910	8,090	35,000	167
168	Decatur Union Elevator Company	″	″	*		2,000	2,000	168
169	Decatur, Light, Heat and Power Company	″	″	*	…	20,000	2,000	169
170	Linne & Scruggs Dry Goods and Carpet Company	″	″	100,000	7,200	2,800	10,000	170
171	Maroa Electric Light Company	″	Maroa	*	…	1,000	1,000	171
172	Municipal Electric Company	″	Decatur	25,000	4,003	997	5,000	172
173	Young Bros. & Maris Company	″	″	125,000	16,815	3,185	20,000	173
174	Carlinville Water Company	Macoupin	Carlinville	75,000	3,660	2,340	6,000	174
175	Alton Gas and Electric Light Company	Madison	Alton	60,000	14,000	1,000	15,000	175
176	Alton Railway and Illuminating Company	″	″	250,000	26,750	8,250	35,000	176
177	Madison County Ferry Company	″	Venice	200,000	16,834	8,166	25,000	177
178	St. Louis Merchants Bridge Company	″	″	…	144,000	56,000	200,000	178
179	Centralia and Central City Street Railway Company	Marion	Centralia	10,000	426	574	1,000	179
180	Centralia Light and Power Company	″	″	31,000	3,100	2,900	6,000	180
181	Nunda Electric Light Company	McHenry	Nunda	2,000	296	204	500	181
182	Bloomington City Railway Company	McLean	Bloomington	…	8,239	7,761	16,000	182
183	Bloomington Electric Light Company	″	″	40,000	11,020	3,980	15,000	183
184	Citizens' Gas Light and Heating Company	″	″	250,000	12,938	7,062	20,000	184
185	Home Telephone Company	″	″	30,000	6,243	757	7,000	185
186	Normal Electric Light and Power Company	″	Normal	12,500	2,332	168	2,500	186
187	Safety Deposit Company	″	Bloomington	10,000	1,200	1,800	3,000	187
188	Keithsburg Bridge Company	Mercer	Keithsburg	600,000	29,950	1,050	31,000	188
189	Hillsboro Electric Light and Power Company	Montgomery	Hillsboro	18,000	1,295	1,205	2,500	189
190	Litchfield Electric Light and Power Company	″	Litchfield	15,000	2,285	1,715	4,000	190
191	Litchfield Car and Machine Company	″	″	200,000	…	1,000	1,000	191
192	Litchfield Light, Heat and Power Company	″	″	50,000	557	7,443	8,000	192

193	Litchfield Mining and Power Company	Montgomery	Litchfield		25,000	1,207	793	2,000	193
194	Litchfield Water Supply Company	"	"	*		....	1,000	1,000	194
195	Nokomis Electric Light and Power Company	"	Nokomis		8,500	1,260	740	2,000	195
196	Prairie Heights Water Company	"	Hillsboro		3,000	182	818	1,000	196
197	Eagle Electric Company	Monroe	Columbia		7,000	2,000	....	2,000	197
198	Jacksonville Gas Light and Coke Company	Morgan	Jacksonville		....	21,685	4,000	25,685	198
199	Jacksonville Railway Company	"	"		33,450	2,763	....	2,763	199
200	Oregon Electric Light and Power Company	Ogle	Oregon		10,000	960	1,040	2,000	200
201	Central Railway Company	Peoria	Peoria		750,000	53,583	11,417	65,000	201
202	Elmwood Electric Light Company	"	Elmwood		8,000	2,954	2,046	5,000	202
203	German Fire Insurance Company	"	Peoria		200,000	410	6,090	6,500	203
204	Peoria Gas Light and Coke Company	"	"		175,000	50,020	14,980	65,000	204
205	Peoria General Electric Company	"	"		150,000	15,867	16,133	32,000	205
206	Peoria Water Company	"	"		1,000,000	43,922	6,078	50,000	206
207	Title Guaranty Abstract and Trust Company	"	"		22,500	....	4,000	4,000	207
208	Wyoming Electric Light and Power Company	"	"	*		....	1,500	1,500	208
209	DuQuoin Light, Heat and Power Company	Perry	DuQuoin		50,000	285	1,715	2,000	209
210	Pinckneyville Electric Light Company	"	Pinckneyvile		2,250	825	175	1,000	210
211	Pittsfield Electric Company	Pike	Naperville		20,000	4,227	773	5,000	211
212	Chester Light, Water and Ice Company	Randolph	Chester		40,000	6,065	935	7,000	212
213	Sparta Natural Gas and Oil Company	"	Sparta		15,000	1,740	260	2,000	213
214	Olney Edison Electric Company	Richland	Olney	*		....	8,000	8,000	214
215	Moline Central Street Railway Company	Rock Island	Moline		20,000	6,803	....	6,803	215
216	People's Power Company	"	Rock Island		300,000	11,778	10,222	22,000	216
217	Rock Island and Davenport Ferry Company	"	"		60,000	1,820	3,680	5,500	217
218	American Aluminum Company	**St. Clair**	East St. Louis	*		....	15,000	15,000	218
219	Belleville Gas Light and Coke Company	"	Belleville	*		....	25,000	25,000	219
220	Blendville Mining and Milling Company	"	East St. Louis	*		....	12,000	12,000	220
221	Carpenter Electric Power and Light Company	"	"	*		....	3,000	3,000	221
222	Citizens' Electric Light and Power Company	"	"		25,000	4,841	1,159	6,000	222
223	City Water Company	"	"		....	15,727	64,273	80,000	223
224	Consolidated Cattle Car Company	"	"	*		....	35,000	35,000	224
225	East St. Louis Belt S. D. and E. Railway Company	"	"	*		....	50,000	50,000	225
226	East St. Louis Dock and Warehouse Company	"	"	*		....	20,000	20,000	226
227	East St. Louis Electric Street Railway Company	"	"		150,000	19,563	....	19,563	227
228	Evans Snider Buell Company	"	Nat. Stock Y'ds		50,000	3,450	550	4,000	228
229	Mascoutah Electric Light Company	"	Mascoutah		5,000	1,085	....	1,085	229
230	Mississippi River and Bonne Terre Transportation Company	"	East St. Louis	*		....	8,000	8,000	230
231	North and South Rolling Stock Company	"	"	*		....	10,000	10,000	231
232	O'Fallon Electric Light, Power, Heat and Water Company	"	O'Fallon		17,000	....	5,000	5,000	232
233	St. Louis National Stock Yards Company	"	East St. Louis		1,250,000	77,582	177,418	255,000	233
234	Star Elevator Company	"	"		10,000	....	10,000	10,000	234
235	Wiggins' Ferry Company	"	"		1,000,000	443,233	131,767	575,000	235
236	Capital Electric Company	**Sangamon**	Springfield		....	1,920	10,080	12,000	236
237	Springfield Consolidated Railway Company	"	"		750,000	26,540	18,460	45,000	237
238	Springfield Electric Light and Power Company	"	"		50,000	8,936	1,064	10,000	238
239	Springfield Gas Light Company	"	"		75,000	25,636	4,364	30,000	239
240	The Abstract and Title Guarantee Company	"	"		23,750	2,400	1,100	3,500	240
241	Rushville Electric Light Company	**Schuyler**	Rushville		12,500	686	2,314	3,000	241
242	Toulon Light and Power Company	**Stark**	Toulon		10,000	1,974	526	2,500	242

Statement 32—Concluded.

Number	Name of Company.	County.	Location.	Amount of capital stock paid up, as reported by company	Equalized value of tangible property assessed by local assessors	Net assessment of capital stock, being excess of equalized value of capital stock and debt over tangible property assessed by local assessors	Total amount assessed being net assessment of capital stock by the board, and equalized value of tangible property assessed by local assessors	Number
243	Freeport Street Railway Company	Stephenson	Freeport	$125,000	....	$20,000	$20,000	243
244	Freeport Light and Fuel Company	"	"	....	$6,024	8,976	15,000	244
245	Freeport Water Company	"	"	150,000	12,402	5,598	18,000	245
246	German Insurance Company	"	"	200,000	75,980	39,020	115,000	546
247	City of Pekin Electric Light and Power Company	Tazewell	Pekin	50,000	2,800	2,200	5,000	247
248	Pekin Gas Light Company	"	"	66,920	4,922	1,078	6,000	248
249	Pekin Water Works Company	"	"	100,000	13,700	6,300	20,000	249
250	Turner Hudnut Company	"	"	125,000	14,055	1,945	16,000	250
251	Danville Gas, Electric Light and Street Railway Company	Vermilion	Danville	250,000	25,503	9,497	35,000	251
252	Danville Telephone Company	"	"	25,000	1,602	898	2,500	252
253	Danville Water Company	"	"	200,000	18,596	26,404	45,000	253
254	Edison Illuminating Company	Warren	Monmouth	10,000	8,225	....	8,225	254
255	Monmouth Gas Company	"	"	30,000	10,000	500	10,500	255
256	Washington Mineral Springs Company	Washington	Okawville	40,000	2,636	3,364	6,000	256
257	Southern Illinois Improvement Company	Wayne	Fairfield	300,000	....	3,000	3,000	257
258	Fulton Electric Light and Power Company	Whiteside	Fulton	20,000	2,490	510	3,000	258
259	Morrison Electric Light and Power Company	"	Morrison	20,000	....	4,000	4,000	259
260	Sterling Gas and Electric Light Company	"	Sterling	39,000	4,728	1,272	6,000	260
261	Sterling Water Company	"	"	35,000	12,971	5,029	18,000	261
262	Whiteside Harrison Telephone Company	"	Morrison	8,400	....	2,000	2,000	262
263	Economy Light and Power Company	Will	Joliet	400,000	47,569	2,431	50,000	263
264	Ingalls' Park Company	"	"	150,000	15,997	4,003	20,000	264
265	Joliet Gas Light Company	"	"	100,000	16,174	3,826	20,000	265
266	Joliet Street Railway Company	"	"	300,000	42,349	9,651	52,000	266
267	Union Elevator Company	"	"	66,500	10,650	2,350	13,000	267
268	Wilmington Electric Light and Power Company	"	Wilmington	21,000	993	1,007	2,000	268
269	Electric Light, Street Railroad and Power Company	Williamson	Creel Springs	*	....	500	500	269
270	Hope Electric Light and Power Company	"	Carterville	8,800	734	766	1,500	270
271	Marion Electric Light and Street Railway Company	"	Marion	*	....	1,000	1,000	271
272	Forest City Electric Light and Power Company	Winnebago	Rockford	80,000	12,403	7,597	20,000	272
273	Forest City Insurance Company	"	"	100,000	55,234	766	56,000	273
274	Insurance Company of the State of Illinois	"	"	100,000	13,940	6,060	20,000	274
275	Holland Ferguson Company	"	"	50,000	1,230	1,770	3,000	275

276	Rockford City Railway Company	"	"	36,000	8,692	8,308	17,000	276
277	Rockford Electric Power Company	"	"	53,000	7,448	2,552	10,000	277
278	Rockford Gas Light and Coke Company	"	"	300,000	14,055	15,945	30,000	278
279	Rockford Insurance Company	"	"	200,000	54,687	15,313	70,000	279
280	Rockford Traction Company	"	"	300,000	6,225	6,775	13,000	280
	Totals			$139,331,694	$10,764,276	$4,030,384	$14,794,660	

* Company failed to make complete return.

No. 33.

Statement of the Equalized Assessment of all Taxable Property in the State of Illinois for the year 1896, as Equalized or Assessed by the State Board of Equalization, showing the valuation of the several classes of property in each County.

Counties.	Assessed in Counties by Local Assessors.						Assessed by State Board of Equalization.		
	Assessed value of lands, lots and personal property, including railroad property, assessed by local assessors.	Average rate per cent. of addition or reduction.		Net amount added.	Net amount deducted.	Equalized value of property assessed by local assessors.	Equalized value of railroad track, rolling stock, and improvements on right of way.	Equalized value of capital stock of corporations other than railroads	Total equalized value of property assessed for year 1896.
		Add.	Ded.						
Adams	$12,604,683		12		$1,513,569	$11,091,114	$773,618	$16,470	$11,881,202
Alexander	2,324,372					2,324,372	243,879	14,525	2,582,776
Bond	2,421,589		2		60,485	2,361,104	370,480	6,000	2,737,584
Boone	3,198,730		6		194,958	3,003,772	377,511	3,500	3,384,783
Brown	1,867,896		2		50,129	1,817,767	150,684		1,968,451
Bureau	10,116,135		19		1,939,288	8,176,847	1,518,586		9,695,433
Calhoun	1,446,922		14		202,593	1,244,329			1,244,329
Carroll	3,815,946		3		143,876	3,672,070	779,490	924	4,452,484
Cass	3,686,024		17		632,757	3,053,267	321,974		3,375,241
Champaign	9,971,448		12		1,128,304	8,843,144	635,882	2,500	9,481,526
Christian	6,660,381		7		445,004	6,215,377	468,812	8,950	6,693,139
Clark	1,602,134	58		$939,316		2,541,450	407,081		2,948,531
Clay	1,702,231		13		218,568	1,483,663	257,577	200	1,741,440
Clinton	2,610,741	13		338,982		2,949,723	385,539		3,335,262
Coles	5,211,102		12		605,894	4,605,208	524,952	7,050	5,137,210
Cook	207,530,692	22		45,213,929		252,744,621	17,476,088	2,720,165	272,940,874
Crawford	1,740,064	3		57,968		1,798,032	127,592		1,925,624
Cumberland	1,147,290	18		201,551		1,348,841	328,770		1,677,611
DeKalb	7,788,484		10		809,467	6,979,017	1,020,187	4,500	8,003,704
DeWitt	3,553,533		4		132,185	3,421,348	326,502	402	3,748,252
Douglas	3,878,970		4		138,634	3,740,336	397,292		4,137,628
DuPage	5,249,437		3		167,744	5,081,693	1,048,675		6,130,368
Edgar	5,331,873		1		78,658	5,253,215	697,573	1,375	5,952,163
Edwards	1,419,671		15		207,086	1,212,585	146,273		1,358,858
Effingham	2,023,823	13		267,485		2,291,308	530,022	4,130	2,825,460

Fayette	2,748,016	3		90,504		2,838,520	400,348	3,000	3,241,868
Ford	3,586,446		15		527,771	3,058,675	441,744		3,500,419
Franklin	1,009,362	13		134,856		1,144,218	127,518		1,271,736
Fulton	7,551,445	3		213,210		7,764,655	807,436	500	8,572,591
Gallatin	868,145	58		505,312		1,373,457	159,036		1,532,493
Greene	4,571,714	1		57,987		4,629,701	536,030		5,165,731
Grundy	3,624,296				2,653	3,621,643	911,282		4,532,925
Hamilton	1,168,546	20		239,772		1,408,318	187,974		1,596,292
Hancock	7,382,182		8		568,692	6,813,490	750,566	13,630	7,577,686
Hardin	725,247		24		177,093	548,154			548,154
Henderson	2,601,038		5		131,948	2,469,090	587,375		3,056,465
Henry	9,939,436		21		2,066,142	7,873,294	1,084,143	4,774	8,962,211
Iroquois	9,061,303		13		1,177,970	7,883,333	806,827	784	8,690,944
Jackson	2,500,632					2,500,632	449,038	350	2,950,020
Jasper	1,635,021	6		105,021		1,740,042	194,660		1,934,702
Jefferson	1,615,580	17		276,586		1,892,166	409,716	973	2,302,855
Jersey	2,904,081	13		374,975		3,279,056	305,568		3,584,624
JoDaviess	3,982,010		12		487,603	3,494,407	515,394	16,006	4,025,807
Johnson	1,454,162					1,454,162	199,958		1,654,120
Kane	13,849,182		11		1,459,002	12,390,180	1,375,968	18,508	13,784,656
Kankakee	4,735,467		6		277,315	4,458,152	917,455	611	5,376,218
Kendall	3,526,940		14		504,328	3,022,612	337,622		3,360,234
Knox	9,824,770		7		713,945	9,110,825	1,193,454	13,545	10,317,824
Lake	7,016,886		9		632,164	6,384,722	1,024,904	100	7,409,726
LaSalle	16,661,162		16		2,709,154	13,952,008	1,808,139	39,291	15,799,438
Lawrence	1,298,639	26		337,576		1,636,215	222,329		1,858,544
Lee	7,311,711		18		1,328,896	5,982,815	686,281	7,497	6,676,593
Livingston	8,834,720		8		682,937	8,151,783	1,592,321	7,347	9,751,451
Logan	6,797,848		7		525,521	6,272,327	580,451	9,729	6,862,507
Macon	10,118,418		16		1,593,485	8,524,933	591,864	54,992	9,171,789
Macoupin	6,439,830	18		1,157,263		7,597,093	967,380	2,340	8,566,813
Madison	10,949,554		5		592,894	10,356,660	1,957,786	73,416	12,387,862
Marion	3,367,369	10		340,926		3,708,295	245,398	3,475	3,957,167
Marshall	3,973,344		10		397,335	3,576,009	564,055		4,140,064
Mason	3,096,957					3,096,957	452,995		3,549,952
Massac	1,531,279	1		21,003		1,552,282	92,764		1,645,046
McDonough	6,458,503		8		494,970	5,963,533	527,081		6,490,614
McHenry	5,675,817		16		935,864	4,739,953	746,571	204	5,486,728
McLean	16,240,201		4		708,971	15,531,230	1,481,271	21,528	17,034,029
Menard	4,106,730		24		1,001,503	3,105,227	312,970		3,418,197
Mercer	4,454,825	4		164,624		4,619,449	485,471	1,050	5,105,970
Monroe	2,531,765		1		33,792	2,497,973	154,505		2,652,478
Montgomery	5,417,747	4		234,391		5,652,138	716,256	14,714	6,383,108
Morgan	11,038,485		35		3,873,730	7,164,755	664,803	4,000	7,833,558
Moultrie	2,419,327	4		95,245		2,514,572	434,837		2,949,409
Ogle	7,186,269		2		176,553	7,009,716	1,092,982	1,040	8,103,738
Peoria	16,373,851		18		2,889,222	13,484,629	1,638,704	62,244	15,185,577
Perry	1,898,425					1,898,425	369,831	1,890	2,270,146
Piatt	4,064,856		10		401,137	3,663,719	561,552		4,225,271
Pike	4,784,464	9		410,735		5,195,199	751,824	773	5,947,796
Pope	1,074,278					1,074,278			1,074,278
Pulaski	940,243					940,243	77,484		1,017,727

Statement 33—Concluded.

Counties.	Assessed in Counties by Local Assessors.						Assessed by State Board of Equalization.		
	Assessed value of lands, lots and personal property, including railroad property, assessed by local assessors.	Average rate per cent. of addition or deduction.		Net amount added.	Net amount deducted.	Equalized value of property assessed by local assessors.	Equalized value of railroad track, rolling stock, and improvements on right of way.	Equalized value of capital stock of corporations other than railroads.	Total equalized value of property assessed for year 1896.
		Add.	Ded.						
Putnam	$1,389,914		11		$150,302	$1,239,612	$61,952		$1,391,564
Randolph	3,294,067	8		$277,722		3,571,789	391,201	$1,195	3,964,185
Richland	1,623,357		2		30,829	1,592,528	199,175	8,000	1,799,703
Rock Island	7,330,175		19		1,372,666	5,957,509	750,227	13,902	6,721,638
Saline	1,391,212		1	16,750		1,407,962	214,939		1,622,901
Sangamon	16,767,008		20		3,353,402	13,413,606	1,257,476	35,068	14,706,150
Schuyler	2,502,023	9		212,964		2,714,987	154,216	2,314	2,871,517
Scott	2,498,190		10		247,134	2,251,056	232,828		2,483,884
Shelby	5,641,634		9		490,639	5,150,995	642,225		5,793,220
Stark	3,205,720		7		216,113	2,989,607	300,531	526	3,290,664
St. Clair	12,672,247		10		1,328,230	11,344,017	2,244,518	568,167	14,156,702
Stephenson	8,754,270		21		1,803,219	6,951,051	724,097	73,594	7,748,742
Tazewell	6,737,587		4		242,686	6,494,901	1,164,755	11,523	7,671,179
Union	1,899,863	11		216,736		2,116,599	166,427		2,283,026
Vermilion	10,944,046		12		1,296,821	9,647,225	1,488,130	36,799	11,172,154
Wabash	1,495,068		24		352,047	1,143,021	162,898		1,305,919
Warren	5,562,643		3		188,145	5,374,498	677,451	500	6,052,449
Washington	2,959,674	12		349,964		3,309,638	229,084	3,364	3,542,086
Wayne	1,806,743	6		114,001		1,920,744	273,954	3,000	2,197,698
White	1,445,692	38		549,223		1,994,915	370,608		2,365,523
Whiteside	7,427,274		16		1,200,503	6,226,771	926,680	12,811	7,166,262
Will	11,965,305		2		215,952	11,749,353	1,068,723	23,268	13,841,344
Williamson	1,777,110	3		52,335		1,829,445	189,919	2,266	2,021,630
Winnebago	12,185,876		19		2,290,400	9,895,476	850,171	65,086	10,810,733
Woodford	6,106,095		10		610,611	5,495,484	437,179		5,932,663
Total	$731,215,488			$53,568,912	$51,131,488	$733,652,912	$78,996,324	$4,030,384	$816,679,620

No.

Statement of Bonds Issued by Counties, Townships, Cities and "An Act to fund and provide for paying the Railroad Debts of

No. of line	Locality—issued by.	Railroad aided.	Date.	Principal—when payable.
	Alexander County:			
1	County of Alexander	Cairo and Vincennes	1872 July 1	1892 July 1
2	" "	Cairo and St. Louis	" Jan. 1	" Jan. 1
3	" "	" "	" " 1	" " 1
4	" "	" "	" " 1	" " 1
5	City of Cairo	Cairo and Vincennes	" July 1	" July 1
6	" "	Cairo and St. Louis	" Jan. 1	" Jan. 1
7	" "	" "	" " 1	" " 1
8	" "	" "	" " 1	" " 1
	Bureau County:			
1	Tp. of Lamille	Illinois Grand Trunk	1870 Dec. 1	1880 Dec. 1
2	" Ohio	" "	1871 Jan. 1	1876 to 1880
3	" Walnut	" "	" " 1	1881 Jan. 1
	Cass County:			
1	City of Beardstown	Rockford, R. I. and St. Louis	1869 Feb. 1	1889 Feb. 1
2	" "	" "	" Nov. 1	" Nov. 1
	Champaign County:			
1	Tp. of Urbana	D., U., B. and P.	1867 Oct. 1	1877 Oct. 1
2	" "	" "	" " 1	" " 1
3	" *Champaign	Monticello	1868 Dec. 1	1878 Dec. 1
	Coles County:			
1	Town of Charleston	Tuscola, Charl'st'n and Vincennes	1880 June 1	1900 on or before
2	" "	" "	" " 1	" "
3	" "	" "	" " 1	" "
4	Tp. of East Oakland	Paris and Decatur	1871 Apr. 20	1881 Mar. 1
5	" "	" "	" " 20	" " 1
	DeWitt County:			
1	Tp. of Clintonia	Gilman, Clinton and Springfield	1871 July 1	1891 July 1
2	" "	H., M. City, L. and Eastern	1872 Sept. 1	1882 and 1892
3	" Creek	" "	1871 July 5	1891 July 5
	Douglas County:			
1	Tp. of Arcola	Paris and Decatur	1871 Mar. 1	1881 Mar. 1
2	" "	" "	" " 1	" " 1
3	" Bowdre	" "	" Apr. 9	" " 1
4	" Bourbon	" "	1873 July 1	1882 July 1
	Effingham County:			
1	Tp. of Moccasin	St. L., V. and Terre Haute	1869 July 1 & aft'r	1894 July & Nov.
2	" Summit	" "	" Nov. & July 1	" "
	Edgar County:			
1	Tp. of Embarras	Paris and Decatur	1871 Apr. 20	1881 Mar. 1
2	" Paris	" "	" Mar. 23	" " 1
3	" Y'ng America	Indiana and Illinois Central	1873 Apr. 10	1883 Apr. 10
	Fayette County:			
1	Tp. of Vandalia	St. L., V. and Terre Haute	1868 July 1	1883 July 1
	Franklin County:			
1	County of Franklin	Belleville and Eldorado	1877 Nov. 13	1897 Nov. 13
	Fulton County:			
1	Tp. of Pleasant	Peoria and Hannibal	1868 Oct. 1	1883 July 1

* Late West Urbana.

34.

Towns, registered in Auditor's office, in pursuance of an act entitled' Counties, Townships, Cities and Towns, in force April 16, 1869.

Interest—when payable.	Rate of interest...	When registered.	Denomination.	No.	Amount.	Amount of principal which has been redeemed and canceled.	Amount outstanding Sept. 30, 1896.	No. of line........
Jan. and July..	8	1872 Dec. 28..........	$1,000 00	95	$95,000 00	$27,000 00	$68,000 00	1
" "	8	1875 Mar. 24..........	1,000 00	61	61,000 00	47,000 00	14,000 00	2
" "	8	" Apr. 9..........	1,000 00	10	10,000 00	7,000 00	3,000 00	3
" "	8	" " 10..........	1,000 00	29	29,000 00	5,000 00	24,000 00	4
" "	8	1872 Dec. 21..........	1,000 00	95	95,000 00	75,000 00	20,000 00	5
" "	8	1875 Mar. 19..........	1,000 00	56	56,000 00	42,000 00	14,000 00	6
" "	8	" Apr. 9..........	1,000 00	10	10,000 00	9,000 00	1,000 00	7
" "	8	" " 10..........	1,000 00	29	29,000 00	26,000 00	3,000 00	8
Dec. 1, ann....	10	1871 Apr. 15..........	1,000 00	40	40,000 00	30,000 00	10,000 00	1
Jan. 1, ann....	10	" " 15..........	100 00	400	40,000 00	37,600 00	2,400 00	2
" 1, "	10	" " 15..........	100 00	400	40,000 00	29,400 00	10,600 00	3
Aug. and Feb...	10	1870 Feb. 24..........	100 00	400	40,000 00	39,700 00	300 00	1
May and Nov...	10	" Apr. 25..........	500 00	22	11,000 00	10,500 00	500 00	2
Oct. 1, ann....	10	1871 Apr. 7 & after.	1,000 00	37	37,000 00	30,000 00	7,000 00	1
" 1, "	10	1869 Dec. 31 "	500 00	70	35,000 00	33,500 00	1,500 00	2
Dec. 1, "	10	1870 Jan. 4..........	1,000 00	40	40,000 00	37,000 00	3,000 00	3
June 1, ann....	6	1882 Feb. 18..........	1,000 00	73	73,000 00	16,000 00	57,000 00	1
" 1, "	6	1883 Oct. 6..........	1,000 00	2	2,000 00	1,000 00	1,000 00	2
" 1, "	6	1885 July 8..........	1,000 00	17	17,000 00	....	17,000 00	3
Mar. 1, "	10	1872 Apr. 11..........	500 00	110	55,000 00	....	55,000 00	4
" 1, "	10	" " 11..........	100 00	200	20,000 00	....	20,000 00	5
July 1, ann....	10	1871 Sept. 14..........	1,000 00	50	50,000 00	48,000 00	2,000 00	1
Sept. 1, "	10	1872 " 21..........	1,000 00	50	50,000 00	43,000 00	7,000 00	2
July 1, "	10	1872 Dec. 12..........	1,000 00	30	30,000 00	24,000 00	6,000 00	3
Mar. and Sept..	10	1872 Mar. 6..........	500 00	160	80,000 00	....	80,000 00	1
" "	10	" " 6..........	100 00	200	20,000 00	....	20,000 00	2
" "	10	" Apr. 12..........	500 00	60	30,000 00	....	30,000 00	3
July and Jan. 1.	10	1873 July 5 & after.	500 00	70	35,000 00	....	35,000 00	4
July & Nov. ann	10	1870 Sept. 1 & Nov. 11	500 00	10	5,000 00	2,500 00	2,500 00	1
" "	10	" " 1..........	1,000 00	10	10,000 00	9,000 00	1,000 00	2
Mar. and Sept..	10	1872 Feb. 22 & after.	500 00	50	25,000 00	....	25,000 00	1
Mar. 1, ann....	7	1871 Oct. 17 "	500 00	100	50,000 00	....	50,000 00	2
Apr. 10, "	8	1873 Apr. 24..........	1,000 00	12	12,000 00	11,000 00	1,000 00	3
July 1, ann....	10	1879 Apr. 29..........	500 00	30	15,000 00	14,500 00	500 00	1
Jan. and July 1.	8	1877 Nov. 23 & after.	1,000 00	149	149,000 00	....	149,000 00	1
July 1, ann....	10	1870 Mar. 15..........	100 00	150	15,000 00	14,600 00	400 00	1

Statement 34—

No. of line	Locality—issued by.	Railroad aided.	Date.	Principal—when payable.
	Gallatin County:			
1	County of Gallatin..	Illinois Southeastern...........	1870 Jan.1 & aft'r	1890 Jan. 1......
2	" " ..	St. Louis and Southeastern.......	1871 Jan. 1......	1891 " 1......
3	City of Shawneetown	" "	1892 " 1......	1892 " 1......
	Hamilton County:			
1	County of Hamilton.	St. Louis and Southeastern.......	1871 Oct. & Nov.	1891 Oct. & Nov.
	Iroquois County:			
1	Tp. of Belmont......	Chicago, Danville and Vincennes.	1871 Mar. 23.....	1881 July 1......
2	" Concord......	" " "	" June 1......	" June 1......
3	" Grenard......	" " "	" Mar. 23....	" July 1......
4	" Lovejoy......	" " "	" " 31....	Various ....
5	" Middleport...	" " "	" " 24....	" ....
6	" Milford.......	" " "	" " 30....	" ....
7	" "	" " "	" " 30....	" ....
8	" Martinton.....	" " "	1892 July 1......	1882 July 1......
9	" Papineau......	" " "	1871 Apr. 13......	Various.........
10	" Sheldon.......	" " "	" June 1......	1881 June 1......
11	City of Watseka.....	" " "	" Feb. 1......	Various.........
	Jasper County:			
1	County of Jasper....	Grayville and Mattoon............	1876 Oct. 19......	1877-8 Oct. 1.....
2	" "	" "	" Nov. 11.....	1878 to '80 Nov. 1
	Johnson County:			
1	County of Johnson..	Cairo and Vincennes'.............	1872 Dec. 3......	1892 Dec. 3......
	Kane County:			
1	Tp. of Aurora........	Ottawa, Ohio & Fox River Valley.	1869 May 1......	Various.........
	Kendall County:			
1	County of Kendall ..	Ottawa, Ohio & Fox Rivey Valley.	1869 May 4......	Various.........
2	Tp. of Fox	" " "	" " 4......	" ....
3	" Kendall.......	" " "	" " 4......	" ....
4	" Oswego.......	" " "	" " 3......	" ....
	Knox County:			
1	Tp. of Rio............	Rockford, R. I. and St. Louis......	1870 Nov. 4......	1890 Oct. 1......
	LaSalle County:			
1	Tp. of Bruce.........	Ottawa, Ohio & Fox River Valley.	1870 Oct. 22......	1890 July 1......
2	" "	Fairbury, Pontiac and N. W.......	1874 Oct. 9......	1891 " 1......
3	" Dayton........	Ottawa, Ohio & Fox River Valley.	1869 May 1......	Various.........
4	" Osage........	" " "	" " 22......	" ....
5	" Ottawa........	" " "	" " 1......	" ....
6	" S. Ottawa.....	" " "	" " 1......	" ....
	Lee County:			
1	Tp. of Amboy........	Chicago and Rock River	1872 Apr. 5......	1881 July 1......
	Macon County.			
1	County of Macon....	Pekin, Lincoln and Decatur.......	1871 Oct. 11......	1891 Oct. 11......
2	" "	Monticello.........................	1873 Sept. 25.....	1893 Sept. 25.....
3	Tp. of Mt. Zion......	Chicago and Illinois Southern....	1872 Dec. 26......	1892 Dec. 26......
	Marshall County:			
1	Tp. of Evans.........	Ottawa, Ohio & Fox River Valley.	1869 May 22......	Various.........

Continued.

Interest—when payable.	Rate of interest.	When registered.	Denomination.	No.	Amount.	Amount of principal which has been redeemed and canceled.	Amount outstanding Sept. 30, 1896.	No. of line.
Jan. and July 1.	8	1870 Mar. 31 and after.	$1,000 00	200	$200,000 00	$197,000 00	$3,000 00	1
" " 1.	7	1871 Jan. 6..........	1,000 00	100	100,000 00	52,000 00	48,000 00	2
" " 1.	8	1872 Feb. 17..........	1,000 00	25	25,000 00	....	25,000 00	3
Jan. and July 1.	7	1871 Nov. 1 & Dec. 5...	1,000 00	200	200,000 00	....	200,000 00	1
July 1, ann....	10	1871 July 6..........	1,000 00	15	15,000 00	....	15,000 00	1
June 1, "	10	" Oct. 20 & 24.......	1,000 00	25	25,000 00	....	25,000 00	2
July 1, "	10	" July 6..........	1,000 00	4	4,000 00	....	4,000 00	3
" 1, "	10	" Sept. 23 & Nov. 29	1,000 00	10	10,000 00	....	10,000 00	4
June 1, "	10	" July 6..........	1,000 00	15	15,000 00	....	15,000 00	5
July 1, "	10	" " 26..........	1,000 00	20	20,000 00	....	20,000 00	6
" 1, "	10	" " 26..........	617 15	1	617 15	....	617 15	7
" 1, "	10	1872 Sept. 10..........	1,000 00	11	11,000 00	....	11,000 00	8
Mar. 1, "	10	1871 Aug. 26..........	1,000 00	6	6,000 00	....	6,000 00	9
June 1, "	10	" Oct. 20..........	1,000 00	25	25,000 00	14,000 00	11,000 00	10
Mar. 1, "	10	" July & Nov......	500 00	20	10,000 00	4,500 00	5,500 00	11
Oct. 1, ann....	10	1876 Oct. 24..........	1,000 00	25	25,000 00	16,000 00	9,000 00	1
Nov. 1, "	10	" Nov. 13..........	1,000 00	25	25,000 00	14,000 00	11,000 00	2
July and Jan. 1.	8	1872 Dec. 7..........	500 00	189	94,500 00	61,000 00	33,500 00	1
July 1, ann....	10	1870 Oct. 13 & after....	1,000 00	60	60,000 00	12,000 00	48,000 00	1
July 1, ann....	10	1870 Nov. 25..........	1,000 00	47	47,000 00	2,000 00	45,000 00	1
" 1, "	10	" Feb. 18 & Mar. 22.	1,000 00	14	14,000 00	....	14,000 00	2
" 1, "	10	" Mar. 22 & after...	1,000 00	22	22,000 00	....	22,000 00	3
" 1, "	10	1871 July 6 "	1,000 00	50	50,000 00	....	50,000 00	4
Oct. 1, ann....	8	1870 Nov. 17..........	1,000 00	30	30,000 00	21,000 00	9,000 00	1
July 1, ann....	10	1870 Nov. 1..........	1,000 00	13	13,000 00	....	13,000 00	1
" 1, "	10	1871 " 3..........	1,000 00	15	15,000 00	....	15,000 00	2
" 1, "	10	1869 " 10..........	1,000 00	12	12,000 00	....	12,000 00	3
" 1, "	10	" Aug. 17..........	1,000 00	20	20,000 00	....	20,000 00	4
" 1, "	10	" " 17..........	1,000 00	150	150,000 00	....	150,000 00	5
" 1, "	10	" " 17..........	1,000 00	30	30,000 00	....	30,000 00	6
July 1, ann....	10	1872 April 8..........	500 00	200	100,000 00	98,500 00	1,500 00	1
July 1, ann....	8	1871 Dec. 12..........	1,000 00	100	100,000 00	96,000 00	4,000 00	1
" 1, "	8	1873 Sept. 26..........	1,000 00	25	25,000 00	24,000 00	1,000 00	2
Dec. 26, "	8	1872 Dec. 26..........	1,000 00	20	20,000 00	....	20,000 00	3
July 1, ann....	10	1869 Aug. 17..........	1,000 00	40	40,000 00	....	40,000 00	1

Statement 34—

No. of line	Locality—issued by.	Railroad aided.	Date.	Principal—when payable.
	Mercer County:			
1	Tp. of Abington	Dixon and Quincy	1870 Dec. 31	1890 Dec. 31
2	" Greene	American Central	1869 Mar. 11	1874 or 1879
3	" Mercer	" "	" " 23	1879 Mar. 23
	Monroe County.			
1	Tp.3S.,range9W3dP.M.	Cairo and St. Louis	1874 Sept. 2	1894 Sept. 2
	Morgan County:			
1	Tp.14N.,R.9W.3dP.M.	Illinois Farmers	1870 Oct. 1	1890 Oct. 1
	Moultrie County:			
1	County of Moultrie	Decatur, Sullivan and Mattoon	1871 Nov. 1	1881 Nov. 1
2	" "	Bloomington and Ohio River	1872 May 27	1882 July 1
3	Tp. of Dora	Paris and Decatur	1871 Apr. 29	1881 Mar. 1
4	" Lowe	" "	" July 15	" " 1
	Ogle County:			
1	Tp. of Pine Rock	Ogle and Carroll County	1871 Apr. 8	1891 Apr. 1
2	" Mt. Morris	Chicago and Iowa	1875 May 3	1885 May 3
3	" "	" "	" " 3	" " 3
	Perry County:			
1	County of Perry	Belleville and Southern Illinois	1871 Jan. 1	1891 Jan. 1
2	" "	Chester and Tam. C. and R. R.	'71 July, '72 Jan. 1	1891 and 1892
	Piatt County:			
1	Tp. of Bement	Bloomington and Ohio River	1871 Dec. 1	1881 July 1
2	" Blue Ridge	D., U., B. and Pekin	1867 Oct. 1	1887 Oct. 1
	Pulaski County:			
1	County of Pulaski	Cairo and Vincennes	1872 Oct. 17	1892 Oct. 17
	Randolph County:			
1	Tp.4 S.,R.8W.3dP.M.	Cairo and St. Louis	1874 June 8	1894 June 8
	Saline County:			
1	County of Saline	Cairo and Vincennes	1872 Oct. 8	1892 Oct. 8
2	Inc. T. of Eldorado	St. Louis and Southeastern	" Jan. 1	" Jan. 1
	Schuyler County:			
1	Tp. of Frederick	Rockford, Rock Island and St. L.	1870 June 1	1890 June 1
	Shelby County:			
1	Tp. of Richland	Bloomington and Ohio River	1873 Dec. 13	1884 Jan. 1
2	" Windsor	" "	1872 Jan. 1	1882 " 1
3	City of Windsor	" "	1871 Dec. 18	1881 July 1
	Stark County:			
1	Inc. T. of Wyoming	Peoria, Dixon and Hannibal	1869 July 1	1889 July 1
	St. Clair County:			
1	City of Belleville	Illinois and St. L. R. R. and C. Co.	1870 Aug. 6	1890 Aug. 6
2	Inc. T. of Freeburg	Belleville and Southern Illinois	" Jan. 1	" Jan. 1
	Tazewell County:			
1	Tp. of Elm Grove	D., U., B. and Pekin	1869 Dec. 1	1889 Dec. 1
2	" "	" "	" " 1	" " 1
	Union County:			
1	County of Union	Cairo and St. Louis	1874 Oct. 6	1894 Sept. 7
2	City of Jonesboro	" "	1872 July 1	1892 July 1

Continued.

Interest—when payable.	Rate of interest...	When registered.	Denomination.	No.	Amount.	Amount of principal which has been redeemed and canceled.	Amount outstanding Sept. 30, 1896.	No. of line.......
July 1, ann....	10	1871 April 15..........	$100 00	100	$10,000 00	$9,900 00	$100 00	1
Mar. 11, "	8	1873 Jan. 13, July 23...	100 00	90	9,000 00	8,800 00	200 00	2
" 23, "	10	" May 31..........	100 00	120	12,000 00	4,300 00	7,700 00	3
Sept. 2, ann....	8	1874 Sept. 3 and 7......	500 00	30	15,000 00	....	15,000 00	1
Oct. 1, ann....	10	1870 Nov. 18	1,000 00	32	32,000 00	....	32,000 00	1
Nov. 1, ann....	8	1871 Dec. 1...........	1,000 00	75	75,000 00	70,000 00	5,000 00	1
July 1, "	10	1872 May 29...........	1,000 00	200	200,000 00	86,000 00	114,000 00	2
Mar. and Sept. 1	10	" Aug. 23...........	500 00	36	18,000 00	....	18,000 00	3
" " 1	10	1873 June 4...........	500 00	60	30,000 00	....	30,000 00	4
April 1, ann....	7	1871 June 5...........	100 00	100	10,000 00	400 00	9,600 00	1
May 1, "	10	1875 Sept. 4 and after.	1,000 00	25	25,000 00	1,500 00	23,500 00	2
" 1, "	10	" " 4 " "	500 00	46	23,000 00	....	23,000 00	3
Jan. 1, ann....	7	1871 Jan. 2...........	1,000 00	100	100,000 00	3,000 00	97,000 00	1
Jan. and July ..	7	" Nov. 17, 1872 Jan. 1	1,000 00	100	100,000 00	....	100,000 00	2
July 1, ann....	10	1871 Dec. 5...........	1,000 00	50	50,000 00	49,000 00	1,000 00	1
Oct. 1, "	10	1870 Feb. 1 and after..	100 00	45	4,500 00	4,400 00	100 00	2
Jan. and July 1.	8	1872 Dec. 23 and after.	500 00	190	95,000 00	66,000 00	29,000 00	1
June 8, ann....	8	1874 July 25...........	1,000 00	50	50,000 00	....	50,000 00	1
Jan. and July 1.	8	1872 Oct. 12...........	500 00	190	95,000 00	....	95,000 00	1
" " 1.	8	" Aug. 3............	1,000 00	50	5,000 00	....	5,000 00	2
June 1, ann....	8	1870 July 6............	500 00	10	5,000 00	4,500 00	500 00	1
Jan. 1, ann....	10	1873 Dec. 15...........	1,000 00	40	40,000 00	....	40,000 00	1
" 1, "	10	1872 Jan. 4...........	1,000 00	50	50,000 00	48,000 00	2,000 00	2
July 1, "	10	1871 Dec. 20...........	1,000 00	20	20,000 00	12,000 00	8,000 00	3
July 1, ann....	10	1870 May 17............	1,000 00	10	10,000 00	....	10,000 00	1
Aug. 6, ann....	8	1871 Dec. 12...........	1,000 00	25	25,000 00	....	25,000 00	1
Jan. 1, "	6	1870 July 8............	1,000 00	15	15,000 00	....	15,000 00	2
Dec. 1, ann....	10	1870 Aug. 6............	1,000 00	4	4,000 00	....	4,000 00	1
" 1, "	10	" " 6............	500 00	6	3,000 00	....	3,000 00	2
Sept. 7, ann....	8	1874 Oct. 13............	1,000 00	50	50,000 00	....	50,000 00	1
July 1, "	8	" " 13............	1,000 00	25	25,000 00	....	25,000 00	2

Statement 34—

No. of line	Locality—issued by.	Railroad aided.	Date.	Principal—when payable.
	Wayne County:			
1	County of Wayne ...	Illinois Southeastern.............	1869 Sept. 9 & 19	1890 Jan. 1 ....
2	" "	" "	1869 and 1870	1889 July 1 ....
3	" "	" "	1870 May 6	1890 Jan. 1 ....
	White County:			
1	County of White	Cairo and Vincennes	1872 Sep.10, Dec.2	1892, Sep. & Dec.
2	Inc. T. of Carmi.....	" "	1872 Dec. 21	1877 to 1892......
	Williamson County:			
1	Co. of Williamson...	Carbondale and Shawneetown....	1872 Jan. 1	1892 Jan. 1 ....
	Total..............	....	....	....

Concluded.

Interest—when payable.	Rate of interest...	When registered.	Denomination.	No.	Amount.	Amount of principal which has been redeemed and canceled.	Amount outstanding Sept. 30, 1896.	No. of line...
Jan. and July ..	7	1869 Sept. 11 & Dec. 7.	$500 00	100	$50,000 00	$31,200 00	$18,800 00	1
" "	7	1869 Dec. 7, 1870 Jan. 24	100 00	500	50,000 00	32,100 00	17,900 00	2
" "	7	1870 May 9............	1,000 00	100	100,000 00	51,000 00	49,000 00	3
July and Jan. 1.	8	1872 Sept. 13 & Dec. 4.	500 00	199	99,500 00	....	99,500 00	1
Jan. and July 1.	8	" Dec. 26...........	100 00	70	7,000 00	6,900 00	100 00	2
July and Jan. 1.	8	1872 Jan. 1............	1,000 00	100	100,000 00	98,000 00	2,000 00	1
....		....	....	....	$4,582,117 15	$1,868,300 00	$2,713,817 15	

No.

Statement of Bonds Registered in

No. of line	Locality—issued by,	Railroad aided.	Date.	Principal—when payable.
	Adams County:			
	City of Quincy	Northern Cross, Quincy and Palmyra, Chicago, Burlington and Quincy and other purposes ...	July 1, 1866-7-8 and after ...	20 yrs. after date
1	" "			20 " "
2	" "			30 " "
3	" "	Quincy and Missouri Pacific......	1871 July 1......	1891 July 1......
4	" "	Quincy, Mo. and Pacific R. R. Co.	1877 " 1......	1897 " 1......
5	" "	" " "	1878 June 8......	1898 June 8......
6	" "	" " "	" " 28......	20 yrs. after date
7	" "	" " "	1879 Jan. 24......	20 " "
8	" "	" " "	" Aug. 21	20 " "
	Hancock County:			
1	City of Warsaw......	Miss. and Wab. and War. and Rock	1865 July 1 & aft'r	20 yrs. after date
2	" "	" " "	" "	20 " "
3	" "	" " "	" "	20 " "
	Henderson County:			
1	City of Oquawka....	....	1871 July 1......	20 yrs. after date
	JoDaviess County:			
1	City of Galena......	Galena and Southern Wisconsin..	1872 July 1......	20 yrs. after date
2	" "	....	1873 Aug. 25 & aft.	20 " "
	Total..............	....	....	....

35.

pursuance of the Act of February 13, 1865.

Interest—when payable.	Rate of interest...	When registered.	Denomination.	No.	Amount.	Amount of principal which has been redeemed and canceled.	Amount outstanding Sept. 30, 1896.	No. of line......
July 1, ann......	6	1866 Sept. 1 and after.	$100 00	300	$30,000 00	$29,900 00	$100 00	1
" 1, "	6	" 1 "	1,000 00	466	466,000 00	463,000 00	3,000 00	2
" 1, "	6	" 1 "	1,000 00	428	428,000 00	16,000 00	412,000 00	3
" 1, "	6	1871 July 19..........	1,000 00	250	250,000 00	131,000 00	119,000 00	4
" 1, "	6	1877 Nov. 30..........	1,000 00	75	75,000 00	....	75,000 00	5
" 1, "	6	1878 June 14..........	1,000 00	50	50,000 00	....	50,000 00	6
" 1, "	6	" " 29..........	1,000 00	25	25,000 00	....	25,000 00	7
" 1, "	6	1879 Jan. 27..........	1,000 00	50	50,000 00	....	50,000 00	8
" 1, "	6	" Aug. 23..........	1,000 00	50	50,000 00	....	50,000 00	9
July 1, ann......	6	1868 July 2 and after..	100 00	101	10,100 00	6,700 00	3,400 00	1
" 1, "	6	" 2 "	500 00	99	49,500 00	22,000 00	27,500 00	2
" 1, "	6	" 2 "	1,000 00	55	55,000 00	47,000 00	8,000 00	3
July 1, ann......	6	1871 July 1 and after...	Various...	42	32,356 68	....	32,356 68	1
July 1, ann......	6	1872 Aug. 1.	1,000 00	57	57,000 00	....	57,000 00	1
" 1, "	6	1873 Sept. 1 and after..	Various...	32	40,232 77	39,964 05	268 72	2
....	..	....	....	....	$1,668,189 45	$755,564 05	$912,625 40	

No.

Statement of Bonds Registered in pursuance of the Act
27, 1877, and

No. of line	Locality—issued by.	For what purpose.	Date.	Principal—when payable.
	Adams County:			
1	City of Quincy	To fund existing indebtedness ...	1882 Sept. 1......	1902 Sept 1......
2	" "	" " " ..	" " 1......	" " 1......
3	" "	" " " ..	" " 1......	" " 1......
4	" "	" " " ..	1886-8 July 1....	1906-8 July 1....
5	" "	" " " ..	" " 1....	" " 1....
6	" "	" " " ..	1886 " 1....	1906 " 1....
7	" "	" " " ..	1890 " 1....	1893-1910 " 1....
8	" "	" " " ..	1891 " 1....	1911 " 1....
	Alexander County;			
1	Co. of Alexander....	To fund existing indebtedness ...	1878 Dec. 1......	1898 June 1......
2	" "	" " " ..	" " 1......	" " 1......
3	" "	" " " ..	1895 July 1......	1915 July. 1......
4	" "	" " " ..	" " 1......	" " 1......
5	" "	" " " ..	" " 1......	1915 " 1......
6	City of Cairo.........	" " " ..	1878 Dec. 1......	1898 Jan. 1......
7	" "	" " " ..	" " 1......	" " 1......
8	" "	" " " ..	" " 1......	" " 1......
9	" "	" " " ..	" " 1......	" " 1......
10	" "	" " " ..	1894 Jan. 1......	1914 Jan. 1......
11	" "	" " " ..	" " 1......	" " 1......
12	" "	" " " ..	" " 1......	" " 1......
	Bureau County:			
1	Tp. of Ohio	To fund existing indebtedness ...	1881 Aug. 8......	1901 Aug. 8......
2	" Walnut	" " " ..	1882 " 7......	1883-1902 Aug. 7.
	Cass County:			
1	City of Beardstown .	To fund existing indebtedness ...	1882 Jan. 1......	1893-1894 Jan. 1..
	Champaign County:			
1	City of Urbana	To fund existing indebtedness ...	1881 July 1......	1893-1901 July 1.
2	Tp. of Champaign...	" " " ..	1893 Jan. 1......	1894-1913 " 1.
3	" " ...	" " " ..	1889 " 1......	Fifteen-tw'nties
4	" Urbana.......	" " " ..	1884 Dec. 1......	1887-1905 July 1.
5	" "	" " " ..	" " 1......	" " 1.
6	" "	" " " ..	" " 1......	" " 1.
7	" "	" " " ..	1889 May 1......	1909 May 1......
	Christian County:			
1	Tp. of Pana..........	To fund existing indebtedness ...	1885 July 1......	Five-twenties ..
2	" "	" " " ..	1887 " 1......	Ten-twenties....
3	" Johnson......	" " " ..	" Jan. 1......	" ...
	Clark County:			
1	Co. of Clark..........	To fund existing indebtedness ...	1880 May 1......	1900 May 1......
2	Tp. of Westfield.....	" " " ..	1885 Sept. 1......	Ten-twenties....
3	" Marshall.....	" " " ..	" July 1......	Optional........
4	" York..........	" " " ..	" Jan. 1......	1890 to 1900 Jan. 1
	Clay County:			
1	Town of Hartr.......	To fund existing indebtedness ...	1881 May 25.....	Five-twenties...
2	Tp. of Louisville....	" " " ..	1882 April 1.....	" ...
	Coles County:			
1	City of Mattoon......	To fund existing indebtedness...	1880 Mar. 22....	1895 Mar. 22....
2	" "	" " " ...	" " 22....	1900 " 22....
3	" "	" " " ...	1890 May 1....	1910 May 1....
4	" "	" " " ...	1895 Mar. 22....	1915 Mar. 22....
5	Tp. of Mattoon.......	" " " ...	1880 May 1....	1890 May 1....
6	" "	" " " ...	1891 July 1....	1911 July 1....
7	Tp. of Seven Hickory	" " " ...	1884 July 10....	1904 " 10....
8	" "	" " " ...	" " 10....	" " 10....

36.

of February 13, 1865, as amended by the Act of April June 4, 1879.

Interest—when payable.	Rate of interest...	When registered.	Denomination.	No.	Amount.	Amount of principal which has been redeemed and canceled.	Amount outstanding Sept. 30, 1896.	No. of line...
Sept. 1, ann.....	5	1882 Oct. 14 & after.	$1,000 00	25	$25,000 00	....	$25,000 00	1
" 1, "	5	" 10 "	500 00	12	6,000 00	....	6,000 00	2
" 1, "	5	" 10 "	100 00	49	4,900 00	....	4,900 00	3
July 1, "	4½	1886-8 June 26-8	1,000 00	224	224,000 00	....	224,000 00	4
" 1, "	4½	" " 26-8	500 00	202	101,000 00	....	101,000 00	5
" 1, "	4½	1886 " 26	100 00	90	9,000 00	....	9,000 00	6
" 1, "	4½	1890 " 20	1,000 00	225	225,000 00	$110,000 00	115,000 00	7
" 1, "	4	1891 " 25	1,000 00	227	227,000 00	226,000 00	1,000 00	8
Jan. and July 1.	6	1880 Jan. 31 and after	500 00	210	105,000 00	....	105,000 00	1
" 1.	6	" " 31 "	50 00	150	7,500 00	....	7,500 00	2
" 1.	6	1895 Sept. 24.........	500 00	75	37,500 00	....	37,500 00	3
" 1.	6	" " 24.........	100 00	100	10,000 00	....	10,000 00	4
" 1.	6	" " 24.........	50 00	150	7,500 00	....	7,500 00	5
" 1.	6	1879 April 11.........	1,000 00	138	138,000 00	118,495 80	19,504 20	6
" 1.	6	1881 Mar. 10.........	500 00	200	100,000 00	85,866 00	14,134 00	7
" 1.	6	1879 April 11.........	100 00	199	19,900 00	17,086 80	2,813 20	8
" 1.	6	" " 11.........	50 00	155	7,750 00	6,654 93	1,095 07	9
" 1.	6	1894 Feb. 1, 9, 23, 28 ..	500 00	97	48,500 00	....	48,500 00	10
" 1.	6	" " 1, 9 & aft'r	100 00	65	6,500 00	....	6,500 00	11
" 1.	6	" " 1, 9 "	50 00	52	2,600 00	....	2,600 00	12
Aug. 8, ann.....	6	1881 Nov. 25.........	1,000 00	57	57,000 00	....	57,000 00	1
" 7, "	6	1882 Sept. 7.........	500 00	80	40,000 00	28,000 00	12,000 00	2
July & Jan., ann	5	1882 Feb. 4 and after	500 00	251	125,500 00	34,500 00	91,000 00	1
July 1, ann......	6	1882 Jan. 9..........	600 00	9	5,400 00	2,400 00	3,000 00	1
Jan. and July 1.	5	1892 Dec. 28..........	500 00	110	55,000 00	4,500 00	50,500 00	2
Jan. 1, ann......	5	1888 Dec. 26..........	500 00	66	33,000 00	....	33,000 00	3
July 1, ann......	6	1885 May 9 and after	1,000 00	21	21,000 00	10,000 00	11,000 00	4
" 1, "	6	" " 9 "	500 00	45	22,500 00	8,500 00	14,000 00	5
" 1, "	6	" July 22..........	100 00	52	5,200 00	2,500 00	2,700 00	6
May 1, "	6	1889 April 29..........	500 00	40	20,000 00	....	20,000 00	7
July 1, ann......	6	1885 July 29..........	1,000 00	102	102,000 00	....	102,000 00	1
" 1, "	6	1887 " 1..........	1,000 00	36	36,000 00	....	36,000 00	2
" 1, "	6	" Jan. 21..........	1,000 00	5	5,000 00	....	5,000 00	3
May 1, ann......	6	1880 May 4..........	1,000 00	30	30,000 00	....	30,000 00	1
July 1, "	6	1885 Sept. 30..........	1,000 00	20	20,000 00	....	20,000 00	2
" 1, "	6	" " 8 & after.	1,000 00	50	50,000 00	24,000 00	26,000 00	3
Jan. 1, "	6	1886 Jan. 2..........	1,000 00	15	15,000 00	10,000 00	5,000 00	4
Jan. & July 1, ann	6	1881 June 9..........	1,000 00	20	20,000 00	....	20,000 00	1
Apr. & Oct. 1, ann	6	1882 Mar. 24..........	1,000 00	19	19,000 00	4,000 00	15,000 00	2
Mar. 22, ann....	6	1880 July 1..........	1,000 00	25	25,000 00	21,000 00	4,000 00	1
" 22, "	6	" " 1 and after	1,000 00	15	15,000 00	....	15,000 00	2
May 1, "	4½	1890 Apr. 28..........	1,000 00	25	25,000 00	....	25,000 00	3
Mar. 22, "	4½	1895 Oct. 21, Nov. 5..	1,000 00	21	21,000 00	....	21,000 00	4
May 1, "	6	1880 May 6..........	1,000 00	50	50,000 00	....	50,000 00	5
July 1, "	5	1891 July 3..........	1,000 00	46	46,000 00	....	46,000 00	6
" 10, "	6	1884 " 22..........	1,000 00	30	30,000 00	....	30,000 00	7
" 10, "	6	" " 22..........	500 00	60	30,000 00	4,000 00	26,000 00	8

Statement 36—

No. of line	Locality—issued by.	For what purpose.	Date.	Principal—when payable.
	Cook County:			
1	Inc. Town of Cicero	To fund existing indebtedness...	1878 Dec. 1...	1898 Dec. 1....
2	" " "	" " " ...	1879 " 1...	1899 " 1....
3	" " "	" " " ...	1880 " 1...	1900 " 1....
4	" " "	" " " ...	1883 July 1...	1903 July 1....
5	" " "	" " " ...	1884 " 1...	1904 " 1....
6	" " "	" " " ...	1885 " 1...	1905 Dec. 1....
	Crawford County:			
1	County of Crawford	To fund existing indebtedness...	1887 Jan. 1...	1902 Jan. 1....
2	Tp. of Hutsonville..	" " " ...	1886 " 1...	1901 " 1....
3	" Robinson.....	" " " ...	1884 Sept. 1...	1904 Sept. 1....
4	" "	" " " ...	" " 1...	" " 1....
	Cumberland County:			
1	Tp. of Sumpter......	To fund existing indebtedness...	1885 June 1...	Ten-twenties...
	DeWitt County:			
1	Tp. of Clintonia......	To fund existing indebtedness...	1882 June 20&aft	Five-twenties...
2	" Creek.........	" " " ...	" July 1...	1883-97 July 1...
3	" Santa Anna..	" " " ...	1886 " 1...	1891-1906 July 1.
4	Town of Barnett.....	" " " ...	1888 " 2...	1889-98 July 1...
	Douglas County:			
1	Tp. of Newman......	To fund existing indebtedness...	1881 July 1...	Eight-fifteens..
2	" Tuscola.......	" " " ...	1896 " 1...	Five-fifteens....
	Edgar County			
1	Tp. of Kansas.......	To fund existing indebtedness...	1880 Jan. 1...	1900 Jan. 1....
2	" Paris	" " " ...	1892 July 1...	1897 July 1....
3	" Ross..........	" " " ...	" Mar. 1 & aft	Five-fifteens....
4	" Shiloh.........	" " " ...	" " 1...	" ....
5	Paris Union S. Dist.	" " " ...	1896 July 1...	1897-1916 July 1.
	Effingham County:			
1	Tp. of Mason........	To fund existing indebtedness...	1882 Oct. 1...	Five-twenties...
2	" West..........	" " " ...	" July 1...	" ....
3	" Douglas......	" " " ...	1883 Mar. 1...	Ten-twenties...
4	" "	" " " ...	1884 " 1...	" ....
5	" "	" " " ...	1885 " 1...	Five-twenties...
6	" "	" " " ...	1886 " 1...	" ....
	Ford County:			
1	County of Ford......	To fund existing indebtedness...	1886 July 1...	1887-1906 July 1
2	Tp. of Drummer.....	" " " ...	1892 Dec. 1...	1893-1912 " 15
3	" Peach Orchard	" " " ...	1891 May 25...	1892-1902 May 25
	Fulton County:			
1	Tp. of Astoria.......	To retire bonds issued to R., R. I. & St. L. Railroad..............	1880 June 1...	Five-twenties ..
2	" Lewistown...	To fund existing indebtedness0..	1882 July 1...	" ..
	Gallatin County:			
1	County of Gallatin..	To fund existing indebtedness...	1885 July 1...	Ten-twenties...
2	City of Shawneet'wn	" " " ...	1881 " 1...	Five-twenties ..
	Greene County:			
1	City of Whitehall....	To fund existing indebtedness...	1890 Feb. 1...	1891-1900 Feb. 1.
2	" " ...	" " " ...	" " 1...	1901-5 Feb. 1....
	Hancock County:			
1	County of Hancock..	To fund existing indebtedness...	1885 Oct. 19...	1889-1900 July 1.
	Henry County:			
1	Tp. of Western......	To fund existing indebtedness...	1890 Oct. 1...	1896-1909 Oct. 1.
	Iroquois County:			
1	City of Watseka.....	To fund existing indebtedness...	1884 July 1...	1897 May 1......
2	Tp. of Sheldon.......	" " " ...	1895 Sept. 1...	1896-1900 Sept. 1
3	" Douglas......	" " " ...	1891 Mar. 1 1...	1906 Mar. 11.....

Continued.

Interest—when payable.	Rate of interest...	When registered.	Denomination.	No.	Amount.	Amount of principal which has been redeemed and canceled.	Amount outstanding Sept. 30, 1896.	No. of line........
June and Dec. 1	6	1879 Jan. 16 and after	$1,000 00	10	$10,000 00	....	$10,000 00	1
" " 1	7	" Dec. 17..........	1,000 00	20	20,000 00	....	20,000 00	2
" " 1	$5\frac{1}{2}$	1881 Sept. 21..........	1,000 00	10	10,000 00	....	10,000 00	3
" " 1	5	1883 Dec. 12..........	500 00	20	10,000 00	....	10,000 00	4
Jan. and July 1	5	1884 July 22..........	1,000 00	10	10,000 00	....	10,000 00	5
June and Dec. 1	5	1885 Nov. 28..........	1,000 00	15	15,000 00	....	15,000 00	6
Jan. 1, ann....	6	1887 Oct. 4 and after	1,000 00	100	100,000 00	....	100,000 00	1
" 1, "	6	1886 Jan. 9..........	500 00	25	12,500 00	....	12,500 00	2
Sept 1, "	6	1884 Dec. 10..........	1,000 00	20	20,000 00	....	20,000 00	3
" 1, "	6	" " 10..........	500 00	20	10,000 00	....	10,000 00	4
July 1, ann....	6	1885 June 16..........	1,000 00	24	24,000 00	....	24,000 00	1
June 15, ann....	6	1882 June 20..........	1,000 00	80	80,000 00	$42,000 00	38,000 00	1
July 1, "	6	" July 8..........	1,000 00	30	30,000 00	28,000 00	2,000 00	2
" 1, "	6	1886 " 2..........	1,000 00	70	70,000 00	19,000 00	51,000 00	3
" 1, "	6	1888 " 2..........	1,000 00	30	30,000 00	24,000 00	6,000 00	4
July 1, ann....	6	1881 June 24..........	1,000 00	12	12,000 00	7,000 00	5,000 00	1
" 1, "	5	1896 July 6..........	1,000 00	20	20,000 00	....	20,000 00	2
July 1, ann....	7	1880 Feb. 26..........	600 00	50	30,000 00	....	30,000 00	1
" 1, "	6	1892 June 24..........	1,000 00	21	21,000 00	18,000 00	3,000 00	2
Mar.&July1,ann	6	" Feb. 25..........	1,000 00	17	17,000 00	14,000 00	3,000 00	3
Mar. 1, ann....	6	" " 25..........	1,000 00	10	10,000 00	7,000 00	3,000 00	4
July 1, "	5	1896 Sept. 11..........	1,000 00	20	20,000 00	....	20,000 00	5
Oct. 1, ann....	6	1882 Oct. 13..........	1,000 00	10	10,000 00	8,000 00	2,000 00	1
July 1, "	6	" June 23..........	1,000 00	10	10,000 00	7,000 00	3,000 00	2
Mar. 1, "	6	1883 " 27..........	1,000 00	32	32,000 00	....	32,000 00	3
July 1, "	6	1884 Mar. 28..........	1,000 00	9	9,000 00	1,000 00	8,000 00	4
" 1, "	6	1885 " 24..........	1,000 00	4	4,000 00	3,000 00	1,000 00	5
" 1, "	6	1886 " 4..........	1,000 00	6	6,000 00	....	6,000 00	6
Jan. and July 1.	5	1886 June 29..........	1,000 00	136	136,000 00	25,000 00	111,000 00	1
July 15, ann....	5	1892 Nov. 22..........	500 00	136	68,000 00	8,000 00	60,000 00	2
" 1, "	6	1891 May 23..........	1,000 00	23	23,000 00	10,000 00	13,000 00	3
June 1, ann....	7	1880, June 8..........	500 00	50	5,000 00	20,000 00	5,000 00	1
July 1, "	6	1882 Aug. 4..........	500 00	90	25 000 00	40,000 00	5,000 00	2
Jan. and July 1.	6	1885 July 24..........	1,000 00	190	190,000 00	....	190,000 00	1
" " " 1.	6	1881 June 30..........	1,000 00	50	50,000 00	....	50,000 00	2
Feb. 1, ann....	5	1890 Jan. 30..........	500 00	10	5,000 00	3,000 00	2,000 00	1
" 1, "	$4\frac{1}{2}$	" " 30..........	1,000 00	5	5,000 00	....	5,000 00	2
July 1, ann.....	5	1885 Oct. 19..........	1,000 00	120	120,000 00	80,000 00	40,000 00	1
Jan, and July 1.	$5\frac{1}{2}$	1890 Sept. 29..........	1,000 00	20	20,000 00	....	20,000 00	1
July 1, ann.....	7	1884 Dec. 27..........	1,250 00	1	1,250 00	....	1,250 00	1
Sept. 1, "	6	1895 Sept. 23..........	1,000 00	15	15,000 00	2,000 00	13,000 00	2
July 1, "	6	1891 Mar. 14..........	500 00	26	13,000 00	....	13,000 00	3

No. of line........	Locality—issued by	For what purpose.	Date.	Principal—when payable.
	Jackson County:			
1	City of Muphysboro.	To fund existing indebtedness...	1887 May 16....	1897 May 16.....
	Jasper County:			
1	County of Jasper....	To fund existing indebtedness...	1887 Oct. 1....	1888-1907 Oct. 1.
2	Town of Fox.........	" " " ...	1882 Sept. 1....	1897 Sept. 1.....
3	" "	" " " ...	" " 1....	" " 2.....
4	Tp. of St. Marie.....	" " " ...	1881 Feb. 1....	1896 Feb. 1......
5	" Wade;	" " " ...	1887 May 1....	Ten-twenties...
	Jersey and Macoupin Counties:			
1	IncTown of Brighton	To fund existing indebtedness...	1880 May 1....	Five-twenties ..
2	" " ...	" " " ...	" " 1....	" ..
3	" " ...	" " " ...	1881 " 1....	" ..
	Jersey:			
1	Sch. Dist. 8, T. 7, R. 12	To fund existing indebtedness...	1885 July 1....	1888-99 July 1...
	Jefferson County:			
1	County of Jefferson.	To fund existing indebtedness...	1887 July 1....	1888-1907 July 1.
2	Tp. of Mt. Vernon...	" " " ...	" " 1....	1907 July 1......
	Kankakee County:			
1	County of Kankakee	To fund existing indebtedness...	1884 July 1....	1904 July 1......
2	Tp. of Ganeer........	" " " ...	1883 Dec. 27....	Ten-twenties ...
3	" "	" " " ...	1896 July 1....	Five-twenties ..
4	" Momence.....	" " " ...	1883 Dec. 27....	Ten-twenties ...
5	" Pilot..........	" " " ...	1884 July 1....	1889-99 July 1...
6	" Pembroke....	" " " ...	" April 1....	Ten-twenties ...
7	" Aroma........	" " " ...	1890 July 1....	Five-twenties ..
	Knox County:			
1	Tp. of Rio...........	To fund existing indebtedness...	1884 May 1....	Five-twenties ...
	LaSalle County:			
1	Inc. T. of Marseilles	To fund existing indebtedness...	1879 Sept. 1....	Five-twenties ..
	Lee County:			
1	Tp. of Wyoming	To fund existing indebtedness...	1881 July 1....	1882-1901 July....
2	" Amboy........	" " " ...	1884 Sept.1 & aft.	1885-97 July 1....
3	" "	" " " ...	1885 July 1....	1890-97 July 1....
4	" "	" " " ...	1891 Aug. 6....	1892 July 1 & aft.
5	" "	" " " ...	" " 6....	1907 " 1 "
6	" "	" " " ...	1893 " 1....	1912 " 1 "
	Livingston County:			
1	Tp. of Amity.........	To fund existing indebtedness...	1883 Oct. 1....	1885-94 Oct. 1....
2	" "	" " " ...	" " 1....	1895-1900 Oct. 1..
3	" Pontiac	" " " ...	1879 July 15....	1884-99 July 15...
4	" "	" " " ...	1890 " 1....	1891-1903 July 1..
5	" Reading......	" " " ...	1878 June 1....	1880-95 June 1...
	Logan County:			
1	County of Logan	To fund existing indebtedness...	1887 July 1....	1892-1901 July 1.
2	Tp. of Atlanta	" " " ...	1882 " 1....	One-twenties...
3	" East Lincoln.	" " " ...	1886 " 1....	Ten-twenties....
4	" "	" " " ...	" " 1....	"
5	City of Lincoln......	" " " ...	" " 1....	1906 July 1......
6	Tp. of West Lincoln.	" " " ...	1890 July 1....	Five-twenties...
7	Sch.Dist. No. 5, Tp. 18 N., R. 2 W. 3d P. M.	" " " ...	1887 Aug. 31....	"
	Macon County:			
1	County of Macon	To fund existing indebtedness...	1879 Oct. 1....	1884-99 Oct. 1....
2	City of Decatur......	" " " ...	" June 1....	1899 June 1......
3	Town "	" " " ...	" Oct. 1....	1884-89 Oct. 1....
4	" "	" " " ...	1894 July 1....	1895-1909 July 1.

Continued.

Interest—when payable.	Rate of interest...	When registered.	Denomination.	No.	Amount.	Amount of principal which has been redeemed and canceled.	Amount outstanding Sept. 30, 1896.	No. of line......
May and Nov. 15, semi-an..	6	1887 June 30.........	$500 00	16	$8,000 00	....	$8,000 00	1
Oct. 1, ann,....	5	1887 Oct. 13.........	1,000 00	80	80,000 90	$32,000 00	48,000 00	1
Sept. 1, "	6	1882 Sept. 27.........	1,000 00	14	14,000 00	....	14,000 00	2
" 1, "	6	" " 27.........	622 53	1	622 53	....	622 53	3
July 1, "	7	1881 Feb. 28.........	1,000 00	11	11,000 00	2,000 00	9,000 00	4
" 1, "	6	1887 Sept. 21.........	500 00	47	23,500 00	....	23,500 00	5
May 1, ann.....	6	1880 Oct. 15.........	500 00	40	20,000 00	4,500 00	15,500 00	1
" 1, "	7	" " 15.........	500 00	16	8,000 00	7,000 00	1,000 00	2
" 1, "	6	1884 April 28.........	500 00	1	500 00	....	500 00	3
July 1, ann.....	6	1885 July 27.........	1,000 00	12	12,000 00	9,000 00	3,000 00	1
Jan.&Ju.1,s-ann	5	1887 June 30.........	1,000 00	100	100,000 00	33,000 00	67,000 00	1
" " "	6	" Oct. 15.........	1,000 00	25	25,000 00	....	25,000 00	2
July 1, ann.....	5	1884 Aug. 1 and after	1,000 00	53	53,000 00	....	53,000 00	1
" 1, "	6	" Jan. 4 "	500 00	60	30,000 00	28,500 00	1,500 00	2
" 1, "	5	1896 July 7.........	500 00	54	27,000 00	....	27,000 00	3
" 1, "	6	1884 Jan. 4 and after	500 00	72	36,000 00	....	36,000 00	4
" 1, "	6	" Aug. 18.........	1,000 00	11	11,000 00	8,000 00	3,000 00	5
" 1, "	6	" Nov. 1.........	500 00	9	4,500 00	....	4,500 00	6
" 1, "	5	1890 July 12.........	500 00	60	30,000 00	4,000 00	26,000 00	7
May 1, ann.....	6	1884 April 23.........	1,000 00	18	18,000 00	....	18,000 00	1
Jan. and July 1.	7	1879 Nov. 21.........	1,000 00	13	13,000 00	11,000 00	2,000 00	1
July 1, ann.....	6	1881 July 26.........	500 00	118	59,000 00	39,000 00	20,000 00	1
" 1, "	6	1884 Sept. 24 and aft.	1,000 00	34	34,000 00	30,000 00	4,000 00	2
" 1, "	6	1887 Apr. 11 "	1,000 00	8	8,000 00	6,000 00	2,000 00	3
" 1, "	6	1891 Aug. 7.........	500 00	163	81,500 00	19,000 00	62,500 00	4
" 1, "	6	1893 Apr. 26 and aft.	500 00	57	28,500 00	....	28,500 00	5
" 1, "	6	" Aug, 6.........	500 00	29	14,500 00	....	14,500 00	6
Oct. 1, ann.....	6	1883 Nov. 1 and aft.	1,000 00	12	12,000 00	10,000 00	2,000 00	1
" 1, "	6	1890 June 20.........	1,000 00	12	12,000 00	4,000 00	8,000 00	2
July 15, "	6	1879 July 15 and aft.	500 00	50	25,000 00	12,500 00	12,500 00	3
" 1, "	5	1890 June 30.........	1,000 00	50	50,000 00	24,000 00	26,000 00	4
June 1, "	$7\frac{3}{10}$	1878 " 11.........	500 00	100	50,000 00	42,500 00	7,500 00	5
July 1, ann.....	5	1887 Sept. 15.........	1,000 00	50	50,000 00	25,000 00	25,000 00	1
" 1, "	6	1882 June 27.........	1,000 00	62	62,000 00	33,000 00	29,000 00	2
" 1, "	5	1886 July 3.........	1,000 00	13	13,000 00	....	13,000 00	3
" 1, "	5	1887 June 29.........	1,000 00	85	85,000 00	10,000 00	75,000 00	4
Jan. and July 1.	5	1886 Aug. 25 and aft.	1,000 00	53	53,000 00	....	53,000 00	5
July 1, ann.....	5	1890 June 23.........	1,000 00	50	50,000 00	10,000 00	40,000 00	6
Aug. 31, ann.....	6	1887 Oct. 28.........	1,000 00	12	12,000 00	3,000 00	9,000 00	1
Jan. and July 1.	6	1879 Nov. 29 and aft.	1,000 00	187	187,000 00	140,000 00	47,000 00	1
June and Dec. 1.	6	" May 30.........	1,000 00	20	20,000 00	....	20,000 00	2
Jan. and July 15	6	" Oct. 17.........	1,000 00	50	50,000 00	39,000 00	11,000 00	3
" " 1	5	1894 July 24.........	1 to 3,000 00	15	25,000 00	2,000 00	23,000 00	4

No. of line	Locality—issued by.	For what purpose.	Date.	Principal—when payable.
	Macoupin County:			
1	County of Macoupin.	To fund existing indebtedness...	1878 July 1 & aft.	20 yrs. or on call
2	" "	" " " ...	" " 1 "	" "
3	" "	" " " ...	" " 1 "	" "
4	" "	" " " ...	" " 1 "	" "
5	" "	" " " ...	1890 July 1....	Ten-twenties....
6	City of Virden.......	" " " ...	1892 Jan. 1....	Five-twenties ..
	Madison County:			
1	City of Edwardsville	To fund existing indebtednes7...	1890 Aug. 1....	1891-1900 Aug. 1.
	McDonough County;			
1	Tp. of Bushnell......	To fund existing indebtedness...	1886 June 1....	Five-twenties ..
	McLean County:			
1	Tp. of Bloomington..	To fund existing indebtedness...	1889 July 1....	1893-97 July 1...
2	Village of Saybrook.	" " " ...	1882 Jan. 1....	1893 Jan. 1.......
	Mercer County........			
1	Tp. of Keithsburg...	To fund existing indebtedness...	1884 July 1....	1885-94 July 1...
2	City of New Boston..	" " " ...	1890 June 23....	1909 June 1......
	Monroe County:			
1	County of Monroe...	To fund existing indebtedness...	1893 June 24....	Four-twenties...
2	" " ...	" " " ...	" " 24....	"
3	" " ...	" " " ...	" " 24....	"
4	" " ...	" " " ...	" " 24....	"
	Montgomery County:			
1	City of Litchfield....	To fund existing indebtedness...	1890 July 1....	Ten-twenties ...
	Morgan County;			
1	County of Morgan...	To fund existing indebtedness ...	1887 June 15....	Ten-twenties ...
2	City of Jacksonville.	" " " ...	1885 April 27....	1905 April 27....
3	" "	" " " ...	" " 27....	" " 27....
4	" "	" " " ...	1889 July 1....	Ten-twenties ...
5	" Waverly	" " " ...	1895 June 1....	" ...
	Moultrie County:			
1	County of Moultrie..	To fund existing indebtedness ...	1882 July 1....	Ten-twenties ...
	Ogle County:			
1	Tp. of Oregon	To fund existing indebtedness ...	1888 Aug. 17....	1893-98 July 1...
2	" Pine Rock	" " " ...	1892 Oct. 1....	1894 Oct. 1 & after
3	" Mt. Morris ...	" " " ...	1894 June 1....	1895 to 1910 ......
4	" " ...	" " " ...	" " 1....	" " ......
5	City of Polo	" " " ...	1895 " 1....	1902-07 June 1...
	Peoria County:			
1	Tp. of Brimfield.....	To fund existing indebtedness ...	1887 July 1....	1890-1904 July 1.
2	" "	" " " ...	1889 " 1....	1891-1909 " 1.
3	" Elmwood	" " " ...	" Nov. 27....	1909 July 1....
4	" "	" " " ...	" July 1....	1892 and after...
5	" Peoria..........	" " " ...	1890 Dec. 1....	Ten-twenties ...
	Piatt County:			
1	Tp. of Bement.......	To fund existing indebtedness ...	1882 Jan. 1....	1883-93 July 1 ..
2	" Blue Ridge...	" " " ...	1884 July 1....	1891-1904 July 1..
3	" " ...	" " " ...	1886 June 15....	1887-1905 " 1..
4	" Goose Creek..	" " " ...	1889 July 1....	1890-94 and 5-20s.
5	" Sangamon....	" " " ...	1882 Mar. 1....	Four-twenties..

—Continued.

Interest—when payable.	Rate of interest...	When registered.	Denomination.	No.	Amount.	Amount of principal which has been redeemed and canceled.	Amount outstanding Sept. 30, 1896.	No. of line.....
July 1, ann.....	6	1878 Mar. 11 and aft.	$1,000 00	865	$865,000 00	$309,000 00	$556,000 00	1
" 1, "	6	" " 11 "	500 00	736	368,000 00	82,000 00	286,000 00	2
" 1, "	6	" " 11 "	100 00	674	67,400 00	53,700 00	13,700 00	3
" 1, "	6	" " 11 "	50 00	221	11,050 00	11,000 00	50 00	4
Jan. and July 1.	4	1890 June 6.........	1,000 00	1000	1,000,000 00	*990,000 00	10,000 00	5
Dec. and June 1	5	1891 Dec. 7.........	500 00	40	20,000 00	6,500 00	13,500 00	6
Feb. and Aug. 1.	4½	1890 Aug. 7.........	1,000 00	25	25,000 00	7,000 00	18,000 00	1
July 1, ann.....	6	1886 May 26.........	1,000 00	50	50,000 00	5,000 00	45,000 00	1
July 1, ann.....	4½	1889 Sept. 27.........	1,000 00	100	100,000 00	78,000 00	22,000 00	1
Jan. 1, "	6	1882 Feb. 15.........	1,000 00	5	5,000 00	4,000 00	1,000 00	2
July 1, ann.....	7	1884 Oct. 9.........	500 00	70	35,000 00	19,000 00	16,000 00	1
June 1, "	6	1890 June 25 & July 8	500 00	39	19,500 00	11,500 00	8,000 00	2
June 24, ann....	4½	1893 June 24.........	100 00	150	15,000 00	....	15,000 00	1
" 24, "	4½	" " 24.........	1,000 00	3	3,000 00	....	3,000 00	2
" 24, "	4½	1894 Feb. 26.........	1,000 00	57	57,000 00	....	57,000 00	3
" 24, "	4½	" " 26.........	500 00	50	25,000 00	....	25,000 00	4
Jan. and July 1.	5	1890 Aug. 5	500 00	62	31,000 00	....	31,000 00	1
June 15, ann....	4	1887 June 10.........	1,000 00	100	100,000 00	....	100,000 00	1
Jan. and July 1.	5	1885 April 29.........	1,000 00	67	67,000 00	....	67,000 00	2
" "	5	" " 29.........	1,000 00	32	32,000 00	....	32,000 00	3
" "	4½	1880 July 1.........	500 00	311	155,500 00	....	155,500 00	4
June 1, ann....	5	1895 Nov. 8.........	1,000 00	30	30,000 00	1,000 00	29,000 00	5
July 1, ann....	5	1882 Aug. 8 and after	1,000 00	245	245,000 00	123,000 00	122,000 00	1
July 1, ann....	6	1888 Aug. 18.........	1,000 00	59	59,000 00	11,000 00	48,000 00	1
Oct. 1, ann....	5	1892 Oct. 26.........	1,000 00	10	10,000 00	4,000 00	6,000 00	2
June 1, ann....	5	1894 June 1.........	500 00	112	56,000 00	7,000 00	49,000 00	3
" "	5	" " 1.........	100 00	16	1,600 00	200 00	1,400 00	4
June and Dec...	5	1895 July 11.........	1,000 00	12	12,000 00	....	12,000 00	5
July 1, ann....	5	1887 July 5.........	1,000 00	40	40,000 00	23,000 00	17,000 00	1
Jan. and July 1.	5	1889 June 21.........	1,000 00	50	50,000 00	6,000 00	44,000 00	2
" "	5	" Nov. 30.........	1,000 00	80	80,000 00	....	80,000 00	3
" "	5	" June 21.........	1,000 00	35	35,000 00	15,000 00	20,000 00	4
Dec. and June 1	5	1890 Dec. 6.........	1,000 00	98	98,000 00	....	98,000 00	5
July 1, ann....	6	1882 Feb. 4 and after	1,000 00	73	73,000 00	35,000 00	38,000 00	1
" 1, "	7	1884 July 22.........	500 00	57	28,500 00	7,500 00	21,000 00	2
" 1, "	7	1886 June 17.........	500 00	50	25,000 00	13,000 00	12,000 00	3
" 1, "	5	1889 July 12.........	1,000 00	45	45,000 00	8,000 00	37,000 00	4
" 1, "	6	1882 March 16	500 00	80	40,000 00	14,000 00	26,000 00	5

* Not sold—canceled by order of County Board.

Statement 36—

No. of line	Locality—issued by.	For what purpose.	Date.	Principal—when payable.
	Pulaski County:			
1	County of Pulaski...	To fund existing indebtedness ...	1880 May 1....	1900 May 1....
2	" " ...	" " " ...	" " 1....	" " 1....
3	" " ...	" " " ...	" " 1....	" " 1....
4	" " ...	" " " ...	" " 1....	" " 1....
5	City of Mound City..	" " " ...	1879 Oct. 1....	1899 Oct. 1....
6	" " ..	" " " ...	" " 1....	" " 1....
7	" " ..	" " " ...	" " 1....	" " 1....
8	" " ..	" " " ...	" " 1....	" " 1....
	Richland County:			
1	County of Richland.	To fund existing indebtedness ...	1884 Jan. 1....	Five-twenties ..
	Saline County:			
1	County of Saline....	To fund existing indebtedness ...	1885 July 1....	Five-twenties ..
2	" "	" " " ...	1894 Mar. 20....	1914 Mar. 20....
	Sangamon County:			
1	County of Sangamon	To fund existing indebtedness ...	1895 April 1....	1902-06 July 1...
2	" "	" " " ...	1891 June 21....	1894 and after...
3	" "	" " " ...	1891 Sept. 15....	1898 " ...
4	City of Springfield..	" " " ...	1880 Sept.1 &aft'r	1900 Sept. 1&aft'r
5	" "	" " " ...	" " "	" "
6	" " ..	" " " ...	" " "	" "
7	Tp. of Springfield...	" " " ...	1890 Feb. 8....	" Feb. 9......
8	" "	" " " ...	1891 June 20....	1906 June 21....
9	" Capital	" " " ...	1890 Feb. 8....	1900 Feb. 9....
10	Tp. of Capital........	" " " ...	1891 June 20....	1911 June 21.....
11	" Cartwright....	" " " ...	" Oct. 1....	1893 and after...
12	" Talkington....	" " " ...	1892 Jan. 1....	" Jan. 1 & aft.
	Schuyler County:			
1	County of Schuyler.	To fund existing indebtedness ...	1888 July 1....	1893-1908 July 1.
2	" "	" " " ...	" " 1....	" " 1.
	Shelby County:			
1	Tp. of Dry Point....	To fund existing indebtedness ...	1883 Jan. 1....	Five-twenties...
2	" "	" " " ...	1885 Sept. 1....	" ....
3	" Prairie.......	" " " ...	1883 " 1....	Ten-twenties....
4	Town of Windsor...	" " " ...	1882 July 1....	Five-twenties...
5	" "	" " " ...	" " 1....	" ....
6	" "	" " " ...	1885 Nov. 2....	1885 Nov. 2......
7	" "	" " " ...	1886 Jan. 1....	1886 Jan. 1......
8	City of Windsor...	" " " ...	1884 Dec. 15....	Five-twenties...
9	" "	" " " ...	" " 15&aft	" ....
10	Tp. of Richland	" " " ...	1885 July 1....	10 years & after
11	Town of Okaw......	" " " ...	1890 Oct. 1....	1900 Oct. 1.....
12	" "	" " " ...	" " 1....	" " 1.....
13	Tp. of Shelbyville...	" " " ...	" April 10....	" April 1.....
14	" Todd's Point.	" " " ...	" Oct. 1....	" Oct. 1.....
15	" "	" " " ...	" " 1....	" " 1.....
	Stark County:			
1	Tp. of Essex.........	To fund existing indebtedness ...	1888 July 1....	1889-1908 July 1
2	" "	" " " ...	" " 1....	1906 " 1
3	" "	" " " ...	1889 " 1....	1891-1909 " 1
4	" "	" " " ...	" " 1....	" " 1
5	" Goshen	" " " ...	1888 " 1....	1889-1908 " 1
6	" "	" " " ...	" " 1....	1894-1903 " 1
7	" Toulon........	" " " ...	" " 1....	1889-1908 " 1
8	" "	" " " ...	" " 1....	1892-1908 " 1
9	" Osceola........	" " " ...	1889 " 1....	1890-1909 " 1
10	" "	" " " ...	" " 1....	" " 1
11	" Penn..........	" " " ...	" " 1....	1891-99 " 1
12	Village of Wyoming	" " " ...	" " 1....	1909 " 1
	St. Clair County:			
1	City of E. St. Louis.	To fund subsisting legal indebtness................................	1888 Sept. 1....	1908 Sept. 1......
2	Village of Brooklyn	To fund subsisting legal indebtness................................	1895 Nov. 15....	1896-1904 Nov. 15

Continued.

Interest—when payable.	Rate of interest...	When registered.	Denomination.	No.	Amount.	Amount of principal which has been redeemed and canceled.	Amount outstanding Sept. 30, 1896.	No. of line........
Jan. 1, ann....	6	1880 June 10 and after	$500 00	100	$50,000 00	$1,000 00	$49,000 00	1
" 1, "	6	" Nov. 1..........	100 00	200	20,000 00	13,900 00	6,100 00	2
" 1, "	6	" June 10 and after	50 00	98	4,900 00	1,350 00	3,550 00	3
" 1, "	6	" " "	25 00	38	950 00	500 00	450 00	4
June 1, ann....	6	" " "	100 00	120	12,000 00	....	12,000 00	5
" 1, "	6	" " "	50 00	96	4,800 00	....	4,800 00	6
" 1, "	6	" " "	25 00	61	1,525 00	....	1,525 00	7
" 1, "	6	1889 Dec. 3.........	50 00	4	200 00	....	200 00	8
July 1, ann....	6	1884 Jan. 8.........	1,000 00	200	200,000 00	101,000 00	99,000 00	1
July 1, ann....	6	1885 Nov 23.........	1,000 00	100	100,000 00	....	100,000 00	1
" 1, "	6	1894 April 12.........	1,000 00	31	31,000 00	....	31,000 00	2
Jan. and July 1.	5	1895 April 1.........	1,000 00	75	75,000 00	....	75,000 00	1
" " 1.	4	1891 June 20.........	1,000 00	50	50,000 00	33,000 00	17,000 00	2
" " 1.	4	1891 Sept. 15.........	1,000 00	91	91,000 00	....	91,000 00	3
Sept. 1, ann....	5	1881 Jan. 22 and after	1,000 00	725	725,000 00	56,000 00	669,000 00	4
" 1, "	5	" " "	500 00	417	208,500 00	....	208,500 00	5
" 1, "	5	" " "	100 00	216	21,600 00	....	21,600 00	6
Jan. and July 1.	4½	1890 Feb. 15.........	500 00	10	5,000 00	....	5,000 00	7
" " 1.	4½	1891 June 23.........	500 00	17	8,500 00	....	8,500 00	8
" " 1.	4	1890 Feb. 24.........	1,000 00	25	25,000 00	....	25,000 00	9
Jan. and July...	4	1891 June 23.........	1,000 00	41	41,000 00	....	41,000 00	10
Oct. 1, ann....	5	" Oct. 26.........	1,000 00	20	20,000 00	6,000 00	14,000 00	11
Jan. 1. "	5½	" Dec. 29.........	1,000 00	20	20,000 00	4,000 00	16,000 00	12
Jan.&July 1, ann	5	1888 May 23.........	1,000 00	50	50,000 00	10,000 00	40,000 00	1
" "	5	" " 23.........	500 00	40	20,000 00	5,000 00	15,000 00	2
Jan. 1, ann....	6	1883 Feb. 8.........	1,000 00	18	18,000 00	4,000 00	14,000 00	1
Sept. 1, "	6	1885 Sept. 2.........	1,000 00	10	10,000 00	....	10,000 00	2
" 1, "	6	1883 Aug. 31 and after	1,000 00	70	70,000 00	8,000 00	62,000 00	3
July 1, "	6	1882 " 29.........	1,000 00	16	16,000 00	....	16,000 00	4
" 1. "	6	1885 Jan. 22.........	1,000 00	34	34,000 00	....	34,000 00	5
" 1, "	6	" Nov. 5.........	1,000 00	5	5,000 00	....	5,000 00	6
" 1, "	6	1886 Jan 25.........	1,000 00	7	7,000 00	....	7,000 00	7
" " "	6	1885 " 2.........	1,000 00	9	9,000 00	....	9,000 00	8
" 1, "	6	" Feb. 18 and after	1,000 00	15	15,000 00	....	15,000 00	9
" 1, "	6	" Aug. 12.........	1,000 00	75	75,000 00	20,000 00	55,000 00	10
April 10, "	6	1890 Oct. 2.........	500 00	12	6,000 00	....	6,000 00	11
" 10, "	6	" " 2.........	293 00	1	293 00	....	293 00	12
" 10, "	6	" Sept. 2.........	500 00	50	25,000 00	....	25,000 00	13
" 10, "	6	" Oct. 2.........	500 00	7	3,500 00	....	3,500 00	14
" 10, "	6	" " 2.........	207 00	1	207 00	....	207 00	15
Jan. & July, ann	6	1888 June 27.........	1,000 00	22	22,000 00	9,000 00	13,000 00	1
" "	6	" " 27.........	500 00	1	500 00	....	500 00	2
" & July 1, ann	6	1889 " 27.........	1,000 00	19	19,000 00	5,000 00	14,000 00	3
" & July, ann	6	" " 27.........	500 00	6	3,000 00	....	3,000 00	4
" "	6	1888 " 19.........	1,000 00	25	25,000 00	13,500 00	11,500 00	5
" "	6	" " 19.........	500 00	10	5,000 00	1,000 00	4,000 00	6
" "	6	" " 19.........	1,000 00	40	40,000 00	10,000 00	30,000 00	7
" "	6	" " 19.........	500 00	9	4,500 00	1,500 00	3,000 00	8
July 1, ann....	6	1889 " 28.........	1,000 00	56	56,000 00	14,000 00	42,000 00	9
" 1, "	6	" " 28.........	500 00	8	4,000 00	1,000 00	3,000 00	10
July and Jan. 1.	6	" " 29.........	1,000 00	28	28,000 00	15,000 00	13,000 00	11
Jan. and July 1.	5	" " 28.........	1,000 00	10	10,000 00	....	10,000 00	12
Sept. 1, ann....	5	1888 Oct. 20 and after	500 00	1300	650,000 00	....	650,000 00	1
Nov. 15, ann....	6	1895 Nov. 20.........	400 00	9	3,600 00	....	3,600 00	2

Statement 36—

Name of line	Locality—issued by.	For what purpose.	Date.	Principal—when payable.
	Tazewell County:			
1	County of Tazewell..	To fund existing indebtedness ...	1890 July 1....	1910 July 1, opt.
2	City of Pekin........	" " " ...	1887 Feb. 1....	Ten-twenties....
3	" "	" " " ...	" " 1....	Five-twenties....
4	" "	" " " ...	1895 July 1....	Ten-twenties....
5	" "	" " " ...	" " 1....	" ....
6	Tp. of L. Mackinaw.	" " " ...	1884 " 1....	Five-twenties....
7	" Mackinaw	" " " ...	1889 Nov. 26....	" ....
8	" "	" " " ...	1894 " 3....	" ....
9	" Delevan.......	" " " ...	1890 July 1....	1896-1900 July 1
10	" "	" " " ...	1890 " 1....	1901-10 " 1
11	" Fremont......	" " " ...	1889 Dec. 1....	1899 Dec. 1, opt.
	Vermilion County:			
1	Town of Danville....	To fund existing indebtedness ...	1886 July 1....	1887-1906 July 1
2	" "	" " " ...	1880 " 1....	1890 " 1
3	Tp. of Butler	" " " ...	1882 Feb. 17....	1885-97 Feb. 17..
4	" Elwood........	" " " ...	" July 1....	1902 July 1......
5	" Grant	" " " ...	1883 Sept. 11....	Five-tens to 15s.
6	" Ross...........	" " " ...	" " 15....	1884-1903 July 1.
	Wabash County:			
1	County of Wabash..	To fund existing indebtedness ...	1881 Sept. 1....	1882-1901 Sept. 1
2	City of Mt. Carmel..	" " " ...	" May 1....	" May 1
3	" "	" " " ...	" " 1....	" " 1
	Warren County:			
1	Tp. of Swan..........	To fund existing indebtedness ...	1881 Dec. 19....	Five-twenties...
2	" Roseville.......	" " " ...	1890 July 1....	1891-99 July 1...
	Wayne County:			
1	Tp. of Lamard	To fund existing indebtedness ...	1881 Sept. 1....	Five-twenties...
2	" Jasper	" " " ...	1883 Oct. 1....	1903 Oct. 1 ......
3	" Big Mound....	" " " ...	1886 July 1....	Five-tw.nties...
	Washington County:			
1	Co. of Washington..	To fund existing indebtedness ...	1885 Mar. 1....	1886-1905 Mar. 1.
	White & Edwards Co's			
1	Inc. Tp. of Grayville	To fund existing indebtedness ...	1895 June 3....	1900-1905.........
2	" "	" " " ...	" " 3....	" ....
	White County:			
1	County of White....	To fund existing indebtedness ...	1885 July 1....	Five-twenties...
2	" " ...	" " " ...	" " 1....	Ten-twenties....
3	Village of Enfield...	" " " ...	1887 Sept. 28....	Five-twenties...
	Williamson County:			
1	Co. of Williamson...	To fund existing indebtedness ...	1895 Jan. 1....	1896 Jan. 1 & aft.
	Total...............	....	....	....

Concluded.

Interest—when payable.	Rate of interest	When registered.	Denomination.	No.	Amount.	Amount of principal which has been redeemed and canceled.	Amount outstanding Sept. 30, 1896.	No. of line
July 1, ann....	4	1890 June 28.........	$1,000 00	194	$194,000 00	....	$194,000 00	1
" 1, "	5	1887 Jan. 27.........	1,000 00	28	28,000 00	....	28,000 00	2
" 1, "	5	" " 27.........	1,000 00	25	25,000 00	....	25,000 00	3
" 1, "	5	1895 June 28.........	1,000 00	70	70,000 00	....	70,000 00	4
" 1, "	5	" " 28.........	500 00	11	5,500 00	....	5,500 00	5
" 1, "	6	" " 25.........	500 00	80	40,000 00	$25,000 00	15,000 00	6
Nov. 26, "	6	1889 Nov. 27.........	1,000 00	8	8,000 00	4,000 00	4,000 00	7
" 3, "	5½	1894 " 23.........	1,000 00	18	18,000 00	....	18,000 00	8
July 1, "	5½	1890 June 30.........	1,000 00	10	10,000 00	2,000 00	8,000 00	9
" 1, "	5	" " 30.........	1,000 00	34	34,000 00	....	34,000 00	10
April 1, "	6	1889 Nov. 22.........	500 00	18	9,000 00	2,500 00	6,500 00	11
July 1, ann....	5	1886 June 30.........	1,000 00	159	159,000 00	80,000 00	79,000 00	1
" 1, "	6	1880 Nov. 16 and after	500 00	66	33,000 00	....	33,000 00	2
Feb. 17, "	6	1882 March 2.........	1,000 00	25	25,000 00	24,000 00	1,000 00	3
July 1, "	5¼	" July 12.........	1,000 00	30	30,000 00	....	30,000 00	4
" 1, "	6	1883 Sept. 18.........	5,000 00	6	30,000 00	20,000 00	10,000 00	5
" 1, "	6	" " 18.........	1,824 00	20	36,480 00	23,712 00	12,768 00	6
Sept. 1, ann....	6	1881 Sept. 1.........	5,000 00	20	100,000 00	75,000 00	25,000 00	1
May 1, "	6	" June 21.........	500 00	60	30,000 00	21,000 00	9,000 00	2
" 1, "	6	" " 21.........	250 00	100	25,000 00	17,500 00	7,500 00	3
July 1, ann....	6	1881 Dec. 20.........	1,000 00	35	35,000 00	32,000 00	3,000 00	1
" 1, "	6	1890 June 27.........	2,000 00	9	18,000 00	12,000 00	6,000 00	2
Sept. 1, ann....	6	1882 April 27.........	1,000 00	10	10,000 00	7,000 00	3,000 00	1
April and Oct. 1.	7	1884 Mar. 19.........	1,000 00	3	3,000 00	1,000 00	2,000 00	2
July 1, ann....	6	1886 Oct. 6.........	1,000 00	5	5,000 00	2,000 00	3,000 00	3
July 1, ann....	6	1885 Feb. 26.........	1,000 00	200	200,000 00	85,000 00	115,000 00	1
July 1, ann....	5	1895 June 27.........	2,000 00	5	10,000 00	....	10,000 00	1
" 1, "	5	" " 27.........	2,500 00	1	2,500 00	....	2,500 00	2
Jan. and July 1	6	1885 Aug. 21.........	500 00	100	50,000 00	....	50,000 00	1
" "	6	" " 21.........	500 00	200	100,000 00	....	100,000 00	2
July and Jan. 1	6	1887 Oct. 3.........	500 00	22	11,000 00	....	11,000 00	3
Jan. 1, ann......	4½	1895 Jan. 22.........	1,000 00	100	100,000 00	2,000 00	98,000 00	1
....	....	....	....	....	13,496,227 53	$4,285,365 53	$9,210,862 00	

No.

Statement of Drainage District Bonds registered

No. of line	Name of District and Location.	Date.	Principal—when payable.
	Bureau and Whiteside Counties:		
1	Greene River Special Drainage District	1894 July 1	1900 July 1&aft'r
	Cass County:		
1	Hager Slough Special Drainage District	1893 Aug. 1	1896 Aug.1&aft'r
2	" " "	" " 1	1900-1901
3	" " "	1896 " 1	1902-1903
4	" " "	" " 1	1904 Aug. 1
	Cass and Morgan Counties:		
1	New Pankey Pond Special Drainage District	1890 Dec. 1	1893 June1&aft'r
	Champaign County:		
1	The Big Slough Special Drainage District	1885 Dec. 2	1896 Dec. 2
2	" " " "	" " 2	" " 2
3	Wild Cat Special Drainage District	1887 May 16	1902 May 16
	Iroquois County:		
1	Union Drainage Dist. No. 1, Ashkum and Danforth **Tps.**	1886 Aug. 2	1887-8-9 Aug. **2.**
2	" " " 2, Danforth and Ashkum **Tps.**	1896 May 1	1898-1901 Aug. **1.**
3	" " " 2. " "	" June 1	" " " **1.**
4	Sp'l Dr. Dist. No. 1 of Onargo, Douglas & Danforth **Tps.**	1886 Nov. 1	1901 July 1
5	Milks Grove Special Drainage District	1888 Nov. 19	1895-6 " 1
6	" " " "	1891 Mar31&aft'r	1898 " 1
7	" " " "	" June 13	" " 1
	Iroquois, Ford and Livingston Counties:		
1	The Vermilion Special Drainage District	1889 May 1	1895-1904 May **1.**
	Jackson County:		
1	Big Lake Special Drainage District	1892 Apr.12&aft'r	1902 July 1&aft'r
2	" " "	1893 Jan. 7	1905-6 July 1
3	" " "	1894 Oct. 30	1906 " 1
4	" " "	" Nov. 21	" " 1
5	" " "	1896 Feb. 1	1907 Feb. 1
	LaSalle County;		
1	Drainage District No. 2, Town of Wallace	1895 July 15	1896-1904 July **15**
	Logan, Macon and DeWitt Counties:		
1	North Branch Lake Fork Special Drainage District	1893 Nov. 1	1895 July 1&aft'r
2	" " " " "	1894 July 1	1900 July 1
	Macon and Logan Counties:		
1	Illini Special Drainage District	1895 Aug. 1	1898-1900 Aug. **1.**
	Mason County:		
1	The Central Special Drainage District	1888 Jan. 1	1898 Aug. 1
	Mason and Menard Counties:		
1	Mason and Menard Special Drainage District	1892 Nov. 19	1897 July 1&aft'r
	Mason and Tazewell Counties:		
1	The Mason and Tazewell Special Drainage District	1885 July 15	1889-99 July 1
2	" " " "	" " 15	" " 1
3	" " " "	" " 15	" " 1
4	" " " "	1886 May 16	1899-1901 " 1
	McLean County:		
1	The Esterbrook Special Drainage District No. 1	1886 Apr.1&aft'r	1890-93 Jan. 1
	Total		

37.

in pursuance of the Act of June 27, 1885.

Interest—when payable.	Rate of interest.	When registered.	Denomination.	No.	Amount.	Amount of principal which has been redeemed and canceled.	Amount outstanding Sept. 30, 1896.	No. of line.
July 1, ann....	6	1894 Sept. 6..........	$500 00	135	$67,500 00	....	$67,500 00	1
Aug. 1, ann....	6	1893 Oct. 5..........	500 00	8	4,000 00	$1,000 00	3,000 00	1
" 1, "	6	1895 Feb. 12..........	500 00	4	2,000 00	....	2,000 00	2
" 1, "	6	1896 May 9..........	500 00	4	2,000 00	....	2,000 00	3
" 1, "	6	" Oct. 10..........	500 00	2	1,000 00	....	1,000 00	4
Dec. 1, ann....	6	1891 Apr. 24..........	500 00	8	4,000 00	1,000 00	3,000 00	1
June and Dec. 2	7	1886 Dec. 8 & after.	500 00	46	23,000 00	....	23,000 00	1
" " 2	7	1888 June 7..........	200 00	10	2,000 00	....	2,000 00	2
Jan. and July...	6	1887 May 20..........	1,000 00	25	25,000 00	....	25,000 00	3
Aug. 2, ann....	7	1886 Aug. 27 & after.	500 00	23	11,500 00	....	11,500 00	1
" 1, "	6	1896 June 18..........	500 00	21	10,500 00	....	10,500 00	2
" 1, "	6	" " 18..........	500 00	9	4,500 00	....	4,500 00	3
July 1, "	6	1886 Dec. 16..........	1,000 00	50	50,000 00	....	50,000 00	4
" 1, "	6	1888 Nov. 26..........	1,000 00	3	3,000 00	2,000 00	1,000 00	5
" 1, "	6	1891 June 17..........	1,000 00	6	6,000 00	....	6,000 00	6
" 1, "	6	" " 17..........	1,200 00	1	1,200 00	....	1,200 00	7
May 1, ann....	6	1889 May 6..........	1,000 00	28	28,000 00	4,000 00	24,000 00	1
July 1, ann....	6	1892 May 14 & after.	500 00	42	21,000 00	....	21,000 00	1
" 1, "	6	1893 Jan. 11..........	500 00	26	13,000 00	....	13,000 00	2
" 1, "	6	1894 Nov. 1..........	468 75	8	3,750 00	....	3,750 00	3
" 1, "	6	1895 Jan. 3..........	7,250 00	3	21,750 00	....	21,750 00	4
Feb. 1, "	6	1896 Feb. 27..........	500 00	18	9,000 00	....	9,000 00	5
July 15, ann....	6	1895 July 19..........	500 00	16	8,000 00	500 00	7,500 00	1
July 1, ann....	7	1893 Dec. 19..........	500 00	40	20,000 00	8,000 00	12,000 00	1
" 1, "	7	1894 July 16..........	500 00	18	9,000 00	....	9,000 00	2
Aug. 1, ann....	6	1896 July 1..........	500 00	6	3,000 00	....	3,000 00	1
Aug. 1, ann....	6	1888 Jan. 7..........	1,000 00	15	15,000 00	....	15,000 00	1
July 1, ann....	6	1893 Feb. 2..........	1,000 00	10	10,000 00	....	10,000 00	1
July 1, ann....	7	1885 July 22..........	1,000 00	131	131,000 00	100,000 00	31,000 00	1
" 1, "	7	" " 22..........	500 00	30	15,000 00	12,000 00	3,000 00	2
" 1, "	7	" " 22..........	100 00	50	5,000 00	4,000 00	1,000 00	3
" 1, "	7	1886 May 14..........	1,000 00	72	72,000 00	....	72,000 00	4
Jan. 1, ann....	7	1886 May 22 & after.	100 00	39	3,900 00	3,800 00	100 00	1
....	..	....	....	....	$605,600 00	$136,300 00	$469,300 00	

No. 38.

Sny Island Levee of Adams, Pike and Calhoun Counties.

* Bonds issued by Commissioners in pursuance of Act of April 24, 1871, in force July 1, 1872: registered in the Auditor's office under Act approved April 9, 1872, in force July 1, 1872, viz.:

What aided.	Date.	Principal—when payable........	Interest — when payable........	Rate of interest.	When registered.	Denomination...	No...........	Amount..........	Amount outstanding Sept. 30, 1896
Sny Isl'd Levee	1872, Oct. 1.	1882 to 1891	July, ann	10	1872 Nov. 12 & aft'r	$500	193	$96,500	$96,500
" "	'72, Oct. 1 } '75, Mar. 1 }	1882 to 1894	"	10	" "	1000	552	552,000	552,000
Total........	....	....	....	..	....	....	....	$648,500	$648,500

* The Supreme Court of Illinois has held that the law under which these bonds were issued is in violation of the State constitution.

No. 39.

Statement of State Treasurer's Accounts with the Different Registered Local Bond Funds, from October 1, 1894, to September 30, 1896, inclusive.

Local Bond Funds. County.	Local Bond Funds. Fund.	Balance in Treasury Oct. 1, 1894.	Amount received from Oct. 1, 1894, to Sept. 30, 1896, inclusive.	Total.	Local Bond Funds. County.	Local Bond Funds. Fund.	Warrants canceled from Oct. 1, 1894, to Sept. 30, 1896, inclusive.	Balance in Treasury Oct. 1, 1896.	Total.
Adams	County of Adams	$1,219 65		$1,219 65	Adams	County of Adams	$1,219 65		$1,219 65
"	Tp. of Keene	148 62		148 62	"	Tp. of Keene		$148 62	148 62
"	City of Quincy	9,525 34	$161,451 39	170,976 73	"	City of Quincy	161,515 24	9,461 49	170,976 73
"	City of Quincy Sinking Fund	224 51	108,107 50	108,332 01	"	" Quincy Sinking Fund	107,981 92	350 09	108,332 01
Alexander	County of Alexander	8,761 04	26,017 86	34,778 90	Alexander	County of Alexander	25,670 63	9,108 27	34,778 90
"	City of Cairo	18,154 17	62,418 19	80,572 36	"	City of Cairo	59,472 40	21,099 96	80,572 36
Brown	County of Brown	141 62		141 62	Brown	County of Brown		141 62	141 62
Bureau	Greene River Special Drainage District		8,373 33	8,373 33	Bureau	Greene River Special Drainage Fistrict	8,182 36	190 97	8,373 33
"	Tp. of Ohio	1,064 94	7,916 43	8,921 37	"	Tp. of Ohio	8,341 88	579 49	8,921 37
"	" Walnut	267 52	5,805 57	6,073 09	"	" Walnut	5,807 87	265 22	6,073 09
"	Village of Buda	93 00	1,046 05	1,139 05	"	Village of Buda	1,139 05		1,139 05
Cass	City of Beardstown	8,595 83	18,495 51	27,091 34	Cass	City of Beardstown	19,768 08	7,323 26	27,091 34
"	Hager Slough Special Drainage District	110 23	2,837 97	2,948 20	"	Hager Slough Special Drainage District	2,727 61	220 59	2,948 20
Cass and Morgan	New Pankey Pond Special Drainage District	293 03	1,556 84	1,849 87	Cass and Morgan	New Pankey Pond Special Drainage District	913 61	936 26	1,849 87
Champaign	City of Urbana	402 51	1,673 79	2,076 30	Champaign	City of Urbana	1,678 70	397 60	2,076 30
"	Tp. of Champaign	7,029 73	8,691 12	15,720 85	"	Tp. of Champaign	11,661 32	4,059 53	15,720 85
"	" St. Joseph	1,377 84	3,450 65	4,828 49	"	" St. Joseph	4,828 49		4,828 49
"	" Urbana	803 28	9,010 07	9,813 35	"	" Urbana	9,156 95	656 40	9,813 35
"	Big Slough Special Drainage District	1,028 54	31,807 28	32,835 82	"	Big Slough Special Drainage District	3,614 03	29,221 79	32,835 82
"	Wild Cat Special Drainage District	1,756 27	3,014 53	4,770 80	"	Wild Cat Special Drainage District	3,030 07	1,740 73	4,770 80
Ch'mp'ign and Piatt	Lake Fork Special Drainage District	306 81		306 81	Ch'mp'ign and Piatt	Lake Fork Special Drainage District		306 81	306 81
Christian	Tp. of Johnson	294 32	1,389 46	1,683 78	Christian	Tp. of Johnson	1,630 19	53 59	1,683 78
"	" Pana	1,043 05	16,599 00	17,642 05	"	" Pana	17,147 89	494 16	17,642 05
Clark	County of Clark	33 37	6,454 16	6,487 53	Clark	County of Clark	6,487 53		6,487 53
"	" Clark Sinking Fund	25,879 12	6,464 23	32,343 35	"	" Clark Sinking Fund	30,000 00	2,343 35	32,343 35

Statement No. 39—Continued.

Local Bond Funds. County.	Local Bond Funds. Fund.	Balance in Treasury Oct. 1, 1894.	Amount received from Oct. 1, 1894, to Sept. 30, 1896, inclusive.	Total.	Local Bond Funds. County.	Local Bond Funds. Fund.	Warrants canceled from Oct. 1, 1894, to Sept. 30, 1896, inclusive.	Balance in Treasury Oct. 1, 1896.	Total.
Clark	Tp. of Marshall	$152 00	$4,694 93	$4,846 93	Clark	Tp. of Marshall	$4,238 54	$608 39	$4,846 93
''	'' Marshall Sinking Fund	11,097 53	6,499 56	17,597 09	''	'' Marshall Sinking Fund	12,000 00	5,597 09	17,597 09
''	'' Westfield	57 07	2,443 44	2,500 51	''	'' Westfield	2,432 39	68 12	2,500 51
''	'' Westfield Sinking Fund	7,588 03	2,173 86	9,761 89	''	'' Westfield Sinking Fund	....	9,761 89	9,761 89
''	'' York	637 38	1,715 49	2,352 87	''	'' York	978 21	1,374 66	2,352 87
''	'' York Sinking Fund	4,094 07	1,624 43	5,718 50	''	'' York Sinking Fund	5,000 00	718 50	5,718 50
Clay	'' Harter	734 86	2,628 08	3,362 94	Clay	'' Harter	2,304 54	1,058 40	3,362 94
''	'' Louisville	3,286 92	2,822 30	6,109 22	''	'' Louisville	5,006 51	1,102 71	6,109 22
Coles	City of Mattoon	2,786 00	5,866 29	8,652 29	Coles	City of Mattoon	6,677 38	1,974 91	8,652 29
''	Tp. of Charleston	304 06	9,293 52	9,597 58	''	Tp. of Charleston	9,151 77	445 81	9,597 58
''	'' Mattoon	331 86	10,674 49	11,006 35	''	'' Mattoon	10,706 37	299 98	11,006 35
''	'' Seven Hickory	343 68	7,113 96	7,457 64	''	'' Seven Hickory	7,156 52	301 12	7,457 64
''	'' Seven Hickory Sinking Fund	1,091 03	2,234 51	3,325 54	''	'' Seven Hickory Sinking Fund	3,000 00	325 54	3,325 54
Cook	Incorp. Town of Cicero	7,450 28	3,931 09	11,381 37	Cook	Incorp. Town of Cicero	8,444 45	2,936 92	11,381 37
Crawford	County of Crawford	6,391 51	12,210 17	18,601 68	Crawford	County of Crawford	12,121 05	6,480 63	18,601 68
''	Tp. of Hutsonville	739 28	1,664 36	2,403 64	''	Tp. of Hutsonville	1,535 09	868 55	2,403 64
''	'' Hutsonville Sinking Fund	8,643 86	2,669 45	11,313 31	''	'' Hutsonville Sinking Fund	....	11,313 31	11,313 31
''	'' Robinson	171 72	3,621 92	3,793 64	''	'' Robinson	3,033 10	760 54	3,793 64
Cumberland	'' Sumpter	103 43	2,904 93	3,008 36	Cumberland	'' Sumpter	2,908 92	99 44	3,008 36
DeWitt	County of DeWitt	1,548 41	18,600 38	20,148 79	DeWitt	County of DeWitt	20,148 79	....	20,148 79
''	Tp. of Barnett	284 44	7,260 33	7,544 77	''	Tp. of Barnett	7,302 60	242 17	7,544 77
''	'' DeWitt	97	....	97	''	'' DeWitt	97	....	97
''	'' Clintonia	3,121 39	4,925 75	8,047 14	''	'' Clintonia	2,135 13	5,912 01	8,047 14
''	'' Creek	206 67	4,564 00	4,770 67	''	'' Creek	4,625 82	144 85	4,770 67
''	'' Nixon	19 32	....	19 32	''	'' Nixon	19 32	....	19 32
''	'' Santa Anna	484 76	13,846 50	14,331 26	''	'' Santa Anna	13,883 13	448 13	14,331 26
DeWitt, Macon and Logan	North Branch Lake Fork Special Drainage District	7 47	14,963 43	14,970 90	DeWitt, Macon and Logan	North Branch Lake Fork Special Drainage District	14,407 26	563 64	14,970 90
Douglas	County of Douglas	6,307 59	5,184 23	11,491 82	Douglas	County of Douglas	10,942 92	548 90	11,491 82
''	Tp. of Bowdre	155 43	....	155 43	''	Tp. of Bowdre	....	155 43	155 43
''	'' Camargo	70 85	6,694 20	6,765 05	''	'' Camargo	6,568 62	196 43	6,765 05

Douglas.....	Tp. of Garrett..........	180 27	4,506 48	4,686 75
"	" Newman.........	23	5,241 71	5,241 94
"	" Tuscola.........	60 91	2,493 54	2,554 45
Douglas & Moultrie..	Union School District No. 7, T. 15, R. 6 and 7.	531 75	....	531 75
Edgar.......	Tp. of Kansas...........	220 14	4,253 60	4,473 74
"	" Paris............	07	1,152 52	1,152 59
"	" Paris Sinking Fund..........	1,991 00	5,628 74	7,619 74
"	" Ross............	313 96	6,902 67	7,216 63
"	" Shiloh..........	372 43	4,629 21	5,001 64
"	" Young America.	280 94	3,513 00	3,793 94
Edwards and White	City of Grayville........	562 35	1,608 61	2,170 96
Effingham..	Tp. of Douglas..........	3,568 13	18,308 78	21,876 91
" ..	" Liberty..........	190 67	62 53	253 20
" ..	" Liberty Sinking Fund..........	545 15	1,454 85	2,000 00
" ..	" Mason..........	1,412 31	2,286 62	3,698 93
" ..	" Moccasin........	1,545 34	....	1,545 34
" ..	" Summit..........	1,009 42	....	1,009 42
" ..	" West............	16 29	2,556 37	2,572 66
Fayette.....	" Bear Grove......	230 04	5,571 51	5,801 55
"	" Vandalia........	1,018 76	11,000 00	12,018 76
Ford........	County of Ford.........	3,570 89	17,510 68	21,081 57
"	Tp. of Drummer........	763 98	9,936 47	10,700 45
"	" Lyman...........	168 00	3,168 30	3,336 30
"	" Peach Orchard..	266 72	5,871 76	6,138 48
Ford, Iroquois and Livingst'n	Vermilion Special Drainage District.....	156 14	7,405 86	7,562 00
Fulton......	Tp. of Astoria..........	1,267 90	....	1,267 90
"	" Lewistown......	109 95	....	109 95
"	" Pleasant........	348 94	....	348 94
Gallatin.....	County of Gallatin......	11,152 71	29,044 44	40,197 15
"	" Gallatin Sinking Fund...	6,285 00	....	6,285 00
Gallatin.....	City of Shawneetown...	2,198 88	6,116 61	8,315 49
Greene......	City of Whitehall.......	463 96	2,193 32	2,657 28
Hancock....	County of Hancock.....	599 44	26,143 56	26,743 00
"	City of Warsaw.........	1,102 17	8,093 83	9,196 00
Henderson.	" Oquawka.........	171 11	....	171 11
Henry......	Tp. of Galva............	348 31	....	348 31
"	" Western.........	1,886 39	4,393 36	6,279 75
Henry and Whiteside	Big Slough Special Drainage District.....	21 85	....	21 85
Iroquois....	Tp. of Concord..........	44 87	....	44 87
"	" Douglas.........	101 17	1,550 82	1,651 99
"	" Martinton.......	379 76	2,512 33	2,892 09
"	" Sheldon..........	87 42	6,264 68	6,352 10
"	City of Watseka........	119 32	2,372 06	2,491 38

Douglas.....	Tp. of Garrett..........	4,449 63	237 12	4,686 75
"	" Newman.........	4,991 01	250 93	5,241 94
"	" Tuscola.........	2,424 46	129 99	2,554 45
Douglas & Moultrie..	Union School District No. 7, T. 15, R. 6 and 7.	....	531 75	531 75
Edgar.......	Tp. of Kansas...........	4,284 47	189 27	4,473 74
"	" Paris............	987 93	164 66	1,152 59
"	" Paris Sinking Fund..........	7,000 00	619 74	7,619 74
"	" Ross............	5,981 81	1,234 82	7,216 63
"	" Shiloh..........	1,454 48	3,547 16	5,001 64
"	" Young America.	3,793 94	....	3,793 94
Edwards and White	City of Grayville........	1,641 02	529 94	2,170 96
Effingham..	Tp. of Douglas..........	6,669 44	15,207 47	21,876 91
" ..	" Liberty..........	187 76	65 44	253 20
" ..	" Liberty Sinking Fund..........	2,000 00	....	2,000 00
" ..	" Mason..........	2,433 52	1,265 41	3,698 93
" ..	" Moccasin........	....	1,545 34	1,545 34
" ..	" Summit..........	942 75	66 67	1,009 42
" ..	" West............	2,550 47	22 19	2,572 66
Fayette.....	" Bear Grove......	5,798 77	2 78	5,801 55
"	" Vandalia........	12,018 76	....	12,018 76
Ford........	County of Ford.........	17,685 29	3,396 28	21,081 57
"	Tp. of Drummer........	10,381 18	319 27	10,700 45
"	" Lyman...........	3,257 05	79 25	3,336 30
"	" Peach Orchard..	5,935 52	202 96	6,138 48
Ford, Iroquois and Livingst'n	Vermilion Special Drainage District.....	7,318 33	243 67	7,562 00
Fulton......	Tp. of Astoria..........	693 45	574 45	1,267 90
"	" Lewistown......	....	109 95	109 95
"	" Pleasant........	....	348 94	348 94
Gallatin....	County of Gallatin......	27,220 51	12,976 64	40,197 15
"	" Gallatin Sinking Fund...	3,515 00	2,770 00	6,285 00
"	City of Shawneetown...	4,613 39	3,702 10	8,315 49
Greene......	" Whitehall.......	1,739 59	917 69	2,657 28
Hancock....	County of Hancock.....	25,658 21	1,084 79	26,743 00
"	City of Warsaw.........	9,077 66	118 34	9,196 00
Henderson..	City of Oquawka.......	....	171 11	171 11
Henry......	Tp. of Galva............	....	348 31	348 31
"	" Western.........	2,257 59	4,022 16	6,279 75
Henry and Whiteside	Big Slough Special Drainage District.....	....	21 85	21 85
Iroquois....	Tp. of Concord..........	....	44 87	44 87
"	" Douglas.........	1,575 55	76 44	1,651 99
"	" Martinton.......	2,892 09	....	2,892 09
"	" Sheldon..........	6,079 02	273 08	6,352 10
"	City of Watseka........	2,375 31	116 07	2,491 38

Statement 39—Continued.

Local Bond Funds.		Balance in Treasury Oct. 1, 1894.	Amount received from Oct. 1, 1894, to Sept. 30, 1896, inclusive.	Total.	Local Bond Funds.		Warrants canceled from Oct. 1, 1894, to Sept. 30, 1896, inclusive.	Balance in Treasury Oct. 1, 1896.	Total.
County	Fund.				County.	Fund.			
Iroquois	Milks Grove Special Drainage District.....	$308 93	$9,600 34	$9,909 27	Iroquois.....	Milks Grove Special Drainage District....	$9,607 67	$301 60	$9,909 27
"	Special Drainage District No. 1 of Onarga, Douglas and Danforth Tps.............	317 63	5,919 17	6,236 80	"	Special Drainage District No. 1, Onarga, Douglas and Danforth Tps............	6,059 59	177 21	6,236 80
"	Union Drainage District No. 2, Danforth and Ashkum Tps.....	....	202 50	202 50	"	Union Drainage District No. 2, Danforth and Ashkum Tps.....	195 97	6 53	202 50
Jackson.....	City of Murphysboro...	32 78	1,215 66	1,248 44	Jackson.....	City of Murphysboro...	970 87	277 57	1,248 44
"	Big Lake Special Drainage District...........	122 97	6,904 59	7,027 56	"	Big Lake Special Drainage District...........	6,669 59	357 97	7,027 56
Jasper.......	County of Jasper.......	7,389 21	12,931 18	20,320 39	Jasper,......	County of Jasper.......	13,491 66	6,828 73	20,320 39
"	Tp. of Fox..............	68 24	1,759 77	1,828 01	"	Tp. of Fox..............	1,791 94	36 07	1,828 01
"	" " Sinking F'nd	3,942 87	7,842 08	11,784 95	"	" " Sinking F'd	....	11,784 95	11,784 95
"	" St. Marie.........	88 76	3,671 78	3,760 54	"	" St. Marie.........	3,566 06	194 48	3,760 54
"	" Wade...........	106 50	2,828 94	2,935 44	"	" Wade...........	2,848 25	87 19	2,935 44
"	" Willow Hill.....	52 86	391 75	444 61	"	" Willow Hill.....	82 36	362 25	444 61
Jefferson....	County of Jefferson	2,841 75	15,999 96	18,841 71	Jefferson ...	County of Jefferson....	16,517 05	2,324 66	18,841 71
"	Tp. of Mt. Vernon......	392 40	1,199 27	1,591 67	" ...	Tp. of Mt. Vernon......	1,211 99	379 68	1,591 67
Jersey.......	School District No. 8, Tp. 7, R. 12...........	101 24	2,538 80	2,640 04	Jersey.......	School District No. 8, Tp. 7, R. 12...........	2,553 35	86 69	2,640 04
Jersey and Macoupin.	Incorporated Town of Brighton	461 26	2,407 57	2,868 83	Jersey and Macoupin.	Incorporated Town of Brighton	2,245 64	623 19	2,868 83
JoDaviess ..	City of Galena..........	2,509 14	16,943 62	19,452 76	JoDaviess ..	City of Galena..........	14,035 40	5,417 36	19,452 76
Johnson.....	County of Johnson......	1,181 38	6 04	1,187 42	Johnson.....	County of Johnson.....	17	1,187 25	1,187 42
"	" " S'k'g F'd	47 90	9 97	57 87	"	" " S'k'g F'd	....	57 87	57 87
Kankakee...	County of Kankakee...	439 68	4,993 39	5,433 07	Kankakee...	County of Kankakee...	5,351 46	81 61	5,433 07
" ..	Tp. of Aroma..........	85 56	7,383 97	7,469 53	" ..	Tp. of Aroma..........	7,393 67	75 86	7,469 53
" ..	" Ganeer.........	137 63	24,671 69	24,809 32	" ..	" Ganeer.........	24,255 17	554 15	24,809 32
" ..	" Momence.........	232 40	4,381 29	4,613 69	" ..	" Momence.........	4,358 50	255 19	4,613 69
" ..	" Pembroke.......	26 09	556 63	582 72	" ..	" Pembroke.......	545 48	37 24	582 72
" ..	" Pilot............	84 58	2,580 96	2,665 54	" ..	" Pilot............	2,555 60	109 94	2,665 54
Knox........	" Rio............	183 51	2,183 72	2,367 23	Knox........	" Rio............	1,397 82	969 41	2,367 23
LaSalle.....	" LaSalle..........	607 98	....	607 98	LaSalle.....	" LaSalle..........	....	607 98	607 98
"	Incorporated Town of Marseilles............	106 66	274 58	381 24	"	Incorporated Town of Marseilles............	282 76	98 48	381 24

LaSalle	School District No. 2, Tp. 33, R. 1, E.	287 50	....	287 50	LaSalle	School District No. 2, Tp. 33, R. 1, E.	....	287 50	287 50
"	Drainage District No. 2, Town of Wallace	....	980 00	980 00	"	Drainage District No. 2, Town of Wallace	980 00	....	980 00
Lee	Tp. of Amboy	1,140 48	22,172 83	23,313 31	Lee	Tp. of Amboy	22,251 21	1,062 10	23,313 31
"	" Hamilton	46 40	1,095 51	1,141 91	"	" Hamilton	1,095 92	45 99	1,141 91
"	" Wyoming	2,966 66	8,084 08	11,050 74	"	" Wyoming	10,648 87	401 87	11,050 74
Livingston	" Amity	3,274 47	5,351 48	8,625 95	Livingston	" Amity	5,594 55	3,031 40	8,625 95
"	" Eppards Point	776 97	1,036 56	1,813 53	"	" Eppards Point	1,813 53	....	1,813 53
"	" Indian Grove	2,534 89	2 70	2,537 59	"	" Indian Grove	2,537 59	....	2,537 59
"	" Owego	185 96	....	185 96	"	" Owego	185 96	....	185 96
"	" Pontiac	699 98	13,703 79	14,403 77	"	" Pontiac	14,403 77	....	14,403 77
"	" Reading	305 17	7,008 39	7,313 56	"	" Reading	3,996 09	3 317 47	7,313 56
Logan	County of Logan	1,078 03	12,757 88	13,835 91	Logan	County of Logan	13,330 03	505 88	13,835 91
"	City of Lincoln	1,541 18	5,323 46	6,864 64	"	City of Lincoln	5,353 12	1,511 52	6,864 64
"	Tp. of Ætna	303 66	4,319 78	4,623 44	"	Tp. of Ætna	4,623 04	40	4 623 44
"	" " Sink'g F'd	203 05	....	203 05	"	" " Sink'g F'd	203 05	....	203 05
"	" Atlanta	552 63	4.318 86	4,871 49	"	" Atlanta	4,061 70	809 79	4,871 49
"	" East Lincoln	570 83	9,723 18	10,294 01	"	" East Lincoln	9,922 14	371 87	10,294 01
"	" East Lincoln Sinking Fund	9,859 61	10,126 35	19,985 96	"	" East Lincoln Sinking Fund	10,000 00	9,985 96	19,985 96
"	" Mt. Pulaski	256 10	4,245 95	4,502 05	"	" Mt. Pulaski	4,383 03	119 02	4,502 05
"	" Oran	4,921 47	5 60	4,927 07	"	" Oran	4,927 07	....	4,927 07
"	" West Lincoln	658 40	14,253 60	14,912 00	"	" West Lincoln	14,845 02	66 98	14,912 00
"	School District No. 5, Tp. 18, R. 2	59 47	1,221 13	1,280 60	"	School District No. 5, Tp. 18, R. 2	970 91	309 69	1,280 60
Macon	County of Macon	18,614 23	36,963 43	55,577 66	Macon	County of Macon	37,212 26	18,365 40	55,577 66
"	City of Decatur	789 65	2,394 97	3,184 62	"	City of Decatur	2,333 02	851 60	3,184 62
"	Tp. of Decatur	1,624 58	13,735 07	15,359 65	"	Tp. of Decatur	8,983 22	6,376 43	15,359 65
"	" Mt. Zion	30 94	....	30 94	"	" Mt. Zion	....	30 94	30 94
Macoupin	County of Macoupin	3,726 62	261,736 59	265,463 21	Macoupin	County of Macoupin	245,031 78	20,431 43	265,463 21
"	City of Virden	1,294 88	1,126 19	2,421 07	"	City of Virden	1,638 76	782 31	2,421 07
Madison	City of Edwardsville	1,067 33	6,685 49	7,752 82	Madison	City of Edwardsville	7,089 55	663 27	7,752 82
Mason	County of Mason	17,767 16	....	17,767 16	Mason	County of Mason	17,767 16	....	17,767 16
"	Tp. of Havana	460 50	....	460 50	"	Tp. of Havana	460 50	....	460 50
"	" Mason City	234 86	367 56	602 42	"	" Mason City	602 42	....	602 42
"	Central Special Drainage District	3,094 11	44,490 09	47,584 20	"	Central Special Drainage District	43,528 84	4,055 36	47,584 20
Mason and Menard	Mason and Menard Special Drainage District	45 85	1,522 03	1,567 88	Mason and Menard	Mason and Menard Special Drainage District	1,567 88	....	1,567 88
Mason and Tazewell	Mason and Tazewell Special Drainage Dist	3,261 49	50,746 76	54,008 25	Mason and Tazewell	Mason and Tazewell Special Drainage Dist	52,081 85	1,926 40	54,008 25
McDonough	Tp. of Bushnell	2,488 54	5,433 85	7,922 39	McDonough	Tp. of Bushnell	7,208 24	714 15	7,922 39
"	" " S'k'g F'nd	....	4,320 19	4,320 19	"	" " S'k'g F'd	....	4,320 19	4,320 19
McLean	" Bloomington	1,759 12	46,132 48	47,891 60	McLean	" Bloomington	46,024 50	1,867 10	47,891 60
"	Village of Saybrook	1,272 61	2,219 86	3,492 47	"	Village of Saybrook	2,312 60	1,179 87	3,492 47
"	Easterbrook Special Drainage District	1,910 30	....	1,910 30	"	Easterbrook Special Drainage District	1,777 05	133 25	1,910 30
Mercer	City of New Boston	84 86	1,039 56	1,124 42	Mercer	City of New Boston	1,119 73	4 69	1,124 42
"	City of New Boston Sinking Fund	776 58	2,037 69	2,814 27	"	City of New Boston Sinking Fund	2 010 80	803 47	2,814 27

Statemennt No. 39—Continued.

Local Bond Funds.		Balance in Treasury Oct. 1, 1894.	Amount received from Oct. 1, 1894, to Sept. 30, 1896, inclusive.	Total.
County.	Fund.			
Merc	Tp. of Abington	$241 66		$241 66
"	" Keithsburg	178 47	$6,935 82	7,114 29
Monroe	County of Monroe	85 30	15,134 34	15,219 64
Montgom'ry	City of Litchfield	747 80	3,269 64	4,017 44
"	" " S'g F'nd	1,968 72	4,291 22	6,259 94
Morgan	County of Morgan	134 46	8,772 85	8,907 31
"	City of Jacksonville	7,260 31	24,573 75	31,834 06
"	" Waverly	3,010 34	35,387 12	38,397 46
"	" " S'g F'nd		1,104 49	1,104 49
"	Tp. 14 N., R. 9, W. 3 P.M.	35 27		35 27
Moultrie	County of Moultrie	2,267 68	95,160 44	97,428 12
"	Tp. of Lowe	139 14		139 14
"	" " Sink'g F'd	2,084 09		2,084 09
"	" Sullivan	7,383 67	10 52	7,394 19
Ogle	" Forreston	312 54	3,720 68	4,033 22
"	" Mt. Morris	637 24	12,663 23	13,300 47
"	" Oregon	378 65	12,206 68	12,585 33
"	" Pine Rock	2,696 88	4,694 71	7,391 59
"	City of Polo		956 70	956 70
Peoria	Tp. of Brimfield	1,607 13	14,865 54	16,472 67
"	" Elmwood	3,573 26	15,450 72	19,023 98
"	" Peoria	2,361 20	10,485 66	12 846 86
Piatt	" Bement	543 39	14,512 22	15,055 61
"	" Blue Ridge	397 97	10,139 13	10,537 10
"	" Goose Creek	253 66	7,057 23	7,310 89
"	" Sangamon	121 12	7,551 88	7,673 00
"	" Unity	1,172 52	1 01	1,173 53
Pike	County of Pike	679 16	62,177 32	62,856 48
"	Pittsfield School Dist.	61 83	7,628 05	7,689 88
Pulaski	County of Pulaski	4,278 83	7,723 34	12,002 17
"	City of Mound City	212 37	2,078 53	2,290 90
Randolph	County of Randolph	929 19		929 19
"	City of Chester	8 34		8 34
Richland	County of Richland	888 08	52,638 29	53,526 37
Saline	County of Saline	21,558 91	4,120 73	25,679 64
"	Inc. Town of Eldorado	25 83		25 83

Local Bond Funds.		Warrants canceled from Oct. 1, 1894, to Sept. 30, 1896, inclusive.	Balance in Treasury Oct. 1, 1896.	Total.
County.	Fund.			
Mercer	Tp. of Abington		$241 66	$241 66
"	" Keithsburg	$6,707 97	406 32	7,114 29
Monroe	County of Monroe	9,284 97	5,934 67	15,219 64
Montgom'ry	City of Litchfield	3,141 85	875 59	4,017 44
"	" " S'g F'nd		6,259 94	6,259 94
Morgan	County of Morgan	8,124 05	783,26	8,907 31
"	City of Jacksonville	23,979 67	7,854 39	31,834 06
"	" Waverly	37,886 93	510 53	38,397 46
"	" " S'g F'nd	1,010 00	94 49	1,104 49
"	Tp. 14, N., R. 9 W., 3 P.M.		35 27	35 27
Moultrie	County of Moultrie	92,843 66	4,584 46	97,428 12
"	Tp. of Lowe	139 14		139 14
"	" " Sink'g F'nd	2,084 09		2,084 09
"	" Sullivan	7,394 19		7,394 19
Ogle	" Forreston	3,729 65	303 57	4,033 22
"	" Mt. Morris	12,871 21	429 26	13,300 47
"	" Oregon	11,269 48	1,315 85	12,585 33
"	" Pine Rock	4,927 97	2,463 62	7,391 59
"	City of Polo	606 28	350 42	956 70
Peoria	Tp. of Brimfield	14,858 08	1,614 59	16,472 67
"	" Elmwood	15,127 26	3,896 72	19,023 98
"	" Peoria	9,901 42	2,945 44	12,846 86
Piatt	" Bement	14,137 76	917 85	15,055 61
"	" Blue Ridge	10,221 41	315 69	10,537 10
"	" Goose Creek	7,005 03	305 86	7,310 89
"	" Sangamon	7,555 31	117 69	7,673 00
"	" Unity	1,062 81	110 72	1,173 53
Pike	County of Pike	61,144 78	1,711 70	62,856 48
"	Pittsfield School Dist	7,347 14	342 74	7,689 88
Pulaski	County of Pulaski	7,920 64	4,081 53	12,002 17
"	City of Mound City	2,004 80	286 10	2,290 90
Randolph	County of Randolph	929 19		929 19
"	City of Chester		8 34	8 34
Richland	County of Richland	39,700 30	13,826 07	53,526 37
Saline	County of Saline	20,884 40	4,795 24	25,679 64
"	Inc. Town of Eldorado		25 83	25 83

Sangamon..	County of Sangamon...	5,697 86	47,869 22	53,567 08	Sangamon..	County of Sangamon...	43,788 75	9,778 33	53,567 08
" ..	City of Springfield	13,097 94	91,388 50	104,486 44	" ..	City of Springfield	93,049 70	11,436 74	104,486 44
" ..	Tp. of Capital	1,746 58	5,401 73	7,148 31	" ..	Tp. of Capital	5,333 41	1,814 90	7,148 31
" ..	" Cartwright......	3,214 97	5,441 38	8,656 35	" ..	" Cartwright......	5,735 70	2,920 65	8,656 35
" ..	" Springfield......	368 77	1,229 62	1,598 39	" ..	" Springfield......	1,227 20	371 19	1,598 39
" ..	" Talkington......	1,117 44	5,477 81	6,595 25	" ..	" Talkington......	4,004 04	2,591 21	6,595 25
Schuyler ...	County of Schuyler	1,925 00	5,471 44	7,396 44	Schuyler ...	County of Schuyler	5,664 81	1,731 63	7,396 44
"	Tp. of Frederick	80 62	...	80 62	"	Tp. of Frederick	...	80 62	80 62
Shelby......	" Dry Point.......	947 96	2,861 24	3,809 20	Shelby......	" Dry Point.......	2,908 71	900 49	3,809 20
"	" Okaw..........	436 92	741 07	1,177 99	"	" Okaw..........	762 63	415 36	1,177 99
"	" Prairie	676 85	12,209 14	12,885 99	"	" Prairie	12,201 58	684 41	12,885 99
"	" Richland	304 55	27,617 23	27,921 78	"	" Richland	27,916 78	5 00	27,921 78
"	" Shelbyville	1,677 07	2,900 67	4,577 74	"	" Shelbyville	3,029 49	1,548 25	4,577 74
"	" Todd's Point....	242 53	445 77	688 30	"	" Todd's Point....	449 29	239 01	688 30
"	" Windsor.........	694 16	17,359 93	18,054 09	"	" Windsor	7,958 55	10,095 54	18,054 09
"	City of Windsor	35 32	3,874 29	3,909 61	"	City of Windsor	3,878 62	30 99	3,909 61
Stark	Tp. of Essex...........	3,765 35	7,837 22	11,602 57	Stark	Tp. of Essex...........	10,423 47	1,179 10	11,602 57
"	" Goshen..........	1,331 48	4,552 12	5,883 60	"	" Goshen..........	5,163 41	720 19	5,883 60
"	" Osceola	229 89	11,180 05	11,409 94	"	" Osceola	11,055 75	354 19	11,409 94
"	" Penn	607 01	6,686 22	7,293 23	"	" Penn	6,902 23	391 00	7,293 23
"	" Toulon	1,442 59	8,309 08	9,751 67	"	" Toulon	8,383 15	1,368 52	9,751 67
"	Village of Wyoming....	288 20	1,024 47	1,312 67	"	Village of Wyoming ...	984 99	327 68	1,312 67
St. Clair....	Village of Brooklyn....	...	439 60	439 60	St. Clair....	Village of Brooklyn....	1 20	438 40	439 60
"	City of East St. Louis..	5,652 95	64,285 29	69,938 24	"	City of East St. Louis..	67,905 07	2,033 17	69,938 24
"	Tp. of Centreville Sta'n	3,522 35	41,884 47	45,406 82	"	Tp. of Centreville Sta'n	44,409 07	997 75	45,406 82
Tazewell ...	County of Tazewell	884 14	16,194 44	17,078 58	Tazewell ...	County of Tazewell	15,963 97	1,114 61	17,078 58
"	City of Pekin	1,169 80	88,959 30	90,129 10	"	City of Pekin	89,567 76	561 34	90,129 10
"	Tp. of Delavan	725 92	8,650 46	9,376 38	"	Tp. of Delavan	8,605 98	770 40	9,376 38
"	" Hittle...........	158 97	...	158 97	"	" Hittle...........	...	158 97	158 97
"	" Little Mackinaw	397 94	10,281 46	10,679 40	"	" Little Mackinaw	10,594 16	85 24	10,679 40
"	" Mackinaw.......	2,669 85	2,699 84	5,369 69	"	" Mackinaw.......	3,862 65	1,507 04	5,369 69
"	" Tremont	577 26	807 26	1,384 52	"	" Tremont	878 38	506 14	1,384 52
Union	County of Union	4,394 06	...	4,394 06	Union	County of Union	...	4,394 06	4,394 06
"	City of Jonesboro	444 41	...	444 41	"	City of Jonesboro	...	444 41	444 41
Vermilion ..	Tp. of Butler	2,629 32	3,007 91	5,637 23	Vermilion ..	Tp. of Butler	4,500 39	1,136 84	5,637 23
" ..	" Danville.........	1,451 75	28,930 54	30,382 29	" ..	" Danville.........	29,219 70	1,162 59	30,382 29
" ..	" Elwood..........	188 31	4,200 40	4,388 71	" ..	" Elwood..........	4,223 15	165 56	4,388 71
" ..	" Grant...........	385 08	12,187 40	12,572 48	" ..	" Grant...........	12,171 43	401 05	12,572 48
" ..	Tp. of Ross............	272 79	5,394 73	5,667 52	Vermilion ..	Tp. of Ross............	5,544 75	122 77	5,667 52
Wabash	County of Wabash	631 72	13,882 80	14,514 52	Wabash	County of Wabash	13,988 91	525 61	14,514 52
"	City of Mt. Carmel.....	311 17	7,508 72	7,819 89	"	City of Mt. Carmel.....	4,936 39	2,883 50	7,819 89
Warren	Tp. of Monmouth	358 67	5,339 20	5,697 87	Warren	Tp. of Monmouth	5,696 80	1 07	5,697 87
"	" Roseville........	199 02	5,100 05	5,299 07	"	" Roseville........	5,110 90	188 17	5,299 07
"	" Spring Grove...	277 01	5,682 32	5,959 33	"	" Spring Grove...	5,957 17	2 16	5,959 33
"	" Swan...........	62 92	1,051 32	1,114 24	"	" Swan...........	970 06	144 18	1,114 24
Washington	County of Washington.	3,641 72	42,969 96	46,611 68	Washington	County of Washington.	35,551 15	11,060 53	46,611 68
Wayne......	County of Wayne	4,788 24	12,308 57	17,096 81	Wayne......	County of Wayne.......	10,351 99	6,744 82	17,096 81
"	Tp. of Big Mound......	76 10	434 35	510 45	"	Tp. of Big Mound......	243 37	267 08	510 45
"	" Jasper...........	52 95	396 94	449 89	"	" Jasper...........	283 38	166 51	449 89
"	" Lamard	72 19	418 75	490 94	"	" Lamard	303 59	187 35	490 94

Statement No. 39—Concluded.

Local Bond Funds.		Balance in Treasury Oct. 1, 1894.	Amount received from Oct. 1, 1894, to Sept. 30, 1896, inclusive.	Total.	Local Bond Funds.		Warrants canceled from Oct. 1, 1894, to Sept. 30, 1896, inclusive.	Balance in Treasury Oct. 1, 1896.	Total.
County.	Fund.				County.	Fund.			
White	County of White	$5,357 58	$18,141 31	$23,498 89	White	County of White	$18,193 46	$5,305 43	$23,498 89
"	Inc. Town of Carmi	42 00	....	42 00	"	Inc. Town of Carmi	....	42 00	42 00
"	Village of Enfield	368 97	1,382 04	1,751 01	"	Village of Enfield	1,333 51	417 50	1,751 01
Whiteside	Tp. of Coloma	1,875 26	5,114 66	6,989 92	Whiteside	Tp. of Coloma	6,329 55	660 37	6,989 92
Williamson	County of Williamson	5,270 99	20,098 59	25,369 58	Williamson	County of Williamson	12,668 16	12,701 42	25,369 58
Woodford	Township of Olio	266 17	5,333 35	5,599 52	Woodford	Tp. of Olio	5,447 52	152 00	5,599 52
Adams, Pike and Calhoun	Sny Island Levee	50 42	....	50 42	Adams, Pike and Calhoun	Sny Island Levee	....	50 42	50 42
	Total Local B'd Funds	$474,160 35	$2,763,513 58	$3,237,673 93		Total Local B'd Funds	$2,744,891 88	$492,782 05	$3,237,673 93
	Total State Funds	1,449,301 72	8,755,079 51	10,204,381 23		Total State Funds	9,810,817 15	393,564 08	10,204,381 23
	Grand total	$1,923,462 07	$11,518,593 09	$13,442,055 16		Grand total	$12,555,709 03	$886,346 13	$13,442,055 16

No. 40.

Statement of the aggregate amount charged on tax books of 1894, on account of Local Bond Funds, the amount of abatements, commissions, etc., the net amount collected, and the amount paid State Treasurer.

Locality.		Amount charged.	Abatements.			Amount paid State Treasurer.
County.	Bond Fund.		Ordinary abatements, including errors, insolvencies, forfeitures, commissions, etc.	Enjoined from collection on property of railroads and other corporations	Total.	
Adams	City of Quincy	$86,324 76	$2,930 17	$873 67	$3,803 84	$82,520 92
"	" Sinking Fund	56,067 65	1,843 66	467 53	2,311 19	53,756 46
Alexander	County of Alexander	13,452 39	545 78		545 78	12,906 61
"	City of Cairo	31,853 19	1,343 62		1,343 62	30,509 57
Bureau	Village of Buda	1,075 86	29 83		29 83	1,046 03
"	Tp. of Ohio	5,225 78	158 36		158 36	5,067 42
"	" Walnut	3,030 40	89 20		89 20	2,941 20
"	Green River Special Drain. District	3,769 29	154 30		154 30	3,614 99
Cass	City of Beardstown	9,960 89	402 69		402 69	9,558 20
"	Hager Slough Special Drain. District	1,376 00	40 08		40 08	1,335 92
"	New Pankey Pond Special Drain. District	448 10	13 44		13 44	434 66
Champaign	Tp. of Champaign	2,906 00	171 03		171 03	2,734 97
"	" St. Joseph	3,548 75	102 06		102 06	3,446 69
"	" Urbana	3,720 22	268 98		268 98	3,451 24
"	City of Urbana	921 29	66 01		66 01	855 28
"	Big Slough Special Drain. District	1,813 00	42 71		42 71	1,770 29
"	Wild Cat Special Drain. District	1,548 00	34 78		34 78	1,513 22
Christian	Tp. of Johnson	1,320 08	39 17		39 17	1,280 91
"	" Pana	9,865 18	387 92	1,122 54	1,510 46	8,354 72
Clark	County of Clark	5,114 08	151 88		151 88	4,962 20
"	" " Sinking Fund	6,706 67	242 44		242 44	6,464 23
"	Tp. of Marshall	1,355 60	87 96		87 96	1,267 64
"	" " Sinking Fund	3,379 41	122 58		122 58	3,256 83
"	" Westfield	1,292 47	47 65		47 65	1,244 82
"	" " Sinking Fund	1,131 14	40 72		40 72	1,090 42
"	" York	1,256 63	48 94		48 94	1,207 69
"	" " Sinking Fund	849 40	38 91		38 91	810 49

Statement 40—Continued.

Locality.		Amount charged.	Abatements.			Amount paid State Treasurer.
County.	Bond Fund.		Ordinary abatements, including errors, insolvencies, forfeitures, commissions, etc.	Enjoined from collection on property of railroads and other corporations	Total.	
Clay	Tp. of Harter	$1,270 45	$46 48	....	$46 48	$1,223 97
"	" Louisville	909 01	30 24	....	30 24	878 77
Coles	" Charleston	4,855 11	190 76	....	190 76	4,664 35
"	" Mattoon	5,833 02	326 76	....	326 76	5,506 26
"	" Seven Hickory	3,673 26	99 52	....	99 52	3,573 74
"	" " Sinking Fund	1,164 69	31 55	....	31 55	1,133 14
"	City of Mattoon	2,183 02	173 65	....	173 65	2,009 37
Crawford	County of Crawford	6,372 73	244 37	....	244 37	6,128 36
"	Tp. of Hutsonville	864 49	38 90	....	38 90	825 59
"	" " Sinking Fund	2,795 17	125 72	....	125 72	2,669 45
"	" Robinson	1,919 99	66 80	....	66 80	1,853 19
Cumberland	" Sumpter	1,528 35	57 89	....	57 89	1,470 46
DeWitt	County of DeWitt	19,258 28	659 40	....	659 40	18,598 88
"	Tp. of Barnett	3,878 46	123 18	....	123 18	3,755 28
"	" Clintonia	2,582 45	88 68	....	88 68	2,493 77
"	" Creek	2,436 23	81 30	....	81 30	2,354 93
"	" Santa Anna	6,734 48	232 77	....	232 77	6,501 71
"	North Branch Lake Fork Special Drain. District	512 08	15 36	....	15 36	496 72
Douglas	County of Douglas	5,375 50	191 27	....	191 27	5,184 23
"	Tp. of Camargo	369 05	12 56	....	12 56	356 49
"	" Garrett	2,313 51	79 25	....	79 35	2,234 26
"	" Newman	595 52	23 01	....	23 01	572 51
"	" Tuscola	1,327 84	46 56	....	46 56	1,281 28
Edgar	" Kansas	2,178 81	78 31	....	78 31	2,100 50
"	" Paris	663 70	18 38	....	18 38	645 32
"	" " Sinking Fund	1,768 17	48 99	....	48 99	1,719 18
"	" Ross	301 04	9 66	....	9 66	291 38
"	" Shiloh	292 19	8 59	....	8 59	283 60
"	" Young America	108 47	7 96	....	7 96	100 51
Edwards	Inc. Town of Grayville	304 11	14 06	....	14 06	290 05

Effingham	Tp. of Douglas	9,275 98	481 55		481 55	8,794 43
"	" Liberty	64 81	2 28		2 28	62 53
"	" Liberty Sinking Funk	555 51	19 49		19 49	536 02
"	" Mason	1,199 19	43 66		43 66	4,155 53
"	" West	326 77	11 21		11 21	315 56
Fayette	" Bear Grove	5,774 55	203 04		203 04	5,571 51
Ford	County of Ford	9,220 45	323 03		323 03	8,897 42
"	Tp. of Drummer	5,026 25	182 19		182 19	4,844 06
"	" Lyman	2,238 50	75 01		75 01	2,163 49
"	" Peach Orchard	3,114 81	104 82		104 82	3,009 99
"	Vermilion Special Drain. District	2,818 13	95 39		95 39	2,722 74
Gallatin	County of Gallatin	12,944 65	488 12		488 12	12,456 53
"	City of Shawneetown	3,303 99	138 18		138 18	3,165 81
Greene	" Whitehall	1,546 72	136 56		136 56	1,410 16
Hancock	County of Hancock	15,474 94	523 59	$936 89	1,460 48	14,014 46
"	City of Warsaw	4,039 64	249 56		249 56	3,790 08
Henry	Tp. of Western	1,122 59	31 29		31 29	1,091 30
Iroquois	" Douglas	864 59	23 84		23 84	840 75
"	" Martinton	2,585 71	73 38		73 38	2,512 33
"	" Sheldon	1,419 28	49 15		49 15	1,370 13
"	City of Watseka	1,208 54	36 97		36 97	1,171 57
"	Milks Grove Special Drain. District	5,678 45	113 57		113 57	5,564 88
"	Spl. Drain. Dist. No. 1 of Onarga, Douglas & Danforth Tps	3,089 36	61 79		61 79	3,027 57
"	Vermilion Special Drain. District	1,203 64	34 90		34 90	1,168 74
Jackson	City of Murphysboro	775 68	33 63		33 63	742 05
"	Big Lake Special Drain. District	2,380 15	93 67		93 67	2,286 48
Jasper	County of Jasper	7,981 80	268 14		268 14	6,713 66
"	Tp. of Fox	929 49	33 13		33 13	896 36
"	" " Sinking Fund	4,041 29	145 05		145 05	3,926 24
"	" St. Marie	784 63	26 56		26 56	758 07
"	" Wade	1,501 60	61 31		61 31	1,440 29
"	" Willow Hill	407 55	15 80		15 80	391 75
Jefferson	County of Jefferson	7,859 83	402 84		402 84	7,456 99
"	Tp. of Mt. Vernon	710 97	48 96		48 96	662 01
Jersey	School District No. 8, T. 7, R. 12	1,361 40	44 61		44 61	1,316 79
"	Inc. Town of Brighton	88 89	2 93		2 93	85 96
Jo Daviess	City of Galena	9,167 26	378 10		378 10	8,789 16
Johnson	County of Johnson	1,227 44	1,221 40		1,221 40	6 04
"	" " Sinking Fund	67 68	57 71		57 71	9 97
Kankakee	County of Kankakee	2,548 45	141 38		141 38	2,407 07
"	Tp. of Aroma	1,962 90	64 98		64 98	1,897 92
"	" Ganeer	1,906 15	62 80		62 80	1,843 35
"	" Momence	2,272 50	78 76		78 76	2,193 74
"	" Pembrooke	271 20	9 52		9 52	261 68
"	" Pilot	1,380 93	46 01		46 01	1,334 92
Knox	" Rio	1,156 39	32 14		32 14	1,124 25
LaSalle	Inc. Town of Marseilles	139 84	4 35		4 35	135 49
Lee	Tp. of Amboy	11,549 79	347 13		347 13	11,202 66
"	" Hamilton	579 61	16 19		16 19	563 42
"	" Wyoming	2,362 93	65 57		65 57	2,297 36
Livingston	" Amity	2,876 63	77 91		77 91	2,798 72
"	" Eppard's Point	1,065 06	28 57		28 57	1,036 49

Statement 40—Continued.

Locality.		Amount charged.	Abatements.			Amount paid State Treasurer.
Counties.	Bond Fund.		Ordinary abatements, including errors, insolvencies, forfeitures, commissions, etc.	Enjoined from collection on property of railroads and other corporations	Total.	
Livingston	Tp. of Pontiac	$7,709 20	$224 57		$224 57	$7,484 63
"	" Reading	3,921 53	121 31		121 31	3,800 22
"	Vermilion Spl. D. D.	4 66	09		09	4 57
Logan	County of Logan	7,233 27	951 52		951 52	6,281 75
"	Tp. of Ætna	4,482 06	162 28		162 28	4,319 78
"	" Atlanta	2,896 62	554 31		554 31	2,342 31
"	" East Lincoln	5,305 02	456 97		456 97	4,848 05
"	" " Sinking F'd	3,424 59	192 21		192 21	3,232 38
"	" Mt. Pulaski	2,220 32	59 18		59 18	2,161 14
"	" West Lincoln	7,920 30	576 69		576 69	7,343 61
"	City of Lincoln	3,724 24	225 55		225 55	2,498 69
"	School Dist, No. 5, T. 18, R. 2	768 56	21 01		21 01	747 55
"	North Branch Lake Fork Spl. D. D.	7,000 00				7,000 00
Macon	County of Macon	20,669 48	805 24		805 24	19,864 24
"	Tp. of Decatur	7,860 19	346 75		346 75	7,513 44
"	City of Decatur	1,565 62	298 74		298 74	1,266 88
"	North Branch Lake Fork Spl. D. D.	1,980 98	41 63		41 63	1,939 35
Macoupin	County of Macoupin	146,289 54	8,674 26		8,674 26	137,615 28
"	Inc. Town of Virden	770 75	87 18		87 18	683 57
"	" Brighton	1,020 53	29 69		29 69	990 84
Madison	City of Edwardsville	4,181 68	138 96		138 96	4 042 72
Mason	Tp. of Mason City	450 31	82 75		82 75	367 56
"	Mason & Menard Spl. Drain. Dist.	729 78	315 97		315 97	413 81
"	Mason & Tazewell Spl. D. D.	24,472 80	6,224 02		6,224 02	18,248 78
"	Central Special Drainage Dist.	27,088 27	5,214 80		5,214 80	21,873 47
McDonough	Tp. of Bushnell	2,853 46	115 10		115 10	2,738 36
"	" " Sinking Fund	2,225 53	74 68		74 68	2,150 85
McLean	" Bloomington	23,772 91	877 43		877 43	22,895 48
"	Village of Saybrook	1,157 66	36 76		36 76	1,120 90
Mercer	Tp. of Keithsburg	4,032 54	232 92		232 92	3,799 62
"	City of New Boston	2,040 52	1,432 87		1,432 87	607 65
"	" " Sink'g Fund	1,475 59	418 21		418 21	1,057 38

Monroe	County of Monroe	10,619 90	600 46		600 46	10,019 44
Montgomery	City of Litchfield	1,814 93	166 86		166 86	1,648 07
"	" " Sinking Fund	2,270 63	208 98		208 98	2,061 65
Morgan	County of Morgan	4,804 27	127 78		127 78	4,677 49
"	City of Jacksonville	12,839 50	355 12		355 12	12,484 38
"	City of Waverly	3,672 16	175 90		175 90	3,496 26
"	New Pankey Pond Spl. D. D	194 84	3 90		3 90	190 94
Moultrie	County of Moultrie	45,925 28	1,598 12		1,598 12	44,327 16
"	Tp. of Sullivan	15 93	11 16		11 16	4 77
Ogle	" Forreston	3,831 53	110 85		110 85	3,720 68
"	" Mt. Morris	6,564 62	189 41		189 41	6,375 21
"	" Oregon	6,548 62	179 40		179 40	6,369 22
"	" Pine Rock	2,599 81	75 35		75 35	2,524 46
Peoria	" Brimfield	6,689 69	199 13		199 13	6,490 56
"	" Elmwood	4,829 06	138 90		138 90	4,690 16
"	" Peoria	6,180 90	186 00	$12 00	198 00	5,982 90
Piatt	" Bement	7,338 91	248 64	239 03	487 67	6,851 24
"	" Blue Ridge	5,520 83	192 49	104 52	297 01	5,223 82
"	" Goose Creek	3,117 56	105 19		105 19	3,012 37
"	" Sangamon	2,202 18	98 58	251 36	349 94	1,852 24
"	" Unity	110 17	03	109 13	109 16	1 01
Pike	County of Pike	65,228 39	3,158 77	162 36	3,321 13	61,907 26
"	Pittsfield School District	4,265 66	230 15		230 15	4,035 51
Pulaski	County of Pulaski	4,444 50	382 16		382 16	4,062 34
"	City of Mound City	1,124 45	105 01		105 01	1,019 44
Richland	County of Richland	7,496 73	290 51		290 51	7,206 22
Saline	County of Saline	2,198 60	100 10		100 10	2,098 50
Sangamon	County of Sangamon	21,377 98	748 89		748 89	20,629 09
"	Tp. of Cartwright	2,852 47	82 33		82 33	2,770 14
"	" Capital	2,777 97	89 85		89 85	2,688 12
"	" Springfield	667 28	33 62		33 62	633 66
"	" Talkington	3,586 79	543 86		543 86	3,042 93
"	City of Springfield	46,366 89	1,564 81		1,564 81	44,802 08
Schuyler	County of Schuyler	4,172 81	200 75		200 75	3,972 06
Shelby	Tp. of Dry Point	1,583 51	53 14		53 14	1,530 37
"	" Okaw	364 26	10 28		10 28	353 98
"	" Prairie	3,867 49	103 70		103 70	3,763 79
"	" Shelbyville	2,664 84	101 56		101 56	2,563 28
"	" Richland	27,186 62	879 28		879 28	26,307 34
"	" Todd's Point	241 65	7 14		7 14	234 51
"	" Windsor	4,257 95	122 81		122 81	4,135 14
"	City of Windsor	2,832 89	85 35		85 35	2,747 54
Stark	Tp. of Essex	3,295 90	120 64	14 98	135 62	3,160 28
"	" Goshen	2,070 39	70 56		70 56	1,999 83
"	" Osceola	6,064 94	209 34		209 34	5,855 60
"	" Penn	6,755 48	227 23		227 23	6,528 25
"	" Toulon	4,394 59	150 34		150 34	4,244 25
"	Village of Wyoming	564 77	21 21	39 62	60 83	503 94
St. Clair	City of East St. Louis	35,835 27	3,760 35		3,760 35	32,074 92
"	Tp. of Centreville Station	21,780 24	1,955 63		1,955 63	19,824 61

Statement 40—Concluded.

Locality.		Amount charged.	Abatements.			Amount paid State Treasurer.
Counties.	Bond Fund.		Ordinary abatements, including errors, insolvencies, forfeitures, commissions, etc.	Enjoined from collection on property of railroads and other corporations	Total.	
Tazewell	County of Tazewell	$7,985 33	$272 78	$22 37	$295 15	$7,690 18
"	Tp. of Delavan	4,623 75	137 46	3 05	140 51	4,483 24
"	" Little Mackinaw	1,158 24	37 66		37 66	1,120 58
"	" Mackinaw	1,687 27	61 14		61 14	1,626 13
"	" Tremont	451 78	12 55		12 55	439 23
"	City of Pekin	7,451 40	330 32		330 32	7,121 08
"	Mason & Tazewell Spl. D. D.	8,039 03	495 31		495 31	7,543 72
Vermilion	Tp. of Butler	2,257 43	61 04		64 04	2,193 39
"	" Danville	15,216 18	503 94		503 94	14,712 24
"	" Elwood	2,193 15	76 68		76 68	2,116 47
"	" Grant	6,558 92	184 05		184 05	6,374 87
"	" Ross	2,885 01	103 14		103 14	2,781 87
Wabash	County of Wabash	7,831 99	195 77	532 56	728 33	7,103 66
"	City of Mt. Carmel	4,152 15	128 09	113 60	241 69	3,910 46
Warren	Tp. of Monmouth	5,543 06	203 86		203 86	5,339 20
"	" Roseville	2,694 63	95 85		95 85	2,598 78
"	" Spring Grove	5,886 74	204 42		204 42	5,682 32
"	" Swan	622 22	20 67		20 67	601 55
Washington	County of Washington	27,646 20	1,024 54		1,024 54	26,621 66
Wayne	County of Wayne	7,837 00	312 04		312 04	7,524 96
"	Tp. of Big Mound	171 12	6 35		6 35	164 77
"	" Jasper	311 09	12 88		12 88	298 21
"	" Lamard	386 12	13 47		13 47	372 65
White	County of White	9,705 18	504 35		504 35	9,200 83
"	Village of Enfield	712 98	36 20		36 20	676 78
"	Inc. Town of Grayville	760 50	42 11		42 11	718 39
Whiteside	Tp. of Coloma	5,267 77	153 11		153 11	5,114 66
"	Green River Spl. D. D	776 43	19 33		19 33	757 10
Williamson	County of Williamson	8,258 42	242 18		242 18	8,016 24
Woodford	Tp. of Olio	3,433 58	125 16		125 16	3,308 42
Totals		$1,416,933 31	$75,923 24	$5,005 21	$79 928 45	$1,337,004 86

No. 41.

Statement of the aggregate amount charged on the tax books of 1895 on account of Local Bond Funds, the amount of abatements, commissions, etc., the net amount collected, and the amount paid State Treasurer.

Locality.			Abatements.			
Counties.	Bond fund.	Amount charged.	Ordinary abatements, including errors, insolvencies, forfeitures, commissions, etc.	Enjoined from collection on property of railroads and other corporations	Total.	Amount paid State Treasurer.
Adams	City of Quincy	$81,487 28	$2,556 81		$2,556 81	$78,930 47
"	" sinking fund	56,089 84	1,738 80		1,738 80	54,351 04
Alexander	County of Alexander	13,730 84	619 59		619 59	13,111 25
"	City of Cairo	33,345 30	1,436 68		1,436 68	31,908 62
Bureau	Township of Ohio	2,926 41	77 40		77 40	2,849 01
"	" Walnut	2,948 53	84 16		84 16	2,864 37
"	Greene River Special Drainage District	3,381 50	79 36		79 36	3,302 14
Cass	City of Beardstown	9,333 28	395 97		395 97	8,937 31
"	Hager Slough Special Drainage District	1,545 77	43 72		43 72	1,502 05
"	New Pankey Pond Special Drainage District	663 25	19 90		19 90	644 35
Champaign	Township of Champaign	6,239 13	282 98		282 98	5,956 15
"	" Urbana	5,923 16	364 33		364 33	5,558 83
"	City of Urbana	890 86	72 35		72 35	818 51
"	Big Slough Special Drainage District	30,807 00	770 01		770 01	30,036 99
"	Wild Cat Special Drainage District	1,537 00	35 69		35 69	1,501 31
Christian	Township of Johnson	115 52	6 97		6 97	108 55
"	" Pana	9,710 68	343 86	$1,122 54	1,466 40	8,244 28
Clark	County of Clark	1,518 24	56 50		56 50	1,461 74
"	Township of Marshall	3,555 75	128 46		128 46	3,427 29
"	" " sinking fund	3,364 41	121 68		121 68	3,242 73
"	" Westfield	1,243 50	44 88		44 88	1,198 62
"	" " sinking fund	1,124 01	40 57		40 57	1,083 44
"	" York	526 06	18 26		18 26	507 80
"	" " sinking fund	843 17	29 23		29 23	813 94
Clay	" Harter	1,460 56	56 45		56 45	1,404 11
"	" Louisville	982 68	39 15		39 15	943 53
Coles	" Charleston	4,837 30	208 13		208 13	4,629 17

Statement 41—Continued.

Locality.		Amount charged.	Abatements.			Amount paid State Treasurer.
Counties.	Bond fund.		Ordinary abatements, including errors, insolvencies, forfeitures, commissions, etc.	Enjoined from collection on property of railroads and other corporations............	Total.	
Coles	Township of Mattoon	$5,579 75	$411 52	....	$411 52	$5,168 23
"	" Seven Hickory	3,638 98	98 76	....	98 76	3,540 22
"	" " sinking fund	1,132 11	30 74	....	30 74	1,101 37
"	City of Mattoon	4,166 61	309 69	....	309 69	3,856 92
Cook	Incorporated Town of Cicero	2,785 10	66 50	....	66 50	2,718 60
Crawford	County of Crawford	6,315 97	234 16	....	234 16	6,081 81
"	Township of Hutsonville	868 73	29 96	....	29 96	838 77
"	" Robinson	1,834 98	66 25	....	66 25	1,768 73
Cumberland	" Sumpter	1,487 80	53 33	....	53 33	1,434 47
DeWitt	Township of Barnett	3,630 84	125 79	....	125 79	3,505 05
"	" Clintonia	2,562 35	130 37	....	130 37	2,431 98
"	" Creek	2,287 05	77 98	....	77 98	2,209 06
"	" Santa Anna	7,632 12	287 34	....	287 34	7,344 79
"	North Branch Lake Fork Special Drainage District	611 99	20 30	....	20 30	591 69
Douglas	Township of Camargo	3,457 75	120 04	....	120 04	3,337 71
"	" Garrett	2,352 82	80 60	....	80 60	2,272 22
"	" Newman	2,771 84	102 64	....	102 64	2,669 20
"	" Tuscola	1,260 17	47 91	....	47 91	1,212 26
Edgar	" Kansas	2,223 77	70 67	....	70 67	2,153 10
"	" Paris	445 03	12 83	....	12 83	432 20
"	" " sinking fund	3,656 38	105 27	....	105 27	3,551 11
"	" Ross	636 79	25 50	....	25 50	611 29
"	" Shiloh	3,449 06	103 45	....	103 45	3,345 61
"	" Young America	3,522 16	109 67	....	109 67	3,412 49
Edwards	Incorporated Town of Grayville	174 70	9 26	....	9 26	165 44
Effingham	Township of Douglas	9,886 08	371 73	....	371 73	9,514 35
"	" Mason	1,175 44	44 35	....	44 35	1,131 09
"	" West	247 15	8 84	....	8 84	238 31
Ford	County of Ford	8,930 44	317 18	....	317 18	8,613 26
"	Township of Drummer	5,287 74	195 33	....	195 33	5,092 41
"	" Lyman	1,040 54	35 73	....	35 73	1,004 81
"	" Peach Orchard	2,963 50	101 73	....	101 73	2,861 77
"	Vermilion Special Drainage District	2,535 63	81 48	....	81 48	2,454 15

Gallatin	County of Gallatin	12,828 65	483 65		483 65	12,345 00
"	City of Shawneetown	3,085 68	134 88		134 88	2,950 80
Greene	" Whitehall	810 78	27 62		27 62	783 16
Hancock	County of Hancock	13,690 76	495 91	$1,065 75	1,561 66	12,129 10
"	City of Warsaw	4,630 06	326 31		326 31	4,303 75
Henry	Township of Western	3.395 44	93 38		93 38	3,302 06
Iroquois	" Douglas	730 29	20 22		20 22	710 07
"	" Sheldon	4,055 35	160 88		160 80	3,894 55
"	City of Watseka	1,236 90	36 41		36 41	1,200 49
"	Milks Grove Special Drainage District	4,117 82	82 36		82 36	4,035 46
"	Spec'l Drain. Dist. No. 1—Onarga, Douglas & Danf'th Tps	2,955 11	63 51		63 51	2,891 60
"	Vermilion Special Drainage District	1,082 06	31 08		31 08	1,050 98
Jackson	City of Murphysboro	499 66	25 95		25 95	473 61
"	Big Lake Special Drainage district	3,680 00	127 72		127 72	3,552 28
Jasper	County of Jasper	6,464 71	247 19		247 19	6,217 52
"	Township of Fox	898 74	35 33		35 33	863 41
"	" " Sinking Fund	4,076 15	160 31		160 31	3,915 84
"	" St. Marie	3,023 79	110 08		110 08	2,913 71
"	" Wade	1,442 73	54 08		54 08	1,388 65
Jefferson	County of Jefferson	8,974 04	431 07		431 07	8,542 97
"	Township of Mt. Vernon	576 72	39 46		39 46	537 26
Jersey	Incorporated Town of Brighton	115 64	3 82		3 82	111 82
"	School District No. 8, T. 7, R. 12	1,262 75	40 74		40 74	1,222 01
JoDaviess	City of Galena	8,533 21	378 75		378 75	8,154 46
Kankakee	County of Kankakee	2,681 61	95 29		95 29	2,586 32
"	Township of Aroma	1,540 49	54 44		54 44	1,486 05
"	" Ganeer	1,836 65	60 36		60 36	1,776 29
"	" Momence	2,264 27	76 72		76 72	2,187 55
"	" Pembroke	305 57	10 62		10 62	294 95
"	" Pilot	1,288 75	42 71		42 71	1,246 04
Knox	" Rio	1,094 13	34 76		34 76	1,059 47
LaSalle	Incorporated Town of Marseilles	143 48	4 39		4 39	139 09
Lee	Township of Amboy	11,324 22	354 05		354 05	10,970 17
"	" Hamilton	546 64	14 55		14 55	532 09
"	" Wyoming	5,967 78	181 06		181 06	5,786 72
Livingston	" Amity	2,620 56	67 80		67 80	2,552 76
"	" Pontiac	6,409 58	190 42		190 42	6,219 16
"	" Reading	3,297 58	89 41		89 41	3,208 17
"	Vermilion Special Drainage District	4 78	10		10	4 68
Logan	County of Logan	7,293 93	817 80		817 80	6,476 13
"	Township of Atlanta	2,036 36	59 81		59 81	1,976 55
"	" East Lincoln	5,229 28	354 15		354 15	4,875 13
"	" " Sinking Fund	3,451 19	128 88		128 88	3,322 31
"	" Mt. Pulaski	2,142 16	57 35		57 35	2,084 81
"	" West Lincoln	7,337 58	427 59		427 59	6,909 99
"	School District No. 5, T. 18, R. 2	486 88	13 30		13 30	473 58
"	City of Lincoln	2,982 14	157 37		157 37	2,824 77
"	North Branch Lake Fork Special Drainage District	4,012 95	116 31		116 31	3,896 64
Macon	County of Macon	17,746 11	646 92		646 92	17,099 19
"	Township of Decatur	6,540 37	318 74		318 74	6,221 63
"	City of Decatur	1,188 95	60 86		60 86	1,128 09
"	North Branch Lake Fork Special Drainage District	1,070 95	31 92		31 92	1,039 03

Statement 41—Continued.

Locality.		Amount charged.	Abatements.			Amount paid State Treasurer.
Counties.	Bond Fund.		Ordinary abatements, including errors, insolvencies, forfeitures, commissions, etc.	Enjoined from collection on property of railroads and other corporations............	Total.	
Macoupin...............	County of Macoupin..................	$132,429 61	$8,308 30	....	$8,308 30	$124,121 31
"	Incorporated Town of Virden..........	520 91	78 29	....	78 29	442 62
"	" " Brighton.........	1,260 99	42 04	....	42 04	1,218 95
Madison...............	City of Edwardsville..................	2,747 52	104 75	....	104 75	2,642 77
Mason...............	Mason and Menard Special Drainage District..........	1,101 41	525 12	....	525 12	576 29
"	Mason and Tazewell " " "	24,103 54	6,529 76	....	6,529 76	17,573 78
"	The Central Special Drainage District..........	28,007 77	5,391 15	....	5,391 15	22,616 62
McDonough...............	Township of Bushnell..................	2,773 18	77 69	....	77 69	2,695 49
"	" " Sinking Fund.........	2,231 86	62 52	....	62 52	2,169 34
McLean...............	" Bloomington..................	24,159 41	949 55	....	949 55	23,209 86
"	Village of Saybrook..................	1,151 08	52 12	....	52 12	1,098 96
Monroe...............	County of Monroe..................	5,297 56	182 66	....	182 66	5,114 90
Montgomery...............	City of Litchfield..................	1,730 77	109 20	....	109 20	1,621 57
"	" " Sinking Fund.........	2,376 95	147 38	....	147 38	2,229 57
Morgan...............	County of Morgan..................	4,199 76	104 40	....	104 40	4,095 36
"	City of Jacksonville..................	12,358 74	269 37	....	269 37	12,089 37
"	City of Waverly..................	1,191 97	34 44	....	34 44	1,157 53
"	" " Sinking Fund.........	1,137 85	33 36	....	33 36	1,104 49
"	New Pankey Pond Special Drainage District..........	293 77	5 88	....	5 88	287 89
Moultrie...............	County of Moultrie..................	52,697 47	1,864 19	....	1,864 19	50,833 28
Ogle...............	Township of Mt. Morris..................	6,477 15	189 13	....	189 13	6,288 02
"	" Oregon..................	6,075 54	238 08	....	238 08	5,837 46
"	" Pine Rock..................	2,234 96	64 71	....	64 71	2,170 25
"	City of Polo..................	679 66	22 96	....	22 96	656 70
Peoria...............	Township of Brimfield..................	8,619 58	244 60	....	244 50	8,374 98
"	" Elmwood..................	11,121 22	360 66	....	360 66	10,760 56
"	" Peoria..................	4,664 87	162 11	....	162 11	4,502 76
Piatt...............	" Bement..................	8,173 49	273 48	$239 03	512 51	7,660 98
"	" Blue Ridge..................	5,192 20	172 37	104 52	276 89	4,915 31
"	" Goose Creek..................	4,185 99	141 13	....	141 13	4,044 86
"	" Sangamon..................	2,044 58	93 58	251 36	344 94	1,699 64
Pike...............	County of Pike..................	1,730 20	1,314 25	145 89	1,460 14	270 06
"	Pittsfield School District..................	3,828 07	235 53	....	235 53	3,592 54

Pulaski	County of Pulaski	4,153 00	492 00		492 00	3,661 00
"	City of Mound City	1,191 27	132 18		132 18	1,059 09
Richland	County of Richland	6,593 99	240 29		240 29	6,353 70
Saline	County of Saline	2,120 93	98 70		98 70	2,022 23
Sangamon	County of Sangamon	25,181 90	754 27		754 27	24,427 63
"	Township of Cartwright	2,751 05	79 81		79 81	2,671 24
"	" Capital	2,804 96	91 35		91 35	2,713 61
"	" Springfield	613 69	17 73		17 73	595 96
"	" Talkington	2,503 60	68 72		68 72	2,434 88
"	City of Springfield	48,153 63	1,567 21		1,567 21	46,586 42
Schuyler	County of Schuyler	1,555 35	55 97		55 97	1,499 38
Shelby	" Dry Point	1,380 83	49 96		49 96	1,330 87
"	" Okaw	399 82	12 73		12 73	387 09
"	" Prairie	8,680 10	234 75		234 75	8,445 35
"	" Shelbyville	352 93	15 54		15 54	337 39
"	" Richland	1,346 15	36 26		36 26	1,309 89
"	" Todd's Point	217 56	6 30		6 30	211 26
"	" Windsor	15,983 36	2,758 57		2,758 57	13,224 79
"	City of Windsor	1,160 18	33 43		33 43	1,126 75
Stark	Township of Essex	4,866 00	189 06		189 06	4,676 94
"	" Goshen	2,642 79	90 50		90 50	2,552 29
"	" Osceola	5,515 98	191 53		191 53	5,324 45
"	" Penn	163 51	5 54		5 54	157 97
"	" Toulon	4,213 56	148 73		148 73	4,064 83
"	Village of Wyoming	583 52	62 99		62 99	520 53
St. Clair	City of East St. Louis	38,217 26	6,006 89		6,006 89	32,210 37
"	Township of Centerville Station	25,132 00	3,072 14		3,072 14	22,059 86
"	Village of Brooklyn	708 76	269 16		269 16	439 60
Tazewell	County of Tazewell	8,808 04	303 78		303 78	8,504 26
"	Township of Delavan	4,295 10	127 88		127 88	4,167 22
"	" Little Mackinaw	1,196 43	35 55		35 55	1,160 88
"	" Mackinaw	1,122 82	49 11		49 11	1,073 71
"	" Tremont	378 77	10 74		10 74	368 03
"	City of Pekin	6,629 35	291 13		291 13	6,338 22
"	Mason and Tazewell Special Drainage District	7,568 51	188 03		188 03	7,380 48
Vermilion	Township of Butler	841 00	24 48		24 48	816 52
"	" Danville	14,655 56	437 26		437 26	14,218 30
"	" Elwood	2,149 20	65 27		65 27	2,083 93
"	" Grant	5,997 19	184 66		184 66	5,812 53
"	" Ross	2,735 65	122 79		122 79	2,612 86
Wabash	County of Wabash	7,593 87	282 17	532 56	814 73	6,779 14
"	City of Mt. Carmel	3,984 61	272 75	113 60	386 35	3,598 26
Warren	Township of Roseville	2,589 53	88 26		88 26	2,501 27
"	" Swan	465 20	15 43		15 43	449 77
Washington	County of Washington	16,964 68	616 38		616 38	16,348 30
Wayne	" Wayne	4,986 23	202 62		202 62	4,783 61
"	Township of Big Mound	281 27	11 75		11 75	269 52
"	" Jasper	102 94	4 21		4 21	98 73
"	" Lamard	47 85	1 75		1 75	46 10
White	County of White	8,906 96	432 06		432 06	8,474 90
"	Village of Enfield	742 04	36 78		36 78	705 26
"	Incorporated Town of Grayville	425 79	17 90		17 90	407 89

Statement 41—Concluded.

Locality.			Abatements.			
Counties.	Bond Fund.	Amount charged.	Ordinary abatements, including errors, insolvencies, forfeitures, commissions, etc.	Enjoined from collection on property of railroads and other corporations	Total.	Amount paid State Treasurer.
Whiteside	Green River Special Drainage District	$839 14	$14 72	$125 32	$140 04	$699 10
Williamson	County of Williamson	12,548 18	465 83		465 83	12,082 35
Woodford	Township of Olio	2,103 95	79 02		79 02	2,024 93
Totals		$1,270,641 55	$71,186 48	$3,700 57	$74,887 05	$1,195,754 50

No. 42.

Statement of the condition of Trust Companies, as shown by reports of the last examination of said companies filed in this office prior to date of this report.

Illinois Trust and Savings Bank, Chicago, Illinois. Last examination, close of business December 31, 1895.

RESOURCES.	
Stocks and bonds	$2,828,798 93
Cash on hand	3,378,096 42
Checks and cash items	1,888,568 85
Due from other banks	1,155,340 19
Demand loans on collaterals	15,602,796 03
Time loans on collaterals	4,876,962 63
Loans on real estate	2,442,684 16
Total	$32,173,247 21
LIABILITIES.	
Capital stock	$2,000,000 00
Surplus fund	2,000,000 00
Undivided profits	150,810 83
Dividends unpaid	60,000 00
Time deposits	14,990,613 77
Demand deposits	12,971,822 61
Total	$32,173,247 21

The Northern Trust Company, Chicago, Illinois. Last examination, close of business December 23, 1895.

RESOURCES.	
Loans and discounts	$7,115,234 72
Overdrafts	36,647 61
Bonds and stocks	1,399,927 69
Due from other banks	1,806,975 34
Cash	1,795,352 44
Total	$12,154,137 80
LIABILITIES.	
Capital stock	$1,000,000 00
Surplus	500,000 00
Undivided profits	92,986 78
Deposits	10,345,250 87
Cashier's checks	85,248 09
Certified checks	130,652 06
Total	$12,154,137 80

Statement 42—Continued.

Chicago Title and Trust Company, Chicago, Illinois. Last examination, close of business December 5, 1895.

RESOURCES.	
Loans	$717,061 33
Bonds and stocks	94,370 66
Cash on hand	4,176 84
Due from banks	125,454 73
Real estate	1,335,780 60
Furniture and fixtures	8,717 54
Abstract plant	300,000 00
Due from sundry persons	45,745 47
Due from sundry trusts	18,895 22
Total	$2,650,202 39
LIABILITIES.	
Capital stock	$1,500,000 00
Undivided profits	144,936 90
Mortgages on real estate	315,000 00
Due to sundry persons	2,970 64
Due to sundry trusts	687,294 85
Total	$2,650,202 39

Security Title and Trust Company, Chicago, Illinois. Last examination, close of business December 14, 1895.

RESOURCES.	
Loans	$481,434 16
Plant	650,000 00
Printed abstracts	118,250 25
Stocks	84,000 00
Cash on hand	534 48
Due from banks	44,646 30
Due from treasurer	50,196 35
Due from sundry persons	65,641 85
Checks and other cash items	1,123 74
Total	$1,495,827 13
LIABILITIES.	
Capital stock	$1,254,610 00
Surplus	150,000 00
Undivided profits	80,084 22
Due to sundry persons	86 00
Due to sundry trusts	11,046 91
Total	$1,495,827 13

Statement 42—Continued.

Title Guarantee and Trust Company, Chicago, Illinois. Last examination, close of business November 27, 1895.

RESOURCES.	
Loans	$461,722 55
Due from banks	128,008 66
Cash	2,165 64
Abstract books, records, etc	1,200,000 00
Stocks and bonds	25,591 25
Due from individuals	68,958 83
Due from sundry trusts	100,341 75
Expenses	299,958 91
Total	$2,286,747 59
LIABILITIES.	
Capital stock	$1,600,000 00
Surplus	100,000 00
Undivided profits	522,233 31
Due to sundry trusts	64,514 28
Total	$2,286,747 59

The Royal Trust Company, Chicago, Illinois. Last examination, close of business October 17, 1895.

RESOURCES.	
Loans and discounts	$1,137,565 10
Overdrafts	745 33
Bonds	76,125 53
Cash on hand	20,016 00
Due from other banks	93,721 27
Checks and other cash items	72,652 63
Total	$1,400,825 86
LIABILITIES.	
Capital stock	$500,000 00
Surplus	100,000 00
Undivided profits	40,228 71
Deposits	744,328 57
Certified checks	13,505 28
Cashier's checks	2,763 30
Total	$1,400,825 86

Statement 42—Continued.

American Trust and Savings Bank, Chicago, Illinois. Last examination, close of business September 21, 1896.

RESOURCES.	
Loans and discounts	$3,315,957 41
Overdrafts	5,749 78
Bonds and stocks	249,075 00
Cash on hand	363,268 57
Due from other banks	852,445 99
Checks and other cash items	290,230 78
Total	$5,076,727 53
LIABILITIES.	
Capital stock	$1,000,000 00
Surplus	200,000 00
Undivided profits	22,795 93
Deposits	2,631,572 44
Due to other banks	1,164,674 50
Cashier's checks	14,104 11
Certified checks	43,580 55
Total	$5,076,727 53

The Equitable Trust Company, Chicago, Illinois. Last examination, close of business September 10, 1896.

RESOURCES.	
Loans	$570,048 51
Bonds	585,800 00
Cash on hand	481 20
Due from banks	7,655 16
Checks and other cash items	1,539 17
Real estate	10,994 09
Due from sundry persons	2,903 50
Due from sundry trusts	73,222 90
Total	$1,252,644 53
LIABILITIES.	
Capital stock	$500,000 00
Surplus	125,000 00
Undivided profits	15,668 64
Deposits	480,517 02
Due te sundry persons	18,930 33
Due to sundry trusts	112,528 54
Total	$1,252,644 53

Statement 42—Concluded.

State Bank of Chicago, Chicago, Illinois. Last examination, close of business September 14, 1896.

RESOURCES.	
Loans and discounts	$2,002,414 75
Overdrafts	367 41
Bonds	500 00
Cash on hand	265,633 28
Due from other banks	501,733 23
Checks and other cash items	139,997 63
Total	$2,910,646 30
LIABILITIES.	
Capital stock	$500,000 00
Surplus	200,000 00
Undivided profits	37,421 58
Deposits	2,112,910 91
Due to sundry trusts	6,797 86
Cashier's checks	17,942 12
Certified checks	35,573 83
Total	$2,910,646 30

INDEX.

PAGE.

Accounts of State Treasurer with the different State funds................................ 162
" " " " Local Bond funds........................355-362
Adjutant General, salary of.. 126
" office of and clerk hire.. 100
Agricultural Board, State and County...109-112
Appellate Court, First District, expenses of.. 16
" Second " " 16-17
" Third " " 17
" Fourth " " 17
Appropriations, special.. 4
" general 5
" made by the 38th General Assembly, unexpended balances lapsed September 30, 1895...148-152
" made by 39th General Assembly, unexpended balances October 1, 1896..153-160
Assessments and Equalization for 1895 and 1896...VII
" of all property equalized for 1895..251-253
" " " 1896..326-328
" live stock, comparison for 1895 and 1896......................................VIII
Assessed value of property in the several counties for 1895............................186-214
" " " " 1896............................254-282
Asylum for Insane Criminals.. 81
Attorney General, salary of 126
" office of and clerk hire.. 99
Auditor of Public Accounts, salary of.. 126
" " office of and clerk hire.......................................98-99
" " fees collected and paid into treasury by.................... 1
Banking corporations, statement 43, inset...XIII-XIV
Biennial report of the Auditor of Public Accounts, introduction to.....................III-XV
Binding, public.. 105
Blind, Institution for the Education of.. 85
Blind, Industrial Home for... 84
Bonded debt of the State.. IX
Bonds registered under acts of 1865, 1869, 1877, 1879 and 1885..........................XII, 330-351
" " drainage and levee law of 1872 and 1885..................XII, 352-354
Board of World's Fair Commissioners.. 132
Canal Commissioners, salaries of.. 5
Central Insane Hospital 83
Capital stock of corporations other than railroad, assessment for 1895....................243-250
" " " " " " 1896....................318-325
Classification of warrants drawn on the easury... VI
Commissioners, Lincoln Monument 96
" Railroad and Warehouse..105-108

PAGE.

Commissioners of Labor Statistics, expenses of, etc 7,8
" of Public Charities, expenses of, etc 8,9
" of Claims, expenses of, etc........ XIV, XV, 5,
" to mark position of State troops at Chickamauga........ 6
" on statutory revision........ 94
Contingent fund of Governor........ 9,10
Conveying convicts to Penitentiary........ 10-13
" " " State Reformatory........ 13,14
" " " " Home for Juvenile Female Offenders........ 14,15
Cotton States International Exposition........ 16
Costs and expenses of State suits........ 15,16
County and State Agricultural Boards 109-112
County, State, City, Town, District, School, and other local taxes levied on assessment of 1894........ 174-176
County, State, City, Town, District, School, and other local taxes levied on assessment of 1895........ 177-179
Court, Supreme, Central Grand Division........ 17
" " Northern " " 17
" " Southern " " 17,18
Deaf and Dumb, Institution for the Education of 85
Debt, of State, bonded IX
Detailed statement of warrants drawn........ 4-143
Disbursements and receipts from all funds........ V,1,2
" " of General Revenue fund 1,2
" " of Special State funds........ 3
" State School fund........ 2,136,139
" Unknown and Minor Heirs' fund........ 147
" and receipts of Local Bond funds 140-143
District, State, County, City, School and other local taxes levied on assessment for 1894........ 174-176
District, State, County, City, School and other local taxes levied on assessment for 1895........ 177-179
Equalization, State Board of 112
Equalized assessment of all property for 1895........ 251-253
" " " 1896........ 326-328
Executive Mansion........ 18-21
Expenses, incidental 87-94
" Insurance department........ 101,102
" estimated, of the State government, from October 1, 1896, to July 1, 1897........ VII
Eye and Ear Infirmary, Illinois Charitable........ 82
Factory and Workshop Inspectors 21,22
Farmers' County Institutes........ 22-24
Feeble-Minded Children, Asylum for the Education of........ 81
Female Offenders, Juvenile, State Home for........ 82
Fees of Auditor, statement of 1-2
Fire apparatus for State capitol building........ 24
Flags for dome of State house........ 25
Fish Commissioners, expenses of 24
Fugitives from justice 25-31
Funds, Local Bond 355-362
Funds in State Treasury, balance October 1, 1896........ VI
General Assembly, 39th 31-33
Governor, salary of 126
" Lieutenant, salary and office expenses of........ 126
" office and clerk hire 97
" contingent fund of 9,10
Heating and lighting State house 33-37

PAGE.

Illinois Asylum for Feeble-Minded Children ... 81
" " Insane Criminals ... 81
" Board of World's Fair Commissioners ... 132
" Central Railroad, gross receipts ... X, XI
" Charitable Eye and Ear Infirmary ... 82
" Dairymen's Association ... 37
" Industrial Home for the Blind ... 84
" National Guard ... 39-81
" Soldiers' Orphans' Home ... 82
" Soldiers' and Sailors' Home ... 82, 83
" State Asylum, Incurable Insane ... 81
" " Historical Library ... 37-39
" " Home for Juvenile Female Offenders ... 82
" " " Soldiers' Widows ... 83
" " Horticultural Society ... 39
" " Normal School—Eastern ... 85
" " " —Northern ... 86
" " Reformatory ... 39
" University of ... 87
Incidental expenses ... 87-94
Insane Hospital—Northern ... 84
" —Central ... 83
" —Southern ... 84
" —Eastern ... 83
" —Western ... 84
Institution for the Education of the Blind ... 85
" " " " Deaf and Dumb ... 85
Interest on State School Fund ... 137, 139, 161
Insurance Superintendent, office of and clerk hire ... 101, 102
" " salary of ... 127
Joint Commission on Statutory Revision ... 94, 95
Judiciary, salaries of ... 127-132
Justice, fugitives from ... 25-31
Laborers, Janitors and Watchmen in State House ... 95
Lincoln Homestead, Trustees of ... 95, 96
" Monument Commissioners ... 96
Local Bond Funds, disbursements of ... 140-143
" " " amount charged on tax books of 1894, on account of—amount of deduction, amount collected and paid State Treasurer, and amount remaining unpaid ... 363-368
Same for 1895 ... 369-374
Levy of 1895 ... VIII
" 1896 ... VIII
Lieutenant Governor, salary of ... 126
Money refunded ... 97
Mine Inspectors ... 96, 97
Normal School—Eastern ... 85
" —Northern ... 86
Normal University, Normal ... 86
" " Southern ... 86
Office of Governor ... 97
" Lieutenant-Governor ... 126
" Secretary of State ... 98
" Auditor of Public Accounts ... 98, 99
" State Treasurer ... 99
" Attorney-General ... 99, 100
" Adjutant-General ... 100, 101

PAGE.
Office of Superintendent of Public Instruction 136
" Superintendent of Insurance 101, 102
Paving and curbing streets 102
Penitentiary—Northern 86
" —Southern 86
" conveying convicts to 10-13
Public Charities, expenses of Commissioners, etc 8, 9
Printing paper and stationery 102, 103
Printer Expert, for salary 102
Public printing 103-105
Public binding 105
Property assessed for the year 1895, in the several counties 186-214
" " " 1896, " " 254-282
Railroad and Warehouse Commissioners 105-108
Railroad property, aggregate equalized assessment of, for 1895 240-242
" " " " " " 1896 315-317
Rates per cent. of additions and deductions on assessments of 1895 .... 215, 216
" " " " " 1896 .... 283, 284
Recapitulation of warrants drawn on the State Treasury 144-147
" " " " Revenue Fund 147
" " " " Special State Fund 147
Receipts and disbursements of all funds, summary .... V, 1, 2, 3
" " General Revenue Fund 1, 2
" " Special State Fund 3
" " State School Fund 136-139
" " Unknown and Minor Heirs' Fund 147
" " Local Bond Funds 140-143
Reformatory, State 86, 87
" conveying convicts to 13, 14
Repairs on Capitol Building 108, 109
Reporter of Supreme Court, salary 109
Reports of Supreme Court 109
Revenue Fund, warrants drawn upon 144-147
" " receipts, disbursements of 1, 2
Salaries, State officers 126, 127
" Judiciary 127
" Judges Supreme Court 127
" " Superior Court of Cook County 127, 128
" " Circuit Court of Cook County 128, 129
" " " Courts 129
" State's Attorneys 129-132
" Reporter of Supreme Court 109
School, College and Seminary Funds 161
" Tax Fund, levied, etc., for 1894 .... 170, 171
" " " " 1895 .... 172, 173
" " and interest on School Fund distributed in 1894 and 1895 163-165
Secretary of State, salary of 126
" " office of and clerk hire 98
Soldiers' Orphans' Home 82
Soldiers' and Sailors' Home 82, 83
Southern Insane Hospital 84
" Normal University 86
Special State Funds, receipts and disbursements of 3-136-139
" " accounts with 162
" " warrants drawn upon 136-139
State assessments for 1894 and 1895, taxes charged upon VIII

PAGE.

State bonded debt........ IX
" School Fund........ 3-136-139
" suits, costs and expenses of........ 15, 16
" Treasurer, salary of........ 126
" " office of and clerk hire........ 99
" Entomologist, salary of........ 127
State agents at East St. Louis, South Chicago, Town of Lake and Peoria, to prevent cruelty to animals, salary of........ 127
" State Board of Arbitration........ 112
" State Board of Live Stock Commissioners and State Veterinarian, salary and expenses of........ 114-125
" and County Agricultural Boards........ 109-112
" Board of Equalization........ 112
" Examiners for mine inspectors, etc........ 113, 114
" Board of Health........ 112, 113
" Library........ 126
" State Historical Library and Natural History Museum, salary of Curator, etc... 125, 126
" Reformatory........ 86, 87
" Treasurer's account with the different funds........ 162
" taxes charged for 1894........ 166, 167
" " " 1895........ 168, 169
" County, City, Town, District, School and other taxes, levied on the assessment of 1894........ 174-176
" County, City, Town, District, School and other taxes, levied on the assessment of 1895........ 177-179
" Government, estimated expenses of from October 1, 1896, to July 1, 1897........ VII
Statement No. 1—Receipts and Disbursements of General Revenue Fund........ 1
Statement No. 2— " " Special State Funds........ 3
Statement No. 3—Detailed Statement of Warrants drawn on the Treasury for all purposes, and to what account and appropriation charged........ 4-143
Statement No. 4—Recapitulation of Warrants drawn on the State Treasury for all purposes........ 144-147
Statement No. 5—Balance of appropriations made by the 38th General Assembly, unexpended October 1, 1894, the amount of warrants since drawn thereon, and the unexpended balances which lapsed into the State Treasury September 30, 1895........ 148-152
Statement No. 6—Appropriations made by the 39th General Assembly, the amount of warrants drawn thereon, and the unexpended balances October 1, 1896........ 153-160
Statement No. 7—Warrants outstanding October 1, 1894, and September 30, 1896........ 161
Statement No. 8—Condition of School, Colleges and Seminary Funds........ 161
Statement No. 9—State Treasurer's accounts with the different funds........ 162
Statement No. 10—Showing the amount of interest on School Fund, and the amount of School Tax Fund distributed to the several counties in the State, for the years 1894 and 1895 and amounts paid County Superintendents from said fund. 163-165
Statement No. 11—Aggregate amount of State Taxes charged on the tax books for the year 1894, the amount of abatements, commissions, etc., the net amount collected and paid State Treasurer........ 166-167
Statement No. 12—Aggregate amount of State Taxes charged on tax books for the year 1895, the amount of abatements, commissions, etc., the net amount collected and paid State Treasurer, and amount remaining due........ 168-169
Statement No. 13—Showing the aggregate amount of School Fund tax charged on tax books of 1894, the amount deducted for abatements, commissions, etc., the net amount collected, the amount paid to each county, etc........ 170-171
Statement No. 14—Showing the aggregate amount of School Fund tax charged on tax books for 1895, the amount deducted for abatements, commissions, etc., the net amount collected, the amount paid to each county, etc........ 172-173
Statement No. 15—Amount of State, County, City, Town, District and other local taxes charged on the tax books of 1894........ 174-176
Statement No. 16—Amount of State, County, City, Town, District and other local taxes charged on the tax books of 1895........ 177-179
Statement No. 17—Showing the per cent. of forfeitures and insolvencies on account of State tax for the years 1894 and 1895 in the various counties........ 180
Statement No. 18—Showing the per cent. of total amount of State tax collected for the years 1874 to 1895, inclusive, paid by each of the various counties........ 181-183

	PAGE.
Statement No. 19—Showing the average rate of taxation in the several counties for the years 1888 to 1895, inclusive	184, 185
Statement No. 20—Property assessed for the year 1895, in the several counties, as returned to the Auditor's office	186–214
Statement No. 21—Rates per cent. of addition to or deduction from the assessed value of each class of property in each county in the State, as determined by State Board of Equalization, on assessment of 1895	215.216
Statement No. 22—Assessed value of railroad property in each county in the State of Illinois, for 1895	217–239
Statement No. 23—Aggregate equalized assessment of the property of Railroads for 1895	240–242
Statement No. 24—Assessment made by the State Board of Equalization upon the capital stock of companies and associations incorporated under the laws of this State, other than Railroad companies, etc., for the year 1895	243–250
Statement No. 25—Equalized assessment of all taxable property in the State of Illinois for the year 1895, as equalized or assessed by the State Boatd of Equalization, showing the valuation of the several classes of property in each county	251–253
Statement No. 26—Property assessed for the year 1896, in the several counties, as returned to the Auditor's office	254–282
Statement No. 27—Rates per cent. of addition to or deduction from the assessed value of each class of property in each county of the State, for the year 1896, as determined by the State Board of Equalization	283, 284
Statement No. 28—Showing the proportion of the total equalized assessments of taxable property in the various counties for the years 1884 to 1895, inclusive, assessed on real and personal property, respectively	285–287
Statement No. 29—Aggregate equalized assessments of taxable property in the several counties in the State of Illinois, for the years 1873 and 1884 to 1896, inclusive	288–291
Statement No. 30—Assessed value of Railroad property in each county of the State of Illinois, for the year 1896	292–314
Statement No. 31—Aggregate equalized assessment of the property of Railroads for 1896	315–317
Statement No. 32—Assessment made by the State Board of Equalization on capital stock of companies and associations incorporated under the laws of this State, other than Railroad companies, etc., for the year 1896	318–325
Statement No 33—Equalized assessment of all taxable property in the State of Illinois, for the year 1896, as equalized or assessed by the State Board of Equalization, showing the valuation of the several classes of property in each county.	326–328
Statement No. 34—Bonds issued by Counties, Townships, Cities and Towns registered in Auditor's office, in pursuance of an act entitled "An act to fund and provide for paying the Railroad debts of Counties, Townships, Cities and Towns," in force April 16, 1869	330–337
Statement No. 35—Bonds registered in pursuance of the act of February 13, 1865	338–339
Statement No. 36—Bonds registered in pursuance of the act of February 13, 1865, as amended by the acts of April 27, 1877, and June 4, 1879	340–351
Statement No. 37—Drainage District Bonds registered in pursuance of the act of June 27, 1885	352–353
Statement No. 38—Bonds issued by Commissioners of Sny Island Levee, of Adams, Pike and Calhoun Counties, in pursuance of an act of April 24, 1871, and registered in Auditor's office under act of April 9, 1872	354
Statement No. 39—State Treasurer's account with the different Local Bond Funds, from October 1, 1894, to September 30, 1896, inclusive	355–362
Statement No. 40—Aggregate amount charged on tax books of 1894 on account of Local Bond Funds, the amount of abatements, commissions, etc., the net amount collected, and the amount paid into the State Treasury	363–368
Statement No. 41—Aggregate amount charged on tax books of 1895, on account of Local Bond Funds, the amount of abatements, commissions, etc., the net amount collected, the amount paid State Treasurer, and the amount remaining unpaid	369–374
Statement No. 42—Of the condition of the Illinois Trust Companies, as shown by report of examination filed with State Auditor	375–379
Statement No. 43—Showing resources and liabilities of each State Bank before the commencement of business September 1, 1896, being the date of the last call made by the Auditor prior to the date of this report. Also total resources and liabilities of all State Banks as reported under each quarterly call during the past biennial period	Inset
Stationery and printing paper	103
Storage rooms, Secretary of State	126
Superintendent of Public Instruction	3–136

RESOURCES.

BANKS.

LIABILITIES.

[illegible]—Continued.

ASSETS—Continued.	Banks.		LIABILITIES—Continued.
[illegible]	Name.	Location.	[illegible]

Statement 49—Continued

RESOURCES—Continued

BANKS

LIABILITIES—Continued

[illegible]

	PAGE.
Supreme Court, Southern Division, expenses of	17-18
" " Central " "	17
" " Northern " "	17
Taxes charged on State assessment for 1894 and 1895	VIII
Taxes—State, County, City, Town, District and School, levied on assessment 1894	174-176
" " " " " " " 1895	177-179
Trust Companies	XII, 380-383
University of Illinois	87
Unknown and Minor Heirs' Fund	139
Warrants drawn on the Treasury	VI
" " " detailed statement of	4, 143
" " " recapitulation of	144-147
Warrants outstanding, statement of	161
Watchmen, Laborers and Janitors in State House	95
World's Fair Commissioners—Board	132-135
Woman's—Illinois Exposition Board	147
World's Columbian Exposition	147

www.ingramcontent.com/pod-product-compliance
Lightning Source LLC
Chambersburg PA
CBHW071358050326
40689CB00010B/1682

* 9 7 8 1 0 1 4 1 5 3 2 5 8 *